Progress As If Survival Mattered

Progress As If Survival Mattered

A HANDBOOK
FOR A CONSERVER SOCIETY

BY FRIENDS OF THE EARTH

EDITED BY HUGH NASH

with an introduction by David R. Brower

FRIENDS OF THE EARTH · SAN FRANCISCO

WE INVITE YOU to join Friends of the Earth® in support of the program described in these pages. Memberships start at $25.00/year; members receive FOE's newspaper, *Not Man Apart*, and discounts on FOE's books. Our address is:
  124 Spear Street, San Francisco 94105

Friends of the Earth gratefully acknowledges permission to reprint from the following sources:

George Alderson and Everett Sentman, from *How You Can Influence Congress.* Copyright © 1979 by George Alderson. Reprinted by permission of the publisher, E. P. Dutton.

Arthur Ashe and Frank Deford, from *Arthur Ashe: Portrait in Motion.* Copyright © 1975 by Arthur Ashe and Frank Deford. Reprinted by permission of Houghton Mifflin Company.

Murray Bookchin, from *Our Synthetic Environment,* by permission of Comment Publishing Project.

Paul Conrad cartoons, from *Pro & Conrad,* © 1979 Conrad Projects, Inc.

Doonesbury cartoons are copyright © 1975, 1976, 1977, 1978, GB Trudeau. Reprinted with permission of Universal Press Syndicate. All rights reserved.

Loren Eiseley, *The Lethal Factor,* reprinted by permission of *American Scientist,* journal of Sigma Xi, the Scientific Research Society.

Peter Harnik, "Cycles in Cities," reprinted with permission from *Sierra* magazine, Vol. 65, Number 2, March/April 1980.

Sid Harris cartoons, from *Chicken Soup,* copyright © 1979 by Sidney Harris, published by Wm. Kauffmann, Inc.

Amory Lovins, L. Hunter Lovins, and Leonard Ross, from "Nuclear Power and Nuclear Bombs," reprinted by permission of *Foreign Affairs,* Summer 1980, copyright by the Council on Foreign Relations, Inc.

Daniel Luten, "Limits to Growth Controversy," from *Sourcebook on the Environment,* published by the University of Chicago Press, 1978.

Daniel Luten, "Progress Against Growth," reprinted with permission from the *Sierra Club Bulletin,* Volume 57, Number 6, June 1972.

Margaret Mead, "Why Our World Will Never Be the Same," first published, *Redbook Magazine,* April 1974. Copyright Mary Catherine Bateson and Rhoda Metraux.

E. F. Schumacher, *Small Is Beautiful: Economics as if People Mattered* [New York: Harper & Row, 1973], copyright © 1973 by E. F. Schumacher. Reprinted by permission of the publisher.

Leonard Silk, *Economics in Plain English,* copyright © 1978 by Leonard Silk, reprinted by permission of Simon & Schuster, a Division of Gulf & Western Corporation.

Wallace Stegner, "Story of a Letter", copyright © The Wilderness Society. Reprinted by permission from *The Living Wilderness,* 1980.

World population estimate maps and charts, by permission of The Environment Fund.

Worldwatch Papers No. 9, 11, 16, 17, 18, 20, 21, 22, 23, 28, 29, and 31, copyright © 1976, 1977, 1978, 1979, reprinted by permission.

CONTENTS

In memory of William O. Douglas,
a great jurist, a great conservationist, and a great human.

THE WILLIAM O. DOUGLAS
WILDERNESS AREA (APPROX.)

SCALE: 1 INCH = ABOUT 10 YRS.

LEGEND
——————— UNIMPROVED ROAD.
– – – – – FOOT PATH
SWAMP
UNEXPLORED
·········· ANIMAL TRAIL

(EASTBOUND)

Foreword to the 1981 Edition

FRIENDS OF THE EARTH and the League of Conservation Voters, initially part of FOE, were founded in 1969 in order to augment programs in conservation publishing, political action, legislative lobbying, litigation, and international environmental efforts that were initiated in the course of my seventeen years as executive director of the Sierra Club. FOE now has nearly 25,000 members in the United States and 175,000 in its sister organizations in twenty-six other countries. We work as closely as we can with senior and junior organizations in all twenty-seven. We are pleased to have had a major hand in forming the Environmental Liaison Center in Nairobi, which brings some fifteen hundred citizen organizations into an environmental network with the United Nations Environment Programme.

Energy, and the social and environmental effects of the search for energy and of its development and use, is one of the predominant concerns of our multinational enterprise, as well as of the Friends of the Earth Foundation and the Foundation's International Project for Soft Energy Paths. Soft paths are Amory Lovins's idea, which FOE has been fortunate to be able to contribute to and help promote; soft energy paths would supply all the energy industrialized and developing societies need, using renewable energy primarily, fossil fuels transitionally, and nuclear power not at all. It is one of the solid routes toward world peace. There needs to be much more attention paid to it by environmental organizations and, indeed, by all American institutions that care about the future.

There isn't enough concern yet. In the debate between John Anderson and Ronald Reagan on September 21, 1980, Mr. Anderson singled out three important problems before the country that until that moment had not been considered in their debate: the danger of atomic war, a policy for using the world's natural resources, and nationalism. Those problems were but feebly considered in the campaign as a whole. Energy is deeply involved in each of the three.

National energy policy has been, for the past decade at least, a policy of strength through exhaustion. Both major parties are in a contest to see which can achieve exhaustion faster.

Our national nuclear-energy policy is leading directly toward nuclear war, and is recklessly fostering the illusion that there can be a limited nuclear war that won't hurt anybody very much, or at least won't hurt buildings very much. This is a race to oblivion that nobody needs.

Our national policy for the world's resources is to use them up as fast as they can be found, insisting that our five percent of the world's population is entitled to one third of the world's resources. We threaten those who disagree, and then are a little perplexed that many countries are beginning to think that they cannot afford the US any more.

Our national policy on nationalism, in a shrinking world that can afford less and less of it, is directly out of Robert Ringer, advocate of taking care of Number One and winning through intimidation. Intimidation is no longer what it once was, before terrorism and taking hostages came into vogue.

We have eight suggestions about energy and ecosystems:

1. The national energy goal needs a new look. Expecting renewable energy to provide only one fifth of our energy budget by the year 2000 is too conservative. The nation is ready, we think, to try harder.

2. If the nuclear investment continues to be so excessively high, we will not persuade less-developed countries that we are serious when we try to persuade them to move to soft energy. The best salesman is the one who uses the product himself. If we don't persuade them, the threat of nuclear proliferation will accelerate and get out of hand, and the danger that the world will stumble into nuclear war, even if it doesn't mean to, becomes unacceptably high.

3. If we continue even our present excessive use of irreplaceable fossil fuels—much less increase that use as our present synfuel excitement would have us do—we endanger the air we breathe, the crops we eat, and the shores we love. The danger is not just from global changes in climate, or from acid rain and snow, but also from the toxic metals fossil fuels release which the earth's life-support system cannot handle. Small cars are not a panacea, even if they get one hundred miles per gallon. Ecosystems can be destroyed as surely by being overrun by mice as they can be by being overrun by rats. Cars, small and big, produce particulate emissions, including rubber, asbestos, and metals. And pavement grows where food ought to.

4. We need to moderate our love affair with the car. It will not be easy. (This I know directly; there was only one of the twelve cars I have owned that I did not love, together with the places they took my family and me.) We are still, too many of us, no more logical than the Vancouver car dealer who defended the big cars he sells by saying, "Why not? The Cadillacs and Rabbits are all going to run out of gas together."

5. Considering the liquid-fuel problem, we should require the Army Corps of Engineers and the Department of Energy to put the trains back on the track (put the tracks back first). We dare not wait too long. The rescue will require energy. The energy budgeted for the disastrous MX-missile proposal could get the trains well under way and add to national security instead of diminishing it.

6. Before going too far on gasohol, we need careful research about just how much energy can be siphoned away from the earth's biomass without *(a)* taking food away from people who cannot outbid big-car owners for it, and *(b)* crippling the essential recycling of nutrients. Energy is needed to fuel "the slow, smokeless fires of decay" which keep the soil alive. We should look harder at what is happening to soil, the most important energy converter of all. If you count food and fiber, which most of us still use, more than half the nation's present energy is solar, much of it filtered through plants. We daily dispose of an unconscionable amount of what it takes to support the photosynthesis that lets us live on this planet. Soil is not old-fashioned. It is essential. Yet we blow it away, wash it away, pave it over, compact it, and strew it with hazardous wastes and witches' brews. We can no longer dare to destroy three million acres per year of our best agricultural soil, and who knows how much more of our forest soils.

7. Remember how much too often the free market has given us its message too late. Ask the passenger pigeon. Ask Detroit. Politically popular though it has been to bad-mouth government, it is still true that government of and by the people still speaks best for the people. For all Madison Avenue's skills, corporations don't yet quite do as well for the people, and probably won't until it is as easy for them to look into the distant future as it is for them to look at the next quarter's bottom line.

8. There clearly are limits to growth. Some new growth must go on, of course. And some old growth must make way. *The Global 2000 Report* (see below) makes this limit seem frighteningly imminent. In its hundreds of pages it documents what a recent Acid Rain Conference was told: "If all the world's a stage, this must be the Gong Show."

Energy and War; Conservation and Peace

Amory Lovins has made an unequaled and much celebrated contribution toward identifying and fostering the kind of growth that will help humanity rather than endanger it. In the book, *Energy/War: Breaking the Nuclear Link,* he and his wife, Hunter, point out the hazards of the once-bright nuclear hope and, more clearly than anyone, how inevitably the peaceful atom (which we cannot afford) serves as cover for the warring atom (which life cannot afford). It is a book that cannot be ignored by anyone who cares for the Northern Hemisphere. After you read it, put your own genius to work on the most important of all issues—ending the race to blow ourselves up. There is no more critical time to think clearly than when it is hardest to do so, like now. We need clear thought like Richard Barnet's: "No nation can increase its security by lessening the security of its opponent." The great powers are doing that to each other, to all others, and to us.

Because the US has chosen to emphasize nuclear, not conventional, weapons, the temptation is to rely on nuclear threats, and such threats are increasing, in spite of the well-buttressed thesis that a "limited" nuclear war would swiftly escalate to a full nuclear exchange. That full exchange would initially and quickly cost the live of about a half billion men, women, and children. Almost no living thing would survive the protracted consequence—to the ozone barrier, for example. Damage to it would peak a year after the exchange and let ultraviolet radiation blister a person exposed forty minutes to the sun. It would preclude the growth of crops. (This projection of full-nuclear-exchange consequences was given us in a Department of State briefing urging environmentalist support of SALT II.)

FOE has sought in several ways to obviate nuclear proliferation and the final war, lest all other environmental concerns become academic. We began with our 1970 Vietnam advertisement, "Ecology and War." We have repeatedly warned about the consequences of the US compulsion to have the grossest national product of all. We have put together our *ECO* at many international conferences, including the UN Conference on Disarmament in New York. In the course of all this we found Amory Lovins and his ideas developed— in *World Energy Strategies,* in *Non-Nuclear Futures,* in

Soft Energy Paths, in *Energy/War,* and in books now in manuscript.

All these books firm up the tread on his soft energy path. They recognize that the nuclear genie is out of the bottle and out of control, but that he can be starved if the US is willing to use its strength wisely, at home and abroad. Using the soft path, the US can back away from nuclear power weapons; we can budget nonrenewable resources, and use them again and again; we can mitigate global inequity. In the process, we can use science and technology better, decentralize more and soon enough, spare the environment, make jobs, defuse inflation by making money available for social needs now given short shrift (conservation, education, health, housing, transportation) in our strange infatuation with kilowatts and killer weapons.

Aware of this new route, we can move toward acceptable, sustainable strategies that can spare the earth the thousands of new Dachaus and Hiroshimas that are otherwise too imminent. The US can pioneer in ending the export of nuclear technology to nations shakier than our own by foregoing it here. We have let the atom become our Maginot Line, and we will not correct that unforeseen error with more reactors and the MX Missile (which would put our Maginot Line on AMTRAK).

Each of us represents total success in the miraculous passing forward of the essential information of life, from its inception on earth some three and a half billion years ago. A tiny bit of each of us now alive is that old, old enough to handle our most important heritage, life, better than we do. That experience, in each of us, is what we now need as never before. Until the superpowers show restraint and back off, they hold the world hostage. The promise inherent in each newborn child is also held hostage.

Getting from Here to 2001

When you next encounter a child, remember that you are meeting a citizen of tomorrow, who, when grown, will be every bit as important as you are now. Wonder for a moment what the child's future will be. Then imagine a world—before the child is ready to vote—with these handicaps, even if nuclear war is prevented:

- Six billion people on an earth already overburdened by four billion.
- Two millon fewer species of plants and animals, freshly extinct, thanks to rapacity in our time.
- One billion children, not just today's half billion, too poorly fed owing to overpopulation to use the genius they were born with.
- Twice the chance to contract cancer, because we have poisoned the earth with a technology that raced ahead of reason.
- Too many other handicaps as well, a depressing list of them, man-caused.

These imaginings are not just fantasy. They are based on the best projections our government, after three years' hard work, could come up with, in *The Global 2000 Report to the President, July 1980.* (See the commentary on it by Anne and Paul Ehrlich in this volume.) These dire events will come to pass unless you join the effort to head these tragedies off at the pass; unless you are willing to accept fewer of today's conveniences and persuade others to do the same, so that this child can have tomorrow's necessities; unless you resolve that this child deserves a chance to know a world no less beautiful, no less livable, no less joyful than ours is; unless you say that the world must be better, with more friends of the only earth we'll ever know, and of all the children we'll never know.

If their survival matters, we need a new kind of progress. When *Progress As If Survival Mattered* appeared in 1977, a few months into the Carter years, we were gratified at the response, especially from *Library Journal:* "As guidebook for citizen action . . . as an all-around introduction to the ills and successes of our planet, it should find its way into the homes of almost anyone who reads more than the Sunday comics." The book went through four printings; became a staple in environmental education programs; got into the hands of hundreds of Members of Congress, Senators, newspaper editors, and activists; and, we hope, showed more than a few people that being an environmentalist meant having plans to make life better now and in the future. We hoped that other countries would adapt the plans to their own needs.

Since then the US has had three further years of Jimmy Carter as President, the election of Ronald Reagan, and almost a year of his presidency; the rise of the New Right, the Moral Majority, and Roth-Kemp economics; Mr. Reagan's appointment of James Watt to the most important environmental office in the world, and a huge outpouring of public protest over that choice. The exploiters' lawyer has been named, as Secretary of the Interior, to guard our nation's parks, wilderness, wildlife, public lands, and dwindling and precious minerals, oil, coal, and soil from these same exploiters. The Strength-through-Exhaustion Department is now administered by people who would seem to require that resources be exhausted before the Second Coming.

The Carter years brought much good. Best of all was the unprecedented achievement in Alaska. They also brought us *The Global 2000 Report,* the projections in which make a new edition of *Progress* vital to environmentalism in the Reagan years. The last few years have brought new diversity to the environmental movement. Professional environmental skills were vigorously sought out by the Carter administration, and influenced early decisions in the State Department, Justice, Interior, Agriculture, the Environmental Protection Agency, and congressional-committee decisions as well. This influence unfortunately was badly eroded as the Carter administration succumbed to the old pressures and went sadly wrong on Tellico Dam, energy policy, Presidential Directive 59 (which added to the insecurity of the super/powers), and the MX-Missile (which promises to do the same).

In this new edition, we have written new chapters, thoroughly revised others, added new readings not only from classic literature, but also from recent writing (in which the Worldwatch Institute's contributions have been outstanding).

Here, then, is *Progress* for the the Reagan years, to help you get to 1984. While his predecessor was in office, people and organizations interested in conservation had access—a favorite word—to the White House, if not necessarily having power there. People left our staff and that of organizations like ours to work in government. Many of them have now been fired by the Reagan administration, and it is the people who are intent on undoing environmental progress who have the access now. As Jeffrey Knight wrote in *The New Environmental Handbook* (FOE, 1980), now is the time for good environmentalists to come to the aid of the earth by going back to the grassroots, renewing their spirit and reestablishing their leadership through their love for particular places. People who do not find the Grand Canyon "tedious," as Mr. Watt did, can campaign again, refreshed, to give earth a chance. Opportunity still knocks. After all, only ten per cent of all Americans voted for Ronald Reagan (the other half of his votes, according to the *New York Times-CBS* poll of voters as they left the booths, were votes against Jimmy Carter). Ten per cent does not constitute a mandate for retreat to the nineteenth century.

The ill wind of the Reagan administration's attack on public welfare, arms limitation, landscape, and resources has blown some good. People all over the country—all over the world—are acutely aware of what these plans mean for themselves and their communities. Their favorite beach may be despoiled with spilled crude, the park they have worked twenty years to get established may be sold off, the open field where their children play may be covered with new sprawl, or a new factory, or a military dump. Their clean air may be traded off for Detroit's convenience, their protection from hazardous wastes traded off for chemical-industry profits, their prospects of peace for nuclear threats.

People are outraged. At this writing conservationists have gathered a million signatures asking for Mr. Watt's resignation and a reconsideration of the Reagan energy and environmental policies. New groups are forming to protest the arms buildup by the superpowers, the ultimate environmental threat. People are joining environmental groups at the rate they did in the late 1960s and early 1970s; the Sierra Club has gone above 223,000 and National Audubon above 450,000. FOE is growing too, and has been augmented by a FOEPAC, a political-action committee to serve its members better in elections to come. With a government so unsympathetic to solving or even considering their needs, people are mobilizing themselves, organizing, building coalitions, joining organizations like ours to fight for their rights, their needs, and their visions for the future. It is up to our allies and FOE to help lead these people, to give point to their alienation and voice to their needs. And we intend to to it.

An old land ethic needs to be rediscovered. Its base is our knowing that we are but brief tenants. We are privileged to enjoy the good things that were left here by predecessors who treated the land as if they trusted us to love it. Those we leave it to are owed the same opportunity: an America as beautiful as ours. A whole world as beautiful.

We can be grateful for the variety of ways that ingenious people have created to save places for themselves and their descendants—special places where what counts is the miraculous interplay of the wild living things that were there, have been spared, and are still there. In humanity's earliest days, such places were safe because people did not yet have the tools to spoil them. Later, when the tools had arrived, places were saved by taboo, or set aside for worship, for kings to hunt in, or for people to be buried in. Some places, of course, were spared by their remoteness or by their hazards, real or imagined. Finally, places were saved by a means that must now be applied with new dedication: the will to share the earth with living things other than ourselves. And shared, too, by the largest human population of all—the people who have yet to arrive on the planet, but whose genes are here now, in our custody.

—DAVID R. BROWER, *Founder*
Friends of the Earth
August 14, 1981

Foreword to the First Edition

*In memory of E. F. Schumacher,
Who showed so much of the way.*

WHAT KIND OF COUNTRY do you want? What kind of world? What kind of neighborhood on a small planet? If you have asked yourself such questions, we think you will like this book. If you haven't, we think you need it.

The kind of country and world a growing number of people want—and indeed, the kind we all require for sheer survival—will be less populous, more decentralized, less industrial, more agrarian. Our anxiously acquisitive consumer society will give way to a more serenely thrifty conserver society, one which relies most on renewable resources and least on the irreplaceables. Recyling will be taken for granted and planned obsolescence won't. Nuclear proliferation will be viewed in retrospect as a form of temporary insanity. We will stride confidently and lightly along the soft solar energy path so ably scouted out by physicist Amory Lovins. Restless mobility will diminish; people will put down roots and recapture a sense of community. Full employment will be the norm in a sustainable, skill-intensive economy, and indoor pollution where we work, now fifty times higher than outdoors, will no longer be tolerated. Medicine's role in curing disese will shrink as preventive medicine grows and leaves less and less disease to be cured. Corporations will no longer demand the right to dispense cancer to you. People will turn on TV less and turn on their own senses more, and be better informed of, by, and for the natural world that made them. Parks and wilderness areas will be recognized as legal "persons," as corporations and ships already are, to ensure their permanent and productive survival. Science (and applied science, or technology) will pay more than lip service to elegant solutions; that is, solutions that achieve desired results with the utmost economy of means. Growthmania will yield to the realization that physical growth is wholesome only during immaturity, and that to continue such growth beyond that point leads to malignancy or other grim devices that keep the planet from being suffocated

with a surfeit. The earth will not swarm with life, but be graced with it.

Whatever kind of country and world people decide they want, the next question is, How can they get it? Probably by gaining a new understanding of politics. Politics is democracy's way of handling public business. There is no other. We won't get the kind of country in the kind of world we want unless people take part in the public's business. Unless they embrace politics and people in politics.

Embrace politicians? Yes. Why not? Theirs is, in essence, an honorable calling. When we treat it accordingly, we will deserve politicians who honor their having been called. There is public business to be done. We need to help the men and women who have chosen to undertake it.

Thoreau asked a transcendent question: What is the use of a house if you haven't got a tolerable planet to put it on? A growing number of people see that the planet is less and less tolerable because its beauty—and let 'beauty' epitomize all the things that make an environment excellent and the earth a rewarding place to live upon—is being lost more and more rapidly.

Suppose that one of this growing number of politicians is a presidential candidate and wished to make excellence of environmental quality *the* campaign issue. What kind of platform would such a candidate choose to run on? Or suppose a new political party arose, dedicated, as Friends of the Earth is, to natural law and order. Suppose that party dedicated itself to preserving, restoring, and equitably using the earth and its resources, mineral and living. And suppose it knew that if 'progress' continued to depend upon wiping out irreplaceable resources, such progress could not last long. Imagine, then, a party dedicating itself to timely rethinking and corrective action. What would the platform be like?

Questions like these occurred to us in 1970 and we tried our hand at a voter's guide for environmental protection. It was pretty good. But just about then environmental books became banalized. Early in 1976 we asked ourselves more questions, better ones. We hoped at first to produce an instant book on the environmental issues of the day, a "platform book," and to challenge candidates in that election to state publicly which of our planks they could stand on and which they feared they would fall between. It is still an appealing idea. It might make the earth's health more of an issue. Since the natural laws upon which environmentalism is based can only be perceived, and can never be amended, a book perceiving those laws well should have lasting value. It could also serve as a yardstick against which to measure the environmental literacy and commitment of a candidate, a party, ourself, and yourself as understanding evolved.

Having determined to proceed, we asked who should write what. We began with what. A few FOE staff members selected handfuls of topics. Which brought us to who. Which who? Outside experts, whose knowledge was already proved but whose likelihood of meeting deadlines wasn't, and whose broad philosophy might prove to be temporarily tangential? Or insiders, who share their philosophy with us, are familiar with our deadlines, and who had proved themselves able to dig hard in the fact mines? It is risky to assume that knowledge is acquired more easily than philosophy. We took the risk, and drew upon the talents of FOE officers, members, staff, and advisory counselors. Some of them are recognized authorities in the fields they write about. All care, and all know how to do their homework.

We recommended a basic chapter outline and suggested that the authors concentrate on what environmentalists believe rather than why. Consequently some parts may read a little the way tablets brought down from a mountain do, but lack divine authentication. We added counterpoint—pertinent material from other sources which, by itself, would make an environmental anthology of lasting value.

The most important challenge to each author was the outlining of feasible, unfrightening, tempting steps toward a sensible goal. It was tough. All environmentalists, it goes without saying, are opposed to evil and in favor of good. If a dam is evil they oppose it. That is a positive action from a river's point of view. But no one should underestimate the difficulty of putting together an appealing series of positive actions. It is easy to trip someone, or to veto, or just to carp and cry. It is hard to get anyone to take a series of steps in a direction you think is right. Most of the public must understand why, how, and when before the whole society will let a politician move to spare its environment and save itself.

It is so hard that the people who put such a series of steps together and stick with them are candidates for

hero and should be included in the sequel to John F. Kennedy's book, *Profiles in Courage.* The greater the number of needed causes you espouse, the greater the chance of displeasing somebody. Cheap shots are easy. You can positively oppose cancer, heart disease, multiple sclerosis, inflation, unemployment, forest fires, and pneumonoultramicroscopicsilicovolcanokoniosis and never lose a vote. But if you oppose exponential economic growth, however lethal it is, you are not liked by the Conventional Widsom set. If you take a position for or against abortion or gun control, you divide your constituency and may conquer yourself.

Conservation organizations, like candidates, have political needs to face. We are aware of the risk to FOE as we try to delineate sound environmental views of the may aspects of society we discuss here. It is perilous to take that risk but more perilous not to. We will pin our faith on your intelligence as a lay citizen who cares. Though you may not share our view in all aspects, we ask you to remember that consensus can be carried too far. It can produce not only a dull world, but also an endangered one. Opinions need to differ. As long as they do, you will know people are alive, awake, and still in honest search of truth. And you will remain young in the important sense—still able to listen, ready to change your mind, and willing to avoid being the Practical Man whom Disraeli worried about, who could be counted upon to perpetuate the errors of his ancestors.

Let us propose a grading system. If you agree with, say, seventy-five per cent of what we propose, we'll give you a passing grade, and you can give us one. That's close enough, and qualifies you and us for working together. We probably should.

We freely concede, and think you will, that getting a world to change course will require powerful motivating forces, and we hope to discern them in time. As Dr. Daniel B. Luten (chemist, lecturer on resources, and a FOE director) has said from time to time: Too many people would rather die than change their habits. Almost all of them think the society exists to serve its economy. Too many of them mistake growth for progress. Almost no one understands the extraordinary demands as we now pass from an empty earth to a full one. We have been slow, as we look at the rising population, to ask how dense people can be. We know the planet is lone and finite and that finite things have limits. But we have preferred denying them to facing them. Or we have looked for an escape to some greener colony in space.

People who sense the humor in Dr. Luten's way of putting the vital questions can be cheered. For surely the dawn of new perceptions is breaking. We see that there are better things to do than polarize ourselves. We do not get anywhere by trading epithets, doomsayer versus doommaker, or charging each other with degrees of elitism. The fatal addictions, whether on one's home lot or one's hemisphere, can be diverted with patience and love, and probably no other way. Before the child in us will give up the lethal toys forged by mindless growth, that child must be offered something else, attractive as well as beneficial.

Our ultimate goal herein is to find an alternative to the most lethal of the Great Powers' toys and to what led the powers to fashion it—to find that alternative in time. Nuclear proliferation is that deadly toy. Nobody wants it. No leading power has lessened the pressure to use. it. The Stockholm International Peace Research Institute has predicted that within nine years thirty-five nations will have the capability of making nuclear weapons and nuclear war will be inevitable. But not if humanity says no.

No, for example, to the export of nuclear reactors, which the United States is encouraging to help a dying industry, perpetuate a myth, and improve a negative balance of payments. This is tantamount to the export of nuclear weapons capability, as Indira Gandhi quickly proved. (And so, experts and *Time* magazine think, could Israel.) Adding new refinements to the ways nuclear weapons kill (our neutron bomb and Russia's inevitable answer to it), devising multilateral alliances that tip an uneasy balance and increase the desperation of anxious rivals, eases no fateful tensions. Pursuing with a Strangelove gleam a radioactive technology that demonstrates its uncontrollability in ever more disconcerting ways helps no one relax. A new danger develops. The worsening prospect produces a fibrillation of will, a sense of futility or of brave acceptance. People who might have sought a way to safety turn back instead. Hope yields to despair. As C. P. Snow admonishes, despair is a sin.

The United States, and we think only the United States, can lead the world back from the nuclear brink to which we led it, with the best of intentions, in the first place. The U.S. can do so, however, only if we step back ourselves and thus persuade other peoples we are to be believed. At this writing we are not stepping back, but rushing forward again to get the business before someone else does.

Nobody needs that business, and those who think they do ought to try to learn a different trade. People can bring about great changes once they construe the difficult problem to be a challenging opportunity. As an example of such public achievement, consider the National Environmental Policy Act (NEPA). It moved the United States from an old danger to a new safety. One of Mr. Nixon's good deeds was to sign the act and name Russell Train to oversee it as the first chairman of the Council on Environmental Quality. NEPA became our finest export.

Environmental victories do not, however, stay won by themselves. They require much vigilance and renewed persuasion. The NEPA victory made many enterprising businessmen so uneasy that they set about trying to weaken it without realizing how important it will be to them in the long run if it is kept strong. The first weakening came when Congress, urged on by the oil companies, left NEPA bleeding after the Alaska pipeline controversy, in which Spiro Agnew broke the tie vote in the Senate the wrong way. NEPA requires strengthening if the environment is to remain whole and productive—a requirement as real for corporations as it is for people. It will pay all segments of society well to look searchingly at the social and environmental consequences of a new proposal to alter a piece of the earth. They should also, as NEPA provides, look as hard at the consequences of a fair range of alternatives designed to serve the broad interest instead of the narrow one.

One alternative, rarely considered, can be "Thanks a lot but forget it," coupled with a list of such benefits as would derive from letting things alone—a list that can sometimes be amazingly long. Another alternative is to consider the advantages of exploiting a given resource later on, or more slowly. Alaska's oil, for instance, could be budgeted to last for the next two or three centuries instead of the next two or three decades. A nation that took from the *Mayflower* until now to get where it is should not rule out, by wiping out, the resources that could get it through another three and a half centuries. Our consideration could well extend to a far-distant future and spare our heirs the need to isolate the nuclear radioactivity generated for our convenience. If Iodine 129 had been so isolated 300 million years ago at the bottom of the Redwall Limestone formation in the Grand Canyon, it would be safe about now to let it touch living things whose genes should be left intact. It would be fair to do for our genes what our genes have done for us. That way we would not tinker with them. We would revere the miracle in them instead.

Such reverence could let us learn from history, especially from recent, telling history in Alaska. There is a poignant moral in that history, as we in FOE, having been involved in it since we began, can testify. Sadly, we predicted present consequences all to well in our books, *Earth and the Great Weather: The Brooks Range* (1971) and *Cry Crisis! Rehearsal in Alaska* 1974). It is useful to remember the things lost to Alaskans and to all others because, while too many citizens were preoccupied, Congress relaxed its own judgment and ruled out the court's opportunity to check the administrators. This brought a host of evils upon us. Alaska's last remaining wilderness can belong to all the generations we can conceive of—people who will need wildness in their civilization. It has been split into lesser pieces. Its greatness cannot now be put back together by any number of generations. Its wildness pours out through the wounds, and the skin shrinks back. Your children may not miss what is gone. Like a fully unraveled sweater, what is gone leaves no trace. We cannot measure our own success proudly if it consists of a growing number of things our children will never be allowed to miss.

The unraveling of the earth's heritage of resources can be stopped, we think, by the attitudes and steps our contributors espouse here. People do not have to go on being profligate with resources that are not to be renewed. We can drop out of the lead in the race to see who can make the earth less livable fastest. We would then have a chance to persuade Russia and Japan, or other contenders, to think the old race is not worth the trouble.

Ours was quite a binge. We were not alone in it. The earth's people can still escape the tensions that continuation of the binge will intensify, tensions that threaten the survival of all we or anyone else care about most. We cannot escape by forging on, resolutely and regardless, driven by the unmitigated inertia of outworn habits, until we have forced ourselves over the brink in the "giant step for mankind" no one needs. When you have reached the edge of an abyss, Alwyn Rees said in Wales, the only progressive move you can make is to step backward. Or turn around, and step forward. Progress, if survival matters, can then become a process that lets people find more joy at less cost to their children and to the earth.

We might even aim at something better than mere survival. As Ivan Illich observes, survival can take place in jail. We can instead seek the steps toward, and

rewards of, applying conservation conscience to many fields of human activity. There is still an opportunity to treat the earth as if we knew we ought to do this, and we have told ourselves that this book will help discover how. So, take it from here, please. Tell us about the gaps that you would like see us try to fill in the next edition.

What kind of country do you want? What kind of world? More of the old Preempt-the-Resources Game? Or one fulfilling the hope Adlai Stevenson crystallized in Geneva, July 1965, in his last speech:

We travel together, passengers in a little spaceship,
dependent upon its vulnerable reserves of air and soil;
all committed for our safety to its security and peace;
preserved from annihilation only by the care, the work
and, I will say, the love we give our fragile craft.
We cannot maintain it half fortunate, half miserable,
half confident, half despairing, half slave
to the ancient enemies of man, half free
in a liberation of resources undreamed of unitl this day.
No craft, no crew can travel safely
with such vast contradictions.
On their resolution depends the survival of us all.

The resources that can be liberated without being exhausted are human spirit and love. They can bring the resolution. You can effect the decision. You have the gift. You can pass it on.

—DAVID R. BROWER, *President*
Friends of the Earth
Berkeley, California, September 4, 1977

Toward a Better Global 2000

ANNE and PAUL EHRLICH
and JOHN HOLDREN

THE GRAVE PROBLEMS highlighted by the *Global 2000 Report* arise from the rapid growth of population and affluence and the consequent degradation of the environment and intensification of competition for resources. We have jointly and separately been teaching, talking, and writing about them for over a dozen years, as have a good many other people. Refining the government's ability to make long-term, integrated projections of global trends should now be a top priority, along with establishing policy and directions to address specifically the problems of population, resources, and the environment.

The goal must be to anticipate problems, to alleviate or avert them *before* they become unmanageable. *Global 2000* clearly showed, for instance, how easy it would be to apply a solution to a problem that would create new problems or worsen existing ones. Short-term solutions often become long-term disasters. A splendid example is the rise in wheat harvests that have been obtained in the Great Plains by irrigating from the underlying aquifer—which in some areas (western Kansas) is already showing signs of exhaustion. Another is abolition of the soil bank to increase our harvest of grains. The grain harvest has marginally increased, and the volume of soil being washed into the oceans has risen dramatically. The CEQ has been a leader in pointing out such things.

Obviously, the government needs to develop better liaison among the various agencies. CEQ could perform part of this function. Connection to the rest of the world must be built into each of them. Agriculture must be constantly aware of energy and resource constraints and trends and of environmental feedbacks, climate changes, and even what is happening in related subsectors (remember the fisheries projections). DOE must be much more aware of environmental consequences of energy use, resource constraints (water, for instance), and conflicts with other essential activities (such as agriculture). Perhaps a continuing series of interagency seminars or retreats could be established to expose decision makers to people inside and outside of government who specialize in keeping track of the big picture.

Beyond this, a fairly massive dose of public education seems in order, both inside and outside the government. The lessons of *Global 2000* should be part of school curriculums, background of many news reports, and taken acount of in myriad private business and governmental actions. News media editors and reporters, corporation presidents, as well as agency heads, governors, and congress-people, need to sit down and study the *Global 2000 Technical Volume*. We hope copies of both Volumes I and II were sent to them, to United Nations representatives and agencies, and to national heads of state around the world.

Possibly a world conference on the human predicament would eventually emerge from that. If it did, it would be of use only if the participants, including the United States, were prepared to face squarely and deal with the thorny issues of our times: the distribution of wealth and intergenerational equity. Secretary Muskie's statement about the 800 million people who will not be getting enough to eat in 2000 was appropriate and compassionate. But what about the 450 million (at least) who are underfed today? Our society—and others—must understand what it is doing now that deepens the predicament rather than eases it. That course, if continued, will produce a future at least as dismal as that projected in *Global 2000* and an even grimmer future beyond that. Society must also discover the things it is doing right and try to do more of them.

Somehow the concept of a sustainable world must take root, replacing the passion for growth that has dominated the industrial age. Humanity has expanded and occupied this planet so fully that we are destroying other life-forms at an unprecedented rate and, in the process, are degrading our own life-support systems. And the human population seems committed at least to doubling in size once more—

unless population is brought down by famine, plague, war, or wisdom. The present system is in no way sustainable for more than a few decades—as *Global 2000* made clear.

We could offer lists of priorities and criteria for choices for various branches of the government, from foreign aid projects to agricultural research to energy development. The basic ideas are simple. Consider what will benefit the most people, especially those most in need, and harm the fewest, over the long term. Consider the benefits and costs in the broadest sense. End population growth and start a slow decline. (The U.S. still has no explicit population policy!) Put the agricultural system on a sustainable, ecologically sound basis. (Let agriculture have much more contact with its parent science, biology). Do much more to protect environments and, especially, recognize relatively undisturbed natural ecosystems for what they are—precious resources. Develop a sustainable system for managing resources and energy to replace the present wasteful, growth-centered system. These should be among the highest domestic and foreign-aid priorities of the United States.

A few issues should have particular attention from the government in the near future. One is the accelerating rate of extinction of species worldwide, a problem that *Global 2000* discussed. (See also *Extinction: The Causes and Consequences of the Disappearance of Species* [Ehrlich and Ehrlich, Random House, 1981.]. The most critical aspect of halting the ongoing erosion of biological diversity is protecting habitat—preserving sufficiently large natural areas to insure the survival of other species. This must be done not only within the United States, but everywhere on the planet, most particularly in the tropics, where the richest store of biological diversity exists. *The World Strategy for Conservation* [International Union for the Conservation of Nature, 1981], provides a blueprint. The United States should implement the strategy at home and do everything it can to encourage its adoption elsewhere.

Another serious problem is the toxic-substances issue, one that has for too long been pushed under the rug. The government is now at last takng some action, but in many places it is too late—the damage has been done, as in groundwater contamination. Prevention of future contamination is possible if action is undertaken promptly. An essential prerequisite is an international registry of toxic substances. No adequate registry now exists because industry—to its shame—has until now opposed its establishment.

An area that abounds in opportunities for government action is that of energy and resources. It is agreed that we need to reduce as soon and as much as possible our dependence on oil imports for many compelling reasons. Yet far too little has been done—and mostly too late. A simple measure that would greatly help would be to require U.S. produced and marketed automoblies to meet vastly improved fuel-economy standards by 1990. The benefits to the U.S. economy and world stability in general would far outweigh the inconvenience to the auto industry—and the government would be justified in helping the industry if necessary (but *not* by being lenient on the standards!).

The resultant reduction in oil imports would conserve that resource, holding down the price for everyone and benefiting developing countries by keeping oil affordable for them. It would enormously relieve our balance-of-payments deficit, which at present generates pressure to export weapons and food. The destabilizing effects of weapons export are obvious. Pressure to export food puts an unhealthy drain on our agricultural system and creates dependence on our exported food in other countries that is also potentially destabilizing. Finally, reduced gasoline consumption would have a salutory effect on domestic and global pollution problems, including two of the most difficult ones detailed in *Global 2000*—acid rain and the carbon dioxide buildup in the atmosphere.

These are only a few of the possible changes in policy that would have desirable results. Obviously, there are many others that would emerge from a reorientation of goals toward a sustainable world system. There is no time to waste. Our generation will create, by default or by design, the world our grandchildren will live in. Default would leave them a wasteland; design, a planet that will sustain them and their descendants. To achieve that design is an awesome burden but it is also a great opportunity.

Thirty Years of Conservation
An Address to The Conservation Foundation

RUSSELL E. TRAIN

IT GIVES ME TREMENDOUS pleasure to participate in this occasion celebrating the thirtieth anniversary of The Conservation Foundation. That these have been 30 years of environmental ferment, few would doubt. I would also maintain that they have been years of extraordinary environmental accomplishment, nationally and internationally.

Looking back over the environmental/conservation explosion of the past few years, one can truly say that The Conservation Foundation was "present at the creation." It was in 1948 that Fairfield Osborn published *Our Plundered Planet*, a major contribution to public awareness of the long-term threat to human existence posed by the abuse of the natural resources of the earth, particulary of the land. Osborn, who founded The Conservation Foundation in that same year, was an articulate and passionate spokesman for the principle that man is part of nature and that human well-being is inextricably interwoven with the health of the soil, the water, the air, and the processes that bind them together, as well as with the plant and animal life associated with them.

It was also in 1948 that Aldo Leopold died, leaving a manuscript that was edited and published a year later as *A Sand County Almanac*. In this beautiful book, Leopold spoke of the need for a new conservation ethic:

"We abuse land because we regard it as a commodity belonging to us. When we see land as a community to which we belong, we may begin to use it with love and respect. There is no other way for land to survive the impact of mechanized man, nor for us to reap from it the aesthetic harvest it is capable, under science, of contributing to culture. That land is a community is the basic concept of ecology, but that land is to be loved and respected is an extension of ethics."

Over the next few years, The Conservation Founda-

tion was at the intellectual center of rising public concern over human population growth and the environmental impact of pesticides. Fairfield Osborn published *The Limits of the Earth* in 1954. Rachel Carson's *Silent Spring*, published in 1962, was greatly influenced by the Foundation's work on pesticides. From its beginning, CF placed strong emphasis on conservation education, particularly through the introduction of ecological principles into the standard curriculum. Indeed, throughout all of these years, The Conservation Foundation, more than any other institution, articulated and gave meaning to the concept of "ecology." Although often misunderstood and misapplied, this concept was, of course, central to the environmental revolution of the seventies.

It is a temptation to continue to dwell on the history of CF and the people who gave it its early strength and character. One thinks particularly, in addition to Osborn, of Sam Ordway, George Brewer, Bill Vogt, and Frank Fraser Darling, among many others. And one thinks also of those whose generosity and sensitivity to environmental needs combined to provide the resources necessary to support the Foundation's work in those early years, especially Laurance Rockefeller and Paul Mellon (sometimes referred to as Fair's "right and left bowers"), and the Scaife family.

Of course, I have not been asked to give a history of The Conservation Foundation, but rather to review the course of the conservation effort as a whole over the past 30 years. In responding to such an assignment, though, a review of some CF history is inevitable, for its development has paralleled and reflected in many ways the evolution of the environmental movement—the building of knowledge in critical areas, the growth of public awareness, and the translation of these into policy and action in both the public and private sectors.

The sense of frustration and even despair that characterizes much of the conservation/environment dialogue of the fifties and early sixties can be attributed to the lack of action and the inadequacy of the governmental response to what many felt was the most critical, long-term problem facing mankind. In the spring of 1965, CF held its Conference on the Future Environments of North America, bringing together an extraordinary group of ecologists and social scientists who spoke to the urgent need for building environmental values into decision making. When I joined the Foundation later that year, it was this same theme that gave direction to our entire program—particularly through demonstrations that environmentally sound land-use planning and decisions can make economic sense as well. One can agree with Leopold that we need an ethic that sees the land not just as a commodity, but as part of a community to which we ourselves also belong. However, until that ethic is more fully developed than it is at present, it will continue to be important to demonstrate the compatibility of environmental and economic concerns. One is even led to wonder whether an ethic reinforced by economic self-interest might not constitute the ultimate unconquerable force.

Perhaps under the influence of almost 20 years of experience in government, shortly after becoming president of CF, I proposed the creation of a body of ecological advisors in the White House—a proposal less significant for its content than for the indication it gives of a new emphasis on institution-building. Subsequently, CF played a major role in the development of legislative proposals which culminated in enactment of the National Environmental Policy Act in late 1969, establishing the Council on Environmental Quality, and requiring environmental impact analysis by federal agencies.

I doubt very much that there has ever been such an outpouring of new legislation on any one subject as that enacted during the seventies to deal with environmental problems. The National Environmental Policy Act, the Clean Air Act, the Federal Water Pollution Control Act amendments of 1972, legislation to regulate pesticides, the Noise Control Act, solid waste management and resource recovery legislation, the Endangered Species Act, the Toxic Substances Control Act, and legislation to regulate surface mining, among others, followed in rapid succession, starting in 1970. The one major casualty among all the environmental initiatives of those years was the proposed National Land Use Policy Act.

This legislative torrent was remarkable not only for its volume. Through the environmental impact statement process, profound changes were brought about in the way federal agencies make decisions. Even more significant changes were introduced into the nation's economy through a vast array of new regulatory requirements designed to internalize the environmental costs of production—costs which heretofore had largely been passed on to society as a whole through polluted air and water, degraded landscapes, human health effects, and adverse impacts on plant and animal life.

It is quite certain that at the time of original legislative consideration, the full implications of this regulatory complex for American society were seldom recognized by the Congress, business, or many others for that matter. One thinks, for example, of the Clean Air Act and its far-ranging implications for land-use decisions, particularly the siting of new industrial facilities. Likewise, the full range of the economic costs of compliance was not always appreciated, and projections of those costs tended to be imperfect. Over time, and as actual implementation has proceeded, analysis of these economic impacts has steadily improved, and increasing attention has focused on the relative values of the costs imposed and the benefits to be secured. Certain of the statutes that have been in place for some time, such as the Clean Air Act and the Water Pollution Act, have already gone through a process of legislative modification based on experience to date, although the basic structure of these acts has remained undisturbed. Other statutes, such as the Toxic Substances Control Act, are only now moving into the implementation phase.

My experience as an ex-administrator of many of these programs confirms that by far the most difficult areas in which to apply environmental regulation effectively are those where the regulation in question directly affects the individual citizen. Thus, transportation control plans under the Clean Air Act, which modestly interfered with America's driving habits in a few urban areas, and pesticide regulation and water quality rules, which impacted on the farming practices of individual farmers (either in fact or in rumor), tended to cause major political uproars. One may speculate from this phenomenon that Americans are all for cleaning up pullution as long as someone else does the cleaning up, although I think this is an oversimplification. As good an explanation as any probably lies in the plain cussedness of human nature.

More to the point for our purposes here is the fact that regulators often tend to be insensitive to the response of the regulated. A government agency may possess all the statutory and other legal authority in the world to impose a particular regulatory requirement but, if it lacks the essential base of public understanding and support, it will never succeed in making the regulation truly effective. Significantly, in the particular examples I have mentioned, the Congress was quick to react by cutting down EPA's regulatory authority.

A comparable case, and one with a similar outcome, involved so-called "indirect sources" of pollution, such as shopping centers and other large public facilities which could be expected to cause unhealthy concentrations of auto emissions. EPA's attempt to regulate the siting of such facilities mandated by the Clean Air Act and the courts, was a predictable disaster, as two of the most cherished rights of Americans—the right to use and develop land and the right to use one's automobile—were threatened. Such experiences underline the vital importance for a democratic society of the broadest possible public consultation in all stages of regulatory development. Much grief could have been avoided in the environmental field if this lesson had been learned sooner.

At the same time we were putting these various statutory mechanisms into place, we were also forming new institutions and new procedures in government for environmental management. As I have mentioned, the National Environmental Policy Act established the environmental impact analysis process which I believe, with all of its imperfections, has brought about significant improvements in government decision making. Given the adversarial proclivities of our society, it has also given rise to considerable litigation and has often been the focal point of conflict between environmental and other interests. Much of this has been desirable and necessary to the implementation of NEPA. At the same time, though, environmentalists, industry, labor, and government alike are increasingly recognizing that nonadversarial approaches to the resolution of environmental issues, such as the use of mediation techniques, should receive increased attention. Environmental impact analysis necessarily must play a central role in such approaches.

The Council on Environmental Quality, also established by NEPA, was largely responsible for putting together the major legislative initiatives that I have mentioned. Over time, as the tidal wave of environmental legislation subsided and emphasis shifted from legislation to implementation, the role of CEQ has tended to diminish. The recent action moving the administration of the environmental impact statement process from CEQ to EPA, while leaving policy direction of the EIS process in CEQ, has further weakened the latter's role. At a time when major issues of government are inherently complex—typically involving interrelationships that cut across many functions and agencies—we badly need integrating mechanisms that can promote comprehensive approaches to problem solving. The EIS and CEQ represent exactly such mechanisms. Given adequate staffing and funding and the necessary backing from the President, CEQ could provide an effective means for helping to balance energy and environmental needs, improving the management of water resources, coordinatng environmental health administration, and promoting the coordination of land-use policies, among other possibilities. At its present level of support, CEQ is largely unable to do any of these.

Toward the close of 1970, the Environmental Protection Agency was established by reorganization plan as an independent agency in the Executive Branch, bringing together the research, standard-setting, and enforcement functions of the various pollution-control authorities of the federal government. At the same time, a unified National Oceanic and Atmospheric Agency was established in the Department of Commerce, which has always struck me as a somewhat incongruous home.

Today, we hear that a new Department of Natural Resources built on Interior, and possibly including NOAA, may be proposed. While I would want to see the specifics of such a plan, I have no objection in principle to it so long as EPA remains an independent agency. Alternatively, consideration might be given to merging essential elements of NOAA with EPA to form a Department of the Environment.

At this point, I must confess to some cynicism about government reorganizations that lead to larger and larger conglomerates in the supposed interest of cutting down the number of agencies and simplifying government. Overall, I suspect that the end result is a more monolithic government which is less responsive to the needs and concerns of the public. At the risk of speaking heresy, I would suggest that more, rather than fewer, agencies, with relatively sharply defined functions—such as EPA— might well be the approach which best serves the public interest, utilizing mechanisms—such as CEQ—to promote interagency coordination.

The U.S. initiatives in establishing CEQ and EPA were followed by a wide variety of similar actions by foreign governments. Moreover, as the pace of international cooperation in environmental matters stepped up in the early seventies, nations found it necessary or convenient to establish focal points within their governmental structures which could provide an effective response to such efforts.

The United States quickly assumed a position of world leaderhsip in promoting environmental protection among nations, bilaterally and multilaterally. It was instrumental in developing the Great Lakes Water Quality Agreement with Canada, the U.N. Environment Programme at Nairobi, the Ocean Dumping Convention, the Convention for the Prevention of Pollution by Ships, the World Heritage Trust Convention, and the Convention on International Trade in Endangered Species; bilateral agreements with the USSR, the Federal Republic of Germany, Japan, Poland, and others; as well as on-going involvement with such multilateral organizations as OECD, FAO, WHO, UNEP, NATO, and so forth. Continuing negotiations for a Law of the Sea Convention have significant implications for the marine environment. Recent initiatives would provide an international framework for the protection of the living resources of Antarctica.

Current discussions are also exploring the possibility of strengthening the international machinery for the protection of whales. This is badly needed. You will recall that in 1972, at the Stockholm Conference on the Human Environment, the United States proposed a 10-year moratorium on *all* whaling. The U.S. proposal was defeated in the International Whaling Commission. The rationale for the moratorium had been the inadequacy of scientific data about whale populations upon which scientifically justified management decisions could be based. Since there has been little improvement in the data, the United States should continue to press for a moratorium on all whaling.

Of course, any recital of major environmental developments tends to miss some of the particular events and issues which gave the last 10 years so much of their environmental flavor—the Santa Barbara oil spill, Earth Day, the SST, the Alaskan pipeline, DDT, the Everglades jetport, Kepone, auto emissions and smog, offshore oil and gas development, the nuclear debate, and many, many more.

It seems to me that the accomplishments over the 30-year span have been extraordinary. We have seen the growth of a high level of public awareness of environmental problems, and the development of a growing body of scientific knowledge about those problems. These have been accompanied by the establishment of strong new institutions for environmental

management and the enactment of a broad array of environmental protection statutes. Much of this pattern has been repeated on other nations around the world, although that picture is mixed. In the U.S., total environmental expenditures are estimated at about $40 billion annually, and are still rising. About half that total represents spending by business. In these 30 years, citizen environmental organizations have grown in numbers and effectiveness, particularly in the United States. Especially noteworthy has been the rapid growth of the public-interest law firms, which have had a major influence on public policy and administration.

Make no mistake about it: we have made significant improvements in the quality of our air and water and in other major environmental areas in recent years. We should note with pride that we have made enormous progess in a very brief time. As our attention is seized by the newer problems, such as toxic chemicals, we tend to overlook these impressive achievements. It would be instructive if we could have a momentary glimpse (and smell!) of our environment—given current levels of development—if tough new environmental requirements had not been adopted in the early seventies. I suspect that the comparison would be quite horrendous. All in all, in the field of environmental quality, we have demonstrated as a society a rather remarkable capacity to bring about basic change in an orderly, participatory fashion. It is clear, of course, that with all the progress made to date, many difficult problems remain. The need for proper land-use policies is high among these. The need for far more effective energy conservation measures, as well as the need to develop renewable, environmentally sound sources of energy, such as solar energy, are of critical importance. Nevertheless, I have a strong sense that the problems here in the United States are going to be manageable, given continued high levels of investment and effort, although slower economic growth will doubtless lead to slower progress on some environmental fronts. The public commitment to environmental protection remains strong. That this concern is no longer at the fever pitch of a few years ago simply reflects the fact that environmental values are now institutionalized and woven into the entire fabric of our society.

Internationally, it is important that we continue to push for comparable levels of effort among the developed countries, particularly our trade competitors. I wish more progress could be made in areas where cooperative international control is essential to solving particular problems, such as the impact of fluorocarbons on the ozone layer. Our apparent inability to achieve effective worldwide protection of whales represents another such area. And we must develop effective international mechanisms with enforcement powers to deal with matters that pose a truly global threat. For example, if current research confirms that carbon dioxide from the burning of fossil fuels, among other impacts, is raising the level of planetary temperature, with significant long-term effects on world climate and agriculture, a strong case would arise for truly international approaches to the problem. After all, the concept of sovereignty cannot deny the physical and biological unity of the earth and its biosphere.

Recent computations suggest that the rapid and accelerating destruction of tropical forests worldwide may be contributing to the buildup of atmospheric carbon dioxide at a level approximating that from the burning of fossil fuel. This leads me to say that, while I am reasonably optimistic about the environmental future in the United States and in the developed world generally, enormous problems in the developing countries are not being adequately addressed. In many of these areas, the growth of the human population, the destruciton of forest, particularly the tropical rain forest, the erosion of soils, the spread of deserts, and the elimination of plant and animal species reflect a massive and spreading biotic impoverishment of the planet which will adversely affect the quality of human life in every nation, north and south, developed and developing alike. I would single out the destruction of tropical forests as the most urgent of all these problems.

There are promising signs of a growing recognition of the long-range significance of such problems among the developing countries themselves. But the pressure to provide short-term answers to immediate human needs, always with totally inadequate resources, makes it doubtful that present destructive trends can be reversed without a major international effort enlisting international agencies, governments, and the private sector, particularly the business community. The need is urgent. The biological stability of the planet provides the ultimate security for mankind.

It was Albert Schweitzer who said, "Man has lost the capacity to foresee and forestall. He will end by destroying the earth." I am not ready yet to join in that dire prediction, but we must agree that the issue is in doubt. Borrowing Fairfield Osborn's phrase, it is clear that "all those who care about tomorrow" still have a great deal of work do to.

Part I: Where the Action Is, the Biosphere

Nearly all of Earth is inhospitable to life. Only its surface, a shallow layer of atmosphere above it, and an even shallower layer of soil below it, can support life. This is the biosphere, a moist film clinging to a small planet. All of human experience has taken place in this skin-deep life zone, and despite the potentialities of space travel, the biosphere is likely to be the only real home that we shall ever have. It takes care of all our needs; and it would be smart of us to take care of it.

NASA photograph.
The only eternal spacecraft fully able to support life, as seen by the Orbiter I unmanned spacecraft in the vicinity of the Moon.

Statement on the Beginning of the Second Environmental Decade

The White House
February 29, 1980

THOSE OF US signing this statement constitute the entire past and present membership of the Council on Environmental Quality. We have served as Chairmen and Members of the Council under three Presidents during the whole of the past decade. Each of us joins in this accounting and affirmation.

In the 1970's Americans decided to reverse generations of neglect and abuse of our natural environment. A commitment, historical in scope, was made to environmental restoration. Now, as we begin the 1980's, we must ask: what has been accomplished, and is it enough? These questions are especially important at a time when environmental concerns compete with energy and economic problems for public attention.

We have, first and foremost, enacted the laws and created the institutions to protect and enhance our environment. Before this past decade there was no National Environmental Policy Act—our nation's declaration of environmental policy. There was no national system for air quality management—the great accomplishment of the Clean Air Act Amendments of 1970. There was no workable program to eliminate water pollution until the Water Pollution Control Act Amendments of 1972. There was no Coastal Zone Management Act committing the nation to the preservation of its shorelines. There was no Toxic Substances Control Act, no Occupational Safety and Health Act, no Surface Mining Control and Reclamation Act, no Endangered Species Act, no Resource Conservation and Recovery Act, no Noise Control Act and no Safe Drinking Water Act. The Institutions on which we now rely at the national level were not there a decade ago. The Council on Environmental Quality, whose tenth birthday we celebrate this month, did not exist. The President had his economic advisers, but none to impress upon him a concern for the environment. There was no Environmental Protection Agency. Instead, the nation's fledgling pollution abatement effort was scattered among many agencies. There was no National Oceanic and Atmospheric Administration, symbolizing and implementing the nation's concern for its coasts and its climate. There was an Interior Department, but one which had not adequately learned to put wise stewardship of the nation's resources above the pursuit of resource extraction.

Laws and institutions are, of course, not ends but means. To a considerable degree, however, the environmental laws of the 1970's have begun to work. Although serious pollution problems remain, the historical trend toward steady deterioration of our air and waters appears to have been largely halted. Improvements can be seen in many areas of our country, as major polluters come into compliance with environmental laws. Through the environmental impact statement process, federal agencies have given increasing attention to the harmful impacts of actions. As a result, hundreds of proposed federal projects that could have caused incalculable environmental destruction have been improved and sometimes dropped altogether where that was the only reasonable course. Much of this success has been attributable to watchdog efforts of private environmmental groups and a judicial system responsive to the welfare of society. Natural areas under the various types of governmental and private protection have increased faster than at any other time in our history, and the osprey and the brown pelican are visible again, which would not have happened without the ban on DDT.

Yet, in none of these areas have we fully accomplished our national objectives, and in many other areas we have hardly begun. Thus, we enter the 1980's with a legacy of old problems and serious new challenges to address. The environmental problems of the coming decade deserve, and will demand, our best efforts. The control of toxic substances in the environment and the workplace, saving Alaska's public lands,

improving the quality of life in our inner cities, the protection of our beleaguered coastal areas and declining farmlands, the pursuit of energy conservation and of renewable energy resources while working to avoid the risks of both plutonium and carbon dioxide buildup—these must be among our major concerns at home in the coming years. At the same time, we must deal on a global scale with the increasing prospect of Earth's biotic impoverishment—a process of spreading deserts, disappearing wildlife, deforestation, and overfished, polluted waters. Successfully responding to these global challenges will require all the attention, generosity and ingenuity of which we are capable.

There is a different level at which progress must also be made in the 1980's. The nation's welfare and security depend on the development, in both public and private sectors, of broad economic and energy strategies that are based on sound ecological facts and relationships. Environmental concern cannot be compartmentalized, nor can environmental progress always be achieved by fine tuning the *status quo*. An ethic of caring about the natural community of which we are a part must permeate decisions in all areas of national life. To bolster this ethic, we must continue to improve our scientific understanding about how Earth's ecosystems operate so that we can propose and enforce wiser management practices.

In retrospect, the 1970's will be seen as an environmental decade, much as the 1930's are characterized by the social legislation of the New Deal and the 1960's by civil rights reforms. These were not transient phenomena. They were the beginnings of permanent national commitments to new directions.

Almost twenty years ago Rachel Carson prefaced *Silent Spring* with a statement by Albert Schweitzer— "Man has lost the capacity to foresee and forestall. He will end by destroying the earth." In the 1970's we

George Hall

regained the capacity to foresee. We are learning how to forestall. We must end by sustaining the Earth.

Russell E. Train   Robert Cahn
Russell W. Peterson   Gordon J. MacDonald
John A. Busterud   Beatrice E. Willard
Charles Warren   Jane H. Yarn
Gus Speth   Robert H. Harris

Third Planet Operating Instructions

DAVID R. BROWER

This planet has been delivered wholly assembled and in perfect working condition, and is intended for fully automatic and trouble-free operation in orbit around its star, the sun. However, to insure proper functioning, all passengers are requested to familiarize themselves fully with the following instructions.

Loss or even temporary misplacement of these instructions may result in calamity. Passengers who must proceed without the benefit of these rules are likely to cause considerable damage before they can learn the proper operating procedures for themselves.

A. COMPONENTS

It is recommended that passengers become completely familiar with the following planetary components:

1) Air

The air accompanying this planet is not replaceable. Enough has been supplied to cover the land and the water, but not very deeply. In fact, if the atmosphere were reduced to the density of water, then it would be a mere 33 feet deep. In normal use, the air is self-cleaning. It may be cleaned in part if excessively soiled. The passengers' lungs will be of help—up to a point. However, they will discover that anything they throw, spew, or dump into the air will return to them in due course. Since passengers will need to use the air, on the average, every five seconds, they should treat it accordingly.

2) Water

The water supplied with this planet isn't replaceable either. The operating water supply is very limited: If the earth were the size of an egg, all the water on it would fit in a single drop. The water contains many creatures, almost all of which eat and may be eaten; these creatures may be eaten by human passengers. If disagreeable things are dispersed in the planet's water, however, caution should be observed, since the water creatures concentrate the disagreeable things in their tissues. If human passengers then eat the water creatures, they will add disagreeable things to their diet. In general, passengers are advised not to disdain water, because that is what they mostly are.

3) Land

Although the surface of this planet is varied and seems abundant, only a small amount of land is suited to growing things, and that essential part should not be misused. It is also recommended that no attempt be made to disassemble the surface too deeply inasmuch as the land is supported by a molten and very hot underlayer that will grow little but volcanoes.

4) Life

The above components help make life possible. There is only one life per passenger and it should be treated with dignity. Instructions covering the birth, operation and maintenance, and disposal for each living entity have been thoughtfully provided. These instructions are contained in a complex language, called the DNA code, that is not easily understood. However, this does not matter, as the instructions are fully automatic. Passengers are cautioned, however, that radiation and many dangerous chemicals can damage the instructions severely. If in this way living species are destroyed, or rendered unable to reproduce, the filling of reorders is subject to long delays.

5) Fire

This planet has been designed and fully tested at the factory for totally safe operation with fuel constantly transmitted from a remote source, the sun, provided at absolutely no charge. *The following must be observed with greatest care:* The planet comes with a limited reserve fuel supply, contained in fossil deposits, which should be used only in emergencies. Use of this reserve fuel supply entails hazards, including the release of certain toxic metals, which must be kept out of the air and the food supply of living things. The risk will not be appreciable if the use of the emergency fuel is extended over the operating life of the planet. Rapid use, if sustained only for a brief period may produce unfortunate results.

B. MAINTENANCE

The kinds of maintenance will depend upon the number and constituency of the passengers. If only a few million human passengers wish to travel at a given time, no maintenance will be required, and no reservations will be necessary. The planet is self-maintaining, and the external fuel source will provide exactly as much energy as is needed or can be safely used. However, if a very large number of people insist on boarding at one time, serious problems will result, requiring costly solutions.

C. OPERATION

Barring extraordinary circumstances, it is necessary only to observe the mechanism periodically and to report any irregularities to the Smithsonian Institu-

tion. However, if, owing to misuse of the planet's mechanism, observations show a substantial change in the predictable patterns of sunrise and sunset, passengers should prepare to leave the vehicle.

D. EMERGENCY REPAIRS

If, through no responsibility of the current passengers, damage to the planet's operating mechanism has been caused by ignorant or careless action of the previous travelers, it is best to request the Manufacturer's assistance (best obtained through prayer).

Upon close examination, this planet will be found to consist of complex and fascinating detail in design and structure. Some passengers, upon discovering these details in the past, have attempted to replicate or improve the design and structure, or have even claimed to have invented them. The Manufacturer, having among other things invented the opposable thumb, may be amused by this. It is reliably reported that at this point, however, it appears to the Manufacturer that the full panoply of consequences of this thumb idea of His will not be without an element of unwelcome surprise.

Bill Oetinger

A Gus Speth Reader

Elihu Blotnick

THROUGHOUT THE PAST DECADE, a wide variety of disturbing studies and reports have been issued by the United Nations, the Worldwatch Institute, the World Bank, the International Union for the Conservation of Nature and Natural Resources, and other organiza- tions. These reports have sounded a persistent warn- ing: our international efforts to stem the spread of human poverty, hunger, and misery are not achieving their goals; the staggering growth of human popula- tion, coupled with ever-increasing human demands, are beginning to cause permanent damage to the planet's resource base.

The most recent such warning—and the one with which I am most familiar—was issued in July of 1980 by the Council on Environmental Quality and the US State Department. Called *The Global 2000 Report to the President,* it is the result of a three-year effort by more than a dozen agencies of the US government to make long-term projections across the range of population, resource, and environmental concerns. Given the obvious limitations of such projections, the *Global 2000 Report* can best be seen as a reconnaissance of the future. And the results of that reconnaissance are disturbing.

I feel very strongly that the *Global 2000 Report*'s findings confront this nation and the other nations of the world with one of the most difficult challenges facing our planet during the next two decades—rivaling the global arms race in importance. Let me briefly review those findings for you. As I do, remember that the *Global 2000* projections are based on the assumption that the policies of governments and private companies stay much as they are today, and that major wars and other catastrophes do not intervene.

The Report's projections point to continued rapid population growth, with world population increasing from 4.5 billion today to more than 6 billion by 2000. More people will be added to the world's population each year in the year 2000 than today—about 100 million a year as compared with 75 million today. Most of the additional people will live in the poorest countries, which will contain about four-fifths of the human race by the end of the century.

Unless other factors intervene, this planetary majority will see themselves growing worse off compared with those living in affluent nations. The income gap between rich and poor nations will widen, and the per capita gross national product of the less-developed countries will remain at generally low levels. In some areas—especially in parts of Latin America and East Asia—income per capita is expected to rise substantially. But gross national product in the great populous nations of South Asia—India, Bangladesh and Pakistan—will be less than $200 per capita (in 1975 dollars) by 2000. Today, some 800 million people live in conditions of absolute poverty, their lives dominated by hunger, ill health, and the absence of hope. By 2000, if current policies remain unchanged, their number could grow by 50 percent.

While the Report projects a 90 percent increase in overall world food production in the 30 years from 1970 to 2000, in South Asia, the Middle East, and the poorer countries of Africa, per capita food consumption will increase marginally at best, and in some areas may actually decline below present inadequate

levels. Real prices of food are expected to double during the same 30-year period.

The pressures of population and growing human needs and expectations will place increasing strains on the Earth's natural systems and resources. The spread of desert-like conditions from human activities now claims an area about the size of Maine each year. Croplands are lost to production as soils deteriorate because of erosion, compaction, waterlogging, and salinization, and as rural land is converted to other uses.

The increases in world food production projected by the Report are based on continued improvements in crop yields per acre, at the same rate of the record-breaking increases of the post-World War II period. These improvements are heavily energy-intensive but the Report's projections show no relief from the world's tight energy situation. World oil production is expected to level off by the 1990s. And for the one-quarter of humanity who depend on wood for fuel, the outlook is bleak. Projected needs for wood will exceed available supplies by about 25 percent before the turn of the century.

The conversion of forested land to agricultural use and the demand for fuelwood and forest products are projected to continue to deplete the world's forests. The Report estimates that these forests are now disappearing at rates as high as 18 to 20 million hectares—an area half the size of California—each year. As much as 40 percent of the remaining forests in poor countries may be gone by 2000. Most of the loss will be in tropical and subtropical areas.

The loss of tropical forests, along with the impact of pollution and other pressures on habitats, could cause massive destruction of the planet's genetic resource base. Between 500,000 and two million plant and animal species—15 to 20 percent of all species on Earth—could be extinguished by 2000. One-half to two-thirds of the extinctions will result from the clearing or deterioration of tropical forests. This would be a massive loss of potentially valuable sources of food, pharmaceutical chemicals, building materials, fuel sources, and other irreplaceable resources.

Deforestation and other factors will worsen severe regional water shortages and contribute to the deterioration of water quality. Population growth alone will cause demands for water to at least double from 1971 levels in nearly half of the world. Industrial growth is likely to worsen air quality. Air pollution in some cities in less-developed countries is already far above levels considered safe by the World Health Organization. Increased burning of fossil fuels, especially coal, may contribute to acid rain damage to lakes, plants, and exteriors of buildings. It also contributes to the increasing concentration of carbon dioxide in the Earth's atmosphere, possibly leading to climatic changes that could have highly disruptive effects on world agriculture. Depletion of the stratospheric ozone layer, attributed partly to chlorofluorocarbon emissions from aerosol cans and refrigeration equipment, could also have an adverse effect on food crops and human health.

Disturbing as these findings are, it is important to stress what the *Global 2000 Report*'s conclusions represent: Not *predictions* of what *will* occur, but *projections* of what *could* occur if we do not respond. If there was any doubt before, there should be little doubt now—the nations of the world, industrialized and less-developed alike, must act urgently and in concert to alter these dangerous trends before the projections of the *Global 2000 Report* become realities.

The warnings, then, are clear. Will we heed them, and will we heed them in time? For if our response is delayed, the costs could be large.

On these matters, I am cautiously optimistic. I like to think that the human race is *not* self-destructive; that it *is* paying, or can be made to pay, attention; that as people here and abroad come to realize the full dimensions of the challenge before us, we will take the actions needed to meet it.

Our efforts to secure the future must begin with a new appreciation for, and then an application of, three fundamental concepts. They are conservation, sustainable development, and equity. I want to take a few minutes to elaborate on each of these elements—because I am convinced that each of them is essential in the development of the kind of long-term global resource strategy we need to deal with the problems I have been discussing.

The first thing we must do is to get serious about the conservation of resources—renewable and non-renewable alike. We can no longer take for granted the renewability of renewable resources. The natural systems—the air and water, the forests, the land—that yield food, shelter, and the other necessities of life are susceptible to disruption, contamination, and destruction.

Indeed, one of the most troubling of the findings of the *Global 2000 Report* is the effect that rapid population growth and poverty are already having on the productivity of renewable natural resource systems. In some areas, particularly in the less developed countries, the ability of biological systems to support human populations is already being seriously damaged by efforts of present populations to meet desperate immediate needs, such as the needs for grazing land, firewood, and building materials. And these stresses, while most acute in the developing countries, are not confined to them. In recent years, the United States has been losing annually about 3 million acres of rural land—a third of its prime

agricultural land—because of the spread of housing developments, highways, shopping malls and the like. We are also losing annually the equivalent—in terms of production capability—of about 3 million more acres because of soil degradation: erosion and salinization. Other serious resource threats here at home include those posed by toxic chemicals and other pollutants to our groundwater supplies, which provide drinking water for half of the American public, and to our commercial and sport fisheries.

Achieving the necessary restraint in the use of renewable resources will require new ways of thinking by the peoples and governments of the world. It will require the widespread adoption of a "Conserver Society" ethic—an approach to resources and environment that, while attuned to the needs of each society, recognizes not only the importance of resources and environment to our own sustenance, well-being, and security, but also our obligation to pass this vital legacy along to future generations. Perhaps the most arrogant attitude of which the human spirit is capable is the notion that the riches of the Earth are ours to plunder or carelessly destroy, that the needs and the lives of those who will follow us on this tiny and fragile planet are of no concern to us. "Future Generations," someone once said, "What have they done for us?"

Fortunately, we are beginning to see signs that people in the United States and in other nations are becoming aware of the limits to our resources and the importance of conserving them. Energy problems, for example, are pointing the way to a future in which conservation is the password. As energy supplies go down and prices go up, we are learning that conserving—getting more and more out of each barrel of oil or ton of coal—is the cheapest and safest approach. Learning to conserve non-renewable resources like oil and coal is the first step toward building a Conserver Society that values, nurtures, and protects all its resources. Such a society appreciates economy in design and avoidance of waste. It realizes the limits to low-cost resources and to the environment's carrying capacity. It insists that market prices reflect all costs, social as well as private, so that consumers are fully aware in the most direct way of the real costs of consumption.

The Conserver Society prizes recycling over pollution, durability over obsolescence, quality over quantity, diversity over uniformity. It knows that beauty—whether natural or manmade—is too precious to be destroyed and that the Earth's wild creatures demand our conserving restraint not simply for utilitarian reasons but because, as part of the community of life that has evolved here with us, they too call this place home.

In this, our nation must take the lead. We cannot expect the rest of the world to adopt a Conserver

Paul Conrad

'The time has come,' the walrus said, 'to talk of many things: of crude—and spills—and tanker ships—of oil cartels—and kings.'

Society ethic if we, here in the United States, do not set a strong, successful example.

But the Conserver Society ethic, by itself, is not enough. It is unrealistic to expect people living at the margin of existence—people fighting desperately for their own survival—to think about the long-term survival of the planet. When people need to burn wood to keep from freezing, they will cut down trees.

We must find a way to break into the cycle of poverty, population growth, and environmental deterioration. We must find ways to improve the social and economic conditions of the poor nations and poor people of the world—their incomes, their access to productive land, their educational and employment opportunities. It is only through sustainable economic development that real progress can be made in alleviating hunger and poverty, and in erasing the conditions that contribute so dangerously to the destruction of our planet's carrying capacity.

One of the most important lessons of the *Global 2000 Report* is that the conflict between development and environmental protection is, in significant part, a myth. Without a concerted attack on the roots of extreme poverty—one that provides people with the opportunity to earn a decent livelihood in a non-

destructive manner—we cannot hope to protect the world's natural systems. It is also clear that development and economic reforms will have no lasting success unless they are suffused with concern for ecological stability and wise management of resources. The key concept here, of course, is *sustainable* development. Economic development, if it is to be successful over the long term, must proceed in a way that enhances the natural resource base of all the developing nations instead of exploiting those resources for short-term economic or political gain.

Unfortunately, the dialogue between the developed and the developing nations suggests that achieving steady, sustainable development will be a difficult process—one that will require great patience and understanding on all sides. For our part, here in the United States, we must resist the strong temptation to turn inward—to tune out the rest of the world's problems and to focus exclusively on our own economic difficulties. We must remember that, relatively speaking, we Americans luxuriate in the Earth's abundance while other nations can barely feed and clothe their people. Unless we act, this disparity between rich and poor will tend to grow, increasing the anger and resentment of those on the short end of the wealth equation—the great majority of mankind. One does not have to be particularly farsighted to see that the trends discussed in *Global 2000* heighten the chances for global instability—for exploitation of fears, resentments, and frustrations; for incitement to violence; for conflicts based on resources.

The *Global 2000 Report* itself discusses some of the destabilizing prospects that may be in store for us if we do not act decisively:

The world will be more vulnerable both to natural disaster and to disruptions from human causes . . . Most nations are likely to be still more dependent on foreign sources of energy in 2000 than they are today. Food production will be more vulnerable to disruptions of fossil fuel energy supplies and to weather fluctuations as cultivation expands to more marginal areas. The loss of diverse germ plasm in local strains and wild progenitors of food crops, together with the increase of monoculture, could lead to greater risks of massive crop failures. Larger numbers of people will be vulnerable to higher food prices or even famine when adverse weather occurs. The world will be more vulnerable to the disruptive effects of war. The tensions that could lead to war will have multiplied. The potential for conflict over fresh water alone is underscored by the fact that out of 200 of the world's major river basins, 148 are shared by two countries and 52 are shared by three to ten countries.

The 1980 Report of the Brandt Commission on International Development Issues is eloquent in its plea for action:

War is often thought of in terms of military conflict, or even annihilation. But there is a growing awareness that an equal danger might be chaos—as a result of mass hunger, economic disaster, environmental catastrophes, and terrorism, so we should not think only of reducing the traditional threats to peace, but also of the need for change from chaos to order.

Barbara Ward, the eminent British scholar, believes that the nations of the world can learn a valuable lesson from the experience of 19th-Century England, where the industrial revolution produced an appalling disparity in the distribution of wealth. It was a time when property owners and industrial managers reaped enormous profits while the laborers and mechanics—and their children—worked themselves into early graves. Today, Mrs. Ward observes:

The skew in world income is as great. The already developed peoples—North America, Europe, the Soviet Union, Japan—are the latter-day dukes, commanding over 70 percent of the planet's wealth for less than a quarter of the population. And in all too many developing countries the economic growth of the last two decades has been almost entirely appropriated by the wealthiest ten percent of the people. The comparisons in health, length of life, diet, literacy, all work out on the old Victorian patterns of unbelievable injustice.

Mrs. Ward recommends—and I heartily agree—that the developed nations of today follow the lead of men like Disraeli, who recognized the need to narrow the gap between rich and poor in 19th-Century England and to create a new social order which allowed every citizen a share of the nation's wealth. Without perceptive leaders like Disraeli and other men of conscience who saw the need for reform, Mrs. Ward argues that the growing pressure for equality and social justice would have torn British society apart. The result would have been similar to that in other nations where far-thinking leadership and compassion were lacking: "social convulsion, violent revolution, and an impetus to merciless worldwide war and conquest."

The situation we face in the world today is all too similar. While the humanitarian reasons for acting generously to alleviate global poverty and injustice are compelling enough in themselves, we must also recognize the extent to which global poverty and resource problems can contribute to regional and worldwide political instability—an instability that can threaten the security of nations throughout the world.

Thus, along with conservation and sustainable development, the development of a global resource strategy will require a much greater emphasis on equity—on a fair sharing of the means to development and the products of growth—not only among nations, but within nations as well.

Secretary of State Muskie made this point well in his defense of the US foreign aid program before the Foreign Policy Association: "It is in our interest to do all we can now to counter the conditions that are likely to drive people to desperation later . . . We would rather send technicians abroad to help grow crops than send soldiers to fight the wars that can result when people are hungry and susceptible to exploitation by others." It should be obvious to all of us by now that the interests of our nation go hand-in-hand with the interests of the rest of the world. In helping others, we help ourselves. In providing generous and effective assistance—grants, loans, technical aid—to nations that are in need, we can make one of our best national investments, an investment that will yield large dividends in the future.

To provide the basis for a strengthened, sustained US response to the *Global 2000 Report*, President Carter in July 1980 established a Presidential Task Force on Global Resources and Environment, which I am honored to chair, and asked that it report back to him with a plan of action early in 1981. The Task Force, consisting of officials from the Department of State, the Office of Management and Budget, the White House Office of Domestic Affairs and Policy, and the Office of Science and Technology Policy as well as CEQ, is pulling together recommendations which could, I believe, place our government in a much better position to assert leadership in finding solutions to the problems discussed in the *Global 2000 Report*. Our work is not yet complete, but I can offer the following thoughts:

— If at some point during the coming months or years, we hear proposals for federal legislation and other programs to improve our national capability to respond to global population, resource, and environmental problems, we should not complain, "Here we go again with another enlargement of the federal government." We should think instead of the kind of world we want in twenty years, and of what could

happen if we don't get moving quickly.

— If we hear that our foreign assistance program should be enhanced, and that the United States should catch up with those European countries which give a much larger portion of their gross national products as development aid than we do, we should not respond, "Yet another wasteful federal giveaway." We should think instead of the investment we can and must make to alleviate human suffering and to ensure the long-term health of our own economy and the peace and stability of the community of nations.

— And if we hear people refer to global resource and environmental constraints, our reaction should not be, "There go those 'limits-to-growth' advocates again." We should remember instead that future economic trends can neither be fully understood nor fully addressed unless we pay much more attention to resources, environment, population, and development needs. They are, as the saying goes, all of a piece.

A Nation of Conservers

TEN YEARS AFTER EARTH DAY, it is appropriate to reflect on what has been accomplished. What we see, looking back, is the American people and their system of government at their very finest. Faced with the increasingly likely prospect of leaving their children a legacy of silent springs, the American people called for action, and their government responded with imagination and creativity.

Imagine a world in which there is no national system for air quality management, no workable program to eliminate water pollution and no legislation to protect the coastal zone; where there are no environmental impact statements; where there is no Toxic Substances Control Act, no Occupational Safety and Health Act, no Surface Mining Control and Reclamation Act, no Endangered Species Act, no Resource Conservation and Recovery Act, no Noise Control Act, and no Safe Drinking Water Act. You are imagining 1969.

I have no doubt that future generations of Americans will recall this decade of environmental renaissance the way we now look back on similar bursts of legislation during the 1930's for the New Deal, and the 1960's for Civil Rights: as among Democracy's finest hours.

Another positive dimension of the past decade involves the actions of individuals and thousands of local and national groups which have contributed so greatly to protecting our environment. The bulk of the

progress we have made so far would not have been possible without these groups and without a far-sighted judiciary informed by a sense of historical perspective about the impact of its decisions.

So, as we turn our heads to look behind us, there is not a person here or anywhere in our country who should not feel a deep emotional satisfaction with how far we have come, and how far even the most recalcitrant have come with us—although it is true that some of the latter have not enjoyed the trip very much.

These recalcitrants—who seem to believe that the environment is a nice place to exploit, but of course no one would want to live there—help to remind us that despite how far we have come, the job is not finished.

It certainly looks that way when we turn our heads forward and look at the upward slope of what yet needs to be done. Ahead of us we see several difficult problem areas: energy, land use, water resources, toxic chemicals, and, most important of all, the global environment. Even though these global issues seem remote from us, we must recognize that they will play an increasingly large role in our lives and that they deserve more of our attention.

We must also continue the momentum behind environmental regulation at home if we are going to address international pollution problems like acid rain and toxic chemicals, and to protect coastal fisheries and endangered species. The fabric of public protection regulation built up over the past two decades is probably more vulnerable than we imagine. It could be seriously damaged by the assaults of various interests now advancing under the banner of regulatory reform. We must make regulation efficient and sensitive to economic considerations, but the fact is that we need to strengthen, not weaken, environmental regulation, as the problems of hazardous waste disposal, groundwater contamination, pollution in our inner cities and the acidified lakes in the Adirondacks and Canada all make plain.

How do we meet these new problems? What do we do at home to put ourselves into a position to give the leadership we must give abroad? Where do we in the United States go from here?

Society of Conservers

"The 1980's," said President Carter, "offer vast potential for conserving energy and natural resources that is both good environmental policy and good economic self-interest. It is time to revive some old-fashioned notions about the wise use of what we have. It is time for a society of consumers to become a society of conservers."

A society of conservers—that is where we must go from here. That is how we can continue to preserve and advance civilization while at the same time addressing the growing rift between rich and poor. It is a goal which can unite city and suburb and farm, black and white, rich and poor. It is a goal that does not elevate greed from a sin to a virtue.

Can the Conserver Society help build bridges between environmentalists and the disadvantaged and those most hurt by our economic problems? I believe that it can. There are important linkages between the problem of environmental destruction and the problem of economic injustice—linkages which we are only beginning, with difficulty, to see. The institutions in our society most concerned with fostering a mindless consumerism apparently have little motivation to *care*—to care either for the disadvantaged or for the environment. Because it needs less, the Conserver Society has more to go around, and is more willing to share. Perhaps as we explore these issues among ourselves and with others, we will see that those who know and understand the problems of the environment and those who know and understand the problems of the disadvantaged and the unemployed have a common calling—to be teachers and preachers together.

Drawing by Ed Koren © 1971, The New Yorker Magazine, Inc.

"They're leaving to be recycled."

The initial rounds in the environmental struggle have clearly been won by those who appreciate the larger costs of continued environmental degradation. But the fight is not over, and it will not be won if we permit ourselves to be guided by illusions.

If we look at the recalcitrants and the adversaries of environmental quality, we see a regrouping of forces, a reassertion of economic clout, and cold-blooded exploitation of such fundamental national character traits as suspicion of government interference with private choice.

These special interests have tried to show that environmental concerns cost jobs, and they have failed.

The latest attack involves a perversion of needed regulatory reform, transforming the necessary elimination of redundant or counterproductive regulatory policies into something entirely different: a drive to pull the teeth from health, environmental, and consumer programs. This attack, best termed the immobilization of truth after one of its leaders, seeks to smother the critical faculties of the American people in a blanket of sophistries.

Given the intensity and power of these efforts to turn back the clock, how do we move toward a Conserver Society?

First, we must keep doing, and keep doing better, those things that have already worked so well—educating, lobbying, suing, working with and within Government at all levels.

That is important, but is no longer enough. The current situation also calls for new departures and new strategies.

These involve:
- building better bridges to our natural allies;
- mobilizing the strong grass roots support undergirding political activity; and
- seeking important structural reforms, such as election finance reform, which are not strictly environmental.

An outreach effort to build bridges is absolutely essential not only to broaden the support for environmental issues, but also to build the kinds of coalitions necessary in achieving structural changes.

Who are the natural allies of environmental progress?

They are the urban poor, for they bear the heaviest burden of ill health and lost beauty and recreation due to environmental degradation.

They are the working men and women, for it is they who so often must unwittingly serve as society's guinea pigs, testing chemical and radiological hazards.

They are the nation's farmers, for it is they whose

land is being lost in the millions of acres each year.

They are the concerned and enlightened businessmen, for it is they whose cooperation is necessary if progress is to continue.

It is the poor, the disadvantaged, the urban minorities who are condemned to live in the most degraded, unhealthy environments. Too often in the past, environmental issues have taken on a slight tincture of elitism, perceived by the poor as just another example of the concerns of the comfortable whose mundane wants were so well satisfied that they could enjoy the luxury of suffering for wildlife—but who could not comprehend, nor take time to sympathize, with the realities of the inner city.

We can no longer delay demonstrating, again and again, that dirty air, destructive noise, tainted water, inadequate recreation, toxic threats of all kinds, dwindling resources, ever-higher prices that mock efforts to move out of poverty, are minority issues and urban issues as well as environmental issues. And we can no longer delay demonstrating, again and again, that our concerns are not bounded by remote wilderness areas which, to the urban poor, might just as well be on the far side of the moon.

We need, then, to go beyond demonstrating to mobilizing—to mobilizing support in every area of our country and segment of our society for a more active involvement in politics. We need, in particular, to elect to public office more people with strong concerns for the environment. We need, in sum, to increase by a hundredfold grass-roots organizing and the kind of activities carried out by the League of Conservation Voters and similar groups.

This is a difficult challenge, but what we have seen so far may be only the foothills of the difficult. Since 1971, changes in the campaign law have permitted profit-making corporations to set up political action committees, and to finance overhead costs for such PAC's out of corporate treasuries. Since then, a veritable avalanche of money has passed through the corporate PAC's to political candidates in order to promote special interest causes.

My good friend Jack Bass, who ran unsuccessfully for a Congressional seat from South Carolina, recently described the power of the corporate PAC's in a *New York Times* article. Bass shows the growth curve of corporate PAC's to be rising dramatically. The increase between 1974 and 1979 was from 89 to 813—160 percent *a year*. Such PAC's poured three times as much money into House and Senate campaigns in 1978 as they did in 1974.

Contributions to House committee chairmen from

PAC's of all types—corporate, trade association and labor—averaged $43,000 in 1978, more than double the 1976 average. The number of House members receiving 40 percent of their campaign contributions from PAC's grew from 78 in 1974 to 155 in 1978.

Thus, in addition to mobilizing our allies and enlisting grass roots support, we must reach out beyond the boundaries of purely environmental issues to involve ourselves, our organizations, and our influence in preventing what is fast becoming the special interest PAC dominance of the political process. I fear Common Cause has a point when it warns that "We are facing government of, by and for the PAC's of America, unless this fundamental flaw in our political system is corrected."

Of particular concern are campaign finance reform and the restoration of the balance destroyed by statutory provisions favoring PAC's. Unless this is done, Congress may one day be incapable of responding to environmental and consumer issues, no matter how important.

This is why everyone who is concerned about environmental quality and a host of other issues must put the partial public financing of Senate and House elections at the top of the legislative priority list.

The point is that these matters are not minor. They involve the way our political system works in practice. They involve who gets elected, and how who gets elected votes. They involve, in the final analysis, matters of life or death for environmental concerns, and hence for the environment, and hence for ourselves and our children.

The question I initially posed is, where do we go from here? In many ways, that is an optimistic question. Some may hope the real question is: Do the environmentalists go from here at all? Yet I believe that is a decidedly minority view. The American people still care deeply about restoring environmental quality and about passing on a safe, livable world to future generations. The leadership *you* provide in the 1980's will be essential to ensuring that these aspirations are realized.

As we proceed into the 1980's, let us remember:
- Never let anyone say that those who are concerned about the environment are a special interest group. Anyone who believes that could not tell a fox from a hedgehog.
- Never let anyone say that environmental concerns are hurting the economy or our energy situation. Anyone who believes that has read too many Mobil ads.
- And never let anyone say that concern for the environment is no longer needed. It is, even more today than ten years ago.

Robin Freeman

Environmental Regulation and the Immobilization of Truth

Those who argue against continuing the environmental momentum of the 1970's have failed to grasp the full severity and dimensions of the environmental problems that continue to face us. The issues that persist today are not just questions of esthetics, or comfort, or an idealized notion of "the good life"; they are clear threats to the health and welfare of the American people. They simply cannot be put aside until a time when it is more convenient to focus on them.

We have gained success in combatting gross threats to our air and water only to discover whole new phalanxes of subtle menaces, whose danger and obstinacy often vary in inverse proportion to their ability to be quickly and easily understood. Thus, we look upon the clarifying water and purified air with satisfaction while, stealthily, four square miles of our most productive farm land are each day consumed by concrete and asphalt and lost from agriculture. Fish are returning to waters they long ago fled, but we are finding their flesh often contains significant amounts of toxic chemicals. Sulfur dioxide pollution is now a major health problem in only a few areas, but partly because we are airmailing sulfur oxides to places far away where it falls as acid rain.

There are few who directly attack our environmental commitment, but a growing number have adopted the strategy of undermining that commitment indirectly. At first the strategy took the form of a refreshing concern for the working man and woman. In a kind of perversion of the Phillips curve once vainly used to explain inflation, the argument seemed to run that unemployment went up as smog and oil slicks went down. But that argument was permitted to die a quiet death when the National Academy of Sciences estimated that the nation's effort to clean up the environment actually accounted for about 680,000 jobs, 30 new jobs for every one eliminated due to decisions by manufacturing firms and others that resulted from environmental requirements. A subsequent study by Data Resources, Inc. showed that air and water pollution controls will stimulate employment during the entire 16 year period from 1970 to 1986.

The negative strategy then moved to the issue of inflation. This has now been looked into as well, and it has been found that between 1979 and 1986, federal environmental regulations will add between one- and two-tenths of one percentage point to the annual infla-tion rate. For 1980, existing federal environmental regulation is predicted to add only one tenth of a percentage point to the rate at which prices increase—a rate that should continue in the period 1984 to 1986.

The first point to note is that, even by standard economic measures, the inflationary impact of environmental programs is quite minor. Moreover, any realistic modification of federal environmental regulations would produce no significant reduction in the overall Consumer Price Index. If the inflationary impact of these requirements could be reduced by a fourth—a substantial relaxation—the CPI's increase would be restrained by less than 0.05 percent: the net effect of even draconian measures could be the difference between a 7 percent and a 7.05 percent increase in the CPI. So we must look elsewhere than environmental regulations for the sources of inflation, and for the proper targets of our anti-inflation efforts.

Following the bankruptcy of these contentions, we have been told and told, and then told again, that environmental regulation is merely one aspect of an already over-regulated society, a society forced to divert increasingly scarce resources and managerial talent from productive and innovative ends. Indeed, some major corporations have undertaken rather large campaigns to convince the American people that government regulation is out of control.

In response, I would simply point out that, in light of the continuing revelations of corporate neglect or worse, much of the current protestation against government regulation rings awfully hollow. Virtually every environmental regulation, for example, has its genesis in some problem, like Love Canal or Kepone or PCB's, that threatened the public and finally brought a legitimate public demand for government action. Regulation is not going to go away until the problems do. The way we regulate can *and must* be improved, but let us face the fact that a continued high level of government regulatory activity is *essential* to national goals of paramount importance—to controlling cancer and protecting health, to preventing consumer fraud and deception, to cleaning up air and water pollution, to reducing oil imports and conserving energy, to protecting us from improperly sited or mismanaged nuclear power facilities—the list, obviously, is very long.

Some [critics] are merely using regulatory reform as a kind of shibboleth masking their real motivation, which is to pull the teeth from health and environmen-

Industrial waste site.   *Photograph by Harvey Columbus.*

tal programs. These critics hide their intentions under a flourish of slick public relations sophistries which, for lack of a better word, I might call the imMOBILization of truth.

Mobil, of course, is the company that has spent hundreds of thousands, if not millions, of dollars over the past few years on a rather strident advertising campaign on the Op-Ed pages of major national newspapers and magazines. Some of the ads give away their true nature by taking the form of fables; others are just as mythical and remote from reality. One such ad attacked government regulators as "new reactionaries," and accused government of trying to "turn back the clock to the detriment of today's standard of living." If I had been writing a headline for that particular ad, my first thought would have been: "Bring Back the Robber Barons."

Since the imMOBILizers are so misleading, I would like to look for a moment at a few of their favorite debating points.

The first is what I call *Zen analysis*. We all know what is purported to be the way Zen Buddhists sharpen their powers of concentration. First you think of the sound of two hands clapping and then you think of the sound of one hand clapping. It is, I imagine, a very soft sound, somewhat like the quality of reasoning employed by those who subject health, safety, and environmental regulation to a form of one-handed analysis that discovers that, lo and behold, these activities entail a cost.

Of course environmental quality costs money. The imMOBILizers want us to overlook the fact that the cost of environmental quality is invariably exceeded by the cost of environmental degradation, and that it is the general public who pays the latter, while the former involves some participation by those who would prefer to continue using America the beautiful as a kind of limitless septic field.

The second form of sophistry employed by the factual imMOBILizers involves careful selection of *targets of opportunity*. This involves telling us in great detail about some regulatory excess, and there are some, or about a particular form of regulation that is made to appear unnecessarily burdensome. What never gets mentioned by this form of imMOBILization is that a great deal of regulation, particularly economic regulation, has come into being because business interests of various kinds *wanted* it or found that it advanced their own goals.

Let me just quote from some remarks by Carol Foreman, Assistant Secretary of Agriculture for Food and Consumer Services. When asked about regulation, she said, "Economic regulation, as practiced by the ICC, and the CAB until recently, and certainly the Securities and Exchange Commission, tends to be heavily supported by industry. Certainly the Packer and Stockyard Administration is heavily supported by industry. Some of that economic regulation tends to raise prices and limit markets, which is exactly what it was intended to do, and the businesses that are regulated love it." And then she added, "Businessmen generally say health and safety regulations are terrible. They've

---

I suspect that if you should go to the end of the world, you would find somebody there going further.

—HENRY THOREAU

---

opposed them. And yet my experience in meat inspection is if somebody were to propose to eliminate meat and poultry inspection, the regulated industries would be the first ones to try to prevent that because we protect them from their competitors who might cheat."

Another favorite way to imMOBILize the truth involves *scapegoatery*. Thus, when U.S. Steel decides to close 16 plants in eight states, this action is not portrayed as what is bound to happen from time to time in a truly competitive system, or that economic history is largely the pageant of firms that decline and firms that advance, or that disinvestment in the uneconomic is just as important to healthy growth as investment in the economic. Instead, the experience of U.S. Steel is perverted into becoming a horrible example of what happens when government regulation requires environmental protection, or permits foreign competition. What is not stated is that Japanese steel, the major competitor, is produced under environmental protection restrictions that are more stringent than our own, or that trade barriers, high or low, are forms of government regulation.

If the critics really want to reduce the burden of government regulation, they must take steps to eliminate the situations that create the need for regulation. That, it seems to me, is the enlightened response to a changing society. And those companies that are increasingly taking this approach deserve our praise, support and thanks. With this approach, we will be well on our way to an age when, in the words of one editorial writer, we will fit our desires to the environment, and no longer ruin the environment to suit our desires.

Toward a Better Bull's Eye
Corporate Responsibility and Accountability

The *Business Week* interviewer had asked the executive of one P.R. firm how he managed to prove that his efforts had produced any tangible gain for a corporate client.

After a certain amount of waffling, the executive said, "Well, I'll give you an honest answer if you promise not to quote me by name." The interviewer agreed, so the executive continued. "We shoot first," he said, "and then we draw the bull's-eye around the hole."

Any discussion of "Corporate Responsibility and Accountability" can easily be diverted into a preoccupation with a superficial form of public relations—with Being Nice on the corporate level. But the real focus of this discussion, I believe, must be on the much more substantive matters of goal and purpose: what kind of target should a corporation aim at? Should it be the same one that executives aimed at 20 years ago, or 5, or even today?

My thesis is that it should not. Indeed, I am convinced that if the American corporation is to survive in the long run in something like its present state, it cannot.

There are something like 1.8 million corporations chartered by the states to operate in this country, a seemingly democratic dispersal of enterprise. But if we select from those 1.8 million those with annual sales of $250 million or more, or more than 10,000 employees, we come up with only 700 firms. The largest 200 industrial firms in this country own about two-thirds of all industrial assets. And, *each* of the top 50 U.S. corporations now has total revenues exceeding those of any one of 39 states, and the GNP of 126 *nations.*

Such concentrations of money, with their attendant power, lend themselves to abuse. They permit a relatively few people—almost invariably men—to make decisions that affect millions of others who have no voice in those decisions.

We have been trying to cope with the corporation's potential for abuse at least since the late 1800's, with passage of the Sherman anti-trust legislation. The collapse of the stock market and subsequent disclosures of broad-scale manipulation brought us the Securities and Exchange Commission, whose first chairman, Mr. Joseph Kennedy, moved with the knowledge of an insider to outlaw practices that had contributed to his own fortune. In more recent years, as the size and

influence of the corporation expanded, so did the pace of legislation to control it: since 1963, Congress—not without reason—has enacted at least 150 major laws to regulate the social impact of business activity.

From the standpoint of the businessman, therefore, it would seem that we have all the regulatory control that any economy can withstand. Indeed, some major corporations have apparently launched a rather large campaign to convince the American people that government regulation is out of control.

And yet . . . and yet, year after year some new piece of corporate neglect or law-breaking either mocks the controls we have, or suggests that they have failed again. I am not talking here about the bush-league infractions that any human enterprise will exhibit from time to time, but serious violations—sometimes condoned at the highest corporate level—both of our laws and of the norms of responsible business behavior. PCB's from General Electric plants have profoundly damaged the mighty Hudson—leading to a ban on commercial fishing—and Life Sciences Products, spinoff of Allied Chemical, discharged Kepone into the James, with disastrous effects on it and the Chesapeake Bay.

Here is one of our major steel companies, under investigation—according to the *Wall Street Journal*—by the Securities and Exchange Commission for using two different sets of numbers in estimating future pollution-control costs: one set for investors and another, with much larger numbers, for the news media and public officials. And over there is a growing number of lawsuits based on corporate records which suggest that asbestos manufacturers suppressed evidence about potentially fatal injury to workers.

In view of one revelation after another of this type, and others beyond the environmental realm, much of the current corporate protestation against government regulation rings awfully hollow—especially when companies and entire industries are quite willing to support government regulation when it suits them. In spite of all the praise lavished upon the concept of competition by business spokesmen and their copywriters, we see the trucking industry today *appalled* at the prospect of deregulation, and gearing up a massive political action campaign to fight it. Now that inflation is the bane of our economy, both government and industry are—quite properly—examining the cost-

Victor Fischer

impact of regulation prices. And yet, as Chairman Michael Pertschuk of the Federal Trade Commission commented in 1978, "The most costly and least justified regulatory burdens flow from economic regulation: regulation by business, of business, for business. More often than not," he said, "such regulations are not sanctioned by law, but rather are carried on in defiance of the law—not as *government* regulation of business, but as anticompetitive and inflationary *business* regulation of business. And where these forms of business-inspired regulation do remain imbedded in the law, it is because those businesses and professions regulated have stoutly defended their ancient right to be shielded from the discomforts of free competition."

Corporate complaints about government regulation are perfectly understandable in a human way. Yet virtually every regulation on the books had its genesis in some problem that threatened the public welfare and finally brought a legitimate public demand for governmental action. Regulation is not going to go away until the problems do. The way we regulate can *and must* be improved, but let us face the fact that a continued high level of government regulatory activity is *essential* to national goals of paramount importance— to controlling cancer and protecting health, to preventing consumer fraud and deception, to cleaning up air and water pollution, to reducing oil imports and conserving energy, to protecting us from improperly

sited or mismanaged nuclear power facilities—and I could go on, as you know, with a very long list.

Both sides—business and government—stand to gain from a new approach which supplements traditional regulation with a new focus on efforts to improve corporate governance. As someone concerned with the effectiveness of Federal programs to protect the environment, I have long felt that external regulation would only provide a part of the answer. Corporations bent on weakening or undercutting government efforts have the technical and economic and legal resources skewed in their favor.

From business' perspective, Secretary of Commerce Juanita Kreps made the point well in testimony before Congress: "To the extent business helps (through improved corporate social performance) to deal with issues that might otherwise prompt government regulation, it serves its own economic interests." Secretary Kreps made another point that every business leader agitated by government intrusion should remember: business cannot responsibly call for less government regulation without also addressing those social issues and needs that prompt the calls for more regulation.

The plea for greater corporate social responsibility is by no means limited to Ralph Nader and government officials; it is being prominently expressed by senior corporate officials themselves. "Large corporations," states John W. Filer, chairman of Aetna Life and Casualty, "can no longer be single-purpose institutions directed solely to economic results. All must . . . be visibly attentive to the public interest *as the public views it.*" Walter Haas, chairman of Levi Strauss & Co., argues that, "Today's corporation must develop practical means of giving human needs *the same* status as profit and production. . . . In the long run, this new task of the corporation will be in its own best interest, since it cannot prosper as fully or as long in a society frustrated by social ills and upheaval." And in April of 1978, a group of prominent business leaders and others, meeting under the auspices of the American Assembly, issued a commendable statement calling on American corporations to become more responsive to social concerns.

In my judgment, business leaders, government officials and the public must work together to put the concepts of corporate social responsibility and accountability into routine practice. A great many of our serious domestic problems will never be solved until corporate managers routinely take into account the human, environmental and social effects of their actions and until corporate ingenuity is consciously directed in socially beneficial ways—not as a constraint on profits, or as a necessary adjunct to soothe the public while the corporation makes profits, but as a goal commensurate with profits in importance.

It is unlikely that this will happen as long as the laws that determine the way corporations conduct their "internal" affairs remain so primitive. As far back as the 1890's, New Jersey and Delaware competed to see who could water down their laws most to attract corporate charters. Delaware won; by 1934, one-third of the corporations listed on the New York Stock Exchange were incorporated in Delaware. By 1971, owing to further relaxations of state law, Delaware was deriving 23 percent of all state revenues from corporate franchise fees and related income; by 1974, 76,000 corporations were chartered there, including 52 of the top 100 corporations and 251 of the largest 500.

This is an astonishing tribute to the "favorable business climate" in one of our smallest states. Delaware seems to be to corporations what Liberia is to tankers.

Partly because of this auctioning-off of corporate controls to attract business, the legal institutions for corporate governance—the stockholders and the directors—function as little more than rubber stamps for management decisions. Those that are affected most by the corporation's decisions—labor, consumers, the community at large—have least to say in its decisions. Moreover, the staff of the Senate Subcommittee on Reports, Accounting, and Management released an analysis showing the staggering number of interlocking directors on the boards of 130 major U.S.

Drawing by Mike Peters, Dayton News.

I remain oppressed by the thought that the venture into space is meaningless unless it coincides with a certain interior expansion, an ever-growing universe within, to correspond with the far flight of the galaxies our telescopes follow from without.

The inward skies of man will accompany him across any void upon which he ventures and will be with him to the end of time.

No one needs to be told that different and private worlds exist in the heads of men. But in a day when some men are listening by radio telescope to the rustling of events at the ends of the universe, the universe of others consits of hopeless poverty amidst the filthy garbage of a city lot. A taxi man I know thinks that the stars are just "up there" and as soon as our vehicles are perfected we can all take off like crowds of summer tourists to Cape Cod. This man expects, and I fear has been encouraged to expect, that such flights will solve the population problem.

—LOREN EISELEY

corporations. These companies had assets of more than $1 trillion—about 25 percent of the assets of *all* U.S. companies.

According to the free market scriptures, these 130 companies are absolutely drenched with perspiration as they battle back and forth in a no-holds-barred competition for the favor and dollars of the American consumer. But my goodness, what a chummy group these gladiators seem to be when the door to the board room closes! The Subcommittee staff found that 123 of these companies "connected on an average with half of the other companies in the study through a total of 530 direct and 12,193 indirect interlocks."

"These facts," the Subcommittee staff concluded, "raise fundamental issues: Such interlocking directorates among the Nation's very largest corporations may provide mechanisms for stabilizing prices, controlling supply and restraining competition. . . . They can bear on corporate responsibilities with respect to environmental and social issues and possibly, control the shape and direction of the Nation's economy."

While agreeing that there are perfectly legitimate reasons for seeking advice on corporate policy from experienced senior executives of other firms, the staff commented that "the use of the interlocking directorate as a management device may have gone too far. . . . It may have already crossed the threshold of private enterprise and entered the domain of private government."

As a solution to these ills, I think it's time for a healthy dose of democracy in corporate decision-making. Two fundamental elements of democracy are participation *by* and accountability *to* the people whose lives the corporation affects. I have two proposals for bringing greater participation and accountability into corporate affairs, and I don't believe either risks the economic benefits that corporations provide. Neither proposal is fully developed or final in my own mind, but they do indicate the type of steps I think are needed. But before offering them, let me stress that I would not be happy leaving these proposals to voluntary implementation by those corporations with public spirited management. The stakes are too high, the issues too important and the pressures to avoid implementation too great to leave these initiatives to voluntary action or self-regulation. Those corporations which will move forward on their own in this area are almost by definition those least in need of this dose of democracy, and I would think the more progressive corporate leaders would see the advantages of an approach which ensures that all corporations above a certain size complied.

The first proposal, then, is that the independence and representativeness of the boards of directors of all large corporations be assured. To accomplish this, every large corporation should be required to have on its board of directors a strong majority of members who come from outside corporate management, so that, say, two-thirds or more of the directors of these companies would be unemcumbered by relationships (such as significant business relations to the corporation) which limit their ability to provide an independent review of management. Of these independent directors, about half—or a third of total directors—should be directly representative of the public communities affected by the company's activities: consumers, environmentalists, employees, citizens from plant towns, and so on. Finally, it seems clear to me that some additional steps are needed to protect against conflicts of interest and other abuses posed by the current use of interlocking directorates.

Regarding the proposal that the company's constituencies be represented on the board, I'm not talking about dragging just anybody in off the street simply because he or she belongs to the Audubon Society. Such "public directors," in addition to being representative of constituencies I've mentioned, would have to wear two hats and share responsibility with other directors for the corporation's profitability. And who is to decide who these directors are? There are several possibilities, but the simplest is to let the shareholders vote for candidates for the potential slots, much as they vote for directors now.

For such a reform to have any meaning, however, the proxy and other machinery through which directors are nominated and elected will have to be reformed. As matters stand, shareholders typically ratify nominees selected by management: what you see is what you get. Today's corporate democracy is too often democracy in name only, and changes should be made that put shareholders in a central role in nominating and selecting directors.

The second proposal is that major corporations be required to prepare a periodic social audit or report which will provide the public with the information needed for determining whether the company is a good citizen and also provide shareholders with the information they need to make socially responsible decisions in buying and voting their shares. Social reports are now required in several European countries where they are viewed in part as an alternative both to central government control and to the traditional market, which is no longer felt to be capable of meeting the broad spectrum of social needs.

Such proposals could be enacted with a minimum of corporate expenditure and a minimum of federal intervention and bureaucracy. All they require is a clear statement of standards for the independence of board members; for the inclusion on boards of "public directors" from specific social constituencies; and for the content of a social audit. Within these broad requirements, corporations could proceed as they choose to implement internal controls aimed at developing genuinely democratic accountability.

Justice Brandeis observed that "sunshine is the best disinfectant." The American public, concerned with evidence of improper dealings by their elected representatives, and by the growth of government bureaucracy, has demanded and received increasing disclosure of information about what goes on in Washington. Like Brandeis, it knows that forced disclosure is a most powerful deterrent to unwanted conduct. It is time, it seems to me, for new disclosure requirements to be applied to our largest corporations. For these concentrations of financial resource have indeed crossed the threshold of private enterprise to become private government. They must be made accountable and responsible, not only to shareholders, but to the citizens who keep them in business. The needed change is mainly a matter of expanding the concept of "profit" to include social goods that every one of you values in his or her own life . . . and then harnessing the incredible resources of today's corporation to achieve these goods. It is, in sum, a matter of shooting second, and drawing a better bull's-eye first.

A Small Price to Pay
Environmental Controls and Inflation

When the OPEC nations suddenly hiked the price of crude oil in 1973, the U.S. began looking for ways to resolve the energy crisis. As any well-informed observer might have predicted, environmental regulations immediately came in for a close look and schemes were quickly hatched to speed the development of new energy sources by revising or outflanking laws.

Then, as the unemployment figure inched upward, environmental regulations were attacked again—this time, as a barrier to creating jobs. Critics of environmental regulation did, indeed, have some numbers on their side: according to EPA's analyses, the costs of pollution control by 1976 had forced the closing of plants employing about 20,000 people. But the defenders of such regulation came back with another set of numbers that deserved attention: air and water pollution control investments forced by local, state, and federal regulation had also *created* more than 600,000 jobs—roughly 30 new jobs for every one they had destroyed.

Today, environmental regulations—having weathered, at least temporarily, the energy crisis arguments and the unemployment arguments—are being criticized on a new ground: as contributing substantially to inflation.

There is absolutely no question that inflation on the scale we confront today demands that we in government take strong measures. At a 10 percent inflation rate, the cost of goods *doubles* within seven years. Consumer goods that cost $100 in the base statistical year of 1967 cost $195 eleven years later.

Inflation at this rate cannot be tolerated. It rewards speculators and penalizes savers as well as those with fixed incomes or limited power to bargain in the marketplace. It can lead to increased personal and family insecurity and a general decline in public confidence that could, together, result in a serious psychological malaise across the country—a sense that the individual has no power to improve or even protect his fiscal future.

But as an administration official with specific responsibilities in the environmental area, I have serious reservations about cutting back on health, pollution, and resource-development controls in the name of combating inflation. *Not,* I emphasize, because I think environmental protection is a sacred cow before which every other national need must bow; rather, because I believe relaxing environmental controls would have very little effect on inflation. Such a relaxation would indeed, increase real social costs that our traditional economic indices do not measure. And finally, such an effort might distract us from the necessary intellectual labor of dissecting a new kind of inflation and confronting its causes while we still have time to do so.

How much do our present environmental protection laws cost us?

To date, only one really comprehensive analysis of the inflationary impact of pollution control regulations has been done. It was performed by Chase Econometrics at the behest of the Council on Environmental Quality. Chase's study indicates that, for the period 1970–1983, federal pollution-control requirements would cause an average annual increase in the Consumer Price Index of between 0.3% and 0.4%. The first point to note is that, even by standard economic measures, any conceivable modification of federal environmental and health regulations would produce no significant reduction in the overall CPI. If the inflationary impact of these requirements could be reduced by 20%—a substantial relaxation—the CPI's increase would be restrained 0.1%: the net effect of even draconian measures could be the difference between a 10.0% and a 10.1% increase in the CPI. Further, even if we were to order modifications in our federal environmental and health regulations tomor-

row morning, the economic effects would not be noticeable for some years—and we do not know what the inflationary pressures will be at that time.

Moreover, we must recognize that the Consumer Price Index, like the GNP, is a very limited measuring stick. It gauges inflation by measuring the price increases of a typical market basket of goods. Expenditures to improve the environment can and do greatly increase consumer welfare—I have in mind improvements in public health, reduced property damage, increased agricultural and resource yields, and enhanced recreation and enjoyment of leisure time—but these benefits to consumers are poorly reflected in the CPI.

Inflation is best understood as an increase in price without a corresponding increase in value. It follows that as long as the full benefits of environmental regulations exceed the full costs—and I believe that this is clearly the case today—these regulations cannot be considered truly inflationary. The Council of Economic Advisers made a similar point in its 1978 *Economic Report to the President* when it noted that insofar as federal regulatory efforts "result in improvements in public well-being, we may simply have taken part of our productivity gains in forms that are not measured in GNP."

Our economics counts up the money we *have* spent; it is just beginning to take account of the money that we did *not* have to spend to repair the consequences of our carelessness.

I believe that we must make every effort to ensure that environmental and health regulations are not unnecessarily expensive and are set after due consideration of economic impacts—and I want to stress that this is required by almost all federal environmental laws and is an integral part of the program of the Environmental Protection Agency and other agencies. We must look elsewhere for the underlying sources of inflation and the appropriate targets for our anti-inflation efforts.

During recent years we have been buffeted by inflationary shocks of unusual magnitude and frequency. The quadrupling of OPEC oil prices, widespread crop shortages, the Soviet grain purchases, the fall in the value of the dollar, and other factors led to double-digit inflation in 1974; we are still living with the impacts of these events as they work their way through the economy. Both price and wage increases are said to be justified by the need to "catch up" with the past wage and price increases in other sectors—a constantly rising spiral of cause-and-effect that has no logical end. Yet the inflationary shocks continued: poor weather conditions, smaller meat supplies, and restricted sugar imports drove food prices up at an annual rate of 16 percent during the first quarter of 1978.

There seems to be a consensus that today's inflation is different. One notable characteristic of current inflation is that it is not restricted to a single nation or region, but is common throughout the industrial world. Another is that, as the Council on Wage and Price Stability pointed out, "the current inflation in the United States differs significantly from our earlier post World War II episodes when excess demand pressures played a prominent role. The current inflation has persisted in the face of the worst recession since World War II." This simultaneous existence of substantial unemployment and strong inflation, in the words of the Council of Economic Advisers, "poses major problems for both economic theory and policy."

Lester Brown, Director of the Worldwatch Institute, sees a pattern in what might otherwise seem to be a random set of inflationary shocks. He believes many of our current economic ills may be rooted in the deteriorating relationship between the world's population, now numbering more than four billion, and the earth's natural systems and resources.

In Brown's view, the OPEC price hike and our increasing food prices are not isolated or one-time events. The rise in food and fuel prices should be viewed—together with the dramatic increases in forest product prices and land values—as too many people chasing a shrinking total of basic goods.

Brown is careful not to ascribe all the current inflation to pressures on resources; he says such pressures are one important new factor that distinguishes today's inflation from the past. But if, as he suggests, we are indeed approaching planetary resource limits, then we can expect that the factors which brought an abrupt end to two decades of decreasing new materials prices will continue to exert their inflationary impact in the future.

If the analyses by Brown and others are correct, and they appear on target to me, environmental regulations aimed at the wise stewardship of our natural resources may be the best investment we can make. Cutting back on such regulations might leave us in the grip of a biologically illiterate economics that could spend us into global bankruptcy.

Waiting for a Philosopher King
Making Cancer Policy Until Certainty Arrives

Environmental cancer is a subject which the "experts" do not fully understand, yet it is one that should be of concern to everyone. In 1900, cancer was eighth on the list of causes of death among Americans, accounting for 64 deaths in every 100,000 members of the population; by 1970, cancer was second only to heart disease, and accounted for 163 deaths for every 100,000 people. An estimated 900,000 new cancers will be diagnosed this year and 360,000 will die of cancer. Eventually, according to the American Cancer Society, one in every four of us will develop cancer; and about two-thirds of those of us who get it will very possibly die of it.

One can take a cynical view of such statistics and attribute the rise in cancer mortality to our success in conquering other forms of disease. We have to die of something, in this view; now that diphtheria and TB are no longer killing us in large numbers, we have to expect an increase in deaths from other causes, such as cancer. But by 1960 cancer mortality in the U.S. was already about double that which might have been predicted on the basis of the increasing age and size of the population. It is clear, from statistics in other countries as well as our own, that something new is loose in

the world.

By comparing various cancer rates, scientists now estimate that as much as 60 to 90 percent of cancer is related to environmental as opposed to hereditary factors. Examples of such environmental factors include smoking habits; alcohol consumption; dietary habits; exposure to various forms of radiation, such as x-rays, radioactive materials, and ultraviolet radiation from the sun; and exposure to a wide range of industrial chemicals and minerals and certain naturally occurring compounds, such as aflatoxins, which are secreted by certain molds.

No one knows for certain the relative importance of these various factors. Today our suspicion is focused increasingly on chemical compounds as the most prevalent cause of cancer. An estimated thirty thousand chemicals are in commercial production in the U.S., and a few hundred are introduced annually into commercial production and distribution. Old and new chemicals are ubiquitous in our environment—as by-products of manufacturing processes, as constituents of packaging, as additives in our food and wastes in our air, land and water.

How do we know which ones are harmful? Of all the

chemicals that have been released into the human environment, we *know* that a small number cause cancer in man. We know this for the best and most tragic of reasons: they *have* caused cancer in man, and we have taken steps to prevent or reduce their further introduction into our environment.

But we cannot patiently wait for other carcinogens to make themselves known in this manner. Cancer has a typical latency period of 15 to 40 years; by the time a carcinogen has been positively identified, many thousands of our population may already have contracted cancer. Hence we have to figure out some way to spot a cancer-causing agent before we expose humans to it.

This latency period—the long delay between exposure and disease—points up another complication. The cancer patterns of today reflect stimuli present in the environment decades ago. We have thus only just begun to experience the results of the surge of new chemicals which began after World War II. The Federation of American Scientists has called attention to one ominous implication of this fact: "In principle it is only too possible to imagine the cancer rate suddenly rising 2%, 3%, or 4% a year—rather than the 1% now being experienced. At these rates, cancer would quickly become far more serious even than it is today. Suddenly, it might be belatedly realized that one or more of many chemicals introduced into the environment decades ago was highly carcinogenic and was, after a twenty or thirty year lag, beginning to show its effects. With the present inability to cure substantial numbers of cancers, Americans would be defenseless—with alarm bells ringing much too late. It is obviously insupportable to continue to run these risks."

We are now spending about $500 per capita annually for medical research and health care—some tens of billions for cancer alone. Despite this investment, we have made only modest progress since the 1950's toward arresting diagnosed cancers and prolonging life. We continue to seek cures, and hope they will be found—but it is obvious that the cure is not just around the corner, and we must turn to other strategies for dealing with cancer.

The lack of a major breakthrough in finding a cancer cure and the belief that a major and increasing portion of human cancer is due to exposure to chemicals in the environment have combined to focus public and governmental attention on preventing cancer by seeking out and eradicating its causes.

Some aspects of preventive strategies can be formulated and carried out by government officials, acting within their respective spheres of authority. In this democracy, however, public policy still rests on the choice of the individual voter. Thus, the ultimate success of any cancer-prevention policy rests on the willingness of voters to explore disputed principles on which an action may be based.

The entire field of carcinogenesis is shrouded in uncertainties. There are substantial areas of agreement among our technically qualified people, but also major issues on which they differ. And then there are difficult value choices that would exist even if the technical issues were resolved. At this point we might wish for the modern equivalent of Plato's philosopher-king—one person whose superior wisdom and pre-eminent virtue made his authority acceptable to all.

Such fellows may have abounded in ancient Greece, but they seem to be rare today—and we cannot defer our choices until one of them arrives. Recognizing that we are faced with uncertainty, we must decide for ourselves—and we must decide *soon*. Having learned all we can from our technicians, we are forced to realize that in this, as in so many complex matters, social value judgments frequently exceed the decision-making prerogatives of any profession or discipline. It is both the glory and the burden of democracy that lay citizens must make the final choice.

Decision Making in the Solar Age

HAZEL HENDERSON

IN ORDER TO CLARIFY my position at the outset, it might be useful to try to clear up the fuzziness which leads many business spokespersons to confuse the large modern corporation with "free enterprise" and even with private property. Luckily the American people, according to surveys, still can distinguish the crucial difference between genuine free enterprise and large, bureaucratized corporations operating beyond the classic checks and balances of Adam Smith's requirements for free markets to function as efficient resource-allocators: i.e., that buyers and sellers meet each other in the marketplace with equal power and equal information and that no "spillover" nuisance effects should be visited on innocent bystanders to the transactions. I need hardly add that such conditions are rarely met in today's industrial economies, except in the babysitter market!

Countless surveys have also shown that while public confidence in large corporations and their management has plummeted, there is as much support as ever for free enterprise and private property rights, and indeed, there is a resurgence of concern and sympathy with the smallest businesses, genuine entrepreneurship, and the growing numbers of self-employed, self-reliant citizens. This clarity on the part of voters is encouraging and bodes well for our form of political democracy, although not surprisingly, it discomfits many corporate managers. Similarly, the US public still appears to understand the difference between the inviolable sanctity of individual, personal property as a bastion of political liberty and to assure personal dignity and security, versus the license to hide behind property rights (encouraged by interpretations of the 14th Amendment to the Constitution in ascribing "personhood" to corporations chartered for only limited *financial*, not social, purposes).

The well-known constitutional lawyer Arthur S. Miller points out the schizophrenia inherent in this definition of corporate "personhood" which permits corporations to enjoy all the benefits of personhood under the law: due process and the equal protection laws under the sanctity of the 14th Amendment, but without the accompanying duties that the rest of us real persons must bear. Thus corporations pose serious constitutional issues as political entities shielded from law.

As we know, today such agglomerations of property, divorced from the control of stockholder/owners, can often deny or conflict with the property rights of individuals. In fact as early as 1814, Thomas Jefferson noted, "I hope we shall crush in its birth the aristocracy of our moneyed corporations, which dare already to challenge our government to a trial of strength and bid defiance to the laws of our country."

This brief clarification is necessary because I believe that all late stage industrial societies such as our own, Canada, those of Europe and Japan, are going through an inevitable transition, resulting from their very success in the past 200 years of the Industrial Revolution in maximizing labor-productivity and the GNP-measured growth of their institutionalized, monetized economies (as opposed to their total productive societies). This economic transition, already well underway, involves an inevitable shift from economies maximizing rates of production and consumption based on non-renewable resources to economies that minimize such wasteful rates of throughput of energy and materials and will be based on renewable resources and managed for sustained-yield, long-term productivity. The symptoms of this great transition include increasing rates of inflation, structural unemployment, the failure of macro-economic management, and growing tax revolts. The transition also marks the end of the Age of Keynes, and the reliance on "trickle-down" theories of stimulating aggregate demand so that greater consumption by the more affluent would trickle down to benefit the poorer groups by increasing sales, profits, investment, and jobs in the private sector. And if more workers were automated out of the private sector, or if private consumer demand faltered, there was always public-works pump-priming and easy credit to fill the gap, while government employment—local, state and federal—became the employer of last resort.

All this worked out quite well, with almost unnoticeable rates of inflation, as long as cheap, abundant energy and resources were available or could be imported. However, in an age of higher global expectations and understandable demands from resource-rich, less-developed countries (LDCs) for a New International Economic Order, cheap resources are now denied to the newly-vulnerable industrial countries, which all face an unavoidable period of retrenchment as they gear down their now-excessive energy and resource-intensity and undergo what I have described as a period of social entropy.

While it is now clear in the travails of most industrial countries that Keynesianism has failed, many are taking another nostalgic detour back to laissez-faire, monetarist remedies, creating recessions, raising interest rates, and creating unemployment in the vain hope of reducing their structural inflation. Since their inflation is related to their excessive resource-intensity and the growing backlog of social and environmental costs now coming due, however, all that these policies will do is to increase inflation. In fact, we are now seeing the new breed of inflationary recessions, with inflation rates following the interest rates, as I have predicted for a decade. The fashionable "supply-side economics" will only make things worse, since "inflation" is a measure of the thermodynamic errors in designing production processes and capital investment decisions that economic theory perpetuates. Thus Mr. Ronald Reagan will be just as unsuccessful as was Jimmy Carter at solving the nation's stagflation syndrome, and his policies of increasing military spending by $20 billion and adding massive tax cuts and further subsidies to capital investment (however abortive in "net energy" terms) will further increase inflation, as will the stimulation of private consumption, much of it wasteful or polluting. The next few years will provide a needed lesson that it is not only Keynesian Liberalism that doesn't work, but also that Monetarist Conservatism won't work either. As voters in Britain are discovering with Mrs. Thatcher's monetarist-advised recession, high interest rates, catastrophic loss of jobs, and whole sectors of the small business economy facing bankruptcy, this has only increased Britain's inflation and may lead to a backlash swing to the far Left.

Indeed, there is an inevitable trade-off in evolution between adaptation and adaptability. Past success constrains future success; growth creates structure and then structure inhibits further growth. Nothing Fails Like Success. Anthropologists state the same proposition as the Law of the Retarding Lead: those cultures most successfully adapted to past conditions will be overtaken by those less committed and overspecialized, as conditions change.

Today we see the maturing industrial societies of the Northern Hemisphere caught in this oldest evolutionary trap, having developed socio-technical configurations superbly adapted to past conditions of vast, unexploited fossil fuel and raw material deposits and fertile or sparsely-populated lands. Today, as countries such as Brazil and others try to emulate their specifically historic growth pattern, these older industrial societies of the North, whether capitalistic, socialist, or mixed, are in shock. They are almost totally unprepared for the Solar Age.

We see fearful evidence that the leaders of these crises-ridden industrial societies, instead of accommodating the necessary feedback and opening up their societies to adapt to change, are rigidifying and redoubling their efforts to shore up their crumbling sectors and no-longer viable institutions by trying to augment the already unresponsive, cumbersome machinery of centralized control. The crises of industralism range from malfunctioning dinosaur technologies, bureaucratized decision-making, paralysis of over-centralization, information-handling bottlenecks, collapsing monetary and trading systems, proliferating pollution, domestic unrest, inadvertent weather and climate modification, overfished and poisoned waters, vanishing agricultural land, loss of productivity and increasing vulnerability caused by resource-dependencies. All this has culminated in increasing militaristic confrontations over resources and the now obvious instability of the existing international system based on the contradiction of mutual deterrence, polarization of the USA and the USSR around the 19th Century debate between capitalism and socialism. Both are forms of industrialism.

It is clear for example, that the crises in the world monetary system auger global restructuring, whether one is a banker in London or New York or a finance minister of a Third World country heavily in debt. However, like most other tightly-linked systems in our crowded, interdependent world, the monetary system is so delicately interwoven (nothing more than an information system operating globally at computerized speed) that it *requires* cooperation, as it is enmeshed in its own feedback. Although the rules of the game were set by industrial countries, they have now transformed the system with their own technology and belief in endless paper profit, which now flouts the basic laws of physics and commonsense. Multinational companies can make more paper profits by trading currencies than by putting up a real factory to produce real goods anywhere in the real world, while private investors look for ever higher paper returns in short-term paper or flee to gold.

Those who live by the monetary illusion may die by the monetary illusion, since they have mistaken money symbols for real wealth. In such a chaotic system, any significant group of Third World debtor countries could bring the whole house of cards crashing down by simply declaring bankruptcy together, while reminding the bankers and financiers of a similar happening when Germany defaulted after the first World War. Thus, there already *is* a "New International Economic Order," since the relationship between debtor and creditor countries is no longer hierarchical in reality, but one of mutal dependence—and only mutual respect and rewriting the rules to fit the new facts will allow a peaceful evolution of the world's monetary and trading system. Thus the task is to correct the inequities and imbalances perpetuated on paper, and rewrite the charter of all global monetary institutions to reflect full participation of all actors in all decision-making: debtors and creditors alike. Thus debtor countries now see their power to "call the bluff" of those who have controlled the monetary system by declaring that they will no longer play the game by an outmoded set of rules that have led to imbalances now verging on disaster for all players.

We must call the bluff of many other keepers of the old order who cannot see what is being born. They say, in effect, "we have created such a dangerously unstable system that you must keep us in power since only we know and can manage the dangers we have created." One can never expect new alternatives to emerge from dominant cultures and their elites. Those who see the new possibilities are usually from groups subordinated and manipulated by the conventional wisdom. This "protection racket" logic of the keepers of the old order must at last be debunked, if we are to see beyond it and create alternative futures for human societies.

One of the best indications of a generalized, systemic crisis is that continuing to apply conventional control mechanisms only makes matters worse, as for example when the traditional stop-go remedies of the monetarist and Keynesian economic planners leave industrial societies exhausted and "stagflated" with ever more pernicious unemployment. Even the question, "Where is the new Keynes?" is wrongly posed, since the remedies lie beyond the discipline of economics.

Today, we see many other instances where redoubling old efforts and applying old mechanisms simply exacerbates old problems while leading to a score of new ones as evidenced with our "add-on" technological fixes. As my dear friend Fritz Schumacher, author of *Small Is Beautiful,* used to say, "industrial societies now need a breakthrough a day to keep the crisis at bay." Take energy policies in most Northern Hemisphere countries. While paying much lip service to conservation, most are re-doubling their efforts to increase supplies of non-renewable energy, rather than reconceptualize their situation as one of energy and resource over-dependence and address the real issues of redesigning their industrial processes and infrastructure for vastly greater thermodynamic efficiency, while committing their investments to an orderly transition to economies based on renewable resources managed for sustained-yield, long-term productivity. Instead of embracing and capitalizing on the inevitable dawning of a new Solar Age, most countries are still hurling their precious capital, research and development funds, and human resources into yet another costly detour into non-renewable energy technologies.

The Soviet Union, France, Germany, and Britain are still backing into a nuclear future, looking through the rear-view mirror, while the USA, its nuclear program stalled by wary Wall Street investors and insurance companies, has now committed $20 billion tax-funds into a wasteful, inept boondoggle in synthetic fuels from coal. This is hailed, not incidentally, by big oil companies who will benefit, and thus recapture most of the $24 billion windfall profit tax just enacted by the Congress! Thus the costly detour through the non-renewable energy past, at the behest of dinosaur industries, continues to prevent adaptation to the future. Meanwhile, the so-called less-developed countries of the world's sun-belt are free to leapfrog the unsustainable technologies and proceed straight to the Solar Age.

I recently attended the World Association for the Study of Social Prospects (Association Mondiale de Prospective Sociale) conference in Dakar, Senegal, where there was much discussion of these multiple crises of the industrial countries, as well as predictions that the next stage would be their stepped-up efforts to export all these crises to the Third World. If German, French, and American citizens prefer safer, renewable energy to nuclear fission, then the nuclear power industry would step up its sales efforts in Brazil, the Phillipines, and Pakistan. If Americans are up in arms about toxic chemical dumps, such as that in Love Canal, New York, then the wastes must be dumped in Africa.

We see further indications of systemic crisis in that

applications of old control mechanisms interact to create such vicious circles as the tragic interaction of energy and military policies. Thus the focus on energy *supply* rather than addressing the structure of *demand* creates tragic absurdities such as US threats to defend "our" oil lifeline in the Mid-East, militarily, if "necessary," but at the cost of exacerbating domestic conflict by re-instating the military draft. Not surprisingly, a whole generation of young Americans, inculcated by advertising with the belief that their patriotic duty consisted of little more than buying a car to "See the USA in Your Chevrolet," voiced misgivings and protest at the idea of fighting a war to preserve their parents' right to drive large cars and vacation in air-conditioned motor-homes. The most obvious contradiction in all this is the even more tragic absurdity that fighting wars over energy supplies wastes even more energy—since war is the most energy-intensive and entropic of all human activities!

All human societies—and other living species, for that matter—sustain themselves by taking ordered, low-entropy resources from their environments and discarding higher-entropy wastes. Thus all our extraction, production, consumption, and recycling processes are entropic and their true efficiency is best measured by their success at minimizing these rates of entropy; they are better accounted for in thermodynamic terms than by economics. In fact, the economists' mystification, "inflation," merely represents all the variables left out of economic models, coming back to haunt us; and a good chunk of industrial economies' persistent inflation is the thermodynamic errors that economic models of efficiency encourage. Thus another symptom of the evolutionary bind of industrial countries is that all their redoubled efforts to continue on the same historic course simply increase their inflation rates, since these resource-dependent societies are simply encountering the boundary conditions of the Laws of Thermodynamics. The harder they struggle, the deeper they will fall into the thermodynamic sink they prefer to call "inflation." Thus the contradictions of industrialism itself are now clear in the escalating destruction of the biosphere itself, whether by socialist commissars or state-owned or "private" transnational corporations.

The task facing industrial societies as they enter the 1980s and 1990s, and their coming "trial by entropy," will be to face up to the unsustainability of their value-systems rather than view their "problems" as deficiencies of nature. This kind of "gestalt switch" out of our infantile, anthropocentric preoccupations is now the prerequisite for our survival and for the sur-vival of our species. We need to begin inventorying all of the world's value-systems, since they represent, in essence, packages of social "software" which produce various mixes of behavioral outputs, technological "furniture," and organizational forms which can be fitted to specific geographical regions and their ecological carrying capacities. We need to learn that value-systems are *resources*—just as real as coal or oil, and provide the key human adaptive mechanism to changes in our environment. Aware leaders might arise from within the institutional arrangements, nations and corporations that comprise the existing, fast-crumbling world order.

The temptation is to throw the dice on one more turn of the old wheel: one more year of good return on investment to dazzle the Wall Street analysts; one more round of high-risk lending of "funny-money" Eurodollars; one more round of escalation of the East-West arms race; or one more round of speculation in gold, commodities, or the world's shrinking land and forests. The rationale is easy to the point of glibness: "If we don't, someone else will," or "If you can't beat 'em, join 'em."

And yet we are all aware that this type of vicious-circle reasoning by individual actors is precisely that which accelerates the disintegration: in systems and operations research theory it is known as sub-optimization. In game theory terms it is encoded in the well-known story of "The Tragedy of the Commons," restated rigorously by Garrett Hardin in *Science*. In feudal England, all peasants grazed their animals on the village green, known as "the Commons," but it did not take long for each peasant to learn that he could maximize his own situation by grazing ever more of his animals on this common land. In a predictably short period the Commons itself became overgrazed and was destroyed for all. Thus the brief 200-year development of an economics which rationalized that each pursuing his own self-interest would culminate in the best outcomes for the group, i.e., the "Invisible Hand" of Adam Smith, can now be seen as coinciding with an equally brief period of rapid, one-time exploitation of fossilized energy, which allowed a temporary expansion of the "Commons." Today, as the Age of Petroleum wanes, we see the much older and diametrically-opposite proposition, i.e., the Tragedy of the Commons, return, based as it is on the First and Second Laws of Thermodynamics and on general systems and game theory.

How then are we to grasp the nature of these proliferating crises, where it seems that all of the planet's major sub-systems are going critical simultaneously, and that these processes appear to be accelerating as

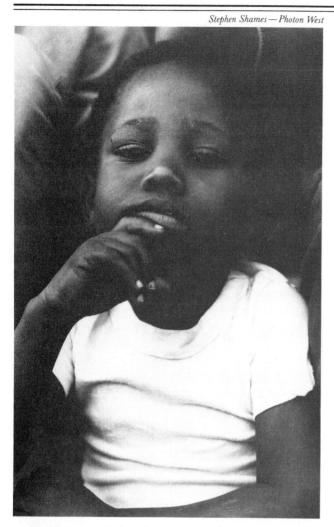

Stephen Shames — Photon West

well? The most helpful model is that of the biological process of morphogenesis, extremely common in nature: the process, for example, by which a chrysalis turns into a butterfly. This kind of model of change allows us to see both the breaking down of old structures and the generation of new, often radically different structures occurring simultaneously. Other characteristics of morphogenetic change are that it is systemic, affecting all parts of the system in transformations and that these processes of change accelerate, governed by exponential, positive feedbacks which amplify the changes and push the systems over thresholds into new states and structural forms. Morphogenetic systems are now becoming of great interest to physicists, chemists, and mathematicians, as we leave the mechanistic, materialist age based on the manipulation of inorganic raw materials and move to the Solar Age, which will be based on the biological sciences. Today the industrial societies misunderstand their problems, as declining "productivity" and "innovation," based on confused economic definitions.

Rather, they must shift attention from the exhausted potential of their past socio-technical configurations, and see the new possibilities opening up in rearranging their institutional forms and value systems growing out of the new worldviews provided by biological, organic models of change and evolution.

Morphogenetic systems have been well described in biology, and have led to breakthroughs in mathematical modelling by Rene Thom (1972), biochemical models of development of living organisms by Ilya Prigogine (1967), and general systems theories of Magoroh Maruyama and Erich Jantsch. Unlike the simple homeostatic cybernetic models that are self-regulating via thermostat-type feedback which keeps them in a structurally-stable, internally-dynamic equilibrium, morphogenetic models are in dis-equilibrium, constantly changing and evolving, as are all living systems. Thus, I believe that what is happening to the human species on this planet today is this kind of awesome metamorphosis of the entire Earthly biosphere, which biochemists James Lovelock and Lynn Margulis have termed "Gaia" after the Grecians' Earth goddess. This global metamorphosis can be seen in the altering of the Earth's atmosphere with increasing carbon dioxide levels, the mostly man-made changes in lands, oceans, and forests as well as the swiftly changing, unmanageable societies of human beings, their technologies, and their values. In a real sense the whole world has changed.

Nations and corporations can, in the short-run, avoid dealing with the new Tragedy of the Global Commons, but in the longer-run, it will engulf them too, and their short-run behavior will govern the length of the intervening time-span. The most immediate form in which this global Tragedy of the Commons presents itself is in growing global starvation and malnutrition. But it is becoming clear that it is no longer enough for good people to work at redistributing food when the global marketplace cannot distinguish between "effective demand" for food and needs, and that it is the working of this economic system that creates obesity in the over-developed countries and starvation in the Third World. The "world market" is a ridiculous abstraction when compared with the reality just described. That dream world of the "world marketplace" is rapidly being impinged upon as we see the limits of competitive, zero-sum games based on growth and expansion of sub-units in a finite, crowded, polluted, depleted planet. And yet only uniformity of constraint and a new set of global rules for the activities of transnational corporations could allow any individual corporation to face up to the global crises as a responsible institutional "world citizen."

Within such a chicken-and-egg, Catch-22 situation for corporate managements, how nevertheless can leadership be asserted? The situation faced by transnational corporations which, on such realistic appraisal of the new global conditions, decide to exert such leadership, is not very different from that of national governments operating in the traditional competitive, expansionist geopolitics of "national security" now so clearly counterproductive to all actors on the global stage. How can they change the context of their malfunctioning relationship from a position within these outmoded systems? Obviously, unilateral actions can merely set one institution at a disadvantage in relation to others not so globally responsible. Thus, there is no substitute for the painstaking quasi-political task of engineering a broad consensus within the existing system of relationships that can provide the underpinnings for a resolution of these "beggar-thy-neighbor," zero-sum dilemmas at the larger, contextual system-level: whether as the new Law of the Sea treaty or a uniform global Code of Conduct for Transnational Corporations called for by the Brandt Commission and many other bodies within the United Nations system.

The choice is either the evolutionary dead end we are facing or the evolutionary succession of shifting to Solar Age economies. This implies a design revolution, the most exciting challenge industrial societies have ever faced—and one that can involve all our citizens able to work, as well as the overhaul and capitalization of new production systems. I do not mean the confused, catch-all slogan "re-industrialization," another rearview-mirror concept which begs the real question: which sectors of our economy should be maintained, and by what criteria shall new sectors be capitalized? In my view, the transition strategy must begin by retrofitting for conservation: everything from inner-city housing to tightening up industrial production processes and redesigning thousands of products while applying full-cost pricing to eliminate some of the most frivolous and energy-wasteful, and applying life-cycle costing to yield true comparisons between traditional energy sources and solar and renewable sources whose initial costs are high, but whose "fuel"—sun, wind, falling water—are free.

I envision not only a design revolution, but also a scientific revolution, beyond the simple "meat ax" technologies of the past, when we could let cheap petroleum do our thinking for us. The next scientific revolution will be orders of magnitude more challenging and sophisticated, more subtle and elegant. A problem of production will not even automatically call up images of factories, machinery, or "hardware," but will involve thinking harder: better "software," so that we first scan the ecosystem and its living, renewable resource-base for processes and capacities we can tap into on a sustained-yielded productivity basis, or that we can augment—for example, redesigning plants to fix their own nitrogen and fertilizers instead of mining the last few tons of our world's dwindling phosphates.

The design revolution involving the bio-sciences and ecological sciences will far supercede the complexity of the physical, inorganic, and mechanical sciences. The new productive and maintenance systems it will engender will all be subjected to environmental impact statements, and will yield positive environmental benefits, such as producing hydrocarbons from plants which bloom in the most arid deserts. This is what I mean by Solar Age decision-making. The Solar Age means a lot more than flat-plate solar collectors now sprouting on suburban rooftops all over the USA. Of course, I mean the broadest possible interpretation of the Solar Age. For many this means remembering that it is the sun which drives every process on our beautiful planet: the hydrological cycles, the nitrogen and carbon cycles, the photosynthetic processes, the climate and weather machine—all of which permit economic processes, based on energy and materials conversion and combustion, to occur. Thus, my definition of the Solar Age includes not only solar thermal and photovoltaic technologies, but windpower, hydro-power, geothermal energy, ocean thermal gradient and tidal power, hydrogen and biomass fuels, bioconversion of wastes, passive-designed architecture. Conservation technologies, from home insulation to better thermodynamically-performing industrial processes and cogeneration of electric power, are even more fundamental to the coming Solar Age, because they imply the need to restructure major sectors of traditional industrial economies, redesign both products and production methods and even major reconfiguration of their basic infrastructures, such as transportation modes and population densities and catering to changing tastes and lifestyles.

Reading and Designs

Designs for the Solar Age imply specific concern with scale, a key criterion in the management of both organizational and physical systems. Thus the popularity of such books as Schumacher's *Small Is Beautiful;* Leopold Kohr's *The Breakdown of Nations,* first published in 1957 and now reissued; Kirkpatrick

Sale's *Human Scale,* an astute analysis of the political realignments occurring around the issue of "bigness" per se, whether of government or corporations; Jaroslav Vanek's *Self-Management* and *The Participatory Economy,* describing the Yugoslavian enterprise model; *The Sane Alternative* by James Robertson, a former British diplomat and high-level bureaucrat, who witnesses eloquently the dis-economies of scale and describes the "informal economy" in Britain; Amory Lovins's *Soft Energy Paths,* describing a renewable energy scenario which allows political and economic decentralization, and which has spurred dozens of similar studies in Sweden, Denmark, Japan, France, and Britain, to name a few.

No reading list on the issue of scale and decentralism is complete without Mildred Loomis's *Decentralism: Where it Came From, Where Is It Going?,* a comprehensive history of this oldest American political tradition from Thomas Jefferson to libertarianism and utopian anarchism. Contributions from Latin America include Ivan Illich's *Tools for Conviviality;* from France, Jacques Ellul's celebrated *The Technological Society;* from Africa, *Poverty: The Riches of People,* by Albert Tevoedjre of Benin; from Sweden, Nordal Ackerman's *Can Sweden Be Shrunk?;* from Canada, Lawrence Solomon's *The Conserver Solution;* from Denmark, the best-seller, *Opror Fra Midten* (Revolt from the Middle) by former education Minister, Helveg Petersen, physicist, Niels Meyer, and journalist Villy Sorenson; from Germany, Joseph Huber's *Anders Arbeiten-Anders Wirtschaften;* and from New Zealand, the manifesto of the Values Party, which won 6 percent of the vote in its first election bid, entitled *Beyond Tomorrow.*

Even the Stanford Research Institute and the Trilateral Commission have found it necessary to prepare reports on the ungovernability of nations and the unmanageability of large organizations. Here again, biological theory is more useful than economics, since the study of scale as it relates to the size, structure, and volume of biological systems (which is also a definition of human societies, their "economies" and technological configuration) is well developed under the theory of allometry. In addition, ecological theory offers an important model: when energy is withdrawn from an ecosystem, it must devolve to a more modular, decentralized configuration. When applied to a sociotechnical structure, the same phenomenon is evident, as petroleum is withdrawn, national and international marketing systems based on cheap energy give way to new regional efficiencies of scale—nowhere more evident than in the food system, where transport, packaging, marketing and distribution become increasingly large cost factors, while the local bread baker enjoys a new boom.

Thus at the dawning of the Solar Age we see two linked phenomena:

1) The "spontaneous devolution" of unsustainable institutions in the older, industrial countries, with citizen movements attempting to recall power once delegated under cheap energy to central governments and large corporations, all summed up as "the new localism"—whether in Spain's Basque region; in the United Kingdom's restive Scottish, Irish, and Welsh groups; in Canada's struggles with Quebec and the oil-rich provinces of the West; or in the Polish workers' struggle against the party bureaucracy and the Soviet Union's problems with its Afghanistan situation, its Muslims, Ukranians, Latvians and other ethnic and religious minorities.

2) At the international level we see the calls for a New International Economic Order and the new economic regionalism of Third World states, now aware of the much greater advantages in forming trading partnerships and monetary agreements with each other in geo-specific regions. At the same time, Third World countries are demanding fair participation and democratic control of the Northern-hemisphere-dominated international monetary institutions, the World Bank and the International Monetary Fund, as outlined in the recent Terra Nova Statement on the IMF signed in Jamaica after former Prime Minister Manley's skirmish with the bank. Export-dependent island economies can no longer ride the roller-coaster of world trade, where domestic economies are now destablized every morning when currency exchange markets open. One could put Adam Smith himself in charge of Jamaica's economy, or Karl Marx, for that matter. It would make little difference. The problem is the need for painful re-structuring for greater self-sufficiency and regional trading and bartering, and reduced dependence on the vicissitudes of world markets beyond their control.

Viable alternative futures are already visible to the rest of us with little stake in the dinosaur industries and the government agencies that cater to them. In the painful birthpangs of global transition, we see what is being born: the planetary societies of the new Solar Age—more communitarian and cooperative, based on sustainable technologies and renewable resources, on multiple-leadership at all levels, on information-sharing and networking, on heterarchy (not hierarchy), firmly rooted in biological science and specific, regional ecological and cultural resources, all linked by pluralistic communications media, diverse patterns of regional cooperation, trade, and exchange, and regulated by global treaties and principles for the use of oceans, space, and all common-heritage resources, and for enforcement and peace-keeping. As growing enclaves in Northern industrial societies are developing and spreading these concepts and activities (in what I have described as the emerging "counter-economy," and others have called the "informal economy," the "dual-economy," the "household economy," and the "convivial economy") they look to the more balanced, traditional communities of the Third World for inspiration. Traditional, communitarian, village lifestyles and values have always been despised by the Eurocentric, industrial societies—viewed as "inefficient" by both capitalists and Marxists. All fell under the spell of progress, "efficiency," and monetization, the basic coefficient by which all was to be judged.

Even today, economists ignore the fact that well over 50 percent of all the world's production, consumption, maintenace, and investment is not monetized; indeed, 80 percent of all capital-formation is not monetized. Thus economists see only half the world's economy. The world's monetized systems are in shock precisely because they have ignored the basic rural, village, agricultural production sectors on which they have been parasitic. They have likewise cannibalized these co-operative, non-monetized sectors, destroying their very roots and the bedrock on which they rest. Today then, we must ask "Will The Real Economy Please Stand Up?"

Contrary to economists' beliefs, the informal sectors of the world's economies, in total, are predominant, and the institutionalized, monetized sectors grow out of them and rest upon them, rather than the reverse. Even in the industrialized nations, this submerged and surprising reality can be documented—although the bias of economic statistics virtually precludes this type of analysis. In France, for example, a 1975 study calculated that while 43 percent of the total working hours of the French population were devoted to formal employment, that 57 percent of the working hours were in the informal sector (Adret, *Travailler Deux Heures Par Jour*, Seuil, Paris, 1977). While it is clearly necessary for any society to have both an institutional and an informal sector in its total economy, the danger has arisen in industrialism's focus on "economic efficiency," measured by money and values derived thereby; the overgrowth of the institutionalized sector has created huge imbalances which now threaten to destroy the informal sector, which is the bedrock of all societies. This cannibalizing of the informal sectors, where the monetized sectors' social

costs have been buried, is most visible, of course, in the "most advanced" industrial societies, and luckily is providing an important object lesson for other countries who want to avoid the same trap. Thus the task is that of re-balancing of societies so that informal sector values and functions are revived and restored, while the institutionalized economy and its money-values are limited and put back in their place.

Evidence of the enormity of the errors of economic statistics were presented by the International Labor Organization at the UN Women's Conference in Copenhagen, July 1980. The ILO reported that on a global basis, women worked two-thirds of all the hours worked (paid and unpaid), received 10 percent of the wages and own one percent of the property, while they produce 44 percent of the food. A re-balancing of the dual-economies in societies is really the only way to reduce centralism, Big-Brotherist bureaucracies, mindless hierarchies, and bottlenecks, as well as the accumulations of power and wealth they always create—which, in turn, have always led to expansionism, institutional aggrandizement, military adventures, technological mischief, fantasies of omnipotence and control, and the inevitable exploitation of subordinated groups and the environment.

I believe that as the centralized power in the old world-system is decentralized and new regional configurations of nations and trading alliances emerge, this will present some great opportunities for defusing the new paranoid, ideological Cold War struggle between the USA and the USSR. The dawning Solar Age makes this scenario inevitable, because our planet's energy bases will be more diffused and the Third World will have enormous solar and renewable energy potential which will be explored at the UN meeting on Renewable Energy and Resources scheduled for Nairobi in 1981. Yet the Solar Age choices too, are in danger of being distorted if these new technologies are bought up by the dinosaur companies, who will load them with their overhead and force them to fit inappropriate corporate structures and short-term profit goals, all aided by mis-shapen government research and development grants and priorities, as was documented in *The Sun Betrayed* by Ray Reece. Misguided programs to subsidize gasohol from carbohydrate and food crops such as corn, may bring a new and ugly collision between world food needs and frivolous driving habits. Worse, there is very little thermodynamic yield from such processes, which have been encouraged politically by government subsidies under the misguided synfuels program.

Many scientists favor using methanol from waste wood and other cellulose wastes, so that the conflict with food crops can be avoided and because the potential feedstocks for this biomass source are much larger and more diverse. Even taking competitive uses into account, there is sufficient waste wood, crop residues, wild grasses, etc., to produce 115 billion litres of methanol in the US. Even more exciting is the potential of hydrocarbons derived directly from plants such as euphorbia lathyris—capable of complete chemical reduction, according to Nobel Prize-winning biochemist Melvin Calvin—which can provide hydrocarbon feedstocks for chemical processes and a high-quality, low-molecular weight crude oil for $40 a barrel. It can be grown without irrigation or fertilizers in scrub areas unsuitable for food production! Thousands of other plant and tree species have similar potential for replacing fossil energy and feedstocks, according to biochemist Ingemar Falkehag, who notes in *Bioresources for Development* (1980), edited by Alexander King and Harlan Cleveland, that there are hardly any products made from, or services performed by, fossil carbon sources for which biomass and renewable resources could not be a substitute. The World Conference on Future Sources of Organic Raw Materials, held in Toronto in 1978 drew similar conclusions, with a wealth of papers from Europe, Asia, Africa, Latin America, and the Eastern bloc countries as well as from several transnational corporations.

Perhaps you can begin to see why I am so excited about the Solar Age, and why so many environmental and appropriate technology advocates are organizing and networking around the planet to see that this bright future for all the world's people is not foreclosed by the blindness of existing leaders in their rush to nuclear destruction. Thus we are impelled to work at creating viable strategies of transition to a new global order. Of course it is a herculean task—with no profits on the bottom line. By comparison, running a transnational corporation is child's play. An economy based on renewable resources, and carefully managed for long-term productivity of all its resources, can provide useful satisfying work and richly rewarding lifestyles for all its participants. However, it simply cannot provide support for enormous, pyramided capital structures and huge overloads, large pay differentials, windfall returns on investments, and capital gains to investors, nor can it finance the overblown executive stock options and already extended pension liabilities, the monstrous office buildings, corporate jet aircraft, country club memberships, art collections, and other "perks" which were subsidized in the receding era by cheap fossil fuels and resources. All of this overhead was masked also by the convenient

economic theories of "externalized" costs, passed on to taxpayers, society at large, the environment, or future generations. Nor, I would add, can renewable-resource-based economies sustain massive nuclear arsenals and permanent war economies or costly space adventures. In the transition, we will simply have to stretch capital, energy, and resources further, cutting the waste from our energy system and combining our precious capital with more productive people in smaller, flatter-structured enterprises that liberate human initiative.

The question arises of world competition. But we must remember that all industrial societies, both market-oriented and centrally-managed, are experiencing similar stresses; and the US, with the richest and most wasteful economy, is in the most advantageous position to cut out flab without cutting into muscle. We must also remember that the flab is at the *top*—not the bottom!

Meanwhile, the demands of tomorrow's labor force for more opportunities for personal development and job satisfaction most often favor the small company, which can be more democratically-managed and which can release human potential and productivity through greater identification with the enterprise. Indeed, our greatest future productivity gains will come from learning to trust people to do a good job. Already, there is heightened interest (because of the worldwide interest in human rights, perhaps) in the whole question of civil liberties for employees, described by David Ewing in *Freedom Inside The Organization* (1978).

All of this is not to say that large corporations will fade away. They will not. We will still need to pour steel and aluminum, maintain telephone systems and electrical grids. But some of these systems may have reached an optimal size already, and the growth of newer sectors of the economy may better satisfy new needs in wholly new ways, for which the old corporations and their existing technological configurations may be quite unsuited. Most corporate leaders were acculturated during the now-receding Age of Petroleum, and they have not yet grasped the fact that the socio-economic transition to the Solar Age will require an economic paradigm shift—an entire shift in worldview. This shift will involve replacing the linear, static logic of market equilibrium economics with a much more realistic general systems view of the larger social and ecological *contexts* of managements' decisions.

The most fatal flaw of traditional "flat earth economics" involves its assumptions of an equilibriating economic system (such as actually existed during 18th and 19th century era of Adam Smith). Today, because of the "fine-tuning" of a generation of activist economic policy-makers and to the development of ever more complex, capital-intensive, socially and ecologically disruptive technologies, we now have created industrial systems that are in chronic states of *dis*-equilibrium. In addition, they are linked globally and both ride on the same international roller coaster of today's world trade and monetary systems. Yet business leaders, while dealing every day with these realities, still heed advice from economists who believe that such complex dynamic economies are still analogous to simple hydraulic systems. Corporate decisions on capital investments and risk assessment are becoming more error-prone, for example, in the insurance industry, where the conceptual foundations of probability theory are now inadequate.

Corporate leaders, still guided by such bankrupt economics, continue to exhort us to simply turn the clock back and de-regulate the economy, without acknowledging that economic processes such as the 200-year development of the Industrial Revolution are not reversible, but evolutionary transformations, as Nicholas Georgescu-Roegen shows in his *The Entropy Law and the Economic Process* (1971). Massive corporations inevitably create equivalently large government infrastructures to coordinate and regulate them, not to mention huge dis-equilibriating global flows of capital between countries, as described in "Stateless Money" (*Business Week*, Aug 21, 1978). Can one imagine for example, the auto industry having attained its preeminence without the Interstate Highway System, bridge-building, the provision of driver and vehicle licensing bureaucracies, not to mention the staggering costs of traffic police systems? Likewise, how does one repeal the tax-supported airport and traffic control system that underpins the airline industry, or the Federal Communications Commission that must, whatever the outcome of current legislative debate, attempt to coordinate the use of the electromagnetic spectrum and communications satellites, and deal with licensing CB radios, ham operators, etc.? It is also axiomatic in economic development theory that LDCs cannot hope to emulate Western-style industrial expansion without the necessary *government-created* infrastructure: roads, railways, telephones, trained bureaucrats, public education for basic literacy, sanitation, ports and air ports. So the growth of government is always symbiotic with the growth and scale of the private sector.

Confused by such economic paradigm shifts, not surprisingly, many corporate leaders are now spear-heading the charge for lowered taxes. The Republican Party (in the past known for excoriating Democrats as fiscally irresponsible) based much of its 1980 election campaign on the tax revolt issue. We can expect that a preponderance of corporate leaders, bankers, and investment advisors and their economists will step up their speaking, lobbying, and proselytizing on the tax-cut, government-spending issue, since so many of them belong to the Republican Party. Public vigilance on corporate-advocacy advertising and grassroots lobbying will be essential. We must hope that business spokespeople take time to re-think their ideological positions on some of these issues, as well as re-assess their own corporate future options. Meanwhile, corporate managers have the prerogatives of their corporate-image advertising budgets and lobbying capabilities to propagate their own political and economic views (not necessarily those of their stockholders). Additional safeguards against such use of stockholders' assets for political advocacy and grassroots corporate lobbying are needed.

I commend to your attention the recent testimony of Professor S. Prakash Sethi of the University of Texas at Dallas before the Sub-Committee on Commerce, Consumer, and Monetary Affairs of the House Government Operations Committee. Professor Sethi, who has authored several books on corporate/consumer/media/government issues, suggests several ways in which the image v. advocacy advertising issue can be codified; how grassroots lobbying can be regulated more efficiently, and how the right of access in media coverage and counter-advertising for consumer groups' views can be assured. Sethi underlines an important legal distinction between the corporation's right to free speech versus the management's right to speak for the stockholders. He proposes that managers legitimate their views in behalf of the corporation by specifically soliciting the views of stockholders (not *stockholdings*) by means of proxies, since as he adds, "unlike property rights, political rights are *not* subject to trade and transfer."

The problem of access to media for consumers is exacerbated by the natural biases of the business press, mindful of its advertisers' interests. *Fortune*, in an article on the "Backlash Against Business Advocacy," Aug 28, 1978, while pointing out that there was a lack of symmetry in allowing corporations and their trade associations to deduct lobbying expenses while foundations and consumers groups have less deductibility and individuals none, nevertheless justified the situation thus: "But it can be reasonably argued that most corporate grassroots lobbying is a legitimate business expense, since it usually has to do with issues directly affecting the profitability of the company." What *Fortune* failed to point out is that this assumes free mar-

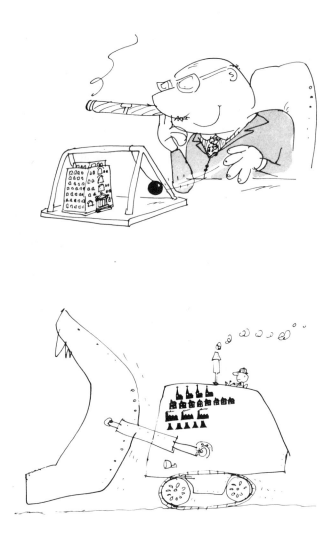

David Myers, Punch

economist Martin Feldstein dismisses the theoretical principle behind the Laffer Cruve, i.e., that at *some* point reducing tax rates increases tax revenues, as "something we teach in the first week of the course on public finance." Most economists agree that the key question is *at what point* on the curve—and that even Laffer can't say where, we are on what can only be described as his Laffable Curve.

The hidden agendas, as always, involve whose oxes are to be gored; and when corporate managers go public with their views on these issues, it usually depends on the business of their corporations. Construction companies don't want the cuts to be made in highway, bridge, and dam-building projects; oil and gas companies don't want to give up tax credits for intangible drilling costs; ship-building firms don't want to give up maritime subsidies; and most of all, aerospace and military-contracting firms don't want to see cuts in the Department of Defense.

Similarly, the North-South dialogue is a way of avoiding the restructuring that now must occur in industrial countries, as well as the value changes now occurring that must be reinforced, rather than countered as they are today, by commercial advertising that still plays on infantile fantasies, greed, and insecurities to sell unsustainable lifestyles and often harmful, addictive products whose manufacture jeoparidzes human health and environmental safety and is even more harmful and disruptive to Third World countries. Although many studies have been made showing that the existing pattern of world trade and monetary systems has harmed, not helped, Third World countries, widening the poverty gap, the most rigorous new study of the destructive nature of the current world economic relationships is that of Graciela Chichilnisky of Columbia University, New York, and the University of Essex, England.

Chichilnisky addresses head-on the conventional development theories such as Richard Cooper's "An International Order for Everyone's Gain," which assumes that the growth of the Northern industrial economies is a precondition for the growth of the South's developing economies. Chichilnisky focuses on differences in technology between industrial and developing countries and their relative capital/labor intensities, and how these readily-observable differences lead to vastly asymmetrical results as to the benefits and costs of world trade. She highlights the subsistence sectors left out of the conventional models of "modernization" (now a curiously old-fashioned word), and she notes that such models fail to explain the fact that during the 25-year post-war period (1945–1970), wealth differences and specialization between the

kets are functioning, while in truth, a powerful corporation can increase its profitability *at the expense* of consumers and taxpayers.

Some corporate leaders are honest enough to admit that corporate agendas may not be coterminous with the public interest. Others are honest enough to admit that lobbying and calling for tax cuts without government spending reductions are sheer irresponsibility. Even Alan Greenspan, former member of the Nixon Council of Economic Advisors, refutes the contention that large tax-cuts would increase economic activity and eventually make up for the loss in higher revenues. This is the reasoning behind Arthur Laffer's now-famous Laffer Curve, which promised such an unlikely pot of gold at the end of the rainbow to the gullible California voters for Proposition 13. Harvard

North and South significantly increased, while the volume of the international market increased in an historically unprecedented fashion. Further, the North-South wealth differentials and the distribution of income within the South did not improve during the period as these theories would predict. Neither gains from trade nor factor price equalization theories can be made consistent with these facts.

An even more graphic example of the end of the old comparative-advantage model of economic development was provided, albeit inadvertently, by a recent article on the new problems inherent in Britain's trade gap in the conservative journal *Now* by its economics analyst, David Smith, entitled "The Invisible Threat To Britain's Fortunes." The article documented the stubborn balance of trade problems in Britain (visible trade in manufactured goods has been in surplus only three years since the Second World War) which have usually been "rescued" by the "invisibles" such as insurance premiums, investment dividends, and tourist payments for an overall balance of payments that has been more manageable. Smith then went on to point out that these "invisibles" that have been mostly in surplus for over a hundred years may now themselves plunge into deficit before the end of 1980. He then outlined the reasons for this historic change, including the strong pound, Britain's contribution to the budget of the European Economic Community (EEC), which Mrs. Thatcher has been trying to reduce, Britain's negative tourist balance, and insurance losses. But the most interesting item was the admission that because of heavy foreign investment in Britain's much-vaunted North Sea oil bonanza, a heavy new volume of profits from these operations are now being repatriated, mostly to the USA—from 1.2 billion pounds sterling in 1979 to an expected 4 billion pounds sterling by the mid-1980s. Thus, we have the case stated baldly: it is better to be an investor in someone else's economy than it is to have investment from abroad in one's own economy. We must give it credence because this analysis of the way international trade and investment actually works comes from the horse's mouth; Britain's colonial preeminence was based on such foreign investments.

Illusions about the efficacy of obsolete, GNP-measured economic growth as a criterion of "development" underlie both the Adam Smith "comparative advantage model" and the new global Keynesianism model of the Brandt Commission. There is now no choice but to address the whole issue of what constitutes "development" from the "basic human needs" approach developed in some UN agencies, the emphasis on human-centered and endogenous development

models now advocated by many Third World countries and codified in the Cocoyoc Declaration, the alternative models of "eco-socialism," and the now-ubiquitous, self-reliant, localized, "people-power" models of development summed up in the title of E.F. Schumacher's *Small Is Beautiful*. Indeed, in most industrialized countries, it is the people who are far ahead of their leaders in raising all these issues as citizen movements for ecological and consumer protection, corporate and government accountability, worker ownership and self-management, cooperative and neighborhood enterprises, and new values of self-restraint; it is the people who explore voluntary simplicity, personal responsiblity for health, vegetarianism, jogging, and holistic self-help; and the people who demand clean, safe, renewable energy, more skills-intensive and capital-saving technologies, economic justice, and conversion of military production to civilian purposes.

In general terms, we are quite aware of the basic principles on which the new world order must be built. Fundamentally, these principles are:

- the value of all human beings;
- the right to satisfaction of basic human needs (physical, psychological, and meta-physical) of all human beings;
- equality of opportunity for self-development for all human beings;
- recognition that these principles and goals must be achieved within ecological tolerances of lands, seas, air, forests and the total carrying capacity of the biosphere;
- recognition that all these principles apply with equal emphasis to future generations of humans and their biospheric life-support systems, and thus include respect for all other life forms and the Earth itself.

Historically, human development can be viewed as many local experiments in creating social orders of many varieties, but usually based on partial concepts. These social orders worked for *some* people at the expense of *other* people, and were based on the exploitation of nature. Furthermore, they worked in the *short*-term, but appear to have failed in the *long*-term. All these experiments in local and partial human development, when seen in a planetary perspective, have been failures in one way or another.

Today, we know that such societies are impossible to maintain and that the destabilizations on which they have built themselves are now affecting both their internal governmental stability and the global stability of the planet. Interestingly, these instabilities can all

Jim Marshall

be stated in scientific terms:

1) In classical equilibrium thermodynamics, in terms of the Law of Conservation and the Entropy Law, that all human societies (and all living systems) take negentropy (available forms of energy and concentrated materials) and transform them into entropic waste at various rates, and that we can measure and observe these ordering activities and the disorder they create elsewhere—e.g., the structuring of European countries in their colonial periods at the price of the concomitant dis-ordering of their colonies, culturally and in terms of indigenous resources.

2) In terms of biology and the evolutionary principle, "Nothing Fails Like Success"—i.e., the trade-offs between short-term and long-term stability and structure.

3) In terms of general systems theory, the phenomenon of suboptimization—i.e., optimizing some systems at the expense of their enfolding systems.

4) In terms of ecology, as violations of the general principle of interconnectedness of ecosystems and the total biosphere—i.e., the continual cycling of all resources, elements, materials, energy, and structures. This interconnectedness of all sub-systems on planet Earth is much more fundamental than the inter-dependence of people, nations, cultures, technologies, etc.

Thus, the aspirations for a new world order are not

only based on ethical and moral principles, important as these emerging planetary values will be for our species' survival. The need for a new world order can now be *scientifically* demonstrated. We see the *principle of interconnectedness* emerging out of reductionist science itself, as a basis, and the concomitant ecological reality that redistribution is also a basic principle of nature. Since all ecosystems periodically redistribute energy, materials, and structures through biochemical and geophysical processes and cycles, all human species' social systems and institutions must also conform to *principles of redistribution* of these same resources that they use and transform, whether primary energy and materials or derived "wealth" (capital, money, structures, means of production, and "power").

The new scientific understanding of *interconnectedness* and the fundamental processes of *redistribution* are accompanied by the emerging paradigms of *indeterminacy, complementarity,* and *change* as basic descriptions of nature. These five principles operate not only at the phenomenological level of our every-day surface realities and in our observance of nature (in the "middle-range" realm of classical physics), but also at the sub-atomic level of phenomena of quantum mechanics.

These five principles emerging in Westernized science itself imply human behavioral adaptation:

- **INTERCONNECTEDNESS** (planetary cooperation of human societies)
- **REDISTRIBUTION** (justice, equality, balance, reciprocity)
- **CHANGE** (re-design of institutions, perfecting means of production, changing paradigms and values)
- **COMPLEMENTARITY** (unity *and* diversity, from either/or to both/and logics)
- **INDETERMINACY** (many models and viewpoints, compromise, humility, openness, evolution, "learning societies")

Thus the new world order can be founded both on scientific *and* ethical principles. We are *discovering* the new world order in science and *remembering* that we know it already, since the new scientific principles are found in all religious, spiritual traditions.

Ethical principles have become the frontiers of scientific enquiry. Morality, at last, has become pragmatic while so-called idealism has become realistic.

Stress is evolution's primary tool—forcing us to grow up at last, to assume our role of fostering the birth of a peaceful, just, humane, ecological world order. Not to "steer" or "manage" the planetary "spaceship" Earth—an arrogant, old-fashioned idea still trapped in our childish fascination with vehicles, transportation, power, and motion. Rather our emerging awareness is of our human species as a conscious *part* of the Earth—no mechanical spaceship, but a living planet—a total, teeming, pulsating, evolving, biological organism: Gaia, the mysterious, self-organizing Earth Mother, nurturer of us and of all life.

What Opinion Makers Expect of the 1980s

THINGS ARE likely to get worse before they get better, but they will get better in the 1980's. Steady pressure in the name of energy development and inflation control will continue in the early 1980's to roll back some standards protecting the environment. We will see further selective erosion of laws and degradation of the environment.

But public awareness of the health, environmental, and economic costs of misusing our air and water and land will not diminish. It will continue the phenomenal growth it had in the 1970's. As more and more citizens—and their elected officials—increase their understanding of the relationship between the environment and human welfare, as the cost of degradation becomes clearer, as people realize that synfuels are not filling their gas tanks while renewable resources take on their share of the job, then we will see a remarkable and permanent nationwide turn toward environmentally sound solutions to our energy and other resource problems. It will bring by the end of the 1980's a reversal of policies and strategies that now threaten the hard-won gains of the 1970's.

— Janet Welsh Brown

The environmental deterioration of the past century is largely energy related. The digging and burning of coal, the transporting and burning of oil, and the indiscriminate cutting and burning of trees, have had a devastating impact on our life-support systems.

The end of the petroleum era is fast approaching. Now is the time to dedicate ourselves to using our remaining fossil fuels more efficiently, while developing renewable solar resources that will provide future generations with safe, clean, endless energy.

This dual approach—more efficient use of energy and development of solar energy—provides an environmentally sound path into the future. Success in this venture will permit us to make the nuclear fission period a brief one and thereby minimize the threats to life currently accumulating from this alternate energy path.

— Russell Peterson

As Americans who stand largely outside the technological establishment, women may be better able to see the cost to this country and this Earth of the drive toward the technological profiteering of the powerful few.

As the majority of community leaders, we are also more likely to support populist concerns within the environmental movement, instead of the more elitist concerns that are important but have limited appeal.

For both these reasons of an outsider's clarity of vision plus inside community involvement, I believe that the women's movement and the environmental movement will and must become more synonymous in the 1980's. Women have always been the troops of environmental work, but have tended to be displaced when salaries, organizations, and hierarchy have been introduced.

In the 1980's, women will be in the leadership as well as in the ranks of environmental preservation.

— Gloria Steinem

I hope the old-line environmentalists will increasingly realize that the worst, most polluted environment is where millions of men and women work. This clean-up of the work place will take the skills and insights of the best environmentalists among us.

— Frank Wallick

Environmentalism in the 1980's will have to become increasingly involved with the needs of people living in urban areas. This is where the majority of Americans are located and where environmental problems pose the greatest danger to health and well-being. And the urban environment has to be seen as more than air or water quality, for it also embraces economic and housing opportunities as well. These latter two elements cannot be viewed as unconnected to environmental issues in the 1980's as they have been in the 1970's, if our cities are to be made liveable for all our citizens.

— Vernon E. Jordan, Jr.

For the most part the laws we need for environmental controls in the workplace and in the general environment are on the books. What remains to be seen is if we have the political resolve to enforce those laws both by retro-fitting existing pollution sources and by assuring that future economic, industrial, and energy development be carried out in an environmentally sound manner.

I fear that our national will to do so is very close to being weakened. Politically attractive calls for regulatory "reform" threaten to beguile us into regulatory paralysis, and energy programs may needlessly be allowed to stampede over substantive environmental safeguards.

A loss of our environmental will would indeed be short-sighted. It would mean more health suffering and other social costs that accompany pollution; it would increase the costs of controls that ultimately will have to be imposed; and it would continue mismanagement of our depletable resources. We have the tools to make the 1980's a decade of solid environmental progress. It only remains to be seen whether we will be forward thinking enough to use them.

— Lloyd McBride

Pamela Valois

With each passing day the public has grown more aware that our natural resources are very limited. And with this realization comes the acceptance that the 1980's will require continued efforts to abate pollution, deal with hazardous wastes, preserve farmlands, encourage wise land use, and influence other major environmental decisions.

A personal environmental ethic has evolved—one which we believe will flourish in the 1980's if nurtured. People no longer talk about energy and environmental conservation in the abstract—they practice it. They recycle solid waste, conserve energy, and do their part to help save our resources.

The public has become increasingly aware of the danger of assuming that major problems we face in coping with high inflation, energy needs, limited food supplies, and other areas can be easily solved at the expense of the environment.

Society will always face conflicting values and needs. But citizens have begun to realize that we must be on guard lest environmental protections be sacrificed in the rush to confront complex national and international problems.

The issues of the 1980's will include: preserving American farmland to insure adequate food supplies; coming to grips with the impact of various forms of energy development; learning much more about hazardous materials; focusing on the impact of diffuse sources of pollution from urban and rural areas on water quality; dealing with the acid precipitation issue.

We have learned through experience that protecting the environment is a dynamic process and citizens must continue to play a role in this vital effort.

— Ruth J. Hinerfeld

I am concerned about the Administration's absorption with the intermediate situation concerning energy production problems in the environment and its failure to first address the immediate problems and then most seriously consider the long term problems. The most counterproductive program with respect to both inflation and the long term problem of environment is a crash program of producing synthetic fuels.

Also, Congress and the Presidency have caught the deregulation fever. The failure to establish standards of control and restraint has already sowed mine beds of hazardous waste and the relaxation of air quality standards now threatens to make of the Earth a poisoned hothouse where life is at best uncomfortable and at worst unbearable. Too much attention has been given to the unpredictable intermediate future and not enough to the observable present and predictable final result of a failure to plan and regulate intelligently.

— Bob Eckhardt

The people of America know full well that environmental protection cannot be sacrificed if we are to remain a thriving, productive Nation.

Farmers, ranchers, and urban dwellers realize that the quantity and quality of water, soil, forests, and other natural resources must not be degraded.

People will not tolerate further pollution that is hazardous to their health.

There are many other benefits from environmental protection, but those which have economic and health values will serve as substantial bulwarks against emerging pressures to gouge our natural resources and lower standards against pollution.

We must dedicate ourselves to carrying out the people's will.

— M. Rupert Cutler

The 1980's will be the either/or decade. We could choose the soft energy path, a concept invented by Amory Lovins. It can lead to a recovery of the senses. It is a world energy strategy for attaining a sustainable global society fueled by renewable energy, phasing out the use of fossil fuels in half a century, and requiring no nuclear energy at all. It minimizes the need for costly electricity, for hard to get capital, for vulnerable overcentralization, and for waste. It matches the energy needed with the most logical source.

Or we could choose the hard path which is just the opposite. Mr. Lovins has made clear the many reasons for choosing without further delay the soft path.

Many individuals and some corporations are already making that choice. By concentrating on energy productivity and conservation, they have made available, in the last five years, two and one half times as much new energy supply as has been provided by alternative hard path routes, including energy imports.

The Congress and the Administration have been slow to perceive the importance of the soft path. They are rushing down the hard path seeking strength through exhaustion, providing energy for a brief America.

A swift change in course, profiting from the soft path energy studies here and abroad, can vastly improve the world's chance to enhance equity, create jobs, reduce the triple threats of inflation, acid rain, and nuclear proliferation, and preserve irreplaceable resources inanimate and living.

— David R. Brower

A fresh breeze is blowing that bodes well for the 1980's. Not only can we understand that statement in its literal sense—our efforts to reduce air pollution are having some effect—but many consumers are thinking "environment" as they evaluate what they buy.

Assuming this trend goes on, we can expect less noise around the home, more small cars and bicycles on roadways, fewer broken bottles and torn plastic packages in our landfills and on our streets.

As the media now animatedly share news and documentaries on environmental traumas such as oil slicks, toxic chemical seepages into backyards and drinking water, so we can expect the media to build such concerns into their television dramas, talk shows, and syndicated columns during the next decade. Affected consumers, themselves, will probably become major media focuses. The viewers/readers will be that much more motivated to act in the interest of their survival, their health, and the ultimate cost that society would incur from not protecting our environment.

The consumer movement may well help our 1980's environment by taking advantage of the economic benefits in returnable containers and recycled products. The more consumers support such choices, the more employment will be generated by environmentally "healthy" business.

— Esther Peterson

I am confident that the 1980's will see a continuation of the progress we have made during the past decade in protecting our environment and natural resources. Despite our short term economic and energy problems, the basic commitment of the American people to a clean, safe, and healthy environment remains strong. Americans want their cities to be free of air pollution, trash, and noise. They want natural areas nearby where they can fish and hunt and hike. They want to be able to work and play without worrying about ill effects from toxic chemicals or nuclear power plants.

More than ever before, the American people appreciate that this is the only planet we have, and that we must walk softly on it.

— Gus Speth

The outlook is positive. The developing countries of the world have changed their perception of environmental concerns dramatically since the Stockholm Conference in 1972. Most now see the necessity of environmentaly-sound development and the pursuit of programs to restore or protect the natural resource base on which future development depends.

The problems and priorities of desertification, water management, deforestation, habitat species loss, and environmental education are gaining widespread recognition. Several developing nations have established ministries of the environment; others are learning more about the extent of their problems.

— Thomas Ehrlich

America woke up in the 1970's to the realization that its life-sustaining resources were endangered. The challenge for the 1980's is to avoid going back to sleep. We are at a dangerous fork in the road. The energy shortages should reinforce our awareness that all of our resources are finite. Yet there is a nasty backlash in the air, aided by the red tape with which some environmental laws have become encumbered. The challenge for the 1980's is to advance environmental protection of our land—a job that has hardly been initiated. The prospects are by no means bleak if we focus on substance.

— S. David Freeman

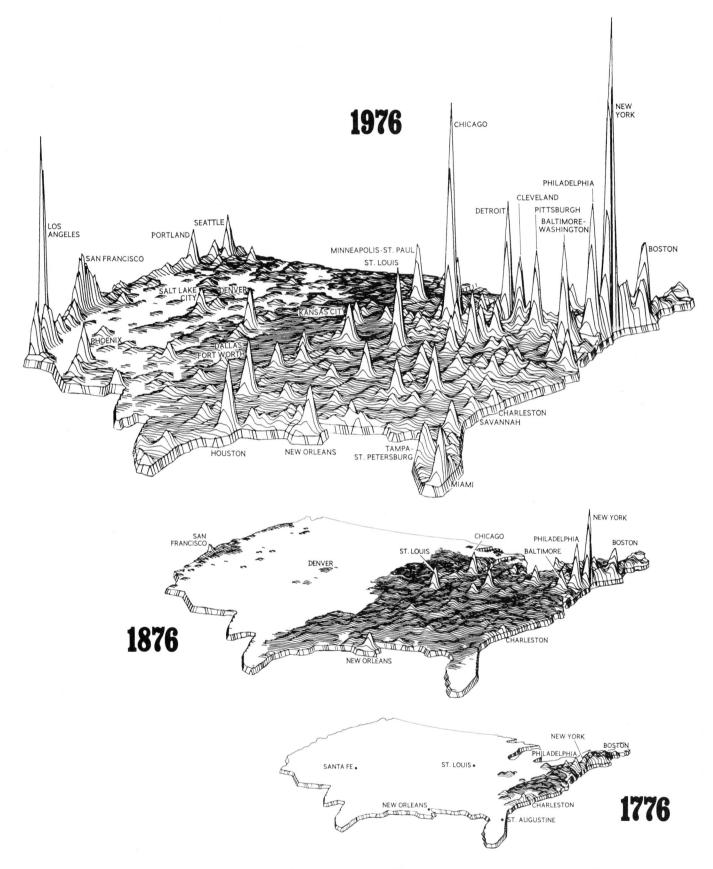

1976

LOS ANGELES
SAN FRANCISCO
PORTLAND
SEATTLE
SALT LAKE CITY
DENVER
PHOENIX
DALLAS FORT WORTH
HOUSTON
KANSAS CITY
NEW ORLEANS
MINNEAPOLIS-ST. PAUL
ST. LOUIS
TAMPA-ST. PETERSBURG
CHICAGO
DETROIT
CLEVELAND
PITTSBURGH
BALTIMORE-WASHINGTON
PHILADELPHIA
NEW YORK
BOSTON
CHARLESTON
SAVANNAH
MIAMI

1876

SAN FRANCISCO
DENVER
NEW ORLEANS
ST. LOUIS
CHICAGO
CHARLESTON
BALTIMORE
PHILADELPHIA
NEW YORK
BOSTON

1776

SANTA FE •
ST. LOUIS •
NEW ORLEANS •
• ST. AUGUSTINE
PHILADELPHIA
NEW YORK
BOSTON
CHARLESTON

Population density maps, generated by Massachusetts Institute of Technology, from National Geographic, *July 1976.*

Part II: Problems We Must Resolve Better

Population

Projections of current growth rates suggest that Planet Earth's population will double (to 8.8 billion) by the year 2016. But many observers think that unlikely. It would require doubling the amount of food, clothing, shelter, and other necessities in a world already resource-short, polluted, and out of control politically. Humanity is all too likely to have its numbers curtailed by famine, epidemic, war, technological disaster, or an amalgam of them all. But today we still have a choice. Intelligent action can probably still save us. We must seek to limit our numbers by all available means. Indeed, for the noble future that *might* be humanity's on Earth, we should set a goal of reducing population to a level that the planet's resources can sustain indefinitely at a decent standard of living—prob-

ably less than two billion. Americans should take the lead in adopting policies that will bring reduced population. Ultimately, those policies *may* have to embrace coercion by governments to curb breeding. But coercion can perhaps be avoided by sufficient provision of incentives, education, careers for women other than childbearing, encouragement of later marriage, and more widespread availability of the means to limit family size. Incentives should certainly include an improved economic status for all the world's poor and provision for their security in old age. Official persuasion might also include revision of the tax laws, replacing their present pronatalist tendencies with subsidies for childlessness. As a first step, we must certainly banish today's social pressures toward childbearing.

Population

STEWART M. OGILVY

"THE POPULATION BOMB" is a phrase invented more than a generation ago by Tom Griessemer and Hugh Moore, who used it to title a pamphlet that described the menace they saw in the growth of human numbers. Medical advances of World War II had helped set population on an unprecedentedly steep climb, and by the pamphlet's publication in 1954, the worldwide increase had already risen to about 1.3 percent a year, or 35 million persons. World population stood at about 2.7 billion.

Two million copies of *The Population Bomb* pamphlet circulated. Its title was recycled when, at David Brower's urging in the late sixties Paul Ehrlich crystallized his own crusade for population restraint into a Sierra Club/Ballantine book. The Ehrlich book sold three million copies in the US, has appeared in five other lands under Friends of the Earth's imprint, and has recently reappeared in a revised US edition.

Despite those efforts and many, many more—literary, scientific, and organizational, by legions of dedicated workers—the population bomb is not yet defused. The globe's population has mushroomed to almost four and a half billion and is exploding at nearly 2 percent, or some 80 million persons, per year. Even if the growth rate continues to slacken as it has recently, we would still, at current rates, have more than eight billion inhabitants on the planet very early in the twenty-first century. That's because there are so many young potential parents in today's population.

Tens, perhaps hundreds, of millions of human beings are jobless, inadequately housed, malnourished if not starving. The projected growth of numbers means that those statistics of agony may be multiplied many times before this century is out. For how can we possibly provide, in the 36 years world population now takes to double, as many new dwellings, hospitals, schools, churches, workplaces, and arable acres as today comprise the legacy of all the generations past? Not to mention the problems of energy, resources, and pollution that eight billion human beings would raise. Nor the matter of providing maintenance for all their buildings and machines, those existing today and others yet to be built.

Many observers say so fast a doubling is beyond the capability of mankind—that the strain on politics, management, resources, energy, medical facilities, and food distribution (if not food production) makes it certain that growth will soon be curtailed by famine,

That's the first thing to do: start controlling population in affluent white America, where a child born to a white American will use about fifty times the resources of a child born in the black ghetto.

—DAVID BROWER

pestilence, nuclear disaster, social chaos, war, or a combination of them. Population growth will certainly be checked within a generation or so, they say, but checked by resurgence of the death rate rather than by reduction of the birth rate. In the meantime, as Hugh Moore, who believed population *can* be checked by intelligent action, put it: "Whatever your cause, it's a lost cause unless we check the population explosion."

The population problem is really several problems. Perhaps the one that deserves first attention is the problem of rate of growth. Exponential growth has continued so long, and we are already on such a steep part of the growth curve, that human reaction-time may be too slow for us to save ourselves. Can we possibly change humanity's culture patterns of procreation fast enough to reduce growth appreciably before intolerable strain sets in? Perhaps not, but we *must* try.

Next, there is the problem of absolute numbers. Are there already too many passengers aboard Planet Earth? Has the "carrying capacity" of the globe already been surpassed? It seems clear that for the long term, it has. But what is that carrying capacity?

Subordinate to those fundamental problems are others. The problem, for instance, of individual freedom: What constraints are permissible to cope with

Elihu Blotnick

population pressure? The problem of human distribution: Should migration be restricted or redirected? If so, by whom and how? The problem of feeding hungry nations: Should it be conditional on each nation's population policy? Should we practice the "ethics of the lifeboat," whereby, to conserve supplies for those most likely to survive if helped, we deliberately withhold food aid from today's direst sufferers from famine because their rescue would breed even more hungry mouths (and suffering) in the future?

Each of the population problems raises practical questions, ethical questions, religious questions, and ultimately, political questions.

The Goal:
Balance After Drastic Reduction

What should the United States do?

We must first of all recognize the urgency of the need for worldwide population action, beginning at home. The US per capita use of the world's resources is far greater than that of any other nation and many times—perhaps 50 times—that of most Third World countries. Today, the US has no explicit population policy.

We must resolve to bring the globe's passenger load into lasting balance with its resources, and we in the US must show ourselves willing to go as far as any nation to bring that about.

Few quarrel with the abstract idea of achieving balance between resources and population. Most recognize its inevitability, though some dream of colonies in space to absorb Earth's masses. When one tries to express the goal of balance in terms of numbers, arguments arise. What *is* the globe's ultimate carrying capacity? Some scientists contend that food and all other necessities can be found or synthesized to support a far larger population. Others deny that and point to "the law of the minimum," which will quench growth when the first resource indispensable to growth runs out. The world supply of phosphate fertilizer has been suggested as the vital resource likely to be exhausted first, and that soon. But there are many other weak links, as the Club of Rome's *Limits to Growth* study dramatized.

Although the American Association for the Advancement of Science and the Population Council set a number of formidable thinkers to ponder the question of optimum population, they reached no agreement. Zero Population Growth, Inc., which first set a flat

If you travel at all, you need only one eye half open to see that population is the only real major issue in the world today. I come back to the States and hear some black people tell me that birth control is some kind of white conspiracy. The Catholic Church says it is a sin, and some blacks say it is cultural genocide. Here are millions of people, millions—black mostly, but that is incidental—starving to death in sub-Sahara Africa, and Black Americans and Catholics are telling me they have a right *to make more babies.*

Dick Gregory, whom I greatly admire, is perhaps the best-known black who supports the genocide theory. As I understand it, he believes that we must keep on producing at a higher birthrate to help ourselves politically. But surely, there must be easier ways of stuffing the ballot box. What does it profit blacks if we gain a bigger share of the agony? Is it really an accomplishment if we are the ones who are presiding at the end of the world?

—ARTHUR ASHE

no-growth population curve as its goal, now advocates an unspecified population reduction. Negative Population Growth, Inc., another membership group, has set its goal as one-half the 1970 population of the planet, or less than two billion people, with all nations sharing proportionately in the reduction. NPG contends that a population of that size would probably be indefinitely sustainable, would be large enough to maintain all the comforts of industrial civilization yet too small to generate its woes.

Our own conviction is that, for both safety and a decent quality of life, the world's population must be vastly reduced. How far depends, not only on physical carrying capacity or the law of the minimum, but also on one's social, ethical, and spiritual values. Is a world crowded to its ultimate carrying capacity the kind we want to live in or leave to our posterity? Would such a world provide sufficient privacy? Sufficient individual freedom? How much does one value wilderness?

Assuming the need for drastic reduction, how do we get there from here? At least since Malthus, there has been substantial intellectual advocacy of curbs on growth. For more than 50 years, "family planning" has been promoted. For almost as long, effective contraceptive materials have been available, at least to those who could pay for them. From the end of World War II, when growth rates began to skyrocket, population limitation has been widely urged. There is some evidence that the urging has had some effect in the US, where it has been coupled with easy access to contraceptives and in some areas to abortion. There are some other areas in the world where population increase is now being slowed significantly, some few where decrease has already set in. But the growth of

numbers worldwide and the continuing overall growth *rate* suggest that mere unofficial advocacy and purely voluntary compliance are far from enough—certainly not enough to stimulate widespread reduction in population in the time we have left before population induced catastrophe. What's more, voluntarism guarantees big families for the ignorant, the stupid, and the conscienceless, while it gradually reduces the proportion of people who, in conscience, limit the size of their families.

As discussion at 1974's World Population Conference in Bucharest made clear, many Third World officials believe that "if we take care of the people, population will take care of itself." That is, they believe socio-economic improvement in the have-not nations will automatically bring about a "demographic transition" from high to low birth rates. US, West European, and Japanese experience does suggest some long-range correlation between industrialization and birthrate reduction. But it is not clear that the transition can occur with anything like the necessary speed. Moreover, worldwide industrialization on the Western model would soon exhaust the planet's clean air, fresh water, and nonrenewable resources.

So conscious policies of birth control, together with policies to enhance the well-being of the poor, must be pursued simultaneously. In lands where high infant mortality encourages parents to continue childbearing, medical care must be improved. Where children are their parents' only security in old age, social security systems must be instituted. Where sex furnishes the most available entertainment, both substitute pastimes and contraceptives must be provided.

Sad to say, coercion will undoubtedly be used by

many governments in the future, as they strive to cope with famine and chaos. That may come sooner than most of us like to think. India instituted a nominal policy of government support for voluntary family planning in 1952, but the growth rate there is now nearly twice what it was then. Recently, India experimented with incentives and penalties that were indeed coercive. The government fell as a result. But China has achieved considerable success in curbing births by decreeing late marriages and by stimulating strong social pressures against large families.

If the less stringent curbs on procreation fail, someday perhaps childbearing will be deemed a punishable crime against society unless the parents hold a government license. Or perhaps all potential parents will be required to use contraceptive chemicals, the governments issuing antidotes to citizens chosen for childbearing.

Steps For Today

To protect ourselves in the US against such far-reaching infringements on liberty, it behooves us to undertake at once such lesser steps as may most surely promote the population decline we need. Certainly, for instance, we must support the Equal Rights Amendment, for it will encourage women to have careers. That need not preclude motherhood, but will perhaps be conducive to smaller families. Further, we should advocate a later marriage age and a longer educational period. We should support all efforts to maintain women's freedom of choice in abortion and make it universally available when contraception fails. We should also support the widest possible availability of voluntary sterilization. Research for better and longer-lasting contraceptives should be encouraged, perhaps supported more heavily by tax money since safety standards have made such research unprofitable for private enterprise. The contraceptives we have now should be made easier to use and more easily available to all sexually active persons of whatever age.

Courses in sex education, sexual responsibility, and the global population problem should be taught throughout the educational system so that no child could reach maturity without a clear understanding of the social imperative, of techniques of contraception, and of his or her own obligations.

In addition to urging a clear and explicit statement by the US government that it seeks to reduce the nation's population size, we should promote federal actions to bring that about. Government institutions such as those suggested by the Commission on Population Growth and the American Future—the "Rockefeller Commission," whose report, which went no further than to advocate zero growth in the future, was torpedoed by Richard Nixon—should be created and charged with implementing the reduction policy. Financial support of birth control clinics and contraceptive distribution should be increased. Tax levies that are now pronatalist should be revised to help discourage childbearing if this can be done without injury to the children involved. Indeed, subsidies might be paid to the childless, and adoption should be encouraged. Pronatalist economic practices such as reduced transit fares for children should be discouraged, perhaps by legislation. And if, by legislation, we can require tobacco ads to warn that cigarettes may be unhealthy for the individual, we should be able to legislate that pronatalist advertising is unhealthy for society and should carry a warning.

The US has heretofore been most generous in welcoming aliens into the country and lax in enforcing the legality of entry. For our own welfare and the globe's, that US policy should be reconsidered, particularly as regards illegal entrants. Every newcomer, legal or illegal, not to mention his or her potential offspring, swells our population problem and encourages the country of origin to defer reduction of its own birth rate. International migration generally should also be controlled in the interest of reducing the "brain drain" that often hampers education and wise planning in Third World countries, with consequent

Third Prize winner, 1974 Population Cartoon Contest.

1980 World Population Estimates

	Mid 1980 Population (millions)[1]	Natural Increase (%)[2]	Birth Rate (Per 1000)[3]	Death Rate (Per 1000)[3]	Increase in Population 1965-70 (thousands)[4]	Increase in Population 1975-1980 (thousands)[4]	Population in Labor Force, 1965 (millions)[5]	Population in Labor Force, 1995 (millions)[5]
WORLD[6]	4,471.0	1.8	30	12	331,679	390,652	1,395.2	2,326.5
AFRICA	477.6	2.8	46	19	44,373	64,182	122.8	248.1
ASIA	2,604.6	2.0	32	12	203,209	250,247	787.1	1,369.9
EUROPE	484.3	0.4	14	10	17,339	10,656	197.5	238.9
NORTH AMERICA	252.4	0.7	15	8	12,625	8,639	86.8	131.9
U.S.A.[18a]	228.4	0.7	15.4	8.5	10,823	7,570	79.4	118.9
U.S.A. (Alternative)[18b]	232.4	1.2	—	—	—	11,570	—	—
LATIN AMERICA	363.6	2.8	36	9	40,228	44,054	79.2	179.7
U.S.S.R.	265.8	0.8	18	10	12,183	11,418	114.5	145.1
OCEANIA	22.7	1.2	21	9	1,722	1,456	7.3	13.0

Explanatory Remarks

This year, we have returned to U.N. estimates. For the majority of countries, U.S. Census Bureau and U.N. figures are about the same. We are constantly amazed, however, at the difference between estimates for certain countries. The difference between estimates from the two sources is more than 10 million in India and more than 70 million in China. If we add to these discrepancies another 4 million in Mexico, it is clear that all total *world* estimates are in serious doubt.

As population pressures build in the underdeveloped countries, the number of uncounted migrants is increasing in many parts of the world. There is also an ever-increasing number of refugees (currently estimated at 14 million). Many of these are counted, and many are not.

It is for these reasons that we once again emphasize that many of these estimates are probably in error by as much as ten percent (10%), and some may be more than that. However, they are the best figures available.

Population figures less than one million are given to the nearest 10,000 persons in order to increase their comparability. All other population figures have been rounded to the nearest 100,000 persons. Countries with 1980 populations of less than 200,000 persons have not been listed separately, although their populations have been included in the regional, continental and world totals.

A dash indicates that no figure was available.

For each column, the world, continental and regional figures are the sum or population-weighted average of the entries for the continents, regions or countries contained therein.

Footnotes

1. Unless otherwise indicated, the individual country 1980 populations are derived from "Population and Vital Statistics Report," Series A, Volume XXXII, No. 1, January 1980, United Nations, New York.

2. Natural increase is equal to births minus deaths, and does not allow for net migration.
Note: In the case of Africa, the continental figure for natural increase does not equal total births minus total deaths because of rounding.

3. Unless otherwise indicated, birth and death rates are from "Population and Vital Statistics Report," op. cit.

damage to their population control programs. International aid should be most generous to nations that conduct effective population-control programs. Aid should also be allocated in such a way as to encourage accurate population statistics. The US contribution to the United Nations Fund for Population Activities should be increased, not cut back. And any steps that can be taken to replace the UN with a democratic federal world government, under which the population problem would become much more tractable, deserve support.

The late Margaret Mead and others have observed that the population explosion demands a worldwide cultural revolution, a new ethic regarding human numbers. In furtherance of the new ethic, we should demand leadership toward a reduced world population by all who run for office. Not only should they promise concrete action after election; they must also help set new social norms and reverse pronatalist peer pressures. They should, for instance, speak out on the advantages of careers for women, later marriage, longer schooling, singleness, and nonparenthood; on the acceptability of abortion to backstop contraception; on the normality of one-child families; on the right to homosexual practice by consenting adults.

What Will It Cost?

The idea of a shrinking population will raise apprehensions. In a world where the number of men in a nation's army or navy was, till recently, a gauge of power, population reduction may seem an abdication

4. 1965, 1970, and 1975 population figures are taken from 1965, 1970, and 1975 United Nations' *Demographic Yearbooks.* In those cases for which no population figure was given for the desired year, the following year's *Demographic Yearbook* (i.e., 1966, 1971, or 1976) was used to supply the missing information. 1980 population figures are taken from column one on this data sheet.

In those cases for which the *Demographic Yearbook* did not supply population figures, the source is: "World Population Trends and Prospects by Country, 1950-2000: Summary Report of the 1978 Assessment," Department of International Economic and Social Affairs, United Nations, New York, 1979.

5. Figures for Population in the Labor Force, 1965 and 1995, are taken from Tables 1 and 4 in *Labor Force Estimates and Projections, 1950-2000.* Volumes 1-4, I.L.O., Geneva, 1977.

Labor Force includes those over 10 years of age who are employed (including housewives doing farm work), and unemployed seeking employment. It does not include unemployables, students, retired workers, and housewives.

6. There is an enormous range of variation between population estimates for China. The most recent U.N. figure puts the Chinese population at 965,000,000 (including Taiwan). Obviously, whatever figures are used for China's population and rate of natural increase *significantly alter the world's total population and rate of natural increase.*

18. As in last year's chart, we are providing two sets of estimates for the United States. The choice of which to use is the reader's.

(a) The first line does not consider illegal immigration. The 1980 population figure in this line is simply the sum of the 1970 census verified undercount (5.3 million) and the midyear 1980 U.S. Census Bureau clock reading (223.1 million) which does not include the undercount. The Census Bureau clock figure of 223.1 million also does *not* include an undetermined number of refugees or illegal aliens. If these figures could be included, both the U.S. population and growth rate would have to be adjusted upward accordingly.

(b) The second line includes the lowest official estimates available for illegal immigration to the United States for the years through 1977 (see our *1978 World Population Estimates*), plus our estimates for 1977-1978 (2,066,000) and 1978-1979 (a nominal 1,000,000. No official estimates have been made since 1976-1977.

Illegals have continued to enter the United States in larger numbers, and an undetermined number of people have entered this country who will eventually be classified as refugees, immigrants, or illegals. Whatever their eventual status, they are here and they presently constitute part of the U.S. population. Therefore, we have added a nominal one million for illegals, plus 200,000 for those of undetermined status, to last year's U.S.A. alternative figure.

The figure in column two of this line (1.2%) is the sum of the natural increase of the United States population from March 1979 to March 1980 (1.568 million, from "Monthly Vital Statistics Report," Volume 29, No. 3, National Center for Health Statistics, U.S. Department of Health and Human Services), and the 1979-1980 estimate for illegal immigration (1,000,000), and the estimate for those of undetermined status (200,000), divided by the 1979 midyear U.S. population (including illegal aliens).

POPULATION DOUBLING TIME

Population Growth Rate %	Number of Years to double Population
0.5	139
1.0	69
1.5	46
2.0	35
2.5	28
3.0	23
3.5	20
4.0	17

Published by
© 1980 THE ENVIRONMENTAL FUND

of position; in an economy that has always been able to count more customers year by year, population reduction may appear threatening.

Nuclear arms have long since made sheer numbers almost irrelevant, however, and in any case, the US cannot hope to outdistance China, the USSR, or India in population. As for the economy, population changes will necessarily come so slowly that adjustment to new market conditions need pose no problem. Every industry is already well accustomed to adjusting to fad, fashion, technology, and acts of God much more rapidly than US population is likely to shift from growth to decline. (Gerber's Baby Food, for example, anticipating a continued falling off in the US birth rate, has diversified into insurance for the elderly. Disposable disapers are finding a new market in pro-

. . . While great wars cannot be avoided until there is a world government, a world government cannot be stable until every important country has a nearly stationary population.
—BERTRAND RUSSELL

liferating old-age homes.) Moreover, growth will almost certainly continue for years even if all the suggestions made in earlier paragraphs were to be adopted tomorrow. Too many young people already stand on the verge of parenthood for instant reversal

United Nations/ILO

Unlike plagues of the dark ages or contemporary diseases we do not yet understand, the modern plague of over-population is soluble by means we have discovered and with resources we possess. What is lacking is not sufficient knowledge of the solution but universal consciousness of the gravity of the problem and education of the billions who are its victims.

—MARTIN LUTHER KING

to be probable.

For centuries to come, population decrease will benefit both the living and coming generations: each individual can share a larger slice of the pie. The labors of those who have gone before us have built a stockpile of resources and of capital goods that can continue to make life easier and more humane if we have the wit and will not to squander it in war. More and more, we can divide and distribute the stock so that none need want materially. More and more, we can divert our economic growth to music and the other arts, sports, science, education, service industries, and the production of fewer but higher-quality material goods.

The result of reducing our population—and the globe's—to some fraction of what it is today can only be a healthier, happier world in which a lot of problems would be turned into a lot of opportunities. It is time we made a determined start toward that goal.

If, by some mischance, we have judged wrong and it is decided in some future generation that renewed growth is desirable, Paul Ehrlich points out that the job of repopulation is one that can be undertaken by un-skilled workers who would enjoy their task. Repopulation is altogether too easy. Our task is more difficult, but not impossible unless we choose to make it so.

Recommended Actions

☐ The President should proclaim, and by a joint resolution of both houses, Congress should reaffirm, that population reduction is an essential long-term goal of the United States.

☐ In the United Nations and other international forums, and through bilateral diplomacy, the US should seek the earliest and widest possible consensus that population reduction is a crucial goal for the whole human community.

☐ The President and/or Congress should appoint a top-level commission to investigate what the carrying capacity of the US may be presumed to be under various reasonable assumptions, and suggest a range of populations within which the optimum population may be presumed to lie.

☐ The State Department should encourage other nations to make similar investigations of maximum and optimum population, and the UN should be urged to carry out such investigations for the world as a whole.

☐ Congress and the state legislatures should repeal provisions of tax codes that discriminate in favor of parenthood; consideration should be given to a gradual reversal of the bias to discriminate in favor of childlessness and small families.

☐ All officials and candidates for US office should support the Equal Rights Amendment because, among other reasons, it would help open up to women careers other than motherhood.

☐ The Department of Education should promote sex education and the teaching at all educational levels of population dynamics and the social and economic problems that result.

☐ Appropriate agencies at various levels of government should increase support of contraceptive research, birth control clinics, and the wide distribution of inexpensive contraceptives.

☐ Abortions should be freely available, as a right, to women who want them, regardless of age and consent of spouse or parent.

☐ Voluntary sterilization of both sexes should be officially encouraged.

☐ Opinion-makers in all walks of life should encourage longer schooling, later marriage, and adoption as an alternative to physiological parenthood; we should all help establish new social norms in which singleness is not regarded as inferior to marriage and childlessness is respected no less than parenthood.

☐ The US should increase its support of the United Nations Fund for Population Activities.

☐ The US should tighten its immigration policy, both to reduce the growth rate in the US and to eliminate the encouragement that a loose policy provides for other countries to neglect birth control.

☐ The US should reduce its own infant mortality rates and assist other countries to lower theirs, since, where mortality is high, parents have many children to assure that one or two will reach adulthood.

☐ Because the poor tend to look upon children as the only form of security available to them in old age, programs to alleviate poverty and universalize social security should be instituted in the US and encouraged abroad.

☐ As our government becomes more conscious of population pressures, congressional and other groups will undertake to study the matter (e.g., regular legislative committees, the recent Select Committee of the House, and the later Select Commission on Immigration and Refugee Policy). Such bodies hold public hearings, at which each of us should make plain our concerns and our suggestions for reducing the nation's and the world's populations to sustainable levels.

Immigration and the American Conscience

LINDSEY GRANT and JOHN H. TANTON

IN APRIL 1980, when Cubans began to arrive in Key West in large numbers, the United States government put on a remarkable display of irresolution. In the eyes of US law, the arrivals were illegal entrants. In late April, the Department of State called attention to that fact, and the Deputy Secretary tried unsuccessfully to enlist Cuban-American leaders in a public effort to call off the boatlift while orderly migration procedures were developed. A day later, the Vice President undercut him with an equivocal statement which failed to call for an end to the boatlift. On May 6, off the cuff, President Carter told a meeting that we would "welcome the Cuban refugees with open hearts and open arms." Eight days after *that,* the President decided to enforce the law; he coupled the announcement with a plea to Castro to allow American ships to bring out the refugees in an orderly procedure. *Time* magazine quotes Presidential Assistant Jack Watson as explaining the delay by saying, "We decided then it would be counterproductive to enforce the laws."

The end product of this confusion of purposes was the acceptance of an unscheduled 140,000 Cuban and Haitian entrants, on top of the existing refugee quota of 221,000, the largest in the world.

Migration is one of the oldest human characteristics and one of the principal forces shaping human geography. The question arises: how could an American government be so unprepared to deal with so basic and predictable an issue?

The easy answer of course is politics: the President did not want to offend Hispanic voters in an election year. There are probably other reasons. The neglect of immigration issues must seem benign to employers seeking cheap labor, or to recent immigrants with a personal or group interest in open immigration. Immigration as an issue has been taboo in world forums; in a world of fragile borders, many of them new and cutting across old ethnic and territorial claims, migration is a topic to be avoided.

Despite its importance, the implications of migration have been blurred in recent centuries by technological advance and the empty spaces of New Worlds ready to absorb it.

Those explanations are still not enough. Among idealistic and liberal Americans, one frequently encounters a trepidation about raising immigration as an issue, as if any proposal to examine it were somehow morally tarnished. The roots of this attitude are partly historical; past efforts to limit immigration have frequently had racist overtones which now are, or should be, repugnant to Americans.

Even more important, however, is a peculiarly American mindset which leads us to universalize our experience. We assume a responsibility for everything, everywhere. The United States has been a frontier and a continent more than a nation-state. Most of us are descendants of historically recent immigration. If people are overcrowded elsewhere, if they are driven from their livelihood by economic or political pressures, do we not owe them the chance we have had? Most new immigrants seem attractive and hard working; why not welcome them? The motive is generous, if sometimes the actions are misplaced; we do well to recognize that nations have responsibilities to each other.

This "world conscience" may, however, conflict with a more immediate and direct obligation to protect and pass on, undiminished, the national patrimony for which we are responsible. If one does not believe in limits, the idea of responsibility to the land and to coming generations is somewhat alien. The ideals of conservation were nearly submerged in a century or more of frantic growth. They are making their reappearance, and they impose obligations on the American conscience which some Americans may forget.

History is an imprecise guide in the problem which the world now faces. To ask whether migration has heretofore been good or bad is to ask the unanswerable; it is too fundamental a part of what mankind now is to permit us to isolate it for analysis. There is however, something qualitatively new. The empty spaces have been occupied, throughout the world. Migration is no longer a solution to population pressures. At the same time, the world seems to be in the beginning of a period of intense pressures generating migration.

It is the authors' purpose in this article to suggest that American complaisance concerning immigration will not help solve the problems which generate the movement, that such complaisance may indeed worsen those problems, and that there are other fundamental obligations which should have at least as good a claim upon the enlightened American conscience as does the obligation to succor the stranger.

The Edge of Anarchy

The issue is not simply theoretical. Movements of people to and from the United States are rising. We cannot count the surreptitious entries, but we do know that in 1960, there were 89 million alien entries into the US through land checkpoints; in 1978, 155 million. Aircraft manifests show 2.4 million total arrivals in 1960 and 17 million in 1978, but they show only 15.8 million leaving in 1978. What happened to the other 1.2 million? In 1978, 9.3 nonimmigrant visa holders arrived, up from 4.4 million a decade before. Which ones decided to stay?

We cannot tell. Responsive to perceived pressures, the US government has progressively abdicated its responsbility to enforce existing immigration laws. Immigration and border patrol operations have deteriorated to the edge of anarchy; *The New York Times* speaks of "virtual bureacratic collapse." The Border Patrol attempts to monitor some 6,000 miles of mostly unfenced border with 2,101 agents—fewer than the New York City Transit Police. The Immigration and Naturalization Service (INS) cannot systematically tell which visitors leave again. It has stopped trying to estimate the number of persons illegally in the United States. A "cautious speculation" by Census Bureau employees, produced at the insistence of the Select Commission on Immigration and Refugee Policy, is 3.5 to 6 million. Private estimates vary from 3.5/5.5 million to 4/12 million. The range itself is a measure of the almost complete lack of information.

The number appears to be rising. The INS, despite its problems, made over one million apprehensions in fiscal years 1979 and 1980, more than ten times the rate in the early 1960s.

Legal immigration in 1980 totaled about 800,000, including the government's decision to regularize the illegal Cuban/Haitian entrants. In light of the magnitudes described above, a guess of 500,000 to one

Had the United States stablized its population in 1970, we could have the same level of energy consumption and standard of living as we do today without *any Iranian oil or a single nuclear power plant.*
—THE ENVIRONMENTAL FUND

million illegal entrants is not unreasonable. Current immigration matches or exceeds the peak levels of the turn of the century, and the US population is growing more than one percent a year, probably the highest growth rate in the industrial world.

America welcomes visitors. It benefits from some migration. It feels compassion for refugees. But what are the implications of this extraordinary influx?

Shocking Projections

Modern technology and modern medicine have generated a population surge unprecedented in human history. By a conservative projection the world's population may grow by 2000 AD to about 6.35 billion, an increase of about 53 percent over the 1975 level. The year 2000 is only twenty years away.

The global figures conceal some fundamental differences. In the industrial world, fertility is already low. The growth rate is still projected at 0.6 percent per year, but population stabilization is in sight—assuming zero net migration.

Not so in the "less developed countries" (the LDC's). Most of the world's population increase—about two billion—is expected to occur in those countries. The African population is expected to more than double, and that of Latin America to rise 96 percent.

The working-age population (15-64 years old) is projected to rise 86 percent in the LDC's. If unemployment is not to increase, job opportunities must almost double, even more so if women enter the work force in large numbers, as they have in he industrial world. By contrast, the working-age population in the industrial countries is expected to rise only 18 percent. This comparison alone suggests the intensity of pressures on labor to move from areas of glut to those of relative scarcity.

The projections are shocking but they are, if anything, conservative. They are predicated upon an anticipated decline of 30 percent fertility in the LDC's between 1975 and 2000. (The Census "high" series assumes only a 24 percent decline in LDC fertility rates, which adds another 348 million to their population by 2000 AD.) There is no assurance, or even very compelling evidence, that declines of such magnitude will occur. In dealing with fertility, one is dealing with fundamental human behavior, and a worldwide change of 30 or even 24 percent in a generation is a very hopeful expectation, indeed.

Some demographers believe they have detected signs of declining fertility in the LDC's. Much of this work has been done by conscientious and reputable demographers, but it is based upon a shaky statistical edifice. Census counts are difficult, commonly inexact, and slow. The recent conclusions are drawn largely from sample interviews. Experience has not yet permitted a systematic verification of these sampling methods. A decline in overall LDC population growth rates has not yet shown up, statistically.

The purpose of this brief foray into a forbidding statistical jungle is to dramatize the magnitude of the

ILO photograph

problem. The LDC's contain three-fourths of the world's population. Even by an optimistic estimate, their growth alone by 2000 AD will be nearly twice the current population of the industrial world and nearly ten times the United States' population.

To believe that a permissive United States view of immigration will significantly contribute to easing a problem of this scope is simply to engage in wishful thinking. Even if such a permissive attitude were shared throughout the industrial world (which it emphatically is not), migration could not accommodate the current surge of population.

Population Growth Is Pivotal

The conscience may argue that, if migration is not a solution to today's crowded world, it may offer at least a palliative, and that we are not justified in withholding the palliative.

It may be a dangerous palliative.

"Be fruitful and multiply" has generally been good advice, to a point. Other species before us have, however, demonstrated the dangers of too much success. Yeasts in a bottle multiply, very successfully, until the alcohol they excrete wipes them out. The Earth is our bottle. Population growth, multiplied by technological change and industrial growth, poses threats that people have not dealt with before. Along the curve of history, we are in the vicinity of the point at which human expansion forces a progressive decline in the Earth's carrying capacity, just when that capacity is needed to support the population growth which undermines it. The longer a basic solution is deterred, the more difficult it becomes.

The Global 2000 study suggests that traditional fishery production has already peaked, and that livestock herds in the LDC's are not increasing as fast as the population. These declines in animal protein availability put an increased pressure on arable land, which is expected to increase in area by only four percent worldwide by 2000 AD and to begin to decline in many regions. Arable land per capita in the LDC's will decline sharply to about 0.17 hectares—about 100 x 225 feet. Food must be cooked. The combination of over-grazing, competition for arable land, and fuel-wood gathering is resulting in the desertification of perhaps six million hectares annually in Africa, Asia, and Latin America.

A parallel process is destroying the world's forests, which have declined about 20 percent since 1956 and are projected to decline at about the same rate through 2000. Commercial standing timber per capita in the LDC's will then have dropped to less than 40 percent of the 1975 level, and in another generation it is expected to effectively disappear.

The problems of industrialization include toxic wastes, the acidification of rain and therefore of soils, and—perhaps the most perplexing uncerainty of all—the accelerating increase of carbon dioxide in the atmosphere. When human activities are each year measurably changing the composition of the very atmosphere in which we live, it should give the race more pause than it does.

One may hope that industrial pollution and the consumption of resources are levelling off in the industrial countries, but a vast increase will accompany any general improvement in living standards of the LDC's. No end of pressures on the environment is in sight.

"Solutions" tend to pose their own problems. The Green Revolution places increasing reliance on pesticides and on a few high-yielding strains, which raises the vulnerability to blight. This process, coupled with deforestation in the tropics, is dramatically narrowing the Earth's diversity. That diversity has helped ecosystems in the past adjust to environmental changes. We are accelerating the change precisely while we diminish the capacity to adjust to it.

Most of the increase in arable land will be taken from grazing areas, woodlands, and wetlands. The problem of scarcity will be shifted, not solved. Substitute biomass for dwindling petroleum stocks; it would help to reduce the carbon dioxide inputs to the atmosphere, but it would raise the question of how the diversion would affect food and forest production, or the green manuring and stubble mulching necessary to preserve the soil. Let the peasant migrate; his move would microscopically reduce the pressure on the land he left, but he would then consume more resources and produce more pollution than before, if he shares at all in the standard of living of the industrial society to which he moved.

The projections will probably turn out to be wrong, for one reason or another. The figures are not important. Given the power of geometric growth at the rates the world is experiencing, an error is likely simply to move the calculations a few years or decades one way or the other. Technology may move them one way, as more benign and less resource-intensive techniques are discovered. Unexpected disasters or changes may move them the other way. If the trends have been correctly described, the basic point is valid. Population growth is threatening to reduce the Earth's productivity.

Capital is needed to provide jobs for the expanding work force, to improve consumption levels, to adjust to the end of the petroleum era, and to ameliorate the environmental damage of economic growth. Yet population growth itself diverts funds from such investment.

Population growth is the pivot, and any "solution" which does not include the solution of that problem is illusory. World Bank President McNamara has repeatedly criticized the "leisurely approach to the population problem that has characterized the past century." Only a few countries have gone beyond the provision of family planning services and occasional exhortation in the effort to stabilize population. Family planning is of limited help if people plan big families, and there is no evidence in any LDC that parents generally want families small enough to stabilize the population.

If we encourage LDC leaderships anywhere to view immigration as an alternative to population limitation, we do them and the planet a serious disservice.

Unrestricted migration to the United States may directly affect the LDC's. The number of grain-exporting countries has steadily shrunk as domestic population growth has eaten up export surpluses. Of the six significant remaining regular exporters, five (the US, Australia, Canada, Argentina and South Africa) were populated in recent historical times. The United States now supplies two-thirds of the grain entering the world grain trade and is the principal source of food aid to the LDC's.

If a faster-than-anticipated population rise in the United States consumes an increasing portion of US grain output, US exports will suffer and the LDC's will be left with no alternative source.

The direct effects of immigration on the immigrant-exporting nation are certainly not all good. Some restless and potentially troublesome unemployed are exported, and some remittances may be gained from abroad, but there is a loss when the skilled, the able, and the ambitious depart. And the exporting country pays the price of raising the immigrant through his dependent years, only to lose him during the potentially productive ones.

These are not areas susceptible to rigorous proof. A sufficient point has been made, if it has been shown that migration is no substitute for a frontal attack on the population problem and that immigration does not necessarily benefit the sending country.

What Sort of Patrimony?

When the ideals of national interest and of a world conscience seem to come into conflict in the American mind, national interest is likely to place second. The order should be reversed to ask: what does the American conscience owe to the United States?

The current *de facto* condition of uncontrolled immigration conflicts with our fundamental obligations to present and future generations of Americans, in two connected ways.

First, we cannot provide the conditions for employment of Americans at a decent wage, under decent conditions, if the labor force is indefinitely expansible. Glut will drive the standards down. As a nation, we have impressive legislation on minimum wages, occupational safety, and labor standards. To the employer, one of the attractions of illegal immigrant laborers is that they will work for lesser wages and conditions. We are witnessing the creation of a sub-class outside our laws, and we are conniving in the undermining of those laws.

Whatever the exact figure, the number of illegal aliens working in the United States is a substantial fraction of the number of Americans unemployed. Apologists have expended considerable ingenuity to show that there is not necessarily a one-for-one relationship. One can accept their argument and yet leave the burden of proof on them to show that there is not still massive displacement. Secretary of Labor Marshall suggested that the nation would be meeting its full employment goals were it not for illegal immigrant labor.

The permissive view of immigration may mask a comfortable short-term middle-class self interest. The people who should address these problems are taken care of. They have their jobs. Most of their contact with illegal migrants is with domestic servants, taxi drivers, and waiters. It is comfortable to have such services inexpensively. The existence of the poor has always been comfortable to the prosperous, until the poor get restive.

In the United States, we had moved past this parochial view to a larger dream of a society which could provide decently for all. Are we now to move backwards?

Most displaced workers are the unskilled, women, the young, and particularly minority youth, with the longest future ahead of them and the least psychological investment in the status quo. As the government's recent emphasis upon youth work programs suggests, the United States has a social stake as well as a humane interest in giving priority to bringing these youth into the American economy. The *laissez-faire* view of immigration strikes at the heart of that effort.

Some argue that migrants will work harder for less, at jobs that Americans won't take. Of course they will. They are running hungry. But if the work ethic is to be instilled in our young, isn't there some approach other than to make them as hungry as the migrants were?

Our second obligation to future Americans is really an extension of the first. What sort of patrimony should we pass on to succeeding generations? Such thoughts come more naturally to Europeans with their limited space than to Americans, for whom there has always seemed to be more room and more resources, but the difference is really one of historical timing; we are coming to a point where the Europeans have been.

At bottom, both these issues are not about the number of immigrants, but the number of Americans. If American fertility were as high as that of the LDC's, this article would be about controlling rather than immigration, and that is where the concern was a decade ago.

Like a forest fire, the population explosion seems to have swept through the Western world. In the United States, fertility reached replacement levels within the last decade—that is, if women have the average number of children they have recently been having, the native-born population will eventually stabilize. Like a forest fire, the problem could re-ignite. There is no particular magic about replacement-level fertility. The United States reached it briefly two generations ago, and then fertility rose again. What with the "baby boom" and immigration in the intervening years, the US population has nearly doubled since then. Fertility may be rising again.

We cannot accept total responsibility for all the world. But we *are* responsible for the United States. We are already stretching some resources thin enough to affect long term productivity in the United States. For example, the Department of Agriculture notes that some three million acres of agricultural land are being converted annually to roads, home, and urban uses; much of this is prime farmland. Erosion is proceeding at more than sustainable levels on some 34 percent of US cropland. Groundwater resources, on which much irrigation depends, are being mined faster than they are recharging in 60 or 106 water resource subregions in the US; 25 percent of our use of groundwater represents net depletion of the resources. Population growth will be a key factor determining whether these pressures will intensify or be brought under control.

We are trying to conserve oil and energy. How much each of us can use will depend upon how many of us there are.

The population/resource bind does not yet press so obviously on the United States as it does on most of the world. In addressing the transition away from petroleum, we have options available to few others: alternative energy resources, land available for biomass production, a living standard high enough to provide the capital to finance a shift to new sources. We can make adjustments if the acid rain and the carbon dioxide problems require it, and the world will benefit, since we are the largest source of those emissions. We can afford the luxury of keeping wilderness and natural areas out of production, which may help to preserve genetic diversity.

The country's optimum population may turn out to be less in the future, with an economy dependent upon renewable resources, than it has been while we have drawn down fossil reserves. We had forgotten that the future is always uncertain. We are relearning that truth, and in the process we should be learning that the greatest good is not necessarily achieved by allowing population to rise to meet the limits of current productivity. The world will be better off if we have some reserve capacity, and the land for which we are responsible may better preserve its productivity for coming generations.

Needed: Population and Immigration Policies

One can hardly be dogmatic as to what immigration levels are desirable. In the face of the formidable lack of information, it is difficult to develop any sense of the demographic implications of different mixes of native fertility and immigration. Information is needed which the United States government does not appear inclined to assemble.

Moreover, the US government has no view as to what population size is desirable. A policy on population would help to shape policies on immigration. A decade ago, Congress created a Commission on Population Growth and the American future, which in 1972 concluded *inter alia* that it saw no advantage in further population growth. That was an election year, and the report was shelved. Now Congress has created a Select Commission on Immigration and Refugee Policy, to report in 1981, safely after the 1980 election. Important hopes ride, somewhat uncertainly, with it.

Certainly, there should be some immigration, if only to widen our horizons and to provide for specific humanitarian cases. (Be it noted that even proposals for zero net migration would permit such a flow, up to the levels of immigration.)

The United States government should at least enforce the existing immigration law. It is imperfect, but it represents the nearest thing to a national consensus. It provides for annual immigration in the 400,000 range, which seems tolerable at least as an interim level. It provides for refugees (though a shift of preference classes in their favor would seem desirable).

This proposal will evoke shock. There will be references to delicate foreign relations and the rights of the illegal immigrants. Considerable negotiation would be necessary to effectuate such a seemingly simple proposal. The critics should step back, however, and consider: what strange and nightmarish time have we entered, when a proposal to enforce the law is regarded as impractical and somehow indecent?

The government lags behind the people. Opinion polls regularly indicate that the public opposes increases in the existing immigration quotas. The leadership should consider the possibility that the public is right. As a nation we have obligations to our own people and to the future of our land which should be balanced against the general urge to help others. No country, not even the United States, can absorb the present population explosion. It can only be met in each country where it is under way. To offer haven to the few who escape is to forget the many who cannot, and an expanding American population does not necessarily advance the common good. To those whose conscience stands in the way, we offer this suggestion: your human instincts may be sending you the wrong message.

China's Drive Toward Population Stabilization

SHARON CAMP

THE PEOPLE'S REPUBLIC OF CHINA has enormous and perhaps singular importance in all future efforts to achieve a global balance between population and resources. More than one out of every five people in the world are Chinese. China's demographic policies thus have greater significance for world population growth than those of any other country. More importantly, the Chinese have pushed population planning further and faster than any other developing country and have achieved striking fertility declines almost unique in the annals of demographic history. While few observers assume the Chinese experience can be fully replicated elsewhere, most would agree with Judith Banister's conclusion that: "The failure of many other developing countries to achieve the same thing may then be attributed to the unwillingness or the inability of their governments to implement the necessary policies. In such countries, there may be some significant political ramifications of China's success in fertility control."

Only a handful of developing countries—among them Indonesia, Thailand, Singapore, South Korea, Mexico, Colombia, and El Salvador—have shown anything approaching China's political will, and while their progress has been encouraging, most can still expect a population doubling in the next 20 to 40 years. As the first country in the world to consider *the possible advantages of negative population growth*, China may also be out in front of most industrialized countries—including the United States, which has yet to adopt any national population policy, and whose population doubling time (taking into account immigration) is still a mere 65 years.

Replacement Level Fertility In Some Provinces?

For the last several years, intense arguments have raged in demographic circles over the precise size and growth rate of China's population—arguments that will not be settled until, in 1981, China completes its first official census since 1953. But the data on current birth rates, much of it brought back piecemeal by visitors or obtained from provincial radio broadcasts, does suggest that in the more advanced provinces, representing about half the national population, China has reduced fertility in just over a decade to rates approaching replacement level—a demographic transition that took close to 150 years in Europe. Experts place population growth for the country as a whole at 1.2 percent in 1980 (compared with 2.5 to 3 percent for most other developing countries), and total population was estimated at 975 million. The 1979 target of 1 percent growth apparently was not reached in 1979 or 1980, however, and the growth rate may even have climbed in some places. This would help explain several tough new anti-natalist measures, including a system of very persuasive incentives and disincentives.

Behind these tough measures are some serious social and economic problems, among them the thin margin between hard-won increases in agricultural production and escalating demand for food, continued pressure on urban housing and employment, and a serious shortage of educational facilities. Chinese leaders are justly proud of the development gains and fertility declines achieved so far; but at the same time, they are concerned that these fall short of the mark.

China's official goal is population stabilization by the year 2000, but for this to happen, fertility rates will have to fall below replacement level in order to counter the effects of an increasing number of reproductive-age couples. Hence the campaign for one-child families, announced in late 1979.

It is too early to judge the impact of the new incentive programs or the one-child family campaign, both of which have in any case little immediate applicability to most other developing countries. There are, however, at least six population program components which appear to be responsible for the substantial success China has already achieved—and which are, in large part, transferable. They are:

- Reliance on a network of paramedics or barefoot doctors to provide most family planning services through a primary health care system that reaches people where they work and live and makes cost-effective use of traditional medicine;
- A wide array of contraceptive methods, including sterilization and abortion and some methods unknown outside China, all provided free of charge;
- An intensive campaign of propaganda and of community peer pressure, in some cases extending to the actual allocation of a planned number of births among eligible couples;
- A single-purpose administrative structure in the form of "Leading Groups on Birth Planning" with representation from all relevant sectors and with enormous political clout;
- Major improvements in the health, education levels, and living conditions of the average Chinese family—and in the status of women—which have helped change traditional values favoring large family size; and
- A well-enforced code of conduct involving very late marriage, abstinence from premarital sex, and the sublimation of energies into work, sports, and study.

Health and Family Planning Services That Reach All The People

Few things about China impress observers more than that country's unique system of primary health care—a system which has, without the benefit of expensive technology or elaborate health care facilities or highly trained personnel, reduced China's death rate from the high level associated with most poor countries to that of affluent Western countries.

The system's remarkable success in reducing infant and child death rates has been of inestimable value to China's birth planning program by making it possible not only to offer contraceptive services in a highly effective manner, but also to assure couples that their existing children will survive to adulthood. While China's population effort reaches considerably beyond the health network, its success cannot be understood without taking this unique structure into account.

Two factors seem to have played a key role in China's health care achievements: reliance on barefoot doctors and other health outreach personnel working at the community level, and willingness to integrate traditional Chinese medicine—herbal remedies and acupuncture—with techniques imported from the West.

China has trained more than 1.8 million barefoot doctors and another 4.2 million health aides and birth attendants, almost all of whom continue to take part in agricultural or industrial production alongside their clients. By 1974, nearly all of China's 50,000 rural communes had their own health clinics, and by 1977, nearly every production brigade had its own health station staffed with two or three barefoot doctors.

All indications are that using this community-based health infrastructure, China has either eradicated or brought under control all the major epidemic and endemic diseases—smallpox, cholera, malaria, ankylostomiasis, bilharzia, and tuberculosis. Improvements in maternal and child health are equally dramatic. In Peking, for example, infant mortality has declined from 117 per thousand in 1949 to about 10 per thousand in 1979.

Family planning services fit directly into this localized health structure and its emphasis on preventive medicine. Contraceptive supplies are available to women in the fields, factories, and even at home through barefoot doctors who are the social equals of their clients. In addition, a well run system of medical supervision and referrals assures that women with complications and those needing sterilization or abortion receive immediate attention from trained physicians. In fact, it is safe to say that no other country puts as much of its health resources into family planning—and no other country has achieved such cost-effective results.

Propaganda Incentives and Peer Pressure

While no effort is spared by the Chinese to put free family planning services within the ready reach of every eligible couple, an equally great effort is exerted to assure that such services will be accepted and used. Propaganda is pervasive and peer pressure at the community level is intense, through individual and group sessions that amount in most cases to effective sanctions against noncompliance. Incentives can be subtle, such as generous paid leave for sterilization and abortion, or explicit. Incentives adopted recently in pursuit of the new one-child-family goal are, for the average Chinese couple, substantial.

In some parts of China, community involvement in birth planning has evolved to the point where annual birth quotas are established and births are allocated among couples. To some observers these methods seem, if not coercive, most certainly a serious invasion of privacy. But most agree that community pressures have been central of the success of China's birth control program.

Birth control propaganda finds its way into every

possible channel of communication: articles in the press explaining the rationale for population planning; vignettes on the radio and ever-present public address systems reporting success stories and popularizing behavioral models; colorful posters and leaflets; cultural performances with specially written birth planning scripts; neighborhood meetings; adult study groups; and household visits. No one escapes this net, and given the strong Chinese sense of community obligations, perhaps no one wishes to.

Of the concrete rewards and sanctions that back up the motivational efforts, some are of local creation, others nationally mandated. In a society of "rationed poverty" even small benefits take on significance—like the nationally mandated 14 days of paid leave following induced abortion (there are a total of only seven official holidays), or the locally instituted nutritional subsidies worth from 10 to 50 percent of average monthly wages. To push the one-child-family campaign, China is now moving toward a scheme of incentives and disincentives similar to those used in Singapore to encourage two-child-families. Some of China's leading provinces and cities have been experimenting with the scheme since late 1979. Local variations remain, and implementation problems (especially in the more backward provinces) appear considerable. For families who commit themselves to only one child, benefits include child-care subsidies

equivalent to about 10 percent of average annual income until the child reaches age 14, housing or private farm plot allocations equal to those permitted larger families, preferential treatment in school admission and job placement for the single child, and a substantial pension for the parents on their retirement.

Community Birth Planning

Perhaps the most interesting innovation in China's birth planning program is community planning of births. While not yet universal, the practice appears to be widespread in a number of provinces. It begins with a series of up and down communications between production team and work brigade, brigade and commune, commune and county, county and province, and province and central government, the purpose of which is to establish a target number of births at each level for the coming year. Once these targets are set, it is up to the production team or neighborhood group to allocate the total planned births among eligible couples. Preference is given to the newly married or childless, and those who have not had a child for at least four years. Fundamental reproductive decisions about the number and timing of children are no longer considered a matter of individual or family choice, but a community responsibility governed by very explicit national norms.

Women Hold Up Half the Sky

Observers of China's population program doubt that such rapid changes in fertility behavior could have occurred without the revolutionary changes that have reshaped Chinese society. Although China remains poor by any standard, most Chinese families have experienced immense improvements in health, educational levels, and general living conditions. These changes, and the new equity in Chinese society, give families the hope that their children will not only survive but prosper as a result of new opportunities for education and employment.

Clearly the most important social change affecting fertility patterns has been in the status of women, especially the full integration of women into the labor force. As one official of the Women's Federation explained it: "The status of women in Old China was very low, since they were under the oppression of the three big mountains—feudalism, imperialism, and capitalism—and also suffered under the authority of the husband." It should be stressed that Chinese officials do not justify female education and employment as a means to population control. Sexual equality is the stated goal, and family planning one of the means for achieving it. China recognizes that women represent half its human resource and that they need to be relieved of "excessive family burdens" if they are to "hold up their half of the sky."

The Constitution of the People's Republic of China provides in Article 53 that "Women enjoy equal rights with men in all spheres of political, economic, cultural, social and family life. Men and women enjoy equal pay for equal work.

"Men and women shall marry of their own free will. The state protects marriage, the family, and the mother and child.

"The state advocates and encourages family planning."

Nearly all Chinese women are expected to work full-time outside the home, and sexual divisions of labor are few compared with other countries. Discrimination is not entirely dead, as evidenced by pay differentials and the fact that women are only 36 percent of all university students. But the condition of women today is certainly startlingly different from those of a generation ago, and their mass participation in the workforce is clearly a major deterrent to large families.

China's Asexual Revolution

In addition to its social and economic revolution, China has also had what might be called a moral revolution. Like the other revolutionary changes, this one has had the full backing of China's particular communist ideology and powerful propaganda machine, both of which stress self-denial, discipline, and devotion to duty. Young people are expected to delay marriage (and sexual activity) until their late 20's, and to channel their energies into building the socialist state. Perhaps because there is little in present-day Chinese society that is even vaguely provocative, and because privacy is almost nonexistent, this code of conduct appears to be widely observed.

Delayed marriage has been one of the principal components of China's birth planning program, accounting for a major share of the fertility declines observed. Many observers question, however, whether this pattern can be sustained indefinitely, especially as liberalization occurs in other aspects of Chinese society. Already there has been some shift away from puritanical communist values, as indicated by new sex education programs in the schools. But with or without sex education, if strong pressure for liberalization continues, the government will be faced with two options: to allow earlier marriage but not childbirth, or to make contraceptive services available to sexually active unmarried individuals.

Recent economic reforms loosening the restrictions on individual initiative, new interest in Chinese culture and in modern Western technology, and other moves away from the doctrinaire policies of the early 1970s all represent serious tests for China's economic and social policies. But one of the severest tests may involve the birth planning program and its ability to survive a major shift in sexual mores.

More Thoughts on Population

IRELAND PROVED to be a perfect laboratory for the new Malthusian science. At the start of the eighteenth century, two million people had lived in Ireland—fairly miserably—on small grains. Then the potato was introduced; it enabled more people to eat better. Infant mortality fell. By 1845 the Irish population had grown to eight million, and the people were living as poorly on potatoes as their ancestors had on grain. But the total amount of misery, one might say, had increased fourfold.

With the potato famine of 1845, 1846, and 1847 the population of Ireland fell. One million died from starvation and disease and one million emigrated. From eight million in 1845, the population dropped to six million people, most of them living barely above the subsistence level. At this point, the cycle should have started all over again, but this time the Irish chose the second Malthusian option—to check misery with the fear of misery. Late marriage became socially approved. The famine had a lasting effect long after the worst years were past. Ireland's population fell to four million in the mid-1920's and is less than three million today.

But the history of Ireland is not—or not yet—the history of the world. In the poor nations of Asia, Africa, and Latin America, improved nutrition and sanitation have led to a popultion explosion. Imported foodstuffs and technological advances have barely kept pace; most of the world's population lives close to a Malthusian equilibrium—at the subsistence level. With bad luck and bad harvests, millions will fall below it.

Even in the rich industrial countries, fears are abroad that the Malthusian problem has not vanished. The human population is bound to the earth, with its finite resources. Will the exhaustion of nonrenewable resources eventually do us in? Or can science somehow help us to escape? Will we be compelled to limit population to far lower numbers? Must we, like the Irish, die or emigrate in large numbers—this time to outer space? Parson Malthus' riddle persists.

—Leonard Silk

If it proves impossible to control population increase, the human race is doomed to early extinction.
— NEIL A. ARMSTRONG

THE FAILURE of many family planning programs over the last decade or two is in part a measure of their failure to approach women as whole individuals. Programs that deal with women merely as reproductive beings can hardly bring about the broad social changes prerequisite to fundamental changes in attitudes toward family size.

Social systems whose positive images of women are all linked to the reproductive role leave women only one path to a sense of purpose and accomplishment. Most societies have gone further, constructing formidable roadblocks along every other path. A constructive approach to controlling population growth would be one that sought to dismantle the roadblocks along women's alternate paths, and indeed helped them open new paths toward fulfillment.

Women have many different kinds of needs, just as men do, such as a claim on economic resources, physical health and comfort, security, approval from others, participation in the life of the community, personal autonomy, love, and recognition. The answer to the perennial question "What does woman want?" is located somewhere in that thicket of needs.

Few women (or men) willingly decide to forgo parenthood altogether. Yet any woman who undertakes to combine motherhood with a career, or some other non-maternal role, will find herself much more likely to succeed in both if she limits the number of children she has. Lack of social services pushes women toward an all-or-nothing choice between committed employment and parenthood.

A sound policy must aim to expand women's choices, on the assumption that women are no more naturally inclined to limit themselves to motherhood than men are inclined to limit themselves to fatherhood.

Among the many reasons for having children, the four mentioned above—status, income, security, and emotional satisfaction—are powerful enough in themselves to constitute a legitimate rationale for childbearing from the individual's point of view. However, from the point of view of the community—whether local, national, or global—continued high fertility is a long-term recipe for disaster. The aim of population policy, therefore, must be to reconcile the interests of the individual with those of the community. In order to do this for women, it is necessary to provide alternative sources of status, income, security, and satisfaction.

—Kathleen Newland

THE INCREASE in human numbers thus far has depended heavily on the product of the earth's basic biological systems—fisheries, forests, grasslands, and croplands. These four systems supply not only all our food but, with the important exception of minerals and petrochemicals, all the raw materials for industry as well. With the exception of croplands, these are essentially natural systems that cannot always be improved by human management.

As world population moves toward five billion, there is widespread evidence of excessive demand. Overfishing is now the rule rather than the exception, forests are shrinking in most countries, overgrazing is commonplace on every continent, and at least one-fifth of the world's cropland is losing topsoil at a rate that is undermining its productivity.

One of the earliest signals of excessive demand is inflation. Overall increases in demand are the product of population growth and rising incomes. To the extent that supply increases are not adequate to cover both, prices rise. When the supply of so many basic resources fails to keep pace with even the population component of increasing demand, it should come as no surprise that inflation rates are accelerating.

Inflation could become a powerful contraceptive force in the future. One way to cope with rising prices is to limit family size and the need for purchased goods.

A fall in the economic growth rate to 2 percent per year would not pose any serious problem for West Germany or Belgium, where population growth has ceased. Indeed, incomes there would still rise by some 2 percent per year. But in Senegal or Pakistan, where population is still expanding by 3 percent or more per year, a 2 percent rate of economic growth would lead to a steady decline in the standard of living. In many societies, the hope of sustained improvement in living standards is slowly evaporating.

As world population pressures mount, governments may find it necessary to ration scarce resources such as food and fuel. If human numbers are not controlled, regulation and regimentation could become a way of life.

Unless the deterioration of the natural systems on which the earth depends can somehow be arrested, and unless the wasteful use of oil can be quickly reduced, the seemingly unmanageable economic stresses of the seventies could become merely the prelude to the cumulative economic stresses and social unrest of the eighties and nineties. The problems that

Iranian workers at population lecture.   *UNICEF photograph.*

We use tax incentives to encourage oil exploration; we use them to encourage the installation of pollution abatement devices; we use them to foster pension plans. Is there any reason why we should not use them to tackle our most critical domestic problem—the population crisis?

—SENATOR ROBERT PACKWOOD

arose as world population increased from three to four billion may seem trivial compared with those in store as human numbers go from four to five billion and beyond.

Bringing population growth to a halt is not in itself likely to solve many of humanity's pressing problems. In many cases, however, it is a necessary prerequisite. If the demographic brakes are not applied soon, overfishing, overgrazing, deforestation, overplowing, and their associated economic stresses are certain to worsen. The rapidly expanding demand for basic energy and food supplies is driving humanity up a rising cost curve. An immediate slowdown of world population growth will buy time to make needed adjustments and to develop new technologies and alternative energy sources.

—Lester R. Brown

THE NATURE OF EXPONENTIAL GROWTH is such that limits can be approached with surprising suddenness. The likelihood of overshooting a limit is made even larger by the momentum of human population growth, by the time delays between cause and effect in many environmental systems, and by the fact that some kinds of damage are irreversible by the time they are visible.

The great momentum of human population growth has its origins in deep-seated attitudes toward reproduction and in the age composition of the world's population—37% is under 15 years of age. This means there are far more young people who will soon be reproducing—adding to the population—than there are old people who will soon be dying—subtracting from it. Thus, even if the momentum in attitudes could miraculously be overcome overnight, so that every pair of parents in the world henceforth had only the number of children needed to replace themselves, the imbalance between young and old would cause

population to grow for 50 to 70 years more before leveling off. The growth *rate* would be falling during this period, but population would still climb 30% or more during the transition to stability. Under extraordinarily optimistic assumptions about when replacement fertility might *really* become the worldwide norm, one concludes that world population will not stabilize below 8 billion people.

The momentum of population growth manifests itself as a delay between the time when the need to stabilize population is perceived and the time when stabilization is actually accomplished. Forces that are perhaps even more firmly entrenched than those affecting population lend momentum to growth in per capita consumption of materials. These forces create time lags similar to that of population growth in the inevitable transition to stabilized levels of consumption and technological reform. Time delays between the initiation of environmental insults and the appearance of the symptoms compound the predicament because they postpone recognition of the need for any corrective action at all.

The momentum of growth, the time delays between causes and effects, and the irreversibility of many kinds of damage all increase the chances that mankind may temporarily exceed the carrying capacity of the biological environment. Scientific knowledge is not yet adequate to the task of defining that carrying capacity unambiguously, nor can anyone say with assurance how the consequences of overshooting the carrying capacity will manifest themselves. Agricultural failures on a large scale, dramatic loss of fisheries productivity, and epidemic disease initiated by altered environmental conditions are among the possibilities. The evidence presented here concerning the present scale of man's ecological disruption and its rate of increase suggests that such possibilities exist within a time frame measured in decades, rather than centuries.

All of this is not to suggest that the situation is hopeless. The point is rather that the potential for grave damage is real and that prompt and vigorous action to avert or minimize the damage is necessary.

In the long run the campaign [against hunger] cannot be won until the planet's millions of wives and husbands voluntarily decide to regulate the number of human births.

—ARNOLD J. TOYNBEE

Such action should include measures to slow the growth of the global population to zero as rapidly as possible. Success in this endeavor is a necessary but not a sufficient condition for achieving a prosperous yet environmentally sustainable civilization. It will also be necessary to develop and implement programs to alleviate political tensions, render nuclear war impossible, divert flows of resources and energy from wasteful uses in rich countries to necessity-oriented uses in poor ones, reduce the environmental impact and increase the human benefits resulting from each pound of material and gallon of fuel, devise new energy sources, and, ultimately, stabilize civilization's annual throughput of materials and energy.

There are, in short, no easy single-faceted solutions, and no component of the problem can be safely ignored. There is a temptation to "go slow" on population limitation because this component is politically sensitive and operationally difficult, but the temptation must be resisted. The other approaches pose problems, too, and the accomplishments of these approaches will be gradual at best. Ecological disaster will be difficult enough to avoid even if population limitation succeeds; if population growth proceeds unabated the gains of improved technology and stabilized per capita consumption will be erased, and averting disaster will be impossible.

—Paul Ehrlich and John Holdren

Energy

Official US reaction to OPEC price increases is mad. To avoid dependence on foreign sources, we hasten the day when *all* petroleum will be foreign by draining our own dwindling reserves at an accelerated rate. We rely heavily on nuclear power despite its manifest dangers and disadvantages — and despite the fact that we are already beginning to depend on foreign sources of uranium. We rely increasingly on electricity although electricity is an expensive, and for most purposes, an inefficient form of energy. And we, the world's most wastefully lavish users of energy, take seriously dire predictions that the bottom will drop out of our civilization unless we use more and more. A sane energy policy must be based on conservation and end-use efficiency.

Countries whose standard of living is fully as high as ours use barely half as much energy per capita—and we used that little ourselves a bit more than a decade ago. Conservation is our best and cheapest short-term "source" of energy. For the long term, we must, and easily can, rely for all energy needs on solar power and solar variants such as wind. During a transition period, our needs can be met by sophisticated fossil-fuel technology applied on a small or intermediate scale. True energy independence, for the individual, consists of being able to tap inexhaustible energy sources locally that no one can monopolize or interrupt. That objective is within reach, but we won't reach it by continuing to rush panic-stricken in the opposite direction.

Rondal Partridge

Soft Energy Paths: Safe Energy at Least Cost

AMORY B. LOVINS

A BIG BILLBOARD in Southern California bears the Biblical injunction: "Ye shall pay for your sins." Underneath somebody had added the fine print: "Ye who have already paid, please disregard this notice."

We haven't paid yet for our energy sins and we can't safely disregard the notice. But there are a lot of exciting things going on at the grassroots level that suggest hope that we are solving the energy problem. That same solution is emerging in at least the fifteen countries where my wife and colleague, Hunter, and I work, and I suspect in a good many more. To explore these recent and very optimistic developments, let us discuss four topics: How much energy do we need? What kinds of energy do we need? Where can we get it? How can such a responsive energy policy be effected?

How Much Energy Do We Need?

No doubt you have heard the conventional wisdom that if we make our houses and factories and cars more efficient, we can be as well off as now with twenty or thirty percent less energy than we use now. But we've discovered lately that the scope for wringing more work out of our energy is much larger than that, even if we save energy only by using technical fixes—well-known and presently economic technical measures with no significant effects on lifestyle.

There are two ways to save energy. One way is to curtail or do without the services it gives you—turn off the lights, adjust the thermostat, leave the car at home, and so on. No such measures are necessary to my argument. The second way of saving energy is to use it more productively, more efficiently, to provide the same services as before, or even more, while using less energy. The two methods of saving energy are quite different: insulating your roof does not mean freezing in the dark. It simply keeps you warmer cheaper.

The first firm indication we had of how much we could do with technical fixes came in Janury 1979 in England, when Gerald Leach and his colleagues published their *Low-Energy Strategy for the United Kingdom*. It's a detailed, ratproof account of how to use energy more productively in about four hundred sectors of the British economy, using technical fixes which are in general cheaper than 1977 North Sea gas. When they were added up, they were enough to treble British energy efficiency. Britain could have three times today's gross national product (which per capita would make it grosser than anybody else's), yet the total energy use would still slightly decrease—just by using the energy in a way that saves money.

In Cambridge, England, David Olivier then asked, "What happens if we use technical fixes that might not be cheaper than today's North Sea gas but that at least would be cheaper than the things we would otherwise have to build to replace the dwindling oil and gas—things like synthetic fuel plants and power plants?" He had no trouble coming up with almost a further doubling of efficiency—more that a five-fold improvement in all—in using both total energy and electricity. He then found that most of the important energy-saving measures he'd looked at were still considerably cheaper than building new power plants. So he still hadn't reached the economically optimal level of investment in more efficient energy use. We don't know what that level is, although it is probably more like an eightfold saving.

This is not a peculiarly British result. We have similar results coming in now from a new German study conservatively showing how to quintuple West German energy efficiency. Similar studies have been done in Denmark, Sweden, Switzerland, France and in North America—quite a range of countries. These studies tend to assume continued, even accelerated, economic and industrial growth. It may well be true that the resulting five-cars-and-a-boat-and-a-helicopter-in-every-garage scenario is "spherically

Elihu Blotnick

senseless"—that it makes no sense no matter which way around you look at it. But my collegues and I assume it anyhow, in order to show that if your goal is to Los Angelize the planet, you can meet the resulting energy needs most cheaply with a soft energy path. If you consider today's values or institutions to be somehow imperfect, or if you have more ecological consciousness, then of course you may wish to assume instead some mixture of technical and social or value changes that would make a soft energy future easier to achieve. But our energy efficiency analyses have not done this: they assume a "pure technical fix."

This new crop of studies done in the past two years shows much larger energy savings than you are accustomed to hearing about, not because it assumes a less frenetic or acquisitive society, then, but for two other reasons. One is that the new studies are simply a lot more detailed. They add up many individually small savings which were previously ignored. Second, they take much fuller account of recent technical progress in raising our energy efficiency.

Technical Progress

Let me give a little flavor of that technical progress. To start with, consider how many BTUs of heat it takes to keep a square foot of your house comfortable for one Farenheit degree-day of cold weather outside. A typical sieve such as most of us live in takes about fifteen or twenty of these units of heat. A newly built sieve is more like ten to fifteen. What the federal government until very recently regarded as a well-

insulated house would need about eight. But that's pretty bad compared with what Gene Leger (an engineer in East Pepperell, Massachusetts) accomplished. He recently built a house that cost the same and looks the same as any other house on the block. It uses one-and-a-third of these units. The best present art in Saskatchewan and elsewhere uses about one quarter of a unit or less anywhere down to zero. The extra capital cost is at most a few thousand dollars, paying back in the first few years. In fact we know how to make cost-effective houses (or other buildings) so heat-tight that they require essentially no heating in a sub-Arctic climate and no cooling in a tropical climate. They are heated by people, windows, lights and appliances and they are cooled mainly by not getting hot in the first place. They are very well ventilated, but they're ventilated through a heat exchanger so you get most of your heat or coolth back again. For a materials cost of about thirty dollars, you can make a heat exchanger which will recover four fifths of the outgoing heat or coolth so you don't have the stuffiness otherwise associated with a tight house. Such heat exchangers are one of the most cost-effective things one can add to a reasonably well-insulated house. Most existing buildings can be cost-effectively fixed up nearly to the efficiency standards I've mentioned.

Let's consider cars. The average U.S. car gets about fifteen miles a gallon. The average new domestic model sold in 1980 got about twenty; the average import got about thirty-two. A diesel Rabbit gets about forty-two mpg. Its successor model gets about sixty-four. Volkswagen has recently tested a four-passenger advanced diesel car with a 3-cylinder turbocharged diesel which shuts off on idle or coast. That got eighty miles a gallon city, 100 highway in an EPA test. That's nowhere near what we know how to do. VW recently took a 3500-pound car and put in it, using off-the-shelf components, what is called a diesel-electric hybrid drive. It did eighty-three miles a gallon the first time they turned it on. A number of European prototypes have done well over one hundred. We can easily do sixty miles a gallon with a big, comfortable car with off-the-shelf technology.

The new generation of jet aircraft now being flight-tested is about forty percent more efficient than most of the planes they replaced and about twice as efficient as the present fleet. The Japanese have recently doubled the fuel efficiency of a merchant ship.

Motor Efficiency

We used to think our industrial electric motors were ninety to ninety-five percent efficient. It turns out that as they are actually used, they are typically about twenty-five to thirty-five percent efficient because they are oversized, badly coupled, and badly controlled. If we do some good housekeeping on the motors, we roughly double their practical efficiency with a payback time of a few years. Just that one saving would more than replace the electrical output of all U.S. nuclear power plants.

Perhaps you remember the old, mainly prewar refrigerators that had the motor up on top. Those motors were about 90% efficient. Nowadays the motors are more like sixty percent efficient, and instead of being on top, they are underneath so the heat goes up where the food is. Your refrigerator probably spends close to half of its effort taking away the heat of its own motor. Then the manufacturers kept trying to make the inside bigger without making the outside bigger. (I suppose, given time, they'd have had the inside bigger than the outside.) This means that they skimped on the insulation, so the heat comes straight in through the walls. Then they designed the whole thing so that when you open the door, the cold air falls out, so it frosts up inside. Most refrigerators have intermittent electric heaters inside to melt out this frost. They also tend to have electric strip heaters around the door to keep it from sticking, because it's too simple to use a nonstick coating as in a frying pan. Then the heat is pumped out the back to a kind of radiator that is often pressed right into that thin insulation so the heat can get back inside as fast as possible. The refrigerator is quite often installed next to your stove or next to your dishwasher so when that goes on, the refrigerator goes on as well. It's hard to think of a dumber way to use electricity. When a refrigerator is designed properly, it will keep the same food just as cold, just as conveniently, with about one-sixth as much electricity as now.

If we were similarly to redesign all household appliances, we would save about three-fourths of our present electric bill (excepting space heating or water heating, which we shouldn't do with electricity anyway). The pay-back time on the extra investment is five or six years, so it's a very good deal.

When you add up these kinds of improvements throughout the economy, you find that it's very hard to avoid a three- or four-fold saving in total energy and in electricity use. This means, by the way, that if we supported the present U.S. economy by using electricity in a way that saves money, then we would not need *any* thermal power stations, old or new—whether powered with oil, gas, coal or uranium—but only present hydro, the readily available small-scale hydro and filling some empty turbine bays in existing big dams. Add a bit of windpower and that would be it. We would use the existing grid but extend it no further.

Energy Conservation: A Growth Field

The kinds of efficiency improvements I've talked about might seem so hopelessly slow that we would need to do other things meanwhile. It turns out, though, that they are by far the fastest-growing component of national energy supply right now, and have been since the 1973 oil embargo

Between 1973 and 1978, more efficient energy use in this country gave us twice as much energy-"supplying" capacity, twice as fast, as the synthetic-fuel people say they can do—at ten times the cost. Just the saving we got in the industrial sector during those five years gave us roughly twice the equivalent of the 1978 full flow of the Alaska pipeline, except it left that much oil in the ground. In 1979, over ninety-eight percent of the economic growth in the U.S. was fueled by energy savings, under two percent by new supplies. Thus millions of individual actions in the marketplace—people trying to save energy to save money—together outpaced all the centrally planned expenditures of energy supply by better than fifty to one. By the end of 1979, the rate of savings since the embargo had reached five or six million barrels a day. Our 1981 rate of net oil imports is about 5,400,000 barrels per day. So our oil problem would have been twice as big as it is, had it not been for the efficiency improvement which we made—during a period, by the way, when the real price of gasoline was still below what it was in 1960. The real price increases only started to hit us in 1980. In that year, real GNP stayed flat while total U.S. energy use fell by nearly four percent. In the future we

"Have you given any thought to what you'll do with your Saturdays when the world's fossil fuels are used up?"

shall probably do still better.

The economic incentives for efficiency are already strong. This was nicely pointed out by Roger Sant in a study called *The Least Cost Energy Strategy,* summarized in May-June 1980 in the *Harvard Business Review.* Sant used to run the U.S. energy conservation program under Presidents Nixon and Ford. He asked in his study how much energy Americans would have used in 1978 if, for about ten years before that, we had simply bought the *cheapest* energy system at each point, compared with what energy was going to cost us in 1978. What if we had known those prices in advance and acted to minimize our total costs? Had we done that, he calculates, then in 1978 we would have bought about twenty-eight percent less oil than we did, which would have cut our imports at least in half; about thirty-four percent less coal than we did, so we wouldn't have started to strip the West; and about forty-three percent less electricity than we did, so more than a third of today's power plants, including essentially all the nuclear ones, would never have been built in the first place. The total net cost of such a program would have been about seventeen percent less than we *did* pay for the same energy services that we actually received. If that was such a good deal in

1978, it's clearly a much better deal today. Sant has recently analyzed a least-cost strategy for the period 1980-2000. Even with massive economic growth he finds that energy needs would barely rise; it would not be economically worthwhile even to finish building most of the power stations under construction; and oil imports, being uncompetitive with efficiency-raising investments, would rapidly dwindle to about zero. Moreover, the function of GNP spent on buying energy services would *decrease,* so that the energy sector, far from driving inflation, would become a net *exporter* of capital to the rest of the economy!

The Demand Curve

To see how quickly our thinking has been changing about how much energy we are going to need, look at Figure One—a sociological matrix showing how much total energy various people thought this country would need in the year 2000. It is measured in quads per year. A quad is a quadrillion British Thermal Unit. In 1980 the U.S. used abut 76 quads.

I've arranged these estimates according to date and source. Huxley said, "All knowledge is fated to start as heresy and end as superstition." So I've shown those

Figure 1

Evolution of Approximate Estimates of
U.S. Primary Energy Demand in the Year 2000

$$(Q/Y = 10^{15} \text{ BTU}/y \approx EJ/y$$

(1980 Rate: Ca. 76 Q/y)

YEAR	SOURCE			
	BEYOND THE PALE	*HERESY*	*CONVENTIONAL WISDOM*	*SUPERSTITION***
1972	125 LOVINS	140 SC	160*** AEC	190 FPC
1974	100 EPP (zeg)	124 EPP (tf)	140*** ERDA	160*** EEI, EPRI
1976	75 LOVINS	89-95 VON HIPPEL & WILLIAMS/ LOVINS**	124 ERDA	140*** EEI
1978	33*-55 STEINHART/LOVINS SPEECHES	63***-77 CONAES I II	95-96-101 DOE/CONAES III/IEA	123-124 DOE/LAPP
1980	10-15 LOVINS, LOVINS, KRAUSE & BACH	49***-54*** STANFORD III/ CONAES CLOP	64-85 SERI; ROSS & WILLIARD/ SANT	97-102 EXXON/DOE

Doubled GNP after 2050
**In "Road Not Taken"— Foreign Affairs*
***With life-style changes*

ABBREVIATIONS: SC Sierra Club; AEC Atomic Energy Commission; FPC Federal Power Commission; EPP Ford Foundation Energy Policy Project; zeg zero energy growth; tf technical fix; ERDA Energy Research and Development Administration; EEI Edison Electric Institute; EPRI Electrical Power Research Institute; CONAES National Academy of Science Committee on Nuclear and Alternative Energy Systems—I, II, and III represent the spread of predictions; SERI Solar Energy Research Institute; IEA Institute for Energy Analysis; DOE Department of Energy.

categories with "Conventional Wisdom" in between and "Beyond the Pale" out in left field. Back before the oil embargo, people like me were saying that 125 quads would be plenty at the turn of the century. The Sierra Club was being pretty heretical suggesting 140, because the Atomic Energy Commission was secure in the conventional wisdom of 160. Other Federal agencies were saying 190. Exxon was around 230—which was really pretty ambitious compared to 76 in 1980.

But then came the embargo and the Ford Foundation's Energy Policy Project, whose 100-quad "Zero Energy Growth" Scenario (a curious misnomer) was still considered beyond the pale and not taken very seriously although there was a lot of argument about their 124-quad "Technical Fix" scenario because it was lower than the government's 140 and the utilities' 160.

Then in 1976 in *Foreign Affairs* magazine I was suggesting that 95 quads would be plenty, but in speeches I was already saying that 75 made better use of the technical fixes we had already discovered by then. Some Princeton analysts came up with a solid 89. The government had by then dropped from 140 to 124.

They had discovered technical fixes; you really *can* weatherstrip your house. The utilities had dropped from about 160 to 140: they had discovered price elasticity, which means that the more they charge you, the less you buy.

In 1978, John Steinhart at the University of Wisconsin was already talking about 33 quads for the year 2050, assuming some arguably desirable lifestyle changes. For the year 2010, a very distinguished National Academy of Sciences panel, assuming a doubled GNP, came up with 77 or 96 quads, which were pure technical fixes, and 63, which could have been. Alvin Weinberg, the granddaddy of the nuclear business is happy with 101. Ralph Lapp, a nuclear advocate who thinks energy and GNP march forever in lockstep, is happy with 124. About six months after I first made this matrix Dr. Schlesinger came out with the Department of Energy's latest forecast. At an oil price which is essentially what we now have (only he thought we wouldn't have it until 2000) he came up with 95 quads. So precisely the number greeted with a certain skepticism just two years earlier when I published it in *Foreign Affairs* was now the Department's conventional wisdom. They also had some low-oil-price forecasts shown in the Superstition column because they need supernatural intervention. Those averaged to 123 quads. Things thus came out roughly where they ought to, as if the matrix had some predictive power. The pattern is diagonal: every two years, everything is neatly popping down one column towards the lower right.

In 1980, two studies considering plausible and already observable trends in social values suggested 49 and 54 quads were plausible for 2010. Roger Sant's analysis showed that 85 quads would result from highly cost-effective efficiency improvements. An even more detailed report by the Solar Energy Research Institute, published by the Commerce Committee of the U.S. House of Representatives after the Department of Energy had suppressed it, showed that with similarly sanguine growth assumptions and more realistic (but still conservatively low) conventional fuel prices, total energy use could *fall* to 62-66 quads by 2000, of which about 10-20 quads would be renewable. Exxon, apparently ignoring recent history, was forecasting 97 quads. The Department of Energy has slipped into the "Superstition" column, forecasting 102 quads, and the President's Commission for a National Agenda for the Eighties called 100 quads "a recent average"—which it had been several years earlier.

Trebling Efficiency

We have nowhere near hit bottom yet. We've only just discovered, for example, that an energy-conscious materials policy would roughly treble our national energy efficiency, but it's not reflected in any of these numbers. Indeed, if you take seriously some of the lastest European results, it looks as though in the long run, even if we're more affluent than now, we ought to be converging on numbers as low as ten or fifteen quads—the current "beyond the pale" estimate.

You don't have to go nearly that far to see where this argument is leading. Consider the illustrative graph I published in *Foreign Affairs* (Fig. 2) in 1976—showing what we now know to be a bloated 95 quads for the year 2000, the same as Schlesinger's number of 1978 and nearly the same as Exxon's of 1980. But even at that level, the U.S. would phase out oil imports and nuclear power fairly rapidly with only a modest and temporary expansion of coal mining, not requiring significant Western stripping. We'd be squeezing down the oil and gas from both sides. That's at 95 quads. But a lot of people now think we'll never get above about 85 (Sant's 1980 estimate) because of the higher prices already with us. In fact, the kind of

Figure 2

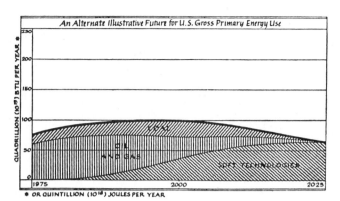

energy and electricity demand we've had the past year or two may turn out to have been the all-time maximum. It may just be stable and a bit downhill from here as the efficiency impovements start to take hold. At 85 quads you don't need coal expansion. With about 60 quads, which I now think is realistic, you can even shut in a lot of conventional oil and gas wells; it isn't going to run away.

What Kinds of Energy Do We Need?

The question of how much energy we need is crucial: it determines whether we ought to be buying more major energy supplies at all. An equally important question which hasn't been much asked is: What kinds of energy do we need? It's important because there are many different forms of energy whose different prices and qualities suit them to different applications. Traditionally we've said that the energy problem is simply where to get more energy, of any kind, from any source, at any price—as if all kinds of energy were alike. This is like saying we're running short on bread and cheese, but that's okay, we'll substitute sirloin steak. It's nice if you can afford it. Some of us have to be a little more discriminating than that.

There is, after all, no "demand for energy" *per se*. Who wants raw kilowatt-hours or barrels of sticky, black goo? What people want is instead energy *services*, such as comfort, light, mobility, ability to bake bread or make steel. We ought therefore to start by asking: What do we want the energy *for*? What are the many different tasks we're trying to do with the energy? And what is the amount and type and source of energy that can do each task cheapest?

If we look at the kinds of energy required at the point of final use in this country, we discover about fifty-eight percent require heat, mainly at low temperatures. Another thirty-four percent are needed as portable fuels to run our vehicles. Only about eight

Parabolic solar collector   *ERDA photograph*

percent represent all the special, premium uses which need electricity and which can give us our money's worth out of it, for electricity is a special, high-quality, and extremely expensive form of energy. The average kilowatt-hour sold in 1980 was priced at five and a half

Figure 3
APPROXIMATE STRUCTURE OF END-USE ENERGY NEEDS, 1975

| | PERCENT OF TOTAL DELIVERED ENERGY | | | |
	U.S.	U.K.	F.R.G.	Japan
Heat	58	66	75	68
of which: <100°C	35	55	50	22
100-600°C	15	6	12	31
>600°C	8	5	14	15
Portable liquids for vehicles	34	26	18	20
Electricity-specific	8	8	7	12
of which: motors	5	4	4	7
other*	3	4	3	5

*electronics, lights, electrometallurgy, electrochemistry, arc-welding, electrical home appliances, electric railways, etc.

cents—equivalent to buying the heat content of oil at about $88 a barrel, or over $2 a gallon, or two and a half times the 1981 OPEC oil price. If you order a new thermal power plant today, the delivered electricity will come in at nearly twice that: $130-160 or so a barrel, 8-10 cents a kilowatt-hour in today's dollars. That's equivalent on a heat basis to *four times* the price of OPEC crude oil. If you could use that extra electricity for electronics, light, motors, appliances, smelters, railways—uses that really need electricity—then it might be worth paying that sort of a high price. But those special uses—eight percent of all our delivered needs—are already filled up twice over by power stations already built. Nationally, we supply today not eight percent but thirteen percent in the form of electricity with more on the way. Almost two-fifths of our electricity today is already being used uneconomically for low-temperature heating and cooling: space heating, water heating, air conditioning. And if we make still more electricity, that's *all* we can use it for—because the premium, electricity-specific uses are already saturated.

This implies that arguing about what kind of power

plant to build is like shopping around for the best buy in brandy to pour into your gas tank, or the best in Chippendales to burn in the stove. It's completely the wrong question. It's asking how to get more of an expensive kind of energy of which we already have far more than we can get our money's worth out of. Our real energy problem, ninety-two percent, is dispersed uses of heat and of portable liquid fuels. More electricity is much too slow and much too expensive ever to be an economic solution to these unsaturated needs, regardless of how efficiently we use it.

That implies in turn that it doesn't matter in the least which kind of new power plant will be able to send out the cheapest kilowatt-hours, because no kind of new power plant can come anywhere near competing with the *real* competitors—the cheapest ways to meet our unsaturated energy needs. Those cheapest methods are of course familiar things like weatherstripping, insulation, heat exchangers, greenhouses, window quilts and shutters and overhangs, venetian blinds, pyrolysis of logging wastes. As a matter of fact, those measures are generally cheaper than the running costs *alone* for even a new nuclear power plant. So if you have just built such a plant, you can save the country money by writing it off and never operating it.

Let me run through that one again slowly. The only task for which the extra electricity that the plant produces can be used is low-temperature heating and cooling, because the premium uses are filled up already. But all that it's worth paying for low-grade heating and cooling is what it costs to do them the cheapest way—efficiency improvements and passive solar. Because those measures cost less than the running cost alone for the plant, you're better off not running it. It's even better than that. Under our tax laws, if you don't run the plant, then you no longer have to pay the future utility profits and the future federal tax subsidies to the plant. It turns out that those add up to about two-thirds of the capital cost which you already paid to build the plant. So if you don't have to pay the future costs, you've got that money back again. You recover the other third of the capital costs by the saving on running costs, provided that your conservation which displaces the plant is at least three tenths of a cent per kilowatt hours cheaper than the plant's running cost (which totals about two cents a kilowatt hour if you count not just the plant but everything it takes to get the energy to you). That means that the target your efficiency improvments has to beat is only about $20 or $25 a barrel. That's easy. Practically anything will beat that. As long as you can do that, you'll save money for the society on both running cost and capital cost. It would have been better not to build the reactor in the first place, but if you built it, it's better not to run it. The same argument applies to plants that are unfinished, partly amortized, or fossil-fueled.

Ask The Right Question

If we do want more electricity, then obviously we ought to get it from the cheapest places first, in order of increasing price. The cheapest source of electricity is eliminating pure waste, like lighting empty offices at headache level. The next cheapest source would be displacing with good architecture the electricity already being used for low-grade heating and cooling. (This is what many utilities, new no-interest conservation loans are doing. It's why they will come in and insulate your electric water heater free: they can then take the saved kilowatt-hours that used to heat your crawlspace and sell them to somebody else without having to build an expensive new plant to get them. But they could go much further. It would probably pay them, for example, to give you a free solar water heater. The next cheapest source is the parable of the refrigerator: make the appliances, lights, motors, smelters and so on technically more efficient.

When you've done those three things, you've saved at least three-quarters of your electricity, with no change in lifestyle or economic output. If you still want more electricity, then the next cheapest sources are industrial cogeneration (making electricity in factories as a by-product of the heat already made there), combined-heat-and-power plants with district heating (the kind of thing Minneapolis is looking at),

Over the next few decades we could reduce the energy required to make things by a third, reduce the energy required to run homes and buildings by 40 percent, and reduce transportation needs by 20–40 percent. Aside from the changes in cars and in added recycling, we'll hardly notice the change in energy use except at the bank; for in addition to saving millions of barrels of oil each day we'll save billions of dollars a year.
—LEE SCHIPPER

solar ponds with heat engines, filling empty turbine bays in existing large dams, wind machines, and small-scale hydro in good sites, and possibly even some new developments in cheap solar cells, although I haven't counted those.

My point is it's only after we have exhausted those first four categories and their various subcategories, that we'd even consider building a new power plant, because that is the slowest and most expensive way we know to replace oil.

It's worth noting, by the way, that nuclear power in this country does not replace much oil. What it mainly does is replace coal, which supplies five times as much electricity as either oil or nuclear power. There's almost a direct correlation between the growth of nuclear power and the decline in capacity factor of coal plants. It's interesting that between the first quarters of 1979 and of 1980, our oil-fired generation in this country went down by twenty-six percent, while the nuclear output *simultaneously* went down by twenty-five percent. That's not exactly what you'd call a substitution of one for the other. The real oil saving came from better end-use efficiency and from gas and coal substitution.

Saving Oil

If you do want to save a lot of oil in a hurry, there are only two important ways to do it: stop living in sieves and stop driving Petropigs. I've already said a bit about the sieves. We could quite straightforwardly fix up the buildings in this country enough in the next ten years to save 2,500,000 barrels of oil a day, equivalent to two-fifths of the 1980 rate of net U.S. oil imports. We could save close to four million barrels a day—the other three-fifths of imports—if somehow within the next ten or fifteen years we could simply replace all our cars with sixty-mile-a-gallon versions. Now, how could we do that? It takes ten years for the car stock to turn over. In fact, it probably takes longer than that now, because as the trade-in value of the gas guzzlers drops toward zero, those cars are filtering down to the poor people who can least afford to run them or to replace them. They and we are stuck with them.

There's a way around that. Rather than building synthetic fuel plants, it would be cheaper and quicker for our country to save oil by having the Treasury pay anywhere from half to all of the cost of giving you a diesel Rabbit or Honda CVCC, or an equivalent American car if Detroit would make one—provided that you would *scrap* your Brontomobile to get it off the road. Alternatively, rather than building synfuel plants, it would be cheaper and quicker to save oil by giving you a cash grant of about $200 for every mile per gallon by which your new car improves on your old car which you scrap. The average payback time against synfuels would be five years. (The saving compared to building reactors would be much greater than that. And if, by the way, you want to scrap your car and *not* replace it, you should also get a bounty for it.) As still another alternative, if Detroit spent as implausibly high a sum as one hundred billion dollars extra to retool immediately to make a sixty mile per gallon fleet of cars and light trucks, then spread that cost over the new fleet they plan to build anyhow in the next ten or twelve years, the extra cost per vehicle would be about $770. If you bought one, you'd recover that extra cost, at 1981 gasoline prices, in *fourteen months*. It makes you wish we had an economically conservative Administration. Such a fleet would save oil equivalent to three and a half North Slopes, all U.S. oil imports at the 1981 rate, or over a hundred big synfuel plants.

To emphasize the importance of thinking clearly about what we want energy for—what's the best tool for the task?—consider this sad little story from France concerning what energy planners call a "spaghetti chart." It's simply a way of showing where energy goes in a country. You feed in on the left-hand side of the chart the different fossil fuels, hydro, wood, nuclear, burning energy studies and so on. Those go through various transformations (the "meatballs" in the middle) and emergeon the right-hand side in different forms doing different tasks—heating buildings, making concrete, running TVs and trucks, and so on. A few years ago the energy efficiency people in the French government correctly started on the right-hand side of the chart. They said, "Our biggest single need for energy in France is heating buildings. What's the best way to heat a building?" They decided that even with heat pumps, the most uneconomical way was with more electricity. They fought their utility; they won; and as a result electric heating in France was supposed to be discouraged or phased out as a waste of money and fuel. Meanwhile, the energy supply people, much more numerous and influential, started on the left-hand side of the chart. They said, "Look at all this nasty imported oil coming into our country! We must replace that oil. Oil is energy," they mused, "we must need some other form of energy. Voila! Reactors give us energy; we'll build reactors all over the place." They didn't pay much attention to what would happen after that, nor to relative prices. So the two sides of the French energy establishment were trying to solve two different, indeed two incompatible, energy problems: more energy of whatever kind versus the right kind for the job. In 1979, they suddenly realized that the only way they can sell that extra nuclear electricity is for electric heating, which they just agreed not to do. All industrial nations are in this position. Which end of

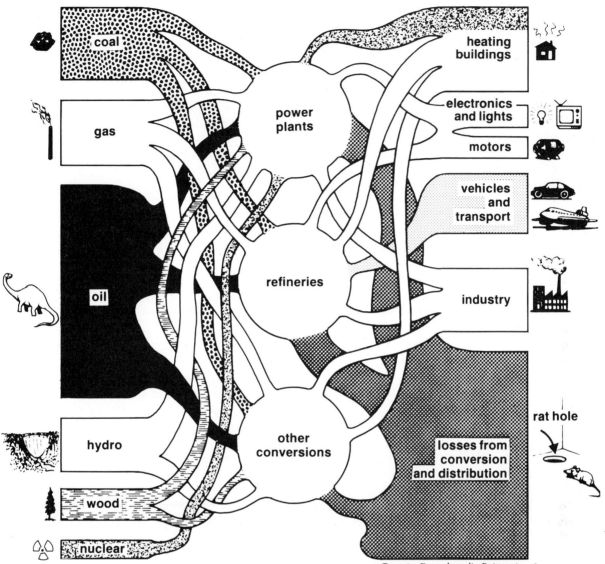

the spaghetti chart you start on, or what you think the energy problem is, is not an academic abstraction. It determines what you buy, and in particular it determines whether you buy reactors or greenhouses; whether you buy synthetic fuel plants or little pyrolyzers for logging waste; and it certainly determines as well whether you buy efficiency improvements or more supply.

Where Can We Get Energy Sustainably?

Where should we get our energy from as the oil and gas decline? I used to assume that although renewable sources are nice, they would be too expensive. But my views changed in the mid-1970s, when I started to shop for the best "soft technologies": the dozens of different kinds of renewable energy sources which run on sun, wind, and water, farm and forestry wastes, but not on depletable fuels. They are relatively under-

standable, to the user, but can still be technically sophisticated. (This is the spirit of the pocket calculator: it is a high-tech gadget; I don't quite know what goes on inside, and don't think I could make one, but what matters to me as a user is that this is a tool and not a machine. I run it. It doesn't run me, or at least not very often. It is not a mysterious giant lurking over the horizon somewhere and run by a technological priesthood whose arcane mysteries I'm not initiated into; it is something I can make up my own mind about; it's accessible to the democratic process.)

Finally, soft technologies supply energy at the right *scale* and *quality* for the tasks they are trying to do, so as to minimize the costs and losses of distributing and converting that energy respectively. I've already explained the importance of matching energy quality to the task. There are likewise many diseconomies of large scale which haven't been counted by people who say that energy systems have to be huge—otherwise we can't afford them. It's quite easy to show, using even a few of those well-quantified effects, that if you were going to build a power plant, it would be cheaper per kilowatt to build it small than to build it big.

The best soft technologies already in or entering commercial service are things that are already here, for which we don't need to wait. They include active and passive solar heating, passive solar cooling, high-temperature solar heat for industry (which we now know how to collect even on a cloudy winter day in Seattle or in Scandinavia), converting farm and forestry wastes (but not special crops) to liquid fuels (being *very* careful to protect soil fertility in the process) present hydro, small-scale hydro, and a bit of wind—maybe for electricity, but in most cases for pumping water, pumping heat, or compresssing air to run machines. The best present art in soft technologies supports two rather surprising conclusions.

First, if we use the best present soft technologies; each to do what it does best, they are more than

enough to meet essentially all our long-term energy needs in every industrial country and locality so far studied. We started with the tough countries like Japan and Denmark and went on to others like Britain, France, Germany, Sweden—countries which are simultaneously cold, cloudy, heavily industrialized, and densely populated. We still found that although these countries are often poor in fuels, they're rich in energy. They have plenty of renewable energy if it's used to advantage.

Speed And Cost

Second, although the soft technologies are not cheap, they are cheaper than not having them. Some cost more and some cost less than today's oil— mostly they cost a bit less. But they are uniformly cheaper even in capital cost, and several times cheaper in the energy price you pay as consumers, than the synfuel plants and power plants which you would otherwise have to build to do the same tasks. As the Harvard Business School study *Energy Future* found recently, the best investments are the efficiency improvements, then the soft technologies, then the synthetic fuel plants. Most expensive by far are the power stations. Nationally we've been taking those priorities in reverse order, worst buy first.

The same argument holds for speed as for cost. Both in theory and in practice, efficiency improvements and soft technologies give more energy, jobs, and money back sooner per dollar invested—for quite fundamental reasons. They're better for jobs and the economy and the environment; much better for Third World development; they don't have risks like climatic change or nuclear proliferation. They also have much lower political costs.

This last point should be stressed. Although soft technologies will outcompete the hard technologies in a free market, synfuels and nuclear power would never even emerge as an option in a competitive market. The synfuels program, like the nuclear program, requires much greater central authority to shield it from democratic forces—authority perhaps embodied in an Energy Mobilization Board. It requires an Energy Security Corporation to shield investments from market forces by underwriting projects which the market quite wisely has never been willing to finance. It requires corporate socialism: industry takes the profits, the public takes the risks. The hard technologies not only require more technocratic decisionmaking, they also give us a more vulnerable energy system which is more easily disrupted, whether deliberately or accidentally. They change the power balance between large and small groups in soci-

Vertical axis windmill   *NASA photograph*

Andrea Entwistle

ety. In contrast, the soft tecnologies make us more resilient against all kinds of surprises.

The Politics of Energy

There is another disturbing feature of the hard technologies. Because they are centralized, they automatically give the energy and the side-effects to different groups of people at opposite ends of the transmission lines, pipelines, rail lines. The energy goes to New York and Los Angeles, while the side effects go to Montana, Navajo country, Appalachia, Georges Bank, the North Slope, the Beaufort and Bering Seas, the Pacific coast. It's an arrangement considered admirable at one end and unjust at the other. As a result we have today more than sixty "energy wars" going on in this country—serious and sometimes violent conflicts between utilities or siting authorities and politically weaker rural people who don't want to live in a zone of national sacrifice for the benefit of slurbians a thousand miles away. The soft technologies don't have that problem. They automatically give the energy and the side effects to the same people at the same time so they can decide for themselves how much is enough.

In fact if you add up the combined political and economic advantages of a soft energy path, they are so overwhelming that if they were allowed to show themselves, a soft path would largely implement itself through the existing market and political process. And that's exactly what is starting to happen very rapidly;

much more rapidly than I would have thought possible. It is happening of course from the bottom up, not from the top down.

If the Department of Energy were to turn into a pumpkin and roll away tomorrow, chances are we wouldn't know for years that anything had happened. The energy problem is made of billions of very different pieces scattered throughout a very diverse society. Central management is therefore much more a part of the problem than part of the solution. The real action is, as it has to be, in the county, city, and neighborhood.

How To Make It Work

How can we make the transition easier so that we end up with a soft path smoothly by choice, rather than disruptively under compulsion of circumstance once we have poured our money into fantasies that didn't work? I think we should be doing mainly three things: First of all we ought to be stopping the tax and price subsidies which now make conventional fuels and power from hard technology look cheaper than they really are by upwards of one hundred billion dollars per year. That's what we are asking conservation and solar to compete against. It's amazing that they can do so at all. It's certainly an unfair thing to expect of them. If we don't have prices that tell the truth, we can't determine how much is enough.

Virtually everyone involved has unconsciously assumed that energy consumption must go on rising year after year to keep up living standards and fuel economic growth. But for advanced Western nations, this assumption is no longer true. Indeed, the nations with the highest per capita energy consumption could over the next few decades reduce their fuel consumption while actually improving living standards and achieving genuine economic growth.   —BARBARA WARD

The second thing we ought to be doing is to move gradually and fairly, as we are not doing, toward charging ourselves for depletable fuels what it will cost to replace them in the long run. Otherwise we are just stealing from our children.

Alternatively, if we want to keep nibbling at the bullet on energy prices, we can allocate most of our capital *as if* energy were already priced at replacement cost, whether it is or not. There's a simple way to do that. Before an electric or gas utility wants to build a new plant, they should have to show it's the cheapest way to meet the incremental end-use needs. If they can show that, then they've got a good argument. But if not, they shouldn't build the plant They should instead lend you the money they would have used to build the plant, at their own cost of money, for any cheaper fuel-saving measure. You then pay it back out of your energy savings. In this way you don't have to come up with any capital to fix up your house or your factory. The utility still comes out well ahead, saving capital and improving its cash flow enormously. It turns over its money so much faster that it doesn't need to go outside for new capital, and it avoids going broke by building more plants than it can pay for. I think the kinds of efficiency loans that some Pacific Northwest utilities have pioneered are a good start; but they are not done in a way that is economically most efficient for themselves or for the consumer. Specifically, the loan should be at the utilities' own cost of money rather than at zero interest, and should not be put into the rate base.

I think there are, in short, ways to remove the capital burden so that people can get out from under their high energy prices. If we make this comparison, so that a utility can't build a new power plant unless it's the cheapest way to do the job, then for the first time we will be directly comparing the costs of conservation and solar with the *replacement* cost represented by that new plant, not with the old cheap gas and hydro. Therefore, even if there is all this temporarily cheap energy sloshing around out there, we will still be allocating most of the capital going into our energy system

as if energy were *already* priced at its replacement cost, but without first having to achieve those unpalatably high prices. In this way we largely can do an end-run around the energy pricing problem.

The third thing we ought to do, especially at a local level, is to identify and systematically clear away all the silly rules and customs—"institutional barriers" or "market imperfections" if you like—which now prevent people from using energy in a way that saves money. There are, for example, obsolete building codes, obsolete mortgage regulations, and zoning rules which may not let you build a greenhouse. There are restrictive utility practices, inequitable access to capital or to information, split incentives: why should the landlord stuff up the cracks around the windows if the tenants pay the utilities? Why should a builder pay a little more to make a building efficient if the buyers are going to pay the running costs? These are all difficult problems. The solutions to them have to be crafted at a local level to match local conditions, but they are not insoluble. There is no energy future free of difficult problems. You just have to choose which kinds of problems you prefer. There is no free lunch, but some lunches are cheaper than others.

Diversity And Consensus

I think it's important politically that a soft energy path can appeal to a wide range of constituencies. If you are an economic traditionalist and you are most concerned with what's cheapest for you, that's OK. You can put up your greenhouse because it's cheaper than not doing it. If you are a worker, you might want to build it because it gives you more and better jobs than building power plants. If you are an environmentalist, you can build it because it is fairly benign. Or if you are a social transformationist, you can build it because it's autonomous. But who cares? It's still the same greenhouse. You don't have to agree before or after about why you built it.

We have a strong consensus today that wise energy use and the benign renewable sources are a good way to go. We have no consensus on anything else in energy policy, and I doubt we ever shall. We ought therefore to add up the bits we mainly agree about, and push them hard, because they are enough. Then we can forget about the bits we don't agree about, because they won't be necessary. We've never tried before to design an energy policy around an existing, broadly based political consensus. But it does seem long past time we started. I think that is what is starting to happen already. As Hunter and I go around the country we find the most exciting things going on at the grassroots level. I'm sure we are not even aware of one percent of what's happening.

In Nova Scotia people weatherized half their housing stock in one year under a simple, no-strings grant program. In Fitchburg, Massachusetts, people were so scared about freezing that by a program of door-to-door citizen action they weatherized over a fifth of their houses in ten weeks. In 1980, Americans spent about $9 billion on energy-saving devices.

There are about half a million solar buildings in this country, of which half are passive and half those were made by adding greenhouses to existing buildings. Fifteen percent of U.S. contractors now offer passive solar designs. In some areas, five to six percent of all space heating, and most of all new housing starts are now solar. In New England, over one hundred fifty factories switched from oil to wood. In many rural areas, upwards of half the households have done the same thing. A handful of stove foundries has become more than 400. Private woodburning has expanded sixfold in five years, and together with industrial use of wood wastes, delivered to the U.S. in 1980 about twice as much energy as nuclear power—which had three decade's head start and over forty billion dollars in direct Federal subsidies. More than half the states have

fuel alcohol programs, some of them very good. Small scale hydro reconstruction is flourishing: Federal permits were sought in 1980 alone for about seventy-five gigawatts of small hydro, or half as much again as all U.S. nuclear capacity operating in 1980. There are upwards of four wind machine companies whose two biggest commercial contributions in 1979, both to state governments on competitive bids, totalled almost a quarter of a billion dollars. In 1980-81, commercial "wind farms" started springing up.

Why are these things happening? Sometimes, as in the Fitchburg case, it's because people are afraid that they can't get the oil or can't afford it. Sometimes it is a particular local decision that focuses people's minds on their opportunities. We've been in little towns in the midwest where the local municipal utility was being asked to buy the next chunk of a coal plant at a capital cost of almost $2,000 for every woman, man, and child in town. That focuses the mind wonderfully. It makes people realize that for that kind of money they could fix up every building in town so it wouldn't need heating or cooling again; and they would have money left over.

Franklin County

Sometimes people come to a soft energy path just because they work out the consequences of *not* doing it. "Bill Moyers' Journal" recently described the poorest county in Massachusetts—Franklin County. It has a lot of trees; it's cold; it's cloudy; there are a lot of people out of work, especially in the old mill town; and farms are rocky and tenuous. Median income, last I heard, was $7,000 or $8,000 a year. And they depend heavily on imported oil. But about fifty people from around the county got together a few years ago to study this

The benefits that will accrue to a society that accepts the low-energy scenario could be most attractive. It could take the rush away from the search for further energy—the rush that has been so costly in the past, that has led to unneeded dams, avoidable oil spills, premature draining of Alaska and drilling of the continental shelf, wanton waste of energy resulting from the dismembering of cities and the paving and overdosing of fertile land, the spoiling of waters, the coloring of air. It could spare us further nuclear risk, and lessen the danger of the ugly fight for the residue of resources at the bottom of the barrel.

If people want a world in which people restrain their numbers and appetites, people can achieve it—and will probably prefer it to the grim alternative waiting in ambush unless they do achieve it.
—DAVID R. BROWER

problem. After a year they had an informal town meeting. The first thing they showed was that the average household in the county every year was sending out of the county more than $1,300 to pay for energy. Somebody held up a bucket with a hole in it, to symbolize the drain of twenty-three million dollars a year from Franklin County to Venezuela. They never see it again. It turns out that twenty-three million dollars a year is about the same as the total payroll of the ten biggest employers in the county. At this point people started to pay very careful attention.

If they were to achieve the *lowest* official forecast of energy need and energy price in the year 2000, things would be four times worse. They would send out $5,300 of today's dollars per household per year not counting inflation, to pay for personal energy needs. To keep that leaky bucket full, the biggest single employer in the county today would have to clone itself every couple of years for the rest of the century. When the utility and the Chamber of Commerce people heard that, they said, in effect, "That's absolutely impossible, We can't do that."

But then people worked out what they could do instead: how to stuff up all the little holes in the houses (totalling a square yard per house), insulate, use passive and active solar heating, run their vehicles on methanol from the sustained yield of some unal—located public woodlots, and meet their electric needs with wind or (six times over) with micro-hydro within the county. They figured that the local machine shops with no work to do could make this equipment for just about the twenty-three million dollars a year they pay now. The difference is that you've just stopped up the hole in the bucket. The jobs, the money, and the economic multiplier effects stay in Franklin County, not in Venezuela. That was what made the Economic Development Commissioner, the County Commissioners, and numerous other groups get behind it. It was obviously the only hope for the economic regeneration of that community. So as a result it is no longer a paper study; it's a project. With various fits and starts, they are doing it. There are at least hundreds and probably by now thousands of communities around the country that are doing that, one way or another. They figured out that it's the only thing they can afford. Nor is this happening only in rural areas,

Solar collector in India   *United Nations photograph*

Under a no-strings grant program, Nova Scotians weatherized half their houses in one year. The people of Fitchburg, Massachusetts, by door-to-door citizen action, did the same in seven weeks, saving a quarter of the town's heating oil. Of the roughly 200,000 U.S. solar buildings, half are passive and half of those are retrofits (greenhouses added to existing buildings). In the most solar-conscious communities, from a quarter to all of the 1978-1979 housing starts were passive solar. More than 150 New England factories, and half the rural households in many areas, switched from oil to wood. Over half the states have active fuel alcohol programs. Small-scale hydro reconstruction is flourishing. More than forty manufacturers of wind machines share an explosively growing market whose two biggest commercial commitments in 1979 totalled $230 million. The size, dispersion, rate and diversity of soft-path activities are now so great that national authorities are only dimly aware of how fast their own targets are being overtaken.

—AMORY LOVINS, HUNTER LOVINS, AND LEONARD ROSS

like the San Luis Valley in Colorado, or in small towns, like Soldiers Grove, Wisconsin, or in suburbs like Davis, California. We are discovering that cities are turning out to be a testing ground for many of these innovations, particularly among low-income people who have no alternatives—who cannot afford to do anything but use conservation and renewables. From the Frontier Project in the South Bronx to the Community Development Corporation in San Bernardino, they are discovering that for people on the margin there is a strong incentive to use initiative and ingenuity in order to capture the benefits of the soft energy path for their own community. And that's why some of the most exciting developments in soft energy have been within our cities. I think we are going to see much more of that.

In short, we are finding—as the Jeffersonians (and market economists) have been try to tell us—that people are really pretty smart, and that if they have incentive and opportunity, and see the energy problem as *their* problem, they can go out and largely solve it, as we have always solved problems. There is nothing mysterious about energy. It isn't too complex or too technical for ordinary people to understand.

We are discovering again in energy something that Lao-Tse told us two and a half thousand years ago:

> *Leaders are best when people scarcely know they exist;*
> *not so good when people obey and acclaim them;*
> *worst when people despise them.*
> *Fail to honor people, they fail to honor you.*
> *But of good leaders who talk little,*
> *when their work is done, their aim fulfilled,*
> *the people will all say: "We did this ourselves."*

Recommended Actions

☐ The President should dedicate himself and his administration to a new energy policy based (1) on conservation and end-use efficiency, (2) on sophisticated fossil-fuel technology, as an interim measure, and (3) on decentralized, small-scale power systems drawing energy from renewable sources.

☐ The President should announce the phasing out of all federal nuclear power programs not only for safety reasons, but also because nuclear power plants use up massive amounts of capital badly needed for other social purposes, because electricity can be generated more efficiently by small decentralized plants located near the consumers they serve, and because nuclear technology absorbs talents and resources needed to attain rational energy goals.

☐ Argonne, Brookhaven, Oak Ridge, and other national laboratories should be ordered to turn their attention from nuclear power to conservation techniques, to more efficient combustion of fossil fuels as a transitional technology, and especially to small-scale systems harnessing solar energy and solar variants such as wind; federal funding of other research and development should also reflect these priorities.

☐ Antitrust laws must be strictly enforced in the energy industry, where a few giant corporations that already control most US fossil fuel reserves are buying up uranium reserves and geothermal leases.

☐ All levels of government must review and revise laws, codes, and regulations that impede the efficient use of energy, such as deterrents to the upgrading of existing buildings to make them energy-efficient.

☐ Public Utility Commissions must be encouraged to rationalize electricity rate structures, which now tend to reward wastefulness and penalize thrift and which charge the poor more per unit of electricity than they charge the rich.

The Arithmetic of Energy Growth

ALBERT A. BARTLETT

WE HEAR POLITICAL LEADERS of the United States speaking of "energy self-sufficiency" and of "Project Independence." We have the vague feeling that arctic oil from Alaska will relieve the energy crisis, and we are told that the US is in good shape in the long run because of our vast deposits of coal. What are the facts?

Rather than take you into the sticky abyss of statistics, I wish to rely on a few data and the pristine simplicity of elementary mathematics.

Mathematical Background: A Review

When a quantity such as the rate of consumption of a resource grows at a fixed percent per year, the growth is exponential. The quantity will grow to twice its initial value in a fixed period called its doubling time. The constancy of the doubling time of the growth means that in one doubling time the quantity will double in size, in two doubling times it will quadruple, in three doubling times it will grow by a factor of eight, in four doubling times it will grow by a factor of 16, and so on.

The Power of Powers of Two

If you place one grain of wheat on the first square of a chessboard, two on the second, four on the third, eight on the fourth, 16 on the fifth, etc., you will have on the 64 squares approximately 500 times the current annual harvest of wheat in the entire world—an amount that is probably larger than all the wheat that has been harvested in the history of the earth. This from a single grain of wheat doubled a mere 63 times.

Populations tend to grow exponentially. The world population today is estimated to be four billion people and it is growing at the rate of 1.9 percent per year. At this rate, the world population would grow by one billion in less than 12 years, the population would double to eight billion in 36 years, the population would grow to a density of one person per square meter on the dry land surface of the earth (excluding Antarctica) in 550 years, and the mass of people would equal the mass of the earth in 1,620 years.

Exponential Growth In A Finite Environment

Bacteria multiply by division. For a certain strain of bacteria, the time for the division is one minute. I put one bacterium in a bottle at 11:00 a.m. and I observe that the bottle is full at 12:00 noon. Here is a simple example of exponential growth in a finite environment. This is mathematically identical to the exponentially growing consumption of our finite resources. Ponder three questions about the bacteria:

Question: When was the bottle half full?

Answer: 11:59 a.m.

Question: If you were an average bacterium in the bottle, at what time would you first realize that you were running out of space?

Answer: There is no unique answer to this question, so let me ask, "At 11:55, when the bottle is only 3 percent filled and is 97 percent empty, how many of you would perceive that there was a problem?"

Suppose that at 11:58 some farsighted bacteria realize that they are running out of space in the bottle and, consequently, they launch a search for new bottles. They look offshore and in the Arctic, and at 11:59 a.m. they discover three new, empty bottles. Great sighs of relief: the magnificent discovery is three times the number of bottles hitherto known. The discovery quadruples the total space resource known to the bacteria. Surely this will solve the problem. Bacterial "Project. Independence" must now have achieved its goal.

Question: How long can the baterial growth continue if the total space resources are quadrupled?

Answer: Two more doubling times, i.e., two minutes.

Let's review the chronology. At 11:58, Bottle No. 1 is one-quarter full; at 11:59, it is half full; at noon, Bottle

No. 1 is full; at 12:01, Bottle No. 1 and Bottle No. 2 are both full; at 12:02 all four bottles are full. Space, a finite resource for the bacteria, has been exhausted.

Quadrupling the resource extends the life of the resource by only two doubling times. When consumption grows exponentially, enormous increases in resources are consumed in very short times.

How Long Will Fossil Fuels Last?

The question of how long our resources will last is perhaps the most important question that can be asked in a modern industrial society. Dr. M. King Hubbert, a geophysicist with the US Geological Survey, is a world authority on the estimation of energy resources and on the prediction of their patterns of discovery and depletion. Many of the data used here come from Hubbert's reports. They are required reading for anyone who wishes to understand the fundamentals and many of the details of the problem.

Available data suggest that we have consumed about 50.8 percent of the total ultimately recoverable oil in the US outside of Alaska—96.6 billion barrels out of an 190-billion-barrel total. Since one-half of our domestic petroleum has already been consumed, the "petroleum time" in the US is one minute before noon.

From 1870 to 1929, the rate of production of domestic crude oil increased exponentially at a rate of 8.27 percent per year, with a doubling time of 8.4 years. If the rate of production was held constant at the 1970 rate (3.9 billion barrels per year), the remaining non-Alaskan US oil would last only 28 years.

In the following table, column one is the growth in the rate of domestic oil consumption, in percent. Column two is the corresponding lifetime of domestic oil reserves (excluding Alaska's). Column three is the lifetime of domestic oil, including Alaska's. Column four is the lifetime of domestic oil, including both Alaska's petroleum and a hypothetical estimate of recoverable US oil shale reserves.

COLUMN ONE	COLUMN TWO	COLUMN THREE	COLUMN FOUR
zero%	28.4 yrs.	31.4 yrs.	62.8 yrs.
one	25.0	27.3	48.8
two	22.5	24.4	40.7
three	20.5	22.1	35.3
four	19.0	20.4	31.4
five	17.7	18.9	28.4
six	16.6	17.7	26.0
seven	15.6	16.6	24.1
eight	14.8	15.7	22.4
nine	14.1	14.9	21.1
ten	13.4	14.2	19.9

Hubbert reports that the oil recoverable from US oil shale under 1965 techniques is 80 billion barrels, and he quotes higher estimates. In preparing the preceding table, I used 103.4 billion barrels so that total reserves in column four would be double those in column three. The table shows that when consumption is rising exponentially, a doubling of the remaining resource results in only a small increase in the life expectancy of the resource. No one who understands the exponential function upon which the table is based can talk glibly of energy self-sufficiency.

Now, let's construct a similar table to show the life expectancy of world oil reserves. My data suggest that 261 billion barrels of an ultimately recoverable 1,952 billion barrels was produced by 1972, or 13.4 percent. A little more than one-eighth of world oil has been consumed. The "world petroleum time" is between two and three minutes before noon, i.e., we are between two and three doubling times from the expiration of the resource.

From 1890 to 1970, world crude oil production grew at a rate of 7.04 percent per year, with a doubling time of 9.8 years. Column one of the following table shows growth of the rate of future consumption ranging from zero to ten percent (zero representing a continuation of the production rate in 1970, which was 16.7 billion barrels per year). Column two indicates the corresponding lifetime of the remaining crude oil. Column three shows the lifetime with an estimate of oil shale production factored in. Column four assumes that reserves of oil shale will prove to be four times as big as currently estimated.

COLUMN ONE	COLUMN TWO	COLUMN THREE	COLUMN FOUR
zero%	101 yrs.	113 yrs.	147 yrs.
one	69.9	75.4	90.3
two	55.3	59.0	68.5
three	46.5	49.2	56.2
four	40.5	42.6	48.2
five	36.0	37.8	42.4
six	32.6	34.1	38.0
seven	29.8	31.2	34.6
eight	27.6	28.8	31.8
nine	25.7	26.8	29.5
ten	24.1	25.1	27.5

The table shows that quadrupling the assumed amount of world shale oil would raise the life expectancy of world oil from 113 to 147 years, at zero rate of growth increase. But if consumption grows 10 percent per year, the life expectancy is extended only from 25.1 to 27.5 years. This illustrates a point of great importance: when we are dealing with exponential growth, we do not need to have an accurate estimate of the size of a resource in order to make a reliable estimate of how long the resource will last.

"What will life be like without liquid petroleum products?" One may think of heating homes with solar energy and traveling in electric cars. But a far more fundamental problem appears when one recognizes that modern agriculture is based on petroleum-powered machinery and on petroleum-based fertilizers. This is reflected in a definition: modern agriculture is the use of land to convert petroleum into food.

From David Pimental we learn that:

"We have now reached the point in US agriculture where we use 80 gallons of gasoline or its equivalent to raise an acre of corn, but only nine hours of human labor per crop acre for the average of all types of produce."

It is clear that agriculture as we know it will experience major changes within the life expectancy of today's students. With these changes could come a major further deterioration of worldwide levels of nutrition. Yet we still have people who proclaim that Malthus has been proved wrong.

It has frequently been asserted that coal will answer US and world energy needs for a long time. What are the facts?

Estimates of ultimate US coal production range from 390 to 1,486 billion metric tons, of which my data indicate that 50 billion metric tons has been produced through 1972. This leaves 34 billion metric tons (low estimate) or 1,436 billion metric tons (high estimate). Let's see how long remaining coal would last under various assumptions as to the rate of increase of coal production above the 1972 level of 0.5 billon metric tons.

GROWTH	HIGH ESTIMATE	LOW ESTIMATE
zero%	2,872 yrs.	680 yrs.
one	339	205
two	203	134
three	149	103
four	119	83
five	99	71
six	86	62
seven	76	55
eight	68	50
nine	62	46
ten	57	42
eleven	52	39
twelve	49	37
thirteen	46	35

The government has set a coal production goal for 1974 to 1980 that amounts to a 13 percent per year increase. You can see that remaining coal wouldn't last long at that rate of growth—less than half a century, whether you choose the high or the low estimate of coal remaining. Even if you assume a comparatively moderate 6.7 percent per year rate of growth, which was characteristic of coal in 1860-1910, before oil and gas took over as the primary sources of energy, remaining coal would last at most three-quarters of a century. Any sizeable exponential growth of the rate of consumption of coal would consume the "vast US reserves" in a very short time.

What Do The Experts Say?

Now that we have seen the facts, let us examine what some branches of our federal government say about coal.

Congressional Research Service: "It is clear, particulary in the case of coal, that we have ample reserves....We have an abundance of coal in the ground. Simply stated, the crux of the problem is how to get it out of the ground and use it in environmentally acceptable ways and on an economically competitive basis....At current levels of output and recovery these reserves can be expected to last more than 500 years."

Here is one of the most dangerous statements in the literature. It is dangerous because news media and the energy companies pick up the notion that "US coal will last more than 500 years" while ignoring the important caveat with which the sentence began: "At current levels of output . . ." It is absolutely clear that the government does not plan to hold coal production constant at current levels.

Energy Research and Development Administration: "Coal reserves far exceed supplies of oil and gas, and yet coal supplies only 18 percent of our total energy. To maintain even this contribution we will need to increase coal production by 70 percent by 1985, but the real aim—to increase coal's share of the energy market—will require a staggering growth rate."

While ERDA tells us that we must achieve enormous increases in the rate of coal production, a government official quoted by the *Boulder Daily Camera* tells us we can increase the rate of production and still have the resource last for a long time.

"The trillions of tons of coal lying under the United States will have to carry a large part of the nation's increased energy consumption, says the Director of the Energy Division of the Oak Ridge National Laboratories....He estimated America's coal reserves are so huge they could last 'a minimum of 300 years and probably a maximum of 1,000 years.'"

Interspersed among news stories like this are advertisements that say coal will last a long time at present rates of consumption—and say at the same time that we must dramatically increase our rate of coal production.

Exxon Advertisement: "At the rate the United States uses coal today, these reserves could help keep us in energy for the next two hundred years....Most coal used in America today is burned by electric power plants [which] consumed about 400 million tons of coal last year. By 1985 this figure could jump to nearly 700 million tons."

Other advertisements talk of a 500-year lifetime for coal without mentioning the rate of consumption.

American Electric Power Company Advertisement: "We are sitting on half the world's known supply of coal—enough for over 500 years."

Some ads stress the idea of self-sufficiency without stating how long we might be self-sufficient.

The AEPC (again): "Coal, the only fuel in which America is totally self-sufficient . . ."

Other ads suggest a lack of understanding of the fundamentals of the exponential function.

The AEPC (yet again): "Yet today there are still those who shrill for less energy and no growth....Now America is obligated to generate more energy—not less—merely to provide for its increasing population....With oil and gas in short supply, where will that energy come from? Predominantly from coal. The US Department of the Interior estimates America has 23 percent more coal than we dreamed of. 4,000,000,000,000 (trillion!) tons of it. Enough for over 500 years."

A simple calculation based on the current production rate of 0.6 billion tons per year shows that the growth in the rate of production of coal cannot exceed 0.8 percent per year if the ad's four trillion tons of coal are to last for the ad's 500 years. Note that the four trillion tons of coal cited in the ad is 2.8 times the "high" and 12 times the "low" estimate of coal reserves reported by Hubbert.

We may *wish* we could have rapid growth in the rate of consumption and have resources last for a long time, but it doesn't take advanced mathematics to prove that these two goals are incompatible. We need to shift our faith to calculations (arithmetic) based on factual data and give up our belief in Walt Disney's First Law, "Wishing will make it so."

Walter Wriston, the top executive of First National City Bank, is probably one of the world's authorities on the exponential growth of investments and compound interest. Yet he contends that "the energy crisis was made in Washington." Ridiculing "the modern-day occult prediction" of computer print-outs and warning against extrapolating past trends to estimate what may happen in the future, he points out that American

free enterprise solved the great "Whale Oil Crisis" of the 1850s. With this example as his data base, he extrapolates into the future to assure us that American ingenuity will solve the current energy crisis if the bureaucrats in Washington will only quit interfering.

Ads by the Edison Electric Institute tell us that "There is an increasing scarcity of certain *fuels*. But there is no scarcity of *energy*. There never *has* been. There never *will* be. There never *could* be. Energy is inexhaustible."

Professor Charles Frush, Colorado School of Mines, offers "proof" of the proposition that "Mankind has the right to use the world's resources as it wishes, to the limits of its abilities. . . ."

The opening sentences of a major scientific study of the energy problem, by J.C. Fisher, American Institute of Physics, read: "The United States has an abundance of energy resources: fossil fuels (mostly coal and oil shale) adequate for centuries, fissionable nuclear fuels adequate for millenia and solar energy that will last indefinitely."

R.L. Bisplinghoff, an educated authority, asserts that there is no problem of shortages of resources. "It is not true that we are running out of resources that can be easily and cheaply exploited without regard for future operations." His next sentence denies that growth is a serious component of the energy problem. "It is *not* true that we must turn our back on economic growth." Three sentences later, he says there may be a problem. "We must face the fact that the well of non-renewable natural resources is not bottomless." Bisplinghoff suggests that lack of "leadership" is part of the problem.

L.G. Hauser's opening paper in an energy conference makes no mention of the contribution of growth to the energy crisis when he asserts that "The core of the energy problem both in the US and world-wide . . . is our excessive dependence on our two scarcest energy resources—oil and natural gas." For him continued growth is not part of the problem, it's part of the solution. "*More* energy must be made available at a higher rate of growth than normal—in the neighborhood of 6 percent per year compared to a recent historical growth rate of 4 percent per year."

The only thing more distressing than the truths revealed by the exponential calculations is the observation that so few of our leaders, educators, policy-makers, and "experts" have performed the calculations or show any sign of understanding the need to heed them.

An Exponential Solution

The exponential function provides an interesting solution to energy and resource problems. If we make the rate of exhaustion of a resource follow the appropriate *negative* growth curve, the total productions from now to infinity is exactly equal to the size of the resource. We can use the resource and have it last forever (but near the end of time, we'd be rationing it out by the atom). This is the ultimate self-sufficiency.

For the "high" estimate of US coal, the production rate would have to *decrease* approximately 3 percent per century in order to assure that US coal would last forever.

A negative-growth program can be applied to any resource. If the ratio of annual petroleum production to the total resource is 1 to 101, then the decline in petroleum consumption would have to be about 1 percent per year to make petroleum last forever.

The greatest act of responsibility we could perform for our descendants for all time would be to put our consumption of coal and other resources on this declining curve. Not only is it proper to save some resources for those who will follow us, but it may also make the difference in national self-sufficiency and ultimately, of national survival.

What Do We Do Now?

We must:

1. Educate all our people to an understanding of the arithmetic and consequences of growth, especially in terms of the earth's finite resources. David Brower has observed that: "The promotion of growth is simply a sophisticated way to steal from our children."

2. Educate people to the critical urgency of abandoning our belief in the disastrous dogma that "growth is good," that "bigger is better," that "we must grow or stagnate," etc., etc. We must realize that growth is but an adolescent phase of life that stops when physical maturity is reached. If growth continues after maturity, it is called obesity or cancer. Prescribing growth as the cure of the energy crisis has all the logic of prescribing cancer as the cure for carcinoma.

As our nation enters its third century, it would be an appropriate time to make the transition from national adolescence to national maturity.

3. Conserve in the use and consumption of everything; outlaw planned obsolescence; recognize that as important as it is to conserve, arithmetic shows clearly that improbably large savings from conservation would be wiped out in short order by even modest rates of growth. Conservation alone cannot do the job.

4. Recycle almost everything. Except for the continuous input of sunlight, the human race must finish the trip with the supplies that were aboard when "spaceship earth" was launched.

5. Invest great sums in research to:

a. Develop the use of solar (including wind) energy.

b. Reduce the problems of nuclear fission power plants. [*Editor's note*: FOE believes the problems of nuclear fission cannot be reduced enough to make fission an acceptable technology.]

c. Explore the possibility that we may be able to harness nuclear fusion and other sources of energy, bearing in mind that the renewable source will serve best.

These investments must not be made with the idea that if they are successful they could sustain growth for a few more doubling times. They must be made with the objective of taking over the energy load in a mature and stable society, one in which fossil fuels are used on a declining exponential curve that will let them last forever as chemical raw materials rather than fuels.

6. Recognize that it is pseudo-science and false technology to promote ever-increasing rates of consumption in the hope that science and technology will rescue us from the consequences of our self-centered folly. It is not acceptable to base our future on the motto, "When in doubt, gamble."

We cannot sit back and deplore the lack of "leadership" and the lack of response of our political system. Every one of us has access to dozens of other leaders who have not yet understood the problem. We must take the message to all the people in a dedicated spirit of education and service.

Some experts suggest that the system will take care of itself and that growth will stop of its own accord, even though they know that cancer, if left to run its course, stops only when the host is dead. My suggestions are offered as *preventive* medicine.

More Thoughts on Energy

THE UNITED STATES is threatened far more by the hazards of too much energy, too soon, than by the hazards of too little, too late.

The hazards of too much, which have been as widely underestimated as the liabilities of too little have been exaggerated, include diverting financial resources from compelling social needs, making hasty commitments to unproved technologies, and generating environmental and social costs that harm human welfare more than the extra energy improves it.

The higher the level of energy use already attained, the more likely it is that the economic-technological benefits of an additional unit of energy will be outweighed by the social and environmental costs. Mounting evidence suggests that the United States is approaching (if not beyond) the level where further energy growth costs more than it is worth.

Critics of conservation are quick to suggest that what is implied here is a return to a primitive existence.

In a society that uses its 5,000-pound automobiles for half-mile round trips to the market to fetch a six-pack of beer, consumes the beer in buildings that are overcooled in summer and overheated in winter, and then throws the aluminum cans away at an energy loss equivalent to a third of a gallon of gasoline per six-pack, this "primitive existence" argument strikes me as the most offensive kind of nonsense.

Finally, less energy can mean more employment. The energy-producing industries comprise the most capital-intensive and least labor-intensive major sector of the economy. Accordingly, each dollar of investment capital taken out of energy production and invested in something else, and each personal-consumption dollar saved by reduced energy use and spent elsewhere in the economy, will create more jobs than are lost.

—John Holdren

WITH THE COMING of the industrial age a sizable portion of the land in many parts of the world was cleared at an accelerated pace, thereby modifying the earth's natural capacity for storing and evaporating moisture and for absorbing solar energy. These human-induced modifications of the environment often slightly altered the local climate from what it had been when the land was in its natural state.

Industrialized peoples, with their higher standards of living, rapidly became dependent on the extensive use of energy to turn their wheels, heat their buildings, produce their electricity, and grow, store, and transport their food. Most of the energy liberated was (and still is) derived from fossil fuels—coal, gas, and oil—whose burning is accompanied by the disagreeable by-products that we now call pollution.

One form of such pollution that affects the entire atmosphere is the release of carbon dioxide (CO_2) gas. Even though it makes up a small fraction (less than one one-thousandth) of the gases that comprise the atmosphere, CO_2 is crucial in determining the earth's temperature because it traps some of the earth's heat (to produce the so-called greenhouse effect). Human activities have already raised the CO_2 content in the atmosphere by 10 percent and are estimated to raise it some 25 percent by the year 2000. . . . This could lead to a 1° Celsius (1.8° Fahrenheit) average warming of the earth's surface, which is roughly equivalent to twice the warming that occurred "naturally" in the first half of this century. This 1°C warming could reduce the masses of ice at the poles, and thereby raise the height of the world's oceans, or affect climate in the temperate zones or other latitudes.

If concentrations of CO_2, and perhaps of aerosols, continue to increase, demonstrable climatic changes could occur by the end of this century, if not sooner; recent calculations suggest that if present trends continue, a threshold may soon be reached after which the effects will be unambiguously detectable on a global basis. Problematically, by that point it may be too late to avoid the dangerous consequences of such an occurrence, for *certain proof* of present theories can come only *after* the atmosphere itself has "performed the experiment."

The processes at work in determining climatic change are simply not yet fully understood. Despite the uncertainty in measurements and in theory, estimates must be given and difficult decisions may have to be made on the basis of the available knowledge. In any case, efforts to develop better estimates and models of potential effects will be absolutely necessary to help us reduce the uncertainties in decision-making to a tolerable minimum. Improvement of the quality of these estimates is the responsibility that atmospheric scientists and their funding agents owe to long-range planners, for the climatic effects of human activities are self-evidently the outer limits to growth. The real problem is: If we choose to wait for more certainty before actions are initiated, then can our models be improved in time to prevent an irreversible drift toward a future calamity? And how can we decide how

Projections still greatly underestimate the technical range and potential use of fully conserving strategies. They are simply not seen as a cheap and effective method of increasing energy supply. It is a strange aberration. If an intensive housing-insulation program lowers the nation's demand for oil, gas, and electricity by 10 percent, this is equivalent to increasing supplies by the same amount. And since the whole process of increasing supplies—especially indigenous energy supplies for counries with no oil— is exceedingly expensive, the range of conservation measures that are cost-effective compared with increasing supply costs is vast.   —BARBARA WARD

much uncertainty is enough to prevent a policy action based on a climate model? This dilemma rests, metaphorically, in our need to gaze into a very dirty crystal ball; but the tough judgment to be made here is precisely how long we should clean the glass before acting on what we believe we see inside.

—Stephen Schneider

THE BASIC REASON for the energy crisis is that nearly all the energy now used in the United States (and in the world) comes from non-renewable sources. As a non-renewable energy source is depleted, it becomes progressively more costly to produce, so that continued reliance on it means an unending escalation in price. This process has a powerful inflationary impact: it increases the cost of living, especially of poor people; it aggravates unemployment; it reduces the availability of capital. No economic system can withstand such pressures indefinitely; sooner or later the energy crisis *must* be solved. And this can be done only by replacing the present non-renewable sources—oil, natural gas, coal, and uranium—with renewable ones, which are stable in cost. That is what a national energy policy must do if it is to solve the energy crisis, rather than delay it or make it worse. But this is a little like saying that all we need to do to cure the ills of earthly life is to enter Paradise. The real problem is whether it is possible to get there from here, and if so, how. The problem is one of transition.

We can now take stock of how the choice between the two optional routes to a renewable energy system is likely to affect the special interests of the different sectors of the economy. The breeder route would favor the electric utilities and the oil companies. The solar route would favor the gas utilities and all the users of energy: industry, commerce, transportation, farmers, labor, and consumers. It seems clear that the self-interest of the preponderant majority would be best served by the solar choice.

Thus the decision to embark at once on the solar transition would mean an unavoidable clash between the national interest and the special interests of the major oil companies and the electric utilities. In the solar transition, the major oil companies, among the richest and most powerful corporations in the U.S., or the world, would lose their dominant position in the economy. For them, the transition would end the attractive prospect of at least twenty-five more years of escalating energy prices, which—given their rights as private entrepreneurs—would enable them to accumulate huge profits and buy up ever larger sectors of the economy. When a solar energy system is in place, and renewable sources have largely replaced oil and natural gas, the oil companies' economic role would become limited to production of stand-by natural gas and raw materials for the chemical industry. (But here, too, if biomass production could be enlarged sufficiently, these biological sources might even replace oil and natural gas as basic chemical feedstocks.) On the other hand, if the interests of the oil companies prevailed and the solar transition is delayed or blocked entirely, they would continue to flourish while the rest of the economy would suffer. Conversely, the rest of industry, and indeed the economy as a whole, would clearly benefit from the solar transition. Damage to the private interests of the major oil companies seems to be a necessary cost of these larger, social benefits.

In a strategy of social governance, public agencies, responsible to the citizens, would decide which solar technologies ought to be introduced, and when. These judgments would rely not only on the technology's immediate cost-effectiveness, or on its profitability to the producer, but more crucially, on its *social* value in fostering an effective overall solar transition. Such a strategy would permit rational planning of the development, testing, and introduction of solar technologies in keeping with the national interest in a smooth, rapid solar transition, rather than conforming only to the narrow criterion of private profitability. But it would challenge the great American taboo against even hinting that social welfare might be a better reason for a new productive investment than private profit.

On the farm, the solar transition means an end to the wasteful, unnecessary use of energy-intensive inputs, producing appreciable amounts of energy without reducing food production—a larger economic output from the same agricultural resources. In the city, the solar transition means replacing inherently inefficient, centralized power plants with local cogenerators, so that homes and shops can be heated, cooled, and lighted more efficiently and more cheaply—a higher standard of living for consumers. In the factories, the solar transition means a more efficient match between energy and the energy-using tasks of production—greater industrial productivity. The solar transition means that economic resources now wastefully tied up in maintaining an energy system that threatens to cannibalize the rest of the economy

can be released and put to useful work: building solar collectors; alcohol plants; methane generators; photovoltaic cells; windmills; cogenerators; electrified railroads, and urban electric trolley systems.

In sum, the solar transition offers the nation a momentous opportunity which, like the decision to abolish slavery, can rebuild the faltering economy. But it is beyond the reach of purely private governance. Society as a whole must be involved, for the solar transition is a great historic passage which only the people of the United States can decide to undertake. What stands in the way of that decision is neither technology nor economics, but politics—the politics of evasion, which, by denying that the problem exists, deprives the American people of the opportunity to solve it.

It will be difficult—some say impossible—to learn how to merge economic justice with economic progress, and personal freedom with social governance. If we allow the fear of failing in this aim to forestall the effort to achieve it, then failure is certain. But if we firmly embrace economic democracy as a national goal, as a new standard for political policy, as a vision of the nation's future, it can guide us through the historic passage that is mandated by the energy crisis, and restore to the nation the vitality that is inherent in the richness of its resources and the wisdom of its people.

—Barry Commoner

Peter Barnes, the Solar Center

THERE IS A source of energy that produces no radioactive waste, nothing in the way of petrodollars, and very little pollution. Moreover, the source can provide the energy that conventional sources may not be able to furnish. Unhappily, however, it does not receive the emphasis and attention it deserves.

The source might be called energy efficiency, for Americans like to think of themselves as an efficient people. But the energy source is generally known by the more prosaic term *conservation*. To be semantically accurate, the source should be called conservation energy, to remind us of the reality—that conservation is no less an energy alternative than oil, gas, coal, or nuclear. Indeed, in the near term, conservation could do more than any of the conventional sources to help the country deal with the energy problem it has.

If the United States were to make a serious commitment to conservation, it might well consume 30 to 40 percent less energy than it now does, and still enjoy the same or even higher standard of living. That saving would not hinge on a major technological breakthrough, and it would require only modest adjustments in the way people live. Moreover, the cost of conservation energy is very competitive with other energy sources. The possible energy savings would be the equivalent of the elimination of all imported oil—and then some.

How could this come about? There is very great flexibility in how much energy is required, and how much is actually used, for this or that purpose. To give a simple example, toast can be made on a barbecue, in a broiler—or in a toaster. The end product is the same—toast—but the methods employed to make it vary greatly in energy consumed and waste produced. The making of toast illustrates the central point of this chapter—that much less energy than is now consumed can be used to achieve the same end.

The barriers to the potential savings through conservation are very great, but they are rarely technological. Although some of the barriers are economic, they are in most cases institutional, political, and social. Overcoming them requires a government policy that champions conservation, that gives it a chance equal in the marketplace to that enjoyed by conventional sources of energy.

But why should the country place greater emphasis on conservation?

Conservation may well be the cheapest, safest, most productive energy alternative readily available in large amounts. By comparison, conservation is a quality energy source. It does not threaten to undermine the international monetary system, nor does it emit carbon dioxide into the atmosphere, nor does it generate problems comparable to nuclear waste. And contrary to the conventional wisdom, conservation can stimulate innovation, employment, and economic growth. Since the United States uses a third of all the oil used in the world every day, major reduction in U.S. demand would have a major impact on the international energy markets.

A firm commitment to conservation is also required for American foreign policy to become credible on energy and nuclear proliferation issues. How can the United States ask the Europeans and the Japanese to give up the fast breeder reactor and reprocessing if it does not hold out some alternative—that is, less pressure on the international oil market? How can the United States ask them to come to the aid of the dollar when American oil imports, a major cause of the dollar's weakness, continue to grow? In fact, foreigners often seem to pay much greater attention than do Americans to the relation between U.S. energy demand and these kinds of issues.

Conservation for the most part involves a multitude of decisionmakers. One major exception does stand out—transportation, and in particular, the automobile. What is involved here is a relatively standardized product used for a standardized activity—moving people about. Only a few producers are engaged in its manu-facture, and they are the key decisionmakers. The automobile is the one and only consumer product that has a disproportionate and indeed massive effect on energy consumption. The transport sector uses 26 percent of the energy used in the United States—half the oil. The private automobile, in turn, consumes over half of the transport sector's energy. Indeed, the American car alone consumes a ninth of all the oil used in the world every day. But the car is amenable to technological fixes—and rather swift ones, since the auto stock turns over more rapidly than most other forms of capital. Because about half of the American automobile population is replaced within five years, an improvement in mileage efficiency, which is a form of conservation, can make itself felt quickly on the international energy market.

But the reader should not be deceived. Nothing will happen automatically, and the obstacles to conservation are manifold. To overcome them in a politically acceptable and nondisruptive way requires adroitness. The movement toward greater energy efficiency, toward greater tapping of conservation energy, will be governed by a complex interaction between government and society. A public policy is required that shapes strong coherent signals, all of which point in the same direction.

It is disheartening to compare the role of public policy in the United States with that of other Western countries, especially when one remembers that the United States is the dominant energy consumer on the world scene. Canada, for instance, has appropriated $1.4 billion to subsidize housing insulation. The program was instituted after comparing the costs of developing new Canadian hydrocarbon resources with the costs of retrofit. The expenditure, given that Canada's population is a tenth of ours, would be the equivalent of $14 billion in the United States. No such commitment has been made here.

The French government, convinced that an "energy transformation" was at hand, embarked on a major energy conservation program, perhaps the most ambitious in any major industrial country. While some of its elements would not be suitable to American society, the program does indicate how a democratic society can make conservation a high priority without being high-handed.

Yet there is something ironic about the French program, for France's energy consumption per capita is only 40 percent of America's. Also, what it does has far less impact on the international energy system, since it uses only about 10 percent of the oil that the United States does.

The best way to conceptualize conservation is as an alternative energy source. As such, we can compare it to other sources in terms of payback, ease of recovery, disruption, and environmental effects. Which is cheaper—a barrel of new production in some distant and hostile terrain, with the risk of a dramatic increase in price, or a barrel saved by insulation? Which is safer—continued reliance on imported oil, or the heat pump? Real choices about direction exist. In general, conservation appears to be the energy source that calls for the greatest emphasis in the short and middle term, since it is often the cheapest, most accessible, and least disruptive. The United States can, in effect, quickly produce millions of barrels per day of conservation energy.

Conservation certainly buys the United States time, and given the difficulties that attend the other sources, provides more immediate relief than do high-capital, high-technology alternatives.

The United States can use 30 or 40 percent less energy than it does, with virtually no penalty for the way Americans live—save that billions of dollars will be spared, save that the environment will be less strained, the air less polluted, the dollar under less pressure, save that the growing and alarming dependence on OPEC oil will be reduced, and Western society will be less likely to suffer internal and international tension. These are benefits Americans should be only too happy to accept.

—Daniel Yergin

Nuclear processes—mining and refining the ore, enriching it, fabricating it and using the fuel rods, storing the wastes—begin to look as though it will cost $2,500 to $3,000 to deliver an extra kilowatt to the consumer. In other words, it can cost $300 to install the nuclear capacity to power one 100-watt light bulb.

—BARBARA WARD

A MAJOR LNG ACCIDENT could kill hundreds of thousands of people. The U.S. Federal Power Commission, as part of its lengthy investigation into the siting of Liquefied Natural Gas facilities on Staten Island, looked into the possibility that a loaded LNG barge might crash in New York harbor. More than *eight hundred thousand people* were in the danger zone, the FPC investigators found; depending on where the crash occurred and how much of the cargo was lost, an "average" of 42,000 people would be killed or hideously burned when the gas ignited.

A number of LNG installations have been built in the middle of populated areas. In Stuttgart, West Germany, for example, an LNG peak-shaving plant was erected in a valley "in the center of a densely populated residential area," with public roads and houses just one hundred meters away. Northwestern Queens, a section of New York City, has an LNG plant in another "high density population area," with a commercial property zone a scant eight hundred feet distant. Millions of people live along approach routes to existing or proposed LNG terminals: on the banks of the Thames east of London; near the industrial complexes of Le Havre and Zeebrugge, Wilhelmshaven, and Tokyo and Yokohama; along the Mediterranean coast near Barcelona, Marseille, and La Spezia, and on the U.S. northeast, southeast, Gulf, and west coasts. How many will die if one of the big new LNG supertankers or storage tanks fails?

—Lee Niedringhaus Davis

IN THE FOSSIL FUEL era, the sun has been largely ignored. No nation includes the sun in its official energy budget, even though all other energy sources would be reduced to comparative insignificance if it were. We think we heat our homes with fossil fuels, forgetting that without the sun those homes would be −240° C when we turned on our furnaces. We think we get our light from electricity, forgetting that without the sun the skies would be permanently black.

While no single solar technology can meet humankind's total demand for energy, a combination of solar sources can. The transition to a solar era can be begun today; it would be technically feasible, economically sound, and environmentally attractive. Moreover, the most intriguing aspect of a solar transition might lie in its social and political ramifications.

Most policy analyses do not encompass these social consequences of energy choices. Most energy decisions are based instead on the naive assumption that competing sources are neutral and interchangeable. As defined by most energy experts, the task at hand is simply to obtain enough energy to meet the projected demands at as low a cost as possible. Choices generally swing on small differences in the marginal costs of competing potential sources.

But energy sources are *not* neutral and interchangeable. Some energy sources are necessarily centralized; others are necessarily dispersed. Some are exceedingly vulnerable; others are nearly impossible to disrupt. Some will produce many new jobs; others will reduce the number of people employed. Some will tend to

The sun is a gigantic fusion reactor in which hydrogen nuclei fuse into helium. The loss of mass is released as the energy that irradiates the solar system.

Only two-billionths of this energy is intercepted by the earth. Yet it is enough to provide the entire globe's basic "space heating." Without the sun, all life on the planet would simply freeze to death. Trees and plants capture one-fiftieth of 1 percent of this radiation. Yet it is enough to ripen every harvest. The sun also powers the planet's cycle of water purification and desalination, which provides the rains that give us the fresh water on which land-based life depends. In a very real sense, we already live in a nuclear-powered economy—fired by a reactor that is a safe 93 million miles away.

—BARBARA WARD

diminish the gap between rich and poor; others will accentuate it. Some inherently dangerous sources can be permitted widespread growth only under authoritarian regimes; others can lead to nothing more dangerous than a leaky roof. Some sources can be comprehended only by the world's most elite technicians; others can be assembled in remote villages using local labor and indigenous materials. Over time, such considerations may prove weightier than the financial criteria that dominate and limit current energy thinking.

Appropriate energy sources are necessary, though not sufficient, for the realization of important social and political goals. Inappropriate energy sources could make attaining such goals impossible. Decisions made today about energy sources will, more than most people imagine, determine how the world will look a few decades hence. While energy policy has been dominated by the thinking of economists and scientists, the crucial decisions will be political.

The kind of world that could develop around energy sources that are efficient, renewable, decentralized, simple, and safe cannot be fully visualized from our present vantage point. Indeed, one of the most attractive promises of such sources is a far greater flexibility in social design than is afforded by their alternatives. Although energy sources may not dictate the shape of society, they do limit its range of possibilities; and dispersed solar sources are more compatible than centralized technologies with social equity, freedom, and cultural pluralism. All in all, solar resources could power a rather attractive world.

Electricity now comprises less than 20 percent of energy use in virtually all countries. If energy sources were carefully matched with energy uses, it is difficult to imagine a future society that would need more than one-tenth of its energy budget as electricity—the highest quality and most expensive form of energy. Today, only 11 percent of U.S. energy is used as electricity, and much of this need could be met with other energy sources.

We are *not* running out of energy. But we *are* running out of cheap oil and gas. We are running out of money to pay for doubling and redoubling an already vast energy supply system. We are running out of political willingness to accept the social costs of continued rapid energy expansion. We are running out of the environmental capacity needed to handle the pollutants generated in conventional energy production. And we are running out of time to adjust to these new realities.

Using small, decentralized, and safe technologies makes sense from a systems-management point of view. Small units could be added incrementally if rising demands required them, and they would be much easier than large new facilities to integrate smoothly into an energy system. Small, simple sources could be installed in a matter of weeks or months; large, complex facilities often require years and even decades to erect. If gigantic power plants were displaced by thousands of smaller units dispersed near the points of end-use, economies of size would become relatively less important vis-a-vis economies of mass production. Technology would again concern itself with simplicity and elegance, and vast systems with elaborate control mechanisms would become extinct as more appropriately scaled facilities evolved.

The attractions of sunlight, wind, running water, and green plants as energy sources are self-evident. Had industrial civilization been built upon such forms of energy "income" instead of on the energy stored in fossil fuels, any proposal to convert to coal or uranium for the world's future energy would doubtless be viewed with incredulous horror. The current prospect, however, is the reverse—a shift from trouble-ridden sources to more attractive ones. Of the possible worlds we might choose to build, a solar-powered one appears most inviting.

—Denis Hayes

Stephen Frisch

. . .Agriculture, still the greatest single activity of man on earth. . .
—E.F. SCHUMACHER

Agriculture, Food, and Nutrition

Amid the technicolored marvels of the American supermarket, the links between agriculture, food, and nutrition fall away. American nutrition is increasingly a branch of industrial chemistry. The newest of American foods are man-made objects to which nutrition can be added. And American agriculture, once a handicraft, is rapidly becoming a large-scale corporate enterprise managed not by sons of the soil but by captains of commerce. That we have gone so far so fast in breaking the chain that binds together earth and the nourishment of man is astonishing. That we should fail to reverse the trend is unthinkable. For the system that supports our curiously baroque food supply has been built upon an unsustainable illusion: that the natural flow of energy and materials in the biosphere can be interrupted indefinitely—with impunity. Mechanized, energy-intensive, chemicals-dependent American agriculture makes inefficient use of two finite and dwindling resources: fossil fuels and arable land. Yields per man-hour are high, but yields per acre or per unit of energy input are not. Contemporary US-style agriculture is inappropriate even for the US under current and future conditions; for Third World countries to mimic US agricultural technology would be suicidal.

Agriculture, Food and Nutrition

JOAN GUSSOW

HUMAN LIFE DEPENDS on some half-a-hundred known nutrients. These, along with nutrients as yet unknown, are acquirable through the ingestion of enough of the right kinds of foods. The production of enough of the right kinds of foods depends very largely on the intentional culture of plants and animals. (Of all human food, some three quarters comes from crop land.) But in the American marketplace, the smells of field and farmyard seem remote. The abundance is dazzling; the produce seasonless, but earth's foods do not predominate here. The aisles are lined with tens of hundreds of "food products" turned out for "fun" (ours) and profit (theirs) by scores of food "manufacturers"—part of the largest single industry in the US.

It is a questionable abundance this system has produced. Food has often been treated like a somewhat inferior raw material that, in the search for profit, is steamed, smashed, extruded, teased, toasted, prodded, and—above all—extended. The resulting "product," its nutritional qualities destroyed, is then patched up by food scientists in the hope that it may once more be capable of sustaining life.

Virtually all processing reduces food's nutritional value. Some losses are tolerable—in canning and freezing produce, for example—since food and its nutrients that would otherwise go to waste are thereby saved and made available out of season. But it is a fair generality that the more a food is processed, the less nutrients it contains. Processing has this overall degrading effect because it eliminates vitamins and minerals—by removal as in refining, or by destruction as in high-heat processing—and because it dilutes the remaining nutrients by adding cheap fillers: water, fats, starches, sugars. Foods so degraded cannot be reconstituted nutritionally for the same reasons that a "complete" food cannot be fabricated *de novo:* because (1) there is no certainty that every nutrient essential for man has been identified, and (2) even if all essentials had been identified, it is not known at what level and in what sorts of contexts many nutrients ought to be restored. Given unlimited funds, unlimited energy supplies, and lots of time, mankind could probably learn to restore to food what we have taken out. We might do this if it were either necessary or rational to do so. Clearly it is neither.

After the subtractives come the additives, accidental and intentional. Some come unbidden from the universal contamination of the food producing environment—pesticides, PCBs, PBBs, chemicals like machinery cleaners and sterilants left over from processing—and are not meant to turn up in the food. But in addition to these inadvertent contaminants, an increasing number of novel chemicals are entering the food supply because someone put them there deliberately. The average American consumed three pounds of intentional additives in 1966, five pounds in 1971, and an estimated nine pounds in 1976, a 200 percent increase in ten years. Even if each additive had been thoroughly tested for *known* hazards—chronic toxicity, carcinogenicity, mutagenicity, teratogenicity—which each has not, their sheer number and the quantities in which they are entering the human diet would indicate an unacceptable level of risk. For hazards as yet unimagined cannot be tested for at all. And it is universally acknowledged that *there is no way of accounting for the interactions of these chemicals*—with each other, with other ingredients of the foods they inhabit, with other foods in the diet, with other chemicals in the environment, with the diversity of human biochemistries and human states of health.

Unmolested foods may also contain unsafe components; rhubarb leaves can kill. But unless it is argued that all risk is acceptable so long as some risk is unavoidable, that fact is not a rational defense of additives, especially when the benefits to the consumer from the most abundantly used additives are so frivolous. Could the possible risk of cancer from the ingestion of Red #2 be rationally weighed against the benefit of a richer brown devil's food cake? (Fortunately, the FDA decided that it could not.)

Most additives are not used, as is often claimed, to protect perishable foods from spoilage. America, with more refrigerators per capita than any other country, also has more additives per capita. More than 90 percent of the additives now in use (both in weight and by

Stephen Frisch

value) are not preservatives. They are colors, flavors, emulsifiers, stabilizers, texturizers, and nutrients designed to replace the colors, flavors, textures, and nutrients destroyed by processing. Additives have also made possible whole new families of food inventions: fake fruit juices, mock eggs, imitation bacon, and mock plastic puddings in plastic containers.

"Progress" in Preparing Foods

Until now, food processing has seemed an inevitable accompaniment to "progress," an investment in the continued growth of the food industry. Since the total amount of food an individual can consume is limited by nature (even for individuals willing to tolerate obesity), a stabilizing population threatened the food industry with zero economic growth. Profits could be increased only be developing substitute foods that used cheaper raw materials or through the addition to raw produce of a benefit, real or imagined, for which the customer could be led by advertising to pay a premium. The food objects this system has created— fruitless jams, imitation margarines, low-calorie whipped creams, purple-marshmallowed breakfast cereals, cholesterol-free eggs, nutrient-free diet cookies and the rest—are not merely nutritionally disastrous and toxicologically questionable, they are ecologically irresponsible. Food is being degraded, nutrition compromised, and energy wasted.

The system that moves food from farms and laboratories to the stove tops of America is absurdly energy-intensive. Food processing and related industries are

sixth among major industrial groups in the US in energy use. Indeed, the total food system utilizes in production, transportation, processing, and storage, roughly ten units of energy for every unit of energy represented by the food itself. For every calorie eaten in the US, in other words, ten calories of fossil fuel have been consumed. Yet unlike the production of steel or aluminum, food production ought logically to be an energy-yielding activity.

To understand why this is so, it is necessary to understand how agriculture and food systems are supposed to work. All human foods that are not laboratory produced are either plants or plant-consumers (i.e., animals). Plants are autotrophs, or self-nourishers. Given the right elements (carbon, oxygen, hydrogen, nitrogen, and a dozen or so minerals), plants can make their own foodstuffs, vitamins, proteins, fats, carbohydrates. Man, like other animals, is a heterotroph. He depends on plants to construct for him many of the complex organic molecules necessary for life. And in order to hunt out, consume, digest, and degrade those substances, then to reconstruct their parts into tissues of his own, man needs energy.

The energy man lives on is solar energy, transduced by plants into substances solid enough to sink the teeth into. Through photosynthesis, plants capture in chemical form some portion of that inexhaustible energy store that streams in daily from outer space, thus providing energy for their own metabolism (including the manufacture of proteins and oils) as well as for the growth and maintenance of man and other animals. In his turn, man degrades plant substance, extracting its energy and releasing back to the environment water, carbon dioxide, and nitrogen so that the cycle can begin again.

All life is ultimately dependent upon the green pigment chlorophyll, the actual compound in plants that uses photons of light energy to transmute water and carbon dioxide into carbohydrate. Man's dependence on this leafy pigment is so profound that it has been called the "green thralldom." Modern man, however, is much more conscious of his dependence upon the sunlight stored in the bodies of ancient plants and animals and transformed over time into petrochemicals. Like industrial progress, agricultural progress has come to be dependent on such fossil fuels. Thus modern crop plants depend for their productivity not only on incoming solar energy, but on fossil solar energy converted into nitrogen fertilizers, pesticides, herbicides, and irrigation, plus tractors, combines, and

technology solution seemed obvious at the time. But rising energy costs have fallen heavily on this energy-hungry agriculture. Moreover, since the method replaces muscle-power (of which developing countries have much) with scarcer fossil fuel power, it has often proved socially as well as economically and ecologically unsound.

Ranked by energy intensiveness, food producing activities range from the labor-intensive, energy-efficient wet paddy agriculture practiced in parts of Asia (yield: 50 calories out for one calorie in) to such incredibly inefficient activities as distant fishing and the fattening of beef on feedlots, which require a subsidy of ten to 15 calories for every calorie of food they produce.

And just as we have encouraged the developing countries to adopt our energy-intensive agriculture, so have we encouraged more developed nations to adopt

other farm machinery and the fuel that propels them. US yields per man-hour are high, reflecting high levels of mechanization. but, contrary to popular assumptions, yields per acre are by no means the world's highest. In 1970, for example, four countries had higher per-acre wheat yields, and three countries had higher per-acre yields of sorghum and rice. American "agricultural efficiency" is really energy-intensiveness.

The Green Revolution That Was

A version of this energy-intensive agriculture was widely exported in the 1960s under the rubric "The Green Revolution," a "miracle" that promised (and in some cases briefly fulfilled its promise) to produce dramatic increases in crop yields in the developing countries by replacing the traditional grain varieties and cultivation methods with a package of inputs including hybrid seeds, fertilizers, herbicides, pesticides, and—ideally—irrigation. Given the urgency of an immediate food-supply increase, the wisdom of this high-

our energy-intensive animal culture; we have promoted confinement cattle-feeding industries abroad so that our potentially price-depressing surpluses of grain and soybeans could be poured down the throats of cattle in other nations as well as ours. Acres of feed grains (from land capable of growing food grains), together with megatons of high protein oilseeds and fishmeals (imported usually from protein-poor countries) have thus been wastefully converted into other megatons of manure, hooves, hides, urine, bones, tallow, and steak. Erstwhile Agriculture Secretary Earl Butz once exulted that we would always be a nation of beef eaters and forecast a per-capita consumption in 1985 of 140 pounds of beef a year—two-and-a-half times the level of 35 years earlier. If the American day is increasingly likely to start with a Breakfast Bar, the Department of Agriculture would encourage it to end with a steak, and instant mashed potatoes.

Thus energy derived from fossil fuels, limited in availability and increasing in cost, has become a major input into food instead of one of its products. Some of

As we move toward a sustainable agriculture, we will necessarily develop an ethic with sustainability at its core.

—WES JACKSON

Persistent pesticides, accumulating in the food chain, have produced—among *known* effects—egg-shell fragility among birds of prey. Some have argued that the food saved more than compensates for the birds lost. The point may be biologically arguable but is probably irrelevant, given the tendency of pesticides to become increasingly ineffective, either because target insects have become genetically resistant or because their natural enemies have been wiped out—by pesticides.

The Factors of Success

But energy and its by-products—economically costly and environmentally polluting—are not all that is required for agriculture. As in any undertaking where a variety of factors contribute to the overall success of the enterprise, the abundance of all other inputs is immaterial as soon as any one becomes limit-

this energy goes into the making and running of large-scale agricultural machinery—machinery that is economical only when it is used to plant and harvest vast acreages devoted to single crops. Machinery-intensiveness encourages larger and larger farms contributing to a decline in the number of small, independent farmers and to an increase in the geographical con-

centration of agriculture. Concentration in turn leads to regional monoculture. With monoculture comes loss of genetic diversity, reduced ecosystem stability, and a host of weed, insect, and disease problems insoluble except (temporarily) with large inputs of herbicides and pesticides.

So another large part of the energy the agricultural system depends on enters the food chain in the form of products for which the ecosphere pays a second price: pollution. Much of the increased yield of modern agriculture comes from heavy inputs of soluble fertilizer materials and complex organic chemicals for weed and insect control. But these inputs have outputs. Fertilizer runoffs pollute the groundwater, and, by feeding algae instead of crops, produce algal blooms and eutrophication in ponds and lakes. (The cattle, swine, and chickens whose manures used to help feed the crops are now fattening far away in confinement, producing concentrations of waste that form a second pollution source.) Herbicides and pesticides alter the flora and fauna of the soil and the growth it supports.

ing. If not energy, what factor will first become limiting in US and world agriculture?

Will we, as some have argued, run out of phosphate, that mineral nutrient more intimately associated with life than nitrogen? Will we, failing to recycle phosphorus from life to life, finally snuff out life itself? Will we run out of water? Will a combination of lowered ground water levels, over-committed surface waters, and changing rainfall patterns turn once productive crop and pasture lands into arid deserts? Is the limiting factor likely to be light itself? Will we so cloud our solar window with the effluents from our polluted society that we reduce the inflow of sunlight, thus hindering the fundamental photosynthetic process? Seeking frantically to satisfy our other consumption "needs," we must recognize how they begin to compete with our food plants and the inputs required to grow them. Increasingly, there is a direct trade-off between using resources for food production or for the production of other goods. The well-publicized competition for fertilizer between croplands in India and sub-

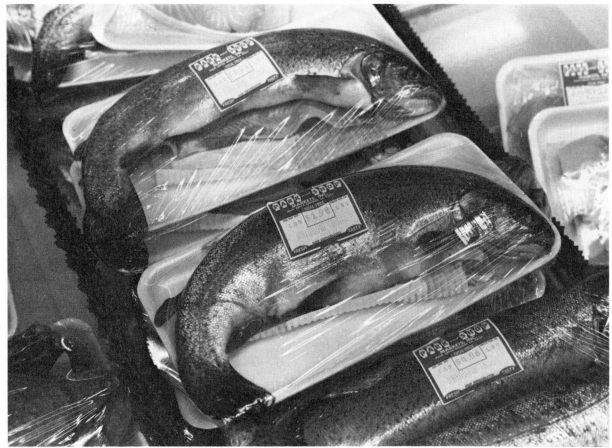

Emilio Mercado/Jeroboam, Inc.

urban lawns and golf courses was a symbol. Even as the world's need for food increases, prime farmland is disappearing at the rate of two-and-a-half million acres a year under those same suburban lawns and golf courses, highways and shopping centers. Less well known is the competition for western land and water between those who would produce food and those who would strip-mine grazing and crop lands in order to get at the coal and shale underlying them—a sacrifice of potential long-term food production for a quick energy fix.

Will the ultimate limiting factor in agriculture turn out to be fertile land? Will we run out of topsoil, a resource present in its greatest abundance at the end of the 350 million years preceding the advent of man during which plant and animal life grew and decayed on this planet? In his book *The Food and People Dilemma,* the noted geographer Georg Borgstrom has documented western education's failure to teach us the extent to which western civilizations have been built and continue to depend on vast reaches of Asian, African, and Latin American topsoil. Yet destruction of the topsoil that supports him has been the mark of civilized man everywhere; and where population pressures build, erosion, desertification, and tragedy have often followed. Man-caused deserts now cover close to

seven percent of the surface of the earth.

In the US, where the resources, the knowledge, and the ability to check erosion and prevent topsoil losses are available, it appears likely that topsoil will continue to disappear. More than a third of the nation's topsoil has been lost in our first 200 years; average annual topsoil loss is estimated at twelve tons per cropland acre and likely to increase. Federal support for rural soil conservation programs has been virtually cut off. Seeking to maximize our farm output in the face of a strong export market, the government has done away with acreage set-asides for the major crops. Farmers, at the urging of the Department of Agriculture, have planted from fence to fence, plowing fields hardly broken since the great dust bowl of the thirties; and faced with record harvest of feed grains, cattlemen have gone back to the feedlots where they could once more pour into the cattle-feeding troughs the product of this all-out production, forced from our dwindling topsoil by ever increasing doses of fertilizer. Yet just as much of the land that blew away in the thirties ought never to have been plowed, since it was incapable of production except when climatic conditions were ideal, so much of the land recently pushed back into production in order to pay for our imported oil is blowing away again in the wake of a dry season. Predictions for an *extended* dry period before the end of the century are widespread.

And the world's population continues to grow at a terrifying rate. The four billion mark was reached in early 1976; predicted doubling time is *less* than 35 years. But will we ever get there? Some think not. Most hope that falling birthrates will make a lie of the prediction before rising death rates do. Thus the world is precariously balanced between an expanding human population and environmentally determined limits on food production. Meanwhile, the great American grain reserves, the source of food price stability in the years following World War II, are gone, sold off with the blessing of a Department of Agriculture that saw rising grain prices in a food-short world as a source of international power and an opportunity to improve the US balance of trade.

In 1970, corn blight wiped out a significant proportion of the US corn crop; yet maintenance of US grain reserves against bad weather, against new strains of insects or diseases, against crop failure anywhere from whatever cause, is currently being left in the hands of the farmers themselves or in the even more willing hands of the multinational grain trading corporations—Cargill, Continental, Cook, Bunge—on whose goodwill in time of need we would be foolhardy to count. Lacking reliable grain reserves anywhere, world food security now depends on a single year's weather.

With the encouragement of the US, the exploding world population has come to depend heavily on the stability of US agricultural output. Some forecasters predict that by the year 2000, 100 percent of all the grain available for export will come from the croplands of the United States and Canada. Yet the agricultural system the world has been urged to emulate, the system that has been the marvel of our time, may not be sustainable. We are perilously close to the brink and running flat out. It would be well if we took off our blinders.

Valid Assumptions

Where do we go from here? Where is it we want to get to? If there is a future, what will it look like?

It is evident that if we do nothing, Parson Malthus will be proved right: population will outstrip food supply, and humanity—in a frantic scramble to feed itself—may well end by destroying the viability of the planet on whose natural systems it depends. "Beware of those 'experts' who appear to advocate the transformation of the ecosphere into nothing more than a food factory for man," warn the authors of *A Blueprint for Survival*. "The concept of a world consisting solely of man and a few favoured food plants is so ludicrously impractical as to be seriously contemplated only by those who find solace in their own willful ignorance of the real world of biological diversity."

What is a viable end point? Clearly it is not, in that fatuous phrase of the Department of Agriculture, "Abundance for all"—not, that is, abundance as represented by the bloated American supermarket in all its gaudy excesses. Prediction beyond ten years, it has been said, is a branch of science fiction. Writing science fiction is always aided by examining the plots that don't work.

Assumption: We will not float alone. Whether it wishes to or not, the developed world will not be permitted to continue to consume the majority of the world's food resources. When the notion was first put forward several years ago that certain countries were "unsalvageable," Egypt was among them. Her friendships with Middle Eastern Oil changed all that. Even those without resources—or wealthy friends—will not float quietly in the water while some of us sail away in our yachts without them. We will not survive as an

In addition to anticipating an American diet that would include a greater proportion of whole grains, dried beans, potatoes, and vegetables generally, we expect that most produce would be grown for local consumption by individuals, by local gardening cooperatives, or by local farmers. It is not difficult to imagine a time when lawns would have very nearly disappeared and suburban houses would be surrounded by gardens and orchards, their residents having gradually come to refuse to pay for high-priced commercial produce. Areas that now look like green residential deserts would resemble the intensely farmed and carefully tended gardens of England or China.

—JOHN STEINHART, MARK HANSON, CAREL DEWINKEL, ROBIN GATES, KATHLEEN LIPP, MARK THORNSJO, STANLEY KABALA affluent enclave in a starving world.

Assumption: Food aid will not prevent babies. People have babies because they want to. If a demographic transition to zero population growth comes, it will not come in response to the provision of food aid without the alteration of other conditions of life. Americans cannot feed the world—and shouldn't even try. The *only* hope of solving the food/population problem is through a restructuring of our economic relations with the developing countries with the goal of moving them toward food self-sufficiency, through improving the agricultural productivity of the rural poor. Population has begun to decline, historically, when death rates among children go down, when the poorest populations have hope that their own lives will be tolerable and their childrens' will be somewhat better, when social planning has provided some alternative to childbearing as the only form of old age security.

Assumption: Wonder foods won't save us. For the foreseeable future, the bulk of mankind will get most of its food from modified versions of existing (though perhaps unexploited) plant and animal sources by modifications of existing cultural methods. New plants will be exploited, new animals may be harvested, but "novel" food sources—algae, yeasts and so on—are not likely, for a variety of social, nutritional, environmental, energetic, and economic reasons, to "solve" the food problem. It is quite possible that some innovative food producing schemes, green-housed hydroponics on the desert for example, may extend food producing capacity and that by the use of on-site solar energy production they may overcome a number of apparent constraints. But not only are many "miracle" food producing schemes energy intensive—synthesis of food materials in the laboratory, for example—they also require energy-demanding machinery com-

Drawing by Ed Koren © *1974,* The New Yorker *Magazine, Inc.*

"No more carbohydrates until you finish your protein."

plexes; and to bring them to a scale that will make them truly economical, they must often be very large, thus requiring large capital inputs that make them highly impractical for the poor countries they are usually designed to help.

Assumption: Food technology will not save us. The more our food derives from solar energy, the less demand food production will put on the rest of the ecosystem. In the present US system, the addition of non-solar energy to food probably has, overall, a nutritionally degrading effect. Grains, for example, contain the nutrients for their own metabolism. Improved milling processes that retained nutrients would provide improved nutrition at much less energy cost than milling white flour and attempting to replace the lost nutrients. Fish protein concentrate, a recent technological triumph, never got off the ground. Supplementation (of sugar with vitamin A, for example) is almost always a temporary "fix," not a permanent solution.

Assumption: The oceans will not save us. We will not "farm" the oceans and produce abundance for mankind. Indeed, if we do not quickly and markedly reduce both overfishing and pollution, we may not even *fish* the oceans. Fish farming on land, or in lagoon-based pounds, will probably increase. Small-scale backyard, rooftop, or basement production of algae-eating fish may, like rabbit or chicken raising, provide supplementary animal protein for many urban and village dwellers. Competition for available ocean fish has already produced a "cod war," a "lobster war," and a "tuna war." Only a few years ago, the resources of the seas were talked of in "unlimited" terms. Now that oceans are being sieved for whatever life they contain, total fish catches have already begun to decline. Harvesting of ocean stocks will have to be closely regulated. The practice of moving down the ocean food chain while moving up the land food chain—i.e., by feeding "trash" fish to livestock—is a wholly irrational activity that should be eliminated on energetic grounds alone.

Assumption: We cannot save half the ecosystem. It is "our" environment. If pressure on the food supply becomes too great, frightening ecological damage will ensue as mankind struggles to eat. Witness the present attempt to turn Brazil's Amazonian jungle, "the lungs of the world," into crop land for the masses of the rural poor; witness the devastating desertification taking place in Africa; witness worldwide soil erosion. It is our mutual life-support system that will be destroyed by the frantic attempts of others to survive.

Assumption: International control of food production and distribution is unworkable. We will not have a "common market" or a "supermarket" world where selected countries produce all of one or another commodity for the rest of us. Only relatively small regions have feedback mechanisms that would permit them to respond quickly to changes in supply or demand, satisfying local demand and minimizing food waste. Only local communities can preserve local ecological systems. Since moving food long distances is energetically wasteful, more food, especially energy-intensive vegetables, will be locally produced. Since most processing is energy-consuming and nutritionally degrading, less food will be processed. Thus the variety of foods available in any one area will be reduced, but since most food will be fresh, the quality will be improved.

Assumption: Improved surveillance technologies will not solve the problem. Even if there were widespread recognition that on the day before the daily-doubling water lilies fill the pond the pond will be only half full, we need long-term planning, not merely the ability to respond to emergencies. Surveillance can only warn of immediately impending large-scale disasters, too late to avert them by, at best, anything other than a questionable technological fix.

Assumption: Research cannot find a "magic bullet,"

We have yet to develop an agriculture as sustainable as the nature we destroy.

—WES JACKSON

---

because there isn't one to be found. The immediate food-and-people problems are much more social and economic than technical and scientific. The solutions require thoughtful social and economic adjustments—moral and political commitments—not "breakthroughs."

Assumption: There is no time to lose. Given the present and projected size of the world population, and the probable carrying capacity of the earth, the world as a whole may not be overpopulated at present, but it will be soon. The only sustainable agricultural systems are those which are ecologically sound, i.e., capable of recycling agricultural, food processing, and household wastes back into the food producing system and not dependent upon biocides. We had all better get started putting them in place before it is too late.

Conclusion: The ultimate goal must be a series of relatively self-sufficient societies whose populations have been stabilized at a level that allows for the production of adequate food for all in a manner compatible with an indefinitely sustained yield. The societies must maintain a system of locally-held food reserves against unexpected crop failures, and must be responsible not only to their own citizens, but to the ecological stability of their regions and the planet.

Recommended Actions

☐ We should urgently develop a system of locally-held emergency food reserves. Since it is believed by many to be unlikely that the world will experience another period of sustained good weather similar to that which allowed the build-up of American food reserves in past decades, additional surpluses must be made available by serious and sustained food conservation in affluent countries.

☐ Governments at all levels should discourage the development of novel food products, including products for pet consumption, for which no clearly defined nutritional need can be established.

☐ Congress should enact legislation requiring that a manufacturer file a Nutritional Impact Statement prior to putting on the market any new food product. Such a statement should take into account the energetic and other ecological costs of the proposed product and provide data demonstrating that the product will contribute to improving the nutritional status of consumers in the US or elsewhere.

☐ State and federal governments should encourage through economic disincentives the elimination of all unnecessary food processing and packaging with the goal of reducing wastes of both nutrients and energy.

☐ Millers should be required over a period of five years to modify the processing of grains to retain the germ and at least a portion of the bran, and to eliminate the use of bleaching and maturing agents.

☐ Congress should mandate the labelling of all packaged foods according to their nutrient content in a manner that is understandable by and useful to consumers. Simultaneously Congress should enact legislation phasing out, over a five-year period, the addition of all synthetic nutrients to food, except where such addition has been demonstrated to have specific public health advantages.

☐ Congress should require the phasing out within five years of artificial colors, flavors, and other chemical additives except for the few that are essential to food preservation and wholesomeness; the Delaney amendment, banning substances which produce cancer, should be extended to include substances which adversely affect the germ plasm.

☐ It should be the policy of the United States to:
a) Restrict food advertising to products that are food conserving and contribute to the public health. Such products would include, but not be limited to, fresh fruits and vegetables, legumes, and unrefined grains and flours (or products made from such flours).
b) Require food advertising to provide consumers with relevant and complete ingredient and nutritional information.
c) Use advertising techniques to promote food responsibility, reduced consumption of animal protein, elimination of food waste, and other behaviors that would reduce demand on world food resources.
d) Prohibit the advertising of cat and dog food.
e) Support efforts abroad to prevent advertisers from promoting wasteful and unnecessary products whose consumption may contribute to malnutrition.

☐ The federal government should mandate the use of a specified percentage of commercial television time for use in educating citizens about the relationships between environmental quality, food supply, and the survival of humanity, and should encourage local authorities to make the teaching of environmentally based nutrition education universal in the schools.

☐ The federal government should develop a model of rational land-use planning (and supportive tax measures) that will ensure the maintenance in best agricultural use of prime farmland in all parts of the country; such measures should include differential farmland assessment, purchase of development rights, changes in inheritance tax laws, and subsidization of best-use farming where it cannot be self-supporting.

☐ It should be national policy to discourage large-scale, geographically concentrated monoculture and to encourage dispersed and diversified family farming operations by:
a) Enforcing maximum acreage laws designed to

broaden the base of land ownership.

b) Promoting maximum crop diversification, within local production constraints.

c) Prohibiting non-farm corporations from producing feed for animals or humans as a way of diversifying their investments, and eliminating tax-shelter farming.

d) Enforcing anti-trust laws and investigating their applicability to non-competitive situations produced by vertical integration.

☐ It should be the policy of the United States to begin a program of research aimed at reducing to a minimum the use of highly toxic, broad-spectrum, and/or persistent insecticides and herbicides, and to convert US agriculture as rapidly as possible to more natural and sustainable methods of insect, disease, and weed control, using predator insects, companion cropping, timed planting, genetically resistant strains, cultivations, mulching, and so on.

☐ Since ruminant animals can utilize grazing land not suitable for agriculture, thus converting humanly inedible substances into high quality protein, it should not be national policy to discourage the raising of animals for human consumption so long as they are not competing for humanly edible resources; it *should* be US policy, however, to regulate animal feedlot operations to eliminate the net calorie and protein loss now associated with confinement feeding.

"*. . . sodium phosphate, di-glycerides, BHT. Warning: The Surgeon General has determined that eating is dangerous to your health.*"

©*1979 by Sidney Harris from* Chicken Soup, *published by Wm. Kaufmann, Inc.*

☐ The federal government should prohibit the use of hormones and antibiotics in animal feeds except, in the case of antibiotics, when they are used in the treatment of short-term illness.

☐ It should be national policy to promote the maintenance and fertility of our topsoil by:

a) Returning to the land the largest feasible amounts of urban and rural wastes such as sewage sludge, processing residues, composted municipal garbage, and animal excreta; such materials should be used not only to fertilize and upgrade existing croplands, but also to help reclaim land degraded by erosion, mining, or other misuse.

b) Prohibiting the exploitation of organic wastes for their energy value unless this is achieved without destroying the value of these materials as fertilizer.

c) Reducing, and in some cases eliminating, the need for high-nitrogen fertilizers by vigorously investigating various methods of exploiting nitrogen fixation by both free-living and symbiotic bacteria.

d) Investigating "least ecological cost" methods of providing essential nutrients to farmlands through local recycling of organic wastes, thus minimizing energy-expensive mining and distribution of fertilizer materials.

e) Enacting a federal soil pollution control act that would set ambient standards below which land could not be degraded in quality.

☐ All levels of government should promote energy conservation in the food chain by:

a) Encouraging the development of various low-energy food preservation technologies—dehydration, fermentation, culturing—to augment more energy-intensive methods such as freezing and canning.

b) Localizing food production and marketing by means of urban farm markets, roadside stands, and consumer cooperatives, thus reducing energy required for transportation and storage.

c) Encouraging production of food in home and community gardens, especially the production of otherwise energy-intensive and perishable fruits and vegetables.

☐ All levels of government should promote water conservation in the food chain by:

a) Discouraging the use of limited ground water supplies to grow fodder crops.

b) Developing a rational water-use policy that will acknowledge agriculture as a first priority taking precedence over competing industrial uses.

c) Encouraging water conservation at the individual farm level.

d) Developing biological systems that clean water by sequestering or metabolizing toxic industrial effluents, and where nutrient pollutants occur in relatively uncontaminated wastewaters, investigating biological systems capable of producing edible end-products.

☐ It must be the policy of the United States to work toward the earliest possible establishment of an international seed bank in which all identified strains of basic food plants will be preserved.

☐ The United States should encourage the development and implementation of a Law of the Seas treaty aimed at:

a) Reducing marine pollution to a minimum.

b) Establishing and enforcing fishery quotas at a level consistent with equitable food distribution and with the survival of various species.

☐ A reoriented Department of Agriculture should:

a) Provide support to groups carrying out serious research in alternative methods of food production such as organic farming, Biodynamic/French Intensive gardening, backyard fish farming, and similar methods that appear to be ecologically sound, high yielding, and hence feasible for small farmers; and it should assess the potential contribution such techniques might make to sustainable food production capacity in the US and abroad.

b) Investigate a system of incentives that would pay a premium for crops of high nutrient content produced in a manner beneficial to local ecological systems.

c) Put increased emphasis on the development of strains of food plants capable of producing high-nutrient crops under a variety of less-than-optimal conditions, and on breeding livestock strains which can function non-competitively in the food chain.

d) Support research to determine the minimum ecological diversity required to maintain stability in a given region.

e) Investigate ways to phase out environmentally unsound large-scale monoculture while sustaining farmers and maintaining total food production at a level consistent with US and world needs.

f) Support the research and development of inexpensive, locally-adaptable, small-scale, "intermediate technology" farm machinery for use in the production and on-farm processing and storage of crops.

g) Design a crop-insurance, price-stabilization system to protect the farmer from the effects of bumper crops and natural disasters, and thereby provide consumers with reasonably priced food.

h) Investigate land and water conserving cultural methods such as multi-level cropping or companion planting that would increase per-acre yields while rebuilding topsoil and reducing erosion.

☐ It must be national policy to reduce the level of US demand on world resources, especially food resources, while helping to sustain the economies of those countries for whom we have represented major export markets.

☐ The US should reexamine its aid and trade agreements and restructure them so that they help foster maximum local food production in developing countries rather than encouraging the production of cash crops which compete for resources with the local food supply.

☐ Americans should support all authentic attempts at social reform that promise to strengthen locally-controlled food production and distribution systems, at home and abroad.

☐ It should be the policy of the US to help other nations develop sustainable agricultural systems appropriate to their own economic, social, and environmental circumstances, providing technical and material assistance and where necessary providing food aid as supplementary support to countries making the transition to food self-sufficiency.

Elihu Blotnick

More Thoughts on Agriculture

THE CHOICE of inappropriate technologies can only exacerbate social, economic, and environmental problems. It is clearly time to shed the notion that the biggest, fastest, most modern technologies are always the best, and to seek alternatives that are more compatible with the changing global conditions of the final quarter of the twentieth century.

Indiscriminate transfer of modern technology from industrial countries to the Third World can cause more problems than it solves. Technological development since the Industrial Revolution has led to the substitution of capital and energy for human labor in the production of goods and services, substitutions that generally reflected the relative availability and cost of capital, energy, and labor in the industrial world. But these capital-intensive, energy-consuming, labor-saving technologies make lavish use of the very resources that are scarce and expensive in the Third World, while failing to utilize much of the Third World's most abundant asset—people.

In a society where only a tiny fraction of the population remains on the land, vast amounts of energy are required for food storage and distribution. In the United States, about four times as much energy is used to transport, process, store, sell, and cook food as to produce it. Production of some foods has become concentrated in specific regions. Commercial vegetable production, for example, is now concentrated in California and Florida, although only a few years ago New Jersey supplied a substantial portion of the vegetables marketed on the East Coast. About 1,150 kilocalories of fossil fuel energy are needed to ship one pound of vegetables from California to New York. That is more energy than most vegetables contain.

If the world's population were fed an American diet, produced with U.S.-style food technologies, production and distribution alone would use up all known global oil and gas reserves in just 13 years. Similarly, if India were to convert its agricultural system to American methods, agriculture alone would require fully 70 percent of the commercial energy that is now used for all purposes in that country.

Energy used to produce chemical fertilizers is now the chief energy input into American agriculture, accounting for more fossil fuel than the gasoline used to power tractors and other farm machines. Chemical fertilizers have taken over almost completely from the manures and leguminous plants that were used as fertilizers just a few decades ago, a substitution made economically attractive by cheap oil and gas. As energy prices rise, however, the economic balance may again favor more extensive use of traditional fertilizers. The use of sewage sludge could also reduce requirements for chemical fertilizers, provided serious questions about the contamination of sludge with heavy metals can be resolved. In addition to saving energy, more extensive use of organic fertilizers like manure would help improve the condition of seriously depleted soils, while recycling sewage sludge on farmlands would reduce the capital and energy costs of constructing new sewage treatment plants.

A particularly striking example of ecologically sound pest management occurred in the Peruvian Canete Valley after problems developed with conventional pesticides. In 1957, farmers in the valley organized an areawide control program that included the introduction of enemies of the cotton pests and more resistant cotton varieties, the rotation of crops, and the use of mineral insecticides only when necessary. Synthetic organic pesticides were banned. Production rose dramatically, almost doubling in seven years. A major incentive for farmers to turn to ecologically more sustainable techniques is the fact that overuse of pesticides has become economically unsustainable.

Some of the technological trends of the past few decades are not compatible with the social needs and resource constraints that lie ahead. Yet choices of technology made today by individuals, communities, corporations, and governments will have lasting impacts on the use of energy and resources. They will affect employment and income distribution for many years to come. Unless consideration of such impacts enters into judgements of which technologies should be developed and employed for particular tasks, some technological choices will lead to more problems than they solve.

The energy-intensity and materials requirements of many modern technologies make their use questionable not only in the developing countries but in the industrial world as well. Moreover, the costs—both in terms of capital requirements and social impacts of massive transfers of technology from rich to poor countries—would be prohibitive. Far from being a technological monoculture, the world of the future will have to be characterized by technological diversity

One cannot claim that the late twentieth century is a time of very general hard physical labor in the developed world. The car and the television set and the growing volume of office work may well have produced the most literally sedentary population human society has ever known. But at the same time, diets stuffed with the proteins and calories needed for a lumberman or a professional boxer have become prevalent. Everywhere, high meat consumption demands grain-fed animals. Meanwhile, what little grain we do eat through bread usually has little nutritional value and roughage, since these are removed when the flour is refined. Thus the human bowel is deprived of the fiber it requires to function easily. The eating of fresh vegetables—which also give necessary fiber—has fallen off by between a third and a half in the last half century. Processed, defibered products have taken their place. The results are literally apparent. In all developed nations, obesity and diet-related illnesses are now a major medical problem.

—BARBARA WARD

if it is to be socially and ecologically sustainable. Each society will have to determine for itself what is appropriate in terms of its own needs and resources. No two societies are likely to need exactly the same mix of technologies.

—Colin Norman

THE QUESTION ARISES of whether agriculture is, in fact, an industry, or whether it might be something *essentially* different. Not surprisingly, as this is a metaphysical—or metaeconomic—question, it is never raised by economists.

Now, the fundamental 'principle' of agriculture is that it deals with life, that is to say, with living substances. Its products are the results of processes of life and its means of production is the living soil. A cubic centimetre of fertile soil contains milliards of living organisms, the full exploration of which is far beyond the capacities of man. The fundamental 'principle' of modern industry, on the other hand, is that it deals with man-devised processes which work reliably only when applied to man-devised, non-living materials. The ideal of industry is the elimination of living substances. Man-made materials are preferable to natural materials, because we can make them to measure and apply perfect quality control. Man-made machines work more reliably and more predictably than do such living substances as men. The ideal of industry is to eliminate the living factor, even including the human factor, and to turn the productive process over to machines. As Alfred North Whitehead defined life as "an offensive directed against the repetitious mechanism of the universe," so we may define modern industry as "an offensive against the unpredictability, unpunctuality, general waywardness and cussedness of living nature, including man."

In other words, there can be no doubt that the fundamental 'principles' of agriculture and of industry, far from being compatible with each other, are in opposition. Real life consists of the tensions produced by the incompatibility of opposites, each of which is needed, and just as life would be meaningless without death, so agriculture would be meaningless without industry. It remains true, however, that agriculture is primary, whereas industry is secondary, which means that human life can continue without industry, whereas it cannot continue without agriculture. Human life at the level of civilization, however, demands the *balance* of the two principles, and this balance is ineluctably destroyed when people fail to appreciate the *essential* difference between agriculture and industry—a difference as great as that between life and death—and attempt to treat agriculture as just another industry.

Instead of searching for means to accelerate the drift out of agriculture, we should be searching for policies to reconstruct rural culture, to open the land for the gainful occupation to larger numbers of people, whether it be on a full-time or a part-time basis, and to orientate all our actions on the land towards the threefold ideal of health, beauty, and permanence.

—E.F. Schumacher

UNDERNUTRITION AND OVERNUTRITION have similar consequences for the individual: reduced life expectancy, increased susceptibility to disease, and reduced productivity. And the number of people afflicted by the modern plague of overnutrition is approaching that suffering undernutrition. In nearly every country in the world, rich or poor, malnutrition of one kind or another contributes to more deaths than does any other factor save, in some countries, age itself.

Through educational, welfare, and agricultural programs, Western governments have long been deeply enmeshed in nutritional concerns, but in a haphazard, often inconsistent way. Thus in the United States, the Department of Agriculture actively promotes increased consumption of high-fat meats and cholesterol-heavy eggs, even as health officials in other federal agencies urge people to cut fat and cholesterol intake. The choice, then, is between this sort of wasteful contradiction and a coherent national nutrition policy that gives priority to public health over special interests.

In wealthy nations, generally high incomes and more or less adequate social welfare programs prevent much of the serious protein-calorie malnutrition of the sort rampant in the developing nations. Yet even in a country as rich as the United States, millions of people live in dire need and some live so far outside the mainstream of national life that government aid programs such as the food stamp program never reach them.

Severe undernutrition in early childhood, a growing body of evidence indicates, can stunt a child's physical and intellectual development. Combined with the social deprivations of poverty, undernutrition can impair reasoning powers, language and motor skills, and social behavior, thereby denying individuals the basic right to realize the human potential carried in their genes. If a child is underfed long enough during a critical period of development, no amount of compensatory feeding or education can fully restore what has been lost.

Both affluent diets and sedentary lifestyles represent radical departures from the conditions under which humans evolved for millions of years. That our bodies should rebel is hardly surprising.

—Erik Eckholm & Frank Record

Andrea Entwistle

Croplands:
The Foundation of Civilization

LESTER R. BROWN

CROPLANDS ARE THE FOUNDATION not only of agriculture but of civilization itself. The first cities did not emerge until the development of agriculture had produced surpluses of food in the countryside. Civilization as we know it today rests squarely on that 10 percent of the earth's land surface that is used to produce crops. When land is scarce, people often go hungry. When soils are depleted and crops are poorly nourished, people are often undernourished as well.

Pressures on the world's croplands have escalated since mid-century as our numbers have increased, raising doubts about long-term food security. Growing populations demand more land not only for food production but for other purposes as well. Even as the demand for cropland is expanding at a record rate, more and more cropland is being converted to non-agricultural uses. Soaring world demand for food since mid-century has led to excessive pressures on vulnerable soils. This in turn has led to soil degradation and cropland abandonment.

Evidence now available raises doubts as to whether it will be possible to get a combination of cropland expansion and yield increases that will satisfy the growth in world food demand expected during the remainder of this century. Between 1950 and 1971, a modest expansion in world cropland area and an unprecedented rise in crop yield per hectare raised world grain production per person from 276 kilograms to 360 kilograms. But since 1971, per capita grain production has levelled off. The result has been rising food prices. If the projected increase in world population materializes, then steep rises in food prices may be inevitable.

The period from 1972 to 1976 was one of insecurity and instability—unprecedented in peacetime—in the world food economy. During the late seventies, however, uncommonly favorable weather and stepped up food production efforts may have lulled the world into a false sense of complacency. The dimensions of the emerging stresses are likely to come into focus the next time two or more of the major food-producing countries have poor harvests. Recent years of good weather have tended to obscure long-term deterioration.

Cropland deterioration and loss are not new prob-lems. The Tigris-Euphrates Valley, described long ago as the Fertile Crescent, may once have supported more people than it does today, and the food-deficit lands of North Africa were once the granary of the Roman Empire. What is new is the scale of cropland loss and soil deterioration, a problem that affects rich and poor countries alike.

Vanishing Topsoil

As population pressures mount, cultivation is both intensified and extended onto marginal soils. Some techniques designed to raise short-term land productivity lead to excessive soil loss. The intensification of farming in the American Midwest has led to continuous cropping of corn, eliminating crop rotations that traditionally included grass-legume mixtures along with the corn. Continuous cropping has been abetted by cheap nitrogen fertilizers that replaced nitrogen-fixing legumes. But while chemical fertilizers can replace nutrients lost through crop removal, they cannot make up for the loss of topsoil needed to maintain a healthy soil structure.

Erosion is an integral part of the natural system. It occurs even when land is in grass or forests. But when land is cleared and planted to crops, the process invariably accelerates. Whenever erosion begins to exceed the natural rate of soil formation, the layer of topsoil becomes thinner, eventually disappearing entirely. When too much topsoil is lost, cropland is abandoned. But the gradual loss of topsoil and fertility that precedes abandonment may take years, decades, or even centuries; although this does not affect the size of the cropland base, it does affect its productivity.

The Soil Conservation Service reports that US farmers are not managing highly erodible soils as well as they were a generation ago. A nationwide survey by the SCS indicated that "in 1975, soil losses on cropland amounted to almost three billion tons or an average of about 22 tons per hectare. Although this was excessive, it was far less than the estimated four billion tons of topsoil that would have been lost in 1975 if farmers had followed no conservation practices at all." The

Rondal Partridge

report concluded that if US crop production was to be sustained, soil loss would have to be reduced to 1.5 billion tons annually, one-half today's level.

The Council for Agricultural Science and Technology reported in 1975 that "a third of all US cropland was suffering soil losses too great to be sustained without a gradual but ultimately disastrous decline in productivity." A summary document prepared for the 1977 UN Conference on Desertification reported that nearly one-fifth of the world's cropland is now experiencing a degree of degradation that is intolerable over the long run. The UN report estimated that productivity on this land has already been reduced by an average of 25 percent.

Few efforts have been made to measure precisely the relationship between loss of topsoil and the fertility of cropland. Luther Carter writes in *Science* that "even where the loss of topsoil has begun to reduce the land's natural fertility and productivity, the effect is often masked by the positive response to the heavy application of fertilizers and pesticides which keep crop yields relatively high." The implications, nonetheless, are disturbing. David Pimental of Cornell University cites three independent US studies indicating that, other things being equal, corn yields decline by an average of "four bushels per acre for each inch of topsoil lost from a base of 12 inches of topsoil or less."

In a world facing an acute shortage of productive cropland, any loss of topsoil should cause concern, for it is essentially irreversible in the short term. Creating an inch of new topsoil can take 100 years; if left to nature, it may take many centuries.

A report from the US Embassy in Jakarta indicates that "soil erosion is creating an ecological emergency in Java. A result of overpopulation, which has led to deforestation and misuse of hillside areas by land-hungry farmers, erosion is laying waste to land at an alarming rate, much faster than present reclamation programs can restore it. In Ethiopia, the deterioration of soils was brought into focus by a drought that culminated in famine in 1974. The US AID mission reports that "there is an environmental nightmare unfolding before our eyes . . . . It is the result of the acts of millions of Ethiopians struggling for survival: scratching the surface of eroded land and eroding it further; cutting down the trees for warmth and fuel and leaving the country denuded . . . . Over one billion—one billion—tons of topsoil flow from Ethiopia's highlands each year."

Historically, as the demand for food pressed against available supplies, farmers devised several techniques for extending agriculture onto land that was otherwise unproductive. Irrigation, terracing, strip-cropping, and shifting cultivation enabled farmers to produce food on land where conventional agriculture would not survive. Today, land farmed with these specialized techniques provides a large share of the world's food supply. Without them, the earth's capacity to feed people would be far lower than it is. Although these practices have withstood the test of time, they are beginning to break down in some areas under the pressure of population growth.

In some parts of the world, the doubling of demand for food over the past generation has forced farmers onto land that is highly vulnerable to erosion. Explosive Third World population growth has forced farmers onto mountainous soils without time to construct terraces. Once the natural cover is removed from unterraced mountainous land, topsoil quickly washes into the valley below, silting streams and clogging irrigation works. In the Andean countries of Latin America, skewed land-ownership patterns aggravate this problem. Wealthy ranchers use the relatively level valley floors for cattle grazing, forcing small landholders onto steeply sloping fields for the production of subsistence crops.

In dryland wheat areas of the world, pressures to reduce the area in fallow could lead to widespread drying up of soils. This proved catastrophic in the US Great Plains during the Dust Bowl of the thirties and in the Virgin Lands of the Soviet Union during the sixties. Except where land can be irrigated, the basic natural constraints on cultivation under low-rainfall conditions cannot be altered substantially.

The Threat to Irrigation

A disproportionately large share of the world's food comes from irrigated land, vulnerable both to ecological forces—waterlogging and salinity—and economic forces that divert water to competing uses. Waterlogging and salinity develop whenever surface water is diverted to irrigate land that has inadequate underground drainage. This gradually raises the water table, and once the water table is within a few feet of the surface, the growth of deep-rooted crops is impaired and the early symptoms of waterlogging appear.

As the water table rises further, water begins to evaporate through the remaining few inches of soil, thereby concentrating minerals and salt near the surface. Eventually the salt concentrations reach a level that prohibits plant growth. Glistening white expanses of abandoned cropland are visible from the air in countries traditionally dependent on irrigation, such as Iraq and Pakistan.

The problem is as old as irrigation itself. Indeed, the decline of some early Middle Eastern civilizations is now traced to the waterlogging and salinity caused by their irrigation systems. Designers of the earliest irrigation systems in the Tigris-Euphrates Valley did not understand subterranean hydrology well enough to prescribe corrective action, but modern irrigation en-

If agriculture is energy-intensive, then fuel shortages must inevitably lead to food shortages.

—RICHARD MERRILL

gineers do. The problem is cost: a recent UN report estimates average salvage costs at $650 per hectare.

Worldwide data compiled in a 1977 UN report indicate some 21 million hectares of irrigated land were waterlogged—one-tenth of the total area irrigated. The productivity on this land had fallen by 20 percent. An estimated 20 million hectares was affected primarily by salinization, with a reduction in productivity estimated to be roughly the same as that caused by waterlogging. Although fully half of the world's irrigation capacity has been developed since 1950, waterlogging and salinity are already impairing the effectiveness of many systems.

In some regions, crop production is threatened not by too much irrigation, but by too little. The diversion of irrigation waters to other purposes is particularly a problem in arid areas with irrigated agriculture and with rapid urbanization and industrialization, such as the southwestern United States. In the western states, farmers must compete for a share of shrinking water supplies. Growing cities, for example, absorb water needed to irrigate farmland. The irrigated area in Maricopa county in Arizona shrank 20 percent from the late fifties to the early seventies as water was diverted to the expanding Phoenix metropolitan area. Despite reduced agricultural demand, ground water levels have continued to drop some 10 to 20 feet per year in that county. In central Colorado, farms are losing water to the needs of Denver. As thirsty Los Angeles requires more and more water, the demand can often be satisfied only by diverting water from far-off irrigation canals. Valleys that were once lush green have turned a dusty brown; fields that were once among the most productive in the world have been abandoned.

In the western Great Plains—Nebraska, western Kansas, Colorado, and Wyoming—the withdrawal of underground water now often exceeds the rate of natural recharge. As water tables fall, pumping costs rise until farmers can no longer afford to irrigate. Efforts to develop coal resources of the northern Great Plains and oil shale resources of western Wyoming and Colorado would necessarily divert more water from agriculture. In Montana, farmers are battling energy firms in the courts to retain water for their fields.

Waterlogging and salinity have long been claiming irrigated land, but the problems associated with whole-sale diversion of water from agriculture are relatively new. During the final quarter of this century, the diversion of water to municipal and industrial uses will continue. Neal Jensen of Cornell University predicts that "western US irrigated agriculture faces gradual elimination as the pressures for higher priority water needs become evident."

Cropland Abandonment

Threats to cropland associated with mounting food demands pose a dilemma for farmers and government planners alike. Economic pressures and political instincts both encourage a short-term focus, a desire to expand output. But this pressure to wring more food out of the land can have devastating consequences for

the soil.

Worldwide demand for cropland is greater than ever before, but the amount of cropland abandoned each year may also be at a record level. The reasons for cropland abandonment—usually the product of economic pressures interacting with ecological forces—include desertification, erosion, waterlogging, salinization, and the diversion of irrigation water to non-farm uses.

Deserts are expanding on every continent. Some 630 million people, or one in every seven of the world's people, live in arid or semiarid areas. An estimated 78 million people live on lands rendered useless by erosion, dune formation, changes in vegetation, and salt encrustation. Desertification has deprived these people of their livelihood.

Fed by human pressures on their fringes—over-grazing, deforestation, and overplowing—virtually all

Rondal Partridge

To be close to the ecological problems of agriculture, the people who live and work on the farms should either own the land or be participants in a land trust system in which everyone's first interest is the conservation of healthy land and water. The bottom line cannot be profit. The land should not be owned by large corporations or wealthy absentee owners but if it is, policy measures should ensure that there is compliance to promote and achieve the best soil and water conservation possible.

—WES JACKSON

the world's major deserts are expanding. As human and livestock numbers multiply, the creation of deserts or desertlike conditions is accelerating throughout the Middle East and in Iran, Afghanistan, Pakistan, and northwestern India. Ecologist J. Vasconcelos Sobrinho reports that the semiarid tip of Brazil's Northeast is being desertified, and similar conditions are developing in Argentina.

A report by the Organisation for Economic Cooperation and Development (OECD) notes that "it is generally agreed that in Italy two million hectares have been abandoned in the last ten years. . . . The farming methods used on this marginal land have led to deterioration of the soil so that the land was consumed in the literal sense of the term." Similarly, in Yugoslavia and Bulgaria during the past two decades, eroded and worn-out soils in farm areas with rugged terrain have been abandoned.

Conversion to Nonfarm Uses

While a significant proportion of the world's cropland shows signs of deterioration or has already been abandoned, other land that remains productive continues to be converted to non-farm uses. The increase in world population and economic activity means that land is needed for urbanization, energy production, and transportation. Each of these sectors is claiming cropland in virtually every country.

The growth of cities is a leading cause of cropland loss. Within the United States, cities are consuming cropland at a record rate. Land-use surveys by the Department of Agriculture in 1967 and 1975 indicated that some 2.51 million hectares of prime cropland "were converted to urban and built-up uses" during the eight-year period. A European study of urban encroachment on agricultural land (grasslands as well as croplands) from 1960 to 1970 found that West Germany was losing 0.25 percent of its agricultural

land yearly, or 1 percent every four years. For France and the United Kingdom, the comparable figure was 0.18 percent per year, or nearly 2 percent for the decade. There is little information on the Third World, where the most rapid urbanization is occurring. But scores of cities in developing countries, such as Lima, Ankara, and Manila, are growing by 5 to 8 percent yearly. Inevitably, some of this growth comes at the expense of cropland.

The UN estimated that the urban population of the world increased by 822 million from 1950 to 1975, and predicts that the increase will nearly double, to 1,580 million, from 1975 to 2000. If it is assumed, perhaps conservatively, that new urban dwellers will need .04 hectares per person, the world's cities may occupy 63 million hectares of land by 2000. Assuming that 40 percent of this total is cropland, expanding cities will cover 25 million hectares of cropland between now and the end of the century. Where cities are situated on the most fertile soils, urban expansion onto cropland represents a disproportionately greater loss to food production resources. A study of changing land-use patterns in Canada reports that "half of the farmland lost to urban expansion is coming from the best one-twentieth of our farmland."

Rivaling the urban sector as a claimant on cropland is the fast-growing energy sector. During the final quarter of this century, the consumption of energy is projected to increase more rapidly than that of food. Like the production of food, the production of energy requires land. Hydroelectric dams often inundate vast stretches of rich bottomland. Electric generating plants can cover hundreds of hectares. More often than not, oil refineries and storage tanks are built on prime farmland along rivers and coastal plains. Strip-mining of coal and the diversion of irrigation water to the energy sector both tend to reduce the area under cultivation.

In the United States, the Senate's Committee on

Interior and Insular Affairs studied the land requirements associated with the development of various energy resources and facilities. Among other things, the committee analyzed President Ford's 1975 State of the Union Address in which he asked for "200 major nuclear power plants, 250 major new coal mines, 150 major coal-fired power plants, 30 major new refineries, 20 major new synthetic fuel plants, and the drilling of many thousands of new oil wells" in the next ten years. The Federal Energy Administration estimated that the program would disturb land on 18 million hectares. The Senate committee noted that "this amounts to a tripling of the amount of land currently devoted to energy thus far."

Although the Senate committee did not estimate the share of this land that would be cropland, some studies conducted at the local level have done so. One such study compiled data on the loss of cropland to the strip-mining of coal in Illinois, a state with some of the most productive land in the Corn Belt. "As of 1976," it reported, "202,422 acres (81,981 hectares) in 40 Illinois counties have been affected by surface and deep mining. Surface mining accounted for over 94 percent (191,874 acres) of this affected acreage." Although mining companies are now required by law to restore land to its original productive state, many people doubt that this will be possible in most situations. Given the extensive resources of coal close to the surface in some 51 Illinois counties, the potential disruption is a matter of great concern.

There are no detailed surveys of the worldwide loss of cropland to strip-mining, but it is safe to assume that the measured loss in Illinois is only a small share of the US total and a minute percentage of the global total. While estimates of future cropland losses to urbanization are difficult, estimates of losses to the energy sector are even more so. The potentially large claims, however, emphatically underline the need for energy conservation programs. To conserve energy is also to conserve cropland.

All transport systems require land but some systems use much more than others. Automobile-centered transport systems are voracious consumers of land. An enormous amount of US cropland has been paved over for the automobile. Millions of hectares are required just to park the nation's 143 million licensed motor vehicles. But even this is rather small compared with the land covered by streets, highways, filling stations, and other service facilities. Moreover, the automobile has encouraged the inefficient uses of land, such as urban sprawl.

Societies moving toward an automobile-centered transportation system should weigh carefully the sacrifice of cropland that is sure to be involved. Almost any other form of transportation requires less land.

Societies with well-developed public transport systems are able to use land far more efficiently than those where most people rely on cars.

Just as rising income increases the per capital demand for cropland, so too it increases the land required for other purposes. High-income man is a space consumer. All the principal nonfarm uses of land are greater among high-income groups than they are among those with low income.

The amount of cropland that will be paved over, built on, strip-mined, or flooded by a dam before the end of this century is unknown. If world population projections materialize, however, 2.3 billion people will be added between 1975 and the year 2000. Given these population projections and the projected gains in income, every nonfarm claimant on cropland—urbanization, energy production, transportation—is certain to be greater during the last quarter of this century than during the third.

Future Cropland Trends

The historical expansion of cultivated land has been closely related to the growth in human numbers. In response to population pressures, farmers moved

---

If differences in the quality and performance of soil are to receive more attention, American farming must be reduced to a human scale. It will become necessary to bring agriculture within the scope of the individual, so that the farmer and the soil can develop together, each responding as fully as possible to the needs of the other.

—MURRAY BOOKCHIN

---

from valley to valley and continent to continent, gradually extending the area under cultivation until, today, one-tenth of the earth's land surface is under the plow. By the mid-twentieth century, most frontiers had disappeared. Up until that time, increases in world food output had come almost entirely from expanding the area farmed. Increases in land productivity were scarcely perceptible within any given generation.

During the final quarter of this century, population is projected to increase by 58 percent; the expected addition of 2.3 billion people would be half again as large as the 1.5 billion added during the third quarter.

As the final quarter of this century began, cropland was being lost to nonfarm purposes at a record rate. The abandonment of agricultural land because of severe soil erosion, degradation, and desertification was at an all-time high. The potential for substantial net additions to the world's cropland base was not good.

How much the world's cultivated area can be expanded has been hotly debated during the past 15 years. Some studies contend that it can easily be doubled, while others assume that the opportunities for adding new land will largely be offset by losses— leading to little, if any, increase in the base. The principal difference between such widely varying estimates is explainable in economic terms. The more optimistic

---

The ultimate resource is the biota—there is no other. And we are destroying it.

—GEORGE M. WOODWELL

---

projections omit economic constraints whereas the less optimistic ones include them. One very rough set of projections by John McHale that incorporates both additions and losses concludes that the former will offset the latter, leading to a cropland base at the end of the century that is essentially the same as that today. A Department of Agriculture model of the world food economy, which assumes a real increase in commodity prices of roughly 50 percent between the 1969–71 base period and the year 2000, shows an increase over the 1975 harvested area of cereals of only 6 percent.

On balance, it is difficult to see how the world can achieve much more than a 10 percent increase in cropland area during the final quarter of this century without a dramatic rise in the price of food. This area increase would be much smaller than the one that occurred during the third quarter of this century. From 1950 to 1975, the increase in cultivated area fell far behind that of population, accounting for only one-fourth of the gain in food output. The projected increase of 10 percent in the harvested area for the final quarter of this century represents an extension of this historical rate of decline.

Barring a pronounced rise in food price—one that would make the cultivation of markedly less fertile soils profitable—a 10 percent net increase in harvested area may represent the realistic upper limit. Combined with the projected growth in population

during the final quarter of this century, such an increase would lead to a *decline* in cereal land per person from .184 hectares to .128 hectares. In absolute terms, this per capita decline of .056 hectares is almost exactly the same as the .057 hectare decline of the third quarter-century, but in relative terms it is much larger. From 1950 to 1975, the area per person shrank by scarcely one-fourth, but during the current quarter the reduction would be closer to one-third.

Projections of world food demand by the UN Food and Agriculture Organisation and the International Food Policy Research Institute indicate or imply that the world demand for food will roughly double between 1975 and 2000. Assuming a modest growth in cropland area of 10 percent, satisfying the projected growth in demand would require an even greater increase in yield per hectare during the final quarter of this century than was achieved during the third quarter.

Unfortunately, recent trends indicate the potential for a continuing rapid rise in crop yield per hectare may be much less than has been assumed in existing projections of world food supply. The postwar trend of rising yield per hectare has been arrested temporarily in the United States, France, and China, each the leading cereal producer on its continent. Aside from the biological constraints on raising crop yield per hectare, pressures to extract ever more food from the land (combined with poor land management) is leading to the slow but steady deterioration of an estimated one-fifth of the world's cropland. For most countries, the mounting demand pressures are of domestic origin, but for food exporters such as the United States and Canada, it is the growth in demand from abroad that is pressing the land beyond its limits.

Meeting the Challenge

Few things will affect future human well-being more directly than the balance between people and cropland. If recent population and cropland trends continue, that balance will almost certainly be upset, leading to economic uncertainty and political instability. Avoiding large, politically destabilizing rises in food prices between now and the end of the century may not be possible without a mammoth effort to protect cropland from nonfarm uses, to improve the management of soils, and, at the same time, to quickly reduce the rate of population growth.

Agricultural land can no longer be treated as an inexhaustible reservoir of land for industry, urbanization, and the energy sector. Cropland is becoming scarce. In a world of continuously growing demand for food, it must be viewed as an irreplaceable resource, one that is paved over or otherwise taken out

Dry land alfalfa hay farming—no irrigation.

of production only under the most pressing circumstances and as a result of conscious public policy.

Historically, land in most countries was allocated to various uses through the marketplace, but unfortunately the market does not protect cropland from competing interests. As cropland becomes more scarce, it can be protected from competing nonfarm demands only through some form of land-use planning. Such planning can occur at the national level, the local level, or both. It can rely primarily on land-use restrictions in the form of legislation or government decrees, or it can rely on incentives such as differential tax rates. Each society will need to employ approaches suited to its own circumstances.

Japan is reported to be the only country with comprehensive zoning nationwide. In 1968, the entire country was divided into three land-use zones—urban, agricultural, and other. In 1974, the plan was further refined to demarcate specific areas for forests, natural parks, and nature reserves. Japan has faced the issue first, and in so doing has developed a model for other countries to follow.

Within the United States, national land-use planning is still at a rather rudimentary level, confined largely to setting aside national parks, forests, and wildlife reserves. Such zoning as does exist is usually at the local level, consisting largely of restrictions on land that can be used for commercial purposes. A number of states are concerned about the need to protect agricultural land, but to date, only a few have done so.

Several European countries—Belgium, France, Germany, and the Netherlands—passed legislation during the sixties establishing national land-use guidelines, but left the actual planning to be done at the local level. In addition to protecting agricultural land as such, their laws addressed such issues as the control of urban sprawl, the need for parks, and the establishment of urban green belts.

Rivaling the loss of cropland to nonfarm uses is the process of gradual soil degradation through erosion. If the loss of topsoil and associated soil degradation are permitted to continue, they will lead to ever higher food production costs. But the effort needed to halt the deterioration of the soils on which humanity depends is staggering.

The one source of cropland degradation and loss officially dealt with at the international level is desertification. The World Plan of Action to stop the spread of deserts, agreed to at the Nairobi conference, concluded that money spent now to halt and reverse desertification and the loss of cropland promised high returns, ones that were competitive with other forms of investment. The plan specified the levels of investment by national governments, the World Bank, the UN Development Program, and the Inter-American Development Bank that would bring the process to a halt within the next decade and a half. The desertification conference estimated that "a net zero desert growth can be achieved within the next 10 to 15 years, provided that the measures are started promptly and are effectively and comprehensively carried out." But achievement of zero desert growth will be possible only with prompt, concerted action by national governments that are, unfortunately, not usually noted for such efforts.

In many countries, the stabilization of soils is such a vast undertaking that it will require a strong national political commitment and a detailed plan of action. Such a program has been outlined for the United States by the Soil Conservation Service. In order to stabilize US soils and bring the annual loss of topsoil down to a level that does not exceed the tolerance factor, the plan calls both for changes in cropping practices and for heavy investments in land improvements. The principal recommendations of the plan include an increase in the terraced land where farmers leave crop residues on the surface from 4.8 million

hectares to 17.6 million hectares, an increase in the amount of strip-cropped land with minimum tillage from about 0.4 million to 14.0 million hectares, and an increase in the strip-cropped land with crop residues left on the surface from 3.2 million to 7.2 million hectares. For land where farmers rely on a combination of contour farming and minimum tillage to keep their soil in place, they recommend a 21-fold increase— from 0.8 million to 16.8 million hectares. The largest suggested increase of all is for land where contour farming and crop residues on the surface are used together—from 3.2 million to 22.4 million hectares.

These prescribed changes in farming practices are monumental in scale, involving half of all US cropland. Adoption of these soil-saving measures would often run counter to the immediate economic interests of farmers and consumers, since they would lead to a 5 to 8 percent increase in food production costs. Some efforts to conserve soil and protect long-term food production might reduce food output as well as increase food prices in the short term. While soil scientists can chart a national plan of action in detail, they cannot generate the political support needed to fund and administer such a plan.

Public support on the scale needed will not be forth-

Courtesy F. Hal Higgins Library, UC Davis

People tend to leave remoter regions simply because they are, in modern transport terms, "remote." If more conserving patterns of farming were to bring back to the countryside skilled men and their families—one can estimate perhaps four extra people for every returning worker—a number of regional centers would revive or grow up, and, "remoteness" being a relative concept the result could be that mixed farms, market gardens, orchards, hill farms, and even intensive restocking of fish in local lakes and streams might be combined to produce an environment at once more productive, more desirable, more attractive, and above all, more populated, than results from the present imbalance between concentrated urban and suburban areas and declining land and emptying villages everywhere else.

—BARBARA WARD

coming without a better understanding of the costs to society of failing to act. R.A. Brink and his colleagues, writing in *Science*, observe that "in our predominantly urban society, it may be difficult to gain the public support needed for funding an adequate soil conservation program." But they predict that "public opinion will shift with the worsening of the world food crisis." Brink wonders whether "as a result of mounting pressures on the land, the need for soil-saving measures is outrunning the capacity of conservation agencies as now financed to assist farmers in meeting it." If this observation applies to the United States, one can only wonder about the future adequacy of efforts to protect cropland in countries that have far less to work with, geographically, institutionally, and financially. Governments that fail to respond effectively will soon be confronted with long-term food scarcity as the cropland base deteriorates.

The future balance between people and cropland is likely to be affected more by population policy than by any other single factor. Growth in human numbers not only generates a demand for more cropland, but it also simultaneously generates pressures to convert cropland to nonfarm uses. Policymakers have assumed that projected increases in population over the final quarter of this century will materialize. But the social costs of remaining on the projected demographic path may become too great.

Convulsive changes in the world food economy dur-

ing the seventies are indicative of growing pressures on the cropland base. They reflect the extension of cultivation onto marginal rainfall areas in the Soviet Union, the encroachment of deserts in Africa, and the flooding in Bangladesh (aggravated by deforestation in the Himalayas). Unprecedented in peacetime, the worldwide food shortages and climbing prices of the early and mid-seventies should be regarded not as an aberration, but rather as a signal that pressures on cropland are becoming excessive. They may in fact be advance tremors warning of a quake to come. For a great many countries, the future promises acute land hunger, grim food shortages, soaring food prices, and widespread social unrest.

Threats to the world cropland base from the nonfarm sector are very apparent, and evidence that the soils on which we depend are deteriorating is overwhelming. What is not nearly so evident is how political leaders will respond—and the time left in which to respond is measured in years, not decades.

The issue is not whether the equilibrium between people and land will eventually be reestablished. It will be. If the deterioration is not arrested by man, then nature will ultimately intervene with its own checks. The times call for a new land ethic, a new reverence for land, and for a better understanding of our dependence on a resource that is too much taken for granted.

Recommended Actions

☐ Congress should require the states to develop statewide land-use plans that recognize the primacy of agriculture, and by means of penalties and incentives, secure implementation of such plans by state and local governments.

☐ The US should propose a United Nations conference on croplands and soil fertility.

☐ The Department of State, in cooperation with the Department of Agriculture and other appropriate federal agencies, should offer advice and assistance to nations that face serious problems of cropland erosion and soil depletion.

☐ Everywhere, educational institutions and religious organizations should promote a land ethic, a tradition of stewardship of the land.

☐ Congress should enact an integrated program of croplands protection and soils management that would:
  • prohibit the diversion of prime agricultural land (and water supplies) to non-agricultural uses;
  • discourage irrigation where irrigation will predictably lead to waterlogging or salinity;
  • encourage farmers to use terracing, contour plowing, and other methods of minimizing soil erosion;
  • encourage farmers to use crop rotations, including legumes, as a substitute for ever-heavier applications of chemical fertilizers;
  • retire marginal croplands and devote them to their best permanently-sustainable use;
  • reclaim eroded or depleted croplands and return them to ecologically sound uses.

Stephen Frisch

Few who have seriously thought of the long term future of food in America doubt for a moment that farming as a way of life needs to be promoted, not for the purpose of providing museum pieces for city dwellers, but because we need stewards on the land. Even the town and urban population, in the not too distant future, will have to look to the land reverently, as the source of their sustenance and health. By then it should have become increasingly clear that stewardship based on economics alone won't do, for if farming continues as a business proposition only, the land is doomed. Eventually short-run economics will dictate the patterns of use. Most small farmers would have it otherwise. Most of them would prefer the farm to be a home or a hearth, a place to live and raise a family. —WES JACKSON

Natural Resources

That our exploitable natural resources are declining in both quantity and quality can hardly be news to anyone. Percentages of minerals and metals imported increase yearly. Estimates of petroleum reserves have been radically reduced. Ore qualities have plummeted. We dig so deep for water that we risk compacting aquifers, pump oil from seas in which fisheries may be destroyed, and contemplate pulverizing mountains for their shale oil. We denude our forested hills. We discourage reclamation and reuse of materials, and we waste more than half the energy we obtain from fossil fuels. In the face of raw material shortages, we discard tens of millions of tons of packaging (much of it superfluous) and of not-so-durable durable goods. Desperately trying to save ourselves by accelerating efforts to get the last usable chunk of ore out of the ground, the last barrel of oil, would merely hasten the decline of our extractive industries. Then, after spending billions of dollars to fritter away resources, undermine industries, and destroy the integrity of our land, we would be left staring into abandoned open-pit mines and wondering how it all happened. Instead, we must begin immediately to eliminate waste, to manufacture durable and reusable products, and to develop recycling systems. *Then* we can worry whether further exploitation of raw resources is inevitable, justifiable, or possible.

Harvey Mudd

Natural Resources

MARY LOU VAN DEVENTER

OUR PARAMOUNT RESOURCE problem is that nonrenewable resources are scarcer than ever, and of lower quality.

The principal nonrenewable resources are iron, ferro-alloy metals used in combination with iron, nonferrous metals, precious metals (such as gold, silver, and platinum), industrial minerals (such as sulfur, asbestos, and borates), and fossil fuels. Some problems are specific to a given resource, but the minerals have three things in common: they are all distributed unevenly throughout the earth's crust, they all cost a lot to obtain in raw form, and they are all decreasing in quality. Richer ores were the first to be exploited.

The National Commission on Materials Policy concluded as long ago as 1973 that the US faced shortages of six of the 13 basic raw materials industry depends on, and by 1985 could expect to rely on imports for another three. Finding domestic reserves of some is improbable, and exploring for others is growing more costly. Many companies estimate that they must spend *at least* $20 million to locate one deposit worth developing; and that doesn't include the costs of evaluating the deposit and preparing to mine.

At constantly growing cost, we find ores of constantly decreasing quality. In the 1920s, it was uneconomic to mine copper ore that assayed less than 1.5 percent copper. In 1975, the corresponding figure was 0.35 percent. Industries have improved their processing techniques to accommodate lower grades of ore, but further advances in technology, while sometimes theoretically feasible, would require scales of operation that are economically unfeasible. In some places, 100,000 tons of ore are already being handled daily. The profit is marginal. To develop technologies to process greater quantities might require capital investments that even governments could not afford.

Processing greater quantities of materials would, in any event, be horrifyingly destructive. Possibly the most destructive course we have contemplated so far is extracting oil from shale. A full-fledged shale-oil industry providing 6.4 quadrillion Btus of energy would require 417 million gallons of water daily, enough to supply the household needs of the entire Washington, DC, metropolitan area. The industry would emit sulfur dioxides equal to thirteen 1,000-megawatt power plants burning western coal without any emission controls, and its solid wastes would be almost nine times the total US residential and commercial solid wastes generated in 1973. Those potential wastes are mountain peaks now; no one can compute the cost of converting vast areas of our grandest mountain country into piles of rubble.

We consider such drastic measures because the import marketplace is unreliable. The oil embargo of 1973 proved that. What we have not yet fully realized is that the markets for other minerals are due for a similar jolt. We rely for essential minerals and nonferrous metals on developing countries that could flex their own resource muscles any time. Charles F. Park, Dean of Mineral Sciences at Stanford University for more than 28 years, said: "If the present trend toward nationalization continues, the industrialized nations will have to depend more and more upon purchases in the open market; they will no longer be able to own their mines and gear production to their needs. Serious problems of supply and pricing may be ahead for the nonferrous metals."

That last sentence could as easily read "ferro-alloy metals," which are used in relatively small quantities but are essential to industry. The US has a surplus of only one of these metals, molybdenum, and we must import a large percentage of the others from less developed nations. That is not to say we should be suspicious of less developed nations. But we must respect their right to begin charging prices that reflect the true value of their resources.

All Earth's resources belong to all its people. The uneven distribution means that some people have custody over some materials, some people over others. We must be careful to distribute those resources so that all people have a chance to use what they really need, no matter where they live—or when. People of all nationalities must be included in the distribution, as must generations yet unborn. When less developed

American cars, ready for shipment to Japan, to be melted down for Japan's steel and auto industry.   Photo by Rondal Partridge

nations charge high prices for raw materials, they are helping to make sure that those who buy them really need them.

As for precious metals, some economists are already trying to deemphasize the role of these metals in monetary systems in order to free them for proliferating industrial uses. We import most of these metals.

Finding substitutes for the precious metals is difficult, if not impossible. The properties that make them valuable are ones that cannot be duplicated. Technological optimists frequently argue that when one material is gone another will be found to substitute for it, but squandering our goods in expectation of the alchemist's remedy is a dangerous strategy. The alchemist cannot change lead into gold if he has run out of lead.

Another aspect of the nonrenewable resource shortage we must face is that public lands are a substantial source both of fuel and nonfuel minerals. The question we must ask ourselves is how much more of our common land we are willing to chew up and shovel into the privately-owned industrial maw.

Renewable Resources Become Nonrenewable

The most important problem with renewable resources is that they are on the brink—some have gone over it—of becoming nonrenewable. The amount of usable land, water, and timber decreases rapidly.

Land disappears into deserts or under pavement. Every year a million and a quarter acres of rural land, a third of it cultivated cropland, are given over to other uses—chiefly urban expansion. (Cities tend to become greedier as they grow; from 1960 to 1970, the land area of urban centers expanded by 40 percent while population grew by 24 percent.) At the same time, formerly good rangeland is deteriorating. The Bureau of Land Management, largest manager of land in the country, says 16 percent of its rangelands are declining.

The next step for declining rangelands—areas where rainfall is too low or erratic to support forests or unirrigated cultivation—is erosion and possibly desertification. Once soil cover is lost from these lands, it can take a century or more to build up another inch of productive topsoil. The United Nations Environment Programme estimates that humanity has changed 9.1 million square kilometers of potentially productive land into desert. This process is what former UNEP Executive Director Maurice Strong called "the relentless march of deserts."

Water is the answer to some soil problems, but we are already having trouble stretching our water supply. North Americans now remove twice as much water from the hydrologic cycle as we return. In 1970 projected American water requirements for 1980 were about 700 billion gallons, but even technological optimists of that time could only come up with a 1980 supply of 650 billion gallons.

To supply water, particularly in the West and Southwest, we have tapped large aquifers—natural reservoirs in underground porous rock. Consequently, water tables have dropped sharply in areas of heavy withdrawal. Some aquifers will take tens or hundreds of thousands of years to replenish, and they may not refill at all if rock from which water was drained is compacted by the earth's pressure. Land in California's Central Valley is already subsiding.

Replenishing trees cut from forests is a similar problem, although the time spans involved are shorter. A prime example of trees becoming nonrenewable resources are the once-vast redwood forests of California. The remnants of those forests are being clearcut rapidly, even to the point of endangering the world's tallest trees inside the boundaries of Redwood National Park. Growing more redwoods the size of the ones we are now cutting would take 800 years or more. Unless man uses unprecedented restraint for many centuries, old-growth redwood is a nonrenewable resource.

Intensive forestry has become the rage in lumbering circles because it provides more wood per acre than other methods. Its practice includes such techniques as clearcutting large tracts and planting even-aged stands of a single species. This is management of trees as a crop, and "tree farm" has come into the language. Anyone can tell where this practice is being carried out, either from peeled hillsides or from rows of trees of uniform height with no underbrush. It is hard to look at trees arranged like soldiers on a parade ground and think of the aggregate as a forest.

Monocultural tree plantations are more than a visual problem, however. Neither short- nor long-term effects of this kind of management are well understood. We do know that the more complex and diverse a natural community is, the greater is its stability. Monocultures are unstable communities that discourage resident wild animals, many of which depend on undergrowth for cover and nourishment. But "tree farms" proliferate. In western forests, removal of old growth exceeds the amount of new growth. In eastern forests, new growth exceeds removal—but only because mature trees (slow growers) have already been cut.

In the early 1970s, nevertheless, a blue ribbon Panel on Timber and the Environment chaired by former Secretary of the Interior Fred Seaton recommended that the Forest Service cut 39 percent *more* timber from public land than it had intended, and that it increase investment in forest "development" by $200 million per year. The panel proposed this intensive development even though the Forest Service is under congressional mandate to manage the forests in accordance with sound environmental practices and in the best multiple-use combination with watershed protection, wildlife and range protection, and outdoor recreation. The conflict of purposes has not been resolved.

Conflicting purposes are also evident in the management of another renewable resource—the only steadily growing one, waste. Inorganic and organic wastes are a $6-billion-a-year problem. It costs us more than five million Btus of energy to collect and dispose of each of the 125 million tons of garbage we generate each year. But a study for the Ford Foundation Energy Policy Project suggests that crop residues, feedlot manures, and urban refuse could actually be used to generate more than four quadrillion Btus. This figure is expected to more than double over the next 20 years or so. Waste conversion could take the place of the proposed shale-oil industry. While our cities debate where to put the next landfill, they ignore the vast potential of the waste they try so hard to hide.

It is easy to understand the main source of our problems with natural resources. When our country was young, we deemed it advantageous to encourage the exploitation of resources. We were even anxious to give away public land to be used for private purposes, believing those uses would benefit the whole country. The country was built with resources virtually given to miners and with tax shelters granted to lumbermen. Now that we have built ourselves a culture and a country, we are slow to take back the concessions granted to resource-exploitative industries, even though the concessions harm us now.

Our Policy a Relic of the Frontier

The Mining Law of 1872 is an example. In the late 1800s, with the smell of industrial revolution in our nostrils, we wanted more minerals to grow with. We provided that anyone who wanted to mine on public land had only to file a claim at the county courthouse and put in $100 worth of work in the claim each year. Miners with a valid claim could gain full title to the

Population, capital, resources, and growth rates, as projected by The Club of Rome, from The Limits to Growth.

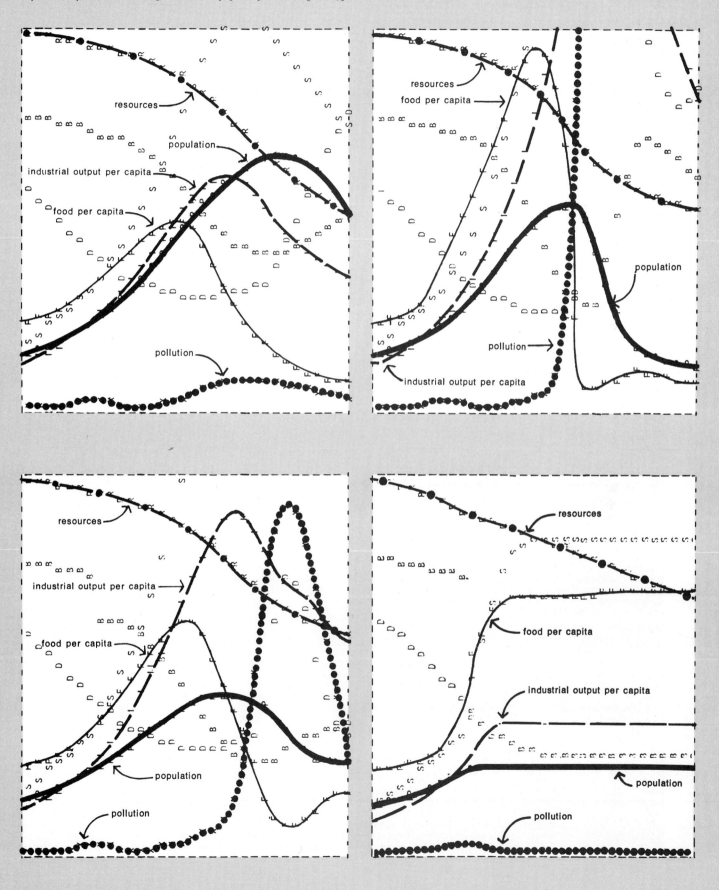

land for a fee of $2.50 or $5.00, depending on the deposit mined, with proof that they had spent $500 in labor or money working the claim and that the claim really had economically worthwhile mineral deposits on it.

Since 1872 we have changed neither the dollar figures nor the requirements for gaining title. Consequently, the federal government has very little control over mining. The 1872 law still applies to gold, silver, iron, copper, lead, zinc, bauxite, uranium, and all the hard rock minerals.

The "new" Minerals Leasing Act of 1920 adopts the philosophy that resources on public lands belong to everyone, but this law applies only to coal, oil and gas, oil shale, phosphates, potassium, sodium, and asphalt. The act contains no environmentally protective features.

Other laws in other areas favor exploitation, too. *Ad valorem* timber laws, which tax remaining stands of trees, encourage clearcutting and sometimes force reluctant owners to cut in order to pay taxes. Capital gains treatment of profits from virgin materials, depreciation schedules, depletion allowances, and other federal tax write-offs subsidize extractive industries to the tune of billions of dollars a year. A staff study done for the congressional Joint Economic Committee concluded that "the subsidies to timber, oil, and other minerals appear to provide incentives to use these resources in greater amounts and instead of other alternatives."

At the same time, federal, state, and local regulations have militated against reusing and recycling. Purchasing specifications based on materials instead of function ("virgin fibers only") have this effect. Labeling standards originally intended to protect consumers ("reprocessed wool") achieve the same result more subtly. Some programs, such as US Department of agriculture subsidies for lime and inorganic fertilizers, discourage the use of organic wastes. Discriminatory railroad rates condoned by the Interstate Commerce Commission make it more expensive to ship ferrous scrap than iron ore. The scrap averages 1.5 times the iron content of the ore.

Closing the Loop

Our fundamental dilemma is that we have built an open system not unlike the digestive tract of an earthworm: one end gobbles up resources and the other end ejects wastes. Were our resources infinite, as the

Supporters of Mono Lake, photograph by Steve Johnson.

Mineral towers at Mono Lake, photograph by Andrew Baldwin

earth must seem to a worm, that would do. But our resources are finite, so we must find ways to approximate the worm Ourobouros, which was said to eat its own tail and never run out of food. We must join the ends of our system so our wastes become resources.

In a closed-loop system, however, our materials are not so useful to us the second time around because of the degeneration of energy described by the Second Law of Thermodynamics. We must hold as many of our materials as possible in the first cycle as long as we can. This is conservation. It will not make our resources infinite; it will only stretch them further. Conservation can be implemented by designing durable goods that can be reused many times before they must be broken down into raw materials for another cycle. We can conserve best by keeping resource requirements to a minimum instead of wantonly generating excesses, as in current packaging. Then, when a product has deteriorated beyond repair, we must recover its materials and use them again. This is recycling, and it is already being practiced by a few infant industries. We must derive our energy for this activity as much as possible from our only nearly-infinite source, the sun.

A Utopian Vision

We picture a society that designs its products well, so it takes years for them to break down. Washing ma-

chines are handed down from parent to child; cars run 15 years or more. Industries that do repairs flourish and employ versatile and skilled workers. When machines do deteriorate beyond repair, we call the municipal recycling agency, which is profitably selling basic materials from discarded goods. A railroad carries sorted scrap to a regional reprocessor, which separates the prinipal ingredients and ships them off to steel mills, glass plants, and other basic industries. There, the scrap is mixed with a small amount of virgin material if necessary to make up for loss of material in the cycle, then sent on to manufacturers who make finished products of it.

On a routine shopping day, we go to the store with cola bottles, a shampoo bottle, an egg carton, and a bread wrapper in hand. At the store we get our bottle deposits back, refill the shampoo container from a jug with a measured-flow spout, choose bread from a yeasty-smelling assortment of loaves at the bakery counter, and select our eggs from crates. We return home in our eight-year-old, classically designed car that has more than 90,000 miles on the odometer and a lot of life left in it—if the store is too far or our purchases too heavy for walking or the bicycle. We turn on lights powered by municipal or neighborhood solar collectors and distribution systems, and put our purchases away. No wrestling with packaging, no trash to throw out. We cook on a stove that burns methane from our sewage reprocessor. After dinner, we stroll down to the river to watch fishermen test the clean water for trout.

How to Get There From Here

Dreaming is one thing, making visions come true is another. We must provide fundamentally sound legislative bases upon which industry can restructure itself in the best interests of the people, and to promote cultural continuity and longevity. Our laws must evolve as we do. The steps in this redirection must be first to eliminate waste wherever possible, then to recycle what wastes we produce.

Eliminating waste is a matter of letting resources' scarcity be reflected in prices, encouraging conservation, and the production of more durable, more reusable goods.

Prices that reflect scarcity are required by the law of supply and demand. We must eliminate artificial advantages for extractive industries. The General Accounting Office recommends that the Mining Law of 1872 be changed to require leases on public lands, and to require detailed exploration, damage-minimization, and land-reclamation plans. Our hard rocks and minerals would be pulled out of the ground more slowly, ensuring that supplies will be available in the future, if needed.

As for fossil fuels, we should eliminate depletion allowances and restrict exploration to safe places. The Gulf of Alaska is one example of an extremely hazardous area that is about to be exploited; grave damage to rich fisheries is unavoidable. That kind of price is simply too high, so exploration should be disallowed. As for land and water, we should tax projects that drain aquifers, tax new low-density urban developments, and grant permanent tax advantages to cropland. And as for timber, we can eliminate *ad valorem* taxes and end the capital gains treatment of profits.

We should encourage conservation by giving loans and temporary tax advantages to urban revitalization projects, to research projects on conservation, and to infant industries that produce conservation-oriented systems. We should end quantity discounts for fossil fuels, electricity, and water.

The ramifications of policies that encourage conservation would be profound. The United States could meet all its new energy needs for the next 25 years, says Denis Hayes, by improving its use of fossil fuels. Industry uses 44 percent of its fossil fuels to produce steam. If the water for that steam were preheated, using elementary solar technology, steam output per unit of fossil fuel would be tripled. If the steam was then used to produce electricity first, before its use in industrial processes, more electricity would be pro-

duced than the entire industrial sector now uses.

We should save energy by retrofitting buildings with conservation-oriented equipment, such as insulation and windows that open and close. The American Institute of Architects estimates that if we adopted a high-priority national program emphasizing energy-efficient buildings, we could save the equivalent of more than 12.5 million barrels of oil per day by 1990.

Conservation of metals and minerals will, in part, be a by-product of high prices for materials and energy. Many short-lived or wasteful products will price themselves out of the market. After the economy has adjusted somewhat to these forces, further conservation can be achieved by systematically encouraging production of durable products. The law against nonreturnable bottles has decreased beverage costs in Oregon and other states without affecting sales. Similar bans could be imposed on nondurable goods. Tax discounts could be given for repairs, especially in housing. Incentives and funding could be granted to cities to establish sewage treatment facilities that recycle detoxified water and use treated sewage as a source of methane and fertilizer.

When we have a good start on conserving, we can step up recycling programs. It is imperative that we design them to prevent dependence on a continuing stream of waste; cities that have sunk capital into facilities that burn wastes as a source of energy are subsidizing waste. Instead, we should concentrate on means of recovering the materials in the waste, then perhaps derive energy from the residue.

A major step would be to end discrimination in freight rates against scrap and used materials. Some recovery industries would become financially feasible immediately, even accounting for high labor costs. To develop others, it would be necessary to grant seed money and temporary tax advantages. Once the industries were established, these incentives should be withdrawn; market conditions would ensure their survival.

Such measures as these will necessitate relocating people who work in industries that now rely on continued exploitation of scarce resources. This is a task that must be done sooner or later in any case. To solve the problem, unions could establish mutually-funded national communication networks that match displaced workers with openings in industries that must grow to balance the production-reclamation system. Construction workers will retrofit buildings with insulation and windows that open. Machinists will manufacture recycling and heat-reclamation equipment. Machine operators will produce electricity from industrial steam. Semi-skilled workers will rip upholstery out of car bodies to facilitate recycling. Unskilled workers will sort and wash bottles. There will be abundant jobs in growing industries, and smart unions will take advantage of the opportunity to broaden their bases. Where unions fail, governments could establish similar placement services.

Within 25 or 30 years, we could redirect our society toward dynamic equilibrium in its use of resources. If we use our resources sparingly, if we design reusable and durable products, if we use energy efficiently, and if we recover the materials in articles that cannot be repaired, we could minimize our dependence on infusions of raw materials. Then we would have designed a pattern of cultural longevity and continuity.

Peeter Vilms/Jeroboam, Inc.

Recommended Actions

☐ The President should proclaim that good husbandry of the nation's natural resources is a national goal and a special mission of the Departments of Agriculture and of the Interior.

☐ The President should appoint Secretaries of Agriculture and of the Interior who are personally committed to stewardship (as opposed to exploitation) of the land and its resources.

☐ The Secretary of Agriculture should order the Forest Service to pay more than lip service to sustained-yield forestry and to cater less to commercial timber interests.

☐ The Secretary should also dedicate his department to the maintenance and rebuilding of topsoil and its fertility.

☐ The Secretary of the Interior should instruct the Bureau of Land Management (and other agencies under his jurisdiction) to put land to its best use (or non-use), not necessarily to the use most profitable to entrepreneurs.

☐ The Corps of Engineers and other water resource agencies should be diverted from damming and ditching to erosion control, aquifer recharging, and water conservation.

☐ The federal, state, and local governments should buy recycled materials for their own use to the greatest extent possible.

☐ The federal and state governments should support recycling research, and through tax incentives and other inducements, should help recycling industries get established.

☐ All levels of government should require that new government buildings be energy-efficient and economical in their use of materials, and wherever possible, should upgrade the energy efficiency of existing government buildings.

☐ An appropriate committee of Congress should draft a totally new mining law ensuring that mining claims in the public domain be leased, not given away, that leaseholders pay royalties to the US Treasury on the minerals extracted, and that the land be reclaimed at the mine operators' expense when mining operations cease.

☐ Congress should repeal all special tax advantages now enjoyed by the extractive industries since these indirect subsidies keep prices artificially low and consumption artificially high.

☐ The President and other opinion-makers should rekindle pride in the traditional American virtue of thrift.

☐ Tax policies should reward the owners of commercial, industrial, and residential property who retrofit energy-efficient equipment such as insulation and openable windows.

☐ Tax policies should also reward owners who help minimize the need for new construction by maintaining existing properties in good repair or rehabilitating rundown properties.

☐ Throwaway containers, a symbol of our wasteful use of resources, should be banned nationally by act of Congress.

☐ The administration should investigate ways to discourage or prohibit excess packaging.

☐ All levels of government should oppose low-density housing developments and settlement patterns, which waste both energy and resources.

☐ Manufacturers of durable goods should be required to design them for easy maintenance and repair, and ultimately, for easy recycling.

☐ The Interstate Commerce Commission should disallow rail freight rates that discriminate against recycled materials.

More Thoughts on Natural Resources

IN A SUSTAINABLE WORLD, what we currently think of as waste will become our major source of high-quality materials for industry and commerce. One important benefit will be the diminishing contribution of rising raw material prices to inflation. Increasingly, virgin ores will merely supplement the existing material inventory. Recycling will become a central organizing principle for the entire economy.

In a society where recycling was the rule rather than the exception, the energy initially invested in refining aluminum might be properly perceived as an energy investment for the future. Only four percent as much energy is required to recycle aluminum as to refine bauxite ore.

Unsound agricultural or silvicultural practices can quickly turn a fertile tract into a disaster area. Because biological resources are renewable, there is a popular tendency to think of them as unlimited. Nothing could be further from the truth. If cultivated carefully, crops can be planted in perpetuity. But if the land is pushed past its carrying capacity or otherwise abused, permanent damage can be done.

There is no question that most consumer durables could be built to last much longer. Two basic strategies toward this end include designing products for longer wear, and designing them for easy and economical repair or remanufacture. In the latter case, it might be sensible to make even the product's exterior replaceable, so that the item could be kept looking relatively new.

To design a society that is truly thrifty in its use of materials, far more than techonological fixes will be required. At a minimum, products must be built to last and be designed in ways that simplify repairs and remanufacturing.

The renovation of dilapidated urban residences, currently inspired in part by rising gasoline costs for commuters, can be thought of as an important form of repairing obsolete existing products. Often these structures were constructed more soundly than many contemporary buildings. If during renovation they were also weatherized and—where possible—outfitted to take advantage of solar energy, the energy benefits would be substantial. No new materials need be constructed for the shell of the building, and a considerable amount of transportation fuel would be saved as well by former commuters.

Of the various "solutions" to the problem of materials scarcity, none is more important than waste reduction. Eliminating things that are unnecessary is better from every perspective than simply recycling them: waste reduction saves materials, reduces energy demands, eases environmental problems, and eliminates some of the clutter in contemporary life in the industrial world. There are already indications of trends in this direction. In many subcultures in Western societies, the ethic of conspicuous consumption is being replaced by one of conspicuous frugality.

Americans spend about $4 billion a year collecting and disposing of municipal solid wastes. In many cities, expenditures on waste management are second only to those on education. To the extent that this volume can be significantly reduced by active source separation and recycling programs, a credit should be received by the recycler for the money saved. Today, only about six percent of municipal solid waste is recovered in any form.

The public may be ahead of its leaders in recognizing that we are entering a new era in which thrift will be a prime asset, and that this development holds more promises than threats. Materialism has failed to provide something for which people hunger, and increasingly they are turning elsewhere. Voluntary simplicity—a central message of every major religious figure from Jesus to Lao-Tzu, from Buddha to Mohammed—is finally acquiring a modern following. And in that fact may lie one of the principal hopes of those who wish to build a sustainable world.

—DENIS HAYES

Rose Skytta

WE PRODUCE 57 million tons of hazardous waste each year. There are more than 750,000 generators of hazardous wastes, 10,000 transporters, and 30,000 treatment, storage, and disposal facilities. At least 90 percent of the hazardous wastes currently produced are disposed of improperly and unsafely. There are up to 50,000 uncontrolled closed and existing sites.

More than 60,000 chemicals are now in common use in this country; thousands more are registered each week. The adverse effects of mismanaged waste can reach us through direct contact, through the air we breathe, the food we eat and the water we drink. It is of critical importance that we keep waste from seeping into ground water. About half of the drinking water supply in this country is taken from groundwater. Twenty percent of the population drinks groundwater untreated.

The arduous, long-term task of dealing with hazardous waste is just beginning. Potentially, there are many things that can be done with hazardous waste besides burying them into a landfill that will meet the Resource Conservation and Recovery Act's requirements. Certain waste can be recycled and sent back for reuse. Other wastes can be used by others without processing. Wastes can be dealt with by incineration, chemical neutralization, separating or blending to yield a useable product or supplemental fuel for firing industrial furnaces, and "biological destruction", in which microorganisms consume the hazardous material and render it harmless.

Ideally, disposal should be the procedure of last resort. Since RCRA's regulations will make this procedure much much more expensive than it's ever been before, eventually the widespread use of other methods should be achieved. For a good while, however, there is no question that the procedure of last resort will be the procedure of first and greatest use. Moreover, proper disposal will be needed even years from now when we will have drastically altered our perceptions and practices with regard to wastes. There will still be a great many materials that are too low in value to recycle, too difficult to degrade or to inject into deep wells and too contaminated with nonflammable mate-

Much of the water supply that we go to such great trouble to purify—about half of it, in fact—is only used to carry off sewage from our toilets. Then we go to great further expense to repurify the same water. —NEIL SELDMAN

The world is threatened by growing population, but it is also, even perhaps to a greater extent, threatened by the exploding appetites of the already rich. —MAURICE STRONG

rials to incinerate.

Proper burial under RCRA will be a far cry from dumping. Serious attention to properly engineered landfills with liners, covers, gas generation techniques and monitoring operations will come into being. The chemical solidification of wastes, now used for only a very small percentage of hazardous materials will no doubt become more popular. And disposal of the wastes will not end the scrutiny process. Disposal site operators will have to monitor and maintain closed sites for many years to make sure that there is no migration into soil or drinking water supplies. There will be liability for each incident of damage that occurs while the site is operating. And money will have to be set aside to close and maintain inactive sites. Violators will be subjected to serious civil and criminal penalties. RCRA calls for truly drastic changes in the way we deal with wastes.

Yet the entire promise and purpose of the Act could be aborted by the strong and widespread public view that treatment and disposal facilities are all right, provided they are located on another planet or at least on another continent.

The solid waste management problem is even more illustrative of the need for sustained and successful public understanding, involvement and criticism than are other environmental issues which received national attention earlier. For decades now, the public has demanded air and water pollution control efforts and the public has paid directly or indirectly for the controls placed on automobiles, industries and municipalities. Even though few members of the public have been personally involved, almost all segments of the public have been represented by public interest groups of all varieties, which in this decade have influenced the development of legislation and its implementation. But air and water pollution problems have not presented anything quite comparable to the dilemma faced by government officials charged with hazardous waste control responsibilities. These public servants must somehow meet the public expectations for protection against a long neglected and insidious problem. Without a high degree of public understanding and participation at the grassroots level, hazardous waste control will not emerge from promise to reality.

—Thomas F. Williams

Elihu Blotnick

THE FORESTS OF AMERICA have been relentlessly plundered ever since Europeans invaded the western hemisphere 500 years ago. The destruction continues almost unabated today—despite the contrary impression that slick, nationally circulated tree-farm propaganda seeks to promote.

The timber industry's campaign to increase cutting on the national forests is evidence that the long-predicated wood famine has finally arrived. Even worse is the growing evidence that for the past 25 years, the Forest Service has been yielding to this pressure by greatly increasing the sale of timber and is now grossly mismanaging the national forests.

In looking at a well-managed forest, one will observe that it is fully stocked with trees of all sizes and ages. It will be obvious that the land is growing about all the timber it can and that most of the growth is valuable older trees. It will be evident that no erosion is taking place. Roads will be stable and attractive: they will look laid on the land rather than cut into it; the soil will be intact; the forest floor will be covered with leaf litter and other vegetative matter in various stages of growth or decomposition. This absorbent layer holds rain and melting snow while it soaks down into the ground through animal burrows, pores such as wormholes, channels dug by ants, and tracks left by decaying roots of past generations of vegetation. This forest becomes

a vast reservoir of water that gradually seeps down through the earth and comes out in springs—clear, cool water. This is how the forest stabilizes stream flow, and this is what is referred to when one reads of the forest protecting watersheds.

One also observes in the well-managed forest that there are frequent small openings stocked with herbs and browse—food close to shelter for wildlife. Finally, one observes that such a forest stays beautiful and will continue to serve our recreational needs as long as it is so managed.

Good forestry means limiting the cutting of timber to the amount that can be removed annually in perpetuity. Good forestry involves cutting selectively where it is consistent with the biological requirements of the species involved. In other cases, good forestry involves keeping the cuts no larger than necessary to meet the biological requirements of the species. Good forestry keeps the full range of naturally occurring species of plants and animals. And—very important—good forestry allows a generous proportion of trees to reach full maturity before being cut.

Forest Service statistics are gathered by sampling techniques, and the people who collect the data do not see the results of their work. The information is forwarded to a computer center, where it is processed and delivered to still others. Management decisions get further and further away from people actually familiar with the particular forest. Basic decisions of how much and which timber to sell are now based on rules and regulations emanating from Washington and depending on data-processing printouts.

The practicing forester has lost touch, and the forests are run by bureaucrats who are closer to industry than to the living forests they control.

With regard to private forest lands, we must recognize that good forestry is not a lucrative business. It never was and never will be; it takes longer than a man lives to grow high-quality timber, longer than anyone can wait for a return on investment. It takes from 75 to 150 years to maximize growth of timber in sizes useful for lumber and plywood. It takes twice that long to grow high-quality wood such as we use for fine furniture and musical instruments. The large spruce trees in Alaska, now being cut and shipped to Japan for piano sounding-boards, for guitars, and for exquisite Japanese residential panelling, are often as much as 1,000 years old.

Owners of timberland, confronted with the choice between a high income for themselves or an even higher income for their heirs, will nearly always choose the former. Few of us can afford to be philanthropists. Firms with large investments will always do what they must do to obtain the highest possible rate of return on

Drawing by Alice Broner

investment, and this decision means growing low-quality timber and cutting trees as soon as they become marketable instead of letting them grow to achieve high quality.

The forester, on the other hand, if he loves the forest and has not confused his role with that of the businessman, will resist the temptation to maximize income and will be more concerned with a wide range of environmental factors. He will want to restrict removal to those trees that can be spared for the sake of improving the health and vigor of the forest. He will want to keep trees growing until they reach their highest value, and he will recognize that maintaining a high inventory of marketable trees is an absolute necessity if the forest is to be managed for recreation, watershed, and wildlife, as well as for the forest industry's raw materials.

For these reasons we require a clear separation of responsibility between the forester and the businessman. The forester alone should have responsibility for the forest. It is quite properly the role of the businessman to make what profit he can from the timber the forester makes available. But the businessman should not be able to set policy or production goals for the forester. Otherwise, forestry cannot be properly practiced.

A satisfactory program for state regulation of forestry on private lands consists essentially of the following:

A law requiring that foresters be licensed and that it be unlawful to practice without a license. The licensing board should comprise people from a cross-section of fields related to managing wild lands. These include aquatic biology, entomology, forest ecology, geology, hydrology, mycology, ornithology, plant and animal ecology, pathology, soil science, and wildlife biology.

There must be no exemptions for foresters who are employed by lumber companies; corporations are frequently the worst offenders.

There should be a sustained-yield law. The best way to achieve this goal is to require states to identify all commercial forest lands and require that all owners file timber-management plans prepared by a licensed forester, with the state division of forestry. A sustained-yield law should include the provisions I have characterized as good forestry: actually practicing sustained-yield, selection management, long rotations, and maximizing diversity of species. A sustained-yield law should establish the precautions necessary to protect the soil from accelerated erosion and leaching of nutrients. These precautions should include standards for design and construction of logging roads, skid trails and landings, and regulation of the kind and size of logging equipment.

Standing timber should be exempt from *ad valorem*

taxes, except for timber cut and removed during the tax year. It is neither fair nor reasonable to require good forest practices on private land unless property taxes on forest land are consistent with those on other properties providing similar net income.

Inheritance and gift taxes should be modified to allow a family to pass a small forest from generation to generation without forcing the family to liquidate immature and unmerchantable timber.

The citizen's right to sue must be preserved. Fifty years of experience with regulatory agencies teaches us that they tend to serve the industries they are intended to regulate, unless they are made accountable by the courts. This is the very essence of our check-and-balance system.

Finally, state laws should emphasize enforcement of water-quality standards for streams originating in or flowing through lands on which logging has occurred. Standards should specify that the water not contain more than normal amounts of suspended matter and nutrients; streams should be monitored regularly to assure that the standards have been met.

—Gordon Robinson

THE MOST STRIKING thing about modern industry is that it requires so much and accomplishes so little. Modern industry seems to be inefficient to a degree that surpasses one's ordinary powers of imagination. Its inefficiency therefore remains unnoticed.

Industrially, the most advanced country today is undoubtedly the United States of America. With a population of about 207 million, it contains 5.6 per cent of mankind; with only about fifty-seven people per square mile—as against a world average of over seventy—and being situated wholly within the northern temperate zone, it ranks as one of the great sparsely populated areas of the world.

It cannot be said, therefore, that—relatively speaking—the United States is disadvantaged by having too many people and too little space.

Nor could it be said the the territory of the United States was poorly endowed with natural resources. On the contrary, in all human history no large territory has ever been opened up which has more excellent and wonderful resources, and, although much has been exploited and ruined since, this still remains true today.

All the same, the industrial system of the United States cannot subsist on internal resources alone and has therefore had to extend its tentacles right around the globe to secure its raw material supplies. For the 5.6 per cent of the world population which live in the United States require something of the order of forty per cent of the world's primary resources to keep going.

An industrial system which uses forty percent of the world's primary resources to supply less than six percent of the world's population could be called efficient only if it obtained strikingly successful results in terms of human happiness, well-being, culture, peace, and harmony. I do not need to dwell on the fact that the American system fails to do this, or that there are not the slightest prospects that it could do so *if only* it achieved a higher rate of growth of production, associated, as it must be, with an even greater call upon the world's finite resources.

Modern economics does not distinguish between renewable and non-renewable materials, as its very method is to equalize and quantify everything by means of a money price. Thus, taking various alternative fuels, like coal, oil, wood, or water-power: the only difference between them recognised by modern economics is relative cost per equivalent unit. The cheapest is automatically the one to be preferred, as to do otherwise would be irrational and 'uneconomic'. From a Buddhist point of view, of course, this will not do; the essential difference between non-renewable fuels like coal and oil on the one hand and renewable fuels like wood and water-power on the other cannot be simply overlooked. Non-renewable goods must be used only if they are indispensable, and then only with the greatest care and the most meticulous concern for conservation. To use them heedlessly or extravagantly is an act of violence, and while complete non-violence may not be attainable on this earth, there is nonetheless an ineluctable duty on man to aim at the ideal of non-violence in all he does.

To get to the crux of the matter, we do well to ask why it is that all these terms—pollution, environment, ecology, etc.—have *so suddenly* come into prominence. After all, we have had an industrial system for quite some time, yet only five or ten years ago these words were virtually unknown. Is this a sudden fad, a silly fashion, or perhaps a sudden failure of nerve?

The explanation is not difficult to find. As with fossil fuels, we have indeed been living on the capital of living nature for some time, but at a fairly modest rate. It is only since the end of World War II that we have succeeded in increasing this rate to alarming proportions. In comparison with what is going on now and what has been going on, progressively, during the last quarter of a century, all the industrial activities of mankind up to, and including, World War II are as nothing. The next four or five years are likely to see more industrial production, taking the world as a whole, than all of mankind accomplished up to 1945. In other words, quite recently—so recently that most of us have hardly yet become conscious of it—there has been a unique quantitative jump in industrial production.

The oil producing countries, meanwhile, are beginning to realise that money alone cannot build new sources of livelihood for their populations. To build them needs, in addition to money, immense efforts and a great deal of time. Oil is a 'wasting asset', and the faster it is allowed to waste, the shorter is the time available for the development of a new basis of economic existence. The conclusions are obvious: it is in the real longer-term interest of *both* the oil exporting *and* the oil importing countries that the 'lifespan' of oil should be prolonged as much as possible. The former need time to develop alternative sources of livelihood and the latter need time to adjust their oil-dependent economies to a situation—which is absolutely certain to arise within the lifetime of most of the people living today—when oil will be scarce and very dear. The greatest danger to both is a continuation of rapid growth in oil production and consumption throughout the world. Catastrophic developments on the oil front could be avoided only if the *basic harmony of the long-term interests of both groups of countries* came to be fully realised and concerted action were taken to stabilise and gradually reduce the annual flow of oil into consumption.
—E.F. Schumacher

SUDDENLY THE MESSAGE has come across loud and clear: We are living beyond our means. As a people we have developed a life-style that is draining the earth of its priceless and irreplaceable resources without regard for the future of our children and people all around the world.

For far too long Americans regarded ecologists—the scientists who study the relationships between living beings and the environment—as just another breed of prophets of doom. Or they treated ecologists' dire predictions as expressions of exaggerated concern by small groups of stubborn people who cared chiefly about wilderness areas and set their love for natural beauty and for lost, idyllic ways of living above the reasonable necessities of our modern, progressive, industrialized world. But now, unexpectedly, we have discovered that it is the ecologists who have been facing the realities—the very hard realities of where the wanton and irresponsible use of natural resources in this country has been taking us.

And instead of receiving clarification from our government as to what resources we have and what we can look forward to, we learned with astonishment that our officials were dependent on industry for information about available reserves, information that industry too often treated as a trade secret. Assurances given in one week were taken back the next week, and regulations intended to protect turned out to be based on the vaguest assumptions about the situation. We have had a babel of contending voices, a proliferation of rumors that distract us from the problems that must be met, assertions refuted by further assertions and arguments instead of answers.

All this has been brought home to us by the energy crisis. . . .

Whatever triggered the energy crisis, we can now plainly see the larger, underlying cause. What has been draining our resources, continually raising our demands for more energy, polluting the earth and the air and the water is what we ourselves have been doing every day as a matter of course. The basic trouble is the way our everyday life is organized, the way each family lives.

Of course no one family causes an exorbitant drain on our resources. But when all the simple, convenient and for the most part, pleasant things we have and use and discard, are multiplied by many millions of users—and by the hundreds of millions more who are longing to become users—it becomes devastatingly clear how the strain on every kind of resource has come about. And it should be clear also that no merely palliative measures, no attempt on our part to become independent of the rest of the world, will solve the problems we face.

It is the life-style of the country—the kind of life each family aspires to and takes for granted as good and desirable—that has placed this incredible burden on the world and has brought us—and all other people who share our aspirations—into crisis.

This, then, is the challenge: how to change our life-style.

To meet the challenge we shall need a very widespread understanding of the real nature of the crisis—a crisis that is no passing inconvenience; no mere by-product of the oil-producing countries using the only weapons they have to make themselves heard; no figment of environmentalists' imagined fears; and no by-product of any presently existing system of government, whether free-enterprise, socialist or communist. Our life-style is the outcome of the inventions made during the last 400 years as we have searched for quicker, easier, more mechanized ways of doing things for ever-growing, more demanding populations. It is the outcome of an implicit belief in the existence of unlimited and unfailing resources on our one small planet and an explicit belief that human beings have the right to exploit every kind of resource as they can and will.

Now we must come to terms with reality. We must develop a life-style based on an understanding that the earth's resources are limited and that use of what we

Photo by Roger Lubin, Jeroboam, Inc.

have must be combined with conservation. A new life-style also can flow directly from the efforts of science and the capabilities of advanced technology. But fundamentally success will depend on an overriding commitment on the part of every adult and on the willingness of families to educate their children to have very different expectations about a good life.

What does all this mean for individuals and families?

As I see it, it means above all that men and women must inform themselves and must demand to be informed. As individuals, as readers of the press, as viewers of television, as members of every kind of organization, as tenants and homeowners, as producers and consumers, as members of communities, as voters in elections at every level of government, we must firmly demand to be given information—demand that governments obtain and pass on to us, as citizens, enough factual information so that we can intelligently judge national policy and act wisely in making local decisions.

The immediate energy crisis should be enough to alert us to this most pressing of all our needs. The information about our resources that is necessary if we are to make viable plans is not wholly available to us, and no legislation now exists that would ensure its availability. Our response could be simply pessimism, confusion and an attitude of each-man-for-himself. But I do not believe Americans would tolerate such an outcome. Nevertheless, we shall get the kinds of information we need—and the kinds of leadership that can provide firm information—only as we make demands and make our demands heard.

—Margaret Mead

Rondal Partridge

Decentralization:

Making Small Places Work Again

Americans should all be able to live and earn their livelihoods in the kinds of environment they prefer, from open country to central cities. In our early history, most work opportunities were agricultural or agriculture-related. People who would have preferred city life stayed on the land instead because cities were dominated by a social elite and because employment opportunities in the city-towns of the day were limited. With the rise of manufacturing and access to mobile sources of power, cities mushroomed as the focal points of industrial activity, and with the mechanization of agriculture, machines displaced more and more farm workers who had no choice but to go where the industrial jobs were. From a nation that was almost entirely rural, we became a nation whose people are nearly three-fourths city dwellers. Many of these people prefer city life; for them, we need only make our cities more livable. But many city dwellers would prefer life in small towns or the countryside; for them, we need to create non-urban residential and employment options. We need to decentralize—not totally, but enough to achieve balance. The decentralist impulse will be reinforced as the energy-intensiveness of large-scale US mechanized agriculture becomes insupportable and as the depletion of nonrenewable natural resources causes the contraction of heavy manufacturing. The choice is not between centralization and decentralization; the choice is between intelligently planned decentralization and random decentralization under the compulsion of inexorable social change.

Decentralization

ANNE and CLAY DENMAN

AMERICA IN THE 1980s continues to be characterized by centralization of population and of power, both economic and political, and the uneven distribution of human and environmental features that contribute to the quality of life.

The most tangible expression of our centralized society is the geographic distribution of our population. In 1970, 73 percent of the American population lived in metropolitan areas; the remaining 27 percent were classified as "rural." The trend of population movement to the cities, the exodus from farms and small towns, the decline of family farms, have become clichés of American life in the last hundred years. Indications that a population reversal might be under way—back to Appalachia, the Ozarks, and other rural and small town areas—have been analyzed with caution, awaiting the 1980 census results.

Most Americans accept the presumed economies of scale associated with centralization and specialization. Making large quantities of widgets permits cheaper widgets; they are also likely to be standardized and of less practical use. We may be given the illusion of variety by polka dots, stripes, sugar-coating, and slick advertising.

The degree of population concentration in urban areas is frequently claimed to be the underlying factor that makes possible the extraordinary character of our society. Economic opportunities, together with industrial complexes, are concentrated in cities; social and cultural activities are regarded as an urban phenomenon; public transportation systems, which serve large centers at minimal cost, serve rural areas and small towns hardly at all.

Production of durable consumer goods and even food is being increasingly automated, certified, mechanized, and centralized before being shipped back to local retailers in forms so standardized that a "fresh" tomato in Possum Gap's chain grocery store may have the same shape and water content as one in Los Angeles, thousands of miles away. Utility companies pull huge blocks of power thousands of miles to urban areas. Television and radio broadcast from urban centers, and when local stations are given time for local programming, they lack the resources to use it; instead, they rely on canned re-runs of network videotapes. In the end, true community withers on the vine.

Is it myth, or fact, that only a few hands are pulling the strings that make us dance our daily rounds? We have been governed by the idea that the most worthwhile activities take place in large cities; we have accepted the assumption that the best talent of a small community will leave it, and that those who stay are by definition second-rate; and we so lack confidence in ourselves that we believe good ideas come only from experts and from the milieu of central cities. These social clichés have led to a self-fulfilling prophecy of community powerlessness that succumbs to outside control.

Centralization has an apparently inexorable effect: we deplore its consequences, and yet we feel powerless to fight it. But like many monolithic problems, it is less formidable when broken into parts. We need to be concerned less with what the system does to us and concerned more with ways we can restructure our lives as individuals within local communities.

What kinds of alternatives to our present centralization are we aiming for?

Some degree of population decentralization is a basic necessity. Too many people are living in urban settlements. Decentralization of people must also involve decentralization of the economic system that their jobs depend on. A revitalized agricultural economy, the regional dispersion of industrial activity, and a revitalization of small-scale business and community-oriented craftsmanship are three necessary and related developments.

Technological innovations can make possible greater self-sufficiency for individuals and for human settlements of all kinds. New developments in agricultural and industrial technology and in the utilization of energy sources have thus far not been explored with the aim of decentralization; they have served centralization alone. A decentralized society, embodying true alternative lifestyles, would involve revitalized community bonds and would harness communication

Decentralization is not merely a logistical or physical solution to concentration and gigantism. Indeed, it is above all a certain sensibility, a way in which people view each other and the natural world. At the very heart of this sensibility is the concept of human scale.
—MURRAY BOOKCHIN

technologies to replace needless physical mobility. A less restlessly mobile society could be well served by better communications instead of motion.

Ultimately, we need to work for the decentralization of economic and political decision-making power. We should consciously seek greater control over our own futures and our own communities. Concentrations of power and economic monopolies or near-monopolies are antithetical to decentralization, whether they affect our television fare, our postal service, our hamburgers and breakfast cereals, or the construction of our houses.

Decentralization Means Variety

A decentralized future includes not merely the revitalization of small communities and rural areas, but also the creation of true diversity—real choice among types of human settlement with the advantages of each type maximized. The quality of life features that have been concentrated in one type of settlement or another should be dispersed among all types. It is commonly recognized, for instance, that open space should not be a unique feature of rural areas but should be introduced into other forms of settlement, and equally, that social and cultural events of high quality should not be an exclusive prerogative of urban centers.

Decentralization, then, should involve the more even distribution of desirable kinds of human activity. Aspects of different settlement forms that are intrinsic to settlements by virtue of their size need to be distinguished from other aspects that are merely historically associated with settlements of a certain size. Given modern transportation and communication potentials, for example, there is nothing to prevent residents of small towns from having access to high quality artistic and musical events. Programs like the 19th century Chautauqua circuit could bring artists, lecturers, and musicians directly to small town people; and television can bring international artists into small town living rooms.

In part, we need to "decentralize" our own thinking patterns to accommodate the acceptance of greater variety. No one could hope to—or would wish to—reduce the US landscape to homogeneity through uniform distribution of population. But we need to recognize the varied histories, sizes, and functions of our diverse communities, and to design policies that loosen the bonds of overcentralization. Significantly, most current classifications continue to lump all varieties of settlement under either "urban" or "rural." But a desirable diversity of settlement types might be visualized in terms of ten settlement categories.

1) *Megalopolis.* This represents dense population concentrations of great size, with economic and cultural variety, multiple centers, and area-wide political structures. It is questionable whether such dense and immense concentrations provide significant advantages to their residents, overall, but such settlement forms are clearly developing.

2) *Cities.* Characterized by large population concentrations, cities have diverse economic bases and a diversity of lifestyles. While they benefit from some economies of scale, they suffer from some diseconomies. Evidence suggests that cities historically do not "replicate" themselves, but rather draw excess population from other areas. Cities grew as trade centers, manufacturing centers, and as centers of financial concentration.

3) *Suburbs.* These have functioned principally as residential centers, although service facilities and "clean" industries have recently moved in. The classic suburb is highly dependent on the city, however, for the financial resources that make possible its comparatively low population density.

4) *Micro-cities.* These settlements lie between large cities and small towns in size, in self-sufficiency and function, and in sense of community. They may serve as significant trade centers and support centers for surrounding settlements.

These four settlement types might all be called urban. Forms that are usually encompassed within the catch-all category of rural include a similar variety. Agricultural engineer G. B. Gunlogson is one of a number of people who have promoted the use of "countryside" as a phrase descriptive of a variety of dispersed settlement patterns. Countryside blends various economic functions that arise more out of local community requirements than out of national or outsiders' needs. A significant portion of our countryside today is devoted to the service of people who are merely passing through on highways; in a decentralized society, local facilities would emphasize the service

Robin Freeman

of local needs.

5) *Small towns.* Most people consider a small town to be any community under 25,000 in population and over perhaps 100. In our work with the Small Towns Institute, we have preferred to use a different criterion: the existence of a *sense of community.* While a sense of community is possible within larger settlements—in city neighborhoods, for example—it is certainly harder to achieve. In the past, many small towns had a high degree of economic self-sufficiency and political autonomy, both of which contributed to a distinct sense of community. Small towns most often grew as service centers for agricultural areas, or grew as places where nearby natural resources were processed.

6) *Dispersed cities.* Geographer John Fraser Hart has suggested that neighboring small towns sometimes function together as a dispersed city. Some specialization among towns creates the overall diversity of economic and population structure characteristic of a city.

7) *Farms.* Use of the land as a productive resource is the basic feature of farming life. Farms are thus residential units associated with the use of the land for agriculture or animal husbandry.

8) *Non-farm rural settlement.* Uses of land by non-farm populations are primarily residential. Non-farm residents may be farm laborers or work in nearby towns and cities.

9) *Hamlets.* We've used this term to refer to a form of settlement that has hardly existed in the US but is common in parts of Europe. Clusters of three or more houses are identified as a village. Larger hamlets may have a café, a small food store, a school, or a dry goods shop. Their past function was as small-scale, concentrated residential areas for farmers and rural craftsmen.

10) *Communal groups.* The defining characteristics of communal groups, which exist as microcosms within rural areas and even within cities, are primarily ideological. Concepts of economic and political self-sufficiency and limitations on settlement size are frequently components of the communal ideology.

11) *Non-settled land.* All thinking people recognize the necessity of closing some portions of our land area to human settlement. Decentralization does not imply that we should end up with the same number of people living on each square mile of the US; instead, decentralization policies must be accompanied by a clear commitment to preserve portions of our landscape from settlement.

Centralization has been reflected in population patterns, economic and political power, and the uneven distribution of factors enhancing the quality of life. Generally speaking, decentralization must involve less concentration in and dependency on megalopolises, cities, and suburbs.

In order to achieve an orderly process of decentralization in the US—of population and of political, economic, and social activities—there must be sweeping changes in the way we apply laws on everything from taxation to environmental protection.

Current laws and administrative regulations favor a continued concentration of power in corporate monopolies, financial institutions, and government bureaucracies. Recent emigration from cities and repopulation of "rural" areas will not necessarily lead to functional communities. We still have many laws that assure the transfer of monopoly economics to the countryside. Administrative regulations and propaganda force rural and small town dwellers to create urban-scale problems so that urban bureaucrats will move in with urban solutions.

Public Policy for Decentralization

To meet the challenge of functional decentralization, we must enact federal and state programs that make monopoly unprofitable and that promote the vitality of individual, group, and community activities. The following six-point program suggests changes that would favor decentralization both of political power and of population.

1. Land Reform

In America, the problem is not only to get land into the hands of individuals who will use it productively in a community context, but also to get it *out* of the hands of monopolies (including government monopolies) without destroying the economic structure that will make individual land ownership possible.

The 160-acre limitation law for irrigated land should be strictly enforced. Legal provisions should be made to allow local planning agencies to enforce other land limitation laws appropriate to regional conditions. For example, 640 acres per person (one section) might be an appropriate limitation in Iowa, while 22,040 acres (one township) might be applicable in parts of Texas. Developers might be limited to speculation on only 160 acres in any one township, thus preventing a single individual or corporation from monopolizing land in areas under development pressure. Railroads that are no longer fulfilling the responsibilities assumed under their original land grants should have the grants revoked; the land returned to public ownership should be opened for or withdrawn from settlement, as appropriate.

With the exception of lands genuinely needed for public purposes, such as wilderness, recreation areas, and wildlife preserves, the vast government-owned lands managed by the Bureau of Land Management and the US Forest Service should be opened for homesteading and subsistence farming. Much of this land is now leased to mining companies, corporate farms, and other large corporations, yielding little benefit to the public.

Mineral rights held separately from the land should be taxed to the owners of such rights. Government-held mineral rights should be placed in the hands of farmers and homesteaders so the inroads of stripmining can be checked by those who live in the community.

2. Financing for a Small Scale

Land reform would make more land available and benefit both existing farmers and future homesteaders by reducing land prices. A central problem would remain: how to get land ownership into the hands of the young, the alienated, the urban poor, and the rural sharecropper.

Much could be done by revitalizing the old homestead laws and enforcing them better. Government could start with its own lands, avoiding the costs of compensation that would be necessary when new forms of land limitation are applied to private lands.

Low-interest loans could be made available to poor people to purchase land from owners of excess acres, such as those in California's Central Valley. Loans at minimal interest would be cheaper than welfare costs, not to mention the costs of relieving urban blight and other related problems. Similar financing could be made available to enable young people to start very small businesses (a natural foods store, for example) or to buy existing businesses in small towns.

3. Restrictive Laws

A great deterrent to people seeking self-sufficiency with small-scale enterprises are the restrictive laws and regulations that are gradually strangling things of human scale in our society. National and state health and safety codes, for example, tend to dictate the specific technology that can be used to achieve health and safety goals. Most of these regulations merely have the effect of promoting specific products and have little to do with health or safety. Some communities ban composting, prohibit the conduct of small businesses in homes (even if they meet zoning requirements), enforce expensive building codes that are imposed on some buildings and not others. One man in Washington State was arrested for building a log cabin because it was not designed by an architect; another was fined for having too many fire extinguishers. In a typical case, fire codes required a building owner to install a fire escape that safety codes condemned as a safety hazard.

Even environmental laws are administered in ecologically unsound ways. Water pollution is encouraged because health codes don't allow composting toilets that produce usable fertilizer; small steam-operated lumber mills are closed down for polluting the air while big firms with tall stacks are permitted to "dilute" their smoke in the upper atmosphere, producing acid rains; farmers are fined for having dusty roads in their fields and are forced to spray oil on otherwise productive soil. To be good, environmental laws must be ecologically sound.

4. Technology and Quality

The decentralization process must take account of the need to bring technology into harmony with people. This means we must encourage technological skills that begin with craftsmanship and culminate in quality.

Centralization robs individuals of diversity, transferring many of their roles to specialists. The process is manifest in gadgetry that we are taught to use but not to understand. As with malfunction lights on auto dashboards, we are not permitted to know that something needs attention until it is too late. With a home appliance that's "sealed for life," there's no way for consumers to extend that life by providing needed maintenance and repair.

Since most people have only a shadow of the knowledge needed for a more self-sufficient life today, programs in schools and colleges need to be expanded for those who want to participate more fully in the decentralization process. Courses on Being a Good Consumer and How to Shop for the Best Buys should be replaced, or at least supplemented, by practical courses in carpentry, mechanics (including foundry work and blacksmithing), ceramic technologies, and horticulture. These courses should focus on such self-sufficient and community-oriented skills as small-scale (including by-hand) milling of lumber; designing efficient small-scale mechanical technologies, and making castings and forgings; growing and preserving food.

5. Research on Appropriate Technology

While it is obvious that most Americans have been alienated from the technology of our society, a major factor in this situation has been the public funds poured into the development of large-scale technologies rather than into more efficient small-scale ones. In agriculture, education, transportation, and other fields, research has led to larger scale technologies and increasingly centralized management.

For more than 70 years, agricultural colleges have focused on development of foods that would conform to mechanized harvesting techniques while neglecting research on plants that would produce yields high in quality and volume on small plots of land. In transportation, research favors the increased profitability of

Elihu Blotnick

vehicle sales rather than more efficient use of fuel and land devoted to transportation facilities. This results in the concentration of technology, marketing, financial capabilities, and even land resources in the hands of monopoly businesses and federal agencies.

Tax structures should favor products manufactured locally and marketed to local consumers. This proposal could be implemented for some products by a tax based on the distance between finished products and their markets. Research funds in agriculture should be increasingly allocated to small groups of individuals working on energy-efficient technologies rather than production "efficiencies."

6. Regionally Oriented Industry

With the development of small-scale technologies appropriate to local ecological conditions, it would be more efficient (as well as profitable) to decentralize industry. Federal and state governments should consider tax incentives for decentralized industries. The "distance tax" would be one example. Decentralization would result in more local employment opportunities, the stimulation of local investment in industry, and a wide diversity of production facilities. A decentralized

The noncommercial urban area comprises about 4.5 percent of all US land. Assuming that the average present development can be represented by a "mixed sprawl" condition, then the switch from current urban land use to one of a high-density planned nature would free about 50 million acres of urban land. This land could be used to slowly decentralize and relocate some of the nation's industrial facilities, thus allowing for shorter trips to work. Such land could also be used to develop community recreation areas, thereby reducing recreational travel needs while focusing individual concern on local environmental quality.
—BRUCE HANNON

industry could ride out crises that would shut down concentrated businesses. Existing conglomerate industry would find it more profitable to disperse its plants as more and more workers showed a preference for countryside environments.

To design public policies working toward decentralization presents something of a paradox in our over-centralized age. We have tended to let centralized government do more for us, rather than less. Many of our policy suggestions are in accordance with an emphasis on the use of existing centralized systems to achieve a decentralized society, but individuals must work hard at the local level for decentralization. The following principles would aid decentralization; they are the basis on which actions in your town, city, or region may be built.

1. See that governments at all levels make strong commitments to decentralization.
2. Where goals can be accomplished locally, make a strong effort to do so with local personnel, funding, and authorization.
3. When you need outside expertise or monetary help, ask for the minimum possible amounts; don't embark on any project without some local matching effort.
4. Make sure legislative requirements allow for variations of scale; don't put up with a million-dollar water treatment plant for your town of 200 people.
5. Seek diverse, innovative solutions to local problems; let solutions grow out of the nature of your community, its particular situation and skills; find out yourself how other towns are coping; don't rely on overworked officials to investigate innovative techniques.
6. Emphasize the uniqueness of your local community through promoting preservation of community character and "sense of place." A community that has preserved parts of its architectural and social

past will be a more effective stimulus to decentralization than a community that represents the Homogenized Franchise ethic.
7. Don't be afraid to force centralized authority to conform to your local requirements instead of the other way around; some towns and cities have successfully pressured national franchises into conformity with local building styles rather than passively accepting standardized design and 50-foot-high signs.
8. Support decentralized institutions in your community; sell to, or buy from, the local farmers' market; patronize businesses that represent local enterprise.

If centralization in our society has come about because of governmental and industrial policies that profit from it, there is no assurance that a short-term political reversal is going to keep massification from happening again. Worldwide, the centralist process has become a part of governments ranging from dictatorial to democratic, from communist to capitalist.

We can work for new legislation as suggested in this chapter, but we must also implement the decentralist society by building practical communities in a decentralist pattern.

The most essential element of decentralization is to get the ownership or control of national resources—the land, minerals, energy, agriculture, finance, everything—into as many hands as possible. Government ownership obviously doesn't bring maximum benefits to the people. Governments already own minerals and land rights, but much of this is leased to giant conglomerates while small farmers (and smaller corporations) are frozen out. Eliminating individuals from economic participation has been a major element of many government programs, from urban renewal to agricultural research.

Groups of people can buy large land holdings and

benefit from economies of scale to become individual owners or hold land in a trust. Eventually, decentralists should acquire scattered ownerships within 25 miles or so to prevent large corporations from moving in on decentralized communities and stimulating tax increases.

Decentralist communities have one advantage over corporate landholders: people can vote, and they can eventually control local government for the benefit of the community and local enterprise.

Economic practices are extremely important in establishing a stable society. Using low-energy technologies, recycling wastes in the local ecosystem, using appropriate "soft" technologies to supplement labor-intensive productivity, a small community can produce food, goods, and services at only a fraction of the costs of food and some other commodities that are produced nationally and transported long distances. Large companies cannot compete with farmers' markets or small local industries—provided that local goods are marketed only to the community and not leaked to outside consumers, thereby exceeding the ecosystem's capacity to provide basic resources. Export your ideas and designs, and educate people who will replicate the decentralist process in their own communities, but don't try to expand production beyond the locality's capacity to support the system.

An essential element of decentralization policy is the maintenance of a steady population. Centralization has come about partly because local citizens produce more than enough children to provide continuity to the next generation. This has been happening for hundreds of years in most of the world's peasant and agricultural societies. Excess children end up in cities where the amount of people overwhelms the amount of useful work to be done. Non-producers gradually build up employment hierarchies of centralist jobs: inspectors, bureaucrats, investigators, record-keepers, government agents—occupations that are either unnecessary or only marginally useful in a true community.

We need to consciously reduce our dependence on centralized federal programs, and the federal government should disburse its project funding in smaller amounts, with reasonable emphasis on demonstration of local commitment through matching funds or community effort. In this way, we residents of this broad nation will again realize our ultimate responsibility for the conditions of our own communities. We will become less beholden to centralized bureaucracies

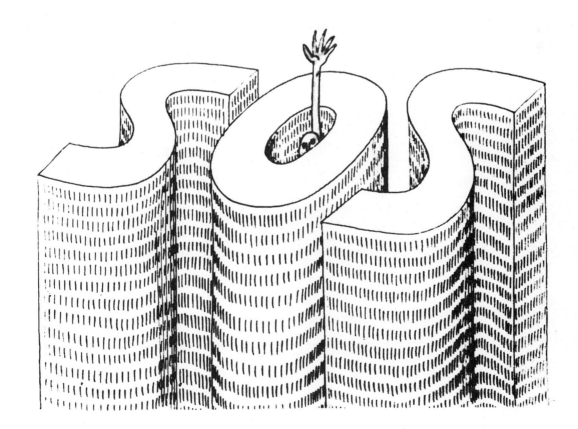

©*Interpress Film—"Attention"*

Bill Owen/Jeroboam, Inc.

that can tell us how wide our streets must be, or how large our sewage treatment plants should loom.

Many recent surveys indicate that Americans are eager to move from large cities to small towns and rural areas, lacking only the assurance of economic opportunity. Public consciousness is increasingly in tune with small-scale, diverse solutions. What sorts of individuals and institutions would experience difficulties in a decentralized society? There seems little doubt that large cities and their residents would suffer most from a decentralization movement. The physical and social facilities representing our current over-investment in urban areas will not be easily wound down.

The Athens of Alcibiades, the Philadelphia of the Founding Fathers, were "big cities" with their fifty thousand inhabitants. But we shall have 273 cities of over a million people by 1985. Perhaps as many as seventeen will exceed the ten million mark.

— BARBARA WARD

The danger is that the wealthy may be the only ones who can afford to decentralize, and the poor will remain. Continued investment in urban areas will surely be necessary to ease the transition to smaller population concentrations, and legislation favoring economic decentralization *must* ensure opportunities for the urban poor. Programs favoring the reuse and recycling of physical facilities in urban areas through conservation and preservation rather than extensive building programs are also a vital strategy. More urban open space can be a result of less severe population pressures. One long-range result of decentralization is sure to be more livable cities as well as more vital small towns and rural areas.

A centralized society not only requires institutions that hold centralized power, it also requires citizens who accede to the demands of that power. There are indications that Americans are becoming wary of centralization. We all know people who are accepting reduced economic rewards but taking advantage of simple opportunities on a small scale and prizing quality of life and a sense of community as parts of the pay-off. Decentralization won't succeed without firm individual and community commitment to the benefits of small-scale as well as large-scale institutions.

Recommended Actions

☐ The President should commit himself to decentralist policies, as should governors, county officials, mayors, neighborhood leaders, heads of families, and individuals.

☐ Lawmakers at all levels should amend or repeal laws that have the effect of encouraging the concentration of population, political influence, or economic power.

☐ Federal homestead laws should be reenacted with tighter enforcement provisions, and public land unsuited to such public purposes as recreation or wildlife preservation should be opened to homesteading and subsistence farming.

☐ Anti-monopoly laws should be vigorously enforced.

☐ Health, safety, and building codes, and similar administrative regulations, should be amended to eliminate arbitrary stifling of individual initiative.

☐ Schools, colleges, and institutions offering adult education should develop courses promoting individual self-sufficiency such as carpentry, organic gardening, handicrafts, accounting for the small shopkeeper, and elementary mechanics.

☐ Incentives to decentralize (and *dis*incentives to centralize) should be built into the tax structure.

☐ Low-interest government loans should be offered to people wishing to buy land or small businesses in small towns.

☐ The law limiting to 160 acres the amount of land irrigated by federal waterworks that can be owned by one landholder should be retained and rigorously enforced; and as the law provides, holders of excess acreage should be required to sell it at pre-irrigation prices.

☐ Federal research-and-development funding should be diverted from "high" technology (especially nuclear fission and fusion) to "appropriate" or "intermediate" technology that is applicable everywhere.

☐ Railroads still holding original land grants should be required either to sell the land and apply the proceeds to the improvement of rail service or to cede such lands back to the federal government; where appropriate, land returned to public ownership should be open to homesteading.

☐ Municipal officials should be encouraged to study ways in which decentralization can be made to work to the advantage of cities and not to their disadvantage.

☐ The urban poor and rural sharecroppers should have highest priority in the homesteading and low-cost loan programs.

☐ Federal project funding should be based increasingly on the principle of providing small amounts of "seed money" to generate local activity. When communities have demonstrated their ability to raise local matching funds, projects may be supported with further funds—but always on a relatively small scale.

More Thoughts on Decentralization

THE KEY TO MEETING basic human needs is the participation of individuals and communities in local problem solving. Some of the most important achievements in providing food, upgrading housing, improving human health, and tapping new energy sources will come not through highly centralized national and international efforts but through people doing more to help themselves. When those most affected by a problem assume the primary responsibility for solving it, they gain the understanding and skill to deal with the broader political and economic issues of their society.

Commercially constructed private homes are beyond the economic reach of more and more people. Public housing has proven too expensive for the government that builds it and often unlivable for the poor who rent it. So where will new housing come from? It may arise from the desire of both rich and poor all over the world to own their own homes, even if they have to build them with their own hands.

Whether judged by yield per acre or by the cost of production, small farms compare favorably with large farms on all continents. Most of the economies of scale associated with size can be achieved on units small enough to be farmed by a family. Numerous studies have borne this out. A 1970 survey for the United States Agency for International Development (AID) showed that small farms in India, Japan, Taiwan, the Philippines, Mexico, Brazil, Colombia, and Guatemala had higher productivity per acre than large farms. A similar study of 40 countries undertaken by the World Bank indicated that small holdings and relatively equitable land distribution were associated with an increase in output per hectare.

An optimal food strategy will obviously include some large-scale farming. But one key element in future food policy must be more production by small farmers and gardeners. Such local food production is an important aspect of the success of Chinese agricultural and nutritional policy. Eighty percent of the vegetables consumed in each Chinese city are grown within ten kilometers of that urban area. Massachusetts, in the United States, imports 85 percent of its food, a tenth of it from 3,000 miles away in California. The contrast could hardly be more striking.

Through small-scale production, local distribution networks, and the involvement of more people in food-growing, the vulnerability of communities to price rises and food shortages can be reduced. In a world where the slack appears to have gone out of the food system, reorganizing production in this manner can help create a margin of safety, a buffer against malnutrition and rising food costs.

—Bruce Stokes

MANY PROBLEMS of the man-made environment are problems of size. Getting out of a city of 100,000 people is relatively easy, even without an automobile; to get beyond the edge of a city of three million, even with an auto, takes a major effort. Air pollution in a city would be less of a problem if it were dispersed over a large area or if cars were restricted in numbers or number of miles travelled—the seriousness of the problem is a function of city size. The magnitude of the problem of solid-waste disposal more than doubles with a doubling in the size of a city, not because the volume of waste more than doubles, but because all of it must be hauled farther for disposal. Economies can result from small scale as well as large.

Today's pattern of extremely high and extremely low densities would, in our scenario, evolve into a pattern of medium-size cities with moderate densities, separated not by suburban sprawl but by farmland and forest. Such cities would be small enough to avoid megalopolitan diseconomies of scale yet large enough to support a vigorous industrial and commercial base and sustain a high level of cultural activity.

A repopulation of rural America would take some pressure off the largest cities and preserve the good aspects of city culture that have been destroyed by urban growth far beyond the human scale. U.S. Census data for recent years indicate that the four fastest growth rates in the United States are in rural areas. Substantial migration out of urban areas, which we have included as part of this scenario, would leave those who stayed behind in possession of cities that could be made very livable.

—John Steinhart, Mark Hanson,
Carel DeWinkel, Robin Gates,
Kathleen Lipp, Mark Thornsjo,
Stanley Kabala

There were only 11 cities of over a million people in 1900, 6 of them in Europe. By 1950, there were 75, with 24 in the developing world. By 1985 there may be 273, and 147 of them will be in the poorer lands. And these statistics of cataclysmic growth leave unmentioned the cities of ten million people—4 of them in 1970, perhaps 17 by 1985, 10 of them in the developing world. When one recalls that in 1820, only one city in the world—London—had a million inhabitants, the scale and speed of the migrations, uprootings, upheavals, and urban cataclysms of the last half century are almost beyond our capacity to grasp.   —BARBARA WARD

TODAY, PERHAPS more so than at any time in the past, millions of Americans sense that gigantism, bureaucratism, and the centralization of power have denied them any control over their social and personal lives.

For more than two decades, millions of Americans have "voted with their feet" against this insidious usurpation of public sovereignty by leaving the cities for suburbs and rural towns where they feel they can understand and exercise some degree of control over the social levers that shape their lives. More recently, sizable numbers of people within the cities have created their own neighborhood institutions, tenants associations, food coops, and cultural centers—a civic world of their own that has already begun to partly replace the official world to which they have been so ruthlessly subordinated.

Whether in the cities, suburbs, or rural areas, these millions are endeavoring to reduce their environments to a comprehensible human scale. They are trying to create a world they can cope with as individuals, a world they correctly identify with the freedom and gentler rhythms of a less mobilized, less massified, and more libertarian society.

The human scale is not only eminently desirable to satisfy our basic human impulses, but indispensable to the integrity of the world of life—including human life. Proper maintenance of the soil not only depends upon advances in our knowledge of soil chemistry and soil fertility; it also requires a more personalized approach to agriculture.

If differences in the quality and performance of soil are to receive more attention, American farming must be reduced to a human scale. It will become necessary to bring agriculture within the scope of the individual, so that the farmer and the soil can develop together, each responding as fully as possible to the needs of the other.

The same is true for the management of livestock. Today our food animals are being manipulated like a lifeless industrial resource. Normally, large numbers of animals are collected in the smallest possible space and are allowed only as much movement as is necessary for survival. Our meat animals have been placed on a diet composed for the most part of medicated feed high in carbohydrates. Before they are slaughtered, these obese, rapidly matured creatures seldom spend more than six months on the range and six months on feedlots, where they are kept on concentrated rations and gain about two pounds daily. Our dairy herds are handled like machines; our poultry flocks, like hothouse tomatoes. The need to restore the time-honored intimacy between man and his livestock is just as pronounced as the need to bring agriculture within the horizon of the individual farmer.

Advances in technology itself have largely overcome the industrial problems that were once invoked to justify the huge concentrations of people and facilities in a few urban areas. Non-polluting means of rapid transportation, electric power, and electronic devices have eliminated nearly all the problems of transportation, communication, and social isolation that burdened humanity in past eras. We can now communicate with one another over a distance of thousands of miles in a matter of seconds, and we can travel to the most remote areas of the world in a brief span of time. The obstacles created by time and space are essentially gone. Similarly, size need no longer be a problem. Technologists have developed remarkable small-scale alternatives to many of the giant facilities that still dominate modern industry.

Thus, almost without fully realizing it, we have been preparing the technological conditions for a new type of human community—one that can be gently tailored to the ecosystem in which it is located. It is no longer fanciful to think of humanity's future environment in terms of decentralized, moderate-size cities that combine industry with agriculture, not only in the same civic entity but in the occupational activities of the same individual. The "urbanized farmer" or the "agrarianized townsman" need not be a contradiction in terms.

But this rounded type of community (what I have often described as an "ecocommunity") with its appropriate "ecotechnologies" presupposes far-reaching changes in human sensibility. This delicate eco-community, viewed merely as the product of physical and logistical changes, would have a tentative future if it were not fashioned by acutely conscious individuals who enjoy a trusting intimacy with each other and are free to fully participate in the governance of the community and its development. Decentralization thus becomes meaningful from an ecological standpoint only if it forms the arena for the widest possible public involvement in every aspect of human affairs, indeed, if it fosters the recovery of the community as a family, not merely as a well-engineered or "well-planned" geographical entity.

For an age that has literally removed mountains, spanned immense gorges, diverted massive waterways, and rebuilt entire nations in the aftermath of war to call this decentralized image of the future human community a mere "utopia" is a libel on human ingenuity and creativity. And if "utopian" this image be, perhaps this critical era in history cannot afford to be anything but utopian. Yet as gigantism dwarfs the human spirit to antlike proportions and induces a terrifying human passivity, as centralization reaches such grotesque proportions that it denies people any sense of control over their destiny, as town and country become polarized against each other in a staggering ecological disequilibrium, as technology is mindlessly employed to undermine the very biogeochemical cycles indispensable for life on this planet— as all of these developments occur at a headlong tempo that is virtually beyond the comprehension of the most informed experts, we must seriously ask: who, in fact, are the mad "utopians" who have lost all contact with the reality of our times and who are the authentic realists?

—Murray Bookchin

SMALL-SCALE OPERATIONS, no matter how numerous, are always less likely to be harmful to the natural environment than large-scale ones, simply because their individual force is small in relation to the recuperative forces of nature. There is wisdom in smallness if only on account of the smallness and patchiness of human knowledge, which relies on experiment far more than on understanding. The greatest danger invariably arises from the ruthless application, on a vast scale, of partial knowledge such as we are currently witnessing in the application of nuclear energy, of the new chemistry in agriculture, of transportation technology, and countless other things.

Why is it so difficult for the rich to help the poor? The all-pervading disease of the modern world is the total imbalance between city and countryside, an imbalance in terms of wealth, power, culture, attraction, and hope. The former has become over-extended and the latter has atrophied. The city has become the universal magnet, while rural life has lost its savour. Yet it remains an unalterable truth that, just as a sound mind depends on a sound body, so the health of the cities depends on the health of the rural areas. The cities, with all their wealth, are merely secondary producers, while primary production, the precondition of all economic life, takes place in the countryside. The prevailing lack of balance, based on the age-old exploitation of countryman and raw material producer, today threatens all countries throughout the world, the rich even more than the poor. To restore a proper balance between city and rural life is perhaps the greatest task in front of modern man. It is not simply a matter of raising agricultural yields so as to avoid world hunger. There is no answer to the evils of mass unemployment and mass migration into cities, unless the whole level of rural life can be raised, and this requires the development of an agro-industrial culture, so that each district, each community, can offer a colourful variety of occupations to its members.

—E.F. Schumacher

SMALL AND MEDIUM-SIZED businesses are, by their very nature, "leaner" users of capital and energy for the simple reason that they lack the resources and the fraternal links with friendly bankers to be lavish in this field. They are also formidable generators of new ideas and new forms of labor-intensive skilled employment. One estimate has put at over 50 percent the share of individuals and their tiny enterprises in the seventy-one key inventions of this century. Indeed, the tendency of large corporations to grow by "agglomeration" has often been admitted to spring from the need for innovation that is no longer provided by giant bureaucracies but is readily bought up from small entrepreneurs who lack the resources for further growth.

One of the most secure and creative ways of lowering unemployment without increasing inflationary pressure would be to subsidize jobs in a wide range of small enterprises and to set up for these enterprises co-operative banks or special accounts in local banks.

— Barbara Ward

How would you like to sign the work you do?

Cooked by Ed Hatcher

Maybe it's a shame that most of us will never get to sign our work. Because as good as we are, it might make us better. And we can afford to be. No matter what kind of work we do, we'd have more to show for it.

More money, for one thing. Because we'd be giving each other our money's worth for the products, the services and even the government we pay for.

For another thing, we'll be giving America better ammunition to slug it out with our foreign competitors. That should help bring the lopsided balance of payments back onto our side. And help make your dollars worth more.

Best of all, as we hit our stride we'll be protecting our jobs here at home. And we'll get more satisfaction out of the jobs we've got.

You don't have to sign your work to see all these things happen. And more.

Just do the kind of work you'd be proud to have carry your name.

America. It only works as well as we do.

Robin Freeman

OUR ATTITUDES toward the future of mankind and the human environment vary considerably with our point of view. Those of us in international organizations are likely to assume a globalist viewpoint. To a globalist, environmental and human problems often appear to be without solution, or their solution involves such massive inputs of money, energy, raw materials, education, and so forth, that any effort seems puny. But only a few environmental problems are really global in nature—and even they usually have solutions which can be applied rather easily at the local level. For example, if we are really threatening the stability of the ozone layer by using aerosol spray cans, it is a simple matter to give them up. They add virtually nothing to the quality of living for any individual, and those who manufacture them can make just as much money doing something else. Similarly, nobody is going to be much affected if the SST never flies again. The future of whales is a global problem, but its solution involves only a change in attitude of comparatively few people in a few countries—and some redeployment of economic effort.

Most conservation problems exist on particular pieces of ground, occupied or cared for by a particular group of people. Attempts to solve them at a global, or even national level often strike far from the mark, because they fail to take into account the attitudes or motivations of the people concerned.

During the past few decades people have been encouraged to look to their nation's capital, or worse yet, to the United Nations, for solutions to problems that had always been considered, in the past, to be local affairs. But the tendency to depend upon the national government for decisions on the management of local resources inevitably creates delay, confusion, and often ends up with the wrong solution for each local community through trying to reach the right solution for all, thus providing water for a nation's population—as viewed from the top—can mean the need to build giant dams and canal systems, costing hundreds of millions of dollars, and taking many years. At the local level providing water may mean only developing some roof-top collectors, storage tanks, and giving some attention to the management of vegetation on the local hills and valleys. It might take a little money, some labor, and a few months of effort to improve the situation. But who will make that local effort if the responsibility lies with the government, and particularly if the government is likely to override such a local initiative? Similarly, the provision of electricity, viewed form the top, may seem to require the installation of a massive, high-risk, nuclear plant, and an environmentally disruptive national grid of power lines. It could also mean, at the local level, the installation of a windmill, or diverting a small stream through an axial flow generator.

Human societies can be divided into two categories, with some transition from one to the other. These are *ecosystem people* and *biosphere people.*

Ecosystem people are those who depend almost entirely upon a local ecosystem, or a few closely related ecosystems. Virtually all of the foods they eat, or the materials they use, come from that ecosystem—although there will be some limited trade with other ecosystem groups. Because of their total dependence on a local system, developed usually over many generations, they live in balance with it. Without this balance they would destroy it, and cease to exist, since no other resources are available. The balance is assured by religious belief and social custom—everything is geared to the rhythms of nature—to phases of the moon, changes of seasons, flowering and fruiting of plants, movements and reproduction of animals. Such people have an intricate knowledge of the environment—the uses of plants for food, fiber, medicine. Every species, every thing, in their environment has some meaning or significance. Recent studies have shown that most such people did not live impoverished lives. Instead they tended to have adequate food, good health, abundant leisure—many of the features of the good life that others today strive for and rarely achieve. Once everybody on earth was in this category. Now only a few so-called "primitive" peoples, living more or less in isolation, survive.

Biosphere people are those who can draw on the resources of many ecosystems, or the entire biosphere, through networks of trade and communication. Their dependence on any one ecosystem is partial, since they can rely on others if any one fails. Drawing as they do on planetary resources, they can bring great amounts of energy and materials to bear on any one ecosystem—they can devastate it, degrade it, totally destroy it and then move on. All of those who are now tied in to the global network of technological society are biosphere people. They are the people who preach conservation, but often do not practice it.

We must aim at selective decentralization. Authority to solve local problems should always be held at the local level. Development should be localized, at a human scale, and intended to solve human problems. . . .

Nothing should be done by the province that can be done better by the village. Nothing should be referred to the nation that can be solved by the province. Those most likely to be affected by development decisions should have the most active role in reaching those decisions. No development decision should be made without full exploration of its effects upon human society and the natural environment. This does not mean that the local, the small scale, should prevail in all activities. Transportation networks need national coordination. Copper mines, smelters, refineries will re-quire massive inputs of energy and labor—they can't be supplied by a few wind generators. Equally, however, one does not need a gigawatt power plant to meet the energy needs of farms and villages. In fact, supplying energy needs in such a way inevitably creates the feeling of alienation and dependence that results when one has no understanding of or control over one's means for survival.

—Raymond Dassmann

Elihu Blotnick

Transportation

The salient fact about transportation is that there's too much of it. Lettuce eaten in Connecticut was grown in California. We are much too mobile, too much attracted to where we aren't and too little appreciative of where we are. Mobility undreamed of before this century is not a God-given right. It is a luxury, and a luxury we grow increasingly unable to afford. The mobility bestowed on us by the auto was bought at a terrible price. Cities and towns were reshaped to suit the auto, and this made them in many ways less suitable for people. The butcher, baker, grocer, and corner drugstore within easy walking distance disappeared, unable to compete with scattered supermarkets and their acres of parking lots. Local merchants of all kinds disappeared too, a victim of regional shopping centers. Employers obtained economies of scale by building a few giant plants instead of many small ones, counting on the auto to bring workers from homes absurdly far away. The auto is a centrifugal force, and our society is in danger of flying completely apart. Fortunately, though, resource scarcity is bringing the era of the auto to an end. We must reshape our cities and towns once more, fitting them to the man or woman on two feet instead of four wheels. No matter how intelligently we rebuild our cities, however, means of transportation will remain essential. Our task is to develop modes of transportation that make efficient use of energy and resources. The railroad is outstanding on either a passenger-mile or a ton-mile basis, and another great age of railroading is surely in the offing.

Elihu Blotnick

Transportation

PETER LAFEN and BRUCE COLMAN

MORE THAN 20 PERCENT of the United States' energy is spent on transportation. This is a sector whose energy intensiveness grew twice as fast as our population during the last quarter century, at more than 3 percent per year. It is a sector in which we are overcapitalized and in which available technology is misused almost as often as it is used appropriately. It is a sector that is almost totally dependent on oil—and increasingly, on imported oil.

Because of this very dependence upon imported oil, we are coming to grips with many of our traditional wasteful practices, not so much through enlightened administrative reform or legislative effort as through the price mechanism as managed by OPEC. The high price of oil is forcing us to conserve fuel, to ride mass transit, and to look carefully at our long distance freight transportation policies. Combined with one of the hopeful aspects of the current anti-regulatory fever sweeping the nation, the changes in our transportation policy that result often are significant improvements.

We have more highways, airports, private automobiles, trucks, and airplanes than can be put to work efficiently. Diseconomies have been perpetuated—in some cases, created—by government institutions that regulate freight rates and passenger fares, and that finance new construction. And the railroads' own regional rate cartels have helped to perpetuate misuse of their own equipment. The Highway Trust Fund is the most infamous financer of wrong-headed construction; the Airport Trust Fund is its high-flying twin.

Deregulation of airline transportation is now well under way, and has already demonstrated some beneficial effects of lifting regulatory protection. Price competition among trunk carriers and the growth of "discount" airlines have benefited the air travel consumer. Aircraft are flying fuller and more efficiently as flights are pared to meet market conditions rather than regulatory requirements. Regional and commuter airlines are springing up to serve markets abandoned by the major airlines—less convenient for the business traveler in some cases, but certainly more efficient from a fuel and equipment standpoint.

Deregulation of the trucking industry can also be attributed at least in part to the pricing pressure on motor fuels. Recently passed legislation calls for the elimination of regulation-required deadheading, the empty backhaul required of a trucker who could haul a commodity to a location but who had to return home empty (leaving a valuable commodity on the loading dock waiting for a certified carrier licensed to carry cargo in the other direction). Furthermore, in areas that remain subject to ICC regulation, it will now be easier for trucking companies to enter the market to compete with other truckers, providing choice and price advantages to shippers.

Rail deregulation will provide rate-making flexibility for railroads, allowing them to recover the costs required to maintain their rail systems as well as pay their costs of operating a given train.

While deregulation will go far toward making our transportation systems economically and environmentally rational, it is not the complete answer. *Greater* regulation and enforcement is needed to guarantee the safety of all transportation systems. Trucks, trains, and airplanes tend to get bigger as fuel costs go up, and the potential for tragedy increases along with size. Eighty thousand pound trucks put greater strains on braking and steering systems. (Fatal accidents involving heavy trucks have gone up significantly since the weight limit was increased in many states.) One hundred ton rail cars overstress rails and railbeds, and the results for a community if the cargo is 100 tons of hazardous materials can be tragic. The air traffic control system and the airworthiness inspection system are stressed to the breaking point. More efficient regulation is needed in all of these areas to make transportation safe as well as efficient.

Government construction and maintenance of certain transportation facilities help to perpetuate many diseconomies as much or more than economic regulation. The Highway Trust Fund is financed by gasoline taxes and used to build highways, needed and otherwise. This benefits truckers and Detroit, but unbal-

Elihu Blotnick

ances our energy budget. The airport Trust Fund builds airports in a massive subsidy to airlines. The Army Corps of Engineers makes waterways navigable and keeps them that way for barge and freight-ship operators. But no comparable government program exists to help the railroads; the rail companies build and maintain their own tracks, roadbeds, and signal systems. Environmentalists won a round in 1975 when Congress opened up the Highway Trust Fund so that some of its monies could, at local option, be spent on public transportation; but the fund remains basically a giant road-building machine.

This road-building machine is running out of fuel. As Americans drive less and drive in more fuel efficient automobiles (again thanks to environmental activists in Riyadh and Tokyo, not in Detroit or Washington), the contribution of fuel taxes from motorists to the Highway Trust Fund is shrinking. Combined with the dramatically increased destructive impact of heavier trucks, the result is a growing crisis in highway finance. The federal government and the states are finding that they cannot pay for highway costs out of current revenue structures. Two responses are possible; only one is desirable.

The states can go ahead and raise gas taxes for individual motorists, either in cents-per-gallon increments or more likely in the form of a percentage sales tax on gasoline. (The latter has the advantage of going up with every gas price increase without further legislative review or action.) If this funding path is taken, we can be sure that the highway machine will grind on as usual, gobbling up land and drinking up energy resources. The alternative is based upon the radical concept that private enterprise should pay its own costs of doing business. Heavy trucks need to be taxed to recover the costs of the damage they do to the highway system. If road taxes for trucks are based not upon fuel (which rewards heavier, more damaging trucks with a lower tax burden) but upon the amount of damage each truck does to road surfaces and bridges, according to well established axle-weight calculations, the results will be beneficial in many ways. Trucks will charge their shippers for the damage that they do to the roads, passing the cost along to consumers of truck-shipped commodities rather than the taxpayers of corridor states. Railroads will be able to compete with trucks on the basis of their naturally greater fuel efficiency without the interference of government subsidies. The damage-based tax system will encourage the use of lighter and safer trucks, resulting in longer lasting highways and fewer accidents.

This country faces the reconstruction of its major transportation systems by the end of this century. The goal of transportation planning should be to move freight and passengers with the least possible waste of resources. More passenger- and ton-miles per gallon should be our aim. We can create a government-subsidized, politically-shaped and inefficient system. Our Highway Trust Fund, Conrail, and Amtrak experiences demonstrate the costs and benefits of that path. Alternatively, we can develop a rational, fuel-efficient system through private investment and evenhanded federal and state policies. The time for decision is now.

Moving to the Future

In the decentralized future, there will be few private automobiles. People will live near their work, and stores will locate near *them*. Cars will remain important in isolated rural areas, but most people will rent cars only when they need them. Vacation and business travel will be largely by train. With better trains, a more relaxed pace to life, and more leisure, Americans won't be so tempted by airplanes. Airlines will be limited to long-haul routes, mainly transcontinental and intercontinental. Improved communications and mail service will make it less necessary for businessmen to travel. The coming revolution in computer technology will reduce the need for office workers to be in offices, and significantly reduce commuter trips.

What cars there are will be long-lived and energy-efficient, designed to accommodate relatively non-polluting fuels such as methanol, derived from agricultural and urban wastes.

The central districts of cities will be car-free zones. Walking and bicycling will be encouraged, with attractive footpaths and bikeways. There will also be free public transportation within car-free zones. Expensive? Not compared to the congestion and pollution it will replace.

Freight will move by rail and barge to points near its final destination. Trucks will link railheads and ports with delivery points that rails and navigable waters don't reach. Containerization will facilitate this. With improved railbeds and more flexible train scheduling, there will be less need to move perishables long distances by truck.

Major transportation services will be handled by consolidated transportation corporations offering highly competitive intermodal passenger and freight services, tailored to meet the specialized needs of travelers and shippers in the least costly and most energy-efficient manner.

This vision of the transportation future is not likely to come wholly true for decades, depending as it does on considerable decentralization and changes in urban settlement patterns. It resembles the visions published in *Popular Mechanics*-type magazines in the past, except this one is predicated on energy conservation rather than science-fiction dreams of near-magical machines.

More modest planning is needed for the near term, planning based on equipment and techniques that are available now. Conservation cannot wait for the technological future. We cannot choose now among various technological options: Wankel versus stratified-charge engines, Turbotrains versus electrically-powered trains, or DC-10s versus L-1011s versus 747s (but will observe here that full jumbo jets get 50 percent more passenger-miles per gallon than full airplanes of the 707 or DC-8 class). We must preserve through research and antitrust vigilance the technological options that may develop in the future.

The highway and airport trust funds should be abolished. Lenny Arrow, a transportation expert in

Someone once suggested that for every child born a tree be planted; for every automobile sold, a thousand, and for every jet airliner built, a hundred thousand.

—WILLIAM BRONSON

Environmental Action's Washington office, advocates replacing them with block grants to the states. Geographic areas that do not meet primary air-quality standards would be required to spend their federal grants on transportation modes other than highways. Such grants should be designed to encourage beneficial secondary effects and mitigate or eliminate longstanding problems. Bike route funding and car pool lanes would be tied to federal highway construction and maintenance grants, for example, and noise control plans would be required as part of any airport expansion or modernization programs. Beyond that, all spending would be at local option. There is no guarantee, of course, that local authorities will choose the most suitable option. But at least the decisions will be made closer to the people affected by them. There will be a better chance to do things right.

Revamping the financing of transportation will create local options so that local needs can be met in the most appropriate way. Revamping transportation regulations will let each mode find its own level, and the rates charged customers will reflect the true, unsubsidized cost of providing service.

Control by one company of production for competing modes should be outlawed. General Motors, for example, should be required to divest itself of either its auto, bus, or locomotive divisions.

Changes in regulations can put more cargo onto carriers that will deliver it most economically, and changes in the same direction are needed for passenger transportation. Travelers and commuters must be coaxed out of cars and airplanes and won back to trains, buses, and mass transit.

American trains should be brought up to the quality of European, Canadian, and Japanese trains. Run-of-the-mill trains abroad give better service than ours, and elite trains far surpass anything we have. First-class trains in Europe and Japan provide comfortable accommodations and good meals; some also offer businessmen office equipment, telephones, and stenographers. Parents can even obtain baby-sitters.

The salesmanship as well as the service of Amtrak seems lacking. Entertainment aboard would help make passenger trains more attractive. Holiday specials—such as ski trains between Boston and New Hampshire or New York and Vermont, or tour trains to other popular holiday areas—are naturals (and ski trains, at least, used to be common). Arranging for passengers either to bring their cars along piggy-back on flat cars or to rent autos at their destinations at a discount, as part of a package deal, are other obvious promotions.

But train rides won't be comfortable, much less en-

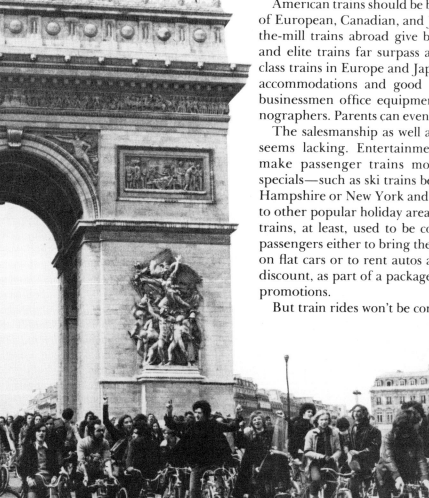

joyable, if our roadbeds aren't improved. They are so rough and poorly kept up that even on our best passenger train, the Metroliner, one sways more wildly than on an ordinary train in Europe; and our potentially fastest train, the New York to Boston Turbotrain, uses only a fraction of its design speed, going no faster than conventional equipment. Train travel should be fast and restful. But freight doesn't care about smooth rides and railroads have seemingly cared about nothing but freight, so roadbeds have been allowed to deteriorate. If train patrons are to become regulars, they must be given tolerably comfortable service.

The federal government should make roadbed repair and upgrading a top priority. Investment tax credits and federally guaranteed loans should lure private investment back to railroad companies that are financially more secure because of deregulation and energy-based cost competitiveness. The resulting employment of large numbers of track personnel would be the corporate equivalent of the Civilian Conserva-

tion Corps of depression years, and far more beneficial than the Army Corps of Engineers' river channeling, dam building, and lock construction activities.

If private enterprise does not get the job done, it may eventually be necessary to nationalize the roadbeds, with their signal systems and field facilities, in order to upgrade them. If so, fine. Virtually all the world's railroads outside the US are government-owned, and nationalization would put railroad rights-of-way on an equal footing with highways, airports, and navigable waterways. Arguments about nationalization are beside the main point, however, which is repair, and they must not be allowed to delay the work.

Repair of roadbeds—leveling bad grades, loosening tight curves, smoothing bumps, and the continuous-welding of all track used by passenger trains—should be a major goal of the Administration. It is a more modest goal than the moon, one achievable earlier than wiping out poverty (which railroad jobs would help to do), and its benefits would last a century or

Harry Dennis

more if we took good care of them.

Bringing our trains up to the standards of the USSR's or Japan's or Europe's would require very hard work; to make them *better* would be a great goal, one with patriotism to fuel it and usefulness besides. We must begin soon. If we don't, costs will escalate as resources dwindle and scarcity drives prices up.

It will take time to wean Americans from the automobile, so we must now mitigate its consequences.

The Interstate Highway System should be declared complete, and no new segments built.

Despite anguished cries and calls for isolationist trade restrictions on foreign automobiles, higher fuel economy standards must be set—in full knowledge that they will probably be exceeded years ahead of schedule by Japanese and European automakers. It is obvious that the only reason American automobile manufactures sell any cars today is because of government-imposed mandatory fuel-economy standards.

Better fuel economy can come about through refinements in engine design, including alternatives to the internal combustion engine that should be vigorously pursued; through limiting car weight; by banning automatic transmissions (except on cars specially prepared for handicapped people); by restricting auto air conditioning to climates where it is a near-necessity, and by making radial tires standard equipment.

Existing cars can be used better. No car should travel in commute traffic that isn't as nearly full as its owner's generosity and sense of community can make it. And there should be inducements to car pooling: toll-free or restricted-access lanes on freeways and bridges have been tried successfully in Boston, San Francisco, and elsewhere. Wherever car pools are rewarded with restricted access lanes, the ad hoc car pool system develops; drivers stop at bus stops en route to work and pick up commuting strangers to take advantage of the faster (and sometimes cheaper) car pool lanes. Their passengers get free rides to work, and the system is more efficiently utilized.

Cars can be made to last longer and get their best performance by proud and loving mechanics, but craftsmanship has left most dealers' service divisions. Craftsmanship is also gone from Detroit. It is not possible on the assembly line. Henry Ford's invention may be responsible for more human misery than any other modern, above-ground industrial institution. The assembly line should be replaced by group assembly shops of the kind Saab uses in Sweden: crews of six or eight or ten are given quotas for certain phases of car-building—engine assembly, let's say—but are free to divide the work and working time any way they like. Or as has already happened in Japan, US automobiles may be constructed by robots, computerized machines that can perform routine tasks effectively without losing a humanity they never possessed. Craftsmanship will be reborn in automobile maintenance. As the cost of materials goes up, auto repair cooperatives and consumer monitoring of auto repair performance will reward quality maintenance. More and more people will be encouraged to maintain their own vehicles.

Whatever changes are possible in Detroit or the internal combustion engine, no more appropriate engineering is possible than the human foot's and no more elegant technology than the bicycle, ski, or shoe. The cyclist who uses two rather than four wheels and leg muscles rather than hydrocarbons to get to work or do errands should be able to deduct the bike's expenses from taxes as one can on one's car. And cyclists shouldn't have to be ever-wary of the heedless motorist or rampaging taxi; bike routes, bike lanes, even bicycle-only streets, would give cyclists greater safety and convenience. Walking in the city should be pleasant, too; walkways and car-free districts should be established soon, and people should be encouraged to walk, not drive, in town.

Ivan Illich says social progress should go at a bicycle's pace. We agree.

Urban mass transit should replace automobiles in commuting, but there is the big question to be faced of what form such transit systems should take. The most advanced new rapid transit system, the Bay Area Rapid Transit District (BART) serving San Francisco and environs, has not been a success. It cost billions of dollars to build, its fares have risen as fast as the Public Utilities Commission would allow, and its service isn't anything like its planners hoped for.

BART *is* about twice as energy-efficient as the average electric commuter train operating in 1970 (leaving out the energy costs of building each), and it is not without redeeming qualities, many of them. The stations are clean, the trains smooth and quiet. Some day BART's bugs will be ironed out, we trust, and it will provide reliably superior transportation.

Meanwhile, transit planners will look closely at BART and its sister-system, the Washington, D.C., Metro, which has similar equipment without such intricate control technology.

We do not expect many new programs like BART. Instead, less aggressively "advanced" technology will more often replace the auto. Suburbs and central cities that are connected by rail lines should put commuter trains on them. (The trains feeding into Manhattan are an example to be improved upon.) Toronto achieved commuter rail service only two years after it was first proposed, a success to be emulated elsewhere. The upgrading of long-haul passenger trains will have obvious spin-off benefits for commuter trains.

It must be recognized that heavy rail commuter

Drawing by Ed Koren © 1976, The New Yorker Magazine, Inc.

"I'd like you to meet Frank Russ. He's just arrived on foot."

systems such as BART, Metro, and others are not only people movers, but city builders. New urban centers are springing up around stations, and economic revitalization is creating jobs and business opportunities wherever these systems are built. One must therefore consider not only the construction and operating costs, but also the beneficial results in real economic terms that may reduce the need for less efficient urban development grants, and perhaps even welfare and unemployment costs.

Care must be taken to avoid the "Lindenwold effect," the explosive growth that occurred in the rural terminal area of the Patco high speed line link in Philadephia with South Jersey. But it is much easier to control station-related growth, of course, than it is to control strip development if a highway is built instead of a rail line.

We must look to the past as well as the future. Combinations of heavy rail subway systems, light rail (trolley cars), electrified buses, and buses utilizing alternative fuels, can provide efficient commuter services to cities and suburban areas of all sizes and densities. Some cities such as Philadephia, Boston, and San Francisco still retain their light rail systems. Many others will find them attractive in the future.

Where rails don't exist and cities don't want to go the BART route, available funds may be spent on commuter and intracity bus service. It is essential to rehumanize our cities by giving everyone access to clean, safe, regular, and convenient public transit, whether by bus, subway, or above-ground trains.

To woo commuters back onto buses, there should be buses-only lanes on freeways and bridges; buses zipping by while you are stalled in bumper-to-bumper traffic are a strangely moving sight. Fare structures should be set so that it costs more to drive than to ride.

For intercity service we must work to convince rail and bus companies that they are far more complementary than competitive. The essential decision that must be made by an intercity traveler is whether to drive, or to go by public transportation. The time factor may dictate the decision between flying and all other modes, but between driving, rail, and bus, the latter two should be seen as a single alternative. Bus service can make rail routes accessible to millions. Buses can act as feeder lines, and intercity buses can provide flexibility in service for smaller numbers of passengers than can be served adequately or efficiently by trains.

The more comfortable, affordable, and available both bus and rail systems are, the more passengers the two systems will lure from the automobile. At that point, the comfort of trains and the flexibility of buses can compete equitably for the passenger dollar.

Saving Energy Aloft

To improve the fuel economy of air service, a hard look at CAB policy is needed—and with it, the adoption of a US policy withholding landing rights from the Anglo-French *Concorde* and its Russian sister in sprints, the Tu-144. When an SST is developed that uses no more fuel per passenger-mile than a standard jumbo jet, is as safe and no noiser, then perhaps we should consider lifting the ban. Until then, we should renounce SSTs as an aberration, a mistake. Our renunciation will have important symbolic value, as did Congress's vote to shelve the American SST in 1971; it will signal our commitment to lowering the energy-intensiveness of transportation.

If the marketplace does not eliminate under-utilized flights, the CAB should order the amalgamation of flights that are going half empty and deny route applications that duplicate train and bus service. The goal should be to fly fewer, but larger, fuller, and more efficient planes on fewer routes. If three airlines were flying partly full between Cincinnati and Dallas, for example, the CAB should order that there be only one flight in any given hour, a wide-body jumbo jet that would be nearly full. A smaller back-up plane might also be indicated in case there weren't enough passengers to load the big one to near-capacity. The three airlines could take turns supplying the plane and crew. Passengers would still be able to buy tickets from any of the three, and accountants could divide the proceeds later. This kind of cooperation is foreshadowed by most airlines' acceptance of each other's tickets in lieu of cash from travelers who change their plans.

Alternatively, license to fly between any two points might be granted on an exclusive basis to a single carrier. There is precious little genuine competition anyway, and with an exclusive franchise, it would be to an airline's advantage to rationalize operations. The CAB would be responsible for seeing that the public was well served. Licenses to fly a route might be for a period of three years, revocable for cause, and renewable if the operator had performed well.

All the advances we can achieve in technology, finance, regulation, scheduling, and competition will be to no avail if the public is not kept informed about

Werner Muller/Jeroboam, Inc.

how best to use the transportation facilities at its disposal. Most Americans know where their local bus service goes and how convenient it is for them. Most do *not* know how it compares for convenience and economy with their own cars. They don't know how much better sense buses or trains make than planes or cars for longer trips. The facts haven't been "sold" to them.

Most traveler education can take the form of conventional advertising. But education about transportation should begin in schools. Many states have driver education requirements; these classes should not so much introduce students to the joys of automobile-mania as place autos in their proper context and steer students toward walking, bicycling, and patronizing more energy-efficient carriers.

In every area of transportation there is room for technological improvement. We need a continual evaluation of the various tools that inventors and engineers want to place at our disposal, and part of our long-term transportation planning should be an office of technology assessment. When something better comes along, it should be put to work to increase efficiency and reduce waste.

Recommended Actions

☐ Declaring it imperative that the US have unsurpassed rail service, the President should call top railroad executives and other authorities together to discuss with him how this can be achieved.

☐ Congress should withdraw all direct and indirect subsidies to energy- and resource-intensive modes of transportation such as airplanes, autos, and long-haul trucks; consideration should be given to subsidizing energy-efficient modes such as walking, bicycling, buses, railroads, and barges.

☐ Congress should ban supersonic transports from US airspace as an egregious example of energy-intensive transportation.

☐ Congress should reorganize the Interstate Commerce Commission and the Civil Aeronautics Board, and give them a mandate to minimize the amount of energy wasted in flying empty airline seats around, for example, or in miles driven empty by trucks that could be loaded.

☐ Congress should raise the miles-per-gallon standard for cars as rapidly as developing technology permits.

☐ Municipal governments must discourage the private car, creating car-free zones and improving mass transit systems.

☐ Cities and towns should do everything possible to promote car pooling, which amounts to mini mass transit.

☐ The President should declare it to be an objective of his Administration to begin decentralizing the nation's settlement patterns, which would eliminate the need for much travel; for recommended actions leading to decentralization, see the chapter on that subject.

☐ The President and other opinion-makers at all levels (including the grass roots) should use their influence to convert us to a nation of walkers and bicyclists who, wherever practicable, *prefer* to get places under their own power.

☐ The President should inform the country of the need to phase out the auto era, and propose to Congress that the US help finance highway projects only in cases where a clear social need has been convincingly demonstrated. Because of the auto industry's importance in the overall economy, the phaseout should be gradual and planned with great care.

☐ The federal government and the states should enact damage-based tax systems to assess heavy trucks their fair share of highway costs, and force them to compete on an equal basis with the unsubsidized and more fuel-efficient railroads.

☐ The President should ask Congress to end the Highway Trust Fund and the Airport Trust Fund.

☐ The President should appoint a commission to study ways in which improved communications, including better postal service, might substitute for travel.

More Thoughts on Transportation

I AM AN URBAN bicycle commuter. Depending on your point of view, that makes me either a bold pioneer or a quaint relic, a dashing trend-setter or an out-of-step fool, a friend of the earth or a menace to society. In order to survive I've had to evolve nerves of steel, lungs of leather, hair-trigger reflexes, an extra reservoir of adrenalin and the ability to turn the other cheek forever. I've looked deep into the various souls of cabbies, bus drivers, tourists, cops, motorcycle delivery boys, jaywalkers—and even other cyclists. I know which red lights to run—and which ones to stop for. I scream obscenities at truck drivers and mumble apologies to pedestrians. Downtown, during the day, no other vehicle can catch me, yet in most people's eyes my form of travel is beneath contempt. I belong to a brother-and-sister-hood of bicycle commuters, that, in the United States, is probably 600,000 strong, but when I'm out on the street it's me alone against all . . . those . . . cars.

And yet, compared to the automobile, my bike is a singularly wonderful machine for the city.

Bikes are quick, nimble, maneuverable and well-suited to "city-size" trips—up to about five miles. Cars are awkward, unmaneuverable and forever getting in each other's way—especially in intersections during rush hour. Although autos are capable of prodigious speed, the average velocity of daytime city traffic is considerably less than 20 miles an hour (in Manhattan it's been clocked at 6 mph), a speed easily equaled by a cyclist.

The efficiency of a bicycle is almost unbelievable. For example, the energy contained in a single slice of bread will propel you and your bike almost four miles, whereas on foot you'd collapse after less than 1700 yards. In contrast, the energy value of a slice of bread wouldn't even *start* a car. (Once started, the auto, which wastes 94% of the potential energy in the gas tank, would travel only 575 feet on that slice of bread.)

The auto is the major urban source of both air and noise pollution. The bike, of course, uses no fossil fuel and so causes no air pollution, and is virtually silent. And, because a bike is some 100 times lighter than an auto, it uses less of such vital natural resources as aluminum, rubber and chrome.

Unlike cars, bicycles are relatively cheap to buy and to fix. In fact, most bike repairs can be done at home. (Last week, when my bike's entire "transmission" system failed, I fixed it for $1.04 with a new gearshift cable.) Furthermore, a bike can last longer than a car.

Because a bicycle takes up only about one fifteenth as much space as a car, the use of bikes sharply reduces congestion on the road and "parking lot pollution" in town. (Downtown Los Angeles today devotes fully two thirds of its space to automobiles.) As a source of exercise, bicycling is unequalled; it strengthens lungs, muscles and the heart while reducing blood pressure (without the damage to knees, ankles and feet often associated with jogging). In contrast, driving—even riding—in a car leads to obesity, hypertension, flabbiness, headaches, low-level carbon-monoxide poisoning and hemorrhoids.

And yet Americans take bicycling only slightly more seriously than roller skating. Americans own 95 million bikes, and 76 million of us ride bikes during the year (making it the second most popular participation sport after swimming), yet transportation planners have given little serious thought to the humble bicycle.

Suzanne Arms/Jeroboam, Inc.

The fact is, bicycles are commonplace. They are affordable, there is little mystique surrounding them, almost everyone learned to ride one as a child, and the styles change little. There's probably a cobweb-covered one in your basement right now.

Yet even with so poor an image, bicycling is on the upswing. And the striking gains are occurring where the case for bike use is indisputable—in the cities, among adults and especially among commuters. Bicycle sales soared phenomenally in the 1970s. In the seven years beginning in 1972, Americans actually bought more bicycles (77 million) than cars (72.5 million)! In 1979, thanks to the gasoline shortage, bike sales surged even more strongly, with factories falling months behind on orders. And these bikes aren't the small-wheel, high-handlebar contraptions you see strewn on suburban sidewalks at dinnertime. Fully 45% are full-size, lightweight machines meant for serious riding.

One indirect cause of the increase in bicycling is the multitude of federal, state and local agencies mandated to "do something" about transportation problems in the cities. The greatest of these problems are air pollution, traffic congestion, urban highway construction and fuel consumption. Translated into policy, their solution requires gradually, inexorably challenging the automobile's special status in our society. Parking bans, higher parking fees and bridge and tunnel tolls, higher gasoline prices, stricter auto-maintenance inspections, carpool-only highway lanes, scaled-down highway construction plans and other measures combine to make cities less hospitable for motorists. And bicycling becomes relatively more attractive.

Unfortunately, however, today's cities could hardly be less geared to bikers. The traffic flow is either too fast or too slow; the air pollution ranges from annoying to debilitating; roadways are torn up by trucks and buses; lanes are the wrong widths; trolley tracks, cobblestones and sewer gratings can be lethal; theft is a problem; and bicyclists rarely are accorded equal rights in traffic. With all our modern urban and energy problems, increased bicycling is an outstanding partial solution—and Americans in many cities seem to be ready for it—but city planners and polticians aren't making the changes needed to stimulate a bicycle renaissance.

In conversations with dozens of cycling advocates and city bike coordinators and planners, several general conclusions have emerged:

- There is an appalling lack of information about cycling. Planners don't know how many people ride, when they ride, what routes they take or what improvements they would like made. (A small part of this deficiency will be remedied soon. Thanks to the efforts of the League of American Wheelmen, the U.S. Census Bureau will ask a specific question about bicycling in this year's census.)
- No large city—no city bigger than, say, Davis, California—can claim the title of "Bike City, U.S.A." Each one is still so wedded to the automobile's needs that bicyclists remain strangers in a strange land.
- Nevertheless, almost every big city has a couple of exciting innovations, experiments or programs to help bicyclists. If all the programs were put together in one place it would mark a quantum leap in bicycle promotion—and use.
- Bicyclists, as a class, are remarkably meek in asserting their desires, needs and rights to the authorities. In particular, most bicyclists seem unwilling to challenge the basic assumption of conventional planners—that cities are to be designed for cars only.

Meekness, however, only delays the period of transition from auto domination, while more bicyclists continue to be injured and killed, assaulted by pollution, and even intimidated back into their cars. It is time for cyclists to take the offensive. Here, then, is a ten-point program that might help to usher in the Bicycle Age.

1. *Restripe auto lanes.* On many downtown streets it would be difficult to build a so-called Class I (structurally separated) or Class II (visually differentiated) bike lane. Yet a bicyclist riding on an average 9-foot-wide lane is either followed by honking cars or is continually passed with only inches to spare. The most inexpensive and politically palatable solution to this problem is to expand the right-most lane to 13 feet by repainting the roadway. That way, during rush hour, cars and bikes can ride side-by-side, but two cars won't quite fit. Wider curb lanes should be bicyclists' minimum demand.

2. *Paint bike lanes.* A bike lane is like a car lane, except cars are not allowed in it. Separate lanes are a better solution than restriping, because they are an explicit statement that cars are no longer kings of the road. Several cities have on-street bike lanes. The most exciting experiment is taking place in New York, where there are eight miles of bike-only lanes in the heart of midtown (down Fifth Avenue and Broadway and up Sixth Avenue). If the test continues to be successful, new lanes are slated to be created in other parts of New York and very likely in other cities. (It is not surprising that bike lanes raise more political problems than restriping; the New York Taxi Association has counterproposed that bike riding be banned in Manhattan altogether!)

3. *Build bike lanes.* This is a better solution because it physically separates bikes and cars by a curb. These lanes exist in some smaller towns, notably Madison, Wisconsin, and Davis, California, but no major city has gone so far. (Of course, in Europe, several cities take

Automobiles and the like are an "efficient" way to get around in our society because our society is designed for the automobile. People once lived near their workplaces and near their merchants: we now have industrial communities, business communities, residential communities, retail communities, educational communities, recreational communities, all "connected" (read: "separated") by highways and roads. Lured by the "freedom" of the automobile, we have made ourselves completely dependent on it.

—GIL FRIEND

such bike lanes for granted.) Constructing curbs is more expensive than repainting, but an Oregon cost-benefit study showed that luring 500 to 700 people from cars to bikes would justify spending $40,000 per mile (in 1972 dollars) on bike lanes.

4. *Design streets for bikes rather than for cars.* Without actually banning cars, some roadways can be made unattractive to auto drivers and appealing to bikers. For instance, streets can be made narrow and curving, lined with trees, flower beds, fountains, benches and outdoor cafes. More important, the speed limits can be reduced to a comfortable 12 miles an hour by police vigilance, speed bumps (with narrow "bicycle slots" in them) or, best of all, rolling traffic lights.

5. *Ban cars from some streets.* This most desirable option is also the most difficult to accomplish politically. Many cities have banned cars—and bikes—from selected pedestrian shopping streets, but few have prohibited autos in favor of cycles. In Seattle, city officials determined that the old 20th Avenue N.W. Bridge was structurally unsound for heavy weights, so they limited traffic to bikes. Washington, D.C., is considering reserving a mile-long, little-used Georgetown street to local-resident traffic only. Perhaps the most remarkable experiment is on Roosevelt Island, in New York City, a thin sliver of land in the East River with a population of 10,000, which has virtually banned cars entirely. Primary access to the island is via an aerial tramway from Manhattan. Residents can drive to the island but must park in a huge garage; nonbicyclists walk or use a shuttle bus. (Islands, of course, have at least a fighting chance of curbing cars. At least three have been successful—Fire Island, New York; Nantucket, Massachusetts; and Mackinac, Michigan—and residents are enthusiastic about the clean air, the quiet, the diminished tension and the sense of community. However, all three are primarily summer resorts.)

6. *Ban cars from park roads.* Urban parks, which were created to provide a respite from the city's noise and congestion, have all too often been usurped by cars. A Sunday bike ride in the park, when it means peddling among sightseers, hot rodders, motorcyclists, multi-car picnic groups and zoo visitors, can be an unpleasant, frustrating experience. Washington, San Francisco and Boston have responded to the problem by closing sections of park roads on Sundays. New York has done better, shutting most of Central Park's roadways all day on weekends and from 10 a.m. to 4 p.m. on weekdays. Seattle is a real leader, having permanently closed the roadway in Seward Park to auto traffic.

7. *Occasionally turn highways and parkways into "pedalways."* There are many parkways that are too busy and important to close to cars permanently, but too beautiful to totally abandon to auto traffic. Chicago's Lake Shore Drive, Manhattan's Henry Hudson Parkway, Detroit's Belle Isle Drive, Washington's George Washington Parkway, Brooklyn's Belt Parkway, Philadelphia's Schuylkill Expressway, Boston's Storrow Drive and many others are all roads that deserve to be experienced for their views, landscaping, smells and sounds in leisurely manner—by bike, on foot or even on roller skates, without the noise, fumes and danger of cars. Certainly our cities could survive if these roads were closed two or three Sundays every year. In the past, the National Park Service closed the lovely George Washington Parkway from Washington to Mt. Vernon one day a year (unfortunately this practice ended when a bike path was built). Seattle has monthly "Bike Sundays" during the summer, with the carpool-only lanes of Interstate 5 closed to cars and with the speed limits of several spectacular scenic roads reduced to 25 miles per hour. In New York City, the American Youth Hostel sponsors an elaborate five-borough bike marathon with 36 miles of streets closed to cars (attracting, in 1978, more than 10,000 participants).

Not all the desirable measures favor bikes over cars. Here are some that even Detroit could support:

8. *Provide bike lockers and better bike racks.* Most bike racks look as though they were designed and placed by the Brotherhood of Hot Bike Dealers. Since theft is a major deterrent to cycling, racks need to become a

Elihu Blotnick

major deterrent to thieves; the fixtures must be designed to protect both wheels and frames (most don't), and they must be located in well-lit areas, much-frequented or even watched by guards (such as parking-lot attendants). In high-crime areas, it may be necessary to provide metal lockers for bicycles.

9. *"Piggy-biking."* There are occasions when it is necessary or desirable to transport a bike on another vehicle. Some cities have bridges or tunnels impassable to bicycles. Others have excellent suburban bike-trail networks that are too far from the city to reach by bike and return in a day. Haltingly, public transit is rising to the challenge. Some West Coast cities, most notably San Diego, have "pedal-hopper" service whereby bicycles can be placed on racks on the rear of buses for some trips. The San Francisco Bay Area Rapid Transit system also allows bicycles in the rear cars of trains during nonrush-hour periods, as does New York's subway from Manhattan to New Jersey. However, many other trains, such as New York's Conrail and Long Island Railroad lines to the suburbs, prohibit bicycles even on weekends.

10. *Plan with common sense.* Often it's the little details of route planning that make all the difference. Many cities erect bikeway signs, but the bicyclists cannot find the route except by stumbling across it. Other cities have lovely bike routes that don't lead anywhere useful. Portland, Oregon, solved that problem with an impressive bicycle map that indicates hills, city bike racks and dangerous trolley tracks, as well as showing which bike routes have heavy bus traffic and which don't. The map even rates streets with a color code, much as ski slopes or canoeing streams are rated. The map takes into account not only traffic volume and roadway width, but even stop signs—and indicates the location of bike shops.

Other common-sense actions to stimulate bicycling are sweeping bikeways free of snow, ice, gravel and broken glass; replacing old sewer gratings that are so aligned as to trap bicycle tires; requiring office and apartment buildings to provide bicycle-storage space (as is now required in Palo Alto, California); passing bottle-bill laws to reduce the amount of broken glass on roadways; and building shower facilities at workplaces for more pleasant midsummer cycling.

Bicycling is good for people. It will make us—individually and as a nation—more self-reliant and independent, healthy and community-oriented. To a growing number of people, that sounds like just the right prescription for these uncertain, changing times.

— Peter Harnik

TRANSPORTATION ENERGY SAVINGS in personal travel and freight hauling described in this scenario would reduce direct energy use per capita to twenty-five percent of present levels. What is more surprising is that no reduction in social interaction or accessibility would occur. The energy savings would result primarily from two factors. First, because redesigned settlements would reduce the length of most car trips and provide alternative modes of transportation, including safe walking and bicycle pathways, the necessity of driving would be markedly reduced. Secondly, for the remaining trips that require driving, the vehicles involved would be smaller and far more efficient in their use of energy per vehicle mile. The same factors would apply to energy used for hauling freight.

The change foreseen in settlement patterns would not reduce the number of trips people would make, but rather reduce the distances spanned and change the modes of transportation. Assuming, for example, a city of circular form with five dwelling units per acre, or 10,000 people per square mile, the distance from the edge of the city to the center would be one mile for a city of 31,000—a twenty-minute walk or a six- to ten-minute bicycle ride. The distance would be two miles for a city of 126,000. This would reverse the trends in social and physical arrangements that began with the widespread ownership of the automobile and the universal willingness to sacrifice 25 to 50 percent of urban areas to the operation and storage of the automobile. The pattern of placing numerous competing food and department stores together in shopping centers and malls accessible only to private autos would be replaced by the neighborhood store. Schools and work places would also be distributed throughout the community. With the emphasis on walking, bicycle, and mass transit, far less land would be given over to roadways, parking, and the associated noise and emissions.

Precedents for this type of transportation future already exist and others are being developed. In Rotterdam, 43 percent of all daily trips are by bicycle. The cities of Runcorn, England (population 70,000) and Port Grimaud, France, are both planned to function without automobiles, providing instead exclusive bus, bicycle, and pedestrian access, except for emergencies and special deliveries.

— John Steinhart, Mark Hanson,
Carel DeWinkel, Robin Gates, Kathleen Lipp,
Mark Thornsjo, Stanley Kabala

THE PROBLEM: how to control the intolerable pollution, congestion, and depletion of resources caused by the automobile and its ever-spreading highways, and to a lesser degree by the airplane and its ever-spreading airports.
THE SOLUTION: provide a balanced transportation system in which railroad passenger service is made so good that many people who now travel by automobile or plane will freely choose to go by rail. Then, when travel by automobile or plane becomes impossibly difficult, or is restricted by law in defense of our environment and our resources, the rail lines will be there.

Travel by rail, it has been found, is 23 times as safe as by automobile, 2½ times as safe as by plane, 1½ times as safe as by bus; it is more dependable than any of its competitors (being nearly immune to bad weather and less subject to mechanical failure when kept in top condition . . .); and it is more relaxing, allowing the traveler to work, read, eat, sleep, or even think while moving at high speed toward his destination. (An automobile commuter was stopped one morning on the New Jersey Turnpike for driving with his elbows while eating a bowl of cereal.)

If we start moving now to balance our transportation system, using democratic devices our forefathers willed us, we can accomplish the partial transition from autos and planes to rails with a minimum of fuss, as free men and women. If we procrastinate like spoiled children, the federal government eventually will have to yank us out of our cars and shove us onto trains, with an inevitable loss of freedom and dignity.

The [Highway] Trust Fund is sometimes defended on the ground that highway users pay the tax and should get highways in return. But its opponents say that this is rather like arguing that the tax on whisky should finance only the building of more whisky distilleries, or the tax on cigarettes the building of cigarette factories.

—Thomas C. Southerland and
William McCleery

PARKLANDS HAVE BEEN TORN, cities have been shattered and rich agricultural lands have been invaded in the process of building the widely heralded and anxiously awaited 12,500-mile California Freeway System. Of the total, 2177 miles are part of the federal interstate system, ninety percent of which is paid for by Uncle Sam. The balance is financed on a fifty-fifty basis by the state and federal governments. The interstate system, like California's freeway system, is a toll-free network, the reason being that only a little more than one fifth of it will carry enough traffic to pay for itself out of toll revenue. What has been boasted as "the biggest construction project in history" is without doubt the largest boondoggle in history, too.

Perhaps the most telling indictment of the highway program is the fact that there is not one mile in a hundred that can be considered anything more than a means to an end. You will find no romance, no beauty, no majesty. There will be no sentimental ballad written for Interstate 5. Where in the freeway system can one find that element of nobility characteristic of man's great works of the past?

In a moment of madness, California State's Division of Highways proposed in 1956 to name a section of new highway in Contra Costa County the "John Muir Freeway," in honor of the great conservationist and founder of the Sierra Club. Naming a freeway for John Muir is about as appropriate as naming a saloon for Carrie Nation.
—William Bronson

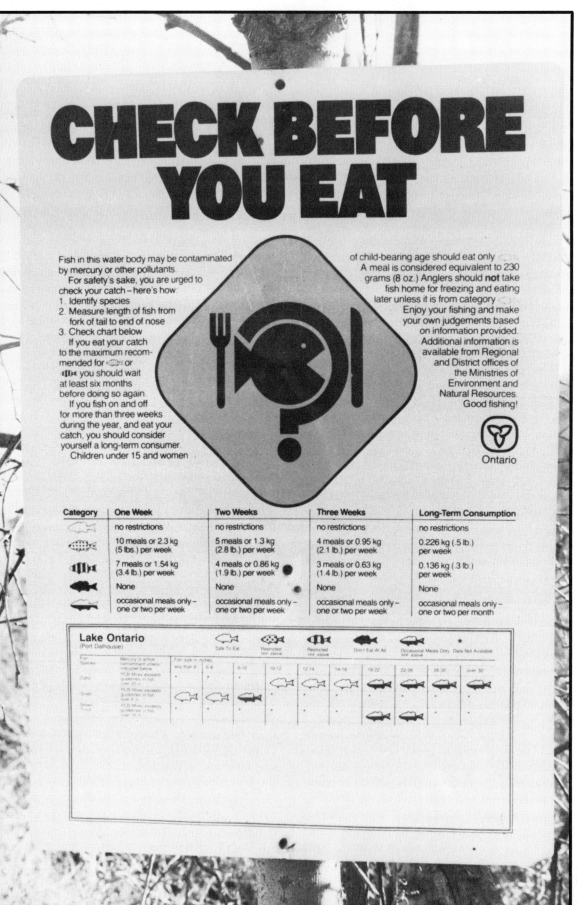

Public Health

Medical practitioners have traditionally gone to heroic lengths to cure sick people, but have done relatively little to keep healthy people well. This was inevitable in medicine's early days, when little or nothing was known about the causes of disease; there wasn't much a doctor could do but wait for people to get sick, then do his best to cure them. But much more is now known about the causes of disease, and preventive medicine should at last begin to come into its own. We are learning that many causes of disease are environmental: air, water, and soil pollution, toxic chemicals, natural and man-made radioactivity, and stresses caused by noise and overcrowding, to name some of the most familiar.

Restoration of the environment to ecological health would be a form of preventive medicine whose importance can hardly be overstated. It would not be enough to eliminate pollution and stresses in the general environment, however. Many farm and industrial workers are exposed to far greater concentrations of toxic pollutants at the workplace than the law permits the general public to be exposed to. This double standard should be eliminated at once. Until environmental hazards are eliminated, health workers will continue to be burdened unnecessarily with the care of millions of Americans whose illnesses were not only foreseeable, but also preventable.

Public Health in the 1980s

MARC LAPPE

AMERICANS ARE GETTING a mixed message about their health. As the decade of the 70s ended, they were told by Julius B. Richmond, Assistant Secretary of Health in HEW, that they were healthier than ever. Richmond cited statistics that showed infant mortality at an all time low in 1978 (13.6 deaths per 1,000 live births) and life expectancy at an all time high (73.2 years). The 1970s marked the first time too that survival from some malignancies had been significantly prolonged, notably for Hodgkins' Disease, leukemia in childhood, and early detected breast cancer.

At the same time, Americans learned of radiation induced cancer on the rise, Love Canal, and unprecedented environmental pollution from toxic wastes and contaminants. New disease entities from environmental exposure appeared to proliferate like flies on the Nile: asbestosis and mesothelioma, vinyl chloride induced angiosarcoma, and other exotic sounding diseases marched from the workplace into American living rooms. What is really going on?

The reality is that the health of Americans is precariously poised between unprecedented well-being and insidious decline. While we stave off death for the aged and pump enormous amounts of taxpayers dollars into evermore sophisticated machinery for monitoring the course and outcome of pregnancy, we are all too vulnerable to the day-to-day wear and tear on our systems that is an inevitable concomitant of living in a technological age. Trichloroethylene and other organic solvents, Iodine[131] along with other radioactive isotopes, and heavy metals are as ubiquitous a part of our lives as was dust and grime in an earlier age. The seemingly salubrious statistics at the beginning and end of life belie the presence of environmental factors that threaten to drastically undercut the hard-won quality of life enjoyed by an increasing majority of Americans.

How do we reconcile Richmond's statement with the growing awareness of environmental degradation? For one thing, the most visible public health achievements are often those most easily enumerated. "Health" tends to be measured in the black and white statistics of life and death, not noisome irritants, excess colds, or just plain malaise. More critically, health data don't yet adequately tabulate birth defects, irreversible neurological damage, or impaired vital capacity—all suspected concomitants of exposure to occupational and environmental pollutants. It should come as no surprise then that significant health efforts tend to concentrate on improving health outcomes that can be readily measured. In the course of improving such outcomes, particularly the genuinely dramatic improvements in fetal and newborn survival, the medical profession can overlook the more subtle effects that often dog their footsteps out of the operating room (caesarean sections are becoming the modus vivendi of American births), and into the pediatric nursery and home.

More and more infants are contracting infections from antibiotic-resistant bacteria while they are hospitalized, and the bottle feeding still done by too many mothers only exacerbates the problem of newborn infections by increasing the kind and resistance of bacteria introduced into the vulnerable neonate. The heroics of the obstetric amphitheater in salvaging premature or low birth weight infants pale when infants are returned to a world where their thyroid function is threatened by radioactive iodine, their neurological development by heavy metals like lead or cadmium, and their immune system by a vast array of potential allergens.

Health data on mortality or longevity, of course, also describe only the norm—not the distribution of vital statistics. Blacks in urban areas like East Oakland, California, Puerto Ricans in South Newark, New Jersey, and Appalachian families in Kentucky and Tennessee, still have an infant mortality rate almost double the national average. And black men can expect to live almost a decade less than their white counterparts. Sudden infant death syndrome (SIDS), which accounts for 8,000-10,000 deaths a year among 2- to 6-month-olds, strikes the children of the poor and non-white far more often than the rich. Stroke and other diseases linked to hypertension are endemic to some urban ghettos. And infectious disease, the scourge of 19th century medicine, still ranks fourth behind the three other horsemen of the apocalypse—heart disease, cancer, and stroke.

Old diseases like gonorrhea, food poisoning (salmonella), typhoid fever, and hemophilus pneumonia are proving increasingly resistant to treatment. Epidemics of previously rare venereal diseases like chlamydial, herpes or trichomonad infections are increasingly common. In fact, the impact of infectious diseases as a whole are of such a magnitude that many observers are questioning whether, on balance, we are any better off in the post-antibiotic era of miracle drugs than we were before they were introduced.

We are uncovering more and more disease entities simply through the assiduous application of newly developed diagnostic techniques. "New" diseases like Legionnaire's, infant botulism and Alzheimer's (senile dementia) often prove to be simply old killers in new guises. While small pox and poliomyelitis may be gone as a result of intensive immunization campaigns, they have been replaced by epidemic outbreaks of hepatitis and antibiotic-resistant bacterial infections. New categories of occupational disease—from vinyl chloride plastic-related diseases such as angiosarcomas and meat wrapper's asthma to chlorinated chemical-caused chloracne and solvent-induced peripheral nerve damage—represent the true newcomers.

The Legacy of Modern Medicine

The continued vulnerability of subgroups in impoverished environments, the failures of some of medicine's previously successful remedies (most notably antibiotics), and the insult of environmental contamination place novel and often unanticipated stress on the ability of some people to adapt to their environment.

By its very success, modern medicine has produced a generation of individuals who would have succumbed to infections, nutritional deprivations, or acute infectious disease in earlier centuries. There is good reason to believe that the net effect of medical advances leading to effective treatment of the insulin-dependent diabetic, life-saving chemo-therapies or operations for early malignancies or childhood immunizations, has meant the survival of many whose genetic constitutions simply would not have withstood the rigors of modern life.

This relaxation of natural selection means that many more of us are being born with genetic constitutions unsuited to the rigors of the modern chemosphere of newly synthesized products of contemporary civilization. Few of us can expect to be genetically prepared to withstand exposure to the unprecedented environmental insult produced by the release of a plethora of new chemicals. In the face of 8,000-10,000 new chemical products added annually to our arsenal of over 140,000 different industrial or agricultural

substances, it is unlikely that either the biosphere generally, or the human body particularly, carries the evolutionary wisdom to fend off the toxic properties of hazardous substances.

Only a portion of us, for instance, carry the hereditary instructions to detoxify the polycyclic hydrocarbons, which, like benzopyrene, are now ubiquitous environmental contaminants. More ominously, those of us who do have this special enzymatic machinery (known as the aryl hydrocarbon hydroxylase system) may in fact be activating the benzopyrene molecule into a carcinogenic chemical in the process of breaking it down!

Similar evolutionary pitfalls exist in the enzymes of the liver's microsome system that detoxifies ingested

---

The importance to good health of personal habits cannot be overemphasized. A study of 7,000 adults in California showed that those who lived longer and healthier lives got adequate rest, ate three meals a day, exercised, did not smoke, and did not overeat or overdrink. Other research suggests that similar life style changes could save more lives among the middle-aged than any conceivable advances in medical science.

—BRUCE STOKES

---

foodstuffs or absorbed poisons. Thus, the microsomal system appears to generate a dangerous epoxide as it breaks down trichloroethylene, a degreasing agent and universal solvent in industry. More than 576 million pounds of this chemical are used annually in the US, so much that wells from places as diverse as Long Island, New York, and the San Gabriel Valley, California, have been uncovered with up to 1,600 parts per billion of this chemical—320 times the EPA-recommended level of 5 ppb.

The Evolutionary Lesson

Because evolution has not prepared the human organism to anticipate its present man-made environment, we are largely unprepared to cope with the onslaught of new chemicals and varieties of infectious

Toxic chemicals being detonated at a waste dump.   *Photo courtesy of the Sierra Club.*

agents produced or encouraged by modern technological innovations. Unfortunately, modern day approaches to public health often gloss over the exquisite vulnerability of some members of the populace to such unanticipated health problems. Whole new specialties like ecologic medicine have sprung up to cope with the hundreds of persons who appear to be allergic to components in the man-made environment. The growing tendency of some industries to screen their workers for genetic susceptibility to hazardous chemicals reflects the level of corporate anxiety about responsibility for work-related disease more than it does good science. Vulnerabilities certainly exist among workers but the solution would appear to be to adjust permissible exposure levels downwards rather than put the onus on the victim's genetic makeup.

More critically, the vulnerabilities that should be of greatest concern to health workers are those that are distinctly centered on particular phases of our life cycle, not individual idiosyncracies. The developing embryo or immune-impaired aged are cases in point. Environmental contaminants as diverse as polychlorinated biphenyls, mercury, and radiation have already left a legacy of congenital malformations and neurological damage among newborns and infants. PCB-contaminated cooking oil in Greece has produced the

"gray baby syndrome" in exposed infants; mercury, the "itai-itai" disease; and radiation, leukemia in exposed children in Japan. American concern about such devastating problems was aroused only after similar findings, albeit on a lesser scale, were uncovered in the United States. A case in point was the tardy concern by the federal government that nuclear testing in the late 1950s probably generated leukemias in children exposed in the southwest corner of Utah. Other environmental contaminants, including chlorinated solvents, heavy metals, and phenoxy herbicides, are only now being recognized as serious threats to the well-being of the young.

Older citizens suffer from nutritional deficiencies in startling numbers. Senility, long thought to be a necessary concomitant of old age, is increasingly recognized as a complex and often treatable constellation of constitutional problems. Environmental insults to the old and infirm are just now being studied for their effects: the increased lifespan so optimistically announced recently by HEW has a hollow ring when we appreciate that more than 80 percent of those 65 or older now live in "warehouses" for the aged, homes without family support systems or the assured incomes needed for autonomy.

These statistics also hide the existence of several

important disease entities that are only recently being understood as complex indices of environmental, nutritional, and dietary factors. For instance, increasing numbers of mentally retarded children are being found to have lead body burdens or nutritional deficiencies that could explain some or all of their problems.

A disease entity that was recognized only in the late 1970s, infant botulism, appears to account for some portion of SIDs deaths. Its cause has been linked to the ingestion of spores of clostridia botulina, a contaminant of some kinds of honey. The discovery of an externally caused and distinct syndrome could have been accelerated had public health officials oriented their thinking towards critical epidemiologic studies.

Cancer

The National Cancer Institute has reported that deaths from cancer inched upwards at about 1.1 percent a year between 1968 and 1978, moving from a rate of 140 per 100,000 population to 160 over the ten-year period. The public has been told that this increase is only marginal, and reflects a trend towards smoking-related increases in lung cancer deaths. In support of this contention, NCI cites the present epidemic of lung cancer among women. Here again, the statistics belie a more serious problem on a local scale. Work-related cancer deaths of the lung and other exposed tissues appear to be increasing at a rate four times higher than that of the population generally. At least, asserts Marvin Schneiderman of the National Cancer Institute, we ought to be recognizing those trends in cancer sites that can't be attributed to smoking. In the workplace, individuals working in professions as diverse as roofing, insulation (asbestos), oil, and pipefitting show a higher cancer death rate than expected from looking at the population as a whole.

Causes

Many farm and industrial workers are exposed to far greater concentrations of toxic pollutants at the workplace than the law permits the general public to be exposed to. Many of these pollutants, like the herbicide 2,4-D, PCBs, or vinyl chloride, have only recently been linked to special syndromes or diseases in people. The continued presence of such environmental hazards at levels above those recommended for safe exposure means that working people will continue to be burdened with incapacitating illnesses that were not only foreseeable, but also preventable.

To date, however, health prevention activities have unfortunately focussed on the health behaviors or life styles of the victims. Cigarette smoking has been sin-

gled out as one such bete noire. While it is true that smoking causes a dramatic proportion of lung cancer and other diseases and contributes markedly to the incidence of stroke and heart disease, much of this contribution can be seen as a result of an overlay of insult on injury.

Smoking exacerbates disease as well as causing it. Pneumonia is worsened by smoking. So are occupationally related asthma and emphysema. Also, a large but unknown portion of lung cancer that is attributed to smoking may in fact result from an underlying injury caused by lung disease, other carcinogens, or asbestos. For instance, prior asbestos exposure dramatically increases the risk to smokers of lung cancer and mesothelioma.

The US government estimates that smoking costs the American public between five and eight billion dollars in health costs. But the solution is not simply an attack on smoking alone. Smoking needs to be seen as part of a larger context. Tobacco companies intent on profit-making and individuals living out their prerogatives to choose hazardous behaviors—as questionable as these activites might be—are just part of the problem. Another part is that society itself creates a common ethos that condones both smoking and environmental pollution as "reasonable" prices for all of us to pay for our technological well-being. A widely run ad carries the message that without chemicals, life itself would be impossible. Other manufacturers imply that chemicals are a necessary concomitant to modern life. These cleverly worded slogans inculcate a belief that we should simply accept a certain level of contamination as the price of sustained growth and economic welfare.

Such an emphasis fails to make a critical distinction between voluntary behaviors like smoking and involuntary ones such as being exposed to other people's smoke or to hazardous concentrations of chemicals on the job. Corporations recognize that it is both more expedient and more economical to attach blame to voluntary behaviors, and to leave involuntary exposures aside. Because of the drive to maximize production and profits, it is axiomatic that occupational and other health hazards generated by the conduct of industry and commerce generally are more resistant to change than are those generated by the consumers themselves.

Pollution Control

Corporate interests are among the first to point out that pollution abatement is subject to the law of diminishing returns: at the beginning, great improvement can be achieved at modest cost; later, it costs a lot to produce even a modest amount of improvement.

They picnic on exquisitely packaged food from a portable icebox by a polluted stream and go on to spend the night at a park which is a menace to public health and morals. Just before dozing off on an air mattress, beneath a nylon tent, amid the stench of decaying refuse, they may reflect vaguely on the curious unevenness of their blessings. Is this, indeed, the American genius?   —JOHN KENNETH GALBRAITH

Since the passage of the Toxic Substance Control Act in 1976, polluters have insisted that the results already achieved are adequate to ensure a modicum of public safety and well-being. But discovery of the health consequences of past abuses, epitomized by the incident at Love Canal in New York, shows that such pronouncements are far from proven.

At Love Canal, residents experienced episodes of birth defects and chemical poisoning as a result of leaching from a vast chemical dump maintained by Hooker Chemical Company of Niagara Falls. The Environmental Protection Agency estimates that at least another 500-800 such sites exist nationwide that pose imminent threats to the public health. Polluters' insistence that further abatement would not be cost-effective has to be weighed against the continued health consequences of inaction. At least one government agency is taking this concern seriously. The EPA has budgeted 500 million dollars to clean up hazardous waste dumps, and states like California have initiated regional plans to ensure that dumping only occurs at properly designated sites.

Many industries have strenuously resisted remedial programs. A case in point is the successful resistance of corporations to the imposition of a stricter standard for benzene in the workplace. Rather than accept the one part per million level proposed by environmental scientists and health officials, industry took the EPA to court and successfully put off implementation of the new standard. Another instance that demonstrates the questionable basis for industry assertions that it could not meet environmental standards centers on vinyl chloride. After the demonstration that vinyl chloride could produce liver and brain cancer in workers, EPA recommended a one-part-per-billion standard. Industry again asserted that the costs of engineering controls would be prohibitive and resisted the change. But instead of the crippling blow that industry predicted, the actual costs of controls were modest.

The Occupational Health and Safety Act of 1970 was passed to help overcome such resistances. Its aim is to "assure so far as possible every working man and woman in the nation safe and healthful working conditions and to preserve our human resources." But farm workers are exposed to insecticides, herbicides, rodenticides, nematocides, fungicides, soil sterilizers, growth regulators, fumigants, solvents, and other toxic chemicals. Many such agricultural chemicals are inadequately tested for their potential danger to exposed workers, and where special precautions are required, they are often neglected. A case in point was the nematocide dibromochloropropane (DBCP), whose use resulted in cases of male sterility. Here, adequate data were available to demonstrate the probability of testicular effects of DBCP years before the human exposures at Lathrop, Calfornia, that caused sterility.

Some industry spokesmen insist that by working where they do, workers tacitly accept any risks associated with the job. There are several troubles with this. For one, industry has seldom been completely candid about the risks its employees are exposed to. For another, workers aware of the risks may face an agonizing choice between known health hazards and. the known hazards of unemployment. If workplace environmental hazards were inherent and unavoidable, it'd be a somewhat different matter. But they're not; their non-abatement merely increases the profits of those whose risks are purely financial at the expense of those whose health is at risk.

Chemical Pollutants

Airborne lead from chemical plants and arsenic from pesticide sprays are especially dangerous pollutants. Lead is capable of profound damage to the nervous system and arsenic is an insidious poison, causing skin cancer and liver damage. Mercury is rendered comparably toxic by activation: bacteria convert mercury to methyl mercury, a compound easily absorbed by organisms in the food chain. Methyl mercury can kill brain cells, and since it can cross the placenta, it can damage fetuses.

Polychlorinated biphenyls (PCBs) were introduced in the US in 1930, but the damage they do was undetected for nearly four decades. It was not until 1968 that the toxic properties of PCBs became known as a result of a poisoning episode in Japan in which 1,291 people were affected. Like DDT, PCBs degrade very slowly and accumulate in fatty tissues. PCBs affect the liver and interfere with enzyme activity. They can also disturb the central nervous system, affect the heart and blood vessels, and cause congenital malformations. The Environmental Protection Agency issued waste-disposal restrictions in early 1972 designed to keep PCB levels low. Nevertheless, EPA's Office of Toxic Substances estimates that at least 4.5 million kilograms of PCBs are dumped into the environment each year. Many fish in the Great Lakes are badly contaminated, as are fish in the Hudson, Milwaukee and Ohio Rivers. In February of 1980, the EPA issued provisional regulations prohibiting the further installation of PCB-containing equipment and machinery.

Radiation

Radiation damage to cellular DNA can kill the cell or cause a mutation. If the cellular progenitors of sperm or ova are damaged, the result can be passed on to subsequent generations. Radiation damage to a fetus at a crucial stage of organ development can cause congenital abnormalities like microcephaly. Exposure to radiation also increases the likelihood of cancer and leukemia. Both effects were seen in the survivors of Hiroshima.

Man-made sources of radiation include the testing (or use) of nuclear weapons, nuclear power plants and associated facilities, nuclear powered ships, and radio-isotopes used in industry, agriculture, medicine, and scientific research. Plutonium 239, a by-product of nuclear power plants and the material of which atomic bombs are made, is the most virulent of carcinogens; it decays very slowly and remains lethal for hundreds of thousands of years. Whether more insidious but faster-decaying radiation like Iodine[131] or Krypton[210] will cause biological damage is being tested in another unintentional experiment: Three Mile Island.

Elihu Blotnick

There is no quiet place in the white man's cities. No place to hear the leaves of spring or the rustle of insects' wings.
—CHIEF SEALTH

Restoration Program

Eliminating the most noxious pollutants and carcinogens from the environment would be the form of preventive medicine that would do the most good for the greatest number of people in the shortest time. Ecologically benign ways of meeting man's material needs do exist, and the appropriate technology movement can discover many more.

Clean air and water, uncontaminated soils, and the decay of man-made radioactivity cannot be achieved overnight. But the further we progress toward those goals, the more we will be rewarded by major improvements in public health. Cleaning up the general outdoor environment will be of limited benefit, however, if workplace environments remain unhealthy and unsafe.

Farming has traditionally been exempt from many of the safety regulations haphazardly applied to other vocations. This seemed reasonable when the family farm was the archetype, perhaps; but in the era of huge agribusiness farms often employing migrant labor, exemption from health and safety regulations is one more subsidy for the rich at the expense of the poor.

Our current practice reflects the philosophy that chemicals are presumed safe until proved to be otherwise. This philosophy has blighted many lives and ended many others. The burden of proof should not rest on the consumer—or even the government—to prove products dangerous; instead, the burden of proof must be placed on the manufacturer to show that his product is safe. No one should be permitted to market a product or introduce a new chemical whose safety is merely assumed and whose possible dangers have not even been investigated. If this means that the deluge of untested new chemical compounds slows to a trickle, no doubt the chemical companies and their customers will manage to survive. It is by no means certain, on the other hand, that either the companies or their customers can long survive if the random introduction of countless untested chemicals continues.

Conclusion

Acting in ignorance, we have discovered that we can significantly alter genetic structures without even trying to do so, merely as an accidental byproduct of some of our other engineering endeavors. Scores of environmental mutagenic hazards exist, from mold products to X-rays, and many more are being synthesized daily.

An unpolluted environment and hazard-free workplace are the foundations upon which public health must rest. Without them, medical practitioners can only palliate illnesses that should have been prevented.

Recommended Actions

☐ The Administration should propose legislation to establish a National Institute for Preventive Medicine.

☐ Congress should strengthen laws to control toxic substances, which must require manufacturers to prove the safety of new chemical compounds before marketing them.

☐ The inappropriate use of antibiotics—their unnecessary prescription by doctors, for instance, or their addition to livestock feeds—should be legislated against (unless the industries and professions concerned voluntarily police themselves).

☐ Congress should enact a law to curb pollution by taxing polluters in proportion to the amount they pollute.

☐ Anti-pollution laws should be more strictly enforced, and to this end, the budget of the Environmental Protection Agency should be increased.

☐ The much higher than average vulnerability of certain sub-groups of the population, such as infants, the aged, the poor, and the sick, should be taken into consideration when setting pollution standards.

☐ An appropriate committee of Congress should hold hearings to determine why the Occupational Health and Safety Act has been less effective than it should, proposing corrective amendments.

☐ Congress should mandate that workplace environments meet the same pollution standards that apply elsewhere.

☐ A committee of Congress should investigate the inadequacy of the Food and Drug Administration's protection of consumers.

☐ The Environmental Protection Agency should set additional noise-pollution standards and strictly enforce them.

☐ Congress should ban supersonic transport planes from US airspace because (among other things) of associated health hazards.

☐ Federal and state government should support municipal initiatives to limit or ban the use of private automobiles in high-density urban areas.

☐ Cities, with federal and state encouragement and support, must create more urban parks for the physical and mental well-being of their residents.

☐ For ways of reducing health hazards associated with mal-distribution of population, see the chapter on decentralization.

☐ For ways of reducing the health hazards of man-made radioactivity, see the chapter on control of the atom.

More Thoughts on Public Health

ALTHOUGH THE PUBLICITY accorded the connection between cigarette smoking and cancer is well deserved, far more of the deaths arising from cigarette smoking involve coronary heart disease—the leading killer in most developed countries—than cancer. Cardiovascular diseases probably account for more than half the premature deaths caused by cigarette smoking. Smokers under the age of 65 are twice as likely as nonsmokers to die of coronary heart disease. Moreover, smoking combines with other major risk factors, such as high blood cholesterol and high blood pressure, to multiply the heart-disease risk manyfold.

In the ambiguity-plagued universe of environmental-health studies, proof of unequivocal links between particular environmental agents and particular diseases rarely emerges. The airtight medical case against cigarettes stands out sharply as an exception. Cigarettes therefore explicitly challenge the capacity of societies to use the conclusions of health research to improve health.

More Americans are killed by cigarettes each year than were killed in combat in all of World War II.

—Erik Eckholm

CAREFULLY CONTROLLED laboratory experiments with animals and statistical correlations in selected groups of humans and in society at large have revealed a great deal about the origins of cancer. Probably the most startling revelation of all is that between 75 and 90 percent of all cancers are related to environmental factors. The term "environmental," in this case, encompasses substances in the food we eat, the air we breathe, and the water we drink, as well as our personal habits, occupations and lifestyles.

Today, the workplace environment unfortunately continues to be the primary laboratory in which the carcinogenicity to humans of certain substances is first revealed.

It has been discovered that virtually every substance (with the notable exception of arsenic) which is carcinogenic to man also causes cancer in animals. This has allowed scientists to identify suspected carcinogens which, although their potential danger is not as clearly established as it would be from direct observation among humans, should be treated with extreme suspicion and caution.

More than any other type of cancer, lung cancer—which in the overwhelming majority of cases is attributable to cigarette smoking—is responsible for the rapid rise in the incidence of cancer in the United States over the past fifty years. In this century the occurrence of several types of cancer, including cancer of the esophagus, prostate, and intestinal tract has remained fairly stable, and cancers of the stomach and uterus have actually declined significantly. Lung cancer, on the other hand, has soared among men and is beginning to rise steeply among women as well.

Despite growing awareness that cancer is largely an environmental disease, scientific testing (and hence meaningful regulation) of chemicals in our environment has lagged far behind. Nevertheless, about 22 chemical substances are generally conceded to be human carcinogens, and a much larger number—about 1,500, according to data from the National Institute for Occupational Health and Safety—are under suspicion.

Vinyl chloride came to public attention in 1974 when several workers who had handled the substance for long periods began developing angiosarcoma, a rare and invariably fatal type of liver cancer. Polyvinyl chloride, which is manufactured from vinyl chloride, is one of the most common plastics in use today, found in everything from toys to food wrappings.

Several pesticides in the chlorinated hydrocarbon family—DDT, Aldrin, Dieldrin, chlordane and heptachlor—have been banned or suspended by the Environmental Protection Agency because they cause cancer in laboratory animals. However, virtually all living Americans still have residues of these chemicals in their bodies. Whether they are dangerous levels is not known. It is worth mentioning that pesticide industry spokesmen and scientists launched a vicious attack of ridicule and vituperation against the late Dr. Rachel Carson when she suggested over a decade ago that some of the chlorinated hydrocarbons should be banned.

The carcinogenic potential of a number of food additives is currently being hotly disputed, with public interest groups and independent researchers often calling for controls on the basis of disturbing but inconclusive tests, and the food industry calling for more testing and a go-slow approach. In the past, the Food and Drug Administration has tended to take industry's side.

Unfortunately, the FDA has been, at best, a rather sleepy watchdog. It has let a number of substances go by without testing them adequately for carcinogenicity, even though the substances should have been regarded with extreme suspicion. A good example is acrylonitrile, a chemical substance which is similar in its molecular structure to vinyl chloride. The FDA has given "interim" approval to a number of plastic beverage bottles made from acrylonitrile monomers without performing itself, or requiring of the manufacturer, any long-term feeding studies on the substance.

The agency is allowed to approve substances without premarket testing if they are Generally Recognized As Safe (GRAS) or if they were on the market prior to 1958 and 1960, when separate amendments strengthening the Food, Drug and Cosmetic Act were passed. However, it must remove any approved substance from the market if new evidence shows that it is unsafe. The FDA's testing program for GRAS substances and those which have been judged acceptable by default is almost ludicrously behind schedule.

The agency's stumblebum performance has been well documented by Ralph Nader and other consumer spokesmen and amply criticized by consumers, environmentalists and some members of Congress, but to little effect. Its problem, according to many observers, is that it is far too much under the influence of the food, drug and chemical industries—the result of decades of pressure from these interests with very little counterpressure from consumer and environmental organizations.

It is time that we forced our regulatory agencies to take a much tougher stance against proven and suspected carcinogens in the environment. Even with existing laws, controls over cancer-causing substances could be considerably more effective than they are today. New laws requiring better premarket testing of chemicals and more comprehensive regulation of toxic substances would, if properly drafted and implemented, be enormously helpful.

Finally, we must face the fact that the "chemical

"Now hear this! Mr. Wetzel is prepared to comply with state and federal emission-control standards if and when they become effective. Until such time, Mr. Wetzel will continue to indulge himself in the manner to which he has become accustomed. That is all."

revolution" of the past fifty years appears to be one of the chief factors behind the rapid rise in the incidence of cancer. And we may only be seeing the tip of the iceberg, because most of the suspected chemical carcinogens did not come into widespread use until after World War II. Ominously, the rate of cancer incidence increased 2 percent last year after rising at a rate of about 1 percent per year for many years. There is no obvious reason why we cannot have a high standard of living without dwelling amid a chemical minefield of cancer-causing agents.

More than any other disease, cancer gives rise to a feeling of hopelessness in all of us, tempting us to throw up our hands and ask, "What can I do?" But if 8 out of every 10 cancer cases are attributable to environmental factors, then it is obvious that cancer is not, except in a minority of cases, inevitable.

Therefore, while we continue to search for a cure, the best remedy is still the oldest one: preventive medicine.
— From the *Newsletter* of the
Natural Resources Defense Council

I WISH TO COMMENT on the misapprehension that medicine has already developed into a full-fledged science, and having matured to this state has already run out of its string. What I hope to persuade you to is, instead, the view that medicine is still the most immature and undeveloped, and, on balance, most unaccomplished of sciences, with a long, long way to go still ahead.

Preventive medicine is being urged on us, from all sides, as though we'd never heard of it, nor ever hankered for it to become, some day, a reality. And if you fail to prevent disease, through some unspecified oversight, then early detection is the thing; if you can check the progress of glaucoma or cervical cancer by early detection, why not do the same for coronary disease, arthritis, diabetes, stroke and all the rest? This has become the public expectation, and it is our misfortune not to have been sufficiently candid about the impossibility of such an expectation, at this state of our knowledge.

We must be careful, in my opinion, not to make promises about preventive medicine as we should have been (but weren't) about curative medicine in the past quarter-century.

For, if the truth be told, we are still at a very early, primitive stage in the development of medical science. There should be nothing shocking or unnerving about this statement. On the contrary, it ought to provide a source for the greatest optimism about the future. It is not that the science has not been getting anywhere, or is stuck somehow; there are the most convincing sorts of evidence that it is moving, and getting ready to

move faster and more productively. But it has to be said that it is just at its beginnings, and most of its new world lies still ahead.

It is often said that as medicine becomes more of a science, the costs of care become higher and higher, but the truth is just the opposite. When the science is really far enough advanced so that the resulting technology can deal directly and decisively with an underlying disease mechanism, the costs go down. The more effective the medical technology, the simpler it is, and the cheaper.

The cost is at its highest, and the technology at its most complex, when we are only halfway along.

We are only halfway, or less than that distance, in our understanding of the causative mechanisms in heart disease, cancer, stroke, nephritis, arthritis, schizophrenia and the others, and what we have for therapy is, correspondingly, a halfway technology, costing enormous sums of money and involving high complexity.

Fifteen years ago, when the biological revolution was just getting under way, things were still quiet and relatively inactive in medicine. Now, the new information is coming in cascades, and it is filled with meaning and astonishment for all of us. And it should not need mentioning that the greatest part of this information has come out of laboratories engaged in the fundamental biological sciences—from the fields of immunology, bacteriophage and microbial genetics, cell biology, membrane structure and physiology, neurophysiology and molecular biology.

Moreover, it is my belief that we are just at the beginning of this.

What is likely to come of this, in the best of possible worlds? Eventually, if all goes reasonably well, nothing less than the control of human disease. If not the outright elimination of disease, at the least a technological capacity to turn it around and govern it when it occurs.

This does not mean as much as it sounds like meaning. It has nothing at all to do with death, beyond the prevention of premature death. No matter how skilled we become at controlling or abolishing the last of our major diseases, we will still die, and probably die by the same, unalterable genetic clock, as always. We will still grow old, although aging will not be the incapacitating and humiliating disorder that it is for most of us, sooner or later, these days.

So things will be significantly better, and the health care system will be very much less a drain on the public purse. But not Utopia. We will still have our other anxieties, our neuroses, our fears of meaninglessness, our problems with each other. We will still be compelled to stare at famine and death on our television screens, trying to think up new excuses. Coping once

School site near Love Canal, Niagra Falls, New York.   *Photo by Victor Fischer.*

and for all with organic disease will not solve any of these, but perhaps it is safe to say that we will be somewhat better at constructing a workable society if we are, at least, physically healthy. Given enough time and patience, and enough good luck in the science, that objective, limited as it may be, is within our grasp.   —Lewis Thomas

SEEMINGLY INNOCUOUS compounds present in the atmosphere can often have dramatic, unforeseen side effects, particularly when they are present in large quantitites. One bizarre example is the recently discovered effect that chlorofluorocarbons (CFCs) have on the atmosphere's ozone layer.

Ozone is a gas continuously created by sunlight in the stratosphere. It not only absorbs most of the ultraviolet radiation of the sun, but also controls the temperature of the stratosphere—and thus indirectly affects the climate at the earth's surface. Removal or substantial reduction of the ozone layer would likely lead to enormous increases in the rate of skin cancer in humans and largely unknown but generally destructive effects in other animals and plants. A National Academy of Sciences publication reported that studies of the effects of a simulated 50 percent decrease in ozone showed that for some species of plants growth

decreased from 20 to 50 percent, chlorophyll content declined 10 to 30 percent, and degenerative changes in cell structures occured. Harmful mutations increased seven- to twenty-fold in some preliminary experiments.

But chlorofluorocarbons may not be the only culprits. Equally perplexing is the recent discovery that the atmosphere contains large amounts of ozone-destroying chlorine atoms in the form of carbon tetra-chloride (CCl_4), a compound that has been used for years as a household cleaner. Thus, CCl_4 might turn out to be just as serious a threat to the ozone layer as the CFCs. The important question is, Where did so much CCl_4 come from and how will its future concentration change relative to that of the CFCs?

Another speculation is that the chlorine compound chloroform may be associated with the purification of drinking water or sewage treatment; both processes often use chlorine. If chloroform could get to the stratosphere and destroy ozone, then the populations of all countries will be confronted with a serious long-term dilemma. If improvement of living and health standards for the growing billions, especially in less developed countries, is to be accomplished and maintained—and I have no doubt that this is an essential international goal—then a massive effort to upgrade water and sewage purification everywhere is impera-

"The doc says I should go East for my lungs."

tive. However, since this could entail a huge increase in the use of chlorine (which in water may react chemically to produce chloroform), there arises the question of potential ozone depletion, which could endanger life on the entire planet.

There is some hard evidence connecting the increased usage of nitrogen fertilizer to an increase in the production of the gas nitrous oxide (N_2O), otherwise known as laughing gas, in the soil. It is known that N_2O can destroy ozone; therefore, when fertilizer-produced N_2O works its way up into the stratosphere, it, too, can reduce our protective shield against ultraviolet radiation. The most difficult question is, How great are these effects? Preliminary calculations suggest that they could be enormous, although there are sitll great uncertainties to be cleared up. Moreover, industrially produced fertilizer is the key ingredient in modern scientific farming, and, indeed, its use is projected to increase by hundreds of percent in the next

twenty-five years. Thus, a discovery and warning that a great increase in fertilizer use could ultimately destroy part of the ozone shield would, if heeded, dash hopes that the developing countries could achieve self-sufficiency in food production soon. Such a discovery could be a staggering blow to those who are counting on expanded use of this particular technology to solve one important aspect of the world predicament.

—Stephen Schneider

IN 1937, A DRUG manufacturer decided the best way to capitalize on the popularity of the new sulfa drugs was to market one of them in a liquid, nonprescription form. He developed a product called Elixir Sulfanilamide, which combined a sulfa compound with diethylene glycol—a commercial solvent used in making antifreeze and brake fluid.

Because the drug control laws of the time did not require safety testing, the manufacturer was free to put his product on the market, and he did so—with devastating results. Although only 2,000 pints of the Elixir were produced, and only 93 were consumed, a total of 107 people died from the effects of the solvent.

The public outcry that followed prompted Congress to pass a new Food, Drug and Cosmetic Act—one that, for the first time, gave the Food and Drug Administration the authority to require the testing of new drug products for safety.

Under the circumstances, the public's outrage and Congress' response to it were scarcely surprising. The trail from cause to effect, in the case of the Elixir, was a short one. No great breakthroughs in the science of epidemiology were required to follow it. Once it was established that all of the victims had consumed the Elixir, the evidence pinpointed diethylene glycol as the cause of death beyond any reasonable possibility of doubt.

Normally, of course, regulatory issues in the health-and-safety area are not posed in such dramatic fashion. This is especially true for environmental regulation. There, the pathway from cause to effect—from the point where a pollutant is discharged into the environment, to the point where it can be positively connected to particular diseases in particular human beings—tends to be a long and circuitous one.

But though we must operate in the absence of scientific certainty, we are by no means without scientific resources. For while we seldom have the kind of proof available in the Elixir episode, we almost always have the scientific equivalent of *circumstantial* evidence. This can take the form, for example, of tests that show how a pollutant affects laboratory animals; or studies of its impact on human beings exposed to it in the workplace, or in food products. Moreover, if we weigh that evidence in a careful and systematic way—the courtroom analogy is giving a suspect pollutant the benefit of due process—we are fully capable of making reasonable judgments about an appropriate degree of regulatory control.

For every pollutant, there comes a point where the scientific knowledge available can offer only guidance for regulatory decision-making—where policy judgments must be made. In regulating air pollutants, for example, the Clean Air Act tells us to allow for a margin of safety—to set the standard somewhat lower than a strict reading of the evidence might seem to call for. And deciding where to set the margin—although reflecting the scientific evidence—ultimately comes down to a question of judgment.

Our approach in making such judgments has been basically this: If the evidence clearly *suggests* the possibility of health damage, but is not conclusive, we will *assume* that the possibility is real.

Why have we adopted this kind of stance? Simply because if we wait for scientific proof before taking firm regulatory action, we will very likely turn out to have waited too long. Thus, with carbon monoxide, we do not have proof that angina leads to permanent heart damage—but there is evidence that it may, and we must take account of that evidence. And the dangers of delay are demonstrated still more graphically by the new class of pollutants that increasingly concern us—pollutants that are products of the post-World War II Chemical Revolution.

We of course have only a limited sense how dangerous these substances are. We assume very few will ultimately turn out to be toxic. Yet the universe of substances we are talking about is a large one—an estimated 5 million chemicals are now known to exist, and 45,000 of these are in commercial use. Moreover, the *quantity* of synthetic chemicals has grown exponentially over the past few decades—with production rising from less than 50 billion pounds in 1950 to more than 300 billion pounds by the late 1970s.

If nothing else, those figures argue for treating these substances with a generous measure of caution. As Love Canal taught us, a careless attitude at one period in history may turn out to impose heavy costs—both in financial and in human terms—more than a generation later.

Given the potential for long-term damage, it seems to me the case for a policy that emphasizes protecting health where the scientific evidence is inconclusive *should* be irrefutable. Yet, as many of you know, it's getting more and more difficult to carry that argument in Washington these days—given the antiregulatory climate in town.

The counter arguments vary. At times, agencies like EPA are accused of failing to do their scientific homework properly; at times of stretching their interpretations of the evidence to support unreasonable regulatory measures. But whatever the particular line of argument, the basic message is the same—we should slow down, wait for more evidence, conduct more studies.

We *do* need to improve our scientific understanding of the links between pollution and health—especially in the case of toxic chemicals, many of which didn't exist a generation ago. But we cannot delay writing sensible, balanced rules governing these substances. We know enough to do that. Moreover, if new evidence emerges to suggest the need for changing our rules, we can change them.

Bill Oetinger

After the final no there comes a yes
And on that yes the future of the world
depends.

— WALLACE STEVENS

Control of the Atom

Peaceful and warlike atoms are not twins, they are one. Fission reactors in commercial power plants produce the stuff of which atomic bombs are made. Proliferation of nuclear power plants in this tinderbox world is an indirect form of nuclear weapons proliferation, and makes a mockery of the Nuclear Nonproliferation Treaty. But the United States still possesses the power to turn civilian nuclear power off, worldwide. Most nuclear installations abroad require US support for their construction, operation, and maintenance. If the US shuts down its own nuclear industry for safety reasons, as it should, the shut-down of nuclear industries in other countries will be a political if not a practical necessity. The US's power to act unilaterally will vanish, however, when nuclear industries in other countries acquire the ability to support themselves unaided. If that is allowed to happen, neither the US nor any other nation will be able to do much on its own initiative to halt nuclear proliferation. We must control the atom in the next few years if we are ever to control it at all.

The Atom

AMORY B. LOVINS, L. HUNTER LOVINS, and LEONARD ROSS

THE NUCLEAR PROLIFERATION problem, as posed, is insoluble.

All policies to control proliferation have assumed that the rapid worldwide spread of nuclear power is essential to reduce dependence on oil, economically desirable, and inevitable; that efforts to inhibit the concomitant spread of nuclear bombs must not be allowed to interfere with this vital reality; and that the international political order must remain inherently discriminatory, dominated by bipolar hegemony and the nuclear arms race. These unexamined *assumptions*, which artificially constrain the arena of choice and maximize the intractability of the proliferation problem, underlay the influential Ford-MITRE report and were embodied in U.S. policy initiatives under Gerald Ford and especially Jimmy Carter to slow the spread of plutonium technologies. Identical assumptions underlay the multilateral, two-year International Nuclear Fuel Cycle Evaluation (INFCE), whose lack of sympathy for those U.S. initiatives is now being cited as a political and technical rationale for dismantling what is left of them. Unfortunately, INFCE'S assumptions were widely represented as its *conclusions*, ostensibly resulting from a careful assessment of alternatives which never actually took place.

Our thesis rests on a different perception. Our attempt to rethink focuses not on marginal reforms but on basic assumptions. In fact, the global nuclear power enterprise is rapidly disappearing. De facto moratoria on reactor ordering exist tody in the United States, the Federal Republic of Germany, the Netherlands, Italy, Sweden, Ireland, and probably the United

This chapter has been adapted from "Nuclear Power and Nuclear Bombs," Foreign Affairs, *Summer 1980. The article, an expanded version of this argument, carries full citation for all quotations and statistics quoted here. The article is also the basis for* Energy/War: Breaking the Nuclear Link *(Friends of the Earth, 1980; Harper and Row, 1981), in which the Lovinses treat the issues of horizontal proliferation, appropriate energy for development, and denuclearization in far greater detail.*

Kingdom, Belgium, Switzerland, Japan and Canada. Nuclear power has been indefinitely deferred or abandoned in Austria, Denmark, Norway, Iran, China, Australia and New Zealand. Nuclear power elsewhere is in grave difficulties. Only in centrally planned economies, notably France and the U.S.S.R., is bureaucratic power sufficient to override, if not overcome, economic facts. The high nuclear growth forecasts that drove INFCE'S endorsement of fast breeder reactors are thus mere wishful thinking. For fundamental reasons, nuclear power is not commercially viable, and questions of how to regulate an inexorably expanding world nuclear regime are moot.

The collapse of nuclear power in response to the discipline of the marketplace is to be welcomed, for nuclear power is both the main driving force behind proliferation and the least effective known way to displace oil: indeed, it *retards* oil displacement by the faster, cheaper and more attractive means which new developments in energy policy now make available to all countries. So far, nonproliferation policy has gotten the wrong answer by persistently asking the wrong questions, creating "a nuclear armed crowd" by assuming its inevitability. We shall argue instead that acknowledging and taking advantage of the nuclear collapse, as part of a pragmatic alternative program, can offer an internally consistent approach to nonproliferation.

Fatalism is becoming fashionable as the headlines show proliferation slipping rapidly out of control. Yet seeking Stevens's courage to affirm, we shall suggest that an effective nonproliferation policy, though impossible with continued commitments to nuclear power, may become possible without them—if only we ask the right questions.

Nuclear Explosives

All concentrated fissionable materials are potentially explosive. All nuclear fission technologies both use and produce fissionable materials that are or can be concentrated. Unavoidably latent in those technolo-

gies, therefore, is a potential for nuclear violence and coercion. Most of the knowledge, much of the equipment, and the general nature of the organizations relevant to making bombs are inherent in civilian nuclear activities, and are largely interchangeable and interdependent for peaceful or violent uses.

All commercial nuclear fuel cycles are fueled with uranium. Natural uranium as mined contains only 0.71 percent of the fissionable isotope uranium-235. Both this concentration and the few percent of uranium-235 present in "low-enriched uranium" (LEU) are too dilute to be explosive. Practicable bombs require concentrations of tens of percent; highly efficient bombs, about ninety percent ("highly enriched uranium" or HEU). A few minor types of commercial reactors, notably the Canadian CANDU, are fueled with natural uranium. The dominant world type, the U.S.-designed light-water reactor (LWR), is fueled with LEU. One prospective commercial type (the high-temperature gas-cooled reactor) and many research reactors are fueled with directly bombusable HEU.

The irradiation of uranium fuel in any reactor produces plutonium, which is a bomb material regardless of its composition or chemical form. The plutonium is contained in the discharged spent fuel, highly diluted and intimately mixed with fission products whose intense radioactivity makes the spent fuel essentially inaccessible for at least a century. The plutonium is thus a proliferation risk only if it is extracted by "reprocessing" the spent fuel behind heavy radiation shielding—chopping up and dissolving the fuel bundles and chemically separating the purified plutonium. It is then in a concentrated, homogeneous and divisible form that can be safely handled, is hard to measure precisely, and is therefore much easier to steal undeteted. Extracted plutonium can be made into bombs so quickly (in days or hours) that even instant detection cannot provide "timely warning," the cardinal principle of safeguards since the start of the nuclear age.

Fuel Cycles

U.S. nonproliferation policy since 1976 has rested on distinctions between proliferation-prone fuel cycles and fuel cycles thought to be proliferation-resistant. LWRs were considered highly proliferation-resistant so long as technologies or services which could further enrich the LEU fresh fuel or extract

The energy panaceas that were being advanced with confidence a decade ago are likely to be a lethal problem in themselves and no solution to any existing problem. Any nation that pursues the nuclear energy alternative not only increases the existing rate of fossil-fuel depletion, but further opens the path to nuclear war, nuclear blackmail and sabotage, the high risk of nuclear-power-plant accident, and finally the impossible task of finding a secure means for disposal of nuclear wastes. The nation that adopts the nuclear option helps to endanger the future of life on earth and almost guarantees the growing restriction of human freedom imposed by the need for increasing security measures. Furthermore, it is no answer to the energy problem, but may militate against finding long-term solutions.
—RAYMOND DASSMANN

plutonium from the spent fuel were not available to non-weapons states. It was considered possible for such states to obtain these technologies on their own, but only at high cost, with great technical difficulty, and with a large risk of timely detection. Reprocessing spent LWR fuel in conventional large plants, for example, is so difficult that no country has yet succeeded in doing it on a reliable commercial basis.

In return for an open-ended fee with no guarantee of performance (estimated costs rose thirteenfold in 1974-78 and are still rising), Britain and France are nonetheless proposing to expand their existing, rather unsuccessful, reprocessing plants to provide export services, thus relieving others of the technical difficulties. However, proposed technical measures to inhibit the use of the extracted and re-exported plutonium in bombs—chiefly by diluting or radioactively contaminating it so that further treatment would be needed—have been shown to be impracticable or ineffectual (especially against governments). International management or weapons-state siting of the reprocessing plant cannot affect how the re-exported plutonium is used.

Because commerce in plutonium therefore poses grave risks to peace, and because neither it nor the reprocessing plants supplying it can be safeguarded even in principle, the United States sought by its own example, and for a time by mild persuasion (but not by exercising its legal veto over reprocessing U.S.-enriched fuel), to discourage Britain and France from breaching the formidable barrier offered by the difficulties of reprocessing. As further recommended by the Ford-MITRE report, the United States also sought to defer as long as possible domestic and foreign commitments to widespread use of fuel cycles requiring reprocessing—recyling plutonium in LWRs and breeding it in fast reactors. "Once-through" (no-reprocessing) LWRs, on the other hand, were encouraged for domestic use and for export because of their alleged proliferation resistance.

Bomb Factories In Disguise

Advocates of reprocessing and plutonium commerce assaulted the U.S. policy on two contradictory grounds: that power reactors did not make plutonium that would be attractive to bomb-makers, and that if they did, commercial reprocessing was not the only way to extract it. The first limb of this argument claimed that the "reactor-grade" plutonium made by normal operation of power reactors—currently some 30 tons (about 10,000 bombs' worth) per yer, a third of it in non-weapons states—could produce only weak and unreliable explosions, and posed exceptional hazards to persons working with it. Countries seeking bombs would therefore pass up this inferior material in favor of "weapons-grade" plutonium whose greater isotopic purity offered optimal performance. Weapons-grade plutonium could be made in existing research reactors (now operating in about 30 countries) or in "production reactors" specially built for the purpose from published designs. This route was claimed to be easier, cheaper, more effective, hence more plausible than using power reactors. Concern over power reactors was thus deemed to be far-fetched.

The technical premise behind this reasoning, however, is false. A detailed analysis of weapons physics has now shown that any practical composition of plutonium—including both "reactor-grade" plutonium and plutonium to which inseparable interfering ("denaturing") isotopes have been deliberately added—can be made by governments or by some subnational groups into bombs equivalent in power and predictability to those made from "weapons-grade" plutonium. Alternatively, power reactors can be so operated as to produce modest amounts of the latter without significantly increasing costs, decreasing efficiency, or being detected.

More sophisticated bomb design is needed to achieve the same performance from reactor-grade as from weapons-grade plutonium, but this may be a small price to pay fo the greater ease of obtaining the former in bulk. The power reactor has an innocent civilian "cover" rather than being obviously military like a special production reactor. It is available to developing countries at zero or negative real cost with many supporting services. It bears no *extra* cost in money or time if one were going to build a power reactor anyhow. And it produces extremely large amounts of plutonium: so large that theft of a few bombs' worth per year is within the statistical "noise" and can be made undetectable in principle, while nearly a hundred bombs' worth per reactor per year— more than from any other option—is available if overtly diverted. Power reactors, then, can be considered large-scale military production reactors with an electricity by-product rather than benign electricity producers with a militarily unattractive plutonium by-product. They are not, as INFCE held, an implausible but rather potentially a peculiarly convenient type of large-scale factory for bomb material.

Of course plutonium in spent fuel from any kind of reactor is unusable in bombs until extracted by reprocessing, and it is here that plutonium advocates mounted their second line of attack. The official U.S. view was that reprocessing is very hard, whereas making bombs is relatively easy, so reprocessing should be inhibited. Plutonium advocates retorted that, on the contrary, making bombs is very hard but reprocessing relatively easy. To support this claim, Oak Ridge scientists developed a conceptual design for a "quick-and-dirty" reprocessing plant which could allegedly separate a bomb's worth of plutonium per week, with only a modest risk of detection during the relatively short construction time (of the order of a year). Restraints on commercial reprocessing (its advocates then argued), and indeed the timely warning concept itself, were futile because any country seeking bombs could build its own crude reprocessing plant and get plutonium from its domestic spent fuel anyhow.

This double-edged argument was inconsistent, however, with the same advocates' reassurances that

providing commercial reprocessing services would dissuade recipient countries from building their own plants; that international safeguards could be relied upon; and that bomb-making could be prevented by returning the plutonium "spiked" with unapproachably radioactive contaminants. (The recipient country could use its crude reprocessing plant to winnow out the plutonium from the spikants even more easily than from the original spent fuel.)

Thus the measures supposed to make reprocessing "safe" do not work. An argument meant to show there was no point discriminating against plutonium technologies showed only the wider dangers of all fission technologies. Far from showing plutonium cycles were safe, it showed only that the rival once-through cycles were nearly as dangerous. For the real implication of the Oak Ridge design was that the reprocessing barrier is not so substantial after all: that both bomb-making *and* reprocessing are relatively easy (if normal requirements of profitablility, environmental control, and worker safety are greatly relaxed).

This conclusion has been reinforced by the recent invention in several countries of unconventional medium- and small-scale methods of plutonium recovery, as yet untested, that are alleged to be substantially cheaper, simpler and less conspicuous than normal reprocessing plants. If, as appears likely, at least one of these new methods or the Oak Ridge concept proves valid, then it does not mean merely the end of the old timely warning concept; it means rather that timely warning can be provided neither for separated plutonium *nor* for spent fuel, so that *all* nuclear fission will be unsafeguardable in principle.

The Ford-Carter policy that reprocessing is very dangerous, therefore, was correct but did not go nearly far enough. By emphasizing that plutonium fuel cycles are *more* dangerous than once-through cycles, it glossed over the risks of the latter. The INFCE findings that there is no technical solution to the plutonium problem, and that once-through fuel cycles are not necessarily far less proliferative than plutonium cycles, are also broadly correct; for they imply, however unintentionally, that reactors of *any* kind are significantly proliferative, and that matters are much worse than the Ford-MITRE analysis and the Ford-Carter policy supposed.

To make matters worse still, more careful scrutiny of the supposedly innocuous front end of the fuel

---

Once man has opted for nuclear power, he has committed himself to essentially perpetual surveillance of the apparatus of nuclear power. —ALVIN WEINBERG

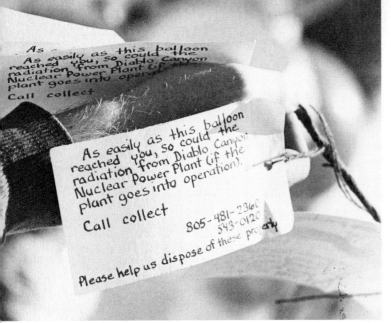

As easily as this balloon
reached you, so could the
radiation from Diablo Canyon
Nuclear Power Plant (if the
plant goes into operation).

Call collect
805-481-2360
543-0120

Please help us dispose of these pr...

Karen Spangenberg

cycle—the use of natural uranium or LEU as fresh reactor fuel—has lately suggested a similar conclusion on independent grounds. Natural uranium can be gradually enriched to bomb-usable concentrations using low-technology centrifuges. LEU can be enriched more than twice as easily. An effective centrifuge design was published 20 years ago. Better versions—much less efficient than high-technology commercial versions, but still adequate—can be, and have been made by a good machinist in a few weeks. Nonnuclear commercial centrifuges may also be adaptable to uranium enrichment. Though tens or hundreds of centrifuges and tons of uranium would be needed for patient accumulation—perhaps requiring years—of even one bomb's worth of HEU, the centrifuges are simple, modular, concealable, relatively cheap, and highly accessible. The uranium, mined in tens of thousands of tons per year worldwide, would be even easier to get. Thus even without assuming any breakthroughs in fast-moving new enrichment technologies—simplified laser methods, or perhpas the newly discovered magnetochemical methods—old, straightforward centrifuge designs suffice to make even natural uranium, as Bernard Baruch noted in 1946, a "dangerous" material.

One Fuel Bundle, One Bomb

There are also disquieting indications that without using any conventional facilities such as LWRs or reprocessing plants, and without serious risk of detection, one unirradiated LWR fuel bundle (about a hundredth of a reactor's annual fuel requirement) could be made into one bomb's worth of separated plutonium in one year by one technician with about one or two million dollars' worth of other materials that are available over the counter and apparently subject to no controls. So far as is publicly known, this novel basement-scale method has not yet been used, but the calculations suggesting its feasibility—unpublished for discretion—appear valid. U.S. authorities were apprised of this method during 1978-79, but no published assessment mentions it. A vivid if indirect confirmation that no fuel-cycle material is officially considered "safe," however, comes from the U.S.-sponsored Convention on the Physical Protection of Nuclear Material. This makes it an extraditable international crime (like genocide or piracy) for unauthorized persons to meddle with any fissionable material other than uranium ore or tailings, and explicitly *including* both LEU (such as LWR fuel) and purified natural uranium.

The proliferative routes just mentioned are only the latest additions to an already long list: conventional enrichment technologies, research and production reactors, direct use of bomb materials of which many tons have been exported (mainly by the United States) for worldwide research, theft of nuclear submarine bomb components. Collectively, both familiar and newly emerging routes to bombs imply that *every* form of *every* fissionable material in *every* nuclear fuel cycle can be used to make military bombs, whether on its own or in combination with other ingredients made widely available by nuclear power. Not all the ancillary operations needed are of equal difficulty, but none is beyond the reach of any government or of some technically informed amateurs. The propagation of nuclear power thus turns out to have embodied the illusion that we can split the atom into two roles as easily and irrevocably as into two parts—forgetting that atomic energy is a-tomic, indivisible.

Can conceivable "safeguards" weaken this stark conclusion? Political arrangements for safeguards must rest on technical measures for materials accounting and for physical security. The former measures are so imprecise and *post hoc* that they cannot, even in principle, provide reasonable assurance that many bombs' worth of plutonium per year are not being removed from a good-sized reprocessing plant. Primary reliance must therefore be placed on physical security measures to limit access to materials and to deter or prevent their removal (or, if they are removed, to recover them). These measures must forestall well-equipped groups, perhaps including senior insiders acting in concert with the host government or a faction of it. Even modestly effective measures would be costly, fallible and intrusive. In the Federal Republic of Germany, for example, they would exceed the authority of the Atomic Energy Act; amending it to permit them would be unconstitutional; and amending

Karen Spangenberg

the Constitution to permit them would conflict with human rights instruments to which the Federal Republic is a party.

Flawed Treaties

The institutional arrangements which rely on these inherently inadequate accounting and security measures are woven around the International Atomic Energy Agency (IAEA), the Non-Proliferation, EURATOM, and Tlatelolco Treaties, and bilateral agreements. Though these are a considerable achievement, they have well-known and collectively fatal flaws, including: non-adherence of half the world's population, including two of the five acknowledged weapons states (France, China), all three suspected ones (India, Israel, South Africa), and all major developing countries except Iran and Mexico; freedom to renounce; no prohibition on designing bombs or

building and testing their non-nuclear components; unsafeguarded duplicate facilities; inadequate inspection staff, facilities and morale; virtual absence of developing-county nationals in key IAEA safeguards posts; high detection threshold; freedom of host governments to deceive, reject, hinder or intimidate inspectors or to restrict their access (especially their unannounced access); unknown effectiveness owing to confidentiality; ambiguous agreements; and unsupported presumption of innocent explanations. The IAEA has already detected diversions of quantities too small for bombs and decided they did not justify even notifying the supplier states concerned. IAEA inspectors "have found many [suspicious] indications and acts . . ., but the IAEA has never taken action on any of them. This will probably continue to be true," according to David Rosenbaum. It is no wonder. All the resources of the U.S. government, in more than a decade of repeated investigations, were unable to determine whether suspected plutonium thefts at the Numec plant in Apollo, Pennsylvania had occurred. Large HEU losses over many years at an Erwin, Tennessee plant crucial to U.S. naval reactor fuel supply led in 1979 to relaxed accounting standards that would make the losses look "acceptable." How, then, could suspected thefts in and perhaps by a recalcitrant foreign country be investigated?

Finally, the momentum and bureaucratic entrenchment of nuclear programs generally prevent effective sanctions against even an obvious, sharp violation, let alone a dimly suspected, creeping one. The breach of EURATOM safeguards by the theft of a 200-ton shipload of natural uranium in 1968 was kept secret for nearly ten years. A decade's advance knowledge of the Indian bomb program by the U.S. and Canadian governments produced only diplomatic murmurs, and the actual test, as Albert Wohlstetter remarks, "inspired only ingenious apologies" from the U.S. State Department—anxious to conceal the U.S. contribution of heavy water—and a congratulatory telegram from the chairman of the French Atomic Energy Commission. As front pages heralded the Pakistani bomb progrm, Pakistan was being unanimously elected to the IAEA's Board of Governors.

In short, we can have proliferation with nuclear power, via either end of any fuel cycle. We cannot have nuclear power without proliferation, because safeguards cannot succeed either in principle or in practice. But can we have proliferation without nuclear power?

Reexamining The Line

It is true that naval reactor fuel and military bombs provide non-civilian routes to more bombs; but that means only that nuclear armaments encourage their own refinement, multiplication and spread, not that there are significant civilian bomb routes unrelated to nuclear power. With trivial exceptions unimportant to this argument—radioisotope production reactors, large particle accelerators, proposed fusion reactors— *every* known civilian route to bombs involves *either* nuclear power *or* materials and technologies whose possession, indeed whose existence in commerce, is a direct and essential consequence of nuclear fission power. Apologists, apparently intending to be reassuring, often state nonetheless that since power reactors themselves are only one of (say) eight ways to make bombs, restraining power reactors is like sticking a thumb in one of eight holes in a dike. But the other holes were made by the same drill. Arguing that reactors have little to do with bombs is like arguing that fishhooks do not cause the catching of fish, since this

can also involve rods, reels and anglers.

The foregoing reasoning implies that eliminating nuclear power is a necessary condition for nonproliferation. But how far is it a sufficient condition? Suppose that nuclear power no longer existed. Again, with trivial exceptions, there would no longer be any innocent justification for uranium mining (its minor non-nuclear uses are all substitutable), nor for possession of ancillary equipment such as research reactors and critical assemblies, nor for commerce in nuclear-grade graphite and beryllium, hafnium-free zirconium, tritium, lithium-6, more than gram quantities of deuterium, most nuclear instrumentation— the whole panoply of goods and services that provides such diverse routes to bombs. If these exotic items were no longer commercially available, they would be much harder to obtain; efforts to obtain them would be far more conspicuous; and such efforts, if detected, would carry high political cost because for the first time they would be *unambiguously military* in intent.

This ambiguity—the ability of countries, willfully or by mere drift, to conduct operations (in Fred Iklé's phrase) "indistinguishable from preparations for a nuclear arsenal"—has gone very far. An NPT signatory subject to the strictest safeguards can quite legally be closer to having working bombs than the United States was in 1947. For example, precisely machined HEU spheres have recently been seen in Japan, doubtless for purely peaceful criticality experiments. But they could also be hours away from bombs.

Bernard Baruch warned in 1946 that the line dividing "safe" from "dangerous" (proliferative) nuclear activities would change and need constant reexamination. No mechanism to do this was ever set up. The variety and ease of proliferative paths expanded unnoticed to embrace virtually all activities once presumed "safe," while most of those activities were enthusiastically broadcast worldwide. Yet their direct facilitation of bomb-making was probably a less grave threat than the innocent disguise which their pursuit lent, and lends to bomb-making. Baruch, noting the importance of adequate "advance warning...between violation and preventive action or punishment," had sought a technological monopoly so that visible operation or possession of "dangerous" steps other than by a special international authority, regardless of purpose, "will constitute an unambiguous danger signal." Today, with dozens of countries on the brink of a bomb capacity, such a neat solution is temporarily forestalled. But the principle remains sound: detection and deterrence of bomb-making require that it be unambiguously identifiable; and for that, phasing out nuclear power and the supporting services it justifies would be both a necessary and a sufficient condition.

The Pakistan Route

Removing the present ambiguity will not make proliferation impossible. Pakistan, both operating and planning power reactors, sought a French reprocessing plant rationalized as aid to energy independence, then, when thwarted, decided to pursue bombs more directly with clandestine centrifuges whose advanced design was stolen (as predicted) from the Netherlands. Pakistan probably did not expect that effort to be accidentally unmasked at an early stage, but was presumably willing to bear the political cost of eventual detection (if there was one: India has not yet been made to bear such a cost). Yet the key point is that the reactors, the uranium supply allegedly needed for them, the hoped-for reprocessing plant, the participation of the Pakistani spy in the Dutch project, the existence of that project and of the uranium mining industry itself—all were justified and cloaked in benignity by nuclear power.

For bomb-making by any route, denuclearization would greatly increase the technical difficulty of obtaining the ingredients, and would automatically stigmatize suppliers as knowing accessories before the fact, hence clear violators of NPT Article I in letter or spirit. By providing unambiguous danger signals, denuclearization would make the political costs and risks to all concerned very high—perhaps prohibitively high. This does not mean that a determined and resourceful nation bent on bombs can by non-military means be absolutely prevented from getting them: much is already out of the barn. But denuclearization would brand as military the use of those escaped resources and inhibit their augmentation and spread. It would narrow the proliferative field to exclude the vast majority of states—the latent proliferators who sidle up to the nuclear threshold by degrees, and those easily tempted.

Yet is not the complete civil (and, in due course, military) denuclearization required to remove every last shred of ambiguity a fantastic, unrealistic, unachievable goal? On the contrary, that goal—and more straightforward interim steps on the way to it—would follow logically and practically from obeying the economic principles to which most governments pay allegiance.

Replacing Oil

Nuclear power has been promoted worldwide as both economically advantageous and necessary to replace oil. Potential proliferation, in this view, is either a small price to pay for vast economic advantages or an unavoidable side effect which we must learn to tolerate

out of brutal necessity. But rational analysis of energy needs and economics strongly favors stopping and even reversing nuclear power programs. Their risks, including proliferation, are therefore not a minor counterweight to enormous advantages but rather a gratuitous supplement to enormous disadvantages.

Replacing oil is undeniably urgent. But nuclear power cannot provide timely and significant substitution for oil. Only about a tenth of the world's oil is used for making electricity, which is the only form of energy that nuclear power can yield on a significant scale in the foreseeable future. The other nine-tenths of the oil runs vehicles, makes direct heat in buildings, and industry, and provides petrochemical feedstocks. If, in 1975, *every* oil-fired power station in the industrialized countries represented in the Organization for Economic Cooperation and Development (OECD) had been replaced *overnight* by nuclear reactors, OECD oil consumption would have fallen by only 12 percent. The fraction of that oil consumption that was imported would have fallen by much more for the United States than for Japan, France, West Germany or the U.K. In practice, U.S. nuclear expansion has served mainly to displace coal, not oil, by running coal-fired plants less of the time: the utilization of their full theoretical capacity dropped from 62 to 55 percent during 1973-78. In overall quantitative terms the whole 1978 U.S. nuclear output could have been replaced simply by raising the output of partly idle coal plants most of the way to the level of which they are

Paul Conrad

practically capable. And, contrary to the widespread assumption that a nuclear shutdown would cause serious regional shortages, an analysis of the balance within each regional power pool found that in 1978 all but 13 U.S. reactors, or all but two if surplus power were interchanged between regions, could have been shut down forthwith without reducing any region's "reserve margin" (spare capacity) below a prudent 15 percent of the peak demand. Further confirming the loose coupling between nuclear ouptut and oil saving, between 1978 and 1979 the United States reduced by 16 percent the amount of oil used to make electricity, while U.S. nuclear output simultaneously *fell* by 8 percent; the oil saving came instead from conservation and coal and gas substitution. Between the first quarters of 1979 and of 1980, total U.S. oil-fired generation fell 32 percent while nuclear output simultaneously fell 25 percent—hardly a substitution.

The OECD calculation for 1975 exaggerates potential oil displacement by nuclear power, partly because reactors take not one night but about ten years to build. Reactors ordered today can replace no oil in the 1980's—and surprisingly little thereafter. The example of Japan, widely considered the prime case of need for nuclear power, illustrates reactors' relatively small eventual contribution to total energy supply. Quadrupling Japan's nuclear capacity by 1990 would reduce officially projected oil import dependence by only about ten percent. An 18-fold increase by the year 2000—costing about a hundred trillion of today's yen

and requiring a large reactor to be ordered every 20 days—could theoretically meet half of all Japan's delivered energy needs then, but fossil-fuel imports would still *incease* by more than two-thirds. "Rate and magnitude" calculations for other countries are equally discouraging.

No Nuclear Panaceas

It may be said that without nuclear power, these examples would look even worse. But even prohibitively large nuclear programs cannot go far to meet officially projected energy needs. The official projections reflect an inability to face the fact that nuclear power cannot physically play a dominant role in any country's energy supply. Solving the oil problem will clearly require, not a nuclear panacea, but a wide array of complementary measures, most importantly major improvements in energy efficiency.

It is therefore necessary to *compare* the elements of this array in costs, rates, difficulties and risks, to ensure that one is displacing oil with the cheapest, fastest, surest package of measures. Just as a person shopping for the most food on a limited budget does not buy caviar simply for the sake of having something from each shelf, but seeks the best bargain in a balanced diet, so every dollar devoted to relatively slow and costly energy supplies actually *retards* oil displacement by not being spent on more effective measures. Nuclear power programs have been justified not by

(translation) "Presumably a shrine for one of their primitive religious cults."

this rational test but by intoning the conventional wisdom stated in 1978 by Brian Flowers of the U.K. Atomic Energy Authority:

> Alternative sources will take a long time to develop on any substantial scale . . . Energy conservation requires massive investment . . . , and can at best reduce somewhat the estimated growth rate. Nuclear power is the only energy source we can rely upon at present with any certainty for massive contributions to our energy needs up to the end of the century, and if necessary, beyond.

Failure to assess *comparative* rates of oil displacement runs the risk that, having like Lord Flowers dismissed alternatives as slow, conservation as costly, and both as inadequate, one may choose a predominantly nuclear future that is simultaneously slow, costly *and* inadequate.

Nuclear power is not only too slow; it is the wrong kind of energy source to replace oil. Most governments have viewed the energy problem as simply how to supply more energy of any type, from any source, at any price, to replace oil—as if demand were homogeneous. In fact, there are many different types of energy whose different prices and qualities suit them to different uses.

This common-sense redefinition of the problem—meeting needs for energy services with an economy of means, using the right tool for the job—profoundly alters conclusions about new energy supply. Electricity is a special, high-quality, extremely expensive form of energy. This costly energy may be economically worthwhile in such premium uses as motors, lights, smelters, railways and electronics, but no matter how efficiently it is used, it cannot come close to competing with present direct fuels or with present commercial renewable sources for supplying heat or for operating road vehicles. These uses plus feedstocks account for about 90 percent of world oil use and for a similar or larger fraction of delivered energy needs. The special, "electricity-specific" applications represent typically only seven or eight percent of all delivered energy needs—much less than is now supplied in the form of electricity.

In most industrial countries, therefore, a third to a half of all electricity generated is already being used, uneconomically, for low-temperature heating and cooling. Additional electricity could *only* be so used. Arguing about what kind of new power station to build is thus like shopping for brandy to burn in the car or Chippendales to burn in the stove.

The economic absurdity of new power stations is illustrated by an authoritative calculation of how much energy Americans would have bought in 1978 if for the preceding decade or so they had simply met their end-use needs by making the cheapest incremental investments, whether in new energy supply or in efficiency improvements. Had they done so, they would have reduced their 1978 purchases of oil by about 28 percent (cutting imports by half to two-thirds), of coal by 34 percent (making the stripping of the Amercian West unnecessary), and of electricity by 43 percent (so that over a third of today's power stations, including the whole nuclear program, would never have been built). The total net cost of such a program: about 17 percent less than American *did* pay in 1978 for the same energy services. Detailed studies of the scope for similar measures throughout the industrial world (and, where data are available, in developing countries) have given qualitatively similar results.

If we did want "more electricity," we should get it from the cheapest sources first. In virtually all countries, those are, in approximate order of increasing price:

1. Eliminating waste of electricity (such as lighting empty offices at headache level).
2. Replacing with efficiency improvements and cost-effective solar systems the electricity now used for low-temperature heating ad cooling.
3. Making motors, lights, appliances, smelters, etc., cost-effectively efficient.
4. Industrial cogeneration, combined-heat-and-power stations, solar ponds and heat engines, modern wind machines, filling empty turbine bays in existing dams, and small-scale hydroelectricity.
5. Central power stations—the slowest and costliest known source.

The notion that despite all constraints—time, money, politics, technical uncertainties—nuclear power stations are at least a source of energy, and as such can be substituted for significant amounts of the dwindling oil supply, has long exerted a powerful influence on otherwise balanced imaginations. But it does not withstand critical scrutiny. It is both logistically and economically fallacious. The high cost of nuclear power *today* limits its conceivably economic role to the baseload fraction of electricity-specific end-uses: typically, about four percent of all delivered energy needs. In purely pragmatic and economic terms, therefore, nuclear power falls on its own demerits.

The Market Test

These arguments concerning the need for nuclear power might a few years ago have seemed remote and abstract. But nuclear power has in these years come under the strictest test of all, that of the market, and been found wanting. Rising costs, falling political acceptance, and dramatically decreased prospects for electricity demand and utility finance have brought nuclear power to a virtual standstill.

Universally—in the United States and in the U.S.S.R., in France and in Brazil, under the most varing conditions of government regulation—the direct economic cost of nuclear power in real terms (corrected for general inflation) have risen unrelentingly since reactors went "commercial." The most detailed cost data available happen to be from the United States, but the same trends and conclusions apply elsewhere.

A recent detailed statistical analysis of all the U.S. data, explaining 92 percent of their variation, has revealed that during 1971-78, real capital cost per installed kilowatt increased more than twice as fast for nuclear as for coal plants and already exceeds the latter by 50 percent, despite investments that decreased coal plants' air pollution by almost two-thirds and will soon have done so by nine-tenths. The same study concludes that for nuclear plants now starting construction, excluding the possible impact of tighter federal regulatory standards in the wake of Three Mile Island, nuclear capital costs will exceed those of coal by 75 percent, indicating, as energy consultant Charles Komanoff writes, "that many of the 90 U.S. [nuclear] units with construction permits could be converted to coal to provide cheaper electricity."

The real costs of operating the nuclear fuel cycle from uranium mining to spent fuel storage have risen even faster. Unexpectedly high estimated costs for waste management, decommissioning nuclear plants after at most a few decades, and cleaning up past mistakes (for example, burying the hazardous tailings left over from uranium mining) add many billions of dollars in liabilities. Erratic reactor performance—poor reliability, cracks in key components, maintenance problems seeming to go with scarcely a pause from the pediatric to the geriatric—has afflicted most countries. And as cumulative losses mount into the billions of dollars, no vendor in the world appears to have made a nickel on total reactor sales.

Failing Credibility

Added to these economic woes is an ever less receptive political climate, punctuated by Browns Ferry, Three Mile Island, and 19-year-old news of a disaster in the Urals. Demolition by peer reviewers compelled the U.S. Nuclear Regulatory Commission to declare that its 1975 Rasmussen Report (claiming that reactors are very safe) was no longer considered reliable, and the Canadian Atomic Energy Control Board to declare its Inhaber Report (claiming that renewable sources are very dangerous) officially out of print. The classically assumed "solution" to the nuclear waste problem—reprocessing, turning the high-level wastes into glass, and burying them in salt—turned out to be technically flawed. The nuclear industry's credibility, heavily committed to these and similar premises, suffered a meltdown that seems irreversible: as Mark Twain remarked, a cat that sits on a hot stove lid will not do so again, but neither will it sit on a cold one. Efforts to repair the effects of past lack of candor or foresight have exacted a high cost in top-level managerial attention—also a scarce resource—out of all proportion to nuclear power's modest potential contribution.

As costs rise and credibility falls, the market for more electricity is quietly evaporating. With the inevitable response to higher prices beginning, forecasts of electricity demand growth in most countries have been falling steadily. Some are nearing zero or negative values. U.S. electricity demand has consistently been growing more slowly than real GNP of late, and all the trends are downward. Forecasters unfortunately responded more slowly than consumers: over the past six years, U.S. private utilities forecast that peak demand for the following year would grow by an average of 7.8 percent, but the actual growth averaged only 2.9 percent. Overcapacity in the United States went over 40 percent in 1980 and has continued to rise (perhaps past the British level of about 50 percent). U.S. overcapacity in excess of a prudent 15 percent reserve margin is already well over twice the present nuclear contribution. It is indeed so large that if *all* U.S. powerplant construction were stopped immediately, growth in peak demand at an annual rate of 1.2 percent—twice that experienced in 1979—would still leave a national reserve margin of 15 percent in the year 2000. Growth by at least 2.2 percent per year could be accommodated if the economically advantageous industrial cogeneration potential were tapped. The market for power stations of any kind is simply imaginary.

Finally, nuclear (or fossil-fueled) power stations and their grids incur such extraordinary capital costs and take so long to build that utility cash flow is inherently unstable. Any utility, whether public or private, regulated or not, which persists in building such plants will sooner or later go broke, and many are already doing so. Funding for new plants is scarce and costly; and even if it is available, building new plants is simply no longer in utilities' financial interest.

These problems, singly and interactively, have taken their toll on industry morale, investor confidence, and resulting expectations. In only six years from 1973, nuclear forecasts for 2000 fell by a factor of five for the world, nearly four for West Germany (no new orders since 1975), and eight for the United States (*minus* 27 net orders during 1974-79). Nuclear forecasts world wide are still plummeting—more for economic than political reasons. The U.S.S.R., for example, achieved only a third of its nuclear goal for the 1970's, half for the past five years. And although there have been essentially no procedural barriers to building reactors in Canada, the pattern of decline in nuclear capacity forecast for the year 2000 has been all but identical in Canada and the United States.

Despite intensive sales efforts and universal subsidies (often up to or exceeding total costs), the drop in expectations for nuclear power has been even faster in developing countries, paced by Iran, which projected 23,000 megawatts for 1994 and will probably get zero, and by Brazil, which projected 75,000 megawatts for the year 2000 and is unlikely to want more than the 2,000 megawatts that are now in serious difficulties. Total nuclear capacity in all developing countries in 1985 is now unlikely to be as much as 13,000 megawatts, or about the present West German level. Even if giveaway offers tempt new customers (perhaps Mexico, Kenya, Turkey, Zaïre) to undertake the well-known problems of integrating gigantic, very costly, complex units into rather small grids in countries poor in infrastructure, that extra "business" would be a tiny fraction of the loss elsewhere. It would not even be profitable business—only a way to inject export-bank funds into the vendors' ailing cash flows.

The collapse of nuclear markets has already sealed the fate of an industry tooled up to meet the inflated expectations of the early 1970s. Even with continued domestic and export subsidies, withdrawals by major firms seem inevitable. While rhetorically the world nuclear enterprise is pressing forward, in reality it is grinding to a halt and even slipping backward. The greatest collapse of any enterprise in industrial history is now underway. Thus, as Harry Rowen and Albert Wohlstetter remark,

> . . . the argument sometimes shifts subtly from the needs of a robust and inexorably expanding industry to the sympathetic care required to keep alive a fragile industry that is on the verge of expiring altogether.

The industry's long-term hope has been "advanced" plutonium technologies. But their first stage, recycling plutonium in conventional power reactors, was officially acknowledged in the U.K. and West Germany in 1977-78 to save too little uranium to pay for the reprocessing and other costs. Even the INFCE study, generally enthusiastic about plutonium, failed to find recycle inviting. Contrary to one of the earlier arguments advanced for reprocessing, INFCE has now concurred in the official positions of Canada, the United States and Sweden that reprocessing is not necessary for waste management. (Some experts believe reprocessing may even make it more difficult.)

Similarly, one of the strongest arguments earlier advanced for reprocessing and plutonium-related technologies—that fission reactors would need so much uranium as to create shortages—is rapidly receding.

Breeder Reactors

In short, the economics of fast breeder reactors look ghastly until far into the next century. There are indications that prospects for funding and finding acceptable sites for the extremely costly next-stage breeder projects range from only fair (in France and the U.S.S.R.) to poor (in West Germany, Japan, the United States and the U.K.). Even sympathetic officials are realizing that the 50-fold potential improvement in uranium utilization that successful breeders might produce cannot in fact be achieved for well over a century because of the time it takes the breeder's fuel cycle to come to equilibrium; for the next 50 to 80 years, the modest uranium savings that could be realized through breeders could be achieved much more cheaply and surely through uranium-efficient thermal reactors instead. Costly, difficult breeder programs are thus looking increasingly like a commercial blunder, akin to pushing the Concorde while others developed jumbo jets. Further attempts to deploy breeder reactors in an already hostile political climate could indeed jeopardized the limited acceptance now enjoyed by thermal reactors.

The loss of momentum for the breeder, and for the nuclear program which it was to culminate, is reflected at the highest political levels in all the main nuclear countries of OECD and beneath the surface throughout the Soviet scientific community. At various times in the past few years, the British, French, and West German cabinets have been sharply split over whether the whole electronuclear program makes sense. Chancellor Helmut Schmidt has even speculated that 20 billion marks may have been thrown out the window.

U.S. Policy: Wrongheaded

How has U.S. policy affected the foreign nuclear debate at all political levels? U.S. technological dominance of the nuclear arena, though still preeminent, is no longer hegemonic; but U.S. political dominance of world energy policy effectively is. So far it has been exercised in exactly the wrong direction.

U.S. policy pretends that the nuclear collapse is not happening, or that if it is, it shouldn't be and deserves no encouragement. The Energy Secretary in 1980 committed two-fifths of his budget for the next five years to nuclear power. The State Department says

drawing by E. Randall Keeney

that *not* using nuclear power would make proliferation worse. President Carter's confirmations of the necessity and the large energy potential of nuclear power bolstered sagging programs in countries poorer in fuels. Promotional rhetoric has given the nuclear industry a license to present in Europe a false but largely uncontested image of a flourishing American nuclear program (and vice versa). The State Department does not know, and seemingly does not want to know, that however monolithic the policy front presented by other countries (an apperance carefully orchestrated by the U.S. nuclear industry), every national nuclear policy is riven from top to bottom by doubt and dissent. Whatever the United States has done, in policy or in rhetoric, has helped one side of those internal debates and hurt the other. Yet the State Department, maintaining a meticulously lopsided neutrality, has never appreciated that the most powerful U.S. lever for affecting foreign nuclear policies in either direction was not blunt instruments like fuel supply, but rather the *political example* of stated and applied U.S. energy policy in its broadest terms.

Ignoring this influence on domestic energy politics abroad, advocates of continuing subsidized nuclear exports have argued that if the United States does not supply sensitive nuclear technologies, others will, so the United States might as well—and that since others can, the United States has no "leverage" to justify abstention. As Harry Rowen and Albert Wohlstetter put it, "We can retain our leverage only if we never use it. A lever is a form of abstract art rather than a tool giving us a mechanical advantage." Today the United States proclaims itself anxious to be seen as a "reliable supplier," spends five billion dollars on a gratuitous expansion of a centrifugal enrichment capacity to take on new fuel export commitments, and seeks to make those commitments irrevocable; yet at the same time it asks itself, half aloud, how much "leverage" it can obtain by exporting more U.S.-fueled reactors as hostages to later sanctions. Both kinds of exports leave the United States in the unpalatable position of vigorously proliferating in the name of nonproliferation, sacrificing for a weak and counterproductive physical leverage a strong and positive political leverage.

The U.S. And Gorleben

How real is that political leverage? The political vulnerability of nuclear projects was strikingly illustrated in 1979 by the West German government's firm commitment, allegedly crucial for national survival, to build an enormous reprocessing and waste-disposal plant at Gorleben in Lower Saxony. The State Department, citing sensitive alliances, had passed up low-cost opportunities to scuttle analogous projects nascent in

the U.K., France, and Japan before still-fluid political commitments to them had solidified. In the German case, they seemed solid already, but inwardly there were doubts, and to defuse local opposition the governor of Lower Saxony commissioned a technical review by an ad hoc panel of 20 independent experts from five countries. Their report was so comprehensively devastating that neither the Chancellor's party in Lower Saxony nor, privately, the project's own promoters could defend it, and Bonn had to cancel it outright. If a mere report and hearing with no official resources behind them can be the catalyst that reverses a supposedly irrevocable national commitment, what political leverage might a country—especially the United States—apply by the example of its whole energy policy?

In sum, the forces of the market—in combination with new and more searching analysis of other factors—have made the future of nuclear power so precarious that a change in policy by the United States, or by several other countries, would greatly hasten the dawning realization that nuclear power has no valid future either in idustrialized or developing countries. The issue is not whether to mantain a thriving enterprise, but rather whether to accept the verdict of the very calculations on which free market economies rely.

Beyond The Nuclear Age

The proliferation problem has seemed insoluble primarily because vast worldwide stocks and flows of bomb materials were assumed to be permanent. Policy never looked beyond the nuclear power age because there was no beyond. But that age may be ending, with proliferation—given pragmatic planning—arrestable just short of total unmanageability.

To abandon nuclear power and its ancillary technologies does not require any government to embrace anti-nuclear sentiment or rhetoric. It can love nuclear power—provided it loves the market more. Governments need merely accept the market's verdict in good grace and design an orderly terminal phase for an unfortunate mistake. That should include the least unattractive and most permanent ways to eliminate from the biosphere (via interim internationally controlled spent-fuel storage) the hundreds of tons of bomb materials already created, and helping nuclear technologists to recycle themselves into work where their talents are more needed. Phasing out reactors would take about a decade and reduce both political tensions and electricity prices.

While collective leadership by other countries is desirable and sufficient, the U.S. example alone would deprive other countries of the domestic political support that an exorbitantly costly bailout of their nuclear industries would require. Interdependent political illusions would quickly unravel. In a period of tight budgets and narrow electoral margins, explicit U.S. recognition that the market has cut short the nuclear parenthesis in favor of more effective means of oil displacement would focus the accelerating swing of public and professional opinion worldwide. To allow the nuclear industry to die without noting and politically capitalizing on its passage would be a signal failure of international leadership.

Beyond the Nuclear Age

Second, as efforts to make the market more efficient hasten the recycling of nuclear resources into the soft path, the United States unilaterally, and interested states (especially nonaligned non-weapons states) multilaterally should freely, unconditionally, and nondiscriminatorily help any other country that wants to pursue a soft path—especially developing countries. Nuclear fuel security initiatives should be turned into energy security intiatives.

Third, these efforts must be psychologically linked to the slower and more difficult problem of mutual strategic arms reduction—treating them as interlinked parts of the same problem with intertwined solutions. All bombs must be treated as equally loathsome, rather than being considered patriotic if possessed by one's own country and irresponsible if by others. A vigorous coalition of non-weapons states to this end is urgently needed. But the key missing ingredient for promoting a psychological climate of denuclearization, in which it comes to be seen as a mark of national immaturity to have or want reactors *or* bombs, is a reversal of the political example now set by the weapons states.

These combined actions, and those outlined . in Amory Lovins's "Energy" chapter, may succeed only if they are taken together and explicitly linked together. Our thesis is certain to be misrepresented as "trying to stop proliferation by outlawing reactors." We have not said that. We have presented the main elements, and many sub-elements, of a coherent market-oriented program, and emphasize that they have a mutually reinforcing psychological thrust—a synergism—essential to their success. Their linkage is also pragmatic, as illustrated by the common and valid argument that if one phased out nuclear power and did nothing else instead, oil competition could worsen. Although the fight against the "vertical" nuclear arms race will be far more difficult than against the "horizontal" spread of bombs, their interlinkages with each other and with nuclear power are so inextricable that they must be pursued jointly and thought of jointly.

Recommended Actions

☐ The President should declare it United States policy (1) to abandon our nuclear power program as unsafe and unwise; (2) to redirect the resources of our nuclear program toward (a) conservation and greater end-use efficiency, (b) sophisticated transitional fossil-fuel technologies, and (c) "soft" energy supply technologies based on renewable sources; (3) to help all other countries that will likewise renounce nuclear power and adopt benign energy strategies; (4) to treat nuclear non-proliferation, control of civilian fission technology, and strategic arms reduction as interrelated parts of a single problem.

☐ The President, speaking before the United Nations General Assembly, should announce that the US will immediately cease exporting nuclear hardware and technology, urging other nations to do the same; he should, at the same time, promise to support the worldwide deployment of environmentally sound energy systems, primarily solar-based, at least as actively as we have hitherto promoted nuclear power.

☐ Nuclear power plants that cannot be shut down immediately without unacceptable consequences, if any, must be operated at well under their nominal capacity in order to improve safety margins; such plants must be decommissioned at the earliest possible time.

☐ The President and the Secretary of State should continue to assign highest priority to strategic arms reduction negotiations, and military projects such as the cruise missile and MX missile system that militate against an agreement should be dropped.

☐ The Department of Energy should be ordered to investigate the orderly phasing out of nuclear power, including the salvaging of the non-nuclear portions of existing nuclear power plants.

☐ The Nuclear Regulatory Commission should be ordered to investigate the safest way to decommission nuclear power plants and to reduce the hazards that already exist as a legacy of our atomic weapons and power programs; all information accumulated should be freely shared with all other nations.

☐ The US ambassador to the UN should be instructed to insist that the International Atomic Energy Agency cease promoting nuclear power and devote itself instead to curbing nuclear proliferation.

☐ Nuclear engineers and technologists who cannot be absorbed by other industries—and their talent assures that they will be few—should be retrained at public expense; they are the victims of their desire to make the atom serve humanity, and they deserve our gratitude and help.

More Thoughts on the Atom

MORE SOPHISTICATED BOMB design is needed to achieve the same performance from reactor-grade as from weapons-grade plutonium, but this may be a small price to pay for the greater ease of obtaining the former in bulk. The power reactor has an innocent civilian "cover" rather than being obviously military like a special production reactor. It is available to developing countries at zero or negative real cost with many supporting services. It bears no *extra* cost in money or time if one were going to build a power reactor anyhow. And it produces extremely large amounts of plutonium: so large that theft of a few bombs' worth per year is within the statistical "noise" and can be made undetectable in principle, while nearly a hundred bombs' worth per reactor per year— more than from any other option—is available if overtly diverted. Power reactors, then, can be considered large-scale military production reactors with an electricity by-product rather than benign electricity producers with a militarily unattractive plutonium by-product. They are not an implausible but rather potentially a peculiarly convenient type of large-scale factory for bomb material.

—Amory Lovins, Hunter Lovins,
and Leonard Ross

EVERY LIGHT BULB lit by nuclear power bears a cost that does not show up on the consumer's utility bill: a dangerous by-product that will need to be guarded for thousands of years. No country has yet found a permanent solution to the problem posed by nuclear wastes. Indeed, much of the mounting international wariness about nuclear energy derives from a growing public recognition that, after a quarter-century of nuclear power, the waste issue remains unresolved.

Ultimately, there is no technical fix for the problems presented by nuclear wastes. Greater degrees of safety can always be provided at greater costs, but absolute and timeless safety can never be assured. While some of the wastes—notably fissionable isotopes of plutonium and uranium—can be recycled, most radioactive wastes can only be isolated from human society in some sort of repository. And the recycling of plutonium and fissile uranium poses more formidable danger than does disposal of these substances with the wastes.

If the benefits of nuclear power are to be enjoyed today, it should be with the understanding that some of the hidden costs will be passed on to our children and grandchildren. And to their children and grandchildren. The growing resistance to nuclear power represents one of the first times that a large part of the population has developed an understanding of an issue of fairness to future generations. Many people seem willing to forego some current consumption in order to avoid placing a burden on their descendants. Currently a major international controversy is raging around the emotionally charged issue of waste disposal. Within the technical community, the debate concerns such issues as the best technology for solidifying the waste, the best medium for long-term storage, and the benefits and risks of recycling plutonium. However, much of the general public is uninterested in the subtleties of the issue. They know only that a dangerous brew is being concocted that must be contained safely for thousands of years, and they have little faith that existing social institutions are equal to the task.

The general public may be closer to the heart of the issue than are the experts. The technological elements of the debate are easier to address, but probably less important, than the social dimensions. The crucial question involves the likelihood of a high degree of international social and political stability for many thousands of years. Unless people are willing to pay the price that such stability implies—probably an unprecedented degree of international authoritarian control—nuclear wastes pose a threat that for all practical purposes is without end.

—Denis Hayes

OF ALL THE CHANGES introduced by man into the household of nature, large-scale nuclear fission is undoubtedly the most dangerous and profound. As a result, ionising radiation has become the most serious agent of pollution of the environment and the greatest threat to man's survival on earth. The attention of the layman, not surprisingly, has been captured by the atom bomb, although there is at least a chance that it may never be used again. The danger to humanity created by the so-called peaceful users of atomic energy may be much greater.

A new 'dimension' is given also by the fact that while man now can—and does—create radioactive elements, there is nothing he can do to reduce their radioactivity once he has created them. No chemical reaction, no physical interference, only the passage of time reduces the intensity of radiation once it has been set going. Carbon-14 has a half-life of 5900 years, which means that it takes nearly 6000 years for its radioactivity to decline to one-half of what it was before. The half-life of strontium-90 is twenty-eight years. But whatever the length of the half-life, some radiation continues almost indefinitely, and there is nothing that can be done about it, except to try and put the radioactive substance into a safe place.

But what is a safe place, let us say, for the enormous amounts of radioactive waste products created by nuclear reactors? No place on earth can be shown to be safe.

The most massive wastes are, of course, the nuclear reactors themselves after they have become unserviceable. There is a lot of discussion on the trivial economic question of whether they will last for twenty, twenty-five, or thirty years. No one discusses the humanly vital point that they cannot be dismantled and cannot be shifted but have to be left standing where they are, probably for centuries, perhaps for thousands of years, an active menace to all life, silently leaking radioactivity into air, water and soil. No one has considered the number and location of these satanic mills which will relentlessly accumulate. Earthquakes, of course, are not supposed to happen, nor wars, nor civil disturbances, nor riots like those that infested American cities. Disused nuclear power stations will stand as unsightly monuments to unquiet man's assumption that nothing but tranquility, from now on, stretches before him, or else—that the future counts as nothing compared with the slightest economic gain now.

No degree of prosperity could justify the accumulation of large amounts of highly toxic substances which nobody knows how to make 'safe' and which remain an incalculable danger to the whole of creation for historical or even geological ages. To do such a thing is a transgression against life itself, a transgression infinitely more serious than any crime ever perpetrated by man. The idea that a civilisation could sustain itself on the basis of such a transgression is an ethical, spiritual, and metaphysical monstrosity. It means conducting the economic affairs of man as if people really did not matter at all.

—E. F. Schumacher

IF WE LISTEN to the technicians actively engaged in nuclear "deterrence" research and development, we gain the impression that no other approach is even conceivable. And this is fundamentally why such tech-

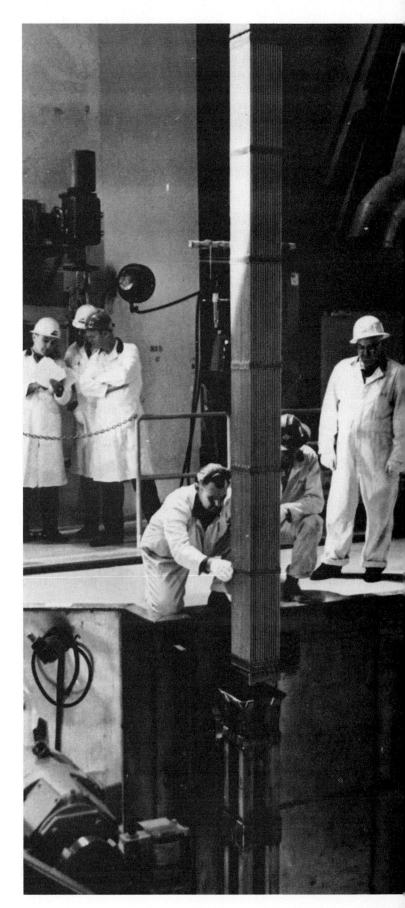

Fueling a nuclear power plant.
Atomic Energy Commission photograph.

nicians are still actively engaged in the work of the nuclear arms race.

But many scientists and technologists, formerly at the very pinnacle of the technical array of nuclear arms specialists, are now of a totally different persuasion. They now recognize that nuclear deterrence via a technologically spiralling arms race is foolhardy and very unlikely to provide security for anyone. They have reached the conclusion that nuclear doom is the most probable result of any further reliance upon weapons for security among nations.

A major requirement for technical excellence is that all *non*-technical considerations *must* be rejected as confusing and detracting from the proper performance of the task at hand. In a field involving the development and deployment of supremely destructive weapons, with the life or death of perhaps one to two hundred million humans at stake, it would be impossible to burden the technicians with human value judgments or moral considerations. Such judgments and considerations are simply inconsistent with execution of the technical responsibility they have accepted.

Men who participate in nuclear weapons and missiles research and development are no moral monsters. It is doubtful in the extreme that any significant number of them would like to obliterate human life massively and indiscriminately through their personal works.

The primary mechanism by which this potential conflict in their minds is resolved in the vast majority of cases is by abdication of the moral and human value judgments *to someone else*. It is reasoned that the appropriate people to make the weighty decisions of human right or wrong are those in the political sphere. It is to the politicians and "statesmen" that the affairs of state, of conflict with other governments, and definition of "vital interests" belong.

The technicians enable themselves, thereby, to feel eminently moral and responsible as human beings and as citizens when they turn over decision-making power concerning human right and wrong to the politicians-statesmen. Any who feel that they have a higher responsibility than that of serving state politics simply do not participate in strategic weapons work.

For USA technicians, "western civilization" is being protected, "the struggle against Godlessness" is being waged, "our way of life" is being preserved, "freedom" is being defended, and the homeland is being protected against prospective hordes of sub-human monsters. Curiously enough, the technicians of the Soviet Union have almost the same slogans to justify *their* abdication of moral and human judgments. The words are a bit different, but the concepts are identical, such as protection of "the Socialist fatherland," the crusade against "capitalist imperialism," and sundry equally soul-satisfying cliches.

A remarkably effective device has been developed during the nuclear era to remove the residual doubts of the technician. This is the concept, carefully nurtured and repeated, that the more effective the weapons development is, the *lower* will be the chance that any such weapons will *ever* be employed.

The adversary will, it is reasoned, have been *deterred* by the terror. This is one of the *most* effective psychological devices in existence for removal of any residual human or moral qualms from the conscience of the prospective weaponeer. He is working to *prevent* horrible holocaust, not to promote it.

Technicians would speak of the time required to get the economy of the country back to the 1950 or 1960 level (after a nuclear exchange between superpowers in 1972). A setback of only 10 years in industrial output would be regarded as minor; a setback to 1900 would be regarded as really effective. Not much deep exploration is made that a human civilization won't be possible at all following a nuclear exchange.

The nature of modern industrial societies, with high concentration of urban populations in relation to industrial plant has, of course, direct implications for the number of human deaths expected to occur in nuclear wars. It generally is calculated that inflicting a reasonably high fraction of industrial disability will be associated with the killing, roundly, of between ten and one hundred million people.

All else failing, the weaponeers can always fall back upon the reassurance that this is what the "other" side thinks acceptable, *not they*. Most of the technicians are very careful to avoid saying *they* would consider initiation of a nuclear exchange without regard for casualties.

There still exists a strange illusion concerning nuclear weapons in the minds of many in the public-at-large. These members of the public feel assured that no one would ever consider nuclear war because "neither side can win." The public has been left far behind in its understanding of what some of the weaponeers mean by *winning*.

Many optimists are inclined to believe that, after all, the technicians in the USA or the USSR do *not* have the last word about the actual *use* of weapons. It is maintained, most hopefully, that the politicians and statesmen can and will overrule technical advice to "go first." We hear such optimistic statements as "reason will prevail" or "the hot line will be used" or other equally unrealistic and naive assertions about the use of a first-strike capability.

There are several very important logical arguments against the proposition that the politicians and statesmen, on both sides, will be able to serve as a brake upon the technical establishment.

NEW!!

Three Mile Island Coffee Mugs

- Made of Heavy Water Proof Plastic
- Won't Melt Down in Washer
- Keeps Hot Things Hot Virtually Forever!
- Available in: Radium White Caramel Tan Atomic Red

Set includes 4 mugs and matching cream and sugar containment vessels

Mail your check, along with this coupon
to: TMI ENTERPRISES, INC.
Box 245-T
Harrisburg, Pa.

Name_____
Street_____
City_____
Color_____

Bill Oetinger

First, it has been made very clear, especially through the writings of Herbert York, that with each step forward in the escalation of nuclear-strategic arms race, the power of decision necessarily passes inexorably *into the hands of technicians,* and worse yet, into the hands of computers and radars operated by the technicians.

In time, if not already, it will be easy for the technicians to bypass the President. The dynamic of the technical approach really *demands* that the President be by-passed, if the technical approach is to be meaningful at all. *The bypassing of the President would represent the supreme manifestation of technical excellence.*

The technicians can reason, at a certain point, that the situation is technically desperate and must, at all costs, not be muddied by fuzzy moral or human considerations.

After all, such reasoning is the very basis of the entire professional structure and outlook when technicians enter the weapons development sphere. Therefore, they can reason that it is their duty to protect the President from his own weaknesses and the country from his weaknesses.

As for the President himself, we must ask ourselves how he could ever *refuse* to accept the technical guidance. He will not himself be technical; he cannot hope to match what he undoubtedly considers the finest in technical expertise.

And this, it can be anticipated, would hold for the technicians versus the political leadership in the USSR as well as in the USA.

If the outlook for the technical approach to security

is as dismal as the foregoing discussion would make it appear to be, why isn't the technical approach abandoned in favor of something more promising?

The technical establishments of the superpowers can certainly not be expected to suggest a non-technical alternative. The very dynamic of their existence and their approach necessarily leads them to suggest more and better technological "fixes."

Who, then, really needs to be convinced and *might* be convinced that the technical approach to security might best be abandoned at an early time? This question is answerable only if another question is asked: "Who hopes to gain by reliance upon military force for resolving conflicts of interest?"

It is the power and privilege elite in nation-states which counts upon military force to protect and extend power, privilege, or both.

Throughout all history up to the present, power-privilege elites have relied upon military force as the ultimate modality for preservation or extension of power and privilege. More than this, such power-privilege elites have looked to the technical establishment for expert guidance. There is every reason to expect they will still look to the technical establishment for such guidance today. And from all that has been

discussed above, the guidance to be expected from this source is *more and better technology.*

It would appear that the highest priority effort should be to ensure an *independent* input of ideas to the power-privilege elite. If this is achieved, it is possible that the technical approach will still be chosen by the elites of the superpowers. But if the prospects for nuclear wipe-out are explained clearly, the power-privilege elites may not like the odds at all. And they might then examine seriously, for the first time, some genuinely alternative approaches.

With their demonstrated skill in mergers, in operations across national boundaries, and in mutually advantageous accommodations, the elites of the superpowers may very well be able to develop a *modus vivendi* with far better prospects for their own security than that offered them by the technical arms race approach. The prospects for humanity in general would improve accordingly.

—John Gofman

IF, AS I AM SUGGESTING here, the disagreement of experts on major aspects of nuclear power is not a temporary condition but, for practical purposes, at

least a semipermanent one, then how is society to proceed? Others have said that nuclear power is too technical an issue to be handled by the public or even by legislators. I believe almost exactly the opposite: the problem is too *nontechnical* to be handled by the technical experts.

I am myself a technologist by training—my background is in engineering and plasma physics—but I have been preoccupied for a substantial part of the past several years with some of the liabilities and shortcomings of technology. One of the biggest of these is our tendency to perceive certain issues as mainly technological, when in fact the fraction of the problem that actually can be illuminated by technical insights is small; the result is to reserve for the judgment of experts' decisions where their expertise is of very limited relevance.

The nuclear controversy is clearly such a case. The toughest questions cannot be resolved by technical expertise. Experts can and should clarify the technical aspects of options and the range of technical uncertainty as best they can. But the public-policy question in the nuclear controversy—how to deal with a situation characterized by uncertainties of these kinds and in these degrees—is not a technical issue. It is a social one. What kinds of risks should be accepted in exchange for what kinds of benefits? With how much uncertainty of specific kinds does the public care to live? How does one weigh the high routine impact of some technologies (for example, burning coal) against the small chance of a big disaster associated with others (for example, nuclear reactors)? The answers to these kinds of questions should be sought in a way that embodies the fullest possible participation of the affected public, and that places the major decisions in the hands of those most directly accountable to the public through the political process.

—John Holdren

Two sides of the nuclear controversy.
LEFT: *A SWAT team at Barnwell, South Carolina, 1978.*   RIGHT: *Protestors at Seabrook, New Hampshire, 1976. Photos by Lionel Delevingne.*

Surely war is civilization's greatest failure.

—LAWRENCE ABBOTT

War and Preparedness

War is the ultimate destroyer. Preparations for war are economically ruinous and tend not to prevent wars but to cause them. In a condition of international anarchy, war is not merely possible but inevitable. The cure for anarchy at the world level is government at the world level. A world government will be federal in form because only a federation can create unity out of diversity, preserve local autonomy, and govern enormous geographical areas effectively. A world federation can not only abolish war and preparations for war, but can also make easier the solution of other global problems such as overpopulation, the despoliation of oceanic environments, and control of the atom. The elimination of war is an environmental as well as a moral imperative.

War

HUGH NASH

WAR IS SYSTEMATIC mass murder, the ugliest manifestation of man's inhumanity to man. Elementary morality demands of us that we work tirelessly to abolish it. And morality aside, war cannot be defended on practical grounds. There can be no victor in World War III; there can only be losers.

Our full military strength cannot be used against another nuclear power without inviting Armageddon. We cannot even use nuclear weapons against a weak non-nuclear power, for small countries have big friends. In the kind of war we still dare to wage, the United States was fought to a standstill in Vietnam by a sixth-rate military power.

We are asked to believe that a burdensome military establishment—which cannot be used rationally in large wars and cannot be used effectively in small ones—is needed to deter Russia. But Russia knows we cannot use our nuclear deterrent unless we are prepared to see tens of millions of Americans killed in the ensuing holocaust.

Such a deterrent is not credible and does not deter. Russia was not deterred in Czechoslovakia, Hungary, or Afghanistan. Nor did Russia's nuclear deterrent dissuade Eisenhower from sending the Marines into Lebanon, Johnson from escalating the war against North Vietnam, or Nixon from conspiring to overthrow by force a duly elected Marxist president of Chile.

It may be argued that the US nuclear deterrent is not expected to restrain Russia in other parts of the world, but simply to forestall a nuclear attack against the United States itself. But a Soviet leader mad enough to contemplate killing 100 million or so Americans would be mad enough to do it regardless of threatened retaliation. The same must be said of any American President mad enough to think of killing 100 million Russians. Deterrents, so-called, do not deter; they merely prolong a precarious balance of terror. Meanwhile, they cost everyone more than anyone can afford.

Politicians who claim that our ponderous military machine is morally or pragmatically justifiable are wrong precisely where it is most necessary to be right.

Preparedness: a Cruel Illusion

Wars would be infrequent indeed if nations were unprepared for them. Preparedness does not diminish, but rather increases, the likelihood, frequency, and severity of war. In theory, all nations might voluntarily agree to enhance their true security by disarming. In practice, however, unanimous agreement to disarm is unimaginable and less-than-unanimous agreement will not suffice.

While war remains possible, preparedness seems essential; and while nations prepare for war, war remains inevitable. If ever there was a vicious circle, this is it.

Cruise missiles mounted on a B52. These weapons may be deployed starting in 1982.   US Air Force photograph.

The circle can only be broken by making warfare impossible, so that preparations for war clearly become superfluous. People everywhere would rejoice in dismantling their military machines if they knew they safely could. The key point, then, is whether war can be made impossible, and if so, how?

War *can* be made virtually impossible, obviating the need for military preparedness. Before we enlarge on that, though, there is more to be said about war, preparedness, and their effects on the environment.

The burden of preparedness is immense; were it not perceived as essential to national survival, we would not tolerate it for a moment. The US defense budget is approaching $150 billion per year, and constitutes about one-third of the entire world's military expenditures.

If preparedness is expensive, war itself is vastly more so. It was President Johnson's attempt to produce both guns and butter without raising taxes—his fight now, pay later policy—that touched off double-digit inflation. Even in a well-managed economy, war and preparedness for war are inherently inflationary; they enlarge consumer purchasing power without producing anything that consumers can buy. The war machine also competes with the civilian economy for raw materials, skilled workers, managerial talent, and capital, thus reinforcing inflationary trends.

A war economy is an economy perennially whipsawed by inflation.

Military hardware is a prodigious consumer of scarce metals and other fast-vanishing resources indispensable to an industrial society. Together with rampant consumerism in wealthy nations, military procurement is a major cause of resource shortages that are reaching crisis proportions.

Even in peacetime, military establishments are ravenous consumers of energy. And wartime energy consumption by military machines beggars the imagination.

Damage to the environment was an incidental by-product of war in the past, and relatively trivial. But modern warfare is the one activity of man that has *as its primary objective* the deliberate degradation of the environment. The United States warred against the environment in Vietnam, defoliating forests that might hide the enemy and destroying crops and croplands that might feed him. Future wars, if we allow them to happen, will be even more ecocidal. Chemical and biological weapons are designed to destroy life-support systems—to poison water supplies, for example. All-out nuclear war might pollute the entire planet with levels of radioactivity that no form of life can endure. Humanity's suicide would be one part of a vaster tragedy. Evolution's promising experiments with terrestrial life would all be snuffed out.

Anarchy and War
Or Government and Peace?

Every cause of war *between* nations also exists *within* nations. Yet war within nations is rare while war between nations is commonplace. The difference is this: anarchy has been superseded by government *within* nations, but *among* nations, anarchy still reigns supreme.

The need for world government is precisely the same in principle as the need for local, state, and national governments. Until anarchy is superseded by government at the world level, war among nations will remain an ever-present menace.

We have in the United Nations a league or confederation, not a government. The distinction is all-important. The constituent parts of a government are its citizens, and law can normally be non-violently enforced because law-breakers are individuals or small groups. But a league's constituent parts are its member states, and when a league's decision is flouted, enforcement (when attempted) necessarily involves coercing a nation-state. There is no non-violent way to do that.

A league is an attempt to square the circle—to keep peace among member states without impinging upon their sovereignty. Since sovereignty is the recognition of no authority higher than one's own, and since national sovereignty's ultimate expression is the asserted right to wage war, every league contains the seeds of its own dissolution. The United Nations does much good where voluntary cooperation is obtainable, but as a keeper of the peace, it is merely the latest in a long line of futile confederations that were designed not to work.

We can have absolute national sovereignty without world peace. Or we can have world peace without absolute national sovereignty. We cannot have both; the two are fundamentally irreconcilable. If peace is our sincere desire, we cannot rationally defend the "sovereign equality of nations."

Sovereign equality is, in any case, a transparent fiction. What real equality is there between Chile and China, Iceland and India, or Romania and Russia? What reality does national sovereignty possess in a world where history's mightiest military power cannot assure the safety of its citizens or its own survival? Any loss of national sovereignty required by the creation of a world government will be the loss of a dangerous

Mock-up of an MX missile on its carriage.   *US Air Force photograph.*

illusion. Which is a gain.

Sovereignty is *divisible*. Nations can be supreme in some respects and not in others. And sovereignty is *transferable*. Sovereignty over matters of importance to everyone alive can be transferred to a world federation without compromising national sovereignty in matters of strictly national concern.

The divisibility and transferability of sovereignty was a discovery of America's Founding Fathers. Under the Constitution, not yet 200 years old, the first federal union was based upon the sharing of sovereignty by the nation, the state and local governments, and their citizens. Americans, of all people, should find world government easy to accept. For a world government is certain to be a federation—an adaptation to the world's needs of the federal principle invented by our Founding Fathers and first applied here in 1789.

The alternative to world federation is endless war and ceaseless preparations for war. World federation alone can eradicate these evils.

The Path to Peace

Establishing a world federation will not be easy. Indeed, we can make it impossible by failing to try hard enough or soon enough. But there is nothing intrinsically impossible about it if we take reasonable steps one at a time. Here are some of the steps that can lead to a federation of the world.

- The President in particular and opinion-makers in general should use all techniques of education and persuasion to obtain support for world federation by a solid majority of the American people.
- By presidential proclamation, world federation by

Each year we spend $400 billion on the means of destroying one another. Our planet—and we ourselves—can be blasted back to little more than the bare and crumbling rock from which, over evolutionary aeons, we emerged. Indeed, so ludicrous is the scale of our "overkill" that we have at our disposal the equivalent of several tons of TNT for every person on the planet.

—BARBARA WARD

So long as peace rests merely upon the continued willingness of potential war makers to behave themselves, the world has made no progress toward lasting peace. Anarchy is still the chief attribute of our international relations.

—VERNON NASH

(or before) 1989, the bicentennial of George Washington's inauguration under the US Constitution, should be made a national goal.

- Intensive, unremitting diplomacy—at home, in the United Nations, and abroad—should aim at winning acceptance of the principle of world federation and winning agreement to sponsor a world constitutional convention.
- Paralleling diplomatic activity, citizens groups should obtain as many signatures as possible on a petition from the *people* of the United States to the *people* of all other countries urging them to join with us in forming a world republic.
- US delegates to a world constitutional convention should be chosen before the convention is called, giving them time to prepare.
- Before the convention assembles, delegates should study governmental institutions and political philosophies, past and present. Although the US precedent is likely to be as closely followed as any other, a world federation will not be a carbon copy of anything. Its founders must be prepared to innovate.
- Nations that have agreed to sponsor a constitutional convention should convoke it as soon as it becomes clear that a majority of the nations of the world, representing a majority of the world's people, will attend.
- The constitutional convention should be open-ended, adjourning only when it has a draft constitution to propose.

Authors of a draft constitution will be anxious not to offend any major powers. They will surely do their best to make the constitution acceptable to the United States. It will not be a perfect instrument, but like the US Constitution, it should be perfectable by amendment.

And like the US Constitution, which took effect when nine of the original 13 states ratified it, a world constitution will doubtless provide for less-than-universal participation at the outset, if necessary. Ratification procedures are certain to be designed in such a way, however, that a federation will not be inaugurated unless it incorporates most of the people and most of the nations of the world. Even from the beginning, the federation will be more powerful than any nation or combination of nations that choose to stay outside. Conscious of its power, the federation can

American GIs exposed to a nuclear bomb blast in the 1957 Smoky test in Nevada.

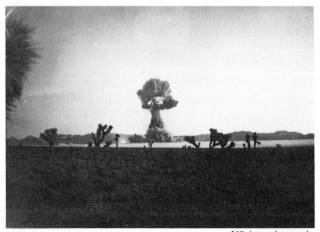

US Army photographs.

afford to woo self-excluded nations with friendliness and generosity, untainted by anxiety.

A balance of power is inherently unstable. The kind of *im*balance represented by a world federation versus a relatively few hold-out nations is far more stable than a precarious balance that the superpowers are laboring to imbalance. Still, an incomplete federation should not rest until it is whole. Only when there is no external threat to any government can all governments buckle down to their real missions: to do, as Lincoln said, what people cannot do at all or cannot do as well for themselves.

An Agenda for Immediate Action

What can be done *immediately?* Assuming a President and a political party sincerely committed to ending war and preparations for war, the following things can be done at once:

- The President, speaking before both houses of Congress with worldwide TV and radio coverage, can dedicate himself and his administration to world peace through world federation.
- Congressional leaders can introduce a joint resolution of House and Senate declaring that world federation is our national goal.
- The President and Congress cooperatively can establish a commission of constitutional scholars and others to study governmental instititutions and political philosophies, past, present, and theoretically possible. The commission's work will help US delegates prepare for a world constitutional convention.
- The President, with the concurrence of Congress, can announce a 5 percent per year *reduction* in the US "preparedness" budget. This can be done with great economic and social benefit, and the risk will be slight so long as we retain overkill capacity. You cannot kill people more than once, and piling overkill on top of overkill is expensively insane.

Our billions of dollars per year saved out of military budgets can be allocated to peace efforts, to foreign aid aimed at making nations self-sufficient in food, and to American citizens whose income is below the poverty level. If we divert money from the arms race to such unchallengeably humane programs, the United States will recapture the moral leadership it has frittered away since World War II.

Disarmament will not come suddenly enough to take defense contractors by surprise. They will have ample opportunity to phase their companies out of war production and into civilian markets bit by bit, over a period of years. If dislocations nevertheless occur, the affected companies and their employees must be helped. The companies can be given preferential tax treatment, for example, and preference in the award of government contracts during a transition period. The various programs to assist the unemployed will be available to displaced war workers, and special programs should not be necessary. The gradual transition from a wartime to a peacetime economy ought to be at least as manageable as the transition following the sudden end of World War II. An end to armaments will be an unmixed blessing.

A New World Without Foreigners

A world from which war, fear of war, and preparations for war have been eliminated will be an altogether new world, totally outside our experience and hard to imagine. Some of the greatest changes will be psychological. When all human inhabitants of the planet feel confident that they will not die in war and that their loved ones won't either, an incalculable weight will be lifted off humanity's heart.

Military adventurism will be a thing of the past. We can rest assured that our governments will not involve us in entanglements we need be ashamed of. A sense of guilt will gradually dissolve as our last foreign excursions fade into history. Love of country can flower into authentic, non-jingoistic patriotism.

There will be no foreigners in a world federation. The basis for xenophobia will be removed. We will live in an opener world where travel and communication are freer. International friendships will multiply, and feelings of separatism will fade. The ancient dream of universal brother- and sisterhood will begin to take on reality.

Today, autocratic governments maintain themselves by pretending to be their nations' only bulwark against external threats, real or imaginary. A world federation will eliminate real threats and reveal imaginary ones for what they are. Even if a world federation is not empowered to push autocratically-governed countries closer to democracy, autocracies will wither on the vine.

The growing gap between rich and poor nations is an explosive issue, and it is hard to see how it can be resolved without resort to war in our present anarchic world. The gap will not magically disappear within a world federation. But if the federation and the nations comprising it dedicate themselves to narrowing the gap, the poorer nations will probably be content to seek gradual, non-violent solutions.

Many of the benefits of federation are economic. The most obvious of these is the reduction to near nothing of worldwide expenditures for preparedness, which now amount to about 400 billion dollars per

Force alone does not guarantee security. A nation can reach a point at which it does not buy more security for itself simply by buying more military hardware. Expenditures beyond that point are not only wasted on defense but will erode the funds available for other essential sectors. By denying that dollar to other essential investments, the process may in the end diminish security rather than bolster it.

If we examine defense expenditures around the world today it is clear that there is a mounting misallocation of resources.

— ROBERT MCNAMARA

year (of which US citizens are saddled with one-third). With a monopoly of military force, the world federation will need very little of it. So nearly the entire 400 billion dollars can be diverted to humane purposes.

Military expenditures, as previously noted, are inherently inflationary. Diversion of hundreds of billions of dollars per year into other economic channels will help curb the inflation that is now pandemic.

Even if a world federation is not given direct authority over international economic matters, it will provide a relatively non-competitive atmosphere in which monetary reforms and other economic activity can be more rationally pursued. Problems involving multinational corporations will be more easily solved.

World federation will produce many environmental benefits. It will end the deliberate destruction of ecosystems not only in war, but also in weapons tests, training maneuvers, and the like—an improvement hard to overstate. World federation will also moderate the resource drain and pollution problems.

Pollutants do not respect boundaries, and many forms of pollution cannot be attacked effectively on a nation-by-nation basis. A world federation can attack pollution problems more systematically, and will be the logical instrument to control the exploitation and pollution of the oceans, our common heritage.

Overpopulation is an intractable environmental

problem in a world of sovereign nations who suspect that population control is a plot to weaken them in relation to potential enemies. Nations within a world federation will soon learn that they have nothing to fear from more populous neighbors—and begin to see more clearly the advantages of a non-growing, sustainable population size. Overpopulation is one of the many problems that can be approached with far greater expectation of success in a less nationalistic, less competitive atmosphere.

At some point, overpopulation tends to be self-limiting through increased death rates. The self-limiting process would be ghastly, but life would go on. Another environmental threat, on the other hand, might turn Earth into a dead planet. Control of the atom would be far easier within the political framework of a world federation, however, and getting the nuclear genie back into its bottle may come to be seen as the most compelling of all reasons for the establishment of a federation of the world.

World federation is not a panacea. Serious problems will persist. But the changes world federation makes, or makes possible, will be wholly salutary.

Historical Footnote

A world federalist movement flourished in the United States (and throughout the western world) during the 1940s and early 1950s. Why did it wither? And what reason is there to suppose it can be revived?

Ironically, the federalist movement split into factions. "Minimalists" believed federalists could advocate a world organization with powers limited to the enforcement of disarmament and the suppression of violence; they favored high-level lobbying in Washington. "Maximalists" believed a world federation should be empowered to promote justice as well as suppress violence, and that it would need legislative, executive, and judicial powers comparable to those of governments at other levels; they felt that grassroots support was a necessary precondition of effective lobbying.

Minimalists triumphed in a struggle for control of United World Federalists, in part at least because most "big names" in the movement were minimalists. It was a costly victory; most rank-and-file members evidently leaned toward the maximalist position, for UWF membership promptly plummeted and the organization never regained its lost momentum.

At about the time UWF eviscerated itself, other events created a climate unfavorable to federalism. Notable among them were the cold war, McCarthyism, Russia's ending of the US atomic monopoly, the Korean War, and the start-up of the United Nations (which, despite the manifest inadequacy of its peace-keeping machinery, siphoned off support from world federation). Even a strong and unified federalist movement would have had trouble holding its own.

There is no guarantee that the federalist movement can be revitalized, but there are grounds for hope. The frailty of the UN's peace-keeping apparatus has been amply demonstrated for several decades. The cold war has thawed considerably, despite continuing tensions. The burden of armaments grows ever more intolerable, and the arms race grows ever more dangerous. Above all, an anarchic world of competing national sovereignties is obviously ill-equipped to control the atom, and failure to control the atom could spell the end of life on earth. The longer federation is delayed, the more urgently it will be needed.

At its peak, the federalist movement won endorsements from hundreds of Members of Congress and hundreds of statesmen abroad. But federation was never unequivocally advocated by a US President. With presidential leadership, support for world federation would swiftly surpass in breadth and depth the promising movement of the forties and early fifties.

Every gun that is made, every warship launched, every rocket fired signifies, in the final sense, a theft from those who hunger and are not fed, those who are cold and not clothed. This world in arms is not spending money alone. It is spending the sweat of its laborers, the genius of its scientists, the hopes of its children.

—PRESIDENT DWIGHT EISENHOWER

Recommended Actions

☐ The President should dedicate himself and his administration to world federation.

☐ The House and Senate should declare that world federation is a national goal.

☐ The administration should establish a commission of constitutional scholars to analyze governmental institutions that might be applicable to a world federation.

☐ The President, Congress concurring, should announce a unilaterial 5 percent per year reduction in military expenditures to prove good faith and capture the imagination of the world.

☐ Opinion-makers from the President down should educate and persuade until a majority of Americans clearly favors world federation.

☐ All diplomatic channels should be used to foster support of world federation in other countries.

☐ A petition bearing as many signatures as possible should invite the people of other countries to join the people of the United States in creating a world republic.

☐ US delegates to a world constitutional convention should be chosen ahead of time so they can prepare carefully for their assignment.

☐ As soon as it becomes clear that a world constitutional convention will be well enough attended, sponsoring nations should announce the time and place of the convention.

☐ The world constitutional convention should remain in session until it has a draft constitution to propose.

☐ The proposed constitution should be ratified or rejected on its merits.

☐ If the proposed constitution is not adopted, a new constitutional convention should be called and another draft constitution should be submitted for ratification.

☐ If a federation begins with less-than-universal membership, the United States should urge non-member nations to join the rest of humanity in a true federation of all the world.

Optic Nerve/Jeroboam, Inc.

Weapons Systems: Trends in Terror

STEPHEN WHEELER

WE ARE, SAD TO SAY, in an age in which the technology of war is developing ever faster, in which both nuclear and conventional weapons are multiplying, and in which international tension and turbulence are likely to increase. The outlook is not bright, unless humanity can learn to live without armed conflict.

The United States and the Soviet Union are seemingly locked, despite attempts at negotiation, in an endless arms race. Enormous defense budgets are being enacted as the US, increasingly worried about its economic strength and leadership position in the world, seeks to reverse its decline by focusing on the military arena.

The tendency in the US is to assume the worst about the Soviet Union, and to plan accordingly. It is, unfortunately, often in the interest of those involved—politicians, weapons contractors, the media—to exaggerate US weakness and Soviet strength, and to look at short-term developments rather than the long-term impacts of new policies and technological advances. Similar forces are undoubtedly at work in the USSR.

The superpowers cannot play their game of chicken forever, in a world of increasing tension and advancing technology. More than any other single factor, the existence of nuclear weapons makes this impossible. In 1980 the US had 9,200 strategic nuclear warheads, and the USSR had 6,000. Even with these numbers deployed, the two countries are increasing their rates of production. And unfortunately, nuclear weapons technology is one of those advancing fastest.

Advances planned for the 1980s in nuclear warfare systems do not have much to do with the sheer power of warheads. Both superpowers tired of building bigger bombs in the sixties, when each routinely deployed single warheads with yields of at least 20 megatons—almost 2,000 times as powerful as the Hiroshima bomb, able to pulverize entire metropolitan areas.

What is being stressed now is accuracy. Precision-guided re-entry systems are being developed for nuclear missiles that will not just land a warhead within a quarter-mile of a target on the other side of the earth, but will actually hit it. Such re-entry vehicles will maneuver right to their targets, making last-minute course corrections based on their own on-board radars and computers. Fitted with relatively low-yield warheads, they will serve precise military functions; in particular, they will be able to knock out opposing missiles lying buried in extremely "hard" underground silos.

Highly accurate systems, development of which the US has consistently taken the lead on, may before long enable either superpower to launch a disarming first strike against the land-based missiles of the other. American military planners have been worrying about the possibility of a Soviet first strike for some time. This is one reason for the massive MX program; the other is to threaten Soviet silos in turn.

The problem will be much worse for the Soviets, because US anti-submarine warfare systems are very good and getting better, and will be able to destroy some or all Soviet submarines before they can fire their missiles, because the US is placing increased emphasis on development of ground- and space-based anti-ballistic missile systems, which could shoot down those Soviet missiles that did get launched, and because the US is developing a range of new systems (most notably, the MX and Trident II missiles) designed specifically to make precise "counterforce" strikes against Soviet missile silos. Soviet planners will have much more reason than we to worry about the first strike problem.

Moreover, US nuclear policy itself has been moving in a "limited nuclear war-fighting" direction, as evidenced by the release of Presidential Directive 59 in the summer of 1980. This evolution of technology and policy raises the possibility that the world will some day be used for a nuclear chess game in which the superpowers trade pinpoint strike for pinpoint strike, or seek to disarm their opponent by striking first. Equally dangerous, the advent of highly accurate delivery systems may push both countries toward a "launch-on-

MIRVs entering the atmosphere during South Pacific test.

warning" policy, in which nuclear missiles are launched when computer systems warn of attack, within the ten- to 30-minute flight time of attacking missiles. Talk of such a policy raises the specter of an accidental nuclear war. US computer warning systems gave three false alarms in 1980 alone.

There has been a prevalent feeling in the world that nuclear weapons are too terrible to be used. Yet military strategists are developing increasingly realistic plans for nuclear weapons employment, plans in which massive strikes on population centers are not envisioned and damage is held to an "acceptable" level, with casualties perhaps only in the millions.

The public, seemingly insulated from the potential horrors of future warfare, and put off by the technical nature of the issues involved, tends to leave questions of nuclear strategy to the experts. This tendency must be reversed, for the possibility that nuclear weapons will somehow be used—whether in a relatively full-scale "strategic" usage or to achieve tactical gains or salvage a losing situation in a "conventional" war—is the greatest single threat humanity faces.

Developments are proceeding rapidly in other forms of weaponry as well. Highly sophisticated conventional weapons—missiles, planes, tanks, etc.—are entering arsenals around the world in growing numbers. World arms expenditures are approaching a trillion dollars a year. The global arms trade is snowballing. As the US, the USSR, and other suppliers ship ever greater quantities of arms overseas, the world grows increasingly militarized and the risks of war increase.

Hundreds of thousands of people are killed every year in major and minor struggles around the world—

in the Middle East and Persian Gulf region, in Africa, in Latin America, and in Asia. Terrorism is on the increase in most parts of the globe. Europe remains heavily fortified. Foreign powers almost always seem to have a finger in Third World conflicts, taking sides and supplying weaponry. The world today is increasingly often compared to the Balkans of 1914.

What can be done? It is, of course, always easier to see problems than to bring about solutions, especially when the issues involved are on such a global scale and reach so deeply into the heart of human nature. A few suggestions:

1. Nations, especially the United States, must re-examine their "defense" establishments, see if their systems and policies are indeed defensive in nature, and eliminate those which are, instead, offensively oriented.

2. The superpowers must lead the way out of the nuclear nightmare; a good starting place would be a comprehensive test ban treaty, or a "freeze" on the production and deployment of new nuclear weapons systems.

3. The international arms trade must be sharply curtailed, the role of the superpowers and their allies in Third-World conflicts re-examined, and US involvement in such conflicts unilaterally restrained.

4. US policy regarding Third-World resources, and our dependencies on those resources (which tend to force US involvement overseas), must be rigorously re-examined. The long-range impacts of US policies and technological developments must be better appreciated, and policy changed accordingly.

More Thoughts on Preparedness

I AM JUST PRIMITIVE enough to hope that somehow, somewhere, a cardinal may still be whistling on a green bush when the last man goes blind before his man-made sun. If it should turn out that we have mis-handled our own lives as several civilizations before us have done, it seems a pity that we should involve the violet and the tree frog in our departure.

To perpetrate this final act of malice seems some-how disproportionate, beyond endurance. It is like tampering with the secret purposes of the universe itself and involving not only man but life in the final holocaust—an act of petulant, deliberate blasphemy.

It is for this reason that Lewis's remark about the widening gap between good and evil takes on such horrifying significance in our time. The evil man may do has this added significance about it: it is not merely the evil of one tribe seeking to exterminate another. It is, instead, the thought-out willingness to make the air unbreathable to neighboring innocent nations and to poison, in one's death throes, the very springs of life itself. No greater hypertrophy of the institution of war has ever been observed in the West. To make the situation more ironic, the sole desire of every fifth-rate nascent nationalism is to emulate Russia and America, to rattle rockets, and, if these are too expensive, then at least to possess planes and a parade of tanks. For the first time in history a divisive nationalism, spread like a contagion from the West, has increased in virulence and blown around the world.

A multitude of states are now swept along in a pas-sionate hunger for arms as the only important symbol of prestige. Yearly their number increases. For the first time in human history the involutional disease of a single civilization, that of the West, shows signs of becoming the disease of all contemporary societies.

—Loren Eiseley

THE U.N.'S PROVISIONS FOR ENFORCEMENT are an at-tempt to apply the vigilante-band system on the world level. To expect "posses" of national contingents to be assembled *ad hoc* after each outrage overlooks an es-sential factor. Whenever armed cowboys of a ranchers' association joined to run down a gang of cattle rustlers, they knew that the outlaws sought by them were merely a small number of men with light arms. The U.N. Charter requires a willingness to go to war; great masses of men with weapons of incredible destructive-ness must hurl themselves against other masses of men who are similarly armed. The difference in degree is sufficient to become a difference in kind.

The whole war system must be eliminated before nations can be greatly improved internally. It is not enough to be able to win total wars; the attempt to keep prepared to do so can ruin us, even if we should be fortunate enough to avoid actual conflict.

It is plain beyond a doubt that a league or confedera-tion (any loose association of fully sovereign states) simply cannot prevent war. In consequence a swift contempt develops for leagues, or—what is even worse—the public becomes entirely indifferent to them. Since no one can be led to trust such a system, each nation insists on keeping the power to defend itself. This very armed might in turn sabotages the league. There is little, if any, hope of avoiding war under the U.N. as presently constituted.

—Vernon Nash

THE OVERWHELMINGLY MILITARY approach to national security is based on the assumption that the principal threat to security comes from other nations. But the threats to security may now arise less from the relationship of nation to nation and more from the relationship of man to nature. Dwindling reserves of oil and the deterioration of the earth's biological sys-tems now threaten the security of nations everywhere.

While the oil supply is threatened by depletion, the productivity of the earth's principal biological systems—fisheries, forests, grasslands, and crop-lands—is threatened by excessive human claims. These biological systems provide all food and all the raw materials for industry except minerals and petro-chemicals. In fishery after fishery, the catch now ex-ceeds the long-term sustainable yield. The cutting of trees exceeds the regenerative capacity of forests almost everywhere. Grasslands are deteriorating on every continent as livestock populations increase along with system. The risk is that petroleum supplies will be squandered frivolously on non-essential uses before an agricultural system can be developed that is not dependent on oil.

The mantle of topsoil covering the earth ranges in depth from a few inches to a few hundred feet. Over much of the earth's surface it is only inches deep, usually less than a foot. Nature produces new soil very slowly, much more slowly than the rate at which humans are now removing it. Thus, once topsoil is lost, a vital capacity to sustain life is diminished. With soil as with many other resources, humanity is beginning to

Elihu Blotnick

ask more of the earth than it can give.

In a world that is not only ecologically interdependent but economically and politically interdependent as well, the concept of "national" security is no longer adequate. Individual countries must respond to global crises because national governments are still the principal human population. Croplands too are being damaged by erosion as population pressures mount. Failure to arrest this deterioration of biological systems threatens not only the security of individual nations but the survival of civilization as we know it.

An all-out conservation program is needed to stretch remaining oil reserves as far as possible and so buy time to shift to renewable energy sources. The challenge is to husband scarce petroleum resources while designing a sustainable and petroleum-free economic decision-makers, but many threats to security require a coordinated international response. The times call for efforts to secure the global systems on which nations depend. If the global climatic system is inadvertently altered by human activity, all countries will be affected. If the international monetary system is not secure, all national economies will suffer. If countries do not cooperate and preserve oceanic fisheries, food prices everywhere will rise. But political leaders have yet to realize that national security is meaningless without global security. —Lester R. Brown

WE HAVE ENDED general lawlessness in human relationships except at the international level. This failure is the one *fundamental* explanation for the frequent recurrence of war. Every other element listed among the major causes of war exists in each community— factors such as greed, prejudice, and ruthless will for power. Yet mob riots which get beyond the control of municipal police are rare, and civil wars within most countries are even more infrequent. Why should wars among nations be a normal, recurring pattern whereas civil wars are exceptional? Lack of enforceable world law is the answer.

What is more paradoxical than a league—designed to keep the peace—which, by its design, can do so only by making war? The ends of the United Nations would be defeated by the only means it can employ to secure these ends. Economic sanctions also punish innocent and guilty alike. The Charter as it stands is unworkable and immoral.

However much civilized countries may wish to expend their energies and wealth on constructive ends rather than on armaments, they feel compelled by world conditions (over which they have no control) to build bombs rather than bridges, jet fighters instead of tractors, and so on. The strongest nations can maintain their relatively greater measure of sovereignty only by ruinous expenditures of blood and treasure. In heaven's name, what kind of freedom is that for sensible men?

If a world government is given sole authority and responsibility for maintaining the peace of the world, and if nations are permitted to retain only such small forces with light arms as are judged by the world authority to be required for the maintenance of internal order within each country, then the military forces of a world government can likewise be reduced to comparably small numbers as soon as all nations have joined. A nuclear world union will doubtless maintain whatever forces may seem to be required by the strength of the countries which chose to remain outside. Once universality has been reached, the military establishment of the world union need only be large enough to provide adequate insurance against possible rebellion. The use of strictly civilian policing methods, backed by mobilizations of militia as needed, can stop preparedness for revolutions or for international war before they reach unmanageable proportions.

A careful study of human history reveals that the assumption that war is inherent in human nature—and therefore eternal—is shallow and faulty, that it is only a superficial impression. Far from being inexplicable or inevitable, we can invariably determine the situations that predispose to war, and the conditions which lead to war.

The real cause of all wars has always been the same. They have occurred with the mathematical regularity of a natural law at clearly determined moments as the result of clearly definable conditions.

If we try to detect the mechanism visibly in operation, the single cause ever-present at the outbreak of each and every conflict known to human history, if we attempt to reduce the seemingly innumerable causes of war to a common denominator, two clear and unmistakable observations emerge:

1. Wars between groups of men forming social units always take place when these units—tribes, dynasties, churches, cities, nations—exercise unrestricted sovereign power.

2. Wars between these social units cease the moment sovereign power is transferred from them to a larger or higher unit.

From these observations we can deduce a social law with the characteristics of an axiom that applies to and explains each and every war in the history of all time.

War takes place whenever and wherever non-integrated social units of equal sovereignty come into contact.

War between given social units of equal sovereignty is the permanent symptom of each successive phase of civilization. Wars always ceased when a higher unit established its own sovereignty, absorbing the sovereignties of the conflicting smaller social groups. After such transfers of sovereignty, a period of peace followed, which lasted only until the new social units came into contact. Then a new series of wars began.

Just as there is one and only one cause for wars between men on this earth, so history shows that peace—not peace in an absolute and utopian sense, but concrete peace between given social groups warring with each other at given times—has always been established in one way and only in one way.

Peace between fighting groups of men was never possible and wars succeeded one another until some sovereignty, some sovereign source of law, some sovereign power was set up *over* and *above* the clashing social units, integrating the warring units into a higher sovereignty.

Once the mechanics and the fundamental causes of wars—of all wars—are realized, the futility and childishness of the passionate debates about armament and disarmament must be apparent to all.

If human society were organized so that relations between groups and units in contact were regulated by democratically controlled law and legal institutions, then modern science could go ahead, devise and produce the most devastating weapons, and there would be no war. But if we allow sovereign rights to reside in the separate units and groups without regulating their relations by law, then we can prohibit every weapon, even a penknife, and people will beat out each other's brains with clubs.

War is the result of contact between nonintegrated sovereign units, whether such units be families, tribes, villages, estates, cities, provinces, dynasties, religions, classes, nations, regions or continents.

We also know that today, the conflict is between the scattered units of nation-states. During the past hundred years, all major wars have been waged between nations. This division among men is the only condition which, in our age, can create—and undoubtedly will create—other wars.

The task therefore is to prevent wars between the nations—international wars.

Logical thinking and historical empiricism agree that there *is* a way to solve this problem and prevent wars between the nations once and for all. But with equal clarity they also reveal that there is *one* way and one way alone to achieve this end: The integration of the scattered conflicting national sovereignties into one unified, higher sovereignty, capable of creating a legal order within which all people may enjoy equal security, equal obligations and equal rights under law.

Democratic sovereignty of the people can be correctly expressed and effectively instituted only if local affairs are

Test-firing the Titan II. A missile like this blew up in its launching silo in Arkansas, October 1980.   US Air Force photograph.

handled by local government, national affairs by national government, and international, world affairs, by international, world government.

Only if the people, in whom rests all sovereign power, delegate parts of their sovereignty to institutions created for and capable of dealing with specific problems, can we say that we have a democratic form of government. Only through such separation of sovereignties, through the organization of independent institutions, deriving their authority from the sovereignty of the community, can we have a social order in which men may live in peace with each other, endowed with equal rights and equal obligations before law. Only in a world order based on such separation of sovereignties can individual freedom be real.

Poles and Russians, Hungarians and Rumanians, Serbs and Bulgars, have disliked and distrusted each other and have been waging wars in Europe against each other for centuries. But these very same Poles and Russians, Hungarians and Rumanians, Serbs and Bulgars, once having left their countries and settled in the United States of America, cease fighting and are perfectly capable of living and working side by side without waging wars against each other.

Why is this?

The biological, racial, religious, historic, temperamental and character differences between them remain exactly the same.

The change in one factor alone produced the miracle.

In Europe, sovereign power is vested in these nationalities and in their nation-states. In the United States of America, sovereign power resides, not in any one of these nationalities, but stands above them in the Union, under which individuals, irrespective of existing differences between them, are equal before the law.

It seems, therefore, crystal-clear that friction, conflicts and wars between people are caused, not by their national, racial, religious, social and cultural differences, but by the *single fact* that these differences are galvanized in separate sovereignties which have no way to settle the conflicts resulting from their differences except through violent clashes.

Just as peace, freedom and equality of the citizens of a nation require within their state specific institutions and authorities separate from and standing above municipal or local authorities—so peace, freedom and equality of men on this earth, between the nation-states, require specific institutions, authorities separate from and standing above national authorities, as well as the direct delegation of sovereign power by the people to these higher world government authorities, to deal with those problems of human relations that reach beyond the national state structure.

—Emery Reves

Growth

Parable Island was shrinking, and the islanders assembled to discuss the crisis. After much inconclusive talk, the venerated Chief Elder rose to speak. "We don't know why," she said, "but at this rate our island will be only half as big in one generation, one-fourth as big in two generations, and one-eighth as big in three. Maybe the shrinkage will stop; but that's not within our control, and it would be foolish to count on it. One thing we *can* control is the number of islanders there will be a generation from now. If our numbers have been reduced by half when the island has shrunk to half its size, everyone will still have as big a garden plot and as much to eat as we do today." Islanders generally have a keen sense of finitude and physical limits, so with little grumbling or dissent, the Parable Islanders adopted the sensible strategy of keeping their population in equilibrium with their shrinking environment.

Our beautiful, blue-green planet is an island in the void. If Earth were shrinking, no one would deny that we Earth Islanders had a problem. But the fact is, Earth *is* shrinking in relation to the human population we impose on it. It is shrinking even faster in relation to the rate at which industrial economies are converting raw materials into products and products into wastes. It is as necessary for Earth Islanders as it is for Parable Islanders to control their numbers and their appetites. Our worlds are finite, and their resources are limited.

George Hall

Growth: More Means Less

DANIEL B. LUTEN

"NO WONDER THEY DISAGREED so endlessly; they were talking about different things." With these words Robert L. Heilbroner, though referring to differences between Robert Malthus and David Ricardo, cautions all participants in the limits-to-growth debate. Seeing all of the problem may, in fact, be the major part of the problem.

Millennia ago at least some of our forebears could see virtually all of the problem simply by scanning the reaches of the single valley that comprised their own territory. What went on outside their own small watershed was beyond concern, had no influence on them, and was not influenced by them. But as men have become progressively more and more involved with mankind, the task of keeping one's eye on all of the problems has increased at an accelerating rate.

Malthus, with whom this discussion begins, had an easier time of it than we do. By means of a few great simplifications of diverse merit, he managed to assemble most of the problem.

Whether any writer, in today's far more complex, more closely woven, more communicative world can do better than Malthus in explaining the problems posed by growth remains doubtful. Surely it is a severe test of genius. We must be warned at every step along the way that any appearance of simplicity is deceptive. The problem *does* appear simple to some of us; the answer fairly shouts at one. And yet others utterly disagree. Are some among us irrational and unwilling to adhere to the rules of human reasoning, or are we "talking about different things"?

With this warning out of the way, we can phrase the basic question: Is this world, for practical human purposes, infinite, or is it finite? It is easily said that of course it is finite, but almost a dozen elements obscuring the answer and largely supporting the opposite view can be identified. These, grouped in five categories, are listed in the following paragraphs.

First, the consequences of growth and interspersal: To primitive men, circumscribed by their valley walls and the unfriendly men beyond, it may well have seemed finite. Many such groups established stable, enduring relationships with those limited environments. As such groups came to be assembled into larger societies with a substantial measure of intercommunication, it is easy to say their world was still finite, with just a larger numerator over a larger denominator. But, in fact, new elements were added:

1. In the primitive, isolated society, innovation diffused slowly to neighboring groups and may often have been abandoned on the way. In the larger, intercommunicating society, innovation diffused faster and with fewer losses.

2. In the larger society, a buffering capacity existed whereby one region could lend support to another during a local spell of ill fortune.

3. Larger societies, if imperialistic, could force a flow of goods from the rim to the heartland—flows that could persist as long as expansion lasted, but not much longer.

Second, the biases of history:

4. Paradoxically, when Magellan circled the earth, he proved it to be physically finite, but also, by hinting at its magnitude and diversity, he may well have lent force to the idea of infinity. Later explorers may have strengthened rather than weakened the conviction of infinity. Because we have never encountered the limits of the earth, we have come to believe there are none. More hubris, even arrogance, has resulted from successful expansion. Is this warranted, or is it simply more people whistling in the dark?

5. Our economic theory began during a period (the eighteenth and early nineteenth centuries) when the world, practically viewed, seemed too large and too rich ever to be seriously impaired by human exploitiveness. The idea of an infinite world is built into economics.

Third, the problem of concern for the future:

6. We cannot possibly be as much concerned for the remote as for the near future, but we differ in the patterns of the decline of our concern with increasing remoteness. Biologists, almost certainly, have a longer vision of the future than social scientists. Economists, among the latter, quantify their declining concern by "discounting the future": the compounded decrement of annual interest subtracted from something of value

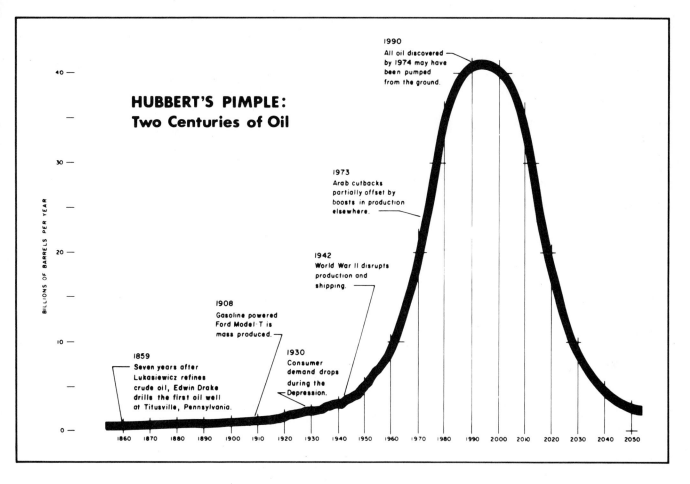

HUBBERT'S PIMPLE:
Two Centuries of Oil

1990
All oil discovered by 1974 may have been pumped from the ground.

1973
Arab cutbacks partially offset by boosts in production elsewhere.

1942
World War II disrupts production and shipping.

1908
Gasoline powered Ford Model-T is mass produced.

1930
Consumer demand drops during the Depression.

1859
Seven years after Lukasiewicz refines crude oil, Edwin Drake drills the first oil well at Titusville, Pennsylvania.

BILLIONS OF BARRELS PER YEAR

in the future. Thus, the present value of a resource that will be used in a century may be quite small: something worth $1,000 in the year 2075 discounted at the rate of 5% per year, modest by today's standards, is worth only six dollars today ($1,000 × 0.95^{100} = $6). Accordingly, economically, one can hardly concern himself with shortages a century from now, and a world with enough for a century is, practically speaking, infinite. Biologists, in asking for a longer concern, are "low discount" people; economists, commonly "high discount" people, are, by that token, concerned only for the near future. Each finds his position so rational as to feel that it requires no defense.

7. Curiously, and again paradoxically, as our economy becomes more hard pressed, interest (discount) rates increase and the period into the future with which economists are concerned shrinks. If such a shrinkage should outrun resource depletion, our economic guides might even be construed as teaching us that the world is becoming more infinite than in the past.

Fourth, the issues of purpose, while not clearly supporting one side or the other, have certainly obscured the debate.

8. Should we seek the welfare of the individual, the society, the nation-state, all of mankind, or all of life? If our concern is for the individual, we must proceed cautiously in exploitation of the planet's resources in order to retain a diversity on this earth to match the diversity of individual needs. If concern is for all of life, extraction of the planet's resources must be restrained. In between these extremes, constraints may be less.

9. Ideas of "optimum" come up and with them the issue of "quality of life." Shall we try for an economic optimum, if we can identify one, or for an even more elusive economic-aesthetic optimum?

10. If we use the criterion of full employment to define the optimum, Keynesian economics suggests that a capitalistic society finds it much easier to achieve happiness while growing. That is, the optimum is not definable as a level of activity but rather as a rate of growth of activity.

Fifth, a matter of the philosophy of science:

11. People assess evidence differently. Some are persuaded more by the plausibility of a principle than by the weight of empirical data; others are not. I suggest that biologists tend to fall in the former category, social

scientists in the latter.

Summing all of this up, like it or not, belief in an infinite world has become an institution. We are concerned in the latter half of the twentieth century with assessing this institution; with luck we shall make up our minds before the century is out—for institutions do not die easily. When they do die, equity is transferred: one man's gored ox is another's prime roast! Insofar as they can see the consequences, the first resists change, the other demands it.

Malthus and His Tormentors

"Every year Malthus is proven wrong and is buried—only to spring to life again before the year is out. If he is so wrong, why can't we forget him? If he is right, how does he happen to be so fertile a subject for criticism?" (Hardin, *Population, Evolution, and Birth Control,* 1964.)

Thomas Robert Malthus (1766-1834) did not initiate concern for the adequacy of the world to meet human needs; he was not the first pessimist. Nonetheless, we can begin with him. Earlier writers have contributed little to the modern debate.

Malthus was basically right: a population with a constant birth rate in excess of a constant death rate will increase exponentially. Additionally, he thought, from examining the new republic across the Atlantic, that the doubling time for unrestrained human population growth must be about 25 years.

Next, the arithmetic increase of food. Here he was cautious, and said only: If, setting out from a tolerably well-peopled country such as England . . .we were to suppose that by great attention to agriculture, its produce could be permanently increased every twenty-five years by a quantity equal to that which it at present produces, it would be allowing a rate of increase decidedly beyond any probability of realization. . . . Yet this would be an arithmetic progression.

Facing the dilemma of geometric versus arithmetic increase, he postulated that two sorts of checks, *positive* and *preventive,* ensure that the population cannot exceed the food supply. Broadly speaking, *positive* checks are those that shorten life and *preventive* checks are those that diminish births. Some checks may be classed as misery (for example, famine); some as vice (for example, wars); and others as moral restraint (for example, postponed marriage with premarital continence). Mention of contraception turns up first in the 1817 edition; Malthus opposed it, largely on the score that its use would magnify the natural indolence of people.

Malthus is commonly damned by social scientists for his opposition to the "poor laws"—laws to provide assistance to the poor. Petersen insists that Malthus has been misread; he was merely trying to point out the adverse consequences of attempts to mitigate poverty by measures so remote from the real causes as the poor laws. But Frank Notestein says flatly, "Malthus is important today as the father of the most regressive social doctrine of our time." At any rate, a great quarrel has ensued.

Bogue has tried to end the debate: "Demographers of the world unite—in burying the population theories both of Malthus and of Marx." But the debate cannot be ended so easily. Perhaps, following Hardin, it is the social scientists who bury Malthus in odd-numbered years, only to have the biologists resurrect him in even-numbered years. In the end, Malthus may be deemed important primarily for having catalyzed (one can hardly say "crystallized," since the waters are still so murky!) the distinction between two schools of thought that we may term *optimism* and *pessimism.* It is worth noting that the optimists have commonly been social scientists allied with technologists; the pessimists have commonly been biologists.

Biologists, less empirical than social scientists and more concerned with law as generalization, know little directly of Malthus. What they do know is that Malthus focused Darwin's attention on the severity of the struggle for existence and led him to understand that the potential for geometrical growth of the populations of organisms means that very few individuals survive long enough to reproduce. Left out of the discussion is any mention of "vice," "misery," or "moral restraint." Few biologists have heard of the poor laws. What remains is simply an idea, a principle, an axiom: "Populations tend to grow geometrically; food arithmetically. Populations press hard against the means of survival."

There are, then, two Malthuses: first, the "disproven" author of "regressive social doctrine," unappealing to empiricists and to the utopian believers in the perfectibility of man; second, the enunciator of an idea that stimulated Darwin, himself the keystone of modern biology.

The Nineteenth-Century Sequels

Of five philosophic threads running through the nineteenth century that affect this discussion, four can be traced back to the beginning of the century and to Malthus. One of these, social science and its optimism, perhaps most active early in the century, we have already mentioned. The second, biological science and its pessimism, latent until long after Darwin, has also been mentioned. A third, neo-Malthusianism, was an immediate response to Malthus. Its proponents were his supporters, and they gave rise in due course to philosophies and programs in support of birth con-

Unless there is a reduction in the rate of population growth, there is no solution to the world food problem. If one projects the present rate of population growth, the charts run off the page. The numbers become not only unmanageable, they become incomprehensible.
—DON PAARLBERG

trol. Although it has become common to refer to all of the pessimists as *neo-Malthusians*, the term is probably best restricted to describe solely those of the nineteenth century. The fourth thread is Marxism; Marx's views on population were sharply antagonistic to those of Malthus. The fifth is the American conservation movement, which, although it has no clear origins until the 1850s and in its early phase has no clearly discernible relations to the population issue, does become involved with it in the middle of the twentieth century.

Societies under Marxist influence have evidenced complex policies on populations, at once utterly liberal on abortion, but denying that anything such as overpopulation could occur in a "properly organized society." Marx refers to the "contemptible Malthus" and argues that "every special historic mode of production has its own special laws of population." In short, he argues that no overriding principle is common to all societal organizations. By and large, it seems that Marx, in common with so many economists, subscribed to the vision of an infinite world. The tradition persists: socialists, including Russian writers on such matters, usually line up on the side of the optimists in the great debate.

The fifth thread, conservation, beginning in the mid-nineteenth century with George Perkins Marsh, became well developed before taking any position on the limits to growth. The history of the conservation movement has been recounted too many times and in too much detail in the geographical literature to be reconsidered here. The post-World War II resurgence of the limits-to-growth issue can be attributed to writers who were as much conservationists as they were biologists.

The Post-World War II Flood

For whatever reason, the literature on the subject became largely American after World War II. Perhaps it was an idea whose time had come; perhaps it reflected a realization of the enormous toll the war had taken of American resources; perhaps the ending of the Western frontier was sinking in. Europe, overwhelmed by the problems of reconstruction, was preoccupied. British writing by no means dis-

appeared, but it was a trickle compared with the stream of American books.

William Vogt gave wings to the controversy with his *Road to Survival* (1948), one of the very few books of this kind (*Silent Spring* is another) to benefit from being a Book-of-the-Month Club selection. Fairfield Osborn followed with *Our Plundered Planet* (1948) and *The Limits of the Earth* (1953). There were rebuttals, among them José de Castro's *The Geography of Hunger* (1952), and counter-rebuttals, such as Karl Sax's *Standing Room Only* (1955). There were affirmations of plenty, such as Kirtley Mather's *Enough and to Spare* (1944). Harrison Brown's *The Challenge of Man's Future* (1954) stands out as probably technically the most competent writing of the period.

The stream of books became a flood during the 1960s. Even to list them becomes impractical. What is truly astonishing is the diversity of arguments they presented. One would think that ultimately the extraneous elements would thin out and the core of the controversy become apparent. That it hardly does so testifies to the complexity of the matter. However, as one examines the record over the past 25 years, one reassurance does appear; the earlier books were factually thin and dilute in content, whereas the more recent ones are packed full of information. The debate has certainly stimulated the compilation and increased the availability of pertinent information. Yet even now we know so little! Only a few of the elements can be examined.

Biologists had noted the rarity of famine in an animal world presumed to be Malthusian (after all, it was the Malthusian image that had stimulated Darwin). Marston Bates and later, others, suggested that pervasive *territoriality*, whether instinctive or cultural, must be a strong deterrent to reproduction in excess of dependable food supply. Individuals unable to claim a territory do not become part of the breeding population; whether in a strictly topographic sense or in some other way, they are forced to the margin of the habitat of the species, the margin where conditions are unsuitable for reproduction. Wynne-Edwards made a related point concerning the colonial nesting of sea birds and hypothesized that the phenomenon might be wellnigh universal. Calhoun strengthened the case by demonstrating in rats the collapse of stable reproductive patterns under conditions of extreme crowding. Ever since, we have been wondering just how ratlike we may turn out to be! Should we, then, consider famine to stem largely from the failure of institutions of territoriality.

Garrett Hardin, an unwavering advocate of the earth's finiteness, elucidated the antithesis of territory, namely the *commons*, a pervasive complication of resource management. Allegorically, the villagers who pasture their cattle on the commons have strong individual incentives for each to increase the number of his cattle while hoping that his neighbors will not. For even when the extramarginal cow that lowers the total productivity of the herd is led onto the commons, the aggressive owner of that last cow stands to gain at the expense of his neighbors. The right to have as many children as one chooses was probably the "commons" uppermost in Hardin's mind. But, pelagic fisheries are also a most conspicuous commons, and the predicament of the great whales bears witness to the tragedy of the commons. Despite such tragedies, if we sought to abolish all commons, we might find ourselves in some new and unwelcome predicaments.

Many demographers have argued that, if we could only accelerate the development of the poor societies, we would catalyze the *demographic transition* and quickly bring them into the condition of Western societies, with low birth and death rates, low growth, and good living conditions and education. Virtually all texts on demography discuss the transition, but Petersen almost alone has questioned it as a predictive law.

Paddock and Paddock, convinced that pandemic famine is imminent, have argued that some societies cannot be saved and that aid from the developed world should be reserved for those poor lands that can be helped through the demographic transition only with outside aid. The analogy is to triage in military medicine: When disastrously overburdened with wounded, ignore those who will recover without medical aid and those who will die even if they are given help, and concentrate the limited facilities on those who can be saved only if helped.

The economists still spoke up for effective infinity. Barnett and Morse, writing with support from Resources for the Future, make the strongest case in *Scarcity and Growth*, 1963. They focus on "Ricardian scarcity," which is the hypothesis that the richest of natural resources are the first to be harvested and that continued increase in demand requires exploitation of less and less rewarding resources. Next, they hypothesize that today's technological society generates technological advance at least as fast as Ricardian scarcity develops. They conclude that costs of raw materials in such a society should not be expected to increase: "Output per capita, as measured by any suitable in-

dexes at our disposal, may conceivably increase into the indefinite future, and our eventual overcrowding is by no means a foregone conclusion."

Barnett and Morse do foresee a possible need for the limitation of population growth, but they regard this as not critical and as a matter that will be manageable through institutional change in due course. Pessimists see the same need but with greater urgency, and they are less assured that control will be easy.

The book by Barnett and Morse is the most carefully written defense of economic cornucopianism. It has been enormously influential. It is in large measure an empirical defense based on extrapolation of existing trends. Schematically, we may express it in these terms: If availability of resources declines exponentially under mounting pressures of population and affluence, still an exponentially increasing technology applied to those waning resources may lead to a slower but still exponentially increasing productivity, plausibly in excess of population growth, and therefore may also lead to exponentially increasing affluence.

Several demurrals may be voiced. Extrapolation of dominant trends will not forecast revolutions, and yet we have revolutions. In the years since the book was written, some trends have broken sharply with tradition. In particular, "energy . . .in unlimited quantities at constant cost" seems more, not less remote.

Again, technological growth must be a function of the number of scientists and technologists. During the last fifty years, pretty much the base period for extrapolation of technological growth, the number of scientists and engineers has also grown exponentially and at such a rate that by early in the next century its continuation would require that all of our children

Rondal Partridge

become scientists and technologists. Disagreeing with Barnett and Morse, I suspect that technology is becoming an activity of diminishing return. Consider for a moment the fruitfulness for human welfare of the basic scientific principles discovered since Copernicus lived. Does anyone care to speculate whether as many more, equally fruitful, will be discovered during the next 500 years? The question is unanswerable, but human destiny demands an affirmative answer if we are to follow the optimists' path.

Finally, Barnett and Morse argue against the conservationsts' concern for the limits of the earth: "By devoting itself to improve the lot of the living, . . .each generation, whether recognizing a future-oriented obligation to do so or not, transmits a more productive world to those who follow."

Colin Clark, an incredibly optimistic Australian economist, thinks the world can readily supply food for 80 billion. Ester Boserup, in a wonderfully terse little book, argues that it is population growth that has forced agricultural progress. This may well be, provided that populations grow slowly enough for adaptive responses. That this has frequently been true in the past does not assure that it will continue to be true. Neither does past experience warrant extrapolation into a quite unknown future for technological agriculture.

But another sort of economist has taken up the cudgels in support of the no-growth economy—for example, Mishan, Johnson and Hardesty, and Daly. The no-growth position differs sharply from that of the optimists by rejecting hopes of ever-expanding production. The penalties of growth, avoided in a steady-state economy, are carefully detailed.

I have merely hinted at the participation of the conservation movement. The Sierra Club, driven by its executive director, David Brower, and stimulated by contributions from Cowles, Luten, Day, and Ehrlich, came in on the side of the pessimists in the late 1960s. Most major conservation organizations have since concurred.

The conservation movement, as another oppressed minority, was at least a lesser darling of the supporters of liberal issues until 1970 when, with Earth Day, conservation or "ecology" took center stage away from civil liberties and the Third World. It thereby engendered substantial resentment and has been under intermittent attack from the Left ever since.

Climaxing, and in a sense terminating the debate of the 1950s and 1960s, was Ehrlich's *The Population Bomb* (1968). Immensely popular, selling more than a million copies, the book was a call to action.

"The Limits to Growth"

In 1972, hard on the heels of the subsidence from the environmental excitement of 1970 and at a time when an optimistic counterattack might have been in order, another pessimistic book appeared. *The Limits to Growth*, by Donella and Dennis Meadows and their colleagues, was carefully framed and phrased. But it was terse and necessarily depended on bold assumptions and sweeping abstractions. It seemed to excite more adverse reviews than any earlier book. Economists clearly disliked it. Conservationists adored it. If Ehrlich reached a naive youthful audience, the Meadows got to the intelligentsia—perhaps for the first time.

The gross national product includes air pollution and advertising for cigarettes, and ambulances to clear our highways of carnage. It counts special locks for our doors, and jails for the people who break them. The gross national product includes the destruction of the redwoods and the death of Lake Superior. It grows with the production of napalm and missiles and nuclear warheads, and it even includes research on the improved dissemination of bubonic plague. The gross national product swells with equipment for the police to put down riots in our cities; and though it is not diminished by the damage these riots do, still it goes up as slums are rebuilt on their ashes. It includes Whitman's rifle and Speck's knife, and the broadcasting of television programs which glorify violence to sell goods to our children.
—ROBERT KENNEDY

The authors identified five major variables important in human subsistence: population, industrial equipment, agriculture, mineral resources, and pollution. They lumped ("aggregated") highly diverse, highly dispersed components, and they postulated functional relationships, including inventories and delays in interactions, both reinforcing and regulatory. Many of the functions are nonlinear. Some of them are very shaky, and the authors admit this. The worst may be the relationship between pollution and life expectancy. No one knows what it is. In one sense, the authors' assumption seems conservative, in another unrealistic. Thus, it almost has to be conservative to imagine that 100 times more pollution than today's would diminish life expectancy by only 50 percent. But it is also unrealistic, for a hundredfold more carbon monoxide on a Los Angeles freeway might well kill its users before they reached an exit.

All of these relationships were assembled as sets of rate equations amenable to computer processing. The authors ran a set through, then changed the assumptions and ran it through again to see what happened. They admitted throughout how uncertain some of the assumptions were, but they thought, and I concur, that the results had meaning nonetheless.

Opponents, including as a class those who would have us take their extrapolations of tradition seriously in this world of revolution, wish also to take *Limits* narrowly and precisely, despite contrary protestations by the authors. Opponents have protested that *Limits* uses a Malthusian model and so of course gets a Malthusian answer. If they had used a non-Malthusian— for instance, one like that of Barnett and Morse—they would have gotten a non-Malthusian result. Granted, but what if it *is* a Malthusian world? Faced with such a choice—even if the arguments in favor of limits were not persuasive—the rational course to follow is to look at the probable results from acting as though we believe the one when the other is actually true. If *we* act as though we believe in infinite expansion, and this turns out to be impossible, we risk an ultimate disaster for humankind. We may well destroy most of the biosphere in our desperate attempts to survive. Indeed, we may well eliminate much of the planet as a suitable place for human habitation. Man-induced expansion of deserts, areas of exhausted and eroded soils, and denuded hill slopes testify to this possibility. Ultimately it may prove impossible to reverse such a trend, for the resources needed to accomplish such a reversal would be unavailable.

If we believe in nonexistent limits and voluntarily restrict our growth—possibly even reduce total population—what losses do we risk? Some geniuses (and some scoundrels) who might have been born will not be born so soon. Perhaps, to compensate, we can better afford to develop the talents of those now neglected. We will have slowed down exploitation of the planet for the benefit of man. We will be faced with serious problems of the equitable distribution of existing goods and services, but at least more could be available per capita, however unevenly distributed. If growth and expansion later prove to be both possible and desirable, it would appear absurdly easy to set the process in motion once again. The resources would still be here. One can do little better here than quote Ehrlich, who strongly urges that we act as though there are limits. "If I'm right, we will save the world. If I'm wrong, people will still be better fed, better housed, and happier, thanks to our efforts."

Limits makes telling use of what we have come to call the "Malthusian corollary" in dealing with nonrenewable resources (the minerals). This is the proposition that if use of such a fixed-stock resource increases exponentially, then the amount used in each doubling interval equals the amount used in past history. Schematically, the amount used in the past, $1 + 2 + 4 + 8 + 16$ equals 31; the amount used in the next doubling period is 32. (Actually, the amount used in a doubling period is the amount used in the first year of the doubling interval times the length of the interval times 1.445). The book's estimates of mineral resource magnitudes may be in error—for example, one wonders whether any estimate can be made for the aluminum resource when most of the earth's crust is quite rich in aluminum. But the authors note, correctly, that so long as you postulate exponential growth—and the optimists are stuck with that—it makes little difference how accurate your estimates of resource magnitudes are; the end is never remote and it comes most abruptly.

The computer results indicated catastrophe, unless we change our ways: a catastrophe that is not imminent, but not remote either—just far enough away so that it cannot be dismissed as preposterous, but close enough to be unsettling: the middle of the next century.

On the limits-to-growth issue there is no place for fence sitters. The world is infinite or it is finite. This time it is wrong for scholars to see "merit on both sides." If my position on the matter has not been clearly revealed, my convictions are these: (1) the earth is finite; (2) the population growth of the past few generations was rare through most of man's history;

(3) the present rate of growth cannot continue for long into the future; (4) at some point there must be no growth at all, for a slower rate, however desirable, merely postpones the day limits are reached; and (5) choosing to limit births to match low death rates is preferable to increasing deaths to match births.

Obviously, however, humanity is not ready to come to a decision. The debate will continue. It is moving now from scholars' desks to national commissions and international conferences; presently the chancelleries will scrutinize it.

The poor nations are castigating the rich nations with charges of resource exploitation; at the same time, the poor lands see population growth as a new bargaining lever. Logic, presumably, has no place in this setting. If the world is infinite, resources are worthless; if it is finite, population growth is a burden. In a related vein, the Arabs are proving to the world that natural resources may be of great value, but they are having doubts on the morality of contraception; perhaps they think the oil resource will never run out. The Russians argue for an infinite world and they can hardly lose, whether it proves infinite or finite, since so much of it is Russian. When the rest of the world goes dry and has to turn to Russia for raw materials, will

they be priced as from an infinite stock or from a finite one?

The consequences of the wrong answer to the great question of the world's finiteness may be of grievous magnitude to humanity, and even more so to the rest of the biota that are our fellow travelers on this planet. Still, we should escape absolute disaster—unless the optimists are almost right. Our best chance, our greatest luck, may be to have the limits of the earth close at hand, perhaps even before we reach a population of five billion. Giddings has argued persuasively that the chances of nuclear war go up as the cube of population, and he guesses, as have several others, that the chance is only one in a thousand per year with today's four billion people. If, however, we should reach 40 billion, then nuclear war would become an even chance each year. How long will biocosmologists persist in their current search for evidence of galactic life

---

Once as President I thought and said that birth control was not the business of our Federal Government. The facts changed my mind. . . . I have come to believe that the population explosion is the world's most critical problem.
—DWIGHT D. EISENHOWER

---

outside the solar system before concluding that all intelligent societies destroy themselves at about the time they become interested in galactic life?

The swords of debate will become tougher and sharper; the debate will grow in complexity, but some issues will be winnowed out. Even if we believe that the earth has limits, we know better than to say we have reached those limits. The world's production of wheat, of maize, and probably of rice has roughly tripled in the last fifty years; who is to say it can't triple again? No one. All that can be said is that it can't triple many more times.

The heraldry of the debate will continue, too—all of the magnificent catch phrases: "geometric versus arithmetic growth"; "standing room only"; "enough and to spare"; "the squeeze"; "the doomsayers"; "for every mouth a pair of hands to feed it"; "for every pair of hands a mouth to be fed"; and so on and on.

Part of the problem in the debate is the intellectual need on the one side to postulate a world that won't happen. The pessimist hopes he is making a self-defeating forecast. Institutions will bend; adjustments will be made. No one will ever know whether the

changes were as fast as they could be, or whether faster change would have helped or hindered. But you cannot argue for a changed course by admitting that you will probably change course. Rather, you must cry, "Rocks ahead; change course!"

The literature will continue to grow, seemingly without limit, but is anything really new added?

I suspect that we witness a quarrel between two faiths: The one is of biologists believing in the reality of constraining principles; seeing mankind at one extreme of a great continuum of life, partaking to some degree of all its attributes for better or worse, and subject to the environment of this world. The other faith is of social scientists, empiricists and skeptical of principle; seeing man as a thing apart and human society as perfectible, given enough study; and seeing man as superior to and capable of controlling the environment of this world.

Finally, a curious and disquieting matter: How large is the earth? Here is an issue profoundly geographical, but to which geographers have made no great contributions. Have they feared to cross swords with those from harder disciplines? Or have they seen all too clearly the size and diversity of the earth and are they appalled at efforts to summarize it in the scope of a single book? One is tempted to cry out, "Only geographers can know the earth is finite. Economists must ask them, 'How big?'; demographers must ask, 'How much room, and where?'"

But if the authors of *The Limits to Growth* are generally right, all this won't make much difference. If the data become firmer, the optimists will have another field day of refined extrapolation. But is it our purpose, anyway, to fill the earth with people? If not, why bother to learn how many it will hold? The critical question is, Do more people today, or in the next generation, or in the next, make a better earth? Both those who feel that the answer is "yes," and those who feel that the answer is "no" will continue to seek supporters.

And so we end up almost where we began: No wonder they disagreed so endlessly; conflicting faiths hid different premises—they were talking about different things!

Economics

A major intellectual revolution now in the making, perhaps as significant to the twentieth century as the Darwinian revolution was to the nineteenth, is the rejection of a nation tacitly accepted by many early economic writers, including Karl Marx, the notion of an infinite earth. The classic phrase was, "For every mouth there is a pair of hands to feed it." No notion came through of a limiting environment. But now we are coming to concede the earth to be finite. The debate has been going on since the Second World War and has had, rather curiously at first sight, strong protagonists and antagonists. This is because the issue has been rather more than the acres of earth; it has also included the question of how much of the future concerns us, and is technology a multiplying factor without limit? Regardless, we have lined ourselves up as either pessimists or optimists, into believers in *Our Plundered Planet* versus believers in a world of *Enough and to Spare*. While, in my observation, the optimists have usually won in face-to-face arguments, they are, nonetheless, wrong.

Quite recently, I believe, they have come to concede that they have been wrong. But they have not been defeated by intellect. If you should ask me, the clinching argument has been the vision of that beautiful, blue-green planet, so little and so lonely, presented in literal photographs taken by the astronauts. So much for the power of the intellect.

Be that as it may, the pessimists have seen, for quite some time now, that population growth must end. And they, the pessimists at least, have agreed that we would prefer population growth to end on our terms, with long life expectancy and small families rather than under the alternative of short lives and large families.

An inescapable consequence of the conclusion that population growth must end is the corollary that economic growth must end. For many of us, this is a far more terrifying and unwelcome proposition that any vision of the end of population growth. Perhaps, in fact, it is economic growth we are hooked on, and population growth as an attractive proposition is entirely subordinate to it.

This aspect struck me hard only in the summer of 1969 on an evening when I had been talking to graduate students in economics at Berkeley on the subject of population. They, all of them interested in environmental issues, asked what they as economists could do about the problems. I suggested to them that the most important problem they could attack was to identify the terms and conditions under which a static economy could operate to our satisfaction. With that, it seemed to me, they all dropped out, lost interest, changed the subject.

David Brower first suggested that I inquire into these matters in 1963. But he also suggested that Galbraith and others of far greater competence than I do so, and I have waited patiently for them to come up with the answers. They have, Galbraith, Boulding and other economists, said repeatedly that there is no reason to need growth. But this is not enough.

Let me observe then, as aggravatively as possible, that if ecology, from *"oikos,"* the *"household,"* and *"logos,"* the *"word"* is the study of the household, then

The world is threatened by growing population, but it is also, even perhaps to a greater extent, threatened by the exploding appetites of the already rich.

—MAURICE STRONG

economics, from *oikos,* again, and *"nemein,"* to manage, to administer, is applied ecology, the subdivision of the study of the household which concerns itself with making decisions on how to manage the household. While many economists will bridle at the notion of being applied ecologists, some of them, God bless them, insist this, in fact, is the task.

As the next observation, please recall that our economic system was not given to us by God, completed and ready to handle any problems which might arise. Rather, it has evolved, beginning with the earliest specialization of human activity, with communication of wants, and with trading among specialists, whether tools for food, arrow flints for salt, aesthetics for subsistence. What it has done for us is to ease enormously the task of deciding what to buy and how much. But it does this better for us with small than with large purchases; it did better when we were poor than now when we are rich.

Today, the obsession with growth which has developed suggests strongly that the economy is in charge of us, not we in charge of the economy.

Well, if we are to talk about a macrostatic economy, what shall be the measure of it? Shall we demand that the Gross National Product cease to grow? I think not; for two reasons.

First, the GNP is no measure of what concerns us; in some respects it is quite unrelated to the finiteness of the world. GNP is a summing up of transactions. Many of these reflect extractions from and impingements on the environment, but many do not. As a trivial example, the gambling enterprises of Reno take money to the bank every evening and this, I suppose, contributes to the GNP. If the legislature were to require that every nickel into a slot machine must go to the bank, and every jackpot, or less, must be paid by check, then the contribution of legalized gambling to the GNP would surely be increased many-fold. Again, the costs of communication, telephoning, for instance, contribute to GNP but they can increase with very little obvious limit and do not appear to be restricted in any substantial way by the finiteness of the earth. A number of people have noted that a growing portion of GNP is for mitigation of malefits. Thus, if I buy gasoline for my car, that purchase is part of the GNP. If, then, to mitigate my share of the smog, I must buy a smog-control device, that also adds to GNP. It has been suggested the GNP may end up composed half of things we did because we liked them and half of measures to counteract the problems created by the first half. That is the first reason for rejecting GNP as a measure of macrostatic economy.

The second reason is that GNP is an index of the happiness of the corporate individual and not of the real individual. The corporate individual, and we must never forget it, has a much simpler purpose than the real individual. It has no legitimate purpose other than to maximize dividends to its stockholders. It has intellectual problems: how much dividends this year, how much in a decade; and how much effort spent on environmental quality or on public relations, will pay off in dividends, now or later? Again, the corporation may be subverted by its managers. They, being real people, may have purposes other than maximization of dividends, and included among these purposes may be the improvement of personal image and the quite unselfish optimization of community amenities. But these, it must be emphasized, are subversions and cannot be the corporate purpose.

GNP, probably being closely related to corporate dividends, is a plausible index of corporate welfare. It is not of great merit as an index of the general welfare, of public good. Accordingly, let the GNP rise as it may wish; this is not our test of the macrostatic economy.

If GNP is not a satisfactory criterion, what is? Perhaps we are in real trouble, if we try to define any optimum in this area. In the case of population, we can easily satisfy ourselves that the earth is finite, that a limit must exist, but if we try to estimate an optimum population, we don't get far. Whelpton, over twenty years ago, thought 90 million people might be optimum for the United States. Currently, estimates for an optimum world population seem to hover around 500 million, about a seventh of the current actual population. But the circumstances which dictate the optimum change by the year. For each who says the optimum is diminishing because of what we have pulled out of place and strewn around the world, there is an antagonist who says it is increasing because of the increasing competence of our technology.

We have worse difficulties with economic activity. It would be easy to accept 500 million people as an optimum population and then to proceed to the requirements for an optimum diet, housing, transportation, cultural and environmental amenities and let it go at that. But the whole thing smacks of an authoritarian management which seems more likely to take the diversity and richness of living out of our lives than to do anything else. Optimum living is not apt to be determined by any authority.

Still, while I do not know how to set optima, this does not mean they do not exist. In the case of population it is generally easy to secure assent to the proposition that a world in which population growth is let go until it is curbed by short life expectancy is a far from optimum world. In similar fashion, if economic activity expands until it is curbed by the rising cost of mitigation of nuisance and destruction, we will be unhappy; the second half of our economic activity will be to rectify the misdeeds of the first half, and any optimum will be utterly missed.

Coming to the issue, if I cannot set an optimum, I can still express the suspicion that we are beyond it, and argue that what we are concerned with is the impact of economic activity on natural resources, including the economic externalities of the environment, what may be called the quality of the environment, but not the aesthetic quality of the landscape. This last exclusion I have tried to justify elsewhere on the score of the incommensurability of aesthetic values with economic values.

The nature of our difficulty is that our economic processes give little concern to the condition of our natural resources. These processes do promote efficiency, but they do not submit to Garrett Hardin's theorem that in any system you cannot maximize both efficiency and stability. They do provide an allocation of scarce resources, but only of immediately scarce natural resources. We have established institutions essentially on the premise that natural resources are infinite.

Garrett Hardin, who comes on strong in this field, has written on this problem in "The Tragedy of the Commons." His parable speaks of the commons where any villager may graze his cattle without charge. But when the commons is grazed to capacity, additional cattle will damage it, will lower its productive capacity. From the collective viewpoint, such additional cattle are a disaster. Nonetheless, an individual villager may find it to his advantage to put an additional cow on the commons. Even though the production of the entire herd is diminished, the return to our individual villager may be increased.

We have left a great deal of our environment in the commons. Examples could range widely, from individual determination of family size to ownership of pelagic fisheries to acquiescence in an extraordinary diversity of pollution. It is hard to escape the conviction that this pattern reflects anything but belief in the infinity of the natural resource base, the infinity of the earth.

In passing, an astonishing and delightful record of early conservation measures in the New England colonies has come to my attention. Within fifty years after

Elihu Blotnick

arrival on this continent, these people were having to restrain their members from taking advantage of the commons in a great many ways: literally pasturing too many cows on the village commons, cutting oak and walnut for inferior uses, overusing fish as fertilizer, fishing out of season, and so on. One wonders if the colonists, freed of the confines and repressions of a crowded England, had felt initially that here no restraints would ever be needed, that here in the New World was an infinitely abundant environment, and that they learned better within their first century here.

The general response to the tragedy of the commons was to accord private ownership of resources. Thus, if the villager owned only his proportionate share of the commons—no longer a commons—the folly of overpasturing should bear in on him. And if not, it was his funeral (or was it only his?).

We did, early, grant ownership in land but this was probably more a matter of strategic location and of the impossibility of several men cropping the same piece of land simultaneously, than of any recognition of limits.

While we have virtually given away almost any of our natural resources that anyone asked for, we have not often granted full ownership of a resource except under the guise of land ownership. You may own a mining claim but this is only a right to recover minerals.

You may have rights to use water, but you don't own it. We seem to have felt ownership to be unimportant; enterprise to develop was the important contribution to the society.

This was a land which was empty and abundantly capable of meeting the resource needs of its scarce inhabitants. They were at the same time poor and with limited wants and limited capabilities for exploiting their resource base. In that situation, we developed a set of resource policies and institutions germane to the time and the place and the people.

Now, we are many, and our wants are immense and we are stuck with an outworn tradition. We are plagued on every front with tragedies of the commons, and perhaps this is more our problem than any absolute ceiling on some index of the economy.

The answer, it seems to me, is fairly straightforward and simple. It is to put a price on those of our natural resources which lead to economic goods and a price sufficient to bring demand for them down to a level which can be sustained. Six categories can be mentioned:

1. *Pelagic marine resources.* By and large these have no owners. By treaties, we have partitioned up fishing rights to some of the harder pressed of these resources. Again, we have decidedly failed on others by

related but less coercive means. The case of the International Whaling Convention and the blue whale is spectacular and dismal. The United Nations would like to claim ownership of resources not already claimed. It would satisfy my criterion if the United Nations succeeded and if they then licensed harvest of those resources which are pressed beyond sustainable yields and exacted fees sufficiently large to reduce harvests to sustainable yields. This is hardly an answer to the world's shortage of animal protein, but overuse of the resources is not an answer, either.

2. The vast resources in the United States which remain in the *public domain*.

a) *Timber*. We sell cutting rights in the National Forests usually at auction. Demand, then, not cost of production, determines price. The volume is large enough to be a substantial factor in determining timber values on private lands, as well. A probable result is that the return from timber sales from private lands is insufficient to permit good management. Recently, Congress was debating a National Timber Supply Act which seemed to view forest productivity in the same light as the productivity of a factory. It provided for more intensive management and increased cutting rates at the expense of other components of the multiple uses of the National Forests. But, in fact, the productivity of a forest differs from that of a factory and depends on the inventory of growing trees as much or more than on the application of management capital and labor.

If you will draw a curve for a growing forest in which you plot the average growth per year per acre since the trees were planted against the age of the forest, this curve must somewhere have a maximum. If you wish to maximize the production of wood from this forest, it should be cut at the maximum. But almost every economic pressure we put on forests hastens the cutting.

Let us, instead, increase the charges for cutting rights in the National Forests until we diminish the demand so that forests will grow at least to the neighborhood of maximum yield before being cut. Doing this will also provide incentive for constructive management of privately owned forests. It will also bring our use of the forest resource down to a sustainable level and thereby approach the macrostatic condition.

b) *Grazing* leases on the public domain have been a wonderful perquisite. They do not dominate the grazing picture to the degree timber from the National Forests does. The Bureau of Land Management has been trying to raise grazing fees, but the grazing lobbies are still ahead. Give these fees the same treatment as cutting prices.

c) *Minerals* have been so much in the public eye on issues of royalties for fuels, but also depletion al-

lowances, that it is hard to ask for much other than pinching down depletion allowances and exacting severance taxes . . .which is perhaps what each of these items comes to.

d) *Water*. No one pays for water; we pay only for its management. If we viewed the resource itself as being as valuable as we say it is, we should not be reluctant to pay for it. So, again, I propose exacting a considerable price for the use of water; let me suggest $25 per acre-foot just to indicate the ball park.

e) *National commercial fisheries*. Exact a severance tax and license rights to harvest so as to do away with the destructive inefficiencies we now impose.

3. *Privately owned productive land*. Exact a land tax based on its productivity or its production, I'm not sure which, but not on its locational value. The latter is not a resource value.

4. The fourth category is the *right to pollute* the environment. We took this for granted when the land was empty. Now, it becomes intolerable. Some success

---

Much of the water supply that we go to such great trouble to purify—about half of it, in fact—is only used to carry off sewage from our toilets. Then we go to great further expense just to repurify the same water.

—NEIL SELDMAN

---

has been had in charging polluters for the costs of cleaning up their effluents. The classical case is in the Ruhr River watershed in Germany. My proposal goes further and suggests charging more than the cost of managing effluents. The matter, of course, goes far beyond water pollution. Tax cars, too, for their pollution. Tax durable containers. Tax noisy motorcycle exhausts.

Please note, in passing, that it is not my purpose in this discussion to abate such nuisances; that is another matter. My purposes here is to limit the impact of the economy on the resource, to direct economic activity away from resource deterioration.

5. The fifth category that comes to mind (you will think of more) is to provide incentive for *recycling of durable unrenewable resources*, most conspicuously to get automobile hulks back to the steel mills with, perhaps, diversions to the copper refineries and aluminum

smelters. "No-deposit-no-return" bottles may be even more conspicuous.

6. The sixth and last category, one which perhaps is only on the margin of the resources picture, is to price services provided by the public sector of the economy so as to limit use to the capacity of the facility. As an example, the two major bridges in the San Francisco Bay area were built at depression prices. They are essentially paid for and the public has become accustomed to tolls. It is claimed new bridges are needed, but new bridges would cost so much that saturation traffic on them would not pay the interest on construction costs. Despite the traffic burden on the existing bridges, we still grant bargain rates to commuters who largely use the bridges at the most crowded hours. This is manifest nonsense; it stems from archaic customs developed in an economy of scarcity when it seems good business to accord diminished prices to large customers. That situation is gone. The land is not empty; it is full. Use of such facilities should be discouraged, not encouraged. Curiously, with that activity cited earlier as having little impact on the resource base, the telephone, we do encourage off-peak use by everyone. With electricity, halfway between, we encourage only the big customers in this fashion. None of this seems paradoxical.

But when we propose similar pricing policy on family size, it is attacked as an outrageous invasion of the sanctity of the family. (It does disturb me, but for another reason: I don't like the vision of children being restricted to the economically acquisitive. The trait might be inheritable. If children are to be taxed, be sure the surtaxes escalate dramatically.) It takes James Reston to reflect that if the State must not constrain the number of children, then surely it must similarly not constrain the number of wives—or husbands.

Revenue from all of these fees might come to a considerable sum. If we may accept a view of the social contract which says that the natural resources of a society are inherently the commonwealth of the members of the society, and if we can accept the view that the society cannot permanently alienate its rights to these resources, then we can argue that this is the revenue which appropriately can go to provide GAI, the guaranteed annual income.

I do not dare suggest that the aggregate of fees, severance taxes, and penalties imposed on the extraction of economic goods from the environment be balanced against the needed GAI, but it does seem a matter worth exploring.

Nothing has been said about the microdynamic aspect of this economy. I see nothing in these proposals to inhibit innovation, and a good deal of stimulus for it.

Brief mention only has been given to those resources which are not economic; to aesthetic resources, wild game, outdoor recreational opportunity, wilderness. These matters are too important to be allowed into the economy.

Finally, in conclusion, perhaps I have vandalized the economic premises enough. Perhaps the economic bosses are a-horseback and will eject me, and the clean-up crews will come along and give us a proper account of teloeconomics and how to achieve a microdynamic, macrostatic economy.

Progress Against Growth

In a young land that has experienced development at an unprecedented pace, it is not surprising that we struggle with the confusion between growth and progress. Historically, growth and progress have been to us almost interchangeable, so much so that even though we may not buy the shopworn idea that bigger is better, we still do not act as though we understand a distinction that seriously affects our lives and will determine the quality of life that our children will live.

Growth can be something other than progress. Our dictionary gives "augmentation" as a synonym for growth—but it also lists "excrescence." There is the rub: growth can go quite beyond healthy increase into the realm of pathology, and here we find that growth is "an abnormal proliferation of tissue, as in a tumor." Here cells lose their stable relationship with the organism, multiply without control, and die for lack of system.

One can demonstrate with simple arithmetic that growth must be a transient condition. While we feel the intellectual need to express growth as a percentage increase for this year over last year's condition, and while many of us fondly imagine that constancy of growth rate is the index of stability, the fact is that the constant rate leads remorselessly to exponential growth and is a measure of revolution rather than stability.

We have dreamed a host of fables about exponential growth: the 600 years to "standing room only" for the world, land and sea; the 1,000 years until the world is one vast book collection, eight stacks of floors with five billion miles of card files; the 200 years until the world is too hot for habitation; the 400 years until the world is vaporized by the energy industries of its people. Though often misunderstood, these fables have a clear purpose—to argue that because the consequences of exponential growth are impossible, the continuance of such growth is itself impossible.

Growth is appropriate to the juvenile condition, not to maturity. Nearly all living organisms adapted to survival go through periods of rapid early growth. But

---

"Progress was OK. It just went on too long."

—OGDEN NASH

---

upon attainment of maturity, control mechanisms come into play to insure that the organism remains of the right size to fulfill its purpose. Lacking such controls, continued growth would lead only to disaster. J.B.S. Haldane, in *Possible Worlds* (1930), has a chapter titled "On Being the Right Size," in which he points up some of the problems of giantism: How big a man can a skeleton made of bone support? Why cannot a blue whale come ashore? How big a bird can fly in an atmosphere as thin as ours? How big can insects be with oxygen brought to their muscles only by diffusion? How big could a warm-blooded animal be before it died of its own metabolic heat?

While living organisms commonly have developed regulatory (usually hormonal) systems which come into play when they reach the right size, human societies have been less successful. Small groups of people living close to the land seem ordinarily to have come to terms with their environment and to have developed institutions for stabilizing their numbers and their impact on the environment. In contrast imperialistic, dynamic, innovative societies have left their mark on the earth but have not long endured. Such societies may not have had the time or introspection to see and accept their own maturity. Could it be that our 20th century conservation movement might become a controlling "social hormone"?

We are told that we must have growth because economists insist upon it. We have listened intently because economists have said what we wanted to hear. Yet John Stuart Mill, over a century ago, saw problems ahead. Today, many others, such as Kenneth Boulding, tell us that indeed we do not need growth—but no one has been able to tell us clearly how to achieve a steady state economy that we will accept. They have, though, illuminated important issues.

Herman Daly has contrasted Adam Smith's "unseen hand" which leads private self-interest unwittingly to serve the general welfare, with the "unseen foot," which kicks to pieces our common interest in the environment. And Mason Gaffney, focusing more narrowly on the growth of cities, has outlined three sorts of "urban containment." The first, ordinarily called "positive planning" and depending heavily on zoning, he calls "negative containment" because he thinks it cannot stand up under the pressures of developers.

The second, "neutral containment," is to have the cities quit subsidizing the suburbs. The third, "positive containment," is close to Henry George's "single tax."

The reality of urban subsidy to suburban growth is clearly shown in a $250 million bond issue passed in 1958 to provide water for the growth of metropolitan San Francisco's East Bay area. Berkeley's burden was some $20 million. What did Berkeley get in return? Essentially nothing, because the growth was not in Berkeley, but in Walnut Creek, Upper Pinole and Lower Slurbovia. But since it was promised that taxes would not increase, Berkeley citizens voted for the bonds four-to-one, without realizing that water rates could be half as high were it not for the need to support new suburban growth. How many cities have paid for their own schools, then chipped in to pay for the schools in successive suburban rings? Gaffney would have the suburbs pay the whole cost of the new services they demand.

It is not surprising that California, the focus of the growth mystique, should generate the strongest opposition to growth. Force begets counterforce. Where the fever of growth is hottest, the antibodies form fastest. The conservation movement grows best on the site of worst abuse. Today, many in California question burgeoning development and when they are told that growth is good, are prepared to look the developer in the eye and ask him how much of that good will end up in his pocket.

Clearly an optimum size must exist. While the optimum size for a metropolis obviously exceeds that for a provincial city, few people who live in the San Francisco metropolitan area could easily identify any progress of importance in the last three decades. Economically and culturally, it is still the same regional center, but the amenities that made it one of the most attractive of great cities are disappearing at an alarming rate.

New York, as almost everyone agrees, has become ungovernable, almost inoperable, neurotic, necrotic, perhaps cancerous.

But those who extol growth keep saying, "growth means jobs." Yes, jobs for today and for immigrants, but none guaranteed to local unemployed. Growth looks good to small business—up to a point. For winners can become losers with frightening suddenness: the local grocery store in a growing neighborhood until the supermarket moves in; the frontage on an increasingly busy street until the freeway bypasses it; the easy drive to work, and then the traffic jam. The longer you ride the tiger of growth, the more dangerous it becomes. The walls of growth press in on the city, shrink room to maneuver, bleed bargains dry, bankrupt the central stores, drain support from schools and libraries. Then the loss of pride, the strife that succeeds sense of community, the rubbish in the streets all suggest a condition where "the mass of men lead lives of quiet desperation." Finally, only friction and litigation can grow.

The consequences of growth so pervade the society that even when we can agree that it should end, a quality of momentum, an inertia, carries it along. We are dismayed to find that we have geared school construction and teacher training to a baby boom now passed, while we never thought of jobs for the adults they have become. Did we not want them to grow up?

How do we turn from pathological growth to humanistic progress?

1. We need more sophistication. When your mayor tells you that growth broadens the tax base, laugh in his face and ask him to count for you the growing cities with growing tax bases—and with declining tax rates. When your antagonists tells you that your love of beauty is emotional, reply that love of money is an emotion, and hunger, too.

2. We need to be more skeptical. When opponents of the Redwood National Park argued that it would destroy Humboldt County's tax base, they sought to play on the gullibility of a public that could not easily check for itself that the loss would be less than five percent. When the power industry warns us that energy needs for environmental protection and mass transit will require great expansion, common sense should tell us that the incremental needs in these areas will be trifling in comparison with the other "growth needs" that the utilities have in mind to promote.

3. We can vote down bond issues, try to limit facilities, but I think this will do more to publicize our feelings than to end growth. Ray Dasmann suggested denying water to Southern California; water control authorities have come close to denying sewers to San Francisco; the Sierra Club suggests denying electric power. Facetiously, it has been said that this won't work but will, instead, trade the present population for one which drinks only alcohol, doesn't wash, and uses outhouses and kerosene lamps. Yet such measures might help if we were to increase water rates to the point were per capita consumption would level off, and if we were to require new developments to pay for all of the services provided rather than only for their incremental costs.

4. Can migration to growing areas be restricted? Probably not. Proposals to exact a California immigration fee of $1,000 would be judged unconstitutional. But what of a carefully measured fee reflective of the facilities available to new residents but paid for by prior residents? If it is a denial of the privileges and immunities clause of the Fourteenth Amendment to restrict interstate migration, is it not a denial of the due process clause to force prior residents to contribute their property to the support of immigrants?

5. We must modify our institutions. They were developed for a juvenile, growing society, a poor society in an empty land. We now have a rich society in a full land, a mature society past its era of growth. The Federal Constitution may require amendment and, if we can identify changes based on sound principle, but expediency, we should not shrink from undertaking them. Would it be a disaster to revise the due process clause of the Fourteenth Amendment to give a man no more than a fair return on investment in land destined for public use? Would it be a disservice to society to exact an almost confiscatory capital gains tax on unimproved land? Its value is generated by the growing society, not by the productivity of its owner. Above all, it is time that we abandon our treasure-hunt philosophy of economics and reward productivity, not opportunism.

6. If growth is to end, we must abandon the growth mystique. Planners, all of them, relish growth. The plan for the San Francisco Bay Area prepared by the Association of Bay Area Governments envisions a persistence of population growth at what is probably a conventional rate for planners. No evidence of effort to restrain growth appears; no effort to reinforce what may be a current magnificent, intelligent, and abrupt decision by the American people to end population growth. Can our generation close its eyes to growth when we know that the next generation must face up to it? Shall we live our lives as addicts to growth and then, having addicted our children, tell them in our wills to kick the habit? Let us say instead, and say it in our plans, that we expect growth to end soon; let our plans cover the period until growth has ended. Let our planning schools begin to produce planners who do not themselves believe in growth.

In California the temper is becoming clear: given a choice between competent plans for growth and competent plans for non-growth, voters will choose the latter. Rarely do they get a choice. Usually, if any choice is granted, it is plans for growth prepared by a competent planning staff against plans for non-growth prepared by overworked amateurs with no experience, working at midnight, with little access to needed details. When voters choose the former over the latter type, it is not because they are for growth, but because they are realistic.

The real power of planners is in their resources and technical competence. Why don't we give the progress-against-growth concept a chance by creating publicly supported groups of technically competent people who are committed to the idea of progress without growth? The cost would be slight, the stakes are large, and the voter would have the chance to decide between workable alternatives.

Part III: Resources We Must Use Better

Education

In the 1980s, America has an educational establishment capable of confounding the principles of government that gave us such a good start 200 years ago and capable, too, of promoting the destruction of what remains of the North American environment. Students are quite lost from view amid the intricate network of policies, credentials, and standardized programs. They learn, more by their experience than their textbooks, that convenience is the goal and insensitivity the means. Remedial help for the educational establishment requires embarrassingly simple programs, the point of which is to put students and teachers in touch with each other, with environments, and with good tools. Humane values and environmental values are learned through close, unhurried contact with people and the land. This requires labor-intensive teaching, low on prepared curricula and paper, high on dialog with people and places. And the structure of the curriculum for a student must make room for skills of the hand as well as the mind, turning labor into craftsmanship, counselling students to enter an age of intermediate technology with competence, critical awareness, and the skill of self-government. Current problems of schools with control, finance, racial animosity, and learning deficiencies all hinge for their solution on decentralization, humanization, and the development of ecologically sound operation—all of which bring student and teacher into the foreground and closer together. Spelling, the art of asking good questions, and the interdependence of a community and a river are all best taught at close range.

Education

MARK TERRY

THE LESSON that has been most mysteriously lost and forgotten during the growth of the education establishment is that children learn. The behavioral prize the primates have been puzzling over and improving on for the better part of 100 million years is learning. Pre-tests, tracking, behavioral objectives, and endless curriculum packages are not nearly as important in the learning process of children as are the behaviors of their elders and peers and the opportunities in their environment. When close contact with elders, peers, and environment is disrupted, children *still* learn—they learn distrust, even terror, and acquire the ability to insulate themselves from their environment.

In light of this long heritage of increasing ability to learn, some of our educational bureaucracy is simply foolish, even amusing. Some slivers of programs and grants have worked to bring students, teachers, and environments closer and to promote learning. But most of the establishment encrustation stands in the way of close personal and environmental contact by design, habit, and sheer size. Children survive in this system by learning how to get by as unimportant individuals in masses tended by administrators, free of responsibility for decisions, insulated from their own capacities, from each other, and from their environment.

It is hardly surprising that problems of support, control, racial hatred, and general apathy flourish. The system is inefficient in traditional economic terms, in its environmental relationships, and especially in terms of the resulting quality of education. The linear passage to higher education, counselled as the only way to get decent jobs, has proved increasingly ineffective and anticlimactic—just a repetition of the high school experience. Grades, held on to tenaciously as the only means to evaluate masses of students, have been soaring to keep the lid on student dissatisfaction, while it is commonly admitted that the quality of student writing has been declining at an equivalent rate.

In 1905 the school building in which I now teach looked out across the bustling new port of Seattle to an uninterrupted view of the Olympic Mountains. Three quarters of a century later, looking out to the moun-tains through a forest of office towers, this old grammar school invites reflection on the variety of goals and techniques of education that have been applied within its walls over the years. As a result of such reflection I am more sure than ever that the education that has mattered—in this building or anywhere—has derived from close contact with other people and with environments: education, to build on Alan Gussow's phrase, that provides a sense of humanity and a sense of place. In these years when we are beginning to understand that Schumacher's economics matters, it is clear that education itself is best as an intermediate technology. It is most efficient, in the quality of student experience, when it is labor-intensive. And its structure and content must support one another.

Walking through these halls I see many elements of the way in which our education system must operate already in place. In fact, we know how schools can best prepare students for the next century—it turns out to be the same way as they might best have prepared us for today. Teachers, for instance, are expected to work with few students, but to know them well. In the early years loads need to be especially light, and at the secondary level no teacher is expected to work with more than about 60 students during a week. Dialog with the student and written evaluation have become much more useful than grades in marking educational progress.

The school is a community of learning, stressing a common purpose for all its members. All personnel are involved with instruction: students are learning from "laborers," in the traditional sense, as well as "teachers"—they learn from custodians, cooks, nurses, secretaries, even administrators. No longer are these people *and their skills* separated from the learning process.

The school has become as self-sufficient in use of resources as possible, stimulating self-sufficiency in the local community as well. Energy and materials come from recycling within the school program and from local sources. The time that such an effort takes is not lost from the educational program, rather it is a major part of it. All students, teachers, and other per-

Andrea Entwisle

sonnel work to lessen the environmental impact and increase the self-sufficiency of the school and its community—and this may be the most important learning activity of all.

Campuses and buildings are destined to remain the focal points of school operation, but the *old* buildings clearly do *not* have to come down to make way for some twenty-first century design. The building I teach in was constructed in 1905 and seemed to many to be ready for demolition for the last 20 years. The programs now being run in the building, however, are attracting national attention and the preservation of the building by the school operating within its walls is seen as a significant benefit to the community. People, their ideas and an opportunity for them to gather to work together make up education, and some of the best work (and education) that can be done is to preserve and enhance an existing structure.

The school moves out from its campus to be involved in the local community. Apprenticeships in trades, services, government, community maintenance, and wilderness preservation form an essential part of the instructional program. And the community greatly increases the efficiency of the school building by using it throughout the year both for instruction and for community functions. Community control of schools becomes strong in a meaningful way when school and community are continually involved in joint programs and planning.

District organizations need to give way to community boards that advise schools in order to maintain an integrated program throughout a student's education, keeping various school faculties in touch with each other's curricula. And higher level advisory groups should facilitate school interaction and exchange programs within broad regions. Such regions might well be political entities with a mandate to gain regional self-sufficiency and ensure maintenance of environmental and economic health; their boundaries might well coincide with those of major watersheds. Within such regions a prime lesson for both communities and their schools—urban, suburban, and rural—will be interdependence and cooperation. School support, beyond each school's own capability for self-support, ought to be provided at the regional level as an integral part of the region's self-maintaining, steady-state economy.

New to the curriculum are thermodynamics, wilderness, political skills, and skills of the hand. Thermodynamics, the principles of energy and order, is threaded through all science teaching, including a required course for all students in technology assessment and science issues. Wilderness, real contact with environments apart from man, is experienced at several points

Steven Rauh

during a student's program, both as an end in itself and as a means to a new perspective of man's role on earth—custodial, not imperial. Political skills, the principles of self-government, are resurrected from the anonymity into which "Citizenship" has fallen and are learned through apprenticeship and application in the local community. And academics, which involve the skills of reading, writing, mathematics, critical thinking, and an introduction to the world's cultures and great ideas, are given *equal* weight in a student's program with skills of the hand—the crafts of building, designing, repairing, maintaining, and all the visual and performing arts.

Graduation from such a school becomes as contingent upon readiness to support oneself with acquired skills as it is upon the ability to read and write and continue learning. There is no automatic expectation of continuance of education in college. It may be much more desirable to enter the community productively and only return to formalized learning when a particular interest emerges.

The preparation and credentialling of teachers and other personnel for such schools need to result from a trial period working with a master teacher. Schools and departments of education at the college level ought to continue to provide opportunities to analyze teaching methods and programs—but all faculty of such institutions should be required to teach elementary or secondary students concurrently, to prevent isolation from the learning process, from real school problems, and from community control.

Powerful Inertia

I am reminded every day how distant a goal such a system is, how powerful the inertia of the present system is. At the university I see class upon class in which a majority of students are turning up for exams only, begging for higher grades, and never questioning the subject matter beyond what is necessary to answer a multiple-choice question on a mark-sense form. Degrees are probably nearer to being simply sold than at any time since the Revolution in this country. And a kind of panic scramble for the professional

Educators, by compressing and organizing knowledge in all areas of the curriculum, have created in the classroom what Paul Tillich has called the fatal pedagogical error—"To throw answers like stones at the heads of those who have not yet asked the questions."

— GEORGE ISAAC BROWN

Some slivers of programs and grants have worked to bring students, teachers, and environments closer, and to promote learning. (Right) But most of the establishment encrustation stands in the way of close personal and environmental contact by design, habit, and sheer size. (Left)
—MARK TERRY

Steven Rauh

and applied programs is commencing as more and more students discover the purely academic degree has no job-generating powers.

Within the large school systems, the greatest part of the inertia derives from the tendency of teachers to teach in the manner in which they were taught. There is also the general assumption, given the present system and economy, that we have a substantial teacher surplus. This works in favor of maintaining older teachers and sending new ones looking for other employment. All of which contradicts the desire of most teachers to work with smaller student loads, knowing the chances of doing a better job are at least greater with smaller numbers.

Reforms Beyond Lesson Plans

Curriculum reform by itself is not a hopeful approach to instituting the new system. It is an easy first step to take, but it rarely leads anywhere, once new materials are in use. There are many examples to be found today of ecologically oriented curricula being taught within traditional school operations, so that the message of the texts is daily contradicted on the grounds, in the lunch room, perhaps even in the use of the course materials themselves. What is wanted is a first step that leads on to others by beginning to alter teacher behavior.

The most effective catalyst is a program that affects the daily operation of schools, affecting all members of the school community and nudging the school toward involvement with the outside community. I believe the most helpful approach is through a program of school self-sufficiency. It will always be attractive economically, and especially so in the light of growing energy consciousness. Federal and state funding incentives could be used to reward schools that can demonstrate:

- that teachers and students, working together with the maintenance staff, have developed an energy conservation and materials recycling program in which all participate;
- that maintenance staff members are giving instruction and supervision on maintenance tasks within the school;
- and that a teacher-student delegation is developing local community contacts to obtain land for school agricultural use.

Such programs should be monitored as they develop and receive additional funds when they demonstrate significant increases in self-sufficiency. Even these steps will threaten some faculty and administrators. When school maintenance becomes a cooperative effort of faculty and students, however, there are noticeable benefits in that elusive educational phenomenon, "school spirit." That, along with increased support from a local community receiving the economic benefits of the school's efforts, should be enough to carry the day and perpetuate the program.

A benefit of employing students and teachers in school maintenance is that the school community becomes much more conscious of itself. And as energy and materials are monitored, an insight critical to all further developments should be realized—teacher-student interaction need not be energy intensive and does not require mountains of materials. Often the best education is built on dialog alone. It is hoped that this will lead teachers toward the development of "lean curricula," curricula that *emphasize* the teacher-student interaction and reduce capital and energy investments in the classroom. Federal and state funds for "lean curriculum" workshops, led by master teachers, should stimulate a move away from the elaborate wares of the educational publishing houses and begin

---

If children do not learn the ropes faster in our society, and even now they learn them faster than we think, it is in part because they do not have to, are not expected to, and do not expect themselves to, and in part because they know that they could not do anything with the knowledge if they had it.
—JOHN HOLT

---

to put teachers back in touch with their own creativity. The more it becomes clear that an unhurried student-teacher relationship is the most productive path to real learning, the more schools will begin to look beyond the myth of the teacher surplus. At this point something like a National Teacher Corps program should help the schools bring in new personnel on apprenticeships under master teachers.

Once the janitorial and dietary staffs begin to be used for advice and instruction in the school self-maintenance program, they should continue to share a responsibility for instruction. It may be a slow evolution, but the idea of a fully participating educational community ought to emerge. The more school operation becomes an acknowledged part of the educational program, the more the experience and skills of all personnel will be sought.

If school-community cooperation on recycling and resource acquisition matures, it will lead to greater community control. The emphasis on self-sufficiency should stimulate a review of existing school structures and building plans. A revolutionary use of state or

federal funds would help here to nudge districts off dead center: reward rehabilitation programs utilizing school personnel rather than traditional building projects. Repairing and refurbishing older buildings will require the assistance of skilled laborers. Funding should be made contingent upon employing these laborers as instructional assistants, thus providing apprenticeships to students within the curriculum. The obvious hope, here, is to further the introduction of a skills curriculum to parallel the academic curriculum.

As community and school become more interdependent in a recycling and maintenance effort, it would be a logical step for the school to make more and more use of people in the community to supplement its programs and for the community to make greater use of the school facilities and personnel on a year-round basis. It is essential that this kind of cooperation develop. Very few of the reforms discussed here can proceed at all far without community support and agreement.

Regionalism in School and Government

The evolution of districts into watershed regional school consortia has little hope unless there is much progress toward regional governments themselves. Incentives can be offered to inter-school programs that disregard current district lines and tie together schools in a region. But real change in school control at this level will depend on hoped-for changes in the political organization and economy of whole regions. It is clear that the current pattern of separate urban and suburban districts and of patchwork solutions to imbalances, such as busing for racial integration, is not working. The search for better solutions is most likely to lead to regional funding and inter-school programs that achieve integration in educational experiences, not simply by moving bodies. It may be that the severity of current problems will be a greater stimulus to change than anything else could be.

If the requirement that schools work with communities on resources and recycling is met, then the stage is set for some important curriculum additions. First citizenship education needs to be resurrected through instruction and practice in the skill of government. Students and teachers should be encouraged to serve in an advisory capacity or directly on local governing bodies as part of the instructional program. Such a use of state and federal funds to stimulate a renaissance in local government might be politically very popular.

The involvement of local artisans in the school maintenance program should also be capitalized upon in the school curriculum. People with skills should be encouraged to enter the teaching program, with incentives again being offered those schools that begin to

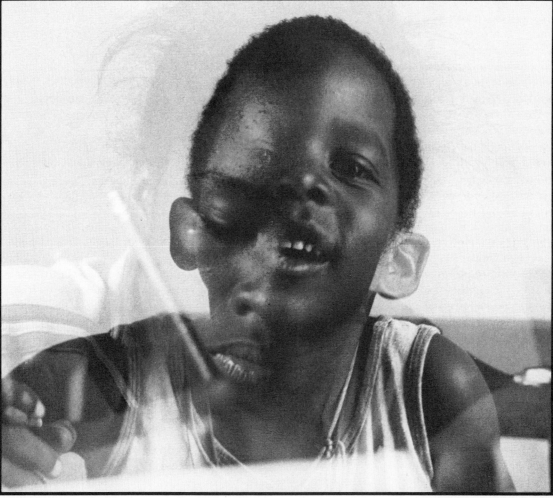

Andrea Entwistle

teach such skills on a par with academics. Scholarship monies, in particular, could be awarded to students graduating with hand skills who will begin a productive role in the community and postpone consideration of college. This balancing of curriculum content will, I hope, develop alongside a general renovation of the respect and support awarded to hand labor as our energy-glutted economy turns toward intermediate technology. It is certainly unlikely that the schools alone can lead such a movement, but they can support it in both their curriculum and their operation.

Clear roles for government incentives in more traditional curriculum development have been left unmentioned until now because structural changes in schools are so much more important and will take so much longer. But it is still to be hoped that funds will be used to support the incorporation of thermodynamic principles in all levels of curricula. Teacher workshops and in-service training programs should stress that teaching the principles of energy and order does not require great amounts of energy and materials. All such workshops should be planned to support the idea of

"lean curriculum" development mentioned earlier. The precise placement of funds, avoiding materials-intensive projects and singling out light educational technology, can do much to foster this development.

Federal and state governments can play essential roles in the development of wilderness education at all levels. The reservation of park and wilderness sites for wilderness curricula is one step, in addition to providing support to schools that ensure that all children have wilderness experience at some time during their program. The National Park Service, for example, should be instructed to take more seriously than ever its educational function and turn more and more to school programs.

The best that can be done for colleges and universities is to offer incentives for the same self-sufficiency programs as the lower schools. Faculty-student maintenance in colleges would be the best preparation for the change in students coming from high schools during the first years of this development. Continued change in incoming students may be expected to stimulate colleges and universities to keep pace, but there is no question that resistance to change increases as you move up from elementary schools to graduate schools.

Those most likely to feel threatened by the evolution of the system described here are established teachers, professors, and administrators. It is difficult to see how the changes can be anything but invigorating for the students, other school personnel, and communities involved. All of these will be discovering ways to take a greater share in the educational system. Teachers and administrators may see their territory threatened. The best hope for gaining their confidence and involvement lies in the prospect of reduced student loads and a less shaky economic picture for the schools. An interim contribution to their understanding and patience with this grand design would be a program of one-year apprenticeships outside the field of education. Teachers and administrators would be supported for a year, with the requirement that they learn some skill quite unrelated to their normal duties. Ideally, all teachers would be required to do this about once in every five years, but perhaps at least a beginning could be made by putting established teachers in touch with the increasingly labor-intensive economy—and giving them, at the same time, a new perspective on their own capabilities and the meaning of teaching.

George Borgstrom replies to questions of what to do given the current environment-energy situation with the simple response: "Become acquainted with the means of your survival." As this becomes increasingly clear because of economic and societal change, teachers will find that developing a system of labor-intensive education will work to their benefit and actually help them accommodate the changes in society around them.

Great encouragement can be taken from the fact that most of the reforms and programs mentioned here are currently in use in schools scattered all over

Intellectual disciplines and categories of knowledge tend to flow into one another unless prevented by artificial barriers. Rather than impeding such flows, universities should recognize and encourage them.

—JOSEPH MEEKER

this country. They are not all to be found in one place as yet, but agricultural self-sufficiency, recycling, maintenance apprenticeships, community control, thermodynamic and wilderness education—all these *can* be found today. Labor-intensive operation and the accompanying increase in the stature of work and hand labor are appearing now, as in the school in which I am writing this in Seattle. Most distant, educationally and politically, is the regional organization of community-controlled schools, but even signs of this can be found today.

In 2076 we can have an educational system suited to perpetuating self-government and a life-giving environment. What is required now is a program to unify the technology and the functioning of schools with the message of self-sufficiency they must teach. Schools can cost less, both environmentally and economically, and teach more if they rediscover the learning potential in the simple teacher-student relationship. The road to this labor-intensive education leads from the involvement of all teachers and students in the maintenance of their schools to an electorate educated with the skills of the hand, of government, and of learning itself. Children learn, and they can certainly learn the means of their own survival.

Recommended Actions

All levels of government should encourage, by all means at their disposal, schools and schooling appropriate to a post-industrial society. In particular, they should encourage:

☐ Decentralization and community control of schools, with maximum interaction between community and school.

☐ Ecologically sound school operation, including a recycling program extending beyond the school into the community.

☐ Maximum self-maintenance and self-sufficiency, involving all students and all school personnel.

☐ Labor-intensive teaching, with more teachers devoting more attention to fewer students per teacher.

☐ Recognition that all school personnel have useful skills, and consequently, that all should be recognized as instructor-advisors in their areas of competence.

☐ Development of "lean curricula" relying more on student-teacher rapport and less on capital equipment.

☐ Within the traditional curriculum, emphasis on reading, writing, mathematics, and critical thinking.

Rondal Partridge

☐ The addition to curricula of thermodynamics, wilderness experience, political skills, and skills of the hand.

☐ Year-round use of school buildings for community as well as educational functions, and maximum rehabilitation of existing structures to minimize the building of new ones.

Science and Technology

Early scientific discoveries were so basic they were hard to misapply. It would be hard to do much mischief with the simple knowledge that all elements are composed of atoms, for example, but it's dreadfully easy to go wrong when you know that atoms can be smashed and rearranged in ways unknown to nature. Modern, big science is not only risky, it's also highly centralized, incredibly costly, and largely incomprehensible to non-scientists. A change is in order, and to see what kind of change we want, we might try turning big science inside out. Then science would be relatively risk-free, decentralized, inexpensive, comprehensible to ordinary citizens, and hence controllable by them. This sounds like a description of Appropriate Technology, which is gaining ground in both developed and undeveloped countries. Of course, big science won't shrivel up and disappear, but it must be brought under more effective control. As a step in this direction, courses in the vocabulary and methods of science should be required in high school and college, and should be available in institutions that offer adult education. Science students should also be required to take courses in the effective communication of technical material in a non-technical manner. After we have taken these steps to demystify science, we can take further steps to democratize it.

Ed Buryn/Jeroboam, Inc.

Science

STEPHANIE MILLS

SCIENCE AND TECHNOLOGY have captivated the American polity since the days of Jefferson and Franklin. In those simpler times, statesmen could also be inventors and experimenters: Franklin with his kite, and Jefferson with his gadgets at Monticello. Today, politicians and scientists have become so specialized in their respective pursuits that communication between them has become difficult—and the evaluation of science policy by the public, even more so. Nevertheless, the optimistic Prometheanism of our science shapes our lives and institutions to an ever-greater degree.

Consider the impact of Sputnik on a whole generation of Americans. We were appalled when it was demonstrated that we hadn't got into space firstest with the mostest, so we mobilized: science education became a priority, aerospace became the surefire career. Our curiosity was directed away from more serious, if mundane, problems. We were knee-deep in garbage, firing rockets at the moon. Only now are we beginning to wonder whether we can afford guns *and* butter *and* NASA.

Lessons like that take time to sink in. We are not in the habit of questioning the beneficence of science, so we assent to an orthodoxy of expertise. We overlook the fact that expertise is often sold to the highest bidder and frequently emerges somewhat the less objective from such transactions.

We cling to the concept of science's objectivity because we must. We yearn for there to be some pure truths—provable, replicable facts to believe in above the subjective mess of sociopolitics. Many of us place more faith in the scientist's lack of bias than some scientists do themselves. Hear what Stephen Schneider has to say in his preface to *The Genesis Strategy:* "I have been unable to avoid injecting my own personal philosophies into some of the discussions, particularly those addressing the question of whether present scientific evidence justifies immediate action. Realizing that total objectivity is impossible, I have tried . . .to state my biases openly and to help the reader separate personal or political philosophy from scientific opinions."

Would that such attitudes were more prevalent. Establishment Science has become so abstracted in purposing to be value-free that it has wished horrors on us. The dispassionate development of the power of the atom, whether for war or peace, is such a good illustration of this problem that it has become a cliché.

The fathers of the bomb were honored because of the mystique, the patriarchy, and the finance of large-scale science. As it stands now, certain kinds of knowledge are inevitably the province of the elites who by talent or good fortune manage to work their way through years of specialized academic discipline and then find support for their ongoing research. Not surprisingly, the market is often defense; that's where the big bucks are in the national budget.

The gulf between scientist and citizen, then, grows ever wider. We wind up taking on faith that the tools and ideas that scientists produce are value-free and ipso facto worth developing.

Maybe a few of us ignorant outsiders are willing to ask questions like "What price are we willing to pay for what knowledge?" or "What if we simply don't do it?" But in this age of technological hubris, we're still blowing in the wind. Science has tooled itself up into a juggernaut and gathered a lot of impetus.

Once we've paid for the big labs and institutes, once we've financed the universities that produce the priesthoods that run the labs, once the "classified" label has

We are reaching the end of technological fixes, each of which gives rise to new, and often more severe problems. It is time that we get back to looking at the land, water, and life on which our future depends, and the way in which people interact with these elements.

—RAYMOND DASMANN

"He's charged with expressing contempt for data-processing."

Drawing by Ed Koren

been applied or misapplied, the juggernaut heads downhill. The religion of objectivity gains momentum, taking over the study of society—once the province of poets, philosophers, and historians—and turning it into sociology, demography, and psychology: give us enough rats and enough paper to graph their behavior on and we can lever the world into predictability. (If we simplify it enough, maybe we really *can*.)

One mustn't be too hard on the hard scientists, because, as Schneider's honesty demonstrates, science is mutable—depending on the scientist, the scale he or she is operating on, and his or her awareness of social concerns.

What Limits to Measuring?

A more cautious, more responsible public attitude toward science, while desirable, will be difficult to arouse. A wealth of invention, native and borrowed, has enabled the US to develop its vast resources quickly, to settle a continent in a few hundred years, to

become the richest country in the world, and to arm itself to the teeth against all contenders for super-power status. Can we begin to question those accomplishments and the attitudes that spawned them? America has been built on a grand scale and so has its science. Science has come to mean a man on the moon, a cure for cancer, and the Green Revolution. Our social policies are statistically analyzed, our welfare is phrased in cost/benefit terms. Our pollution has been weighed, mass spectrographed, and proclaimed an investment opportunity. Quantification, sometimes necessary, is always seductive. Putting numerical values on anything—triumph or disaster—makes it more comprehensible, less affecting.

Quantification aside, we've got to find ways for the public to assess the value judgments implicit in scientific and technological developments before they get under way (and rapidly out of control). We as tax-payers are bankrolling the bombs and missiles and cyclotrons and rat cancers and experiments that watch what terminal syphilis does to people or observe whether a plutonium injection will hasten death. Perhaps one reason why we still feel that science has been an unalloyed blessing is that the typical nonscientific education communicates this message: that we probably couldn't understand the issues around science if we tried, and that we would therefore be unqualified to participate in decision-making.

So education is part of the problem, both for the scientist and the non-scientist. Non-scientists feel no need to master the vocabulary and concepts of science any more than most Americans feel the need to learn a second language. Scientists are all too often sequestered (or remove themselves) from society; too often they become narrowed in their disciplines and head for the labs, perhaps never to participate directly in the communities their work affects.

Quantum Leaps in Scientific Gear

Lavoisier's laboratory was little more than a hearth. Fleming's laboratory would be considered inadequate by the average high school biology teacher today. Fermi conducted the first controlled nuclear reaction in an olive barrel. We might even look upon Newton's apple as a bit of god-given apparatus.

Since then there have been quantum leaps in the elaboration (and cost) of the tools of science. Perhaps the greatest blessing that has resulted is that wherever the radio telescopes and electron microscopes are trained, they reveal ever more infinite realms to investigate. What they really reveal is that we'll never know it all. Unfortunately, this has engendered precious little humility.

Through government and industry, America finances a highly centralized, elaborately equipped, and generally short-term goal-oriented science. "Respectable" research is conducted primarily by three sorts of institutions: universities, national labs, and free enterprise think tanks. Because of a shrinking economy, subsidies for university research—particularly the sort that addresses long-range questions and promises no immediate breakthrough or fiscal benefit—are becoming scarcer. If we are to continue to finance academic research, we should permit it to take a longer view; we should encourage interdisciplinary approaches and leave immediate-return R&D to private industry.

There may be some initial difficulty in reconciling this need for long-term research that addresses big, broad questions (the planet's carrying capacity, for example, or the amount of abuse the ecosphere can endure) with the need for more public participation in setting priorities for science and technology and assessing their possible impacts. Without first opening up a better dialog between science and the citizen, public

scrutiny of some projects might result in curtailing inquiry that seems to lack immediate value. Newspapers preside over an annual event: uncovering a slew of seemingly ridiculous research projects that are being carried on with public funds. It is easy to make a mockery of abstruse scientific pursuits to a public that prefers to regard science as a good gray monolith and does not wish to be troubled with the details.

If our science is to be democratized, then the citizen must begin to take some responsibility for thinking about it, not seek sweet oblivion by letting Werner or J. Robert or Jonas do it. We could all use a better understanding of the scientific method and vocabulary, and this is something we should demand of our educational systems and the news media. If we could develop this understanding and an awareness that there are more scientific styles than just the western style, then we'd begin to be in a position to evaluate and make trade-offs.

Do we want to feed people, do we want to be able to incinerate them all twice, or do we want to see golf balls whacked across the lunar landscape? (There are still a lot of people who refuse to believe that the last ever happened; some diehards of the flat-earth ilk steadfastly cling to the conviction that NASA is a film studio in Utah. While this extreme disbelief may strike us as funny, it illuminates the need for scientists to make what they're doing more comprehensible and not seek the showy accomplishment of a media blitz or the refuge of an ivory tower.)

Only when the dialog between scientist and citizen has begun in earnest can the importance of long-range projects be justified in human terms. When that dialog begins, science may begin to serve people better, and with their consent. Universities and research institutes should be able to pursue some lofty abstractions, but they also need to become much more responsive to their locales. Greater citizen participation in scientific and technological decision-making might well lead to some scaling down of research, demystification of science, and humanization of its goals.

Congress has established an Office of Technology Assessment, which has a citizen's advisory council. This acknowledgement that some technological innovations have far more sweeping influence on the public than legislation ever can is long overdue. Legislators often wind up cleaning up technological messes which—given a more democratic, better informed planning process—might never have been made. Perhaps the people who are to endure the impacts or enjoy the benefits of publicly financed (or tacitly condoned) technologies should be allowed to ask that question: "What if we simply don't do it?" Perhaps they should be given the benefit of knowledgeable counsel on the pros and cons of proposed developments that would affect them.

When one considers traditional societies, with their backbreaking labor, killing plagues, high infant mortality, early death, and recurrent crises of near famine, it should have been a safe prophecy that the application of science and technology to man's and perhaps especially woman's daily work would bring with it a vast improvement in the human condition. Some of the world's greatest thinkers certainly expected it.

Yet in fact the first impact of industrialism was to produce some of the vilest conditions ever endured by a humanity not wholly inexperienced in the realities of misery. —BARBARA WARD

And (without any perhaps this time) their answers should be heeded and acted upon.

Needless to say some scientists are beginning to worry that they won't be able to *pioneer* if their work is to be subject to public scrutiny. There is a tendency on the part of such scientists to look down on non-scientists. This attitude is exemplified by Dixie Lee Ray, former head of the late Atomic Energy Commission, who dealt with non-scientists as children, uninformed and quaking in their boots at the thought of a world wired up to nuclear energy—a world with more than enough plutonium to add a touch of whimsy to the evolutionary process through random mutations. Some scientists wish we would have more faith in their particular judgments and overlook the value questions. But what are we to do when the experts are obviously deadlocked, as they have been for years now on nuclear power?

Here is a political question rather than a political proposal: How can we encourage a more benign, more accessible science—a science which understands that all new technology raises value questions that must be answered before the technology, for better or worse, is turned loose?

Our Goals Should Lead Our Work

Do we want better, more costly scrubbers on ever-higher "beautytubes" or do we want homesteads that are energy self-sufficient? Do we want more kidney machines or do we want to create working conditions and settlement patterns that promote healthy kidneys in healthy bodies?

Some of the answers to those questions will be provided by the rapidly developing Appropriate Technology movement. AT is the application of science and engineering to local problems in ways that are simple and affordable. It includes things like village water purification systems, solar collectors, windmills, modest agricultural equipment. (One AT networker recently described the invention of the shovel in a remote village in India.) It also makes possible the devolution of large-scale manufacturing processes that are currently highly centralized, such as steel and glass furnaces. More importantly, Appropriate Technology is the concrete expression of a decentralist philosophy. Its ideas are neatly explained in E.F. Schumacher's *Small Is Beautiful.* (Schumacher is rightly regarded as a founder of the movement, although he acknowledges a debt to Gandhi for his description of an appropriate scale of production and technology: "not mass production but production by the masses.")

It is perhaps more meaningful to think of AT as ideas rather than a collection of cheap, non-destructive tools. The tools themselves will have to be developed everywhere by the people who will use them, but technical advisers will be helpful. AT is almost like re-inventing the wheel, except that it involves the invention of many different kinds of wheels for thousands of different uses. It is the creation of tools that can help people in developing countries to lead better lives without paying the price of massive cultural disruption that follows the centralization of production. It is a way of enabling people in industrialized countries to detach themselves from central systems and reclaim a measure of self-reliance and control of their own lives. It may catch on faster in the developing world, because here, in the developed countries, it means that we'll have to change our lives enough to be able to do some real, honest-to-god, healthy physical work.

Since Appropriate Technology in all its possible applications is still a nascent body of thought, it's not surprising that a lot of information necessary to users of it is either nonexistent or not yet taught in high schools, colleges, and universities. Consider the plight of the young farmer who would like to learn organic methods at a state agricultural college. In all likelihood, he or she will be disappointed because agribusiness calls the tune, or because what little applicable research there is is scattered and beyond the pale of academe. As a consequence of this lag in the educational system, much of the information needed has to be dug out and passed on by the individuals who need it. While the existence of such networks is a good thing, surely our institutions could begin to acknowledge the importance of Appropriate Technology and abet its development and dissemination.

Another possibly beneficial consequence of this academic neglect is that there are not a number of individuals and small, non-profit organizations conducting fairly rigorous (albeit scaled-down) scientific research, much of it having to do with decentralized approaches to energy and food production, housing, and health. Renegade scientists, engineers, and amateurs are taking upon themselves the responsibility of researching local alternatives. This is true to the classic mode of invention, which is rarely accomplished in large establishments.

While this sort of innovative research is currently most likely to be financed by philanthropy or the inventors themselves, the government might try to figure out ways to help without requiring that the innovators also be skilled grantsmen. Imagine what could be accomplished if the cost of a single modern bomber were scattered across the country in the form of $2,500 no-strings-attached grants to help finance the development of aquaculture projects, roof gardens, windmills, solar collectors, companion-planting experiments, pedal-powered workshops, and the like. No doubt many such projects would fail, but that's usually the case with experimentation regardless of the scale on which it is carried out. And the value of a few successes would be tremendous.

The advantages of encouraging small-scale basic research into alternative methods of food and energy production, energy conservation, housing, and transportation are the promotion of diversity and the creation of greater opportunities for public participation in the discovery process. At the very least, such approaches would spare us the trauma of huge financial commitments to single-option crash programs (like nuclear power, disneylandish rapid transit systems, and fossil-fueled agriculture revolutions) which all too often do crash—and increasingly have the potential to take whole regions down with them when they go.

Deciding how funding for conventional, high-technology, academic research and for Appropriate Technology should be apportioned should be up to the taxpayers. Decisions should be based on the clearest information possible as to the relative merits (and impacts) of the alternatives. This suggests a whole new set of processes for budgeting, and would probably involve a regionalization of federal spending and a localization of state spending. It would require that elected officials seek suggestions from representative groups of citizens—and that means a statistically valid sample of the people, not just Kiwanis or Junior League members appointed by the mayor. These citizens should have access to experts, generalists, and proponents acting in an advisory (and adversary) capacity.

All this may sound drastic, but is it really that drastic to trust *ourselves* with the responsibility to make sensible decisions about the developments that will shape our lives?

Recommended Actions

☐ The President should appoint advisors familiar with the theory and practice of Appropriate Technology, and should be wary of multi-billion-dollar Big Science proposals.

☐ Congress, too, should be suspicious of grandiose research and development schemes that too often do more for the national ego than for the national welfare.

☐ The President or Congress should charge an appropriate agency of the executive branch with responsibility to dispense grants in support of small-scale, decentralized research into various facets of Appropriate Technology.

☐ Citizens' panels should be empowered to recommend how research grants should be allocated in their regions.

☐ Educators should also require (or strongly encourage) science students to take courses in the effective communication of technical material to non-technical readers (and technologists in other fields of specialization).

☐ Cross-sectional panels of citizens (perhaps chosen like jurors) should be empowered to assess proposed technological developments in their localities, reporting their findings to politicians and the public.

☐ Educators and officials concerned with education at all levels of government should work to make the methods and vocabulary of science part of the required curriculum for all students.

"Congratulations, you're the first victim of recombinant DNA"

The Rights and Responsibilities of Scientists and Engineers

DAVID R. BROWER

THE CODE WORD for criticism of science and scientists these days is "hubris." Once you've said that word, you've said it all; it sums up, in a word, all of today's apprehensions and misgivings in the public mind—not just about what is perceived as the insufferable attitude of scientists themselves but, enclosed in the same word, what science and technology are perceived to be doing to make this century, this near to its ending, turn out so wrong.

—LEWIS THOMAS
The Medusa and the Snail

At its annual meeting in January 1980 the American Association for the Advancement of Science considered a series of formal Responsibilities of Scientists and Engineers. FOE's Chairman was asked to comment on the draft.

"SCIOLIST" IS A WORD as obscure as "hubris" was only a few years ago, and I should introduce myself as a sociolist with hubris, and walk quickly away without defining either. A sophomore dropout at Berkeley in the depression that came by surprise, I did eleven years' penance as an editor at the University of California Press, where I gained an editor's tentative knowledge of several fields—eleven years minus three, these three spent learning other fields in World War II. Then, for the 17 years I was executive director of the Sierra Club I attended the University of the Colorado River, unaccredited but rather more informative than I had expected. Founding Friends of the Earth ten years ago, I received further education from encounters with supersonic transport and other excesses of speed limits; among them, those in nuclear and genetic inquiries.

I also encountered John McPhee, who told me what Russell Train had told him: "Thank God for Dave

Brower. He makes it so easy for the rest of us to appear reasonable."

Whereupon I have met responsibility number 3 in the draft for members of the scientific community (which I am not): "When practical or when called upon to do so, to identify the limits of uncertainty, personal biases, significant sources of support and possible conflicts of interest which are relevant to [members'] opinions or conclusions."

Except that I was perhaps correct in not waiting, before identifying my limits, biases, and other problems, until it was practical to confess them, or until I was called upon to do so.

And therein, I now discover, lies my principal concern about Science, one that is more and more widely shared, I fear: the apparent dictum "be ethical when it's practical."

Throwing chronology to the winds, let me explain that concern better. On December 14, 1977, Lewis Thomas wrote me to resign from the Friends of the Earth Advisory Council because FOE had filed civil action against the National Institutes of Health on the recombinant DNA question and he did not agree at all with our arguments. With typical speed in answering correspondence, I began drafting a reply between July 5 and 9, a year and a half later, when I was in Verona, Italy, babysitting with our latest book, *Wake of the Whale*. Years ago I had read and admired Dr. Thomas's *Lives of a Cell* and on the way to Verona had read *The Medusa and the Snail* and admired it too. I think Dr. Thomas is great, and I was in no hurry to disagree with him, and I am still in no hurry. I have not completed the draft yet. But let me allude to some of my notes, some jotted down in the hotel bar, others noted in a pad by my hotel bedside when jet lag found me stark awake at three in the morning. My draft begins: "Dr. Thomas: You've ruled out 'hubris.' 'Arrogant' is name-calling, and to ask anyone to feign fallibility is assuming, oneself, a touch of divine assignment. How about 'smug'?

"You argue persuasively (in *Science*, in *The New Yorker*, in *The New England Journal of Medicine*, and in *The Medusa and the Snail*) that Science must be free to inquire. Professor Richard Delgado thinks (in *The Bulletin of the Atomic Scientists*, January 1979, pp. 60–62) that 'courts will hold that scientific inquiry is entitled to recognition as a first amendment activity,' to be accorded 'the deference that the courts apply when fundamental freedoms, traceable to our colonial heritage, are involved.'

"But free to inquire without limits? What is good for Science is good for the country? So let none but Scientists define the limits?

"To give away my argument to begin with, the moth is free to explore the flame, and pays all the costs of its curiosity. When a child explores flame by striking matches (and Science is even now in its infancy—the latest merest blink of time in the long story of life), the child can run away scared and others in the building may pay dearly.

"Late in that last blink of time we played, in our scientific infancy, with the ultimate fire. I was told by one of his colleagues that when James Bryant Conant was witnessing the first atomic blast in New Mexico, having been party to the calculations that predicted the duration of the alternate sun's flash, he was alarmed to observe that the flash did not end when it was supposed to lest it ignite the earth's atmosphere. 'My God, we've done it!' he exclaimed. We are all witness, alive as we are, to his misapprehension. The atmosphere did not ignite and return the earth to its airless beginnings. The flash winked out, more slowly than planned, but out.

"The story would be better if I had asked Dr. Conant and heard it in his own words. But I waited too long to act, a chronic frailty of mine. If any of you know of this firsthand, please let me know, or put it in your oral history. What I report as hearsay evidence could have happened then, and the likes of it could happen now. We are all given lots of curiosity, a fair amount of restraint, and none of the infallibility required for total prescience and the concomitant ability to foresee all possible consequences. Unfortunately, we are not well endowed with curiosity about our fallibility. Other creatures may sense this.

"It is not being Luddite, but logical instead—for whatever political value logic may have these days—to maintain that for all the scientific brilliance around us, we have a lot to learn about DNA. The natural engineering that, with no scientist's help, has for three and a half billion years kept life going at no hour-cost at all, and that in each of us can organize and operate trillions of cells for each person's lifetime, has something going for it that research and publication and understanding will someday perhaps catch up with. That something that is going for it could be related to what nostalgia tells us about, or to what emotion flavors, or taboo sometimes commands us not to do. Nostalgia, emotion and taboo can also get us as screwed up as any other informants, but they have been working far longer, with recorded success, than our latter-day scientific intuitions have. They all have limits, and our challenge is to discern these limits.

"So we have arrived at the sensitive point. Limits, like nuclear reactors, are fine in someone else's backyard. But everybody, I should like to submit, is in someone else's backyard, there is no away any more, and now is the time for all good men to take limits seriously. Good women have, already."

There my draft petered out, on July 8, 1979. I had not figured out how to include a contentious note, scrawled at 3:30 the morning before, about his discrediting of the few environmental organizations that had taken the time to disagree with his DNA perceptions.

There followed some heiroglyphics about how medicine and good intentions could help too much. I remembered, on the one hand, the disaster in my lepidopterous days when I tried to help western swallowtails from their crysalids out of kindness, and thereby crippled everyone I tried to help. And how on the other hand, without medicine's help, I would not have survived because my mother had to undergo a successful mastoidectomy or I would not have been able to show up a month later, nor my wife to survive infancy without someone's midnight dash for oxygen, nor my oldest son his infancy without penicillin, nor my other sons without medical rescue from serious accidents. Only our daughter didn't need extra help, but how could she have existed if her parents had not survived childhood?

That particular survival having been something I approved of, for all the incipient genetic erosion in the long run, I dropped the subject, and at three in the morning, July 9, jotted down a list of things science should feel a little humility about. It was a list of science-knows-best mistakes. I titled it:

Clay Foot Department

wild oats
lantana
eucalyptus
radiata
ARCO grass
rabbits, Aust. & NZ
English sparrows
starlings
mongoose in Hawaii
opposum in NZ
treatment of freezing
Heathrow, the vector
Apollo waste water
Who unblew the DNA whistle? Why?
Medical government by AMA and pharmaceutical people
CETUS and Cohen
UC and AEC
The US Customs form: "anything live?" and mitochondria

Ten minutes later, I added a note about Dr. Teller: "You wear laurels from having helped the US win in one of the preliminaries in man's race to oblivion— The Talk Loudly & Carry a Bigger Stick School: If you don't agree, I'll blow you up."

I ended on a cooler, reasonable note: Monoculture. Miracle wheat. Miracle Trees. Dow. A quicker life through chemistry. And a note about Sky Lab, then floundering in the sky, hoping none of its pieces would hit Three Mile Island.

If anyone wishes to stay after school, I could explain, in a paragraph or two, any of the items in the Clay Foot Department. Some of them are self-explanatory, but the last one is not. The US Customs form requires returning citizens, upon pain of fine or jail, to confess if they are carrying anything alive into the country except themselves, which means that our own government requires us to lie if we want to get home. Everybody is bringing resident *E. coli* along, and the knowing ones are hoping that the recombinant DNA people have not tinkered with theirs. Only your leucocytes will tell what strangers they are battling at the moment. My temptation, however, has been to say:

"Yes. I am bringing a trillion or so mitochondria in with me, and what are you going to do about it?" My knowledge of this foreign creature comes entirely from Lewis Thomas, and I thank John Updike, and his review of *Lives of a Cell* in *The New Yorker* for bringing mitochondria and Dr. Thomas my way.

I would like the Eighties to be a decade of pause and reorganization in the world of science and technology, of concentrating on ameliorating the disturbances of the universe before hastening to disturb more. Of not waiting until it is practical, or one is called upon to do so, to be ethical about confessing uncertainties, biases, and conflicts of interest. Of having the stature to admit that peers who differ may be right, and reporting the difference. Of realizing that the public pays the costs of the mistakes that may benefit scientists who err. Of permitting the intelligent lay public to be intelligently informed and intelligently listened to. Of compensating for the enormous power of the ubiquitous political action committees (PACs) and the pitifully inadequate perspective of so many of their goals. Of comprehension, at long last, of the larcenous quality of economic growth (and population growth) as presently practiced. Of the frightful penalties that will ensue if we continue to violate the natural laws governing a sustainable ecosystem, so few of them yet grasped.

James Reston's article, entitled "Plunging into the Eighties" in the December 30, 1980, *San Francisco Chronicle*, said many things that bear repeating here, of which I pick one: "The world is being changed, not primarily by the ayatollahs or even by the contemporary leaders of the principal industrial states. The world is being changed by the fertility of the human body and the mind; by ordinary people who produce more children than they can feed and educate; by science that preserves life at the beginning and prolongs it at the end, leaving to the politicians the problem of finding remedies for the deluge.

This deluge needs to be illustrated by a similar graph of the roots of population peaks: how far must these excesses reach for sustenance, at whose cost? Without waiting for MIT to produce the illustration, we can well imagine what the roots would look like, and how they grew, from the tentative tendril of US beginnings to the massive conduits it takes to bring one third of the world's resources to the homes, supermarkets, and highways of one-twentieth of the world's people. Imagining this contorted maze of roots to sustain the peaks of New York, Chicago, and Los Angeles, we can understand, perhaps, the comment of a black lawyer in Michigan a few months ago: "A lot of countries around the world are thinking,

Whoever can read the DNA language can also learn to write it. Whoever learns to write the language will in time learn to design living creatures according to his whim. God's technology for creating species will then be in our hands. . . . Can man play God and still stay sane? In our real world, as on the island [of Well's Moreau], the answer must inevitably be no.

—FREEMAN DYSON
Disturbing the Universe

'Maybe we can't afford the United States any more.' "

This concept has apparently entirely escaped the notice of the subject and author of the recently completed *New Yorker* series, "Master of the Trade." It is a profile of Hans Bethe. By my counts, the profile in part III, violates eleven of the responsibilities of members of the scientific community in the draft before you. Whether the violations are the scientist's, the journalist's, or both, bears investigation. I consider it despicable, and fully worthy of the kind of analysis Professor John Holdren, in 232 pages, has given the infamous Inhaber Report. Some of the highlights are reported in "The Inhaber Affair" in the current *Omni*, in a piece by an author I am often critical of but more often partial and gave penicillin to, Kenneth Brower. Professor Holdren had described the Inhaber Report, in vexation, as "by far the most incompetent technical document I have ever known to have been distributed by grown-ups." It was "the shabbiest hodgepodge of misreadings, misrepresentations, and preposterous calculational errors I have ever seen between glossy covers." *The Wall Street Journal* criticized the invective. Holdren and his colleagues wrote: "We believe that the integrity of the whole process of intellectual inquiry and rational debate is too fragile and too precious—and the costs of misinformation too high—to dismiss so blatant an abuse with a shrug." Dr. Bethe, please note.

Kenneth Brower's final paragraphs become mine:

"Science *is* fragile. It depends, like the rule of law, on the cooperation and integrity of the people involved. It is not impossible that science, though it leads the way, will be our weak link, the first institution to fail under the pressures of the complex new age it has helped us usher in. Perhaps the end will announce itself as scattered breakdowns in scientific integrity—little cancer cells of myth in the body of science.

"In our scenarios the deranged scientist who ends the world is always a genius, a Dr. Strangelove. In reality, it may be the opposite. Perhaps the scientist who rings in the End will be a spectacular nongenius."

No, on second thought, I'll close by myself. With those lines from Tom Lehrer, as I remember them:

The rockets go up
And where they come down,
"That's not my department,"
Said Werner von Braun.

And with the story, from the recent acid rain conference in Toronto, about the scientific solution to the loss of Adirondack fish from that rain: "Produce an acid-resistant fish." A critic, remembering coal-mine gas and canaries, remarked, "That's like producing a gas-resistant canary." Or, I might suggest, solving the problem of nuclear proliferation by genetic manipulation, and thus creating radiation-resistant people. That would probably be a better solution than the MX missile, which I think amounts to putting the Maginot Line on Amtrak.

Let the principles of scientific freedom and responsibility have this goal: That Science is the search for truth; that truth is beauty, which Science ought not destroy; and that Science will not be the convenience of Enterprise, but will instead be a public trust.

More Thoughts on Science and Technology

TO CHALLENGE "endless" scientific and technological progress amounts to a kind of secular heresy. Yet thermodynamic limits, limits to knowledge, and practical limits to the use of technology are clearly discernible; the end of the scientific and technological frontier (and thus compound-interest material growth as well) may be visible.

At some point even the most ordinary technological solutions become physically self-contradictory. For example, no matter how ingenious our technology, we cannot use coastal waters both for extensive mining or petroleum production and for maticulture; we cannot reap greater production from farmlands and still strip mine the coal underneath them; we cannot continually expand energy production without eventually cutting into the room we need to grow food or supply our other necessities; and so forth. In sum, the thermodynamic costs attached to technological fixes seem to be becoming more and more onerous, and at some point in the not-too-distant future we are likely to be unwilling or unable to pay them.

The substitution of one ever-more-efficient form of technology for another cannot continue forever, and we have already reached the limits of technological scale in many areas. Indeed, expenditures in research and development reveal diminishing returns. The millions spent by modern physicists compare unfavorably with the modest budgets of the great turn-of-the-century experimental scientists (to say nothing of Isaac Newton). In effect, the better our current technology, the harder it is likely to be to improve on it.

Even if we were to assume that ways of evading the thermodynamic limits more or less indefinitely can readily be found and that necessity always proves to be the mother of invention, the feasibility of continued technological growth is not assured. For one thing, the management burden thrown on our decision-makers and institutional machinery by continued growth will be enormous and will extend across the board. The rates of growth now prevailing require us to double our capital stock, our capacity to control pollution, or agricultural productivity, and so on every 15 to 30 years. Since we already start from a very high absolute level, especially in the "developed" nations, the increment of new construction and new invention required will be staggering.

Technology cannot be implemented in a vacuum. Something like the ecological "law of the minimum," which states that the factor in least supply governs the rate of growth in the system as a whole, applies to social systems as well as ecosystems, and technological fixes cannot run ahead of our ability to plan, construct, fund, and man them—as engineers who examine the macroproblem and not just isolated projects readily admit.

Our ability to achieve the requisite level of planning effectiveness is especially doubtful. In the first place, we cannot foresee with certainty what the consequences of our technological acts are likely to be. As Weinberg points out, virtually none of the critical decisions we confront can be made scientifically. For example, no certain answers to such "trans-scientific" questions as the risks attached to nuclear energy or to the use of certain chemicals can be found in advance. The only way to determine the risks empirically is to run an experiment on the population at large, and such decisions must therefore be made by prudent men—that is, politically.

Not only must we reach and carry out decisions more quickly than in the past, but we must also be very sure that our decisions and actions are the right ones, for we may not get much of a second chance. Indeed, the growing vulnerability of a highly technological society to accident and error is probably our most intractable management problem. The main cause for concern is, of course, some of the especially dangerous technologies we are beginning to employ.

To count on perfect design, perfect skill, perfect efficiency, or perfect reliability in any human enterprise is folly. In addition, all man's works, no matter how perfect as self-contained engineering creations, are still vulnerable to earthquake, storm, drought, and other acts of God, and some of these are bound to happen in just the wrong place at just the wrong time. Nevertheless, we seem headed toward a society in which nothing less than perfect planning and management will do.

Even massive amounts of money, enormous effort, and supreme technological cleverness can never guarantee accident-free operation of our technological devices, and it is indeed strange that technologists—who discovered the infamous Murphy's Law, which states that "if something can possibly go wrong, it will"—should so often assume to the contrary that they can make their creations invulnerable to acts of God or fool proof in normal operations.

To proceed on the assumption that we can achieve standards of perfection hitherto unattained may be to

A few months ago I read casually in my evening newspaper that our galaxy is dying. That great wheel of fire of which our planetary system is an infinitesimal part was, so the report ran, proceeding to its end. The detailed evidence was impressive. Probably, though I have not attempted to verify the figures, the spiral arm on which we drift is so vast that it has not made one full circle of the wheel since the first man-ape picked up and used a stone.

I saw no use in whispering behind my hand at the club, next morning, "They say the galaxy is dying." I knew well enough that man, being more perishable than stars, would be gone billions of years before the edge of the Milky Way grew dark.

—LOREN EISELEY

fall victim to the overweening pride preceding self-destruction that the Greeks called hubris.

The days of "muddling through" in a basically laissez-faire socio-economic system are over. Indeed, to ask only whether continued technological growth is possible without also asking whether it is humanly desirable is to evade the most important question. Yet all-too-many who talk glibly about "exponential technological growth" virtually ignore the social and political consequences of modern technology.

In a crowded world where only the most exquisite care will avoid the collapse of the technological Leviathan we are well on the way to creating, the grip of planning and social control will of necessity become more and more complete. Accidents cannot be permitted, much less individual behavior that deviates from technological imperatives.

We must ask ourselves, therefore, if continued technological growth will not merely serve to replace the so-called tyranny of nature with a potentially even more odious tyranny of man. Discussions of technological growth as a response to our environmental predicament that do not take such political issues into consideration are fatally defective.

— William Ophuls

PHYSICISTS WHO FORMULATED the theories necessary for energy development and industrial growth have served humanity, but they have also influenced the rapid depletion of natural resources and have provided the world with levels of air, water and radiation pollution unknown in any previous period of history. Those scientists who have served humanity through agriculture have developed new crop strains, in-creased productivity, brought us the Green Revolution, and disrupted nearly every agricultural pattern of land use that had been developed empirically over the several thousand years of agricultural history preceding their influence. Scientists who developed an atomic bomb to end the suffering of World War II contributed generously to the psychological and political chaos of life in a nuclear era. Very few areas of scientific inquiry are free of damaging consequences which arise from their technological applications.

The good intentions of scientists over the past few centuries have produced far too many destructive and unacceptable results. We resemble the highly-skilled disciplinary Brahmans of the Indian fable who found the bones of a dead lion in the forest, and decided to apply their scientific scholarship by reconstructing it. One knew how to assemble the skeleton, another knew how to create the skin and flesh and blood, and the third said he could give it life. The fourth companion, who was not a scientist but merely a man of sense, objected, reminding the others that if you create a lion he will probably kill you. The scholars argued that their accomplishment would amount to a scientific breakthrough for all mankind, and would of course be good for their reputations. The man of sense prudently climbed a convenient tree. When the lion was brought to life, it rose up and ate the three scientists. The story concludes in verse:

Scholarship is less than sense;
Therefore seek intelligence:
Senseless scholars in their pride
Made a lion; then they died.

Science has served humanity's self-indulgent whims during the honeymoon of the industrial era, but now a more stable relationship is needed if the marriage is to endure. Technological applications of scientific theories are increasingly suspect because of their often unforeseen and unacceptable consequences, and because many have discovered that they do not in fact improve human life or the natural environment in significant ways. Humanity's most valuable cultural achievement grew from societies that knew nothing about automobiles, petroleum by-products, electrical energy, nuclear reactors, bacteriology, or the many other sophisticated offspring of the mating between science and technology.

New admiration has arisen for ways of life that are free of technological science. Increasing numbers of people are studying and experimenting with Oriental and primitive religions, with the social lives of hunting/gathering peoples, with agricultural communes, with personal crafts, and with interpersonal relationships, all of which offer alternatives to the shallowness of technological society. This is not mere escapism, but an affirmative search for ways of living which satisfy the deep human needs which science has deliberately neglected.

Non-technological cultures, past or present, still need *science*. They must have accurate and detailed knowledge of natural things and processes. Carleton Coon has estimated that the most successful Eskimo hunters have more precise and complete knowledge of the tundra environment than any professor with a Ph.D. in arctic biology. The Sahelian natives may know better the ecology of arid lands than do agricultural experts trained in great European universities. When scientific knowledge is integrated with the total social, psychological, and cultural life of a people, it is able to serve real human needs and to adapt human life better to its natural environments.

The human mind needs vast and complex scientific knowledge of the world, but it also needs more than that. It needs challenge, perhaps even danger, as well as the security and convenience that technology offers. It needs those close social ties with other humans which come through love, family closeness and friendship. It needs joy and it enjoys beauty. And it needs what is known as identity, or a sense of the self. Identity is acquired through both scientific and spiritual knowledge of the *otherness* of the world, and through understanding of the meaning of the self in relation to all that otherness.

And what does the world need from the human mind? Not much, it seems. All that is required of us or any other species is that we learn to adapt to our environmental circumstances. The reward for success is merely more life, and the penalty for failure is extinction. The human mind is our best means toward winning more life, providing we can get it all together.

— Joseph W. Meeker

THERE WAS A TIME, not too many centuries ago, when to be active in scientific investigation was to invite suspicion. Thus it may be that there now lingers among us, even in the triumph of the experimental method, a kind of vague fear of that other artistic world of deep emotion, of strange symbols, lest it seize upon us or distort the hard-won objectivity of our thinking—lest it corrupt, in other words, that crystalline and icy objectivity which, in our scientific guise, we erect as a model of conduct. This model, incidentally, if pursued to its absurd conclusion, would lead to a world in which the computer would determine all aspects of our existence; one in which the bomb would be as welcome as the discoveries of the physician.

Happily, the very great in science, or even those unique scientist-artists such as Leonardo, who foreran the emergence of science as an institution, have been singularly free from this folly. Darwin decried it even as he recognized that he had paid a certain price in concentrated specialization for his achievement. Einstein, it is well known, retained a simple sense of wonder; Newton felt like a child playing with pretty shells on a beach. All show a deep humility and an emotional hunger which is the prerogative of the artist.

—Loren Eiseley

SCIENTIFIC OR TECHNOLOGICAL 'solutions' which poison the environment or degrade the social structure and man himself are of no benefit, no matter how brilliantly conceived or how great their superficial attraction. Ever bigger machines, entailing ever bigger concentrations of economic power and exerting ever greater violence against the environment, do not represent progress: they are a denial of wisdom. Wisdom demands a new orientation of science and technology toward the organic, the gentle, the non-violent, the elegant and beautiful.

Man cannot live without science and technology any more than he can live against nature. What needs the most careful consideration, however, is the *direction* of scientific research. We cannot leave this to the scientists alone. As Einstein himself said, "almost all scientists are economically completely dependent" and "the number of scientists who possess a sense of social responsibility is so small" that they cannot determine the direction of research. The latter dictum applies, no doubt, to all specialists, and the task therefore falls to the intelligent layman, to people like those who form the National Society for Clean Air and other, similar societies concerned with *conservation*. They must work on public opinion, so that the politicians, depending on public opinion, will free themselves from the thraldom of economism and attend to the things that really

Elihu Blotnick

matter. What matters, as I said, is the *direction* of research, that the direction should be towards nonviolence rather than violence; towards an harmonious cooperation with nature rather than a warfare against nature; towards the noiseless, low-energy, elegant, and economical solutions normally applied in nature rather than the noisy, high-energy, brutal, wasteful, and clumsy solutions of our present-day sciences.

Nature always, so to speak, knows where and when to stop. Greater even than the mystery of natural growth is the mystery of the natural cessation of growth. There is measure in all natural things—in their size, speed, or violence. As a result, the system of nature, of which man is a part, tends to be self-balancing, self-adjusting, self-cleansing. Not so with technology, or perhaps I should say: not so with man dominated by technology and specialization. Technology recognizes no self-limiting principle—in terms, for instance, of size, speed, or violence. It therefore does not possess the virtues of being self-balancing, self-adjusting, and self-cleansing. In the subtle system of nature, technology, and in particular the super-technology of the modern world, acts like a foreign body, and there are now numerous signs of rejection.

The type of work which modern technology is most successful in reducing or even eliminating is skillful, productive work of human hands, in touch with real materials of one kind or another. In an advanced industrial society, such work has become exceedingly rare, and to make a decent living by doing such work has become virtually impossible. A great part of the modern neurosis may be due to this very fact; for the human being, defined by Thomas Aquinas as a being with brains and hands, enjoys nothing more than to be creatively, usefully, productively engaged with both his hands and his brains. Today, a person has to be wealthy to be able to enjoy this simple thing, this very great luxury he has to be able to afford space and good tools; he has to be lucky enough to find a good teacher and plenty of free time to learn and practice. He really has to be rich enough not to need a job, for the number of jobs that would be satisfactory in these respects is very small indeed.

We may say, therefore, that modern technology has deprived man of the kind of work that he enjoys most, creative, useful work with hands and brains, and given him plenty of work of a fragmented kind, most of which he does not enjoy at all. It has multiplied the number of people who are exceedingly busy doing a kind of work which, if it is productive at all, is so only in an indirect or 'roundabout' way, and much of which would not be necessary at all if technology were rather less modern. Karl Marx appears to have foreseen much of this when he wrote: "They want production to be limited to useful things, but they forget that the production of too many useful things results in too many useless people," to which we might add: particularly when the processes of production are joyless and boring. All this confirms our suspicion that modern technology, the way it has developed, is developing, and promises further to develop, is showing an increasingly inhuman face, and that we might do well to take stock and reconsider our goals.

As Ghandi said, the poor of the world cannot be helped by mass production, only by production by the masses. The system of *mass production,* based on sophisticated, highly capital-intensive, high energy-input dependent, and human labour-saving technology, presupposes that you are already rich, for a great deal of capital investment is needed to establish one single workplace. The system of *production by the masses* mobilizes the priceless resources which are possessed by all human beings, their clever brains and skillful hands, *and supports them with first-class tools.* The technology of *mass production* is inherently violent, ecologically damaging, self-defeating in terms of non-renewable resources, and stultifying for the human person. The technology of *production by the masses,* making use of the best of modern knowledge and experience, is conducive to decentralization compatible with the laws of ecology, gentle in its use of scarce resources, and designed to serve the human person instead of making him the servant of machines. I have named it *intermediate technology* to signify that it is vastly superior to the primitive technology of bygone ages but at the same time much simpler, cheaper, and freer than the super-technology of the rich. One can also call it self-help technology, or democratic or people's technology—a technology to which everybody can gain admittance and which is not reserved to those already rich and powerful.

It is my experience that it is rather more difficult to recapture directness and simplicity than to advance in the direction of ever more sophistication and complexity. Any third-rate engineer or researcher can increase complexity; but it takes a certain flair of real insight to make things simple again. And this insight does not come easily to people who have allowed themselves to become alienated from real, productive work and from the self-balancing system of nature, which never fails to recognize measure and limitation. Any activity which fails to recognize a self-limiting principle is of the devil.

It is widely accepted that politics is too important a matter to be left to experts. Today, the main content of politics is economics, and the main content of economics is technology. If politics cannot be left to the experts, neither can economics and technology.

I have no doubt that it is possible to give a new direction to technological development, a direction that shall lead it back to the real needs of man, and that also means: *to the actual size of man.* Man is small, and, therefore, small is beautiful. To go for giantism is to go for self-destruction. And what is the cost of a reorientation? We might remind ourselves that to calculate the cost of survival is perverse. No doubt, a price has to be paid for anything worth while: to redirect technology so that it serves man instead of destroying him requires primarily an effort of the imagination and an abandonment of fear.

The idea of intermediate technology does not imply simply a 'going back' in history to methods now outdated; although a systematic study of methods employed in the developed countries, say, a hundred years ago could indeed yield highly suggestive results. It is too often assumed that the achievement of western science, pure and applied, lies mainly in the apparatus and machinery that have been developed from it, and that a rejection of the apparatus and machinery would be tantamount to a rejection of science. This is an excessively superficial view. The real achievement lies in the accumulation of precise knowledge, and this knowledge can be applied in a great variety of ways, of which the current application in modern industry is only one. The development of an intermediate technology, therefore, means a genuine forward movement into new territory, where the enormous cost and complication of production methods for the sake of labour saving and job elimination is avoided and technology is made appropriate for labour-surplus societies.

— E.F. Schumacher

"Apparently some of the additives cause a nerve disorder, but some of the additives cure it."

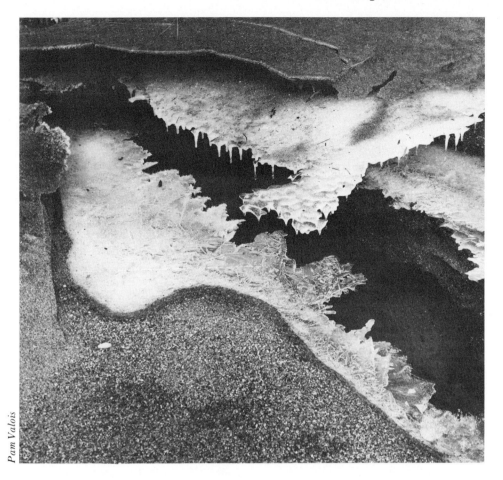

Pam Valois

WE ARE THE INHERITORS of an aggressive culture which, when the great herds disappeared, turned to agriculture. Here again the magic of fire fed the great human wave and built up man's numbers and civilization.

Man's first chemical experiment involving the use of heat was to make foods digestible. He had cooked his meat; now he used fire to crack his grain. In the process of adopting the agricultural way of life he made his second chemical experiment with heat: baking pottery. Ceramics may have sprung in part from the need for storage vessels to protect harvested grain from the incursions of rats and mice and moisture. At any rate, the potter's art spread with the revolutionary shift in food production in early Neolithic times.

After man had learned to change the chemical nature of clay, he began to use fire to transform other raw materials—ores into metals, for instance. One measure of civilization is the number of materials manipulated. The savage contents himself with a few raw materials which can be shaped without the application of high temperatures. Civilized man uses fire to extract, alter, or synthesize a multitude of substances.

By the time metals came into extended use, the precious flame no longer burned in the open campfire, radiating its heat away into the dark or flickering on the bronzed faces of the hunters. Instead it roared in confined furnaces and was fed oxygen through crude bellows. One of the by-products of more intensified experiments with heat was glass—the strange, impassive substance which, in the form of the chemist's flask, the astronomer's telescope, the biologist's microscope, and the mirror, has contributed so vastly to our knowledge of ourselves and the universe.

We hear a good deal about the Iron Age, or age of metals, as a great jump forward in man's history; actually the metals themselves played a comparatively small part in the rise of the first great civilizations. While men learned to use bronze, which demands little more heat than is necessary to produce good ceramics, and later iron, for tools and ornaments, the use of metal did not make a really massive change in civilization for well over 1,500 years. It was what Leslie White of the University of Michigan calls the "Fuel Revolution" that brought the metals into their own. Coal, oil, and gas, new sources of energy, combined with the invention of the steam and combustion engines, ushered in the new age. It was not metals as tools, but metals combined with heat in new furnaces and power machinery that took human society off its thousand-year plateau and made possible another enormous upswing in human numbers, with all the social repercussions.

Today the flames grow hotter in the furnaces. Man has come far up the heat ladder. The creature that crept furred through the glitter of blue glacial nights lives surrounded by the hiss of steam, the roar of engines, and the bubbling of vats. Like a long-armed crab, he manipulates the tongs in dangerous atomic furnaces. In asbestos suits he plunges into the flaming debris of hideous accidents. With intricate heat-measuring instruments he investigates the secrets of the stars, and he has already found heat-resistant alloys that have enabled him to hurl himself into space.

How far will he go? Three hundred years of the scientific method have built the great sky-touching buildings and nourished the incalculable fertility of the human species. But man is also *Homo duplex*, as they knew in the darker ages. He partakes of evil and good, of god and of man. Both struggle in him perpetually. And he is himself a flame—a great, roaring, wasteful furnace devouring irreplaceable substances of the earth. Before this century is out, either *Homo duplex* must learn that knowledge without greatness of spirit is not enough for man, or there will remain only his calcined cities and the little charcoal of his bones.

—Loren Eiseley

RESEARCH AND DEVELOPMENT is now a $150 billion global enterprise employing some three million scientists and engineers. This expansion has been so swift that about 90 percent of all the scientists who have ever lived are alive today.

Yet there is little public knowledge of or understanding about the nature of the world's R&D enterprise—its aims, its priorities, and its international dimensions. Few governments publish accurate, up-to-date figures on research and development conducted within their borders—particularly that carried out by private corporations—and much of the world's scientific work is deliberately cloaked in secrecy, either for military or commercial reasons. Nevertheless, the chief priorities in the global research and development budget are clear.

The largest single item by far is the advancement of military technology. More than $35 billion a year, roughly one-fourth of the world's investment in research and development, is swallowed up by military programs, and over a half million scientists are believed to be working on the development of new weapons.

It is evident that military programs alone account for more financial and intellectual resources than are devoted to R&D on health, food production, energy, and environmental protection combined. Moreover, some of the world's most pressing problems, particu-

larly those facing the bulk of humanity in the developing countries of Africa, Asia, and Latin America, are receiving relatively little attention. The global research and development enterprise is overwhelmingly geared to meeting the political and economic goals of industrial nations.

Investments in the development of new technologies in areas such as energy production and agriculture are likely to have a major influence on future policies by opening up some choices and foreclosing others. The heavy investments in the research and development of nuclear power during the fifties and sixties, for example, coupled with the relative neglect of other potential sources of energy, largely shaped the energy policies of the industrial world in the seventies.

Leaders in many Third World countries have expressed alarm at the widening gulf between rich and poor countries in R&D investments. The global research and development budget is, in fact, not global at all. It is concentrated in a handful of industrial countries. "We are witnessing a shift towards the use of access to modern technology as the main vehicle for exerting control over the productive activities of Third World countries," argues Francisco Sagasti, a Peruvian economist who recently completed a five-year study of science policy in developing countries. "A few hundred people in the highly industrialized nations now make decisions on who is going to get which part of new technologies at the world level, and under what conditions.

As long as the world's R&D capacity remains highly concentrated in the industrial world, the focus will continue to be largely on the problems of the rich countries, and the developing world will remain dependent on imported—and often inappropriate—technology for its economic development.

While substantial amounts of public funds are channeled into research and development in every industrial country, each country has its own set of scientific priorities. Perhaps the most significant difference between countries is the share of the government R&D budget devoted to military science. In three countries—Britain, France, and the United States—military programs take the largest single slice of public research funds. They undoubtedly take up a predominant share of the Soviet Union's R&D budget as well. In the United States and Britain, more tax revenues are spent on the development of military technology than on all other government-supported R&D programs combined.

Nuclear R&D claimed more than 70 percent of the energy research budgets of Britain, Canada, Germany, and Japan in 1977, and even in those countries where nuclear programs take less than half the

"Our computerized telecommunications system is higgledy-piggledy."

total, such as the United States, they still account for the largest single slice of the energy R&D budget. In every country, government support for nuclear research completely dwarfs that for solar energy and other renewable resources, and Sweden stands alone in devoting a large chunk of its national energy research program to the development of conservation technologies.

Driven by the political and commercial motivations of governments and corporations in the industrial world, the global research and development system is poorly attuned to the needs of the developing countries in general and the requirements of the poorest people in those countries in particular. Not only does the lack of R&D capacity in Third World countries perpetuate their dependence on imported technology, but it also means the technologies produced are overwhelmingly geared to the economic environment of the industrial countries—they are capital-intensive, labor-saving, and adapted to large-scale enterprises.

Government R&D priorities have indeed been

changing over the past decade, as the share of funds devoted to military science and technology has declined in most countries, and as outlays on programs related to energy, health, and similar areas have increased. Such trends have been most marked in the United States. Yet spending on military R&D by the US Government still exceeds that on energy, health, environmental protection, agriculture, transportation, basic research, and the social sciences combined.

Many innovative technologies that rely on renewable energy resources, and that are suitable for use on small farms, in small-scale industries, and by community organizations, are being developed by groups outside the traditional R&D establishment. Such appropriate technology groups are reaching people who have been left out of the development process in the past, and are working on technologies that have been ignored by government and corporate researchers. They have proliferated in rich and poor countries alike in recent years, but their work has won little recognition from funding agencies.

There have been a few signs of interest by some governments recently, however. In the United States, a National Center for Appropriate Technology has been established to channel federal funds to such groups, and the Department of Energy has set up a program to provide funding for proposals costing less than $50,000 apiece—proposals that are unlikely to be funded by traditional grants and contracts from an agency used to dealing with multi-million dollar projects. An international agency, Appropriate Technology International, has also been established in the US to support the work of appropriate technology groups in developing countries. And in Britain, Intermediate Technology Development Group, an organization founded by E.F. Schumacher, has recently received a small government grant to aid small-scale industrial development in the Third World. Such initiatives are likely to be stepped up as the need to channel R&D into areas neglected by traditional science and technology agencies becomes more widely recognized.

Reordering the world's R&D priorities by channeling more money into neglected programs, new organizations, and Third World laboratories will not be sufficient, by itself, to solve the world's problems, however. Many tasks are too urgent to wait for R&D to provide solutions and many cannot be solved by science and technology alone. Indeed, when new knowledge is used to bolster and extend the power of governments, corporations, and ruling elites, it can aggravate the social injustices that lie at the root of many of the world's most urgent problems.

Nevertheless, there are many areas in which R&D can play a key role in determining how society responds to the problems that will present themselves in the decades ahead. The world's research and development program now reflects the needs of the fifties and early sixties. Major changes are needed to make it more relevant to the needs of the eighties and nineties.

—Colin Norman

As we all know, the science of ecology was founded in 1969, about 45 minutes after the Santa Barbara blow-out. It has made enormous strides since then, rising above its humble origins in disaster to take on the status of a secular religion. The word *ecology* itself has taken on new meanings. I recently heard, for example, one well-intentioned public figure state that paper-recycling "is good for the ecology." In similar fashion, savings accounts are good for the economics, using a slide-rule is good for the mathematics, and riding a bus to work is good for the internal combustion. I have also discovered, over the years, that a regular paycheck is good for the matrimony.

The public is exposed to so much emotion and so little compensatory science that I'm afraid ecology is in danger of becoming synonymous with a soft-headed desire to repeal technology and re-invent the Garden of Eden. And the problem is that when ecological concerns come into conflict with other social needs or appetites, policy makers in industry and government tend to regard ecological health as a desirable but dispensable extra. In competition with economic concerns, an improved environment is viewed as a sort of

---

It is very seldom that the same man knows much of science, and about the things that were known before ever science came.

—LORD DUNSANY

---

dessert on the social menu. In other words, environmental protection is nice if we can afford it—but let's make sure we can buy the meat and potatoes first.

On the contrary, our biosphere is the meat and potatoes of human life. It is the other things, the supposedly "fundamental" and "practical" concerns of society which are the "extras" made possible by man's primeval success at securing the most favorable niche in the chain of life. That niche was awarded to man largely by the form of good luck known as evolution—

but evolution offers no guarantees to any creature, and man will need more than luck to preserve his place in the world.

Unless we stop counting on future technologies to save us from present distress, one day the problem will beat the solution to our door. Man, having devoted more and more of the interest on his ecological capital simply to staying alive, will finally—as is usually the case with spendthrifts—be forced to go into capital, and to turn his ecological system on a course of irreversible decline.

The wonderful American economic machine began by satisfying needs—and it so excelled at this function that before too long it had enough extra capacity to start satisfying appetites—the things that are not absolutely necessary to life, but make it more attractive. Now this extraordinary machine, having satisfied the appetites of the affluent among us, is more and more devoted to *creating* appetites. "Okay," goes the American sales promotion rationale, "We've sold everybody electric lights, air-conditioning, a refrigerator, a freezer, two TV's, an electric carving knife, and a gadget that turns on a light at dark. Now . . .what else can we make that uses electricity.

I composed that list carefully: I own every item on it. It is not American industry which is the only villain of this homily, but the American consumer—me, and 100 million well-meaning persons like me. And it is not just the American businessman who must be bludgeoned into changing his ways, as if he had deliberately chosen to pollute the water and air, to coat the Mallard with oil, to amplify our wastes with no-deposit, no-return bottles that have to be returned *some*where. *All* of us have elected environmental damage, albeit unwittingly, by voting for convenience with our dollars, and we will all have to change our ways—either unwillingly, in helpless response to one shortage after another, or willingly, in rational, deliberate response to the twin perceptions that everything affects everything else, and that we are spending not only our dollars, but our earth.

Our deepest, most abiding problem is to convince those who make decisions, and those who must accept them, that conservation is more than a short-term tactic calculated to solve a temporary problem. Conservation is a strategy, for the long-term; we must accept it as our new mode of life.

Science has gotten into trouble because it has tried to divide nature into distinct *classes* of things—to divorce things as they exist from their surroundings, and to isolate them for study.

This approach to science has taken us far.

But the paramount insight of ecology is that things do *not* exist in isolation; they exist in *community*. You cannot yank a cell out of a culture, or a bug out of an ecosystem, or cheap oil out of a city, without altering the nature of the system you are examining. You must—if you are to remain true to the distinctive insight that ecology offers—take on the enormous burden of studying that ecosystem as it exists.

Technology has been our servant, but it is threatening to become our master. We have, as Frankel commented, learned to do a thousand things—but we have lost our sense of what all these things are worth doing *for*. The humanists—the historians, the philosophers, the scholars of literature and law and political science—seem utterly incapable of dealing with a world in which our technical grasp exceeds our philosophical reach. And some scientists seem to have lost any sense that the purpose of technology is to serve man.

We need a science that reminds us that the earth is one, and that—though precision may require us to break it down into pieces to facilitate our study—all the pieces form an interdependent whole, and can only be understood as a sensitive, vulnerable unity.

Ecology, in sum, is not a bumper-sticker passion, nor a trendy religion, nor a sudden lamentation for the Snail Darter. It is a science.

It is a science—much more than a technology. It must help man to know not only *how* to do things, but *whether* to do things.

—Russell W. Peterson

MAN, AS A TWO-HANDED manipulator of the world about him, has projected himself outward upon his surroundings in a way impossible to other creatures. He has done this since the first half-human man-ape hefted a stone in his hand. He has always sought mastery over the materials of his environment, and in our day he has pierced so deeply through the screen of appearances that the age-old distinctions between matter and energy have been dimmed to the point of disappearance. The creations of his clever intellect ride in the skies and the sea's depths; he has hurled a great fragment of metal at the moon, which he once feared. He holds the heat of suns within his hands and threatens with it both the lives and the happiness of his unborn descendants.

Man, in the words of one astute biologist, is "caught in a physiological trap and faced with the problem of escaping from his own ingenuity." Pascal, with intuitive sensitivity, saw this at the very dawn of the modern era in science. "There is nothing which we cannot make natural," he wrote, and then, prophetically, comes the full weight of his judgment upon man: "there is nothing natural which we do not destroy."

—Loren Eiseley

National Parks

One of the United States' most important contributions to world culture is the national park concept, born when Yosemite Valley was set aside as a state park in 1864 and formalized in 1872 with Yellowstone National Park. The idea of preserving large areas of wilderness for the benefit of the public has blossomed into a worldwide system of nature sanctuaries; and preserving areas of scenic, scientific, and historic importance is finally being recognized as an essential part of our national and global heritage. Our purpose is not so much to celebrate what is right and good as to identify what is wrong and bad—and to propose remedies. Accordingly, the following chapter is often negative. It is worth noting, however, that the chapter's author is making a career out of helping to save parklands and wilderness—not, we may assume, because he considers matters hopeless. Disneyfication is not inevitable, and where it has already occurred, is not necessarily irreversible. Within a mile or two of the commercial vortex of many of our national parks are wildlands of indescribable splendor. No human agency can make them better. But population and commercial pressures conspire to make them worse, or make them less. Further popularization and commercialization of our parklands would be tragic and must be resisted.

Canyonlands National Park. Photograph by Philip Hyde.

National Parks

CHUCK WILLIAMS

THE NATIONAL PARK and Wilderness Preservation Systems are invaluable not alone for their aesthetic and recreational qualities, but also as scientific preserves containing native plants and animals that have elsewhere disappeared. As a nation proud of its past, hopeful about its future, and concerned about the ecosphere upon which we are totally dependent, we should:

- Protect existing parks and wilderness areas, removing as much development and commercialization as possible and allowing visitors to experience the natural beauty.
- Protect the boundaries of existing parks by expansion, buffer zones (such as national recreation or scenic areas), and other means.
- Preserve remaining *de facto* wilderness areas under the Wilderness Act or similar safeguards.
- Expand the National Park System to include more exceptional areas and representative examples of each of our country's varied biomes so as to save genetic diversity for the future.
- Provide for the educational and spiritual growth of park visitors, and the use of these national treasures as demonstrations of ecologically sane lifestyles.
- Preserve and instill pride in cultural diversity and important historical resources, including agricultural diversity.
- Manage our home as Earth National Park and help the World Heritage Trust to recognize and protect natural, cultural, and historical resources of international importance.

Not Much Is Really Sacred

The United States can be proud of its parks and wilderness, but much remains to be done. Few Americans are aware of the battles fought to save wild areas, and most assume that parklands are now safe. But most "protected" natural areas are menaced either by such traditional threats as logging and mining or by internal problems: overcrowding and overdevelopment.

There are traffic jams in parks. It is sometimes difficult to avoid the noise of cars, logging trucks, mining equipment, motorcycles, motorboats, airplanes, snowmobiles, and generators. Some scenic areas are overrun by luxury resorts, motels, trailer courts, beauty parlors, trinket shops, parking lots, and golf courses. Conglomerates are buying concessions in parks and using their political influence to push parks toward development. "Civilization" has often brought to parks the crime and other problems that they should provide relief from. High fees discourage the poor from using some areas, and lack of transportation prevents them from visiting others.

Strong pressure continues to dam the Colorado River in Grand Canyon and excise part of that park for grazing interests. Water vital to the Everglades is being drained away. Conservationists have to fight incessantly against new roads in Great Smoky Mountains National Park and commercial jets in Grand Teton National Park. Smog and strip mining caused by power plants in the Southwest are threatening the greatest concentration of parks and monuments in the country. At Glacier National Park, a nearby Anaconda aluminum smelter pollutes the air with fluorides and a river's water quality is jeopardized by mines across the boundary in Canada.

Many of the country's ecosystems have no representation in the National Park System. Almost no prairie and very little coastline are protected. While a growing population demands (and needs) more parks, the National Park Service has trouble obtaining funding for additional personnel, and crucial land acquisition funds have been dried up by the Reagan administration.

Developments and Concessions

Parts of the national parks have been commercialized and turned into what congressional critics call "honky-tonk resorts." The trend began in the early days when slow transportation required that accommodations be placed nearer to prime attractions, but many facilities can no longer be justified given modern transportation and overcrowding. In Yosemite Val-

Kansas' proposed Tallgrass Prairie National Park.

National Park Service photograph.

ley—before a start was recently made to clean it up—were 1,176 permanent buildings, 200 tent-cabins, a luxury hotel, motels, a bank, a dentist, a beauty shop, nightclubs with entertainment, tennis courts, a small golf course (fenced to keep out deer), swimming pools, curio shops, even a jail. Critical locations in other parks are overrun by similar urbanization.

Developments in parks, as elsewhere, have far-reaching side effects. Much of the water used by the "villages" on the South Rim of Grand Canyon comes from the North Rim. In spite of a model water recycling program, five tons of coal per day must be strip mined (partly from nearby Indian reservations) for the electricity to drive the 600-horsepower pumps of the 15-mile long, six-million-dollar pipeline. More building is planned for the arid South Rim.

Giant conglomerates, including Music Corporation of America (MCA), Amfac, Trans World Airlines (TWA), and General Host, have bought concessions in national parks and used their political power to affect Park Service planning. After MCA purchased the Yosemite concessions and gave then-President Richard Nixon more than $180,000 in secret campaign contributions, it was given a permit to use the park for filming *Sierra,* a TV series on park rangers, which was actually an advertising scheme to bring more visitors to Yosemite and create a "demand" for more tourist facilities in the park. (MCA painted rocks in Yosemite to make them more photogenic, among other things, and got higher authority to overrule the park superintendent's refusal to allow MCA to use the Park Service's emergency helicopter for filming.) The Park Service and MCA attempted to construct new facilities before the legal planning requirements were completed. MCA was allowed to rewrite parts of the park's master plan and change it into a pro-development document. Public outcry led to the resignation of Ronald Walker, the Nixon-appointed Director of the National Park Service. The Yosemite planning process had to be begun anew, this time with public involvement from the start.

In tiny Zion and Bryce Canyon National Parks, the unneeded overnight accommodations were scheduled to be removed and the new concessioner, TWA, signed a contract agreeing to phase-out. But TWA and Utah politicians then forced the Park Service to allow the lodges and Zion's 135 run-down cabins to remain. TWA later bought the concessions in its fifth park, Crater Lake, already tarnished by illegal concessions construction.

"Possessory interests" allowing concessioners (in essence) to own park facilities, and monopoly contracts with automatic renewals, have kept small businesses out of the larger parks, led to 30-year contracts, and prevented the Park Service from being able to effectively regulate concessioners. "Our investigation thus far," says Congressman Henry Reuss, "suggests that the concessioners, not the National Park Service, are running the parks." A congressional report on Park Service concessions management noted that no other federal land agency gave such lucrative contracts, and chided the Park Service for renting buildings to MCA for next to nothing. An in-house Interior Department study of Park Service concessions operations confirmed the charges and recommendations being made by environmentalists and congressional committees. The Park Service has made many concessions reforms

---

If we are going to succeed in preserving the greatness of the national parks, they must be held inviolate. They represent the last stand of primitive America. If we are going to whittle away at them, we should recognize, at the very beginning, that all such whittlings are cumulative and that the end result will be mediocrity. Greatness will be gone.
—NEWTON DRURY

---

in recent years, including terminating the contract of the Yellowstone concessioner, but conservationists generally believe that reform legislation will be required, especially since Interior Secretary James Watt wants to turn many NPS functions (such as campgrounds, fee collection and interpretation) over to the private concessioners.

Government ownership of facilities seems necessary to effectively regulate operations and permit shorter contracts. Funds needed to buy possessory interests could be paid back by increasing the small share (0.75-3.0 percent) of concession revenues now returned to the government, and would be a good investment. Small businesses and non-profit organizations should be encouraged to operate concessions. The Park Service should have control over the transfer or sale of contracts, and no corporation should operate the concessions in more than one park. Concessioners' financial records should be public since they have no competition, and the public should have a voice in the

awarding of contracts. Concessioners' billboards and advertising, often used to attract conventions to parks, should be controlled.

Where possible, facilities (including housing) should be moved out of parks, or at least away from the main attractions. Park Service policy, though too seldom followed, is clear on this matter. "If adequate facilities exist or can be developed by private enterprise to serve the park visitors' needs for commercial services outside of park boundaries, such facilities shall not be provided within park areas." Remaining concessions should have non-imposing architecture or be situated in historic structures, and should be sound ecological models that tacitly repudiate the throwaway ethic.

Artificial attractions and activities not related to the parks' unique features—golf courses, tennis courts, night-clubs, water-skiing—should be removed from national parks and monuments. The Park Service should help educate the public about reasons for preservation, the special nature of park preservation, and about non-park lands available for recreation.

Overcrowding problems often result from the machinery that park visitors bring along. Local businessmen and others arguing for more and faster roads point to the need to provide access for those unable to hike, but private automobiles and trans-park roads are not necessary to provide access to the representative features for the elderly and handicapped.

The Park Service has replaced private vehicles with free shuttlebusses in a few crowded park areas such as the east end of Yosemite Valley. The experiment is successful as an educational tool, in addition to reducing congestion, smog, and noise. Petrified Forest National Park, for example, is ideally suited for mass transit—and this would reduce thefts of petrified wood, estimated to total 12 tons a year. Instead of banning bicycles, as was done in Glacier, the Park Service should provide them to visitors as a non-motorized alternative on shuttlebus roads; Everglades National Park would be an ideal starting place.

Destructive roads have been built across Yosemite and Mount McKinley parks and along the entire rims in Crater Lake and Bryce Canyon. In Canyonlands, a paved road to the center of the park is half built—thanks to Utah's anti-conservation Congressional delegation. Environmentalists have been kept busy repelling attempts to build more roads in Great Smoky Mountains and Assateague Island. The forces that Edward Abbey calls "Industrial Tourism" are pushing for a road through the heart of the Escalante region of Glen Canyon, a Park Service recreation area where the once-wild Colorado River has been turned into a highway for motorboats.

There should be a moratorium on the construction of new roads and the upgrading of existing slow roads in parks. Some existing roads should be torn up, and major highways should be rerouted outside of parks wherever possible (such as US 101 through Redwood National Park). To avoid huge parking lots at the entrances and provide for those without private cars, mass transit *to* the parks will be a necessary complement to the shuttlebus systems within parks. Railways that once served parks can be revitalized.

Speeding logging trucks dominate many roads in Olympic and Redwood National Parks. Motorboats ruin the tranquility of some park waterways and kill the rare manatees of the Everglades. Park Service tramways planned for Guadalupe Mountains and North Cascades National Parks have been derailed, at least for now. But thousands of snowmobiles invade Yellowstone and other parks in winter.

It is nearly impossible to escape the noise of airplanes, and the military sometimes uses parks such as Death Valley for war games, destroying the peace and park resources with sonic booms. A major battle is raging over allowing commercial jets to land *within* Grand Teton.

Money, Money, Money

The National Park Service, one of the least powerful government agencies, is often bullied by powerful members of Congress and sister-agencies of the Interior Department with bigger budgets. The Park Service is an easy mark for budget-cutters and must often get along with far fewer personnel than Congress authorized.

The Land and Water Conservation Fund was established in 1964 to use government revenues from campground and entrance fees and the like, and from offshore drilling leases, to purchase lands for federal, state, and local parks. Presidents Nixon and Ford fought congressional attempts to enlarge the fund, and even impounded existing funds, causing a backlog of hundreds of millions of dollars worth of authorized parklands and inholdings unpurchased. (This ten-year acquisition backlog became another excuse to oppose new park proposals). Big Thicket National Preserve was logged because funds to acquire it were held up. President Carter and Congress tripled the Land and Water Conservation Fund—a much-needed step—but the fund was later decimated in the budget-cutting frenzy—thanks especially to Alaska Senator Ted Stevens. Now the Reagan administration has totally decimated the land acquisition fund, causing major crises in new parks such as Big Cypress National Preserve and Santa Monica National Recreation Area.

Fees in many parks are increasing, and rangers often spend more time collecting them than protecting and interpreting the parks. The rationale is to limit use and make users "pay their own way," but when a $40 room in Yosemite's Ahwahnee Hotel is rented, only 30 cents goes to the government and MCA keeps $39.70. The number of visitors often needs to be limited, but high fees are the most discriminatory method of regulation. They deny access only to the poor, who already have trouble getting to most parks. To justify high fees, the Park Service's undeveloped campgrounds have been nearly totally eliminated in favor of huge "instant suburbs" with paved sites, hot water, flush toilets, electricity, streetlights, and so on. More equitable ways of reducing visitation and improving its quality would be to simply limit numbers (as is done with tours of Mesa Verde ruins) and to use "built-in frictions" such as slow roads, mass transit, less frills, and dead-end instead of loop roads.

The Park Service is under heavy pressure from private campground operators to charge high fees. Highly developed campgrounds, including all with utility hookups, should be left to private operators outside the parks. The Park Service should return to a policy of providing free or low-cost walk-in and primitive campsites in the parks. Campgrounds within parks should not be operated by the concessioners, as has been done in some parks with bad results.

Animal and Plant Life

The national parks and monuments are the last havens for many endangered plants and animals, but they often don't offer enough protection for migrating animals and need to be enlarged. Developments should never be permitted in prime wildlife habitats, as was done when Yellowstone Canyon Village complex was built at a location favored by grizzlies. Non-native plants and animals must be removed wherever possible to protect the native flora and fauna. For example, goats, introduced late to Hawaii, are destroying endangered plants in the islands' parks. Where feasible, native plants and animals should be reintroduced into parks and wilderness where they have been eliminated by humans. This was done at Zion with the desert bighorn sheep—but it is too late for the many native species now extinct.

The Interior Department (under heavy pressure from developers) is foot-dragging on bringing endangered and threatened plants under the protection of the Endangered Species Act. Smog is damaging the flora in Sequoia and Death Valley, and we mentioned earlier the Anaconda problem at Glacier Park. Legal Action should be taken against such outside causes of injury to parks, as was done for the Devils Hole pupfish, which survives only in a remote Nevada spring that is part of Death Valley National Monument. The spring was being drained by nearby wells of ranchers and subdividers—until they were stopped by a federal lawsuit. Some sheriff's cars in Nevada sported "Kill The Pupfish" bumper stickers, but the Supreme Court ruled in favor of the fish.

Interpretation

Interpretation is an important function of the Park Service, but is one of the first services to suffer from budget cuts. In spite of budgetary restrictions, however, the Park Service has expanded its valuable environmental education programs.

The preservation role of the parks must be empha-sized in interpretive programs, which should be used to explain ecological concepts to a largely urban population (especially school children). Ranger-led overnight camping trips could provide an unforgettable experience for visitors afraid to set out on their own. Shuttlebus systems in parks can be used to expand interpretive services to captive audiences. Park buildings should demonstrate needed soft technologies, like solar heating and cooling.

Wilderness

David Brower has said: "Wilderness is the bank for the genetic variability of the earth. We're wiping out that reserve at a frightening rate. We should draw a line right now. Whatever is wild, leave it wild . . . Liv-

Zion National Park.   *Photo by Phillip Hyde.*

ing diversity is the thing we're preserving."

The Wilderness Act provides for federal lands to be set aside by Congress, after study by the managing agency and public hearings, to be left in a wild state, not vulnerable to administrative whims. This landmark act set the precedent for public involvement in public land management decisions, and Congress has often passed citizens' wilderness proposals larger than the agencies' recommendations.

Most of the National Park System remains unprotected under the Wilderness Act. The Department of the Interior has tried in the past to thwart the intent of the Act, omitting "wilderness enclaves" and large "management zones" around park boundaries and roads. Conservationists are asking that millions of acres more than the Park Service proposes be designated as wilderness. Burying utility lines along roads could further increase the eligible acreage. The Park Service has recommended *no* wilderness for some parks such as White Sands and Mammoth Cave (where conservationists want both caverns and the surface in wilderness) and has ignored others such as Acadia and Virgin Islands. Concessioners in Mammoth Cave and other parks have mounted media campaigns against wilderness designations in "their" parks even though existing facilities wouldn't be affected. Fortunately, both the Park Service wilderness recommendations and public support have been increasing year by year.

Parks Under Siege

At the southern tip of Florida lie the Everglades, where the tropics meet the temperate zone and produce one of the country's broadest spectrums of life. The heart of the region is a river with nearly no gradient flowing slowly from Lake Okeechobee to Florida Bay and the Gulf of Mexico, 100 miles to the south. Everglades National Park, a seemingly endless expanse of sawgrass dotted with forested islands called hammocks, together with Big Cypress National Preserve, protects a portion of this river as it flows through mangrove swamps and exceptionally productive estuaries.

The Everglades were dying and are still threatened. Water essential to this ecosystem has been diverted for urban water supplies and agriculture. Land speculators trying to subdivide swamps divert water away from the 'Glades directly into the sea. Two large corporations are diverting water away from Taylor Slough, the park's most popular area, and are clearcutting along the park boundary.

More than "just the park" is ruined when fresh water is diverted and salt water seeps further inland. Salt now threatens the water supplies both for agriculture and for Miami. Wild areas west of the park are being developed. These are estuarine breeding grounds essential to a multi-million-dollar seafood industry.

Many areas being altered by commercial interests were originally to be part of Everglades National Park, but were deleted. Powerful pressures to delete and drain more of the park still continue. Farmers covet the park to make up for farmlands lost to suburbia. Big Cypress has finally been remade a preserve, but more federal, state, and local action is needed to protect the other water supplies by expanding the park and creating recreation areas and preserves adjoining it. Otherwise, the Everglades will continue to dry up; this amazing display of animal and plant life, already severely damaged, will be decimated.

Starting in 1971, Tenneco, Johns-Manville, Pfizer, Cyprus Industrial Minerals, and American Borate have strip-mined for borates and talc (minerals that are plentiful elsewhere) in Death Valley National Monument. They exploit a loophole intended to allow "single-blanket jackass prospectors" to remain in the Monument. Tenneco even staked out world-famous Zabriskie Point, refraining from stripping it only in the face of outraged public protest. The Park Service was outspoken in defense of Death Valley, but the Interior Department (under President Ford) refused to fulfill what environmentalists believed was a "legal duty to stop this official vandalism." Legislation to prohibit *new* mining claims in Death Valley, Glacier Bay, and the four other parks where mineral entry was permitted, finally passed in 1976, but the future of *existing* mines and claims is yet to be resolved.

A related problem is mineral *leasing* in recreation areas and preserves. The Park Service and Bureau of Land Management granted uranium leases to Exxon in a portion of the Grand Canyon that is in Lake Mead National Recreation Area and under study for wilderness protection and addition to the park. Environmentalists threatened legal action and the leases were finally cancelled. Offshore drilling threatens some parks (especially Padre Island National Seashore), and oil wells along the border of Theodore Roosevelt National Park, in the North Dakota Badlands, are drilled at an angle to remove the oil underlying it. Resource exploitation of Park Service lands is being promoted by other agencies of government. Legislation is needed to close numerous loopholes that have accumulated to the benefit of special interests.

Reservoirs should not be allowed to inundate parts of parks. This was done in Yosemite, almost happened in Grand Canyon and Dinosaur, and has now occurred in Bandelier and Rainbow Bridge National Monuments. In the latter, the reservoir called Lake Powell is being allowed to flood the base of the world's largest natural bridge despite congressional promises to the contrary. Existing dams that compromise parks, such as the one flooding Yosemite's Hetch-Hetchy Valley, should be removed and the natural landscape reclaimed.

Parks such as Bryce Canyon and Capitol Reef will be little more than parkways through stripped landscapes if their boundaries aren't protected against strip mining for the power projects planned for "Utah National Sacrifice Area." Recreation areas and scenic areas adjoining some existing parks would, in addition to serving as buffer zones, allow the Park Service to provide for recreational activities incompatible with wilderness parks.

Private inholdings in parks have been subdivided, logged, and mined because funds to buy them were lacking. When land acquisition funds were finally forthcoming, many landowners within parks rebelled at the thought of regulation. an inholders' organization formed, but has become a lobby against new parklands, using false information and exaggerations to scare local residents near proposed parks, instead of trying to find a fair balance between public good and private exploitation of lands within parks.

New Parks

Agricultural and grazing lands of the Midwest were once a wild prairie inhabited by millions of buffalo, pronghorn antelope, and prairie dogs. The grasses and wildflowers ranged from the shortgrass plains in the rain shadow of the Rockies to grasses that grew taller than humans on the humid eastern edge. Prairie parks, wilderness areas, and other preserves are needed to protect and restore samples of diverse prairies such as the tallgrass prairie, northern plains, Nebraska's Sand Hills, the coastal prairie of Texas, and the Central Valley of California—once a poppy-covered plain.

The tallgrass prairie once covered parts of eleven states but is now almost gone. The remaining areas that have national park potential are in the Flint Hills of Kansas and northern Oklahoma, and have survived because of rocky soil that hindered plowing. But these remnants are being eaten away today by over-grazing, plowing, freeways, power lines, dams, and second-home subdivisions. The Park Service is studying the remaining tallgrass, but high land prices, fierce local opposition, and a lack of appreciation for grasslands have so far prevented establishment of a Tallgrass Prairie National Park.

The rush to build the Alsakan pipeline made the environmentalists' "doomsayer" predictions appear conservative in retrospect, but it did trigger a one-time opportunity to preserve many of that state's areas of park caliber. Environmentalists, having learned the futility of trying to protect and manage less-than-whole ecosystems, are working for the protection of more than 100 million acres in national parks, monuments, wildlife refuges, forests, reserves, and wild rivers. Conservationists' proposals were drawn along nat-

Columbia River Gorge.   *Photo by Chuck Williams.*

ural boundaries where possible in an effort to protect whole ecosystems, watersheds, and wildlife habitats—and avoid many of the problems plaguing parks in the lower 49 states.

Thanks to the Carter administration and the largest grassroots conservation campaign ever, Congress finally passed the Alaska National Interest Lands Conservation Act late in 1980. Although the Senate weakened the strong House bill, the landmark act doubled the size of the National Park System and protects some of the least-altered landscapes left on Earth. The fight is not over, however, as graphically illustrated by Interior Secretary Watt's efforts to hinder planning and regulations for the new units and to rush oil and gas exploitation regardless of the effect on wildlife. Another major campaign will be needed to properly implement the legislative victory.

Numerous new national monuments should be established and some existing ones, such as Death Valley, should be expanded and elevated to national park status. The practice of transferring the most spectacular Forest Service lands to the Park Service (where they would *usually* receive better protection) has waned, but deserves revival. The Wheeler Peak area of Humboldt National Forest in Nevada, for example, could be set aside with surrounding desert as the Great Basin National Park. A Mohave Desert National Park is also needed.

Remaining free-flowing rivers (including important fishing streams) need to be given the protection of the Wild and Scenic Rivers Act. More national trails should be created for those still wishing to see the country on foot, and existing ones such as the Appalachian Trail need further protection.

The coastline is a precious national resource that must be preserved, if for no other reason, because of its important role in the web of life. Only four percent of the nation's shoreline is accessible to the public, and there is a struggle now to save remnants of the seashores recommended for protection by an ignored Park Service study completed two decades ago. Island Trusts (on the Martha's Vineyard model) should be established to control development and ensure public access to islands that are primarily in private hands, like those around Acadia National Park. Representative Phil Burton's Barrier Islands legislation, if enacted, would help protect the rapidly-disappearing hurricane buffers along the Atlantic and Gulf Coasts.

Although (and because) the majority of the US population is in the East, most of the natural parks are in the West. Congress has recently begun establishing national seashores and lakeshores and recreation areas in remaining nearly-natural lands and waters near population centers. It is sometimes argued that the Park Service shouldn't administer recreation areas near cities—especially because of the costs—but the few that already exist are very popular. The executive branch touted the program to "bring parks to the people" in the early 1970s and recommended 14 urban parks for starters; later, it opposed the concept, arguing that it is inflationary, and anyway, a local responsibility. But it seems that only the federal government is capable of creating the large parks needed to save these areas, to take a load off existing parks, and to provide outdoor experiences for those unable to travel far. Now Interior Secretary Watt wants to deauthorize many of the new urban parklands, such as Gateway and Golden Gate National Recreation Areas.

National Parks for the Future, the Conservation Foundation's study of park problems, recommends that land ruined by activities like strip mining, and hence cheap, be purchased by the government and reclaimed by public service employees for future parklands.

The national park idea has spread around the world. Many nations, however, did not have the options of the US; their wilderness had already nearly vanished. In Japan and many European countries, the national park concept evolved to include mixed public and private lands, with a continuation of compatible uses, such as farming. Now the US, by necessity, must look to these variations of an idea born at Yosemite and Yellowstone. A start has been made. Farming and grazing are part of the newer national recreation areas, and President John F. Kennedy, with Cape Cod National Seashore in 1962, expanded the National Park System to include scenic communities. In 1978 Congress authorized a prototype "greenlike park," Pinelands National Reserve, to protect New Jersey's million-acre Pine Barrens with a minimum of federal acquisition. These new parklands are not a panacea, however, and are definitely not a substitute for the traditional wilderness parks. The bitter controversies that surround Adirondack State Park, a huge area in New York that mixes publicly-owned wilderness with private lands regulated by a commission, show how difficult the path will be.

The Columbia Gorge, Big Sur, Jackson Hole, and Lake Tahoe all should have been national parks, but that option has been blocked by "progress." These still spectacular semi-wild areas, all imminently threatened, should be protected as the country's first national scenic areas—creative mixtures of public and private lands and uses involving federal-state-local partnerships.

World Heritage Trust

The World Heritage Trust expands the national park concept to an international level, recognizing that

Yellowstone National Park.   *Photo by Philip Hyde.*

exceptional natural, cultural and historic resources are of global importance. The US should continue to support this United Nations program, which will offer financial, training, and public information assistance to qualifying areas.

The US must dedicate itself to a reverence for the natural world that created and sustains us, and to the preservation of its natural, cultural, and historical heritage. Existing units of the splendid National Park and Wilderness Preservation Systems must be kept inviolate for future generations. New Areas need to be added to these systems and the World Heritage Trust in order to preserve the miraculous living diversity of planet Earth. Remaining wild areas must be left as wilderness. In the words of Edward Abbey: "Wilderness is not a luxury but a necessity of the human spirit, and as vital to our lives as water and good bread. A civilization which destroys what little remains of the wild, the spare, the original, is cutting itself off from its origins and betraying the principle of civilization."

Recommended Actions

☐ The National Park Service should:
☐ Standardize rules governing concessions, taking care that its contracts benefit the public and the government no less than they benefit concessioners ☐ Move artificial attractions, extraneous activities, commercial developments, and other non-essential facilities outside park boundaries ☐ Refrain from building new roads or upgrading existing ones ☐ Extend shuttlebus services and discourage private motor vehicles ☐ Use "built-in frictions" instead of high fees to regulate the number of visitors ☐ Recommend to the President and Congress ways to establish (or reestablish) public mass transit from nearby population centers and transportation hubs to the parks ☐ Encourage bicycle use on shuttlebus roads within parks ☐ Reduce highly developed and high-cost campsites, and restore low-cost, primitive campsites ☐ Exclude developments from prime wild animal habitat ☐ Remove non-native species of animal and plant life wherever practicable and reintroduce native species that have been unnaturally displaced ☐ Protect *all* de facto wilderness in units of the National Park System and recommend that they be formally protected as Wilderness. ☐ Appoint minorities, environmentalists and young people to the Secretary's Advisory Board ☐ Follow-up on a recent report outlining problem areas around existing park boundaries ☐ Continue to study potential new parks and help state and local agencies to protect areas not of national significance ☐ Educate the public as to the importance of wilderness and historic preservation, and stress that the parks are needed to protect genetic diversity, not just to provide recreation.

☐ Congress should:
☐ Propose any legislation necessary to assure that the Park Service vigorously pursues the foregoing objectives—unimpeded by other agencies ☐ Restore cuts made in the Land and Water Conservation Fund ☐ Fund the Urban Recovery Program to provide inner city parks ☐ Enact the American Heritage Act to further protect historic sites and natural landmarks ☐ Establish Tallgrass Prairie, Mohave Desert, Great Basin, Louisiana Bayou and other national parks needed to protect threatened types of ecosystems ☐ Protect the Alaska National Interest Lands ☐ Establish the Columbia Gorge, Big Sur, Jackson Hole and Lake Tahoe National Scenic Areas and other "areas of national concern" ☐ Protect the areas surrounding existing parks ☐ Reform existing concessions legislation ☐ Fund additional park rangers ☐ Enlarge some parks, including Grand Canyon and Everglades ☐ Protect more wild and scenic rivers, hiking trails ☐ Protect the fragile barrier islands and establish island trusts ☐ Protect all *de facto* wilderness in parks ☐ Create an agency or charge an existing one with responsibility for continuing study of ways to dismantle unwanted dams and restore reservoir areas, to restore strip-mined land, and in general, to return devastated lands to something like a natural state.

☐ The US delegation to the United Nations should work to assure the continued and complete cooperation of the US with the World Heritage Trust, Man and the Biosphere, and similar international efforts.

Wilderness

In wildness is the preservation of the world. —HENRY DAVID THOREAU

Elihu Blotnick

The wilderness holds answers to more questions than we yet know how to ask.
—NANCY NEWHALL

Wilderness

JOHN M. KAUFFMANN

WILDERNESS IS THE MATRIX in which mankind evolved on Earth, and we require wild surroundings to sense ourselves in the context of Earth's wholeness and system. "When man obliterates wilderness," a physicist has noted, "he repudiates the evolutionary force that put him on this planet."

Despite our feeling of sophistication in modern-day sciences, we are only beginning to discover the intricacies of Earth's grand natural design. Many environmental subtleties are still beyond our comprehension. If we destroy the remaining natural systems, how can we learn from them? One biologist recently estimated that we are probably exterminating another species of life in the world's shrinking tropical forests every day. What have we lost that might have helped us to prosper, to survive? The gene bank of wilderness is the most important source of the vital organisms that form the chain of life.

The late Justice William O. Douglas reminded us: "Man's greatest mission is to preserve life, not to destroy it. When the wonders of creation have been destroyed, youth has no place to go but the alleys, and a blight lies across the land." Wilderness is as important a place for appreciation of nature and personal communication with self as it is for our scientific inquiry. As novelist Wallace Stegner put it, "Wilderness as opportunity and as idea . . .has helped to make an American different from and, until we forget it in the roar of our industrial cities, more fortunate than other men. For an American, insofar as he is new and different at all, is a civilized man who has renewed himself in the wild. The American experience has been the confrontation of old peoples and cultures by a world as new as if it had just arisen from the sea. That gave us our hope and our excitement, and the hope and excitement can be passed on to newer Americans, Americans who never saw any phase of the frontier. But only so long as we keep the remainder of our wild as a reserve and promise."

The Wilderness Act of 1964, unique in the world, was the product of years of efforts to have the United States legally recognize the importance of preserving an adequate amount of the nation's wildland heritage.

In retrospect, the immediate goal of the act's advocates seems a modest one: to designate as wilderness most of the acreage in the big national parks and monuments as well as those national forest areas already administratively classified as "wilderness," "wild," and "canoe." All this amounted to perhaps 60 million acres. Unconsidered were the Bureau of Land Management's vast domain and much *de facto* wilderness in the national forests.

Slightly more than nine million acres of the national forests were put into our National Preservation System when the act was signed, with an additional 5 million to be reviewed during the ensuing decade. Now, 16 years later, some ten million acres have been added—three million in the national parks, three-fourths of a million in the national wildlife refuges, and the remaining seven million in the national forests.

Congress is considering proposals to place another 10.2 million parkland acres in the wilderness system, and the National Park Service has four million other acres under review. About three-quarters of the large natural and recreational units of the park system have been covered to date, not counting the new national monuments in Alaska.

In 1979, the US Forest Service completed the second of two Roadless Area Reviews to ascertain what should be recommended for the Wilderness System. The service found 46 million acres outside of Alaska to be qualified—but recommended only 9.5 million, with another eight million relegated to further study. Another three million acres, administratively classified as primitive areas, await action as mandated by the Wilderness Act.

The US Fish and Wildlife Service has completed all the more than 100 studies that were required under the Wilderness Act. The service is holding up further reviews until Congress has acted upon the first batch.

The Bureau of Land Management was not mandated by the Wilderness Act to conduct wilderness studies of the 174 million acres of public land it administers in the lower 48 states or the vast domains of Alaska. The Federal Land Poilicy and Management Act of 1976 did direct such studies, however, and the

Tom Turner

bureau began inventorying its lands outside Alaska in 1978. It has already eliminated 120 million acres from further consideration and is now looking at only 53 million acres as possible wilderness study areas.

With a few small exceptions, none of the land management agencies took much notice of the vast reaches of Alaskan wilderness until the 1971 Alaska Native Claims Settlement Act (sparked by oil development) called for park, refuge, forest, and wild river studies. The Carter Administration has recommended 50 million acres of Alaska wilderness. The Alaska Lands bill passed overwhelmingly by the House of Representatives calls for 67 million acres of wilderness. Legislation recommended by the Senate Energy and Natural Resources Committee cuts that by half, while a substitute measure backs the House-passed figure. The Senate was to debate the matter in July 1980.

Huge as Alaska is, its wilderness character is fading fast. A pipeline slices through, and Alaskans clamor to have the road that serves it opened to tourism. More roads are on the drawing boards. The state is pressed to offer large tracts for private use, and Native corporations plan development of their vast land holdings. Meanwhile, the battle over the fate of the national interest lands—land retained in public ownership— has been raging.

Elsewhere, much of America's remaining store of wilderness has evaporated in a generation. In 1921, for example, the late Aldo Leopold proposed six national forest wild areas in New Mexico and Arizona, each of more than half a million acres. Today, only one is left of that caliber: the Gila Wilderness Area and adjoining Black Range Primitive Area in New Mexico. But they are split by a road, and another road penetrates to a national monument. The others? About half of the Blue Range region remains wild. The Jemez Mountains wilderness is down to about 50,000 acres. A 7,000-acre Mount Baldy Wilderness is all that is left of the once-wild White Mountains, Arizona's most extensive high region. The broad wilderness that used to stretch intact across the Kaibab Plateau has been reduced to a few side canyons of the Colorado River. Of the Mogollon Rim, virtually nothing is left wild.

As late as 1930, some 50 million acres of national forest wildlands outside Alaska could be counted in units of 300,000 acres or more. The recent Roadless Area Review found less than that all told in units of any size. The only large chunks left are already in the system or proposed for it, plus some *de facto* wilderness, mostly consisting of areas administratively classified as primitive. The remaining big areas now totals less than 17 million acres.

Until recently, wilderness on the public lands was forgotten. Few people knew much about it. Few were interested. It became victim of a war of attrition. Roads and power lines thrust through, ranch improvements ate into it, dams flooded it. "We've seen millions of acres disappear," remarked Dave Foreman, Southwest regional representative of The Wilderness Society. "The Bureau of Land Management's wilderness inventory came 20 years too late."

It is not surprising, therefore, that wilderness has dwindled alarmingly on the lands administered by BLM. A decade ago, the Red Desert of Wyoming, once home of our largest pronghorn antelope herds, amounted to more than 400,000 acres. Since then it has been cut to pieces by energy prospecting and development. Only five or six small shards aggregating less than 100,000 acres could perhaps qualify as wilderness. Even in southeastern Utah, where much has been protected, the eight-million-acre expanse of wilderness proposed as a park in the late 1930s has been chopped apart. And a fragmented wilderness, even though the aggregate area is large, cannot duplicate the ecological integrity of an undivided whole.

Why has wilderness evaporated so quickly? Some reasons are obvious: more people with more material needs and wants. There is needless predation, however, and dereliction of duty toward wilderness seems evident among many of its should-be protectors.

The timber industry heads the list of wilderness predators. The national forests were once thought of as conservation areas for timber. Their management was largely custodial, and in the early 1900s their yield, mostly for railroad ties and steam engine fuel, amounted to little more than a billion board feet per year. Since World War II, the timber industry has come to view the the national forests as timber mines, cheaper to exploit than industry's own lands, and the cut has climbed to 12 billion board feet annually. As with mining, loggers started with the best. As a result, the remaining wild areas are marginal timberlands: remote, steep, often sparsely stocked—the kind least able to regenerate, most likely to suffer irreparable environmental damage. As long as industry can count upon the government to build access roads and offer cheap stumpage prices, it is eager to log the last pockets and fringes.

Some view the Forest Service as the true ringleader in this tragic tree mining, with industry just an accomplice. In a recent article elucidating a Natural Resources Defense Council study of the selling of US timber below cost, Peter Troast of Friends of the Earth explained that stumpage is priced by a method that deducts logging costs and a profit margin. This "residual pricing" system reduces the stumpage for hard-to-get-out timber to practically zero. Moreover, costs of management and reforestation are not added in. Were it not for this bargain-basement inducement to log our last wild pockets, it would be more economical to let the trees stand than to pay the true cost of logging them. In some places, Troast points out, taxpayers get less than 20 cents back for every dollar they spend on timber sales. Only in the Pacific Northwest do the timber sales seem really profitable, and that is because they involve areas of old-growth timber that commands top dollar. Once the old trees are cut, however, regeneration will be very slow, so their harvesting is tantamount to timber mining.

This practice of "cut it no matter" is in line with a philosophy frequently encountered among land managers: management means doing something with and to the resources, not merely "letting them be." A tree that dies a natural death, for example, is too often regarded as a tree lost and useless. Foresters have been known to tell the public, "If we didn't cut the trees, they'd become old and diseased, blow down, cause fires, infect other trees and there would be no forest any more."

Notice, sometime, the Forest Service's multiple-use

emblem, a five-branch tree. It symbolizes the five purposes enumerated in the Multiple Use-Sustained Yield Act of 1960: Timber, Range, Outdoor Recreation, Water, and Wildlife and Fish. Wilderness is not mentioned as a purpose, but the law, which dates from pre-Wilderness Act times, does state that wilderness is not inconsistent with multiple use. In 1976, the National Forest Management Act made wilderness a full partner with other national forest values.

Nevertheless, wilderness is scarcely considered a peer with the other national forest objectives by many within the Forest Service, which has been accused of resisting wilderness designations in a number of subtle ways. One was to set purity standards so high that many areas could be disqualified from consideration. This was particularly enraging in the East, where many beautiful places have recovered to wildness after early-day impacts. The Eastern wilderness legislation enacted in 1975 helped to rectify the "purity" problem, but the Forest Service reportedly has allowed recreationists to infer that wilderness spells a prompt end to back-country facilities. It has been charged also that stiffened regulations for western wilderness areas have fueled wilderness antipathy among ranchers. Hunters are allowed the mistaken opinion that wilderness status somehow precludes hunting, whereas it is only wilderness in parks, monuments, and some refuges that is so closed. Such closures are in accord with park or sanctuary designation, not wilderness status.

Would-be wilderness advocates are often scared off by predictions that wilderness status will bring publicity and consequent crowding in places that local users once had largely to themselves. Yet it is naive to assume that beautiful areas will long remain "undiscovered." Moreover, concern about over-use marks a failure of the land managers in not controlling use to maintain the quality of the environment and of the experience it offers. Just as poor land use, not rivers, causes flooding, so management, not wilderness designation, crowds and erodes our wildlands.

BLM seems less than sanguine about wilderness preservation, and the agency has been accused of stacking the deck against wilderness in its study processes. The bureau made a good initial inventory of its potential wilderness. Since then, however, rather than recommending wilderness study designation for many qualifying areas, it is finding wilderness qualities less than outstanding where other resource values may exist. That conveniently settles the question of further study.

One might assume that the National Park Service, a world leader in natural-area preservation, would be an enthusiastic protector of wilderness. The famous NPS organic act of 1916 mentions leaving parklands "unimpaired for future generations." What clearer wilder-

It is not given to any man to create wilderness. But he can make deserts, and has.

—WALLACE STEGNER

ness mandate could there be? The original Wilderness Act protagonists counted 90 percent of the national parklands in their initial wilderness system objectives. However, NPS-watchers claim park managers have not registered enthusiasm over wilderness designation. Convinced that they are already doing a good protection job, they doubt if wilderness status is urgent. Furthermore, it might restrict management practices and the placement of roads and facilities.

Important as it may be to save park wildness from the park managers, wilderness designation of parklands sometimes has the unfortunate effect of jeopardizing wildlands elsewhere. Some congressmen use park wilderness legislation to appease conservationists. The legislators realize that it doesn't take any resources off the market; they're already off, and the action diverts attention from wilderness in jeopardy on other public lands.

Managers of the national wildlife refuges obediently finished their wilderness studies, but often apparently without much enthusiasm. Like the foresters and park managers, they like the freedom to manage in their bureau's own best judgment—which often means habitat manipulation, including even clearcutting, that wilderness status would preclude. Although vulnerable to some resource extraction, the refuges are not under such pressure from industry as are the national forests and the public lands under BLM. But USFWS tends to share the purity biases of the Forest Service.

The threats to our remaining wilderness involve much more than the timber industry, which finds it cheaper to cut the public forests with government encouragement and at taxpayers' expense than to utilize its own or other private timber holdings. Three hysterias now beset us. One of them, thirst for water, has been with us for years, created often by pressure to farm marginal land or sell real estate that would be worthless without water. A false water supply argument flooded beautiful Hetch Hetchy Canyon in Yosemite National Park years ago, and now every river flowing westward from the Sierra Nevada has been impounded. A reservoir has engulfed Glen Canyon, "The Place No-One Knew," once part of an eight-million-acre wilderness. A dam project threatened to destroy the Green and Yampa rivers in Dinosaur Na-

"This peak has never before been scaled by a group."

Drawing by Ed Koren

tional Monument.

The Heritage Conservation and Recreation Service has estimated that 20 percent of the nation's river mileage is now impounded. A once-wild river, the Tennessee is now entirely slack. The 6,000 miles of rivers preserved free-flowing in national and state Wild and Scenic Rivers Systems are a pittance compared with losses over the past 50 years. More than 55,000 major dams (25 or more feet high and impounding more than 10 acres) have been identified by the Army Corps of Engineers, which has been responsible for much river destruction. Most of these dams have been built since 1900. Dam building is proceeding at the rate of 1,500 per year, and that rate is increasing. More than 6,000 new sites have been located.

Most of the dams have gone in at the expense of either agricultural lands or wildlands. Pumped-storage facilities, 500 sites for which have been identified in the northwestern states alone, threaten high mountain basins. In the East, all the new dam sites in Pennsylvania are located on rivers ranked 1-A in the state's Wild and Scenic Rivers Program. Even Maine's St. John, unique in the East in its length and wilderness quality, is under threat. The two proposed Dickey-Lincoln School dams, one of the largest dam projects in the world, would operate only 2.5 hours a day to produce peaking power, saving less than one percent of New England's oil consumption and costing an estimated billion dollars. Conservation and power load management can save three times the power Dickey-Lincoln would produce, and the dams would destroy forever 278 miles of wild free-flowing streams, 30 wild ponds, and 88,000 acres of prime timberland.

This boondoggle betokens our thirst not only for water itself but also for energy, and the increasingly hysterical search for depletable energy sources is putting much of our remaining wilderness on death row. Much has already been executed. The Red Desert of Wyoming, mentioned earlier, has been chopped up by the roads and other developments of uranium, oil, and gas prospectors. In Alaska, some people are eager to trade the last great caribou herds for just a little more oil. The possibility of oil in the great "Overthrust Belt" that stretches from Baja California to Canada has apparently panicked the Forest Service and the BLM into writing off much wilderness from further consideration. The government's zeal to spur development of synthetic fuels from oil shale and coal is threatening extensive wild areas; one is the Piceance Creek Basin of northwestern Colorado, winter range of the nation's largest mule deer herd.

Threats to wilderness as a result of energy hysteria come in three waves. First, good areas are eliminated from wilderness recommendation when energy potential is suspected. Second, industry seeks mining law extension or exceptions to environmental laws and regulations. Third, wherever fuel conversion processing is established, air pollution will taint western fastnesses where clean air now washes a pristine landscape.

A new hysteria besetting the West is the alleged need to use a vast territory to deploy defensive missiles. The Air Force's MX Missile System would create a gigantic prairie-dog village of missile silos occupying half of Nevada and a large part of western Utah. Much of this land is in our dwindling stock of wilderness. The environmental effects would be devastating, and there are no substitutes for wildlands lost.

Perpetuating the opportunity to find solitude and self-renewal in pristine country is a basic purpose of wilderness preservation, but some recreationists are hurting our remaining wilderness as much as they are helping to secure it. Once industry has tempted us into buying a macho-machine of some kind, we resent not being able to use it wherever we wish. We are loath to return to the paddle and hiking boots that once gave us healthful pleasure. And of course, machines shrink our outdoors: a lake ten miles long is an ocean to a canoe, a pond to a motorboat. We advocate opening up the country and then wonder why a favorite place is fished out or crowded. Anti-wilderness land managers are clever at implying that we may have to sacrifice our favorite man-made recreational facilities if we opt for wilderness designation, and that wild lands can accommodate everybody and somehow survive.

The charge is often made by those unfriendly to preservation that wilderness recreation is somehow "elitist." The old, simple ways are impugned as aristocratic. Recreation by means of expensive, destructive machines is touted as the common man's democratic way. Wilderness use requires much leisure, we are told, and such leisure implies wealth. Yet even a wilderness trip in Alaska can be fitted into a standard two or three-week vacation for less cash than would be required at a resort.

Decriers of wilderness say it shuts out the old and infirm, as if nearly all of us have had no life to live except in old age and debility. Would a city recreation department shut down its ball fields and playgrounds in favor of park benches and gardens alone? Of course not. Adventuring grounds are needed, and most people are able-bodied and energetic enough to enjoy wilderness for at least half their lives. Their descendants will also be, and will rightly reproach us if we irreversibly eliminate from our land—and theirs— adequate opportunities for wilderness adventure and challenge. There is, of course, an unfortunate minority that is not able-bodied, but there is more beauty for the handicapped to experience by conveyance than anyone can enjoy in a lifetime. And they are probably

among the last to discourage wildlands protection, wanting others more fortunate than they to have opportunities that they lack.

Critics imply that wilderness is undemocratic in not providing for enough people, although wilderness can only be designated by law and is therefore among the most democratic of land allocations. Paradoxically, the critics also warn that too many people will crowd in if choice areas are publicized through wilderness designation. "'If you want to keep an area secluded, don't advertise it with a wilderness label," the argument goes. It is true that the publicity of wilderness designation spotlights recreational opportunity, and all of us like to keep our favorite places secret. The only solution to saving wild country in the long term, however, is not secrecy but regulation of use. Yes, we've come to that and must face it. Much has been said extolling what Bob Marshall half a century ago called "freedom of the wilderness," and it has been charged that regulation destroys that very freedom that is such an essential ingredient of wild country. Perhaps so, but the fact is that we have bred ourselves out of the right to wander withersoever we choose in unlimited numbers. Moreover, many of us are ignorant and untrained in outdoor conduct, and no standards of conduct are insisted upon.

Quality cannot stand overuse. Touch the painting too often and the portrait disappears. Crowd the wilderness and its texture wears away; its ambience fades. We shall be compelled to limit use by requiring reservations and permits, distasteful as they may be, or else wilderness will become shopworn and shabby and, like weak wine, its experiences faint of taste and faintly felt. What was once a right must become a privilege—one earned not by money or influence, however, but by planning and patience. We necessarily impose use limits in other dimensions of our lives both for safety and for quality. Not everyone who might want to can see the championship game or the hit show. Quality wilderness experience must also be earned, by turns, by planning ahead.

Of course, this line of reasoning is anthropocentric in that it assumes that wilderness is a purely recreational resource, set aside only for the inspiration and enjoyment of human beings. It ignores the biocentric view—that wilderness has its own right to life as a community of living things. If they had a say in the matter, they might tell us to watch and learn how nature works without meddling, moving in, and trampling around.

It is hard for us Americans to change our cultural mind-set that the New World is still largely a frontier, with plenty of everything, including miles and miles of wild country. This myth of superabundance is especially evident in frontier-minded Alaska, where some

Alaskan natives protest the North Slope oil lease sale.   *Photograph courtesy of the Anchorage Daily News.*

doubt that wilderness can ever run out. "Many Alaskans feel that we should wait until the need is more evident before additional wilderness is preserved, not realizing that when everyone is convinced that such action is necessary, the opportunity will have been lost." So wrote an Alaskan scientist, Dr. Robert Rausch, 20 years ago.

Many Alaskans have bitterly opposed conservationists' efforts to protect more than 60 million acres in Alaska as wilderness in national parks, forests, and wildlife refuges. Alaska, although no substitute for wilderness in other life zones of North America, is our

last great wildland treasury. There is no further frontier, and in Alaska the wilderness is of a scale to sustain itself with minimal impact from outside influences. The proposed acreages sound huge, but a different scale applies to a land where a grizzly bear needs 100 square miles of habitat, a one-pound grayling may be years old, and it takes a quarter of a century to grow a sapling. In the north, the old "lower 48" ways of using country can be devastating.

Alaska's fewer than half a million citizens have been given a state land apportionment the size of California, and their lands contain most of Alaska's resource

I am glad that I shall never be young without wild country to be young in. Of what avail are 40 freedoms without a blank spot on the map?
                    —ALDO LEOPOLD

riches. Yet a cry comes for more and says to hell with the rest of the nation that has owned the land since 1867 and might like to save some of it for future generations. "Alaska is remote, only for rich folks to enjoy. Don't lock it up. Leave it open for us to pillage and we'll send you some oil." So goes the refrain. But how many of us dream of a wild Alaska, and what if all those dreams were dashed?

There are frightening hope-dashers abroad in the land these days who insist that America decide right away, once and for all, what its ultimate wilderness system should be and release all other unreserved public lands to exploitation—no chance for reconsideration; no room for error or oversight; no comfort in hoping that a few years hence, when more people are enlightened and aware, a remaining wild corner can yet be saved. Do it now, or never. Sierra Club President Theodore A. Snyder, Jr., has pointed out that "such clear and immediate allocations...would change the review process that Congress has relied on over years when considering wilderness proposals. This careful process is area-specific, allowing deliberate review of individual proposals, with citizen participation and local hearings."

What to do? "Everybody loves children, conservation, and wilderness—and America the beautiful. But just try to save some of it—really save it." So wrote Dave Brower, FOE chairman, before the Wilderness Act became law. It's still true, alas, despite the pronouncement of a former national parks director who said: "This nation is not so poor that it must expend its beauty, nor so rich in beauty that it can afford to."

Really saving wilderness cannot be a quickie, one-shot deal, with every area not successfully protected let go forever. We must proceed in our wilderness preservation labors with deliberate speed, examining resources carefully, one by one, as we perceive our requirements and evaluate what wilderness we have left. We need a thorough review and inventory at regular intervals. Special care and attention must be given our few remaining virgin areas, and to sections of the country that are wilderness-poor. To date there has been emphasis on wilderness where recreational opportunities are great—spectacular alpine regions. But there is need to have all kinds of ecosystems represented in our National Wilderness Preservation System: lowlands, coastal areas, swamps, deserts, and grasslands as well as mountains, forests, and rivers.

We must insist on a fair economic accounting when exploitation of our public resources is proposed. There is no sense in paying to have our wilderness destroyed. If the costs of timbering exceed the value of the wood, for example, that alone should dictate that we leave it wild and more intensively manage the more productive lands.

Gnawing at our land for fossil fuel is no substitute for the soft energy solutions that can sustain us and the energy conservation measures that can drastically cut our consumption and its costs. Nor should massive boondoggles that destroy our land masquerade as "necessary for national defense."

Our public-land managers are not leading us toward protection of our wilderness heritage. Some whisper that our interests will suffer if we tie their managerial hands; others abdicate leadership and ask us what we want.

We must tell them. Everything that's still wild should stay wild, especially in Alaska. No matter that it's far away; it's part of our "geography of hope." We must remember that every pristine acre we lose is gone forever. Let's never have to tell our children "You're too late," never have to say "We're sorry."

Saga of a Letter

The Geography of Hope

WALLACE STEGNER

WHEN I WROTE my "wilderness letter" to David Pesonen 20 years ago, I had probably been prompted to do so by David Brower. He was usually the cattle-prod that woke me from other preoccupations and from my workaholism and directed my attention to something important. In this case what he woke me to was close to my heart. I had been lucky enough to grow up next to wilderness, or quasi-wilderness, of several kinds, and I was prepared to argue for the preservation of wilderness not simply as a scientific reserve, or a land-bank, or a playground, but as a spiritual resource, a leftover from our frontier origins that could reassure us of our identity as a nation and a people. The Wilderness Bill, already debated for years and the subject of hundreds of official pages, had not yet passed. The ORRRC report,* with its inventory of what remained of our outdoors and its promise of reorganization of the bureaus managing it, seemed a good place to put in a word.

By luck or accident or the mysterious focusing by which ideas whose time has come reach many minds at the same time, my letter struck a chord. Before it had time to appear in the ORRRC report, Secretary of the Interior Stewart Udall had picked it up and used it as the basis of a speech before a wilderness conference in San Francisco, and the Sierra Club had published it as a document of that conference. It was published in the Washington *Post* and the ORRRC report, and I included it in my collection of essays, *The Sound of Mountain Water*. Before long, some friend of mine saw it posted on the wall in a Kenya game park. From there, someone in South Africa or Rhodesia carried it home and had an artist named C. B. Cunningham surround it with drawings of African animals and birds, and turned it into a poster which

the Natal Park Board, a Rhodesian kindness-to-animals organization and perhaps other groups have distributed all over south and east Africa. A quotation from it captions a Canadian poster, with a magnificent George Calef photograph of caribou crossing river ice; and I have heard of, but not seen, a similar Australian poster issued with the same intent. The Sierra Club borrowed its last four words, "the geography of hope," as the title for Eliot Porter's book of photographs of Baja California. Altogether, this letter, the labor of an afternoon, has gone farther around the world than other writings on which I have spent years.

I take this as evidence not of special literary worth, but of an earnest, world-wide belief in the idea it expresses. There are millions of people on every continent who feel the need of what Sherwood Anderson called "a sense of bigness outside ourselves"; we all need something to take the shrillness out of us.

Returning to the letter after 20 years, I find that my opinions have not changed. They have actually been sharpened by an increased urgency. We are 20 years closer to showdown. Though the Wilderness Bill in which we all placed our hopes was passed, and though many millions of acres have been permanently protected—the magnificent Salmon River wilderness only a few weeks ago—preservation has not moved as fast as it should have, and the Forest Service, in particular, has shown by its reluctance and foot-dragging that it often puts resource use above preservation. Its proposed wilderness areas have consistently been minimal, and RARE II was a travesty.

Nevertheless, something saved. And something still to fight for.

And also, since the BLM Organic Act, another plus-minus development. It is now possible that out of the deserts and dry grasslands managed by the BLM there may be primitive areas set aside as wilderness, as I

*Outdoor Recreation for America, A Report to the President and to the Congress by the Outdoor Recreation Resources Review Commission, U.S. Government Printing Office, January, 1962.

suggested in my letter to Pesonen and as some of us proposed to Secretary Udall as early as 1961. Unhappily, the Organic Act was contemporary with the energy crisis and the growing awareness that the undeveloped country in the Rocky Mountain states is one of the greatest energy mines on earth. That discovery, at a time of national anxiety about energy sources, has brought forward individuals, corporations, and conglomerates all eager to serve their country by strip mining the BLM wasteland, or drilling it for oil and gas. Economic temptation begets politicians willing to serve special economic interests, and they in turn bring on a new wave of states'-rights agitation, this time nicknamed the Sagebrush Rebellion. Its purpose, as in the 1940s when Bernard DeVoto headed the resistance to it, (it was then called Landgrab) is to force the transfer of public lands from federal control to the control of the states, which will know how to make their resources available to those who will know what to do with them. After that they can be returned to the public for expensive rehabilitation.

The Sagebrush Rebellion is the worst enemy not only of long-range management of the public lands, but of wilderness. If its counterpart in the 1940s had won, we would have no wilderness areas at all, and deteriorated national forests. If it wins in the 1980s we will have only such wilderness as is already formally set aside. Federal bureaus are imperfect human institutions, and have sins to answer for, and are not above being influenced by powerful interests. Nevertheless they represent the public interest, by and large, and not corporate interests anxious to exploit public resources at the public's expense.

In my letter to David Pesonen 20 years ago I spoke with some feeling about the deserts of southern Utah—Capitol Reef, the San Rafael Swell, the Escalante Desert, the Aquarius Plateau. That whole area has been under threat for nearly a decade, and though the Kaiparowits Complex was defeated and the Intermountain Power Project forced to relocate northward into the Sevier Desert near Lynndyl, the Union Pacific and 13 other companies are still pushing to mine the coal in the Kaiparowits Plateau, surrounded by national parks; and a group of utilities wants to open a big strip mine in Alton, four miles from Bryce, and a 500-megawatt power plant in Warner Valley, 17 miles from Zion, and a 2000-megawatt plant north of Las Vegas, and two slurry pipelines to serve them. The old forest road over the Aquarius is being paved in from both ends, the equally beautiful trail over the Hightop from Salina to Fish Lake is being widened

Joseph E. Holmes

and improved. Our numbers and our energy demands inexorably press upon this country as beautiful as any on earth, country of an Old Testament harshness and serenity.

It is in danger of being made—of helping to make itself—into a sacrifice area. Its air is already less clear, its distances less sharp. Its water table, if these mines and plants and pipelines are created, will sink out of sight, its springs will dry up, its streams will shrink and go intermittent. But there will be more blazing illumination along the Las Vegas Strip, and the little Mormon towns of Wayne and Garfield and Kane Counties will acquire some interesting modern problems.

What impresses me after 20 years is how far the spoiling of that superb country has already gone, and how few are the local supporters of the federal agencies which are the only protection against it. They would do well to consider how long the best thing in their lives has been preserved for them by federal management, and how much they will locally lose if the Sagebrush Rebellion wins. Furthermore, the land that the Sagebrush Rebellion wants transferred, the chickenhouse that it wants to put under the guard of the foxes, belongs as much to me, or to a grocer in Des Moines, or a taxi driver in Newark, as to anyone else. And I am not willing to see it wrecked just to increase corporate profits and light Las Vegas.

Los Altos, Calif.

Dec. 3, 1960
David E. Pesonen
Wildland Research Center
Agricultural Experiment Station
243 Mulford Hall
University of California
Berkeley 4, Calif.

Dear Mr. Pesonen:

I believe that you are working on the wilderness portion of the Outdoor Recreation Resources Review Commission's report. If I may, I should like to urge some arguments for wilderness preservation that involve recreation, as it is ordinarily conceived, hardly at all. Hunting, fishing, hiking, mountain-climbing, camping, photography, and the enjoyment of natural scenery will all, surely, figure in your report. So will the wilderness as a genetic reserve, a scientific yardstick by which we may measure the world in its natural balance against the world in its man-made imbalance. What I want to speak for is not so much the wilderness uses, valuable as those are, but the wilderness *idea,* which is a resource in itself. Being an intangible and spiritual resource, it will seem mystical to the practical-minded—but then anything that cannot be moved by a bulldozer is likely to seem mystical to them.

I want to speak for the wilderness idea as something that has helped form our character and that has certainly shaped our history as a people. It has no more to do with recreation than churches have to do with recreation, or than the strenuousness and optimism and expansiveness of what historians call the "American Dream" have to do with recreation. Nevertheless, since it is only in this recreation survey that the values of wilderness are being compiled, I hope you will permit me to insert this idea between the leaves, as it were, of the recreation report.

Something will have gone out of us a people if we ever let the remaining wilderness be destroyed; if we permit the last virgin forests to be turned into comic books and plastic cigarette cases; if we drive the few remaining members of the wild species into zoos or to extinction; if we pollute the last clear air and dirty the last clean streams and push our paved roads through the last of the silence, so that never again will Americans be free in their own country from the noise, the exhausts, the stinks of human and automotive waste. And so that never again can we have the chance to see ourselves single, separate, vertical and individual in the world, part of the environment of trees and rocks and soil, brother to the other animals, part of the natural world and competent to belong to it. Without any remaining wilderness we are committed wholly, without chance for even momentary reflection and rest, to a headlong drive into our technological termite-life, the Brave New World of a completely man-controlled environment. We need wilderness preserved—as much of it as is still left, and as many kinds—because it was the challenge against which our character as a people was formed. The reminder and the reassurance that it is still there is good for our spiritual health even if we never once in ten years set foot in it. It is good for us when we are young, because of the incomparable sanity it can bring briefly, as vacation and rest, into our insane lives. It is important to us when we are old simply because it is there—important, that is, simply as idea.

We are a wild species, as Darwin pointed out. Nobody ever tamed or domesticated or scientifically bred us. But for at least three millennia we have been engaged in a cumulative and ambitious race to modify and gain control of our environment, and in the process we have come close to domesticating ourselves. Not many people are likely, anymore, to look upon what we call "progress" as an unmixed blessing. Just as surely as it has brought us increased comfort and more material goods, it has brought us spiritual losses, and it threatens now to become the Frankenstein that will destroy us. One means of sanity is to retain a hold on the natural world, to remain, insofar as we can, good animals. Americans still have that chance, more than many people; for while we were demonstrating ourselves the most efficient and ruthless environment-busters in history, and slashing and burning and cutting our way through a wilderness continent, the wilderness was working on us. It remains in us as surely as Indian names remain on the land. If the abstract dream of human liberty and human dignity became, in America, something more than an abstract dream, mark it down at least partially to the fact that we were in subtle ways subdued by what we conquered.

The Connecticut Yankee, sending likely candidates from King Arthur's unjust kingdom to his Man Factory for rehabilitation, was over-optimistic, as he later admitted. These things cannot be forced, they have to grow. To make such a man, such a democrat, such a believer in human individual dignity, as Mark Twain himself, the frontier was necessary, Hannibal and the Mississippi and Virginia City, and reaching out from those the wilderness; the wilderness as opportunity and as idea, the thing that has helped to make an American different from and, until we forget it in the roar of our industrial cities, more fortunate than other men. For an American, insofar as he is new and different at all, is a civilized man who has renewed himself in the wild. The American experience has been the confrontation by old peoples and cultures of a world as new as if it had just risen from the sea. That gave us our hope and our excitement, and the hope and excitement can be passed on to newer Americans, Americans who never saw any phase of the frontier. But only so long as we keep the remainder of our wild as a reserve and a promise—a sort of wilderness bank.

As a novelist, I may perhaps be forgiven for taking literature as a reflection, indirect but profoundly true, of our national consciousness. And our literature, as perhaps you are aware, is sick, embittered, losing its mind, losing its faith. Our novelists are the declared enemies of their society. There has hardly been a serious or important novel in this century that did not repudiate in part or in whole American technological culture for its commercialism, its vulgarity, and the way in which it has dirtied a clean continent and a clean dream. I do not expect that the preservation of our remaining wilderness is going to cure this condition. But the mere example that we can as a nation apply some other criteria than commercial and exploitative considerations would be heartening to many Americans, novelists or otherwise. We need to demonstrate our acceptance of the natural world, including ourselves; we need the spiritual refreshment that being natural can produce. And one of the best places for us to get that is in the wilderness where the fun houses, the bulldozers, and the pavements of our civilization are shut down.

Sherwood Anderson, in a letter to Waldo Frank in the 1920s, said it better than I can. "Is it not likely that when the country was new and men were often alone in the fields and the forest they got a sense of bigness outside themselves that has now in some way been lost. . . . Mystery whispered in the grass, played in the branches of trees overhead, was caught up and blown across the American line in clouds of dust at evening on the prairies. . . . I am old enough to remember tales that strengthen my belief in a deep semi-religious influence that was formerly at work among our people. The flavor of it hangs over the best work of Mark Twain. . . . I can remember old fellows in my home town speaking feelingly of an evening spent on the big empty plains. It had taken the shrillness out of them. They had learned the trick of quiet. . . ."

We could learn it too, even yet; even our children and grandchildren could learn it. But only if we save, for just such absolutely non-recreational, impractical, and mystical uses as this, all the wild that still remains to us.

It seems to me significant that the distinct downturn in our literature from hope to bitterness took place almost at the precise time when the frontier officially came to an end, in 1890, and when the American way of life had begun to turn strongly urban and industrial. The more urban it has become, and the more frantic with technological change, the sicker and more embittered our literature, and I believe our people, have become. For myself, I grew up on the empty plains of Saskatchewan and Montana and in the mountains of Utah, and I put a very high valuation on what those places gave me. And if I had not been able periodically to renew myself in the mountains and deserts of western America I would be very nearly bughouse. Even when I can't get to the back country, the thought of the colored deserts of southern Utah, or the reassurance that there are still stretches of prairie where the world can be instantaneously perceived as disk and bowl, and where the little but intensely important human being is exposed to the five directions and the thirty-six winds, is a positive consolation. The idea alone can sustain me. But as the wilderness areas are progressively exploited or "improved," as the jeeps and bulldozers of uranium prospectors scar up the deserts and the roads are cut into the alpine timberlands, and as the remnants of the unspoiled and natural world are progressively eroded, every such loss is a little death in me. In us.

I am not moved by the argument that those wilderness areas which have already been exposed to grazing or mining are already deflowered, and so might as well be "harvested." For mining I cannot say much good except that its operations are generally short-lived. The extractable wealth is taken and the shafts, the tailings, and the ruins left, and in a dry country such as the American West the wounds men make in the earth do not quickly heal. Still, they are only wounds; they aren't absolutely mortal. Better a wounded wilderness than none at all. And as for grazing, if it is strictly controlled so that it does not destroy the ground cover, damage the ecology, or compete with the wildlife it is in itself nothing that need conflict with the wilderness feeling or the validity of the wilderness experience. I have known enough range cattle to recognize them as wild animals; and the people who herd them have, in the wilderness context, the dignity of rareness; they belong on the frontier, moreover, and have a look of rightness. The invasion they make on the virgin country is a sort of invasion that is as old as Neolithic man, and they can, in moderation, even emphasize a man's feeling of belonging to the natural world. Under surveillance, they can belong; under control, they need not deface or mar. I do not believe that in wilderness areas where grazing has never been permitted, it should be permitted; but I do not believe either that an otherwise untouched wilderness should be eliminated from the preservation plan because of limited existing uses such as grazing which are in consonance with the frontier condition and image.

Let me say something on the subject of the kinds of wilderness worth preserving. Most of those areas contemplated are in the national forests and in high mountain country. For all the usual recreational purposes, the alpine and forest wildernesses are obviously the most important, both as genetic banks and as beauty spots. But for the spiritual renewal, the recognition of identity, the birth of awe, other kinds will serve every bit as well. Perhaps, because they are less friendly to life, more abstractly nonhuman, they will serve even better. On our Saskatchewan prairie, the nearest neighbor was four miles away, and at night we saw only two lights on all the dark rounding earth. The earth was full of animals—field mice, ground squirrels, weasels, ferrets, badgers, coyotes, burrowing owls, snakes. I knew them as my little brothers, as fellow creatures, and I have never been able to look upon animals in any other way since. The sky in that country came clear down to the ground on every side, and it was full of great weathers, and clouds, and winds, and hawks. I hope I learned something from knowing intimately the creatures of the earth; I hope I learned something from looking a long way, from looking up, from being much alone. A prairie like that, one big enough to carry the eye clear to the sinking, rounding horizon, can be as lonely and grand and simple in its forms as the sea. It is as good a place as any for the wilderness idea to happen; the vanishing prairie is as worth preserving for the wilderness idea as the alpine forests.

So are great reaches of our western deserts, scarred somewhat by prospectors but otherwise open, beautiful, waiting, close to whatever God you want to see in them. Just as a sample, let me suggest the Robbers' Roost country in Wayne County, Utah, near the Capitol Reef National Monument. In that desert climate the dozer and jeep tracks will not soon melt back into the earth, but the country has a way of making the scars insignificant. It is a lovely and terrible wilderness, such a wilderness as Christ and the prophets went out into; harshly and beautifully colored, broken and worn until its bones are exposed, its great sky without a smudge of taint from Technocracy, and in hidden corners and pockets under its cliffs the sudden poetry of springs. Save a piece of country like that intact, and it does not matter in the slightest that only a few people every year will go into it. That is precisely its value. Roads would be a desecration, crowds would ruin it. But those who haven't the strength or youth to go into it and live can simply sit and look. They can look two hundred miles, clear into Colorado*: and looking down over the cliffs and canyons of the San Rafael Swell and the Robbers' Roost they can also look as deeply into themselves as anywhere I know. And if they can't even get to the places on the Aquarius Plateau where the present roads will carry them, they can simply contemplate the *idea*, take pleasure in the fact that such a timeless and uncontrolled part of earth is still there.

These are some of the things wilderness can do for us. That is the reason we need to put into effect, for its preservation, some other principle than the principles of exploitation or "usefulness" or even recreation. We simply need that wild country available to us, even if we never do more than drive to its edge and look in. For it can be a means of reassuring ourselves of our sanity as creatures, a part of the geography of hope.

Very sincerely yours,
Wallace Stegner

---

*Not any more, thanks to the power plants at Four Corners and Page.—W.S.

Recommended Actions

In general . . .

☐ Remind your Representative and Senators that wilderness is scarce and bound to get scarcer, that there cannot possibly be too much of it; request that they vote to enlarge the Wilderness Preservation System at every opportunity, and urge them to oppose any proposed legislation that would set an arbitrary time limit beyond which further additions to statutory wilderness could no longer be made.

Specifically . . .

☐ Join an environmental organization and act according to the information it provides. (Because each wilderness proposal is unique, specific recommendations cannot be given here. Two of the broad-spectrum organizations most concerned about wilderness are Friends of the Earth and the Sierra Club, while The Wilderness Society, as its name implies, concentrates exclusively on wilderness issues.)

Kent Reno/Jeroboam, Inc.

More Thoughts on Wilderness

ON THE MAPS of the old voyageurs it is called *Mauvaises Terres,* the evil lands, and, slurred a little with the passage through many minds, it has come down to us anglicized as the badlands. The soft shuffle of moccasins has passed through its canyons on the grim business of war and flight, but the last of those slight disturbances of immemorial silences died out almost a century ago. The land, if one can call it a land, is a waste as lifeless as that valley in which lie the kings of Egypt. Like the Valley of the Kings, it is a mausoleum, a place of dry bones in what once was a place of life. Now it has silences as deep as those in the moon's airless chasms.

Nothing grows among its pinnacles; there is no shade except under great toadstools of sandstone whose bases have been eaten to the shape of wine glasses by the wind. Everything is flaking, cracking, disintegrating, wearing away in the long, imperceptible weather of time. The ash of ancient volcanic outbursts still sterilizes its soil, and its colors in that waste are the colors that flame in the lonely sunsets on dead planets. Men come there but rarely, and for one purpose only, the collection of bones.

It was a late hour on a cold, wind-bitten autumn day when I climbed a great hill spined like a dinosaur's back and tried to take my bearings. The tumbled waste fell away in waves in all directions. Blue air was darkening into purple along the bases of the hills. I shifted my knapsack, heavy with the petrified bones of long-vanished creatures, and studied my compass. I wanted to be out of there by nightfall, and already the sun was going sullenly down in the west.

It was then that I saw the flight coming on. It was moving like a little close-knit body of black specks that danced and darted and closed again. It was pouring from the north and heading toward me with the undeviating relentlessness of a compass needle. It streamed through the shadows rising out of monstrous gorges. It rushed over towering pinnacles in the red light of the sun or momentarily sank from sight within their shade. Across that desert of eroding clay and wind-worn stone they came with a faint wild twittering that filled all the air about me as those tiny living bullets hurtled past into the night.

It may not strike you as a marvel. It would not, perhaps, unless you stood in the middle of a dead world at sunset, but that was where I stood. Fifty million years lay under my feet, fifty million years of bellowing monsters moving in a green world now gone so utterly that its very light was traveling on the farther edge of space. The chemicals of all that vanished age lay about me in the ground. Around me still lay the shearing molars of dead titanotheres, the delicate sabers of soft-stepping cats, the hollow sockets that had held the eyes of many a strange, outmoded beast. Those eyes had looked out upon a world as real as ours; dark, savage brains had roamed and roared their challenges into the steaming night.

Now they were still here, or, put it as you will, the chemicals that made them were here about me in the ground. The carbon that had driven them ran blackly in the eroding stone. The stain of iron was in the clays. The iron did not remember the blood it had once moved within, the phosphorus had forgot the savage brain. The little individual moment had ebbed from all those strange combinations of chemicals as it would ebb from our living bodies into the sinks and runnels of oncoming time.

I had lifted up a fistful of that ground. I held it while that wild flight of south-bound warblers hurtled over me into the oncoming dark. There went phosphorus, there went iron, there went carbon, there beat the calcium in those hurrying wings. Alone on a dead planet I watched that incredible miracle speeding past. It ran by some true compass over field and waste land. It cried its individual ecstasies into the air until the gullies rang. It swerved like a single body, it knew itself, and, lonely, it bunched close in the racing darkness, its individual entities feeling about them the rising night. And so, crying to each other their identity, they passed away out of my view.

I dropped my fistful of earth. I heard it roll inanimate back into the gully at the base of the hill: iron, carbon, the chemicals of life. Like men from those wild tribes who had haunted these hills before me seeking visions, I made my sign to the great darkness. It was not a mocking sign, and I was not mocked. As I walked into my camp late that night, one man, rousing from his blankets beside the fire, asked sleepily, "What did you see?"

"I think, a miracle," I said softly, but I said it to myself. Behind me that vast waste began to glow under the rising moon.

—Loren Eiseley

When the last corner lot is covered with tenements we can still make a playground by tearing one down, but when the last antelope goes by the board, not all the playground associations in Christendom can do aught to replace the loss.

—ALDO LEOPOLD

Wildlife

The accelerating worldwide extinction of species is causing permanent impoverishment of life on this planet. By the late 1980s, we stand to lose species at the rate of one per hour; from 500,000 to 2,000,000 species of plants and animals will cease to exist between now and the year 2000 if we continue our assault on them.

Advanced technologies pose an unprecedented threat to previously untouched ecosystems. Antarctica, the Southern Ocean, the moist tropical forests, and the Beaufort Sea are a few of the areas that face massive exploitation to satisfy our lifestyles and provide for a burgeoning human population.

Habitat destruction, the greatest single threat to wildlife, continues at a breakneck pace. Which species shall we thoughtlessly nominate for oblivion as we add billions of humans to the planet and preempt a larger and larger share of Earth's resources? Can our covetousness fail to result in our own downfall?

There is a desperate need for us to expand our concern beyond those species that capture our imagination; our concern must encompass entire sustainable habitats. We need to graduate from single-species management and learn to understand the ecosystem approach, to embrace a global ethic that recognizes the essential nature of species diversity and the habitats in which it can endure and prosper. A place must remain for the wildness we share the planet with, and from which we came.

William Curtsinger

Wildlife

DAVID PHILLIPS and DAVID R. BROWER

"THE RED DATA BOOK" published by the International Union for the Conservation of Nature and Natural Resources (IUCN) lists more than one thousand species of mammals, birds, amphibians, reptiles, and fish known to be threatened with extinction. The US Fish and Wildlife Service has listed nearly two hundred vertebrate species as threatened or endangered in the US alone. Countless species of plants, the indispensable link in all food chains, are also under threat.

The sad history of wild species driven to extinction during the past century and the staggering number of species now menaced are not the result of natural, evolutionary events. Wildlife is being destroyed by humans, often inadvertently but sometimes willfully. Species after species has disappeared because of the lifestyles we have chosen.

Commercial exploitation of valuable species and international trade in wildlife products are major causes of the decline of many species. High profits and insatiable markets have led to the decimation of whales, rhinoceros, spotted cats, turtles, and crocodiles, to name a few. Exotic birds and tropical fish are depleted by an expanding worldwide trade in household pets. The international trade in wild primates for scientific research is on the rise, as is the collection of life specimens for zoos.

Direct assaults on wildlife are very damaging, but worldwide destruction of habitat is more serious still. Clear-cutting in the tropics for forest products and clearing of land for cultivation deprives myriad wild species of shelter and food.

Norman Myers, an internationally recognized expert on tropical deforestation, has shown that man's appetite for raw materials is taking a heavy toll. Although moist tropical forests cover less than one-tenth of Earth's surface, they contain nearly half the species living on land. At current rates of destruction, the tropical forests and their associated wildlife would be virtually destroyed within the next 40 years. Myers states that:

"The depletion of tropical moist forest stems, in part, from market demand on the part of affluent nations for hardwoods and other specialist lumbers from Southeastern Asia, Amazonia, and West/Central Africa. In addition, the disruptive harvesting of tropical timber is often conducted by multinational corporations that supply the capital, technology, and skills without which developing countries could not exploit their forest stocks at unsustainable rates. . . . Similarly, the forests of Central America are being felled to make way for artificial pasturelands in order to grow more beef. But the extra meat, instead of going into the stomachs of local citizens, makes its way to the US, where it supplies the hamburger trade and other fast-food businesses. This foreign beef is cheaper than similar-grade beef from within the US—and the American consumer, looking for a hamburger of best quality at cheapest price, is not aware of the spillover consequences of his actions. So whose hand is on the chainsaw?"

Practices in the US are increasingly disruptive to wildlife. Dams block the migration of some fishes and change stream characteristics in such a way that hosts of other species cannot be supported. Pesticides wreak havoc on the reproductive success of eagles, hawks, falcons, and other birds. Acid rain from the burning of fossil fuels, accompanied by the toxic metals in fly ash, renders lakes incapable of supporting life.

Too often, these practices are carried on without knowledge of their long-term effects. Short-term economic benefits are assumed to outweigh wildlife protection. The continued loss of wild species, however, impairs or destroys our ability to understand ecosystems and risks their instability, be they local or global. This loss is the antithesis of a survival ethic and can be redressed neither by those who live on the planet now nor by all future generations to come.

E.O. Wilson of Harvard says that "The one process ongoing in the 1980s that will take millions of years to correct is the loss of genetic and species diversity by the destruction of natural habitats. This is the folly our descendants are least likely to forgive us."

We believe the challenge lies in managing human activities rather than pretending we can, or should,

Baleen for sale, Barrow, Alaska. Photo by Elihu Blotnick.

manage living systems. The human goal should be to watch for warning signs rather than rail at them. To solve the problem of acid rain by breeding acid-resistant fish would be like breeding gas-resistant canaries for miners to take down into the mines. Likewise, the answer to the California Condor's precarious plight in a threatened habitat is not to relegate the species to decades in captivity while we look for someplace to put them. As Kenneth Brower remarks, "When the vultures watching your civilization begin dropping dead from their snags, it is time to pause and wonder."

Rational human activities can permit wild species to survive in a natural habitat. Efforts to regulate trade in endangered species, such as the Convention on International Trade in Endangered Species (CITES) and the Migratory Species Convention, need support. Internationally, consumers can exert considerable leverage to stem the senseless slaughter. As a teenager suggested a decade ago, "Furs look better on their original owners." Every year, hundreds of thousands of products made from wild species are purchased for souvenirs without thought of what animal deaths cost the Earth.

Case I: Mismanagement vs. Marine Life

The history of the fishing and whaling industries is a history of mismanagement and overexploitation. The United Nations Food and Agriculture Organization's review of the state of the world's fishery resources recently determined that overfishing has decreased the annual world catch by nearly 25 percent. Crashes in the North Atlantic cod and herring fisheries, and successive collapses in the Peruvian and Chilean anchovy fishery, underscore the shortsightedness of fishing practices and the inability or unwillingness to develop sustainable operations.

The whaling industry is a particularly striking example of poor management, with the result that most whale species are in decline. Despite the formation of the International Whaling Commission (IWC), long after much damage had already occurred, little has been done to prevent wholesale mismanagement. Blue, bowhead, gray, humpback, and right whales have been exploited to the point of extinction before receiving any protection. This has led Sydney Holt, a respected authority on cetaceans, to sound an alarm:

"There are far fewer forests in the world now, more

Perhaps the world can get along without whales; perhaps not; but it is not the sort of thing one wants to find out empirically. The nearest analogy we do know about concerns the ecological stability of grasslands, which collapses if one removes the large herbivores. Whales are the marine analogy—they are the great grazers of plankton. If, having killed all the whales, we find the world will not work well without them after all, it will be too late. We cannot create whales.   —THE WHALE MANUAL

of the fishes are overfished, and wildlife species steadily diminish—owing primarily to overconfidence in our ability to predict the behavior of complex living systems and to weakness of the institutions through which people of many nations seek to achieve common goals. As Michael Graham, a pioneer in conservation, said to the first United Nations conference on whaling in 1947, 'The world does not stand still while specialists put their minds in order.' The whaling industry likewise has not stood still. After eliminating the big whales, it moved on to the sei whale, to the much smaller minke, and began to look eagerly at the sei's subtropical cousin, the Bryde's whale.

The whale tribe as a whole is now far worse off than it was in 1959 when, with a few others, I was asked to help the International Whaling Commission out of a crisis. We blew the whistle in behalf of the blue whales and humpbacks. Six years later, the IWC declared those species protected. Some whaling countries, however, were not bound by IWC rules, and some other countries lent their flags to still other whaling vessels. The whales were poorly protected, but scientists continued unwittingly to nurture optimism. . . . The state of the art of assessing the state of the whale could thus be seen to consist of some hard data, some soft theory, a little knowledge, and a heap of speculation."

Concerted efforts within the international environmental community have focused attention on the mismanagement of commercial whaling and must continue to do so. The 1979 meeting of the IWC brought unprecedented action to ban factory-ship whaling of all whale species except the small minkes. This resulted in sperm whale quotas 77 percent below 1978 levels. Further action was taken to designate the Indian Ocean as a sanctuary, thus prohibiting whaling within an area of about 40,000 square miles. Expanding the sanctuary concept in other areas throughout the world can further protect marine habitat. A total moratorium on commercial whaling is within reach. Gains made by the elimination of commercial whaling could be undermined, however, by new threats more difficult to control. The whales' food base is being

depleted, and whales are harassed by boat traffic in some places. Oil slicks, chemical wastes, radioactive dumping, and other pollutants are degrading the marine environment. Jacques Cousteau has estimated that ocean life has decreased by one-half during his lifetime.

The three-quarters of Earth's surface that is thinly covered by oceans requires a new human determination to avoid extending the tragedy of the commons to all the life at sea.

Case II: The Untrammeled Places

David Brower notes that "Freedom, for one of Romaine Gary's characters in *The Roots of Heaven*, is a place so open and wide and untrammeled that elephants can roam untroubled there from horizon to horizon and beyond. Elephants once knew that freedom. So did buffalo, wolf, and caribou, all in our own time.

"The condor once had that kind of freedom in the California sky. From the Coast Ranges south of Monterey, eastward along the Tehachapis, and north to the old sequoias of the Sierra Nevada, an array of thermals and knowledge of how to use them kept the huge birds aloft by the hundreds, even in the lifetime of some of us, and let them patrol their vast mountain arc.

"And the great whales knew the one great ocean, with its coves of many names, for the countless eons when there was true freedom of the seas.

"Then the different flood came, as humanity reached its first billion and passed it—the flood that seemed to need no stemming. That flood, as it surged ever higher, extinguished old freedoms. What replaced them was not a few freedom, but license, an arrogant assumption that no title to a place was valid unless written in a newly invented language by one of the most recent arrivals on the planet.

"For this new flood there was no new Ark. It is already too late for a horde of splendid creatures—and for how many lesser ones we never knew?—to find sanctuary. The miraculous flow of information in

California condor. Photo by Carl Koford.

their wild genes, their unique chemistries, and their love of life will not be known again. We banished them forever with a wanton wave of the hand."

Antarctica and its surrounding ocean is an untrammeled place. The coldest, driest, most inaccessible, and least known of all the continents, Antarctica sees little or no daylight for six months a year and feels winds of 200 miles per hour or more. As early as 1815 it was the scene of large-scale exploitation of seals and whales, but Antarctica still represents one of the most unspoiled areas known to man. It may also be the largest natural laboratory for the study of natural habitat and the effects of global pollution. It is among the most productive marine ecosystems in the world: whales, seals, penguins, squid, crab, fish, and a small crustacean called krill are all found abundantly in the Southern Ocean.

Antarctica should be protected as a common heritage of all mankind. Up to now, the 13 member nations of the Antarctic Treaty have kept the continent free of military operations and protected from overexploitation of living marine resources. As worldwide fish stocks decline and shortages of oil and mineral resources become more acute, however, more covetous attention is being focused on Antarctica.

Exploiters, having decimated the great whales, now look to an unlikely target: the two-inch krill. If unregulated, the harvest of krill could increase dramatically during the 1980s. Krill, the basis of an extremely short food chain, are fed upon by almost all larger marine organisms in the Southern Ocean, including blue, fin, sei, humpback, and minke whales; seals; penguins; other seabirds; and fishes. So little is known about interactions among members of the Southern Ocean ecosystems that improper management could not only deplete krill populations, but could also upset sensitive balances and adversely affect the entire system. It could be a major set-back for endangered whale populations.

A regime is being formulated by the Antarctic Treaty powers to regulate the exploitation of living resources. It is essential that investigations of exploiting krill take into account not only the krill population itself, but also all the other species that are dependent upon krill. Interim quotas on krill need to be low until it can be shown (if it *can* be shown) that larger harvests will not upset this fragile ecosystem.

The prospect of habitat destruction from oil development in Antarctica looms large. Technology for drilling in this harsh environment doesn't yet exist; but

North Slope Eskimo whaling boat. Photo by David Phillips.

many nations, including the US, have plans to begin exploration. Oil spills could be devastating to the great whales and to the entire marine ecosystem. All mineral exploration and development should be strictly prohibited until it can be shown (if it *can* be shown) that resources can be extracted without unacceptable harm to the environment.

Case III: Endangered Species, Endangered Culture

The threat of extinction is not limited to wildlife. Humans and their ways of life can be endangered, too; sustainable and diverse human ecosystems need protection. It is for this reason that we support a limited subsistence hunt of the endangered bowhead whale by Alaskan Eskimos—and involvement of Eskimos in efforts to build back the bowhead population and to defend its environment.

Eskimos have sustained their culture for several millenia. We have endangered ours in two centuries. Although birds, seals, walrus, whales, and caribou have long sustained the Eskimo culture, a growing population and non-Eskimo technology have added new stresses to a lifestyle very different from ours—one heretofore characterized by a most rational use of their surroundings. Further stress has resulted from exploitation of their resources by non-Eskimos and the disruption of their traditions by massive and sudden infusions of inedible cash.

At one time the bowhead population was thought to be as high as 18,000, but the current best estimate is fewer than 2,500. The Bering Sea bowhead stock was exploited relentlessly for whale oil and baleen plates in the 18th and 19th centuries. When, in 1915, the population could no longer support commercial whaling, the operation ended.

To the Eskimos, the bowhead hunt has been a prime

source of nutrition and an integral part of their cultural tradition. Since time immemorial, Eskimo whalers have camped on ice floes during the spring, keeping a 24-hour vigil for the whales. When a whale surfaced close enough to the edge of the pack of ice, crews gave chase in sealskin boats called umiaks and the whales were struck with hand-held harpoons. Though records are incomplete, the average historical take was less than 20 whales per year. The Eskimos were not responsible for the depletion of the species, but now have to live with the consequences.

The situation is not an easy one for environmentalists. Biologically, the hunt may well further endanger an already severely depleted species. For the past four years, the International Whaling Commission has recommended that no bowheads be taken. Animal protection groups have called for a termination of the hunt. They have not, however, brought enough pressure to bear to block a far more serious threat to the bowhead—oil and gas exploration in the Beaufort Sea. It is not likely to be possible, and it would surely be unethical, to enforce a bowhead ban without the cooperation of the Eskimos while pressing forward with a corporate attack on an environment critical to the bowhead whale's survival.

Since 1977, the IWC has established quotas to minimize the risk to the bowhead. Eskimos feel that the quota has been too low to serve their cultural and nutritional needs and is not scientifically justified. The quota has nonetheless allowed the Eskimo way of life to continue whle providing time for research on the bowhead's growth rate, feeding habits, social structure, and population dynamics. To date, the quotas have been adhered to and self-regulation by the Eskimos has been successful within the limits—severe ones—of arctic communications. Compromise and cooperation are essential while better data are sought by all concerned. One study, alarming if substantiated, indicates that even with no subsistence hunt at all the bowhead is doomed. Recruitment data—bearing on the population of calves—may well be too inaccurate to project from, however.

It is far too easy, by pointing fingers at Eskimos, to divert attention from the planned oil exploration and development in the Beaufort Sea. Neither the US government nor the conservation community as a whole have recognized that this development poses a far greater threat to the survival of the bowhead than the Eskimo subsistence hunt. The Final Environmental Impact Statement on the Beaufort Sea lease sale indicates that a serious oil spill during the bowhead migration could exterminate half the population. Protection of the bowhead's habitat has been neglected both by the IWC and by the US government. Without such protection, efforts to save the bowhead whale are farcical.

The Eskimos, meanwhile, have maintained that if their activities can be shown to be immediately perilous to the survival of the bowhead whale, they will stop the hunt. In light of the scarcity of such data, it would be unwise and unfair to impose a zero quota. It is clear that the Eskimo culture is seriously stressed. The impacts of western technology are severe. The Native Claims Settlement, the Alaska pipeline, the cash economy, and many western values are in direct conflict with those of subsistence lifestyles. The answer will not consist of perpetuating policies that destroy a way of life, defeat self-reliance, and necessitate unwanted outside support. For when the oil is gone and the pipelines are closed down, what future is in store? David Brower imagines it in *Cry Crisis: Rehearsal in Alaska* (FOE, 1974):

"The North Slope, 1994. A lone caribou tries to pick its way through the maze of small feeder lines, gravel pads, drilling pads, old storage tanks, oil drums, and thawed tundra quagmire, all residue of the collecting net that drained the North Slope oil quickly, in the name of national security and self-sufficiency. The oil is gone, the wells have died. The "poor boys" could not afford to stay in Alaska, much less shut the wells. A mile away, on the porch of an arctic ghost town, an Eskimo man looks up from his newspaper to see the caribou against the skyline. He looks longingly after it. The Eskimo is youngish still and strong, though a little lean now, and with strangely vacant eyes. His small son sees the caribou too, and watches the animal as it makes its way through the obstacle course.

"Scattered in the street below, rusting where they died, are the remains of snowmobiles. Across the street are the ruins of a filling station, with a sign posted on one of the pumps: "Out of gas. Out of oil, too." The paper on the Eskimo's lap, folded neatly to a back page, is the *Fairbanks News-Miner*, very thin and two months old. (The plane does not call as often as it once used to.)

"The boy looks from the caribou to his father. The Eskimo feels his son's questioning eyes on him, but pretends not to. He is trying desperately to remember what he heard from old people about hunting caribou. He cannot. He is as ignorant of that as he is of driving dog teams. It's all like one of those memories of a previous life."

Case IV: Endangered Species vs. "Progress"

How can wildlife be protected and the rapid disappearance of species be stopped? Some basic steps are necessary:

The land is one organism. Its parts, like our own parts, compete with each other and cooperate with each other. The competitions are as much a part of the inner working as the cooperations. Only those who know the most about it can appreciate how little is known about it. The last word in ignorance is the man who says of an animal or plant: 'What good is it?' If the land mechanism as a whole is good, then every part is good, whether we understand it or not. If the biota, in the course of eons, has built something we like but do not understand, then who but a fool would discard seemingly useless parts? To keep every cog and wheel is the first precaution of intelligent tinkering.

—ALDO LEOPOLD

(1) Broaden public concern for large and attractive animals such as whales, mountain lions, and eagles, to include the more difficult task of protecting *all* species. Avoid trying to choose whom to share the planet with: every species has its own right to live and is part of the health and stability of its entire ecosystem.

(2) Protect the ecosystem rather than try to manage single species. Complex interdependencies exist within ecosystems. The extinction of one plant, insect, or minnow may not have repercussions on the rest of the system, but there is no certainty about this. Too little is known. The more we learn, the more we see how well stable ecosystems can handle weather, pests, and the recycling of energy and nutrients.

(3) Promote understanding of endangered species, now far too limited. According to a recent study, only one American in four knew that a manatee was not an insect. Fewer than one in five were familiar with the controversy over the Tellico Dam and the snail darter. Ignorance of this kind leads people to contend that protecting endangered species gets in the way of progress. A public that is aware of the fact that human survival is inextricably tied to the proper functioning of large ecosystems will insist that resource development be ecologically sound. Until then, clashes between those who would protect life-support systems (including wildlife) and those who develop resources will continue to intensify. The Endangered Species Act, the most substantive of the legislation that protects wildlife and it habitat, suffered weakening amendments in 1978 and 1979. The Marine Mammal Protection Act and the Marine Sanctuaries Act can be expected to face attack too. It is essential that they remain strong.

(4) Halt the willful consignment of any species to extinction—what might be called the "Bakerizing of a species" in memory of Senator Baker's deliberately pushing the snail darter over the brink in the Tellico Dam controversy. What had once been more than 2,000 miles of the Tennessee River had been eliminated, stretch by stretch, by dams built by the TVA. The last unspoiled stretch, and the last remaining habitat of the endangered snail darter, disappeared when the Tellico Dam project was exempted from all legal restraints (including the Endangered Species Act, the National Environmental Policy Act, the Fish and Wildlife Coordination Act, the Historic Preservation Act, and the Clean Waters Act). Proponents of the project argued that a $120 million energy-producing project should not be held up by a useless minnow.

Congress, at Senator Baker's urging, passed the exemption even though the review committee established to weigh conflicts between development and species protection had unanimously recommended that the dam not be built, even though income produced by the dam had been shown to be less than its maintenance costs, even though the dam would have no electrical generating capacity, and even though experimental attempts to transplant the snail darter to other habitats failed in two out of three instances. Despite all this, Congress exempted the Tellico project and the floodgates were lowered in November 1979.

Biologist Paul Ehrlich commented: "The extermination of this small fish alone will probably not precipitate an ecosystem collapse. But no more purposeful extinctions by humanity can be permitted. A firm line must be drawn *now*. Because sooner or later a Tellico Dam or its equivalent will threaten every population of nonhuman organisms on the face of this planet. Sooner or later, each body of water will be needed as a source or a sink for some human activity that will be lethal to its natural occupants. Perhaps, indeed, every species will be found to occupy a piece of land that could be plowed, grazed, mined, logged, paved, or otherwise disrupted by someone who sees profit in it."

(5) The goal is to protect species in the wild. Captive breeding, gene pools, animal farms, menageries, zoos, pets, and museums can play only a minor role in the protection of wildlife. The major role is the role played by the whole environment. Each species is an expression and a manifestation of the wild place that created and shaped it. The objective is to prevent the danger to endangered species rather than cause it. The answer is not to put condors in captive breeding pens, snail darters in aquaria, or bears in waiting lines for hand-outs. A wild animal without a wild place to live in has lost its miracle. Ultimately, the question is not whether we can "manage" wildlife; the question is, can we man-age our own activity in ways that allow room on the planet for others than ourselves? As Ken Norris points out: "Wildlife management is largely a matter of human management. We talk about managing animals and their environment because it is the easy thing to do. Dealing with our fellow humans and our institutions, on the other hand, can stir up immediate responses, often not very peaceful."

A world in which the only nonhuman species existed by our sufferance or because of our benign neglect is not a world in which most humans would care to live— assuming, indeed, that such a world would be habitable by humans at all. Concern for wildlife is not simple sentimentality; it springs, instead, from the enlightened self-interest of a species that cannot go it alone.

Michael Shandrick

Recommended Actions

☐ The President, or Congressional leaders, should propose legislation based on the premise that whatever is still wild should remain forever wild. Such legislation would apply to areas that may not qualify for formal designation as Wilderness.

☐ Governors, county officials, and municipal leaders should propose similar laws and ordinances within their jurisdictions.

☐ Congress should enact national land-use legislation recognizing that it is more profitable (in a societal sense) to rehabilitate land that humans have already abused than it is to develop "new land"; smaller political jurisdictions should follow suit, prodded by their constituents.

☐ The President should order his Secretary of State to seek worldwide preservation of wildlands and wildlife through the United Nations and its specialized agencies, through other international organizations, through multilateral and bilateral treaties, and through ordinary diplomatic channels.

☐ The President should order his Secretaries of the Interior and of Agriculture to direct the land-management agencies—the Park Service, Forest Service, Bureau of Land Management, and Fish and Wildlife Service, in particular—to make the preservation of wildlife habitat a primary objective; Congress should support presidential initiatives with complementary legislation. (Or Congress should take the initiative and compel, if necessary, presidential acquiescence.)

☐ Congress should pass legislation offering inducements to states and local jurisdictions to preserve wildlife habitats and wildlife, for the local jurisdictions can assess the opportunities for preservation far better than Congress or the Administration can.

☐ Although Congress and the Administration should accept the preservation of wildlife habitat everywhere as a guiding principal, certain critical areas should receive priority consideration. Among these are Antarctica, tropical forests, the Southern Ocean, and the Beaufort Sea. None of these is subject to exclusive US control, but the US does (or can) exercise considerable influence in each case.

☐ The President and the State Department should work to have Antarctica designated a world nature preserve; moreover, the US should ratify the Living Resources Regime of the Antarctic Treaty and insist on limiting the harvest of krill.

☐ Because more than two-thirds of Planet Earth's wildlands lie under saltwater, the Department of State should work for a strong Law of the Seas Treaty to inhibit the unwise exploitation of animate and inanimate marine resources—and the President should urge its ratification by the Senate.

☐ The President should enlist support both from members and non-members of the International Whaling Commission for an indefinite moratorium on commercial whaling.

Ali Pears

☐ The Secretary of the Interior (under presidential orders, if necessary) should cancel oil leases within the migratory path of the bowhead whale in the Beaufort Sea.

☐ The National Oceanic and Atmospheric Administration (NOAA) should expand research on the bowhead whale, enlisting maximum cooperation from the world's foremost experts on the bowhead, Eskimo whalers.

☐ Under provisions of the Packwood-Magnuson Act, the Secretary of Commerce should ban fishing within the US 200-mile zone by countries that violate regulations of the International Whaling Commission.

☐ The President and congressional leaders should urge expansion of the Marine Sanctuaries Program.

☐ Congress should defeat, or the President should veto, any bill that would exempt any federal project from protective laws such as the Endangered Species Act. State and local officials and agencies should similarly resist the waiver of protective laws and ordinances for the enrichment of special interests.

☐ Citizens should discourage the indiscriminate slaughter of nonhuman predators that compete with us for a certain amount of lamb, veal, salmon, or abalone; nonhuman predation promotes the survival of the fittest in accordance with evolutionary laws, while humans tend to degrade the species they prey upon by giving the least fit individuals as great a chance for reproductive success as those who would certainly die without our medications and ministrations. A world without predators and prey would be unthinkable; a world without nonhuman predators would be a world impoverished by our greed not merely to compete successfully, but to eliminate all competition. Only in some myopic eyes would a world without humans seem less desirable than a world in which humans tolerated competition from bears, coyotes, eagles, grasshoppers, mountain lions, sea otters, snails, and

wolves. Maybe it is all right for us to aspire to pre-eminence in nature's scheme, but can it possibly be all right for us to cancel nature's scheme and substitute our own?

☐ Citizens should discourage eradication of plants and killing of animals for anything less than subsistence purposes; if killing appeals to you as sport, at least eat the flesh and utilize everything but the squeal.

☐ Citizens should refrain from buying furs, skins, or other products derived from carcasses of wild animals, whose pelts must have felt better on the animals they grew on.

Giant otter, in captivity. Photo by D.W. Golobitsch.

More Thoughts on Wildlife

OF ALL MARINE ANIMALS, whales and dolphins have been the most conspicuous in literature and remain the most exciting to watch. They are superbly adapted to their world and are living indicators of its health. If their well-being is assured, then ocean life is likely to be secure. When the cetaceans are in danger, the ocean is too, and so is all life, including our own.

It is hard to imagine any natural danger to the great whales throughout the era preceding history except time, the enemy of all living things that follow the sexual route to diversity and continuity of line. But cetaceans have contended with time successfully.

Throughout all but the last moments of their evolution, whales never met with any natural phenomenon like man. When they met him, according to Melville and others, they resisted him. The day after Captain Scammon took two gray whales on the first day in his lagoon, whales that could not avoid his boats promptly turned and attacked them, and were thereupon called devilfish. Young whales still approach boats until warned by their mothers that it is unwise to address strangers. Fear of man seems to have been learned by cetaceans, not acquired by instinct.

Our own times can bring a change. The blue whale has now become the symbol of a world-wide movement to reverse the processes of environmental destruction. The gray whale's recovery is a fine example of how past wrongs can be righted by decisive protective action. But the bare survival of the right whale, the humpback, and the blue, even under protection, serves as a grim warning that the damage caused by the ignorant or wanton may not be reversible.

The heart of the matter, however, is that whaling is by no means the only threat to whales. Pollution is another. Oil spills do not help. Baltic seals abort their pups from excess of PCBs; perhaps dolphins do too. Whales entering the Mediterranean are likely to be badly burned by chemical wastes. Dumped radioactivity, explosives, and chemical weapons must surely affect the deep-living species, such as the bottlenose and sperm whales. Fishing is an immediate and perhaps greater threat. Seals, dugongs, dolphins, and whales get entangled in fishing nets and drown. Joanna Gordon Clark has predicted, in considering the proposed krill fishery in the Antarctic, that if the fishery really gets going, baleen whales may be classed as pests. All over the world, fishermen and even navies are out gunning for marine mammals: for dolphins off Greece and Japan, for sea lions frolicking in ringe-nets off Southern Africa, for orcas in the North Atlantic. Fishing could also, in the long run, reduce food supply so much as to prevent whales from recovering from previous depletion. Oceanaria are a danger. To catch one orca for exhibition may mean that several are killed or detrimentally harassed.

No single threat need be fatal, but together the threats may well be. The dangers stem from the triumph of what Ray Dasmann calls the Biosphere People, who live within the limits of their own.

One good thing about keeping orcas, belugas, and dolphins in tanks for our amusement is that it helps us see how fast they can learn when they choose to. Helpful too have been those few adventurous souls who in recent years have jumped into the sea with them, and with humpbacks too, to see what people can learn, when they choose to, about what cetaceans have known so long. This knowing leads to a search that may provide what Donald Griffin calls "a window on the minds of animals," and may tell us something about how they feel, sense, and think. It may contribute remarkably to reintegrating ourselves with the rest of the natural world from which we were becoming alien, and lead to one of the most exciting adventures on which man has ever embarked.

—Sidney Holt

World fisheries present an instructive, readily measured example of what happens when too much if demanded of a food-producing ecosystem. —ERIK ECKHOLM

WHAT STRIKES ME in our society is the literal veneration with which we surround certain syntheses of high complexity and uniqueness. I mean the works of great artists—painters, sculptors, musicians. To contain them we build museums, which are akin to the temples of other societies. We would think it disastrous, a universal catastrophe, if the entire works of Rembrandt or of Michelangelo were to be destroyed. We would feel—quite rightly, of course—that something irreplaceable had gone.

But when it comes to those infinitely more complex and infinitely more irreplaceable syntheses which are living species, whether plants or animals, we act completely irresponsibly, quite casually. It's just possible to imagine that if the entire *oeuvre* of Rembrandt disappeared, another painter might appear whose work would, in a different way, succeed in filling that void—a purely theoretical hypothesis. On the other hand it is totally (and, this time, I would say metaphysically) out of the question that a vanished plant or animal species could be replaced by an equivalent species on the time-scale of human existence.

I have often been accused of being "anti-humanist", but I don't believe it is true. What I have stood out against, and what I regard as being deeply harmful, is that kind of humanism run riot which derives (on the one hand) from the Judeo-Christian tradition and (on the other, and closer to ourselves) from the Renaissance and from Cartesianism, which makes man into a master, and absolute lord of creation.

I have the feeling that all the tragedies we have lived through—first with Colonialism, then Fascism, then the Nazi Extermination Camps—all of that counts not against or in contradiction to the alleged humanism we have practised for several centuries, but I would say rather as its natural extension. Because in some way it was one and the same impulse—it made man start by tracing between himself and the other living species the frontier of his own rights—and then go on to shift the frontier inside the human race, separating certain categories, recognised as the "only truly human" ones, from others which then undergo a demotion determined on the same lines as those used to discriminate between humans and nonhuman living species. Here is the true original sin that drives humanity to its own destruction.

Respect for one's fellow men cannot be based on certain special dignities that humanity claims for itself as such, because then one fraction of humanity will always be able to decide that it embodies those dignities in some pre-eminent manner. We should rather assert at the outset a sort of *a priori* humility. If he started by respecting all forms of life in addition to his own, man would be shielded against the risk of not respecting all forms of life within humanity itself.

—Claude Levi-Strauss

Drawing by Ed Koren © THE NEW YORKER, INC.

"Great news! 'Tarzan' is out in paperback!"

THE CABIN had not been occupied for years. We intended to clean it out and live in it, but there were holes in the roof and the birds had come in and were roosting in the rafters. You could depend on it in a place like this where everything blew away, and even a bird needed some place out of the weather and away from coyotes. A cabin going back to nature in a wild place draws them till they come in, listening at the eaves, I imagine, pecking softly among the shingles till they find a hole, and then suddenly the place is theirs and man is forgotten.

Well, I got the door open softly and I had the spotlight all ready to turn on and blind whatever birds there were so they couldn't see to get out through the roof. I had a short piece of ladder to put against the far wall where there was a shelf on which I expected to make the biggest haul. I had all the information I needed, just like any skilled assassin. I pushed the door open, the hinges squeaking only a little. A bird or two stirred—I could hear them—but nothing flew and there was a faint starlight through the holes in the roof.

I padded across the floor, got the ladder up and the light ready, and slithered up the ladder till my head and arms were over the shelf. Everything was dark as pitch except for the starlight at the little place back of the shelf near the eaves. With the light to blind them, they'd never make it. I had them. I reached my arm carefully over in order to be ready to seize whatever was there and I put the flash on the edge of the shelf where it would stand by itself when I turned it on. That way I'd be able to use both hands.

Everything worked perfectly except for one detail— I didn't know what kind of birds were there. I never thought about it at all, and it wouldn't have mattered if I had. My orders were to get something interesting. I snapped on the flash and sure enough there was a great beating and feathers flying, but instead of my having them, they, or rather he, had me. He had my hand, that is, and for a small hawk not much bigger than my fist he was doing all right. I heard him give one short metallic cry when the light went on and my hand descended on the bird beside him; after that he was busy with his claws and his beak was sunk in my thumb. In the struggle I knocked the lamp over on the shelf, and his mate got her sight back and whistled neatly through the hole in the roof and off among the stars outside. It all happened in fifteen seconds and you might think I would have fallen down the ladder, but no, I had a professional assassin's reputation to keep up, and the bird, of course, made the mistake of thinking the hand was the enemy and not the eyes behind it. He chewed my thumb up pretty effectively and lacerated my hand with his claws, but in the end I got him, having two hands to work with.

He was a sparrow hawk and a fine young male in the prime of life. I was sorry not to catch the pair of them, but as I dripped blood and folded his wings carefully, holding him by the back so that he couldn't strike again, I had to admit the two of them might have been more than I could have handled under the circumstances. The little fellow had saved his mate by diverting me, and that was that. He was born to it and made no outcry now, resting in my hand hopelessly by peering toward me in the shadows behind the lamp with a fierce, almost indifferent glance. He neither gave nor expected mercy and something out of the high air passed from him to me, stirring a faint embarassment.

I quit looking into that eye and managed to get my huge carcass with its fist full of prey back down the ladder. I put the bird in a box too small to allow him to injure himself by struggle and walked out to welcome the arriving trucks. It had been a long day, and camp still to make in the darkness. In the morning that bird would be just another episode. He would go back with the bones in the truck to a small cage in a city where he would spend the rest of his life. And a good thing, too. I sucked my aching thumb and spat out some blood. An assassin has to get used to these things. I had a professional reputation to keep up.

In the morning, with the change that comes on suddenly in that high country, the mist that had hovered below us in the valley was gone. The sky was a deep blue, and one could see for miles over the high outcroppings of stone. I was up early and brought the box in which the little hawk was imprisoned out onto the grass where I was building a cage. A wind as cool as a mountain spring ran over the grass and stirred my hair. It was a fine day to be alive. I looked up and all around at the hole in the cabin roof out of which the other little hawk had fled. There was no sign of her anywhere that I could see.

"Probably in the next county by now," I thought cynically, but before beginning work I decided I'd have a look at my last night's capture.

Secretively, I looked again all around the camp and up and down and opened the box. I got him right out in my hand with his wings folded properly and I was careful not to startle him. He lay limp in my grasp and I could feel his heart pound under the feathers but he only looked beyond me and up.

I saw him look that last look away beyond me into a sky so full of light that I could not follow his gaze. The little breeze flowed over me again, and nearby a mountain aspen shook all its tiny leaves. I suppose I must have had an idea then of what I was going to do, but I never let it come up into consciousness. I just reached over and laid the hawk on the grass.

He lay there a long minute without hope, unmoving, his eyes still fixed on that blue vault above him. It must

DO NOT APPROACH BEING REHABED FOR THE WILD

Bob Clay/Jeroboam, Inc.

have been that he was already so far away in heart that he never felt the release from my hand. He never even stood. He just lay with his breast against the grass.

In the next second after that long minute he was gone. Like a flicker of light, he had vanished with my eyes full on him but without actually seeing even a premonitory wing beat. He was gone straight into that towering emptiness of light and crystal that my eyes could scarcely bear to penetrate. For another long moment there was silence. I could not see him. The light was too intense. Then from far up somewhere a cry came ringing down.

I was young then and had seen little of the world, but when I heard that cry my heart turned over. It was not the cry of the hawk I had captured, for by shifting my position against the sun, I was now seeing farther up. Straight out of the sun's eye, where she must have been soaring restlessly above us for untold hours, hurtled his mate. And from far up, ringing from peak to peak of the summits over us, came a cry of such unutterable and ecstatic joy that it sounds down across the years and tingles among the cups on my quiet breakfast table.

I saw them both now. He was rising fast to meet her. They met in a great soaring gyre that turned to a whirling circle and a dance of wings. Once more, just once, their two voices, joined in a harsh wild medley of question and response, struck and echoed against the pinnacles of the valley. They were gone forever somewhere into those upper regions beyond the eyes of men.

—Loren Eiseley

I DID NOT REALIZE at first what it was that I looked upon. As my wandering attention centered, I saw nothing but two small projecting ears lit by the morning sun. Beneath them, a small neat face looked shyly up at me. The ears moved at every sound, drank in a gull's cry and the far horn of a ship. They crinkled, I began to realize, only with curiosity; they had not learned to fear. The creature was very young. He was alone in a dread universe. I crept on my knees around the prow and crouched beside him. It was a small fox pup from a den under the timbers who looked up at me. God knows what had become of his brothers and sisters. His parent must not have been home from hunting.

He innocently selected what I think was a chicken bone from the untidy pile of splintered rubbish and shook it at me invitingly. There was a vast and playful humor in his face. "If there was only one fox in the world and I could kill him, I would do." The words of a British poacher in a pub rasped in my ears. I dropped even further and painfully away from human stature. It has been said repeatedly that one can never, try as he will, get around to the front of the universe. Man is destined to see only its far side, to realize nature only in retreat.

Yet here was the thing in the midst of the bones, the wide-eyes, innocent fox inviting me to play, with the innate courtesy of its two forepaws placed appealing together, along with a mock shake of the head. The universe was swinging in some fantastic fashion around to present its face, and the face was so small that the universe itself was laughing.

It was not a time for human dignity. It was a time only for the careful observance of amenities written behind the stars. Gravely I arranged my forepaws while the puppy whimpered with ill-concealed excitement. I drew the breath of a fox's den into my nostrils. On impulse, I picked up clumsily a white bone and shook it in teeth that had not entirely forgotten their original purpose. Round and round we tumbled for one ecstatic moment. We were the innocent thing in the midst of the bones, born in the egg, born in the den, born in the dark cave with the stone ax close to hand, born at last in human guise to grow coldly remote in the room with the rifle rack upon the wall.

But I had seen my miracle. I had seen the universe as it begins for all things. It was, in reality, a child's universe, a tiny and laughing universe. I rolled the pup on his back and ran, literally ran for the nearest ridge. The sun was half out of the sea, and the world was swinging back to normal. The adult foxes would be already trotting home.

For just a moment I had held the universe at bay by the simple expedient of sitting on my haunches before a fox den and tumbling about with a chicken bone. It is the gravest, most meaningful act I shall ever accomplish, but, as Thoreau once remarked of some peculiar errand of his own, there is no use reporting it to the Royal Society.
—Loren Eisely

National Park Service photograph

ONCE MAINLY THE concern of animal lovers and bird-watchers, the worldwide loss of species now poses a major ecological and social challenge. If allowed to occur, the massive biological impoverishment projected for the next few decades will change the nature of life on this planet for all time.

At risk, the scientists say, are not just hundreds of familiar and appealing birds and mammals. Examination of the survival prospects of all forms of plant and animal life—including obscure ferns, shrubs, insects, and mollusks as well as elephants and wolves—indicates that huge numbers of them have little future. Not hundreds, but hundreds of thousands of unique, irreplaceable lifeforms may vanish by the century's end.

Within sight is the destruction of plant and animal species, and of the genetic heritage of eons they embody on a scale that dwarfs the combined natural and human-caused extinctions of the previous millions of years. Should this biological massacre take place, evolution will no doubt continue, but in a grossly distorted manner. Such a multitude of species losses would constitute a basic and irreversible alteration in the nature of the biosphere even before we understand its workings—an evolutionary Rubicon whose crossing *Homo sapiens* would do well to avoid.

The overriding conservation need of the next few decades is the protection of as many varied habitats as possible—the preservation of a representative cross section of the world's ecosystems, especially those particularly rich in life forms.

If the world's extant species and gene pools are the priceless heritage of all humanity, then people everywhere need to share the burdens of conservation according to their ability to do so. Not only do people in developed countries share the long-term benefits of tropical conservation, but they also, because of their penchant for consuming tropical agricultural and forest products, share responsibility for tropical ecosystem destruction.

—Erik Eckholm

I SPEND A considerable portion of my time observing the habits of the wild animals, my brute neighbors. By their various movements and migrations they fetch the year about to me. Very significant are the flight of geese and the migration of suckers.... But when I consider that the nobler animals have been exterminated here,—the cougar, panther, lynx, wolverine, wolf, bear, moose, deer, the beaver, the turkey, I cannot but feel as if I lived in a tamed, and, as it were, emasculated country. Would not the motions of those larger and wilder animals have been more significant still? Is it not a maimed and imperfect nature that I am conversant with? As if I were to study a tribe of Indians that had lost all its warriors. Do not the forest and the meadow now lack expression, now that I never see nor think of the moose with a lesser forest on his head in the one, nor of the beaver in the other?

When I think what were the various sounds and notes, the migrations and works, and changes of fur and plumage which ushered in the spring and marked the other seasons of the year, I am reminded that this, my life in nature, this particular round of natural phenomena which I call a year, is lamentably incomplete. I listen to a concert in which so many parts are wanting. The whole civilized country is to some extent turned into a city, and I am that citizen whom I pity. Many of those animal migrations and other phenomena by which the Indians marked the season are no longer to be observed.

I seek acquaintance with Nature,—to know her moods and manners. Primitive Nature is the most interesting to me. I take infinite pains to know all the phenomena of the spring, for instance, thinking that I have here the entire poem, and then, to my chagrin, I hear that it is but an imperfect copy that I possess and have read, that my ancestors have torn out many of the first leaves and grandest passages, and mutilated it in many places. I should not like to think that some demigod had come before me and picked out some of the best stars. I wish to know an entire heaven and an entire earth.

—Henry David Thoreau

AT DAYBREAK I am the sole owner of all the acres I can walk over. It is not only boundaries that disappear, but also the thought of being bounded. Expanses unknown to deed or map are known to every dawn, and solitude, supposed no longer to exist in my country, extends on every hand as far as the dew can reach.

Like other great landowners, I have tenants. They are negligent about rents, but very punctilious about tenures. Indeed at every daybreak from April to July they proclaim their boundaries to each other, and so acknowledge, at least by inference, their fiefdom to me.

This daily ceremony, contrary to what you might suppose, begins with the utmost decorum. Who originally laid down its protocols I do not know. At 3:30 a.m., with such dignity as I can muster of a July morning, I step from my cabin door, bearing in either hand my emblems of sovereignty, a coffee pot and notebook. I seat myself on a bench, facing the white wake of the morning star. I set the pot beside me. I extract a cup from my shirt front, hoping none will notice its informal mode of transport. I get out my watch, pour coffee, and lay notebook on knee. This is the cue for the proclamations to begin.

At 3:35 the nearest field sparrow avows, in a clear tenor chant, that he holds the jackpine copse north to the riverbank, and south to the old wagon track. One by one, all the other field sparrows within earshot recite their respective holdings. There are no disputes, at least at this hour, so I just listen, hoping inwardly that their womenfolk acquiesce in this happy accord over the status quo ante.

Before the field sparrows have quite gone the rounds, the robin in the big elm warbles loudly his claim to the crotch where the icestorm tore off a limb, and all appurtenances pertaining thereto (meaning, in this case, all the angleworms in the not-very-spacious subjacent lawn).

The robin's insistent caroling awakens the oriole, who now tells the world of orioles that the pendant branch of the elm belongs to him, together with all fiber-bearing milkweed stalks nearby, all loose strings in the garden, and the exclusive right to flash like a burst of fire from one of these to another.

My watch says 3:50. The indigo bunting on the hill asserts title to the dead oak limb left by the 1936 drought, and to diverse nearby bugs and bushes. He does not claim, but I think he implies, the right to out-blue all bluebirds, and all spiderworts that have turned their face to the dawn.

Next the wren—the one who discovered the knot hole in the eave of the cabin—explodes into song. Half a dozen other wrens give voice, and now all is bedlam. Grosbeaks, thrashers, yellow warblers, bluebirds, vireos, towhees, cardinals—all are at it. My solemn list of performers, in their order and time of first song, hesitates, wavers, ceases, for my ear can no longer filter out priorities. Besides, the pot is empty and the sun is about to rise. I must inspect my domain before my title runs out.

We sally forth, the dog and I, at random. He has paid scant respect to all these vocal goings-on, for to him the evidence of tenantry is not song, but scent. Any illiterate bundle of feathers, he says, can make a noise in a tree. Now he is going to translate for me the olfactory poems that who-knows-what silent creatures have written in the summer night. At the end of each poem sits the author—if we can find him. What we actually find is beyond predicting: a rabbit, suddenly yearning to be elsewhere; a woodcock, fluttering his disclaimer; a cock pheasant, indignant over wetting his feathers in the grass. . . .

I can feel the sun now. The bird-chorus has run out of breath. The far clank of cowbells bespeaks a herd ambling to pasture. A tractor roars warning that my neighbor is astir. . . . We turn home, and breakfast.

—Aldo Leopold

"What surprised me was not that we're endangered species, but that we're snail darters."

Homo sapiens, a single species, threatens the survival of the countless thousands of plant and animal species through its numbers and activities. The addition of three-quarters of a billion people to the world's population over the last decade has, in many regions, upset the balance between human, plant, and animal life. The very size of the human population is altering natural environments: rural habitats are urbanized, forests are turned into farmland. The chemical wastes from manufacturing and commerce, and the widespread use of pesticides and fertilizers to improve nature's productivity threaten to break the life cycles of many species.

The process of extinction is not solely an aesthetic problem. Many plants and animals are vitally important to human well-being. Plankton form the crucial foundation of the ocean food chain, but oceanic pollution is growing faster than man's ability even to analyze its effects, much less control it.

It is difficult to predict which plants might prove helpful to man in the future. The cinchona tree of Latin America was considered useless until it was discovered that quinine, which can be extracted from it, effectively suppresses malaria.

It is tragically ironic that in many countries where increases in agricultural production are most needed, population growth is even now destroying important native plant species. At a time when millions of dollars are being spent to develop food crops that can be grown in the Andes or in desert environments, the world can little afford the loss of those species that have already adapted to harsh habitats.

The risk to man posed by the extinction of plant and animal species cannot be easily quantified. When extinction is a slow natural process, human beings and the environment can adjust. As more and more species are jeopardized by man's increased numbers and ecologically disruptive activities, the odds mount that the complex web of life that supports man may be dangerously and irrevocably disrupted.

—Lester Brown, Patricia McGrath, and Bruce Stokes

Eyes of the Yanomamo

KENNETH BROWER

IF MANKIND PERSISTS on his present course, between 500,000 and 2,000,000 of Earth's plant and animal species will become extinct by the year 2000—their departure not God's work, but our own. So predicts an early draft of Global 2000, a study commissioned by President Carter. The study was supposed to have been published in 1978, but it has been delayed, perhaps because its news is so bad.

Numbers like 500,000 and 2,000,000 are difficult to grasp simply as arithmetic. The enormity of a biological loss on that scale is even harder to come to grips with.

A few years ago, the Bronx Zoo attempted to give some sort of shape to extinction. "This red symbol," reads a sign at the entrance, "calls attention to endangered species. Look for it around the Bronx Zoo. And think about what it means—the final emptiness of extinction." We have yet to build, anywhere on Earth, the zoo big enough to house all the creatures now slated for oblivion. Imagine that zoo. Our present zoological gardens can be depressing places, but they would have nothing on the nearly endless avenues, moats, cells, howls, growls, grunts, sniffles, shrieks, chirps, drummings, trumpetings, and ceaseless caged wall-to-wall pacing of that zoo of red symbols. Your feet would get sore walking the miles of it, to say nothing of your heart.

Of course, some hearts would be fine. There are those who argue that extinction is not so lamentable. Species come and species go, and have done so since the beginning of life, they point out. Look at the big die-off at the end of the Pleistocene! These things happen. Strong animals—and man is proving to be the strongest—fill the niches of weak animals; it's in the natural order of things.

It might give these good Darwinists pause to realize that the red symbol stands now beneath the figurative cages of a number of *human* tribes. All over this planet, mini-races of Homo sapiens are regularly slipping into non-existence. Sometimes fighting, sometimes no longer caring, they lose their grip on the edge and drop into the great worse-than-cold of extinction.

Nowhere are more of us departing than in Brazil. In 1500, when Pedro Alvares Cabal first set foot there, the Indian population of that land was between six and nine million. Today 200,000 survive, an attrition rate of 2½ million per century. Part of that die-off has been the result of diseases accidentally introduced, but much of it has been, and continues to be, deliberate genocide. In 1900 there were 230 known tribes of Brazilian Indians. At last count, in 1957, there were 143. There are fewer now in 1980, and by the year that Global 2000 anticipates, there are certain to be fewer still.

In this century, in Amazonia alone, more than 90 whole *peoples* have exited the planet. More than 90 cosmologies have gone, more than 90 world-views, more than 90 ways of saying "hello" and "thanks" and "please pass the anaconda."

It is true that all men are brothers; it is also true, as anyone who has lived outside his own culture knows, that we are all alien. The Yanomamo Indians, an endangered tribe living on the Brazil-Venezuela border, do not, when looking out of the dark, vaguely oriental eyes in their painted faces, see the same planet we see. Yanomamo eyes, after millenia of peering into the muted green of the rain forest and squinting down the barrels of blowguns, have evolved a Yanomamo way of seeing. Yanomamo shamans, like those of many Brazilian tribes, use psychedelic drugs. The visions of those shamans are far stranger than any in Carlos Castaneda's Don Juan books, for those are simply the imaginings of one of us.

It is odd, or perhaps not odd at all, that as Western civilization destroys real societies—whole, self-contained worlds—in Brazil and elsewhere, one of its literary crazes has been the creation of whole, self-contained imaginary worlds complete with their own societies and languages. Our Tolkiens and Le Guins and Huxleys can't manufacture fictional worlds at the rate actual ones are disappearing.

We have no way of even guessing at how much we're losing in the way of human experience and lore and wisdom. We do know one talent that we are losing. The

Kenneth Brecker

only people who have ever figured out how to live in the dense, stifling, treacherous, fragile jungle of the Amazon Basin are the Indians there. Scheme after scheme for the exploitation and habitation of Amazonia has failed after encountering some new reality about that region's tricky ecosystem, a reality the indigenes likely knew for centuries.

"Since the Amazon jungle is the most complex, richest, and least understood ecosystem in the world, the Amerindians' knowledge of it is of inestimable value," write Robert Goodland and Howard Irwin. "We remain in abject ignorance of the identity, location, and mode of use of myriad Indian drug plants, cures for specific ailments, contraceptives, abortifacients, arrow poisons, and fish-stunning substances. Our ignorance of seasonality, migration and succession in the jungle is almost total."

Is there a drug-wise tribe on some backwater of the Amazon whose people never die of cancer? Perhaps we should let them grow old enough to find out. *Was* there once such a tribe? That we'll never know.

"At the present moment, a silent war is being waged against the aboriginal peoples, innocent peasants, and the rain forest ecosystem in the Amazon Basin," writes Shelton Davis. This is not hyperbole. If anything, it's understatement, for the war is not always silent. The war is being conducted by the Brazilian government and by the private sector of that country, both of which have been responsible for bombing Indian villages and finishing off the survivors with guns or by passing out infected clothing and arsenic-laced sugar. It is being financed by the World Bank, whose loan made possible the 5000-kilometer Transamazonica Highway, which has invaded the territories of the Juruna, Parakana, Arara, Asurini, and Kararao Indians, among others. Flying cover for the invasion was Earth Satellite Corporation and Litton Industries/Westinghouse Corporation, which provided aerophotometric studies for the highway. The war is being prosecuted by USAID, whose grant helped push the Santarem-Cuiaba Highway through the Xingu Indian National Park, and by the U.S. Geological Survey, Swift-Armour King Ranch, Volkswagen of Brazil, Overseas Private Investment Corporation, Fiat, Komatsu, and Eaton Corporation, among others, all of whom in one way or another invaded the territories of the Caiapo, Kaapor, Xicrin-Kayapo, Pianokoto-Tirio, Warikyana-Arikena, and Parukoto-Tirio tribes, among others.

On the frontiers, it's a way of skirmishes. The Arara of the state of Para, for example, first met white men—jaguar hunters—in the 1960s. The jaguar hunters attacked them and fed them poisoned candy. They fled into the jungle and were rarely seen again until the Transamazonica was punched through their land, at which, dwindling rapidly from disease, they fled again.

The Parakana, another tribe in Para, had its women raped first by Transamazonica construction workers, starting in 1970, then by the National Indian Foundation agents sent to aid them. In 1972 a Brazilian doctor diagnosed venereal disease in 35 Parakena women and two National Indian Foundation agents. And so on and so on. The skirmishes in sum become genocide.

Isn't it strange that our environmental organizations spend so much energy in saving a small, drab animal like the snail darter and so little in saving a big, bright-painted creature like the Yanomamo? Isn't it odd that our Jewish organizations, so skillful at keeping alive the memory of their holocaust, haven't done better at making the empathetic leap into the skins—the foreskins, even—of those jungle tribes presently suffering a holocaust of their own?

There are signs that our indifference is changing. In spring of 1979, a group of citizens in Sao Paulo formed the Committee for the Creation of the Yanomamo Indian Park. They are pressuring their government to form a 16-million-acre park for that largest of surviving Brazilian tribes. In Canada, the World Council of Indigenous Peoples is in the process of organizing itself. In New York, Survival International, a London-based outfit concerned with tribal peoples all over the world, has been operating out of a small Fifth Avenue office for a year. In Boston, the Anthropology Resource Center serves as an information clearing house.

"For years the wire services have been carrying stories," says Shelton Davis of Anthropology Resource Center. "'Another Indian Tribe Destroyed along the Highway.' It sort of becomes a filler. With the Yanomamo Park, we're really beginning to do something about it."

"We don't like to speak in terms of successes," says Judith Tucker of Survival International. "The problem is complex and long term. The fact that a tribe manages to survive for a couple of years doesn't mean

As we lengthen and elaborate the chain of technology that intervenes between us and the natural world, we forget that we become steadily more vulnerable to even the slightest failure in that chain. The time has long since passed when a citizen can function responsibly without a broad understanding of the living landscape of which he is inseparably a part. —PAUL SEARS

they'll survive forever. But one of the first projects that Survival International undertook was with a small group of Indians in Colombia, the Andoke, and it worked. The Andoke were living in debt bondage to a rubber planter there. They needed $1000 to buy themselves out of bondage and buy their own tools. We raised it. It illustrates that in some cases you don't need huge resources to help."

To the social Darwinists, the fate of the forest tribes may seem unfortunate, but just one of those things. He is the sort of dullard who has to send to know for whom the bell tolls. He needs to summon from somewhere the imagination to take a walk through that zoo of red symbols; past all the cages; past the golden feline eyes with their vertical pupils; past the multiple eyes of the insects; past the lizard eyes mounted like periscopes; past the kindly anthropoid eyes of the *orangutan*, the "jungle man" named so by the Dayaks of Borneo; past the brown eyes of the Dayaks themselves, endangered, along with the ape, by the relentless logging of Borneo's rain forest; past the Amazonian eyes of the Xavante and the Xicrin-Kayapo, to the cage on the end, where the eyes looking out are his own.

Is there a doubt whether a common government can embrace so large a sphere?
Let experience solve it . . . It is well worth a fair and full experiment.
—GEORGE WASHINGTON

The United Nations and World Order

The United Nations Charter enshrines the principle of absolute national sovereignty, which is another way of saying it enshrines anarchy. For absolute sovereignty and anarchy both consist, essentially, in refusing to acknowledge any authority higher than one's own. Despite its congenital defects and the contempt in which many hold it, however, the United Nations has many important achievements to its credit. It has encouraged decolonization; it has, in many cases, secured more humane treatment of individuals and minorities by their own national governments; it has helped eradicate diseases and has relieved the plight of disaster victims; it has convoked a series of conferences, beginning with the 1972 Stockholm Conference on the Human Environment, that compelled all nations to confront vital problems; and it has prevented or shortened wars. Indeed, we cannot be certain that without the UN's moderating influence, World War III would not have broken out. When all is said and done, however, the UN depends wholly upon voluntary cooperation by member-states whose assertions of absolute national sovereignty amount to a warning that cooperation may be withheld at any time. There is a move afoot within the UN to amend and strengthen its Charter. The official US reaction to date has been negative. This is a national disgrace. Had not the similarly defective Articles of Confederation been succeeded by the US Constitution in 1789, we would not have survived as a nation long enough to celebrate our bicentennial.

The United Nations

MILDRED R. BLAKE

THE UNITED NATIONS IS a great but obsolescent institution that does not fit the world it was designed to protect. From the beginning in 1945, it has always been precariously balanced on several mistaken and impractical assumptions:

1. That its major task of peacekeeping can rest on the unanimous action of the great powers (the permanent members of the Security Council);
2. That the most serious problems facing mankind are international disputes;
3. Than an annual meeting of diplomats, with equal votes for all nations, the majority of them small and powerless (the General Assembly), can deal effectively with international and world affairs;
4. That important international disputes will be submitted to a World Court, even though all parties must first consent, and that without enforcement power anywhere in the whole system, a World Court's decisions will be obeyed;
5. That recommendations from such faulty and weakly-constructed institutions can substantially affect the actions of major powers, or manage the vital problems of mankind;
6. That while unregulated national sovereignty is obviously the chief stumbling block to world peace and sane planetary management, it is both sacred and monolithic; that it cannot be regulated, or divided between internal and world affairs, without loss to the individual citizen's freedom and influence.

Nevertheless, while laboring under all these plainly false assumptions, the United Nations has important accomplishments to its credit.

Some Peacekeeping Achievements

The United Nations has prevented, concluded, or stalemated several minor wars, which might have become major, as in the Congo, Cyprus, and the Middle East. In so doing, it has invented and proved viable the international peacekeeping force, demonstrating that fears about language difficulties and struggles over command were groundless.

Colonialism Ended

The UN has encouraged, and in some cases presided over, the elimination of colonial domination throughout the world, so that in only a few places outside the communist dictatorships are populations of size and conscious discontent living under the domination of alien masters.

Standards Raised on Human Rights

The UN has set higher standards for government treatment of the individual and of minorities through its Human Rights Declaration, so that such ancient evils as slavery, torture, and systematic racial discrimination are no longer openly practiced in most of the world.

Health Promoted, Disasters Relieved

Through its specialized agencies, the UN has carried on philanthropic enterprises of unprecedented scope and success. For example, it has announced the complete and final eradication of smallpox, which made its last stand in the highlands of Ethiopia. Thus ends an agelong scourge whose threat no national effort could ever completely remove. Earthquake, famine, and the distress caused by war, persecution, and economic dislocation have all been mitigated by UN action.

Fairer Distribution of Wealth

The UN has proposed a "New Economic Order" to make new arrangements for world trade favorable to poor countries, reduce world unemployment, and prevent exploitive or corrupt practices by transnational corporations. There has been recognition that this program necessitates some reorienting of the UN's own Development Program to reach poorer populations, not just ruling classes, in developing countries. Fulfillment of this ambitious project depends, like peace and progress generally, on a new world *political* order providing for the processes of compromise and agreed-upon enforcement.

Conferences on Planetary Problems

Perhaps most significant of all UN actions in the last decade is the series of special conferences set up to deal with rising dangers to mankind and all life on this planet, dangers fully as menacing and lethal as war. Of these conferences, the most successful, and an example for those that have followed, was the Conference on the Human Environment in Stockholm, June 1972.

Where previously environment was of minor importance to most governments, today there are few important nations that do not have government ministries or agencies to handle environmental problems. The UN's favorable influence, however, has been dimmed by the fact that its new Environment Programme (UNEP) has never been properly funded and has been much pressured to turn its small funds to the ends of development rather than to its appropriate tasks of preservation, restoration, and monitoring of the Earth's water, air, soil, minerals, plants, and animals.

Under UNEP's aegis, concern for the polluted Mediterranean finally produced protocols signed by 12 nations at Barcelona in 1976 to clean up and prohibit pollution and dumping, but as usual, lack of united enforcement has minimized results.

A Long List of World Crises

Other UN conferences on world problems of equal gravity have been the Population Conference at Bucharest, which seems to have alerted the Chinese and perhaps others to their overpopulation perils, the Food Conference in Rome, and the (more or less at a standstill) Law of the Sea Conference. Others have included the 1975 Conference for the International Woman's Year, followed by conferences on human settlements, the world's water supplies, the problem of expanding deserts, and the effects of science and technology (foremost of which must be counted nuclear proliferation and the arms race).

The World's Real Business

At a glance, it can be seen that the range of problems presented at these world conferences are the world's real business. They simply dwarf the sputtering belligerence, the name-calling, the generally disregarded resolutions (whether censorious or bland) of the General Assembly.

In the light of perils to the whole of humanity and the livability of planet Earth, most of the Assembly's headline-making agenda looks to be taken up with old, mutually-damaging regional feuds. Much of the oratory is based on the shibboleths of back-home foreign offices rather than hope of persuasion.

A Void of New Ideas

In fact, only a few UN resolutions produce division. Scores are passed by consensus or without objection. Most of these are also void of fertile new ideas. They endorse what everyone endorses, and condemn the man-eating sharks that everyone condemns. Often, it seems that the best thing the Assembly does each year is to authorize real debate—somewhere else. And even there, without united action and enforcement, actual results are painfully small and slow; about all that can be accomplished is to publicize the issues.

A Search for What's Wrong Begins

Beginning in August 1975, and continuing year by year since, a Special Committee on the Charter of the United Nations and Strengthening the Role of the Organization has held a series of meetings. So far, nothing of substance has been produced.

A General Assembly resolution in 1979 called for review of the great-power veto in the Security Council, but it was coupled with so many denunciations of the great powers' "racist regimes, foreign domination, and occupation" that the United States, the Soviet Union, Britain, and France united firmly against it. The veto will naturally never be given up while the General Assembly's one-nation-one-vote structure is so unrepresentative of the real population and power in the world. The Third World has yet to come to grips with this situation.

Meanwhile, the rise of the OPEC powers and the outbreak of terrorist and fanatic lawlessness, challenging what meager "international law" exists, has made every foreign office nervous and uncertain.

Bureaucratese for "Nothing Doing"

The US State Department seems to be mired in inaction and indifference, which it expresses in opaque statements such as "It is not a violation of our duty to think charter review is a bad idea."

Internal and external uneasiness about the UN's future has also spread to the Secretariat and the Secretary-General, who feel obliged to remind the public that the United Nations is not a world government. They no longer invariably add that it should not be, and that the principle of absolute national sovereignty (which guarantees world anarchy) must never, never be given up. Being for the most part intelligent men with some experience in successful administration on behalf of successful governments, they must know quite well what the United Nations lacks: the power to make, adjudicate, and enforce world law. They simply despair of making the world's peoples and their governments willing to provide such power. So they do their best with what they have and do not agitate for more or better.

Only Postponing Catastrophe

What powers the United Nations has, like those of the League of Nations before it, will obviously only postpone, not avert, disaster. Not all of today's threats to human life will materialize, but only one needs to. Without determined, enlightened, and united planetary management, the odds on civilized survival are not good.

Obligations in the Face of Disaster

What then is the obligation of the people and leaders of the nation that is still the most powerful member of the United Nations?

Here is a nation that has celebrated more than 200

International Labour Office

years of *e pluribus unum*. Have we so little Latin that we have forgotten that our national motto means "out of many, one"?

What should it take to apply to the world the principles of "liberty and union, now and forever, one and inseparable"—principles that have worked so long, and on the whole so well, for us?

The Way to Start

We cannot start by asking what other nations would agree to. The first thing to ask is what we of the USA would agree to. *We would not agree to a simple reproduction of today's US-type governmental institutions in the United Nations.* We would not agree even if other nations would accept the US system, which is highly questionable.

The twentieth century has seen too much abuse of the one-man-leader principle for us to accept a world Executive as strong as our Presidency. We ourselves have had a close brush with an attempt by a President to destroy his political opposition and put himself above the law. Moreover, attempts to transfer our system to nations of different political experience, in Latin America, for instance, have not been notably successful.

A World Parliamentary System?

The world as a whole would be more likely to accept the parliamentary system—a prime minister and other ministers rising out of the majority party in the legislative body—and so, it seems probable, would we.

As to a world legislative body, we certainly would not agree to be bound by laws enacted by any body resembling the present unrealistic one-nation-one-vote General Assembly. We would require a body much more representative of population and, certainly at first, of economic contribution. We would require that its powers be strictly confined to matters of worldwide effect and concern. It follows then that the representative unit should be world geographic regions, not nations.

Geographic Regions as Units

Each region should have at least two representatives, voting as individuals and elected at different times. Such a regional Assembly of Peoples might be added to the present General Assembly of Nations, thus producing a familiar institution of a two-house legislative body.

"International disputes" could not be brought into such a legislative body for political tugging and hauling. They would have to be submitted to the jurisdiction of a system of regional, appellate, and superior world courts. Final decisions would be enforceable on individuals, avoiding any attempt at enforcement on

Internationalism does not mean the end of individual nations. Orchestras don't mean the end of violins.

—GOLDA MEIR

nations—just as courts inside nations enforce laws on individuals and so never have to make war on cities, provinces, or states in the name of law-enforcement.

Restrictions on World Power

We would require a World Bill of Rights, guaranteeing all the freedoms we now have and protecting the agreed-upon reserved rights of individuals and of local and national governments from infringement by world institutions or their officers.

Pooled Armament

For some time, we would cautiously insist on maintaining a fairly high level of national armament. Meanwhile, there would be a *pooling* of some armament to make a modest stockpile for reinforcing of world law and world court settlements. But as soon as the new world institutions had proved their ability to operate within their guidelines, our nation and others would naturally begin to cut down on the excesses of overkill that now absorb so much of our national income, disarming eventually to the level required to maintain domestic order.

This is certainly the only way, short of general catastrophe, in which disarmament can come about. People will not give up national power, which they trust (however mistakenly) to protect them, until they have come to trust a worldwide power that has proved it can and will protect them.

How Do We Get There?

If such a thorough revision of the United Nations Charter is to be attained—and nothing much short of that is likely to be adequate to the crises ahead—what should the United States be doing now? For a partial answer to that very large question, see the Recommended Actions that follow.

Recommended Actions

☐ The United States should cease its opposition to Charter review in the Special Committee on the Charter and bring in a bold, constructive plan such as that outlined earlier. The Special Committee is waiting for leadership. The US representative should fill the vacuum at once with a plan that will command worldwide attention.

UN reform is being considered in the Senate and House. The United States should urge all other nations to join in proposing far-reaching revision of the UN Charter or the calling of a new World Constituent Assembly. If a majority of the great, medium-sized, and small nations would work together, the advantages of the resulting institutions would be immense and obvious, and would eventually bring in the others.

☐ The United States should set an example of adequate funding for the UN Environment Programme, urging all other nations to do likewise and using its influence to keep UNEP funds from being diverted to purposes other than environmental protection.

☐ Foreign aid (non-military) and international development loans should be maintained to raise the standard of living of poor countries throughout the world and help finance environmental and population-control programs.

☐ The "New Economic Order" should receive United States attention and cooperation. A rise in world standards of living accompanied by population control is in the interest of the USA as well as the Third World. The climate of Third World opinion is more favorable to proposals from the United States (as of 1980) than it has been for years.

☐ The United States should use all its influence to obtain a strong treaty and Law of the Sea. The world heritage of the oceans, their marine life, and the wealth of the deep ocean bottoms should be protected for all mankind and for future generations. The US's unilateral extension to 200 miles of its national rights offshore is justified for the protection of its coastal waters and fish stocks, but the US should offer to bring its position into conformity with an adequate Law of the Sea treaty.

☐ The United States should support UN action to increase food production in poorer countries, provided that these programs use environmentally sound agricultural practices. This means less dependence on chemical fertilizers and mechanized agribusiness methods, more reliance on natural soil-enrichment and better tools and training for individual rural workers.

☐ The United States should not only support efforts throughout the world to control excess population, this nation should also adopt policies to reduce its own population, at least for a number of decades.

☐ The United States should act to reverse the decay of its own cities, and to halt excessive urban growth both here and abroad by improving the quality and opportunities of rural life. We should not accept as inevitable the fantastic evils of doubling the present world population, nor the migration trends that swamp the cities and destroy the countryside.

☐ The United States should support efforts to improve the status, education, health, and working conditions of women—in much of the world an under-privileged half of the human race. Through subsistence farming, women provide a large part of the labor for the world's food production, and everywhere their equipment, literacy, living standards, sex education, and right to family planning, self-determination, and respect should be brought into the modern age.

☐ Finally, the United States should shake off the indifference toward the UN shown by recent administrations. As President John F. Kennedy said, "If we did not have the United Nations, we would have to invent it." But if we did not quickly reassume our former leadership, with some meaningful and far-reaching reform proposals, we will wake up some day to find that we *do not* have the United Nations. It will be late in the day then to invent it. Perhaps too late to save any of the things that have been most precious to us.

More Thoughts on International Matters

WE ARE PAYING a heavy price for having accepted, "as the best we could get" at San Francisco, a form of world organization which falls far short of the minimum needed. The United Nations can act decisively only when it can obtain unanimity among heavily armed nations which inherently have acute conflicts of interest. There is only the remotest chance of ever getting such unity. Civilization—perhaps the very existence of the human race—depends upon our being willing and able to convert the U.N. promptly from a futile league into a world federal government adequate to maintain peace.

The value of open discussion which can reach no definitive end is grossly exaggerated. Blunt talk under such circumstances is more likely to exacerbate feelings than to relieve tensions. Men in a New England town meeting tend to speak and act responsibly because all are conscious that their deliberations may lead to a decision by which *all* the participants will be equally bound. This element is completely lacking in the General Assembly of the United Nations.

Similarly, discussion within our nations in open forums, on and off the air, operates under awareness that the debates can influence legislative bodies empowered to enact statutory law which is enforceable. This makes a very great difference in the attitudes of the disputants toward debate.

We apply the term "law" to international agreements which are unenforced and unenforceable. We call a world arbitration tribunal a "court," though it lacks compulsory jurisdiction and there is no provision for the enforcement of its decisions. The very name of our world organization contains a specious word. Union is implied by "united," and there is not even a vestige of merged sovereignty in the so-called United Nations. As one contemplates the international scene, the impression mounts that here above all other places is the arena where it is most important to follow the advice of Justice Holmes that we "think *things*, not *words*."

Aversion to the idea of world government arises mainly from two false assumptions. The first is that national governments would be abolished, or entirely subordinated, in the creation of a world state. The second is that nationality would thereby be wiped out. Both fears are baseless. We do not need to end nationalism; we need only modify the present absolute nature of national sovereignty.

The unqualified status of nationalism must be ended, but nations can and should retain complete control over all matters that are exclusively national in scope or character.

The suggestion that the federal form of government seems best suited to the world's need is not a call for a world constitution patterned closely on that of the United States or on any one of the other existing federal systems; it is merely pointing out the remarkable applicability of the principle.

Specifically, the powers of central governments in existing federal systems fall within five categories: citizenship, defense, currency, trade and communications *among* the parts, and a common judicial system. Each citizen of a member state is also a citizen of the whole. The common government assumes responsibility for the security of all and therefore controls all military establishments, armaments, and the like. Each federal union has a common currency; each regulates interstate trade and communications. A supreme court with subsidiary circuit and district courts is maintained for the adjudication of disputes among the parts; the union has power to compel all to use these courts rather than to resort to violence. It is probable that a world government would need no more extensive powers than these; conversely, it will be dangerous to attempt to operate a world authority with any less power.

There is little danger that we shall give a world government too much power. To seek for the minimum adequate powers, and then to provide for these and no more, is certain to be one of the guiding principles of a world constitutional convention. There is far greater danger that we shall transfer too little power to a world government in the first instance, and thus force it to begin its work under the same handicap which now vitiates the United Nations and which doomed the League.

No mysterious, freakish realm is entered as we try to deal with world problems on a global scale. There the same kind of human beings operate and the same types of conflict threaten harmonious relations which we have learned to control or prevent elsewhere. In other areas of life we create and uphold political agencies with authority and power to determine what solutions shall be tried from among those suggested by the experts; we must establish and maintain in essentially the same way in international equivalent of our municipal, state, and national governments. *The world must be governed.*

—Vernon Nash

We have repeatedly expressed our opinion in favor of the development of an international organization or some kind of world government which gives full autonomy to its various national units and which at the same time removes the causes for war and national conflict. —PANDIT NEHRU

OPINIONS VARY widely about the responsibility of the industrialized world to assist third world development, but few would defend policies that inhibit attempts by poor nations to accomplish their own development. If, as poor nations strive to better their lot, we are perceived as outbidding them for scarce resources, conflict is a likely result. How much better to offer developed solar, wind, and geothermal technologies that may be adapted more easily to labor-rich third world countries than to offer capital-intensive nuclear plants or oil-dependent machinery. In any case, eliminating United States fuel imports would help preserve remaining stocks for developing nations.

We have no illusions about any voluntary redistribution of the world's wealth, but this scenario offers the chance for a future profitable to both rich and poor. The alternative may mean confrontation between the rich few and the destitute many.

—John Steinhart, Mark Hanson, Carel DeWinkel, Robin Gates, Kathleen Lipp, Mark Thornsjo, Stanley Kabala

EVERY SOCIETY, global or local, is in part what it is because of the inner history of its own development, and as the twentieth century draws to a close, the global society built up by four centuries of colonialism, two centuries of industrialism, and a few decades of advanced communication and space technology is an extraordinary mixture of the traditional and the unprecedented. It is unprecedented, as we have seen, to abandon the idea of the legitimacy of empire. But it is totally traditional to lapse back into accepting the absolute sovereignty and inward-looking self-interest of individual states. It is unprecedented to set up a global system of institutions, from the Security Council to the latest, humblest recruit to the United Nations family. It is traditional to leave all large decisions to the greatest powers and most smaller ones to local states. It is unprecedented to spend a whole decade within the United Nations system discussing the fundamental issues of the planet's common life—environment, population, food, the role of women, employment, settlements, water, the deserts—as though joint strategies and agreed-upon policies offered the only hope of secure survival. It is traditional to leave the global

system very much unchanged in the meantime, and in practice, if not in rhetoric, to give to virtually only one aspect of global unity the attention which realism commands—that aspect being the world-wide market system largely inherited from the colonial years.

The basic reason for this predominance of world-wide economic connections and interests is of course quite simple. The nations cannot escape from them. Centuries of mutual trade underpin them. The internationalization of investment grows more intense, and with it goes a steady adaptation of new types of production in one set of countries to developing patterns of demand in others. Cumulatively, in spite of political decolonization and bitter ideological disputes, all these threads of economic interdependence—in price, in supply, in services, financing, and management—have woven the continuous fabric of a single planetary economic system. No amount of political rhetoric or wish fulfillment or simple benign neglect can conjure away a bedrock economic reality. The world's economic life has a genuinely and inescapable planetary element. Of virtually no other organized human activity is this even remotely true.

The planet we are creating is one in which no nation, no race, no culture, can escape a truly global destiny. There is no choice about this fact. The only choice available is to recognize it—and to do so in time.

—Barbara Ward

MOST NUMEROUS now are adherents of the specialized-function approach to world problems. A host of issues, highly publicized in recent years, such as environmental pollution, control of multinational corporations, overpopulation, food scarcity, shortages and maldistribution of energy and other depletable resources, and exploitation of the seabed have led to growing clamor for separate world authorities to cope with these intractable subjects. The tendency of these single-problem specialists is to go their isolated ways. And while their pseudo-parliaments of experts perform the careful technical work of a government department preparing important legislation under a parliamentary system, their proposals must go to as many as one hundred thirty-eight governments and must wait months, years, or sometimes forever for ratifications. For enforcement they must rely on the various governments, whose performances may vary from good to bad to none at all. And like the United Nations itself, each of these specialized agencies or authorities must go hat in hand to beg its funding from the member governments. Another nagging problem with such dispersion is that the small, impoverished nations can ill afford the costly disparate representation in these numerous pseudo-parliaments and their growing bureaucracies. This method not only perpetuates the present showy, often wasteful, galaxy of specialized agencies but also has the effect of fragmenting the public pressure needed to attain any substantial transfer of governmental power to the United Nations. Advocates of increasing use of this approach may succeed in getting a little something—to be touted as a mighty triumph—but the overall situation will continue to deteriorate. This piecemeal granting of would-be authority over each separate world problem, commended as the easier approach, has proved a failure. Even a village would find it next to impossible to function if it had first to establish a separate administration over every local concern. Proponents of this method are advocating procedures at the world level they would never tolerate in their own locality.

Today's problems are too large and too pressing to be dealt with by the gradual development of the Charter through amendment and judicial interpretation, as in the case of the United States Constitution. World government—federal and democratic in its own structure—needs to be created fully mature and can profit by the long experience of existing federal practice. Fortunately it can also begin with assets never before available. For example, the vast research capacity of the United Nations and the array of scientific and technical specialists it is able to mobilize have already pinpointed many of the problems, amassed the information, and indicated possible solutions. It is the power to act that now must be combined with all this knowledge.
—Edith Wynner

MAURICE STRONG: Let us just look at the way man himself has developed. We've seen and talked about the Rift Valley. But as man has evolved over this approximately three million years that we know he's inhabited the earth, his loyalties have been gradually enlarged. His willingness to cooperate within larger and larger frameworks has been demonstrated by the fact that he has moved and his loyalties have moved from the family to the tribe to the village to the town to the city to the city-state and now to the nation-state. And each time—this hasn't been because he's suddenly been struck with a wave of idealism; it's because his growing self-interest has required it.

As man has advanced technologically and industrially, the interdependencies of man on man have grown. And if he's going to take advantage of the technological civilization, he's got to enlarge the circle within which he cooperates with other people.

Now, the interesting point here, that as man's loyalties have grown, up to the point of the nation-state, for example, he hasn't had to completely shed his loyalty to his family. You're loyal to your home town. You're loyal to your state. You're loyal to the United States of America. There's no real conflict between this hierarchy of loyalties.

But now we've got to take the ultimate leap, all of us. We've now got to give our loyalty, as well, to planet earth. And this doesn't mean that we give up our loyalty to all the other groupings to which we owe our loyalty. It simply means that we have to modify them. We have to make room for that new dimension of loyalty to planet earth.

MOYERS: Maurice, there is blood being shed in Northern Ireland right now, in the Middle East right now. There are conflict-creating tensions and animosities all over the earth that fly in the face of that leap, because we don't see ourselves as citizens of planet earth. What gives you any hope that this fine statement of a goal that you've set forth has any practical possibilities of realization?

STRONG: It has the practical possibilities simply because it's the only guaranty of survival. We simply must make that leap. There is no alternative to making it, and man all through history has shown that when there is no alternative, he can rise above these petty jealousies.

You know, the changes in man's loyalties that I've described haven't come about easily. They haven't changed the basic nature of man. Man is still aggressive; he's competitive. But when his self-interest does force it, he is prepared to be cooperative.

Now, we may not make it. Perhaps our petty greeds, our petty loyalties, our narrowness of vision, they may possibly consume us. We may not make it. But we certainly won't make it unless we act on the basis that when the chips are down, we will have the guts, we will have the enlightenment, we will have the wisdom to do what is best and what is necessary for us.
—Interview broadcast on
Bill Moyer's Journal

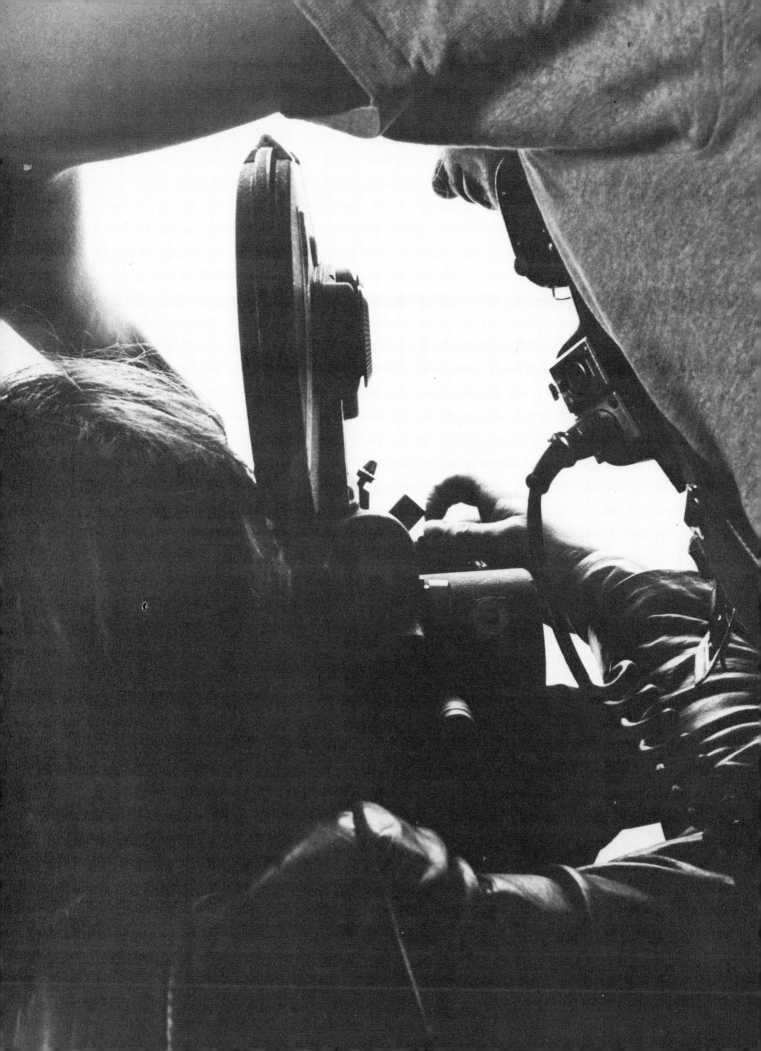

The Media's Conflict of Interests

It is impossible to effect needed social change if the need, the events, and the views for and against aren't reported in the news. If the news media—television, radio, the newspapers and news magazines—fail to report on an event or an idea, the life of communities goes on as if it had not occurred. A free press is vital to the life of a free people, but the media are increasingly guilty of reporting a diminishing amount of the most lively and important of our country's business. The reasons are many. Government interference is usually obvious, always (when recognized) protested against, and frequently driven back. More insidious are the media's own threats to responsible journalism. With fewer newspapers in business every year; television (the most effective medium, if the intellectually thinnest) dominated by show business values; and the remaining outlets being owned by fewer and fewer individuals and corporations, fewer opinions are being expressed, fewer stories are being covered, and there is a growing conspiracy of silence—of which retributions against reporters who do their jobs too well form no small part. The major news organizations fear social ideas and actions, and distort and black out news at the behest of the advertisers who support them. The public's need to know is approaching a tragic confrontation with the press's right to operate without government controls.

Peeter Vilms/Jeroboam, Inc.

Media

JERRY MANDER

The following are excerpts from Four Arguments for the
Elimination of Television, *published by William Morrow
and Company.*

THE FIRST REALLY SHOCKING burst of figures appeared in newspapers in the early 1970s.

It was reported that in the generation since 1945,
99 percent of the homes in the country had acquired at
least one television set. On an average evening, more
than 80 million people would be watching television.

In one generation, out of hundreds of thousands in
human evolution, America had become the first culture to have substituted secondary, mediated versions
of experience for direct experience of the world.
Interpretations and representations of the world were
being accepted as experience, and the difference between the two was obscure to most of us.

Human beings no longer trust personal observation,
even of the self-evident, until it is confirmed by scientific or technological institutions; human beings
have lost insight into natural processes—how the
world works, the human role as one of many interlocking parts of the worldwide ecosystem—because natural processes are now exceedingly difficult to observe.

Most Americans spend their lives within environments created by human beings. This is less the case if
you live in Montana than if you live in Manhattan, but
it is true to some extent all over the country. Natural
environments have largely given way to human-
created environments.

Places formerly as diverse as forest, desert, marsh,
plain and mountain have been unified into suburban
tracts. The human senses, seeking outward for knowledge and stimulation, find only what has been pre-
arranged by other humans.

In many ways the same can be said of rural environments. Land which once supported hundreds of
varieties of plant and animal life has been transformed
by agribusinesses. Insect life has been largely eliminated by massive spraying. For hundreds of square
miles, the only living things are artichokes or tomatoes
laid out in straight rows. The child seeking to know
how nature works finds only spray planes, automated

threshers, and miles of rows of a single crop.

In transforming natural environments into artificial
form, the United States is the most advanced country
in the world. This is not an accident. It is inherent in
our economic system.

To the capitalist, profit-oriented mind, there is no
outrage so great as the existence of some unmediated
nook or cranny of creation which has not been converted into a new form that can then be sold for
money. This is because in the act of converting the
natural into the artificial, something with no inherent
economic value becomes "productive" in the capitalist
sense.

An uninhabited desert is "nonproductive" unless it
can be mined for uranium or irrigated for farms or
covered with tracts of homes.

A forest of uncut trees is nonproductive.

A piece of land which has not been built upon is
nonproductive.

Coal or oil that remains in the ground is nonproductive. Animals living wildly are nonproductive.

Virtually any land, any space, any material, any time
that remains in an original, unprocessed, unconverted
form is an outrage to the sensibilities of the capitalist
mind. Iron, tungsten, trees, oil, sulphur, jaguars and
open space are searched out and transformed because
transformation creates economic benefits for the
transformers.

It is, then, the nature of profit seeking to convert as
much as possible of what has not been processed and
exists in its own right into something which has the
potential for economic gain.

Advertising exists only to purvey what people don't
need. Whatever people do need they will find without
advertising if it is available. This is so obvious and
simple that it continues to stagger my mind that the ad
industry has succeeded in muddying the point.

The only need that is expressed by advertising is the
need of advertisers to accelerate the process of conversion of raw materials with no intrinsic value into commodities that people will buy.

In 1960, at the moment when our economic growth
rate was near its highest point and the nation had been
totally wired in to television, the trade publication

Advertising Age commented, "Network television, particularly, is largely the creature of the 100 largest companies in the country."

In that year, the one hundred largest advertisers in the country accounted for 83 percent of all network television advertising. The top twenty-five of these accounted for 65 percent of the 83 percent. Since that time, the ratio has scarcely altered.

The domination of the one hundred largest is most apparent in network television, but it applies in other media. In 1974, for example, the top one hundred accounted for 55 percent of *all* advertising in all media, 59 percent of all network radio advertising, and 76 percent of network television ads. Since virtually all media in this country depend upon advertising for survival, it ought to be obvious that these one hundred corporations, themselves dominated by a handful of wealthy people, can largely determine which magazines, newspapers, radio stations and television stations can continue to exist and which cannot.

We are speaking of control by 100 corporations out of 400,000. The interest of the other 399,900 are irrelevant as far as television is concerned. As for the thoughts, wishes and feelings of the noncorporate segments of American society—nearly 250 million human beings whose perspectives are as varied as the Indian, the artistic, the humanistic, the ecological, the socialistic, to name a very few—these are not of the slightest importance.

Broadcast television, like other monolithic technologies, from eight-row corn threshers and agribusiness to supertankers, nuclear power plants, computer networks, hundred-story office buildings, satellite communications, genetic engineering, international pipelines and SSTs, is available only to monstrous corporate powers. What we get to see on television is what suits the mentality and purposes of one hundred corporations.

While purporting to be a mass technology available to everyone, because everyone can *experience* it, television is little more than the tool of these companies. If four out of five dollars of television income derive from them, then obviously, without currying their favor the networks would cease to exist.

The corollary is also true. Without such a single, monolithic instrument as television, the effective power and control of these huge corporations could not be harnessed as it presently is. Monolithic economic enterprise needs monolithic media to purvey its philosophy and to influence rapid change in consumption patterns. Without an instrument like television, capable of reaching everyone in the country at the same time and narrowing human needs to match the redesigned environment, the corporations themselves could not exist.

The spread of television unified a whole people within a system of conceptions and living patterns that made possible the expansion of huge economic enterprise. Because of it, our whole culture and the physical shape of the environment, no more or less than our minds and feelings, have been computerized, linearized, suburbanized, freewayized, and packaged for sale.

The Inherent Biases of Television

To have only businessmen in charge of the most powerful mind-implanting instrument in history naturally creates a boundary to what is selected for dissemination to nearly 250 million people. There can be little disagreement with the point that if other categories of people had control, then the choices would be different. If television is a medium of brainwash, then a more diverse brainwash would surely be an improvement over the sort we get at present.

The kind of people who control television is certainly a problem. But this is only the beginning. While our field of knowledge is constrained by their venality and arrogance, the people who run television are constrained by the instrument itself.

Television is no open window through which all perception may pass. Quite the opposite. There are many technological factors that conspire to limit what the medium can transmit. Some information fits and some doesn't. Some information can pass through, but only after being reshaped, redefined, packaged, and made duller and coarser than before. Some ways of mind can be conveyed and some cannot.

The wrinkle in the story is that what *can* be conveyed through television are the ways of thinking and the kinds of information that suit the people who are in control. This is why they like it so much. It is obviously efficient for them to concentrate their communications within a medium that is good at conveying their forms of mind, just as a person with a drive for power is more apt to express that in politics than in gardening. Conversely, it is logical that the medium will not respond well to people or attitudes that defy its limits. It will throw them off, or distort their messages, as a computer would shun anyone who wishes to use it to express feelings of loving tenderness. It might program such a message, but only the words will come out on the tape; not the loving tenderness.

Information Loss

Because of all the preceding it ought to go without saying that any messages that are dependent upon sensory understanding and interaction are not going to work on television.

This is very unfortunate for the ecology movement.

It always surprises me whenever any attempts are made to show wilderness or wildlife on television. The fuzzy image previously described is the first problem: forests become blurs, ocean depths are impossibly foggy, the details of plants are impossible to see. So the viewer depends on the voice-over to know what's going on. Because of the blur, naturalist programs focus on such objective behavior as playing, fighting, mating, eating, just as they do with human sitcoms and soap operas. There are more animal programs than plant programs because animals come through better on the fuzzy medium, and the larger and more rambunctious the animal the better.

But even if TV images were not as coarse as I have described them, there would still be no way to understand a forest or swamp or desert without all the senses fully operative, receiving information in all ranges, and freely interacting with each other.

An interesting recent illustration of the problem was a news feature concerned with a decision that a town council had to make. A land developer sought a permit to convert a large marsh area into a new community of homes. Should the permit be okayed?

It was quite a thoroughgoing, earnest report. Considering the subject, not ordinarily conceived as "good television" by producers, it was also an extraordinarily lengthy report, about eight minutes of an evening newscast.

The report presented interviews with the council members, interviews with the developer, and interviews with a local conservation group that opposed the project. It presented several minutes of images of the plants in the marshland, flocks of birds, nesting grounds, all with the appropriate wild-sounding calls.

Having worked as a publicist for many years, in fact, as a publicist for environmental groups, I knew how much work the environmentalists had to put into this program and how important they felt it to be. In the end, though, I knew they had failed no matter how this particular vote came out, because if there is anything which cannot be conveyed on television it is a feeling for a marsh. I suspected that the result of the program would be to decrease concern for marshes.

The great majority of viewers watching the program had never visited this marsh or any marsh. These images and words about marshes were probably more than they had ever seen or heard before. Since the news report told them interesting things they did not know—how many varieties of creatures lived there, for example—they may have considered it quite a complete story. In terms of popular media, indeed it was. However, while the viewers knew more than before, they were not likely to be aware of what they did not know and were not getting. As the images of the

marsh went hurtling into their brains, accompanied by a news reporter's description of an egret nesting ground, they probably assumed that most of the relevant data were in hand, that they had learned enough to make a judgment.

Images and words about a marsh do not convey what a marsh is. You must actually sense and feel what a strange, rich, unique and *un*human environment it is. The ground is very odd, soft, sticky, wet and smelly. It is not attractive to most humans. The odor emanates from an interaction between the sometimes-stagnant pools and the plants that live in the mud in varying stages of growth and decay. If the wind is hot and strong, there can be a nearly maddening mixture of sweet and rotting odors.

To grasp the logic and meaning of marsh life, the richest biological system on Earth, one needs to put one's hand into the mud, overturn it, discover the tinylife forms that abound. One needs to sit for long hours in it, feeling the ebbs and flows of the waters, the creatures and the winds.

Television cannot capture very much of this. The attempt to push the information through television goes flat. It doesn't work. The viewer is left to evaluate aspects of the experience that television *can* capture, and these reduce to objective facts like the arguments among opposing viewpoints as to the best *use* of the area. People need homes. The developer has a right to profit. The tax base of the community is affected. Meanwhile, the ecologists speak of flyways and breeding grounds, endangered plants and nearly extinct creatures.

A whole world of sensory information has been abandoned, and yet it is in this world that real understanding of marshes exists. And without the understanding who can care about the marsh? Taxes become more important. Birds can be seen elsewhere. Images of mud and reeds do not inspire the mind, especially compared with the hard facts of our world. People need jobs building the houses. Nobody ever "uses" swamps anyway.

It is possible that viewers of that program had a greater feeling for swamps when the swamps resided totally in their imaginations, where, at least, they had the richness that fantasy can create. On television, the fantasy is destroyed and the perspective is flattened.

What was true for this news report is true for all television programs that concern nature. Seeing the forests of Borneo on television makes one believe that one knows something of these forests. What one knows, however, is what television is capable of delivering, a minute portion of what Borneo forests are. It cannot make you care very much about them. When Georgia-Pacific proceeds to cut down hundreds of thousands of acres of Borneo forest, as it has so many

other forests in the Pacific Basin, one remains un-moved. The wood is needed for homes. The objective data dominate when only objective data can be communicated.

Meanwhile, sitting in our dark rooms ingesting images of Borneo forests, we lose feeling even for the forests near our homes. While we watch Borneo forests, we are not experiencing neighborhood forests, *local* wilderness or even *local* parks. As forest experience reduces to television forest, our caring about forests, *any* forest, goes into dormancy for lack of direct experience. And so the lumber company succeeds in cutting down the Borneo forest, and then, near to home, it also succeeds in building a new tract of condominiums where a local park had been.

In my opinion, the more the natural environment is conveyed on TV, the less people will understand about it or care about it, and the more likely its destruction becomes. Ecologists would be wise to abandon all attempts to put nature on television.

During February of 1977, public television carried a National Geographic special, "The New Indians," which was billed as exploring the emerging attitudes among Indian people who, while recovering their civil and political rights, also wish to rediscover and re-affirm the old Indian ways. Robert Redford narrated.

The first five minutes of the program attempted to convey a sense of the beauty of traditional Indian life-style and perception. The camera panned to mountains, rivers, fields of grass dotted by circles of teepees. Redford spoke of the Indian conception of the "oneness of things," the equality of all creatures, the desire to keep in harmony with the Great Spirit. We heard Indian chanting and drumbeats.

Sitting in my living room, I kept track of the technical events. No single shot lasted longer than ten seconds. Keeping the images jumping was a very wise decision on the part of the producers, because the mountains were too far away to be seen in anything beyond outline, the rivers were only a blur, and the fields of grass became a background haze in which the teepees were the only visible highlight. If we had been left to gaze at these images for more than ten seconds, an awareness of boredom would have developed. It was impossible to get a sense of the mountains, rivers, and fields which, so the narrator said, were the central forces in Indian awareness.

Later in the program we see some rare footage of the Potlatch ceremonies of the Kwakiutl people, which were suppressed by the Canadian government until recently. We see Indian dances; people dressed as animals; Indians in canoes led by an eagle-man, his arms flapping in a mock attempt to move the boats forward. We watch totems being carved. The goal is to immerse us, the viewers, in the Indian experience, to convey the beauty and mystery of their art and its organic, naturalistic meaning. But on television, cut at an average of ten technical events per minute, the ceremonials are practically impossible to follow. They are as fuzzy as the natural surroundings from which theyhave emerged. We get no sense of the dance. It passes in and out of the frame of the camera. We see only this piece of it or that one. The fine details of the costumes blur like the tiny seeds of the flower. We cannot smell the burning fire or the sweat of the dancers' bodies or the dirt of the floor. We cannot feel the coldness of the air.

Our exposure comes in ten-second pieces, at most. Whatever understanding we develop comes from Redford's words, which describe what we cannot actually see or intuit.

As I sit at home in my living room, watching these scenes with my family, the program takes on the quality of carnival or Mardi Gras or gigantic costume party. A reenactment. It looks like a production staged by the local museum auxiliary. Its reality is impossible to get. The whole ceremony enters the realm of artifact.

The information loss is virtually total. Aura is utterly destroyed. Time is fractured. The sensory information is lost. The context is deleted. The gestalt of intuitional experience is cracked. The details are gone. The mood is impossible to convey. The process is invisible, as is the source. No magic. Not enough is conveyed to develop any feeling of caring about what might happen to these people because the heart of their belief remains invisible, despite the attempt to convey it to me. This is not to say I don't care what happens. But I cared before I saw these scenes. If these scenes had been my total exposure to these cultures, they would only have confirmed the uselessness of trying to sustain cultures that obviously don't fit the world today.

The program shifts. We go to a Navajo reservation in the American Southwest. A group of young Indian lawyers are struggling to prevent the expansion of power plants in the Four Corners area. The traditional way of life of Navajo sheepherders, suddenly disrupted by roads, noise, soot and ash from the power plants, would be sacrificed to the expansion. The camera follows an old woman, a shepherd, whose land is threatened. The narration says, "She and the land move as one . . . she wants to keep her life as it is . . . she came from the land and she is part of the land." We hear the woman say, "We live in harmony with the Great Spirit."

What Great Spirit could she possibly be talking about? I couldn't see any great spirit there. Could she mean that fuzzy-looking desert, or the scrawny sheep? Could she mean that little mud house with no wiring? Really. What does she expect? It's nice to preserve cultures, but how can a few highways bother that?

Ann Kelley

The program that followed immediately after "The New Indians" was called *In Search of America,* hosted by Ben Wattenberg. A six-part series, the show was intended to look at the bright side of America. "How can a nation that believes it hasn't done anything right or bold or creative in the recent past, do anything right or bold or creative in the immediate future? . . . All we hear today is that big business rips us off, the blacks are losing ground, work is meaningless, we're feeding a bloated military-industrial complex and that we oppress developing countries and rape their resources. All that is mostly inaccurate," Wattenberg said.

The program concentrated on the virtues of big business. "For all its flaws, big business has provided more people with more needs and more luxuries."

Compared with what preceded it, this was quite a simple show; narrow in conception, direct, featuring very simple, straightforward imagery: Wattenberg talking, interviews with corporate economists, and, amazingly, actual footage from advertising commercials, showing how much research corporations undertake in order to improve their products on behalf of all of us. No sweeping (incomprehensible) vistas, no attempts at conveying ways of mind, no talk about Great Spirits. This show was about "needs" (products; easy to photograph); research for a better America (we saw Gillette engineers working night and day to improve our shaving); freedom of choice (twenty-one "shaving systems"); and the satisfaction of American "tastes." The show, of course, was about life-style, but it was a life-style that couldn't have been simpler to convey. And it was conveyed simply, clearly, boldly; the way it is in commercials. No information loss. It was a highly efficient program.

I had wanted the Indian show to dominate, but I already knew that it couldn't and didn't. A stupider, grosser, more simplistic but cleaner and clearer (more highlighted) presentation—better suited to the medium by several orders of magnitude—had achieved an equality, actually a superiority, even in my own biased mind. I reminded myself for the fiftieth time that if there are polar opposites in what television can communicate and what it cannot, at the pole of non-communication would be cultural forms such as the American Indians'. At the pole of total communication would be cultural forms such as American business's.

Naturally, television has been used more successfully for the latter cultural forms than the former. Also naturally, the American population develops more of a feeling for products and a life-style suitable to business than it does for a sensitive, subtle and beautiful way of mind that theoretically offers an alternative. The more people sit inside their television experience, the more fixed they become in the hard-edged reality that the medium can convey.

To use the computer, one must develop computer-mind. To use the car, car-mind. To build the bomb, bomb-mind. To manipulate the media, one must be manipulative. To use television, which broadcasts flatness and one-dimensionality, it is necessary to think flatly and one-dimensionally.

It so happens that print media, while not perfect, can convey a lot more about Indian ways of mind than electronic media can because print can express much greater depth, complexity, change of mood, subtlety, detail and so on. Books, especially, can be written in much slower rhythms, encouraging a perception that builds, stage by stage, over the length of a long reading process that may take many hours, or days.

This is not to say that these books are sufficient. Only direct experience is. But if the battle were fought in books, Indians might win. If print were the only media in the world, the natural advantage of today's dominant forms—corporate, military, technological, scientific—over concrete ways of thinking would be vastly diminished. In a wider information field, the Indian mind would have greater validity. So people who are interested in celebrating and saving Indian cultures, like people interested in the arts or ecology or any nonhierarchical political forms, might be well advised to cease all efforts to transmit these intentions through television and devote greater effort to undermining television itself and accelerating the struggle within other information fields.

By unifying everyone within its framework and by centralizing experience within itself, television virtually replaces environment. It accelerates our alienation from nature and therefore accelerates the destruction of nature. It moves us farther inside an already pervasive artificial reality. It furthers the loss of personal knowledge and the gathering of all information in the hands of a techno-scientific-industrial elite.

Television technology is inherently antidemocratic. Because of its cost, the limited kind of information it can disseminate, the way it transforms the people who use it, and the fact that a few speak while millions absorb, television is suitable for use only by the most powerful corporate interests in the country. They inevitably use it to redesign human minds into a channeled, artificial, commercial form, that nicely fits the artificial environment. Television freewayizes, suburbanizes and commoditizes human beings, who are then easier to control. Meanwhile, those who control television consolidate their power.

Television aids the creation of societal conditions which produce autocracy; it also creates the appropriate mental patterns for it and simultaneously dulls all awareness that this is happening.

David Brower, president of Friends of the Earth, has argued that unlike human beings accused of crimes, all technologies should be assumed guilty of dangerous effects until proven innocent. No new technology should ever be introduced, he has said, until its ultimate effects are known and explained to the population. This is necessary, he feels, because once it has been introduced, getting rid of any technology is practically impossible—so much of life gets reorganized around it and so much power and vested interest

Robin Freeman

attaches to its continuance.

Of course what Brower envisions is itself practically impossible. Many technologies are too technically complex for the average person, like myself, not technically trained, to understand them. Also, in many instances it is impossible to identify all effects of a technology in advance of its introduction, especially those which do not lend themselves to scientific proofs and evidences. But where does this leave us? Since it is impossible fully to grasp or explain many technologies, do we then go ahead with them? Do we trust our industrial leaders? Do we merely let them shoot craps with our existence? And if we do foresee undesirable effects from a technology, what means exist for then getting rid of that technology? Are there any? And what does all of this mean to the ultimate control of our lives?

I have raised the possibility of an alternative way of thinking about the problem. If we believe in democratic processes, then we must also believe in resisting whatever subverts democracy. In the case of technology, we might wish to seek a line beyond which democratic control is not possible and then say that any technology which goes beyond this line is taboo. Although it might be difficult to define this line precisely, it might not be so difficult to know when some technologies are clearly over it. Any technology which by its nature encourages autocracy would surely be over such a line. Any technology that benefits only a small number of people to the physical, emotional, political, and psychological detriment of large numbers of other people would also certainly be over that line. In fact, one could make the argument that any technology whose operations and results are too complex for the majority of people to understand would also be beyond this line of democratic control.

Can we really say any longer that a reason to go ahead with a technology is that it is too complex for people to grasp, or too clumsy or difficult to dismantle? Either we believe in democratic control or we do not. If we do, then anything which is beyond such control is certainly anathema to democracy.

But a central argument here is that television, for the most part, cannot possibly yield to reform. Its problems are inherent in the technology itself to the same extent that violence is inherent in guns.

No new age of well-meaning television executives can change what the medium does to people who watch it. Its effects on body and mind are inseparable from the viewing experience.

As for the political effects, if we switched from the commercial control of television to, say, governmental control, as in Sweden or Argentina or Russia, this would not change the essential political relationships: the unification of experience, the one speaking to the

many, the inevitable training in autocracy that these conditions engender.

Similarly, no change in programming format from the present violent, antisocial tendencies to the more "prosocial" visions of educators and psychologists will mean much compared with the training in passivity, the destruction of creativity, the dulling of communicative abilities that any extended exposure to television inevitably produces. This is even assuming that the programming *could* be substantially changed which, as we have seen, is highly doubtful.

No influx of talented directors or writers can offset the technical limits of the medium itself. No matter who is in control, the medium remains confined to its cold, narrow culverts of hyperactive information. Nothing and no one can change this, nor can anyone change how television's technical limits confine awareness. As the person who gazes at streams becomes streamlike, so as we watch television we inexorably evolve into creatures whose bodies and minds become television-like.

True, if we banned all advertising, that would allay many negative effects of the medium and diminish the power of the huge corporations that are re-creating life in their image.

True, if we banned all *broadcast* television, leaving only cable systems, that would reduce the effect of the centralization of control. More kinds of people might have access to the medium, but they would still have to submit to the dictates of the technology. As they used the machine, they would find their material and their own consciousness changing to suit the technological form. The people who use television become more like each other, the Indian who learns television is an Indian no longer.

If we reduced the number of broadcast hours per day, or the number of days per week that television is permitted to broadcast, as many countries have, that would surely be an improvement.

If we eliminated all crime shows and other sensational entertainment, it would reveal what an inherently boring medium this is, producing awareness of artificial fixation despite boredom.

If we banned all nature shows or news broadcasts from television, due to the unavoidable and very dangerous distortions and aberrations which are inherent in televising these subjects, then this would leave other, better-qualified media to report them to us. The result would be an increased awareness of far more complex, complete and subtle information.

If we outlawed networks, there would be a new emphasis on local events, bringing us nearer to issues upon which we might have some direct personal effect.

All of these changes in television would be to the good, in my opinion, and worthy of support, but do you believe that they'd be any easier to achieve than the outright elimination of the whole technology? I don't think so. Considering how difficult it has been merely to reduce the volume or the kind of advertising that is directed at our children, and considering the overwhelming power of the interests who control communications in this country, we might just as well put our efforts toward trying for the hole in one.

The Long Loneliness

MAN'S GREATEST EPIC, his four long battles with the advancing ice of the great continental glaciers, has vanished from human memory without a trace. Our illiterate fathers disappeared and with them, in a few scant generations, died one of the great stories of all time. This episode has nothing to do with the biological quality of a brain as between then and now. It has to do instead with a device, an invention made possible by the hand. That invention came too late in time to record eyewitness accounts of the years of the Giant Frost.

Primitives of our own species, even today, are historically shallow in their knowledge of the past. Only the poet who writes, speaks his message across the millennia to other hearts. Only in writing can the cry from the great cross on Golgotha still be heard in the minds of men. The thinker of perceptive insight, even if we allow him for the moment to be a porpoise rather than a man, has only his individual glimpse of the universe until such time as he can impose that insight upon unnumbered generations. In centuries of pondering, man has come upon but one answer to this problem: speech translated into writing that passes beyond human mortality.

Writing, and later printing, is the product of our adaptable many-purposed hands. It is thus, through writing, with no increase in genetic, inborn capacity since the last ice advance, that modern man carries in his mind the intellectual triumphs of all his predecessors who were able to inscribe their thoughts for posterity.

All animals which man has reason to believe are more than usually intelligent—our relatives the great apes, the elephant, the raccoon, the wolverine, among others—are problem solvers, and in at least a small way manipulators of their environment. Save for the instinctive calls of their species, however, they cannot communicate except by direct imitation. They cannot invent words for new situations nor get their fellows to use such words. No matter how high the individual intelligence, its private world remains a private possession locked forever within a single, perishable brain. It is this fact that finally balks our hunger to communicate even with the sensitive dog who shares our fireside.

Most of the intelligent land animals have prehensile, grasping organs for exploring their environment—hands in man and his anthropoid relatives, the sensitive inquiring trunk in the elephant. One of the surprising things about the porpoise is that his superior brain is unaccompanied by any type of manipulative organ. He has, however, a remarkable range-finding ability involving some sort of echo-sounding. Perhaps

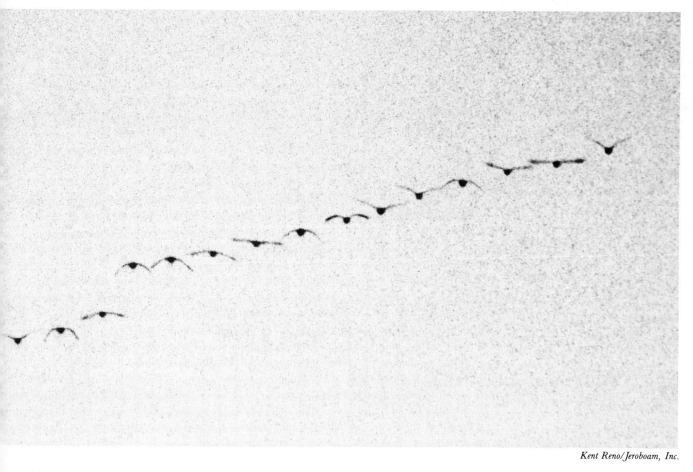

Kent Reno/Jeroboam, Inc.

this acute sense—far more accurate than any man has been able to devise artificially—brings him greater knowledge of his watery surroundings than might at first seem possible. Human beings think of intelligence as geared to things. The hand and the tool are to us the unconscious symbols of our intellectual achievement. It is difficult for us to visualize another kind of lonely, almost disembodied intelligence floating in the wavering green fairyland of the sea—an intelligence possibly near or comparable to our own but without hands to build, to transmit knowledge by writing, or to alter by one hairsbreadth the planet's surface. Yet at the same time there are indications that this is a warm, friendly and eager intelligence quite capable of coming to the assistance of injured companions and striving to rescue them from drowning. Porpoises left the land when mammalian brains were still small and primitive. Without the stimulus provided by agile exploring fingers, these great sea mammals have yet taken a divergent road toward intelligence of a high order. Hidden in their sleek bodies is an impressively elaborated instrument, the reason for whose appearance is a complete enigma. It is as though both man and porpoise were each part of some great eye which yearned to look both outward on eternity and inward to the sea's heart—that fertile entity so like the mind in its swarming and grotesque life.

If man had sacrificed his hands for flukes, the moral might run, he would still be a philosopher, but there would have been taken from him the devastating power to wreak his thought upon the body of the world. Instead he would have lived and wandered, like the porpoise, homeless across currents and winds and oceans, intelligent, but forever the lonely and curious observer of unknown wreckage falling through the blue light of eternity. This role would now be a deserved penitence for man. Perhaps such a transformation would bring him once more into that mood of childhood innocence in which he talked successfully to all things living but had no power and no urge to harm. It is worth at least a wistful thought that someday the porpoise may talk to us and we to him. It would break, perhaps, the long loneliness that has made man a frequent terror and abomination even to himself.

—Loren Eiseley

Readings in Economics

Conventional American economic theory assumes that natural resources are inexhaustible and that perpetual economic growth is possible, desirable, and indeed, essential. Based on these premises, conventional economics is innately anti-ecological. Fortunately, there is a new breed of economic thinkers who are in closer touch with reality. They hold that a steady-state economy is essential in a finite world, and that economics, like everything else, is subject to physical laws (in particular, to the Second Law of Thermodynamics). We offer here some writings by thinkers of this persuasion. Any legislator who fails to heed the steady-state economists does himself and his constituents a disservice; any President who fails to heed them does the nation and the world a disservice.

Kent Reno/Jeroboam, Inc.

A Steady-State Economy

HERMAN E. DALY

A STEADY-STATE ECONOMY (SSE) is defined by four characteristics: a constant population of human bodies; a constant population of artifacts ("extensions" of human bodies); the two populations or stocks are maintained constant at chosen levels that are sufficient for a good life and sustainable for a long future; the rate of throughput of matter-energy by which the two stocks are maintained (i.e., the entropic flow of matter-energy from mines and wells to garbage dumps and environmental sinks) is reduced to the lowest feasible level.

The only things held constant are the two physical stocks: population and total artifact inventory. Knowledge, goodness, information, technology, design and mix of artifacts, genetic characteristics of population, distribution of wealth, etc., are *not* held constant. Progress in the SSE takes the form of qualitative improvement rather than quantitative increase. The goal of technical progress in particular becomes two-fold: to maintain the physical stocks with the least throughput cost (depletion and pollution); and to design, allocate and distribute the constant stock of physical artifacts so as to maximize the service (want-satisfying capacity) of the stock. The concept of GNP is irrelevant to the SSE. A reduction of throughput, other things equal, would imply a lower GNP, which is totally acceptable. If GNP decreases when efficiency increases, then that is a problem for the concept of GNP, not for the SSE.

The standard, somewhat ponderous, definition of economics found in the textbooks is "the study of the allocation of scarce means among competing ends where the object of the allocation is the maximization of the attainment of those ends." In other words, how to do the best with what you've got. But that definition has the virtue of emphasizing the fact that economics is about ends and means. The problem with conventional economics is that it focuses only on the middle of the ends-means spectrum where limits are not apparent. If we expand our vision to the whole ends-means spectrum and include ultimate means and ultimate ends as well, limits become visible. This is illustrated in the following diagram.

Ends-Means Spectrum

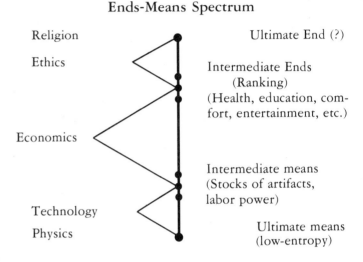

From this diagram economics growth can be defined as the creation of ever more intermediate means for the purpose of satisfying ever more intermediate ends. Orthodox growth economics recognizes that individual resources might be limited, but does not recognize any general scarcity of all resources together. The orthodox dogma is that technology can always substitute new resources for old, without limit. Since intermediate means have grown over the last century it is taken as empirically verified that technology is a limitless source of means. A longer run empiricism would reveal that man has lived in a near SSE throughout most of his history and that the growing industrial economy is an aberration, not a norm. But more of that later.

Growth economists also recognize that any single intermediate end or want can be satisfied for any given individual. But new wants keep emerging (and new people as well) so the aggregate of all wants is held to be insatiable, or infinite in number, if not in intensity. So the growth economists' vision is one of continuous growth in intermediate means, which requires continual growth in throughput, with no limits in sight.

A consideration of the ultimate poles of the ends-means spectrum, however, gives us a different perspective. It forces us to raise two questions: (1) What precisely are our ultimate means, and are they limited in ways that cannot be overcome by technology? (2) What is the nature of the Ultimate End, and is it such that, beyond a certain point, further accumulation of intermediate means (people and artifacts) not only fails to serve the Ultimate End but actually renders a disservice? It will be argued below that the answer to both questions is yes. The nature of ultimate means limits the *possibility* of growth, and the nature of the ultimate end limits *desirability* of growth. Moreover the interaction of possibility and desirability provides the *economic* limit to growth.

The branch of physics known as thermodynamics teaches us that the ultimate means is low-entropy matter-energy. Economist Nicholas Georgescu-Roegen (*The Entropy Law and the Economic Process*) has drawn some important implications from this fact. We have two sources of low-entropy: terrestrial stocks of concentrated minerals, and the solar flow of sunlight. In materials, low-entropy means structure, concentration, order. Dispersed, randomly scattered molecules of any material are useless (high entropy). In energy, low entropy means the capacity to do work, or concentrated, relatively high temperature energy. Energy dispersed in equilibrium temperature with general environmental sinks is useless (high entropy). The terrestrial source of low entropy is obviously limited in total amount, though the rate at which we use it up is largely subject to our choice. The solar source is practically unlimited in total amount, but strictly limited in its rate of arrival to earth for use. Both sources of ultimate means are limited—one in total amount, the other in rate of use.

There is an enormous disproportion in the total amounts of the two sources: if all the earth's fossil fuels could be burned up, they would only provide the energy equivalent of a few weeks of sunlight. The sun is expected to shine for another five billion years or so. This raises a cosmically embarrassing economic question. If the solar source is so vastly more abundant, why have we over the last two centuries shifted the physical base of our economy from overwhelming dependence on solar energy and renewable resources, to overwhelming dependence on non-renewable terrestrial minerals? An important part of the answer is that terrestrial stocks can, for a while at least, be used up at a rate of man's own choosing—i.e., rapidly. Solar energy and renewable resource usage is limited by the fixed solar flux, and the natural rates of growth of plants and animals. This provides a natural constraint on economic growth. But growth can be speeded up for a time at least by consuming geological capital—by running down the reserves of terrestrial low entropy. If the object is growth, then it can be achieved most easily by using up terrestrial stocks rapidly. As population and per capita consumption grow beyond the capacity of renewable resources and solar energy to support, then we have all the more pressure to rely on terrestrial stocks, or geological capital.

The difficulty is twofold. First, we will run out of terrestrial sources eventually. Second, *even if we never ran out* we still would face problems of ecological imbalance caused by a growing throughput of matter-energy. Mankind is the only species that lives beyond the budget of solar income. The whole biosphere has evolved as a complex system around the fixed point of a given solar flux. Now man, in escaping the common constraint, has got badly out of balance with the rest of the biosphere and runs the considerable danger of destroying or at least inhibiting the complex life support systems that all life and wealth depend on. As stocks of people and artifacts have grown, the

---

As energy prices keep going up, and as we start running into serious shortages of some natural materials, and as we face up to putting our large numbers of unemployed to work, I think we shall see a shift to a technology that will put man rather than the machine at the center of industrial economics. To employ, to conserve, and to recycle will be the battlecry of the future.

—RUSSELL PETERSON

---

throughput has had to grow also, implying more depletion and more pollution. Natural biogeochemical cycles become overloaded. Exotic substances are produced and thrown wholesale into the biosphere—substances with which we have had no evolutionary experience, and which are consequently nearly always disruptive.

But are we not giving insufficient credit to technology in claiming that ultimate means are limited? Is technology not itself a limitless resource? All technologies, nature's as well as man's, run on an entropy gradient—i.e., the total entropy of the outputs of the process must always be greater than the total entropy of inputs. If low entropy sources are limited then so is technology. It is ironic to be told by growth boosters that technology is freeing man from dependence on resources. It has done nearly the opposite. Modern technology has made us ever more dependent on the *scarcer* of the two sources of ultimate means. The entropy law tells us that when technology increases order in one part of the universe it must produce an even greater amount of disorder somewhere else. If that "somewhere else" is the sun (as it is for nature's technology and man's traditional preindustrial technologies), we need not worry. If "somewhere else" is on the earth then we had better pay close attention. The throughput flow maintains or increases the order within the human economy, but at the cost of creating greater disorder in the rest of the natural world, as a result of depletion and pollution. There is a limit to how much disorder can be produced in the rest of the biosphere and still have it function well enough to support the human subsystem.

Although man's technology cannot overcome these limits it could achieve a better accommodation to them, and could work more in harmony with nature's technology than it has in the past. In so doing it may be that welfare can increase forever, even though physical stocks are constant. But this improved accommodation cannot be achieved in a growth context, in an economy that would rather maximize throughput than reduce it. It requires the framework of a SSE.

From these considerations about ultimate means, I conclude that there are limits to the possibility of continued growth and that a SSE will sooner or later become necessary. And likely sooner when we consider the growing evidence of ecosystem disruption.

Let us turn now to a consideration of the Ultimate End and the limits it imposes on the desirability of growth. What is the Ultimate End? The fact that one does not know the answer is no excuse for not raising the question, because certainly it is *the* question for all of us. Only a kind of minimum answer to such a maximum question would be likely to command consensus. As a minimum answer, let me suggest that whatever the ultimate end is, it presupposes a respect for, and the survival of, the evolutionary process through which God has bestowed upon the gift of self-conscious life. Whatever human values are put in first place, their further realization requires the survival of human beings. It may be a noble thing to sacrifice the remaining years of one's own personal life to a higher cause, but to sacrifice the whole evolutionary process to some "higher cause" is surely fanaticism. This minimum answer begs many questions: Survival and evolution of life in what direction? To what extent should the evolutionary process be influenced by man and to what extent should it be left spontaneous? I leave these questions aside. The only point is that survival must rank very high in the ends hierarchy and consequently any growth that is made possible only by the creation

of means that threaten survival should be strictly limited. Is the further growth made possible by the development of breeder reactors and multi-ton quantities of plutonium really desirable? The distinguished Committee of Inquiry on the Plutonium Economy of the National Council of Churches believes that it is not desirable, and I certainly agree. Others disagree on this specific question. But surely *some* kinds of growth are limited by their undesirability, even though they may be possible. But what about growth per se? Are *all* kinds of physical growth subject to desirability limits? Is there such a thing as "enough" in the material realm, and is enough better than "more than enough"? Certainly all organic needs can be satiated, and to go beyond enough is harmful. The only want that seems insatiable is the want for distinction, the desire to be in some way superior to one's neighbors. The main avenue of distinction in our society is to have a larger income than the next fellow and to spend more. The only way for everyone to earn more is to have aggregate growth. But that is the rub. If everyone earns more then where is the distinction? It is possible for everyone's *absolute* income to increase, but not for everyone's *relative* income to increase. To the extent that it is higher relative income that is important, growth becomes useless. As E.J. Mishan has expressed it,

> In its extreme form—and as affluence rises we draw closer to it—only relative income matters. A man would then prefer a 5% reduction in his own income accompanied by a 10% reduction in the income of others, to a 25% increase in both his income and the income of others. . . .The more this attitude prevails—and the ethos of our society actively promotes it—the more futile is the objective of economic growth for society as a whole. For it is obvious that over time everyone cannot become relatively better off ("Growth and Anti-Growth: What are the issues?" *Challenge*, May/June, 1973, p. 30).

So even if one's ultimate end is merely to have more than his neighbor, aggregate growth is limited in its capacity to satisfy that end. If one's concept of the Ultimate End is more noble than winning one more round in the materialistic rat race to keep up with the Joneses, then aggregate economic growth is even less able to serve it. It is as futile as the arms race—if each side achieves the capacity to annihilate the other side twenty times over instead of only ten times over, nothing has really changed, except that a lot more resources have been absolutely wasted without altering relative positions.

I conclude that growth beyond some point becomes undesirable, even if still possible. Therefore a SSE

"We found the most marvelous little place where they sell gasoline."

becomes desirable.

The actual point at which economic growth should stop is determined by the interaction of desirability and possibility limits. We do not satisfy ends in any random order. We satisfy our most pressing needs first. We do not use our low entropy means in any random order. We use the highest grade and most accessible resources first. This elementary rule of sensible behavior underlies the law of diminishing marginal benefit, and the law of increasing marginal cost. As growth continues, at some point the curve of falling marginal benefits of growth will intersect the curve of rising marginal costs. At that point growth should cease. Growth economists would not deny the logic, but would rightly object that the analysis is too static. Technology shifts the whole cost curve downward. New wants can push the whole benefits curve upward. Looked at statically the curves have opposite slopes and will certainly intersect. But considered dynamically, technical and psychological change will push the curves apart so fast that, although they still intersect, their intersection will forever remain far ahead of us. That is the faith of the growth economist.

But our consideration of ultimate means and the ultimate end has raised insuperable problems for the growth economist. Technology is limited in its ability to lower costs. Technology uses up ultimate means and cannot create them. New wants in affluent societies tend to be relative wants of distinction, and aggregate growth cannot make everyone relatively better off. Growth can of course continue to make some people relatively better off, but then the price of continuing growth would be increasing inequality. The nature of ultimate means limits the downward shift of the cost curve. The nature of the ultimate end limits the upward shift of the benefits curve. The curves shift but the domain in which they can shift is limited.

I think the case for the necessity and desirability of the SSE must be admitted. But we have not said when. Maybe it won't be necessary for another thousand years. Maybe we can grow for a long time yet. Maybe we have not yet reached the optimum size?

Even if we have not yet reached the optimum size, we should still learn to live in a SSE so that we could remain at the optimum once we got there, rather than grow through it. If we achieve a SSE at one level we are not forever frozen at that level. If we later discover that a larger or smaller stock would be better we can either grow or decline to the preferred level, at which we would again be stable. (Growth or decline would then be a temporary adjustment process, and not a norm.) I believe, however, that we have passed the optimum and will in the future probably have to reduce population and per capita consumption. But the issue of optimum level is very difficult to handle, because a number of related questions must be answered simultaneously: (1) What size population do we want, (2) living at what level of per capita resource consumption, (3) for how long, and (4) on the basis of what kinds of technology? Also we must ask whether the level we choose for the US should be generalizable to the world as a whole. With 6% of the world's people we now consume in the US about 30% of the world's annual production of nonrenewable resources. To generalize the US standard of per capita consumption to the entire world requires a sixfold increase in current resource throughput. In addition, to supply the rest of the world with the average per capita "standing crop" of industrial metals already embodied in the existing artifacts in the ten richest nations, would require more than 60 years' world production of these metals at 1970 rates (Harrison Brown, "Human Materials Production as a Process in the Biosphere," *Scientific American*, Sept. 1970). The ecological disruption caused by the next sixfold increase will be much greater per unit of resource produced because of diminishing returns. Even technological optimists like Dr. Alvin Weinberg recognize the heat limit to energy use.

> Man was increasing his production of energy by about 5% per year: within 200 years at this rate he would be producing as much energy as he receives from the sun. Obviously, long before that time man would have to come to terms with global climatological limits imposed on his production of energy. Although it is difficult to estimate just how soon we shall have to adjust the world's energy policies to take this limit into account, it might well be as little as 30 to 50 years. (*Science*, 18 Oct. 1974).

These considerations make me doubt very strongly that present US levels of living are generalizable, either to the world as a whole, or to very many future generations. Attempts at such generalization are likely to embrace unacceptable technologies. So I think the sooner we move to a SSE, the better.

A SSE is not a panacea. Even a SSE will not last forever, nor will it overcome diminishing returns and the entropy law. But it will permit our economy to die gracefully of old age rather than prematurely from the cancer of growth-mania.

Given that continuous growth is neither feasible nor desirable, how can we stop it, how can we achieve a SSE without enormous disruption? The difficult part is mustering the political will to do it. The technical problems are small by comparison. People often overestimate the technical problems because they identify a SSE with a failed growth economy. A situation of nongrowth can come about in two ways: as the success of steady-state policies, or as the failure of growth policies. Non-growth resulting from the failure of a

growth economy is chaotic beyond repair. But that is a shortcoming of the growth economy, not the SSE. The fact that airplanes fall from the air if they stand still does not mean that a helicopter cannot stand still.

In an effort to stimulate discussion on policies for attaining a SSE I have suggested three institutions which seem to me to provide the necessary control with the minimum sacrifice of individual freedom (cf., H.E. Daly, ed., *Toward a Steady-State Economy*, W.H. Freeman Co., San Francisco 1973). First we need a *distributist institution* which would limit the range of inequality to some functionally justifiable degree. This could be accomplished by setting minimum income and maximum income and wealth limits for individuals and families, and a maximum size for corporations. Since aggregate growth can no longer be appealed to as the "solution" to poverty, we must face the distribution issue directly. The maximum and minimum define a range within which inequality is legitimate, and beyond which it is not. The exact numbers are of secondary importance, but let me suggest a minimum of $7,000 and a maximum of $70,000 on income.

Second, aggregate depletion of each of the basic minerals would be limited by *depletion quotas*, to be auctioned, in conveniently divisible units, by the government. The resource market would become two-tiered. First the government, as a monopolist, auctions the limited quota rights to many buyers. Resource buyers having purchased their quota rights then confront many resource sellers in a competitive resource market. The competitive price in the resource market will tend to equal the average cost of the marginal producer. More efficient producers will earn differential rents, but the pure scarcity rent resulting from the quotas will have been captured in the depletion quota auction market by the government monopoly. The total price of the resource (quota price plus price to owner) will be raised as a result of the quotas. All products using these resources become more expensive. Higher resource prices will force more efficient and frugal use of resources by both producers and consumers. But the windfall rent arising from higher resource prices is captured by the government and becomes public income—a partial realization of Henry George's single tax on rent. It would not be a "single tax," but it would permit the elimination of some other taxes whose effects cause greater resource distortions. Allocative efficiency is improved to the extent that a rent tax, or in this case its equivalent in the form of auctioned quotas, replaces, say an income or a sales tax. But the major advantage is that higher resources prices result in increased efficiency, while the quotas directly limit depletion (increase conservation), and indirectly limit pollution. Pollution is limited in two ways, first because it is simply the other end of the

The monopolists denounce a "planned economy" as heresy. But what they really oppose is not planning—for the most part our economy is already shaped by a handful of officials. Raw materials are used or abused, prices are set and profits are maintained not by the operation of free market forces, but by the bureaucrats of the corporate structure. What the monopolists object to is any measure of planning for the public good instead of private profits. What they say is that we are restricting free enterprise; what they mean is that they want unrestricted power to manipulate an unfree enterprise system.
                                                    —GEORGE MCGOVERN

throughput from depletion, so that limiting the input to the pipeline naturally limits the output. Second, higher prices will induce more recycling, and will push technology toward greater reliance on the abundant solar source and away from excessive use of the scarce terrestrial source of low entropy. The revenue from the depletion quota auction can be used to help finance the minimum income part of the distributist institution, thus offsetting the regressive effect on income distribution of the higher resource prices. Higher prices on basic resources are absolutely necessary and any plan that refuses to face up to this is worthless. Back in 1925 economist John Ise made the point in these words:

> Preposterous as it may seem at first blush, it is probably true that, even if all the timber in the United States, or all the oil or gas or anthracite, were owned by an absolute monopoly, entirely free of public control, prices to consumers would be fixed lower than the long-run interests of the public would justify. Pragmatically this means that all efforts on the part of the government to keep down the prices of lumber, oil, gas, or anthracite are contrary to the public interest; that the government should be trying to keep prices up rather than down *(American Economic Review,* June 1925, p. 284).

Ise also went on to suggest a general principle of resource pricing: that non-renewable resources be priced at the cost of the nearest renewable substitute. Thus virgin timber should cost at least as much per board foot as replanted timber; petroleum should be priced at its Btu equivalent of sugar or wood alcohol, assuming that they are the closest renewable alternatives. If no renewable substitutes exist, then the price merely reflects the purely ethical judgment of how fast the resources should be used up—i.e., how important are future wants relative to present wants. Renewable resources are assumed to be exploited on a sustained

yield basis and priced accordingly. These principles could be used in setting the aggregate quota amounts to be auctioned. For renewables the quota should be set at an amount equivalent to some reasonable calculation of maximum sustainable yield. For non-renewables with renewable substitutes the quota should be set so that the resulting price of the non-renewable resource is at least as high as the price of its renewable substitute. For non-renewables with no close renewable substitute the quota reflects a purely ethical judgment concerning the relative importance of present versus future wants.

In addition to Ise's rules, which deal only with depletion costs, one must be sure that the quotas are low enough to prevent excessive pollution and ecological disruption. Pragmatically quotas would probably be set near existing extraction levels initially. The first task would be to stabilize, to get off the growth path. Later we could gradually reduce quotas to a more sustainable level, if present flows proved too high. Resources in abundant supply and whose use is not environmentally disruptive would have generous quotas and hence relatively low prices.

Depletion quotas would capture the increasing scarcity rents, but would not require expropriation of resource owners. Quotas are clearly against the interests of resource owners, but not unjustly so, since rent is by definition unearned income resulting from a price in excess of the minimum supply price. Additionally, incentive to new exploration could be provided by a system of cash bounties for actual discoveries, or by a public enterprise, since geologic exploration has many characteristics of a natural monopoly.

The remaining institution in our model must provide a mechanism of population control. A stationary population can be achieved by various means that are consistent with the first two institutions. My own favorite is the *transferrable birth license scheme,* first proposed by Kenneth Boulding. But, important as it is, for this occasion I will treat population control as a separate issue and not try to argue for a specific plan, since the depletion quota and distributist institutions could function with a wide range of population control programs, and in no way require the transferrable license scheme (For a defense of transferrable licenses, see H. Daly, *op cit.;* and David Heer, "Marketable Licenses for Babies: Boulding Proposal Revisited," *Social Biology,* Spring 1975).

Two distinct questions must be asked about these proposed institutions for achieving a SSE. First would they work if people accepted the goal of a SSE, and, say, voted these institutions into effect? Second, would people ever accept either the steady state idea, or these particular institutions? I have tried to show that the answer to the first question is probably "yes."Let the critic find the flaw—better yet let him suggest an improvement. The answer to the second question, today, is clearly "no." But in the future the mounting costs of our failing growth economy will make a SSE look better and better. The sooner we realize this the less we will suffer.

The Convergence of Environmental Disruption

MARSHALL GOLDMAN

MOST CONSERVATIONISTS and social critics are unaware that the USSR has environmental disruption that is as extensive and severe as ours. Most of us have been so distressed by our own environmental disruption that we lack the emotional energy to worry about anyone else's difficulties. Yet before we can find a solution to the environmental disruption in our own country, it is necessary to explain why it is that a socialist or communist country like the USSR finds itself abusing the environment in the same way, and to the same degree, that we abuse it. This is especially important for those who have come to believe as basic doctrine that it is capitalism and private greed that are the root causes of environmental disruption. Undoubtedly private enterprise and the profit motive account for a good portion of the environmental disruption that we encounter in this country. However, a study of pollution in the Soviet Union suggests that abolishing private property will not necessarily mean an end to environmental disruption. In some ways, state ownership of the country's productive resources may actually exacerbate rather than ameliorate the situation.

Comparing pollution in the United States and in the USSR is something like a game. Any depressing story that can be told about an incident in the United States can be matched by a horror story from the USSR.

Because the relative impact of environmental disruption is a difficult thing to measure, it is somewhat meaningless to say that the Russians are more affected than we are, or vice versa. But what should be of interest is an attempt to ascertain why it is that pollution exists in a state-owned, centrally planned economy like that of the Soviet Union. Despite the fact that our economies differ, many if not all of the usual economic explanations for pollution in the non-Communist world also hold for the Soviet Union. The Russians, too, have been unable to adjust their accounting system so that each enterprise pays not only its direct costs of production for labor, raw materials, and equipment but also its social costs of production arising from such byproducts as dirty air and water. If the factory were charged for these social costs and had to take them into account when trying to make a profit on its operations, presumably factories would throw off less waste and would reuse or recycle their air and water. However, the precise social cost of such waste is difficult to measure and allocate under the best of circumstances, be it in the United States or the USSR.

In addition, almost everyone in the world regards air and water as free goods. Thus, even if it were always technologically feasible, it would still be awkward ideologically to charge for something that "belongs to everyone," particularly in a Communist society. For a variety of reasons, therefore, air and water in the USSR are treated as free or undervalued goods. When anything is free, there is a tendency to consume it without regard for future consequences. But with water and air, as with free love, there is a limit to the amount available to be consumed, and after a time there is the risk of exhaustion. We saw an illustration of this principle in the use of water for irrigation. Since water was treated virtually as a free good, the Russians did not care how much water they lost through unlined canals or how much water they used to irrigate the soil.

Similarly, the Russians have not been able to create clear lines of authority and responsibility for enforcing pollution-control regulations. As in the United States, various Russian agencies, from the Ministry of Agriculture to the Ministry of Public Health, have some but not ultimate say in coping with the problem. Frequently when an agency does attempt to enforce a law, the polluter will deliberately choose to break the law. As we saw at Lake Baikal, this is especially tempting when the penalty for breaking the law is only $55 a time, while the cost of eliminating the effluent may be in the millions of dollars.

The Russians also have to contend with an increase in population growth and the concentration of much of this increase in urban areas. In addition, this larger population has been the beneficiary of an increase in the quantity and complexity of production that accompanies industrialization. As a result, not only is each individual in the Soviet Union, as in the United States, provided with more goods to consume, but the resulting products, such as plastics and detergents, are more exotic and less easily disposed of than goods of an earlier, less complicated age.

Like their fellow inhabitants of the world, the Russians have to contend with something even more ominous than the Malthusian Principle. Malthus observed that the population increased at a geometric rate but that food production grew at only an arithmetic rate. If he really wants to be dismal, the economist of today has more to worry about. It is true that the population seems to be increasing at accelerated rates, but, whereas food production at least continues to increase, our air, water, and soil supplies are relatively constant. They can be renewed, just as crops can be replanted, but, for the most part, they cannot be expanded. In the long run, this "Doomsday Principle" may prove to be of more consequence than the Malthusian doctrine. With time and pollution we may simply run out of fresh air and water.

In addition to the factors which confront all the people of the earth, regardless of their social or economic system, there are some reasons for polluting which seem to be peculiar to a socialist country such as the Soviet Union in its present state of economic development. First of all, state officials in the Soviet Union are judged almost entirely by how much they are able to increase their region's economic growth. Thus, government officials are not likely to be promoted if they decide to act as referees between contending factions on questions of pollution. State officials identify with the polluters, not the conservationists, because the polluters will increase economic growth and the prosperity of the region while the antipolluters want to divert resources away from increased production. There is almost a political as well as an economic imperative to devour idle resources. The limnologists at Lake Baikal fear no one so much as the voracious Gosplan (State Planning) officials and their allies in the regional government offices. These officials do not have to face a voting constituency which might reflect the conservation point of view, such as the League of Women Voters or the Sierra Club in this country. It is true that there are outspoken conservationists in the USSR who are often supported by the Soviet press, but for the most part they do not have a vote. Thus the lime smelters continued to smoke away behind the resort area of Kislovodsk even though critics in *Izvestiia, Literaturnaya Gazeta, Sovetskaia Rossiia, Trud,* and *Krokodil* protested long and loud.

Until July 1967, all raw materials in the ground were treated by the Russians as free goods. As a result, whenever the mine operator or oil driller had exploited the most accessible oil and ore, he moved on to a new site where the average variable costs were lower. This has resulted in very low recovery rates and the discarding of large quantities of salvageable materials, which increase the amount of waste to be disposed of.

As we have seen, it is as hard for the Russians as it is for us to include social costs in factory-pricing calculations. However, not only do they have to worry about social cost accounting, they also are unable to reflect all the private cost considerations. Because there is no private ownership of land, there are no private property owners to protest the abuse of various resources.

The Russians, however, under their existing system, now only have to worry about accounting for social costs, they lack the first line of protection that would come from balancing private costs and private benefits.

The power of the state to make fundamental changes may be so great that irreversible changes may frequently be inflicted on the environment without anyone's realizing what is happening until it is too late. This seems to be the best explanation of the meteorological disruption that is taking place in Siberia. It is easier for an all-powerful organism like the state than for a group of private entrepreneurs to build the reservoirs and reverse the rivers. Private enterprises can cause their own havoc, as our dust bowl experience or our use of certain pesticides or sedatives indicates, but in the absence of private business or property interests, the state's powers can be much more far-reaching in scope. In an age of rampant technology, where the consequences of one's actions are not always fully anticipated, even well-intentioned programs can have disastrous effects on the environmental status quo.

Amidst all these problems, there are some things the Russians do very well. For example, the Russians have the power to prevent the production of various products. Thus, the Soviet Union is the only country in the world that does not put ethyl lead in most of the gasoline it produces. This may be due to technical lag as much as to considerations of health, but the result is considerably more lead-free gasoline. Similarly, the Russians have not permitted as much emphasis on consumer-goods production as we have in the West. Consequently there is less waste to discard. Russian consumers may be somewhat less enthusiastic about this than the ecologists and conservationists, but in the USSR there are no disposable bottles or disposable diapers to worry about. It also happens that, because labor costs are low relative to the price of goods, more emphasis is placed on prolonging the life of various products. In other words it is worthwhile to use labor to pick up bottles and collect junk. No one would intentionally abandon his car on a Moscow street, as 70,000 people did in New York City in 1970. Even if a Russian car is twenty years old, it is still valuable. Because of the price relationships that exist in the USSR, the junkman can still make a profit. This facilitates the recycling process, which ecologists tell us is the ultimate solution to environmental disruption.

It should be remembered that, while not all Russian laws are observed, the Russians do have an effective law enforcement system which they have periodically brought to bear in the past. Similarly, they have the power to set aside land for use as natural preserves. The lack of private land ownership makes this a much easier process to implement than in the United States. As of 1969, the Soviet Government had set aside eighty such preserves, encompassing nearly 65,000 square kilometers.

Again because they own all the utilities as well as most of the buildings, the Russians have stressed the installation of centrally supplied steam. Thus, heating and hot water are provided by central stations, and this makes possible more efficient combustion and better smoke control than would be achieved if each building were to provide heat and hot water for itself. Although some American cities have similar systems, this approach is something we should know more about.

In sum, if the study of environmental disruption in the Soviet Union demonstrates anything, it shows that not private enterprise but industrialization is the primary cause of environmental disruption. This suggests that state ownership of all the productive resources is not a cure-all. The replacement of private greed by public greed is not much of an improvement. Currently the proposals for the solution of environmental disruption seem to be no more advanced in the USSR than they are in the United States. One thing does seem clear, however, and that is that, unless the Russians change their ways, there seems little reason to believe that a strong centralized and planned economy has any notable advantages over other economic systems in solving environmental disruption.

George Hall

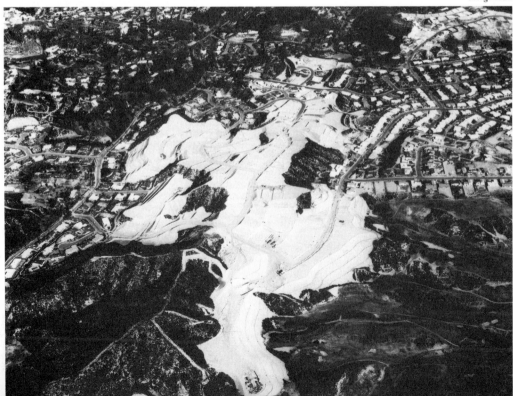

Production in Service to Life

E. F. SCHUMACHER

THE IDEA OF UNLIMITED economic growth, more and more until everybody is saturated with wealth, needs to be seriously questioned on at least two counts: the availability of basic resources and, alternatively or additionally, the capacity of the environment to cope with the degree of interference implied.

It is only necessary to assert that something would reduce the 'standard of living,' and every debate is instantly closed. That soul-destroying, meaningless, mechanical, monotonous, moronic work is an insult to human nature which must necessarily and inevitably produce either escapism or aggression, and that no amount of 'bread and circuses' can compensate for the damage done—these are facts which are neither denied nor acknowledged but are met with an unbreakable conspiracy of silence—because to deny them would be too obviously absurd and to acknowledge them would condemn the central preoccupation of modern society as a crime against humanity.

It is hardly an exaggeration to say that, with increasing affluence, economics has moved into the very centre of public concern, and economic performance, economic growth, economic expansion, and so forth have become the abiding interest, if not the obsession, of all modern societies. In the current vocabulary of condemnation there are few words as final and conclusive as the word 'uneconomic.' If an activity has been branded as uneconomic, its right to existence is not merely questioned but energetically denied. Anything that is found to be an impediment to economic growth is a shameful thing, and if people cling to it, they are thought of as either saboteurs or fools. Call a thing immoral or ugly, soul-destroying or a degradation of man, a peril to the peace of the world or to the well-being of future generations; as long as you have not shown it to be 'uneconomic' you have not really questioned its right to exist, grow, and prosper.

But what does it *mean* when we say something is uneconomic? . . . The answer to this question cannot be in doubt: something is uneconomic when it fails to earn an adequate profit in terms of money. The method of economics does not, and cannot, produce any other meaning.

The judgment of economics, in other words, is an extremely *fragmentary* judgment; out of the large number of aspects which in real life have to be seen and judged together before a decision can be taken, economics supplies only one—whether a thing yields a money profit *to those who undertake it* or not.

Do not overlook the words 'to those who undertake it.' It is a great error to assume, for instance, that the methodology of economics is normally applied to determine whether an activity carried on by a group within society yields a profit to society as a whole. Even nationalised industries are not considered from this more comprehensive point of view. Every one of them is given a financial target—which is, in fact, an obligation—and is expected to pursue this target without regard to any damage it might be inflicting on other parts of the economy.

Economics, moreover, deals with goods in accordance with their market value and not in accordance with what they really are. The same rules and criteria are applied to primary goods, which man has to win from nature, and secondary goods, which presuppose the existence of primary goods and are manufactured from them. All goods are treated the same, because the point of view is fundamentally that of private profit-making, and this means that it is inherent in the methodology of economics *to ignore man's dependence on the natural world.*

To press non-economic values into the framework of the economic calculus, economists use the method of cost/benefit analysis. This is generally thought to be an enlightened and progressive development, as it is at least an attempt to take account of costs and benefits which might otherwise be disregarded altogether. In fact, however, it is a procedure by which the higher is reduced to the level of the lower and the priceless is given a price. It can therefore never serve to clarify the situation and lead to an enlightened decision. All it can do is lead to self-deception or the deception of others; for to undertake to measure the immeasurable is absurd and constitutes but an elaborate method of moving from preconceived notions to foregone conclusions; all one has to do to obtain the desired results is to impute suitable values to the immeasurable costs and benefits. The logical absurdity, however, is not the greatest fault of the undertaking: what is worse, and destructive of civilization, is the pretence that everything has a price or, in other words, that money is the highest of all values.

Having established by his purely quantitative methods that the Gross National Product of a country has risen by, say, five percent, the economist-turned-econometrician is unwilling, and generally unable, to face the question of whether this is to be taken as a good thing or a bad thing. He would lose all his certainties if he even entertained such a question: Growth of GNP must be a good thing, irrespective of what has grown and who, if anyone, has benefited. The idea that there could be pathological growth, unhealthy growth, disruptive or destructive growth is to him a perverse idea which must not be allowed to surface.

It is of course true that quality is much more difficult to 'handle' than quantity, just as the exercise of judgment is a higher function than the ability to count and calculate. Quantitative differences can be more easily grasped and certainly more easily defined than qualitative differences; their concreteness is beguiling and gives them the appearance of scientific precision, even when this precision has been purchased by the suppression of vital differences of quality. The great majority of economists is still pursuing the absurd ideal of making their 'science' as scientific and precise as physics, as if there were no qualitative difference between mindless atoms and men made in the image of God.

There is universal agreement that a fundamental source of wealth is human labour. Now, the modern economist has been brought up to consider 'labour' or work as little more than a necessary evil. From the point of view of the employer, it is in any case simply an item of cost, to be reduced to a minimum if it cannot be eliminated altogether, say, by automation. From the point of view of the workman, it is a 'disutility'; to work is to make a sacrifice of one's leisure and comfort, and wages are a kind of compensation for the sacrifice. Hence the ideal from the point of view of the employer is to have output without employees, and the ideal from the point of view of the employee is to have income without employment.

While the materialist is mainly interested in goods, the Buddhist is mainly interested in liberation. But Buddhism is 'The Middle Way' and therefore in no way antagonistic to physical well-being. It is not wealth that stands in the way of liberation but the attachment to wealth; not the enjoyment of pleasurable things but the craving for them. The keynote of Buddhist economics, therefore, is simplicity and non-violence. From an economist's point of view, the marvel of the Buddhist way of life is the utter rationality of its pattern—amazingly small means leading to extraordinarily satisfactory results.

For the modern economist this is very difficult to understand. He is used to measuring the 'standard of living' by the amount of annual consumption, assuming all the time that a man who consumes more is 'better off' than a man who consumes less. A Buddhist economist would consider this approach excessively irrational: since consumption is merely a means to human well-being, the aim should be to obtain the maximum of well-being with the minimum of consumption.

Buddhist economics is the systematic study of how to attain given ends with the minimum means.

The economics of giantism and automation is a left-over of nineteenth-century conditions and nineteenth-century thinking and it is totally incapable of solving any of the real problems of today. An entirely new system of thought is needed, a system based on attention to people, and not primarilty attention to goods—(the goods will look after themselves!). It could be summed up in the phrase, 'production by the masses, rather than mass production.'

What is the meaning of democracy, freedom, human dignity, standard of living, self-realisation, fulfillment? Is it a matter of goods, or of people? Of course it is a matter of people. But people can be themselves only in small comprehensible groups. Therefore we must learn to think in terms of an articulated structure that can cope with a multiplicity of small-scale units. If economic thinking cannot grasp this it is useless. If it cannot get beyond its vast abstractions, the national income, the rate of growth, capital/output ratio, input-output analysis, labour mobility, capital accumulation; if it cannot get beyond all this and make contact with the human realities of poverty, frustration, alienation, despair, breakdown, crime, escapism, stress, congestion, ugliness, and spiritual death, then let us scrap economics and start afresh.

When I first began to travel the world, visiting rich and poor countries alike, I was tempted to formulate the first law of economics as follows: 'The amount of real leisure a society enjoys tends to be in inverse proportion to the amount of labour-saving machinery it employs.' It might be a good idea for the professors of economics to put this proposition into their examination papers and ask their pupils to discuss it. However that may be, the evidence is very strong indeed. If you go from easy-going England to, say, Germany or the United States, you find that people there live under much more strain than here. And if you move to a country like Burma, which is very near to the bottom of the league table of industrial progress, you find that people have an enormous amount of leisure really to enjoy themselves. Of course, as there is so much less

It is the responsibility of the environmental movement to become involved in the issue of the environment inside the workplace.

Unless the environmental movement takes up this commitment, it will be hard to enlist the interest of working people in what appears to many of them as the much less immediate health problems of the general environment.

—LEONARD WOODCOCK

labour-saving machinery to help them, they 'accomplish' much less than we do; but that is a different point. The fact remains that the burden of living rests much more lightly on their shoulders than on ours.

The strength of the idea of private enterprise lies in its terrifying simplicity. It suggests that the totality of life can be reduced to one aspect—profits. The businessman, as a private individual, may still be interested in other aspects of life—perhaps even in goodness, truth and beauty—but *as a businessman* he concerns himself only with profits.

Everything becomes crystal clear after you have reduced reality to one—one only—of its thousand aspects. You know what to do—whatever produces profits; you know what to avoid—whatever reduces them or makes a loss. And there is at the same time a perfect measuring rod for the degree of success or failure. Let no one befog the issue by asking whether a particular action is conducive to the wealth and well-being of society, whether it leads to moral, aesthetic, or cultural enrichment. Simply find out whether it pays; simply investigate whether there is an alternative that pays better. If there is, choose the alternative.

It is no accident that successful businessmen are often astonishingly primitive; they live in a world made primitive by this process of reduction. They fit into this simplified version of the world and are satisfied with it. And when the real world occasionally makes its existence known and attempts to force upon their attention a different one of its facets, one not provided for in their philosophy, they tend to become quite helpless and confused. They feel exposed to incalculable dangers and 'unsound' forces and freely predict general disaster. As a result, their judgments on actions dictated by a more comprehensive outlook on the meaning and purpose of life are generally quite worthless.

General evidence of material progress would suggest that the *modern* private enterprise system is—or has been—the most perfect instrument for the pursuit of personal enrichment. The *modern* private enterprise system ingeniously employs the human urges of greed and envy as its motive power, but manages to overcome the most blatant deficiencies of *laissez-faire* by means of Keynesian economic management, a bit of redistributive taxation, and the 'countervailing power' of the trade unions.

Can such a system conceivably deal with the problems we are now having to face? The answer is self-evident: greed and envy demand continuous and limitless economic growth of a material kind, without proper regard for conservation, and this type of growth cannot possibly fit into a finite environment. We must therefore study the essential nature of the private enterprise system and the possibilities of evolving an alternative system which might fit the new situation.

We shrink back from the truth if we believe that the destructive forces of the modern world can be 'brought under control' simply by mobilizing more resources—of wealth, education, and research—to fight pollution, to preserve wildlife, to discover new sources of energy, and to arrive at more effective agreements on peaceful coexistence. Needless to say, wealth, education, research, and many other things are needed for any civilization, but what is most needed today is a revision of the ends which these means are meant to serve. And this implies, above all else, the development of a life-style which accords to material things their proper, legitimate place, which is secondary and not primary.

The 'logic of production' is neither the logic of life nor that of society. It is a small and subservient part of both. The destructive forces unleashed by it cannot be brought under control, unless the 'logic of production' itself is brought under control—so that destructive forces cease to be unleashed. It is of little use trying to suppress terrorism if the production of deadly devices continues to be deemed a legitimate employment of man's creative powers. Nor can the fight against pollution be successful if the patterns of production and consumption continue to be of a scale, a complexity, and a degree of violence which, as is becoming more and more apparent, do not fit into the laws of the universe, to which man is just as much subject as the rest of creation. Equally, the chance of mitigating the rate of resource depletion or of bringing harmony into the relationships between those in possession of wealth and power and those without is non-existent as long as there is no idea anywhere of enough being good and more-than-enough being evil.

Toward a Human Economics

Drafted by Nicholas Georgescu-Roegen, aided by Kenneth Boulding and Herman Daly, and signed by more than 200 economists

THE EVOLUTION of our global household earth is approaching a crisis on whose resolution man's very survival may depend, a crisis whose dimensions are indicated by current rates of population expansion, runaway industrial growth, and environmental pollution, with their attendant threats of famine, war and biological collapse.

This evolution, however, has not been determined solely by inexorable laws of nature, but by the human will operating within nature. Man has shaped his destiny through a history of decisions for which he is responsible; he can change the course of that destiny by new conscious decisions, by a new exertion of will. To begin with, he requires a new vision.

Basic to our function as economists is the description and analysis of economic processes as we observe them in operation. Increasingly over the last two hundred years, the economists have been called upon, and have undertaken, not merely to analyze, theorize, describe and measure the economic scene, but also to advise, to plan, and to take an active part in the conduct of affairs. The power of the economists, and therewith their responbsibility, has become very great indeed.

In the past, production has been regarded as a benefit. But production also entails costs that have only recently become apparent. Production necessarily drains our finite stock of raw materials and energy, while it floods the equally finite capacity of our ecosystem with the wastes of its processes. The economist's traditional measure of national and social health has been growth. But continued industrial growth in areas already highly industrialized is a short-term value only; present production continues to grow at the expense of future production, and at the expense of the delicate and evermore threatened environment.

The reality that our system is finite and that no expenditure of energy is free, confronts us with a moral decision at every point in the economic process, in planning and development and production. What do we need to make? What are the real, long-term costs of production, and who is required to pay them? What is truly in the interests of man, not in the present only, but as a continuing species? Even the clear formulation from the economist's perspective of the choices before us is an ethical task, not a purely analytical one, and economists ought to accept these ethical implications of their work.

We call upon our fellow economists to embrace their role in the management of our earth home, and to join the efforts of other scientists and planners, indeed, of other men and women in all areas of thought and endeavor, to ensure the survival of man. The science of economics, like other fields of inquiry in search of precision and objectivity, has tended in the last century increasingly to isolate its domain from others. But the time when economists could fruitfully work in isolation is gone.

We must have a new economics whose purpose is the husbanding of resources and the achievement of rational control over the development and application of technology to serve real human needs rather than expanding profits, warfare, or national prestige. We must have an economics of survival, still more, of hope—theory and vision of a global economy based on justice, which would make possible the equitable distribution of the earth's wealth among its people, present and future.

It is clear that we can no longer usefully consider apparently separate national economies apart from their relations to the larger global system. But economists can do more than measure and describe the complex interrelations among economic entities; we can work actively for a new order of priorities that transcends the narrow interests of national sovereignty and serves instead the interests of the world community. We must replace the ideal of growth, which has served as a substitute for equitable distribution of wealth, with a more humane vision in which production and consumption are subordinated to the goals of survival and justice.

Currently, a minority of the earth's people enjoy an inordinate share of resources and industrial capacity.

These industrial economies, capitalist and socialist alike, must find ways to cooperate with developing economies to correct the imbalance, without pursuing ideological or imperialist competition, and without exploiting the people they propose to aid. In order to achieve equitable distribution of wealth throughout the world, the people of the industrialized countries must relinquish what now seems an unbounded right to consume whatever resources are available to them, and we as economists must play a role in the reshaping of human values toward this end. The accidents of history and geography must no longer serve as rationale for injustice.

The task for economists is therefore an extremely novel and difficult one. Many people now look at the available data—the trends of population growth, pollution, resource depletion, and social upheaval—and lose hope. We have already passed the point of no return toward our rendezvous with disaster, they say gloomily; nothing can be done. But despair is a position we must reject. The moral imperative is for us to create a new vision, to make a road to survival through a treacherous country where there are no roads. At the present moment, man possesses the wealth and the technology not only to save himself for a very long future, but to make for himself and for all his children a world in which it is possible to live with dignity and hope and comfort; but he must decide to do it. We call on economists to join in framing the new vision that will enable man to use his wealth in his own interests, disagreeing, perhaps, on details of method and policy, but agreeing emphatically on the goals of survival and justice.

Nicholas Georgescu-Roegen:

Entropy the Measure of Economic Man

NICHOLAS WADE

NASHVILLE STYLES ITSELF the Athens of the South, and sports a perfect concrete replica of the Parthenon to establish the point. Another local temple, the Hall of Fame, attests to Nashville's position as the national focus of country music. Yet despite its 14 centers of higher learning, the city cannot even support a decent orchestra, grumbles Nicholas Georgescu-Roegen, a long-time resident who is [retired] professor of economics at Vanderbilt University.

Georgescu-Roegen, a Romanian by birth and a statistician by early training, is himself one of the ornaments of Nashville, though probably few of its citizens have ever heard of him. Only in the last few years has his name become known beyond the select fraternity of mathematical economists. There he has long been regarded as one of the specialty's pioneers. His colleagues consider his work to be Nobel Prize material. Nobelist Paul Samuelson of the Massachusetts Institute of Technology, in the foreword to a collection of Georgescu-Roegen's essays, describes him as "a scholar's scholar, an economist's economist," a man whose ideas "will interest minds when today's skyscrapers have crumbled back to sand."

In the last few years Georgescu-Roegen has left the ivory tower altitudes of the pure theory of consumer choice and begun to adumbrate a theory of Malthusian comprehsiveness and all-but-Malthusian gloom. It implies, in brief, that unless man can reorient his technology and economy toward the energy that comes directly from the sun, his life as a species will be sharply limited by his "terrestrial dowry" of low entropy materials.

The theory has received less attention than it almost certainly merits. For one thing, Georgescu-Roegen believes that economic activity must not merely cease to grow, as the Club of Rome suggested in its *Limits to Growth,* but will eventually decline. Neither sentiment is at the pinnacle of economic intellectual fashion. For another, the full implications of the thesis became apparent only during 1974. Its theoretical basis was laid out in 1971 in *The Entropy Law and the Economic Process*, a stimulating but difficult book which is probably more often praised than read. The practical consequences are described in "Energy and economic myths," a paper published in January, 1975, in the *Southern Economic Journal*. The thesis has received resounding accolades from Georgescu-Roegen's intellectual allies, but has so far been largely ignored by orthodox economists. "The behavior of the economic growth people has been like the Sherlock Holmes case of the dog that barked in the night—strangely silent," comments Herman Daly of Louisiana State University. The thesis' claim to public attention, in other words, rests at present on its merits and on its author's formidable scholarly reputation, rather than on the unanimous plaudits of the economic profession.

The starting point of Georgescu-Roegen's theory is the entropy law, or second law of thermodynamics. The law is a broad, almost philosophical concept which has had many formulations in its 110-year history. Central to all of them is the notion of irreversibility, that certain processes go in one direction only and can never be repeated except at far greater cost on the whole. A given lump of coal, for example, can be burned only once. There is of course the same amount of energy in the heat, smoke, and ashes as there was in the lump of coal (that is stipulated by the first law of thermodynamics governing the conservation of matter-energy), but the energy bound up in the combustion products is so dissipated that it is unavailable for use, unlike the "free" energy in the coal, and the process cannot be reversed.

Entropy is a measure of this bound or dissipated energy. The entropy law says that the entropy of a closed system always increases, the change being from free energy to bound, not the other way about. Entropy is also a measure of disorderliness (dissipated energy represents a more chaotic situation than that before the lump of coal was burned). So the entropy law is also saying that the natural state of things is to pass always from order to disorder. Whence the notion of entropy as time's arrow.

The idea of entropy as an index of disorder underlies the description of certain materials as possessing low entropy. An ingot of copper has low entropy because its atoms are disposed in a more orderly state than they were in the original copper ore. Did the refiner create low entropy in making the ingot? No, because in the smelting he engendered far more high entropy by converting free energy to bound. All man's activities, says the entropy law, end in deficit; you cannot get anything except at a far greater cost in low entropy.

There is one more tentacle of the entropy law to examine before considering how Georgescu-Roegen deploys it against the foundations of conventional economics. For a deep law of physics, the entropy law's distinction between free and bound, available and unavailable energy may sound strangely anthropomorphic. And indeed it is anthropomorphic. A pure intellect would not comprehend the distinction: it would just see energy shifting about. The difference is important only to living organisms, because they exist on the slope between low entropy and high. They absorb low entropy by feeding, directly or indirectly, on sunlight, and they give out high entropy in the form of waste and heat.

All species depend on the sun as their ultimate source of low entropy except man, who has learned also to exploit the terrestrial stores of low entropy such as minerals and fossil fuels. Life feeds on low entropy; and so does economic life. Objects of economic value, such as fruit, cloth, china, lumber, and copper, are highly ordered, low entropy structures. For low entropy is the true taproot of economic scarcity.

What Georgescu-Roegen is saying is both profound and yet very simple. He asserts that the entropy law rules supreme over the economic process. The physics student who considers that an obvious truth should try looking for it in an economics textbook. He won't find it, because standard economists (says Georgescu-Roegen) assume a physical model of the world in which everything is perfectly reversible, in which after every disturbance the system comes back into equilibrium and all goes on as before. Standard economists teach that economics is a closed, circular process, an endless pendulum movement between production and consumption in which the exhaustibility of natural resources raises no problem, and the cure-all for pollution is simply to get prices right. Such conceptions are based on the mechanistic framework which economists borrowed long ago from physics, and which they have never revised to redress its basic omission, that of the law of entropy.

Once we recall that none of man's activities eludes the entropy law, the economic process appears in a very different light. For one thing, the process can now be recognized to be not circular and timeless, but irrevocable. It consists quintessentially of the continuous and irreversible transformation of low entropy into high. The basic inputs are drawn from the solar flow of low entropy and from the terrestrial stocks. The material output is high entropy in the form of pollution and dissipated matter and heat. The true—that is, the intended—output of the economic process is in fact an intangible: the enjoyment of life.

This is a radically different view of the economic process from that in the textbooks and, not surprisingly, it stresses different aspects. It places paramount emphasis on the inputs to the process (energy and natural resources) and on the output (pollution). Both are aspects which for long escaped serious attention, says Georgescu-Roegen, because of the propensity of standard economists (and of Marxists) to ignore the natural environment.

The economic process being by the entropy law irrevocable, Georgescu-Roegen is led also to stress its place in history, particularly the way in which the present pattern of economic activity will affect that of future generations. Because the terrestrial dowry of ordered material structures is finite, every Cadillac or every Zim we make today, let alone any instrument of war, "means fewer plowshares for future generations, and implicitly, fewer human beings too." Economic development, Georgescu-Roegen considers, "is definitely against the interest of the human species as a whole if its interest is to have a lifespan as long as is compatible with its dowry of low entropy."

Mechanized agriculture, including the Green Revolution, is also against the long-run interest of mankind, because of the vastly different abundances of solar and terrestrial low entropy. The earth's outstanding recoverable reserves of fossil fuel are estimated to be the equivalent of about 2 weeks' sunlight. Yet the modern method of agriculture replaces the water buffalo and its manure (both the product of solar energy, which is almost a free good) with the tractor and chemical fertilizer (both derived from terrestrial sources of low entropy). In doing so, it substitutes scarce elements for one that is abundant. This is why the Green Revolution, even though it is the only way to feed populations now, is in the long run such a bad deal for mankind.

Mechanized agriculture allows a larger population to survive now at the expense of a greater reduction in the amount of future life. What of the life-span of mankind as a species? If the worst befalls, when his terrestrial dowry is completely exhausted, could not man revert to the cave and survive as once he did by berry picking? The thought ignores that, evolution being irrevocable, steps cannot be retraced in history. Mankind, Georgescu-Roegen believes, has become addicted to his "exosomatic" instruments, those organs which are part of his evolution but not part of his biological constitution. Man's exosomatic instruments, which economists call capital equipment, and which are the ultimate cause of the social conflict that distinguishes the human species (the advantage derived from their improvement became the basis of inequality between individuals and groups), are comforts that man will never give up.

How are we to preserve their share of the terrestrial dowry for future generations? "Standard" economists might suggest that the price mechanism will offset scarcities. But, says Georgescu-Roegen, prices are only a parochial expression of value unless everyone concerned can bid—and future generations are excluded from today's market, which is why oil, for example still sells for the merest fraction of its true value. The only way to protect future generations from the present spasmodic squandering of our energy bonanza is "by reeducating ourselves so as to feel some sympathy for our future fellow humans."

The monopoly of the present over future generations would be substantially reduced in an economy based primarily on the flow of solar energy. Such an economy would still need to tap the terrestrial dowry, especially for materials, and the depletion of these critical resources must therefore be rendered as small as possible. How is this to be accomplished? Georgescu-Roegen has proposed a "minimal bioeconomic program" which, though admittedly utopian, points in what he considers the right directions:

—Production of all instruments of war should be prohibited completely.

—With the productive forces thereby released, industrial nations should help the underdeveloped na-

Budd Gray/Jeroboam, Inc.

tions to arrive as quickly as possible at a good (but not luxurious) life.

—Mankind should gradually lower its population to a level that can be adequately fed only through organic agriculture, a burden that will fall most heavily on the underdeveloped nations.

—Until direct use of solar energy becomes a general convenience or controlled fusion is achieved, all waste of energy—by overheating, overcooling, overspeeding, and so forth—should be avoided, if necessary by regulation.

—Consumption for the sake of fashion, such as getting a new car each year, should be regarded as a bioeconomic crime; manufacturers should focus on durability, designing their products for long life and ease of repair.

"Will mankind listen to any program that implies a constriction of its addiction to exosomatic comfort? Perhaps the destiny of man is to have a short, but fiery, exciting and extravagant life rather than a long, uneventful and vegetative existence. Let other species— the amoebas, for example—which have no spiritual ambitions, inherit an earth still bathed in plenty of sunshine."

Georgescu-Roegen's bioeconomic program, even if utopian, is a surprisingly practical platform for a man who has spent most of his academic life as a pure scholar. But Georgescu-Roegen has been through some very practical experiences. Born in Constanza, Romania, in 1906, he was turned toward mathematics

Adherence to the idea of aggregate economic growth may have its justifications, but the belief that it helps to alleviate poverty is among the poorest. The "trickle-down" theory, if it works at all, is neither fast enough nor equitable enough to meet the needs of all people in the short time we have available to make the transition to a low-energy economy. In a future of energy and materials austerity, the sort of GNP growth we as a nation have come to expect will be impossible to maintain, and will hardly lend itself to the redistribution of income.
—JOHN STEINHART

by his father, a retired army officer. He won a government scholarship to study in Paris, and was advised to choose statistics, a specialty in short supply in Romania. His dissertation was on a method for discovering cycles in irregular phenomena. (He didn't apply it to business cycles, although that was the original inspiration, because of an intuition, which he later proved correct, that business cycles are not truly cyclical.) Georgescu-Roegen then studied in London under Karl Pearson, the founder of mathematical statistics, before returning to Romania where, at the age of 26, he obtained a professorial chair in statistics at Bucharest.

While in London he had applied for a Rockefeller fellowship to study with a program called the Harvard economic barometer. He took up the scholarship in 1934 only to discover on arrival that the barometer had perished long ago: it had issued, on the eve of the Black Tuesday that heralded the great stock exchange collapse, a public prediction that the economy was set fair. Instead, he studied with Joseph Schumpeter, the great economic theorist, and developed an interest in economics.

Despite Schumpeter's pleas, Georgescu-Roegen returned to Romania before World War II. He did statistical jobs for various ministries, acquired some reputation as an administrator, and after the war was appointed secretary-general of the armistice commission, the only Romanian authority the Russians would deal with. The period was not without strain. Requests that Russian soldiers would desist raping women and children were threateningly dismissed as insults to the honor of the Red Army; Georgescu-Roegen was powerless to complain when his own sister-in-law was killed trying to escape from Russian soldiers. He was also head of the Romanian delegation negotiating the payment of the crushing reparations demanded by the Russians—$300 million at 1938 prices. On the day fixed for signing the agreement, the Russians denounced the head of their own delegation as an impostor and the whole negotiation had to start all over again.

Some months after these events, Georgescu-Roegen stowed away with his wife, Otilia, on a boat bound for Istanbul. He returned to Harvard, but the university could not immediately offer him a tenured position. At that stage, he wanted not to move again, and accepted a tenured post from Vanderbilt University.

In conversation, Georgescu-Roegen speaks animatedly of his new theory and of the failure of the would-be critics among his colleagues to come out and debate with him. Asked the reason for his critics' muteness, he replies with a Romanian proverb—'Don't mention the cord in the house of the hanged.' "I am very unpopular with economists," he says, comparing his attack on standard economics to the action of a man who confiscates marbles from children. "They will never forget that, but the next generation of economists will speak only my language."

Coming from a lesser man, the prediction might sound vainglorious. But Georgescu-Roegen inspires favorable reviews from independents and sky-high praise from those who agree with him. Economist Kenneth Boulding, in a review of *The Entropy Law and the Economic Process (Science,* 10 March 1972), wrote that the book had real defects but that "If . . .the right 500 people were to read it, science perhaps would never be quite the same again." Joseph J. Spengler of Duke University, a past president of the American Economic Association, believes that this and Georgescu-Roegen's earlier book "will come to be recognized as two of the greatest books we have had in the first three quarters of this century." According to Herman Daly, a proponent of the steady-state economy, Georgescu-Roegen's new thesis has not yet been fully digested but when it has been, "it will win him a place as one of the most important economists of our time. What he has done is to tie economics back to its biophysical foundations— it is that divorce that has led to many of our current problems such as pollution."

Alvin Weinberg, director of the Institute for Energy

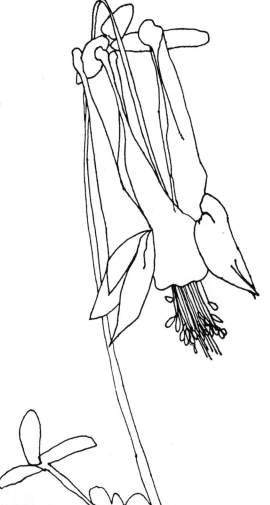

Cheryl Nichols

Analysis and a man whose outlook on energy might be expected to make him an opponent of Georgescu-Roegen's, describes him as a "highly original thinker" whose views people are now beginning to take more seriously. But Weinberg begs off detailed discussion of the thesis, saying he is not an economist. Similarly economist Paul Samuelson professes incompetence to judge Georgescu-Roegen's ideas on entropy, but adds that his tennis partner, a scientist, informs him they are essentially sound. Samuelson finds "everything he writes extremely stimulating," but notes that, as with Malthus, "there is not much refutable about 'Just-you-wait' statements."

Georgescu-Roegen is willing to put more urgency into his "just-you-wait statements" in conversation than he is in print. He regards man's present place in history as being near the end of an unrepeatable bonanza of cheap fuel. "When the bonanza disappears, we may get into the kind of experience similar to that of species like fish which find they have to adapt to living in shallower waters. But in our case it would be a political and sociological change, not a biological modification. Evolution, even exosomatic evolution, is not reversible—man would rather die in the penthouse than live in the cave."

Pressed to say how and when the crisis may come, Georgescu-Roegen replies, "For the near future, I don't know. But in 50 or 60 years the world might find itself in a half anarchic state. I am not saying there will not be a government in the United States. But the tendency for the state to become more and more important in the individual's life will reverse. People will live in isolation from the state. These hippies maybe an avant-garde pre-adaptation. People would have to educate their children at home because there would not be enough taxes for schools. The population might have to go down, I don't know how—it might be from the disorganization in the means of communication or of hospital care."

Whether or not this verbal presentiment turns out to be accurate, Georgescu-Roegen's general theory is a powerful and ambitious synthesis that would seem to deserve more attention than has yet been its lot. Though some of his general conclusions have been touched on by others (notably by Kenneth Boulding in his 1966 essay "The economics of the coming spaceship earth"), Georgescu-Roegen has developed the scholarly underpinning of a broad theoretical framework. The theory offers potential support to many of the ideas of ecologists, environmentalists, advocates of zero population growth, opponents of economic growth, alternative technologists, and other critics of the established economic order. Here at least, if not also among "standard" economists, Georgescu-Roegen should find an increasing following.

Environmental Decision-Making in A Participatory Democracy

An Address to the Stanford Business School

J. IRWIN MILLER

MY REMARKS THIS EVENING will be addressed to those of you present who are students. While we will be exploring some territory different from that covered earlier, it will not be unrelated to the subject of this symposium, and I hope will not be without interest to you.

To remind ourselves one final time, it says in our program:

"The purpose (of this symposium) is to explore the processes by which businesses incorporate the needs of the natural environment and the economic goals of development and growth into their decision-making."

Each of these phrases, "the needs of the natural environment" and "economic development and growth," can be usefully considered as *means* to an end, rather than *ends* in themselves. I would like, therefore, to talk about the end itself, as I perceive it, and the kinds of shapes you will have the opportunity to give to that "end" during your lifetimes.

I come to the subject with a complex of biases. I am biased by the particular decades in which I have lived, by the kind of education I received. I am also biased by the influence on me of the business in which I have been engaged for 40 years. Diesel engines move the freight. They use petroleum products ever more efficiently. They also emit to the air nitrogen oxides and particulates, technical problems which have not proved easy and may be expensive to solve. Finally, I am biased by having been a manager for so long—and by being relatively privileged economically.

You may consider such a basket of biases either disqualifying—or a collection of useful experiences. As you listen and judge, however, bear something else in mind: Each of you is also biased. You are biased by the fact that you are only 24 or 28. You have known the Great Depression and Hitler and World War II only through books, and you have in actuality experienced mainly the 60's and 70's.

The point of all this is that no one of us, recognizing his personal state of affairs or set of experiences, ought to be so sure of his own opinions or so confident of himself that he is not open to the possibility of a better opinion or a new look at the future. I should never be too sure that a long experience of somewhat complex responsibilities gives me access to absolute truth. You should not be certain that a life lived only in the latter half of the 20th Century and devoted, so far, more to learning than to doing, necessarily purifies and validates your outlook. Beware of certainties, and beware of ideology, whether that ideology be "free enterprise," "environmentalism," "consumerism," "the moral majority," Shiite Islam, or the quick disparagement of the motives of any person who disagrees with us.

So, with a mutual spirit that is not too sure of itself, and with some willingness to entertain varieties of opinions, let us proceed, and we will begin with the word, "DECISIONS."

You know a great deal about decision-trees, and about cost-benefit analyses, and about all the other phrases and concepts which I find a little strange, but also most impressive. This is surely useful knowledge. Economics and decision-trees and cost-benefits get into environmental decision-making, but something else gets into it too; and, if I spend more of my time than you think I should talking about this "something else," that will be because I think that, in most schools of business, less time is spent than ought to be spent in understanding and thinking about the "something else."

Let us now look at two interesting kinds of environmental decisions. The first is the Grand Canyon of the Colorado. I believe that virtually everyone in this room would agree that this area should be preserved as nearly as possible in its natural state, including the natural balance of flowers and animals, and that all should be done with reasonable access by human beings, so that men and women could see and enjoy in its natural form this most remarkable area. So much for the Grand Canyon. . . . Now let us consider our second example, the American Midwest (where I live). Less than 200 years ago it was a vast hardwood forest with oak, walnut, hickory, and poplar trees averaging 120 feet high. The foliage was so dense that sunlight seldom reached the ground. There was little or no undergrowth, and early settlers could drive their wagons through it as if through a great park. The area was full of buffalo, deer, otter, beaver, bear, fox, squirrel, as well as rattlesnakes, water moccasins, all kinds of fish, malarial mosquitoes, poison ivy, and a few Indians. The fertile topsoil ran more than 40 feet deep, and there was no other place quite like it on earth.

Now—if we had the chance, what would our environmental decision be on the preservation of this other unique piece of nature? The Midwest decision would give our society more trouble, would it not? There might be a few who would be for leaving it untouched, but I think they would be in the minority. Most people, in varying degrees and in various ways, would be for clearing this extraordinarily fertile area and raising on it food to feed humans. Some would leave a few more trees than others. All of us would favor a better compromise with the Indians than simply driving them out. But almost no one would favor leaving the area totally in its natural state, as most of us would advocate for the Grand Canyon. And we would make this decision about the Midwest in the face of the unavoidable fact that the buffalo, bear, wild turkey, otter, beaver, fox, rattlesnakes—and the Indians—would either be destroyed, or would be greatly diminished in number, or would leave the area.

How can we make such contrary decisions about our environment, about animals, about other human beings? I think we would have to agree that these two decisions are not as contradictory as they first seem, for each one is made on the same premise: The needs and desires of men and women come first. We have taken over the planet, and our concern is not to preserve its environment just for the sake of preserving the environment; it is to preserve and maintain what

we consider to be a good environment *for mankind.* I guess it is this final environment about which I propose to talk.

In environmental decision-making, people on all sides put man first, and perhaps each puts his own group slightly ahead of mankind in general. Where we differ is in our ideas of what puts man first. The cartoon figure of the typical businessman says that he puts short-term profits and the prosperity of his corporation first, and the comparable caricature of the environmentalist has him putting hiking and camping first. At either end of the spectrum, however, the position, the stand, the decision always places some desire or purpose of *man* first. No one really proposes leaving Alaska to the grizzlies and never allowing a human to enter—ever again. Even our occasional enthusiasm for the snail darter is less a concern for the fish itself and more often a ploy to defeat a group with whom one is in emotional disagreement.

Man has thought this way for a very long time. Each of us in his own way agrees with the psalmist:

"Thou has given (man) dominion
  over the works of thy hands,
Thou has put all things
  under his feet,
All sheep and oxen, and also
  the beasts of the fields,
The birds of the air, and the
  fish of the sea."

Our disagreements are about *how* we exercise "dominion," and very little or not at all about *whether* we exercise it. In all our talking about "rights," we talk very little indeed about the rights of animals. (We are meat-eaters after all.) Or the rights of bushes, or the rights of the smallpox virus. We are selectively benevolent or hostile to each of these according as we perceive them affecting for good or ill the kind of local and planetary environment we think best for ourselves.

I mention this because I believe it is important to acknowledge that we are driven to our subject by the prod of self-interest. We differ as to how that self-interest ought to be defined, but Business Roundtable, Sierra Club, AFL-CIO, and the Mudlark Garden Club all come to problems of the environment out of concern for mankind, not out of concern for the environment for its own sake.

I think that all this may be based on a subconscious fear. After all, it is not the environment which is fragile; it is man who is fragile. In the long ages of the planet, the environment always recovers. Species, so far, almost always disappear. We can never quite forget this.

There is a second characteristic of our subject to which I also wish to call attention: Environmental problems are intertwined with almost all other problems, each of which in turn affects, for good or ill, mankind. Environmental problems are entwined, for a single example, with our energy problems. The availability of large supplies of energy has made possible the general material well-being of the 220 million Americans alive today. Before you remind me, I will confess that this material well-being could, of course, be more evenly or fairly distributed, and that a good deal of the energy is wasted. But despite the validity of all equity and efficiency charges, it remains true that our generally high standard of living nevertheless hangs upon a liberal and imaginative use of energy. It is energy that extends what a man can do. The energy required to heat a cup of tea, for example, would require a man to pedal a bicycle as hard as he could for fifteen minutes. By ourselves, with nothing but our hands, we can't accomplish much.

Our use of energy has been increasing at a compound annual rate of close to 3.5 percent for the past one hundred years. This energy comes almost entirely from non-renewable sources. So, as is often said, for a hundred years we have been consuming finite resources at an exponential rate. Herman Kahn, Elliot Janeway, and others tell us not to worry. There is plenty that remains, and all we have to do is go and get it, which will probably happen, they feel, if Government will just bug off. But at some time, exponential growth must be tamed, or we must tap renewable sources, or, better, yet, infinite sources.

All this is not impossible, but *time* gets in the way. From virtually zero in 1880, oil and gas in 1980 constitute 72 percent of our energy consumption, a condition which nothing is going to change significantly in even a generation. Since the Oil Embargo of 1974, new finds have failed to keep pace with consumption, and, for the USA, in the same time period our oil imports have doubled in percent. As if this weren't alarming enough, the share of imports which comes from the Middle East, the politically least stable area on earth, has increased about four times. Loss of 20 percent of our oil, the possibility of which will remain very real indeed for at least the next twenty years, could effectively shut us down as a functioning nation.

Our energy problem then is more a critical short-term problem, and less a long-term one. Given the political forces at work in today's world, nationalism, liberation movements, religious movements, and, given that all these forces are at work with special intensity throughout the major oil-producing countries of the Middle East, our energy problem becomes, "How do we reduce our energy dependence on the Middle East as rapidly as possible—and in time?" Avoidance of World War III hangs on our doing this. The maintenance of employment opportunity in a society more and more of whose members want to work hangs on it, and probably our own internal domestic stability as well.

Right here our energy concerns for our people and our environmental concerns for the same people meet head on: Clean air vs. World War III; a ravaged landscape vs. mass unemployment. That is, of course, raising the confrontation to levels of hysteria, but something like that is not unlikely to be the way we will approach our environment/energy decisions.

It is the way we increasingly approach too many decisions today. The pro-abortionists say a woman should have the say about her own body. The anti-abortionists say, "We are opposed to murder." A Senator makes a brilliant speech proclaiming that only he and his embattled followers favor solving inflation and unemployment simultaneously (without bothering to say how). An anti-gun-control group meets with its Congressman and assures him that his stands pro or con on welfare reform, or inflation, or Salt II, or energy, or even support of local industry and agriculture mean nothing to them. If he does not vote against gun control, they will use all the influence they can muster to defeat him.

A young MBA, doing well in a corporation, has the strongest possible feeling as to the strategic program the corporation should adopt. He makes his pitch to the management committee, and, after hearing him out, management rejects his program and chooses another. As the company then embarks on this other program, our young MBA continues to disparage it to his peers, gives lukewarm or perhaps no cooperation in its implementation, and will be secretly overjoyed if it fails.

These examples, varied as they are, are cited to help me make a point. In an interdependent society, if everyone is shouting and nobody is listening, we are in for trouble. Because of our complexity, every single decision, every single stand, alters, for good or bad, in ways great or small, almost every other decision or complex of decisions. Such interactions, if not taken into account, can, more often than not, be disastrous. Further if we do not take account of them in a useful and responsible way, and if we do not seek some intelligent balance, the results can be equally disastrous.

To "take account" of them properly, we must first of all be responsible to fact. Our data must be solid and unbiased. We must be forever open to its implications. This is not the direction in which we seem to be heading. We have elevated opinions and the new word, "values," to a status at least on a par with truth. Opinions and values have a high emotional and subjective content. All too often they can be maintained only by means of a cavalier disregard for facts. It is a truth that "truth" will always escape us, but it is another truth that we approach ultimate truth only by means of a respect for facts, by an open-minded, humble pursuit of factual knowledge, and by a constant willingness to be led by facts and never to manipulate facts. The ultimate example of the trend which I deplore is the statement of a lofty government bureaucrat to a friend of mine, "In politics, facts are negotiable."

A society which convinces itself that one man's opinions or one man's values are just as good as any other man's opinions or values; a society which gives only a passing nod to the importance of relevant facts, which is impatient with the time required to discover facts, and which considers facts to be like golf clubs (one first decides on the shot one wishes to make, then searches for the best club [or fact] to make that shot); such a society will end only in head-to-head controversy, will be unable to resolve its problems, and somewhere down the road will invite a strong man to take over.

By contrast, a society which is sensitive to its delicate interdependence, to the interactions which will destroy any casually contrived program; a society which values better and better facts and data, which is especially responsible to them precisely when they do not support one's own bias; a society which has an eternal concern for the other fellow, his needs, his point of view; such a society, however it has organized itself, has a more than fair chance to achieve a workable consensus, to cooperate, to solve its problems, to prevent its disasters—to create and sustain a good environment for its people.

What does all this add up to? Environment, energy, inflation, unemployment, fiscal balance, monetary stability, and social progress are all intertwined. If we act on one item or one concern alone, we probably screw up one or all of the others. The only action that will keep the society in any kind of balance is one which tries to take thoughtful account of all serious interactions, and all serious needs and points of view, to reach best possible compromise, and to achieve democratic consensus as it does so. Such a society, one must note, is a cooperative society, not an adversary society. . . . Today we seem to be proceeding more and more toward adversary solutions, and to have less and less competence in cooperating.

Other speakers have expressed similar concern about our growing predilection for using the adversary approach. It is not too early in your careers to sound a warning.

An adversary society is a negative society. In an adversary society, as we now see, any group and sometimes a single person can stop almost anything from being done. To accomplish a great program, however, requires a sophisticated degree of cooperation, of intellectual generosity, and of responsiveness to fact. This is not our national characteristic just now.

If some of you are agreeing with me, let me ask a question: Are you automatically assigning in your minds responsiblity for this state of affairs to someone else: to my own stupid generation, to Congress, to leaders everywhere?

Today we seem to find villains everywhere but in our own circle—the dinosaur corporations, stupid government, reactionary universities, an apathetic and greedy public—everybody but us. If I have led you to believe that the villains are elsewhere, you have missed my point. Each of *you* is already a part of this act. Each of you will carry into your job a set of attitudes which will in some degree leave a mark on the company or community in which you find yourself. Since there is scarcely one of you who does not intend to be a chief executive officer somewhere, sometime, each of you before you reach the graveyard will have an exceptional degree of influence on your times. Each of you will soon be that "other fellow" about whom the nation's youth will then complain.

It is an interesting question to ask oneself: Would you hire your present self when you become chief executive officer, knowing yourself as well as you do? Would you like to manage a company composed of persons like yourself?

I am now going to lapse into the kind of language which you have come to recognize as straight bull, and which would be considered embarrassingly naive if introduced into any business school class. Since I am a little defensive about it, you must first note something: The language of your classes has become today an academic language, a professional language. The purpose of a professional language has, since the Middle Ages, never been clarity, but rather exclusivity, to be mysterious to those outside the profession. No self-respecting doctor would ever tell a patient that he has a stomach ache; his profession requires the use

of the term, "mild gastro-enteritis." And so it is with the other professions; law, sociology, theologians, and finally teachers of business, one of the latest arrivals among the learned professions. This professional language is carried over into business with enthusiasm by junior management, but it is not at all a language used by senior management, even by those who in their day were business school graduates. Professional language is not all bad, but in a sense it is an adversary language, a means of excluding rather than including.

Now comes the other kind of language.

You can have a lot of fun reading *Who's Who* nowadays. The management of this publication has recently permitted invitees to add a sentence or two of comments. These sentences have a fascination for me, even though they range from mostly dull and pompous to a few exciting and provocative ones. They are worth your perusing. If you make CEO, you too will wind up in *Who's Who,* and you too will be making "meaningful' comments. Listen to some of today's batch.

A professional accountant writes: "To be understanding of difference of opinion and thought; to be willing to give oneself to serve others less fortunate."

A professor: "In the pursuit of success, to be vigilant not to infringe on the happiness of others or confuse the means with the end."

A doctor: "Never guess. Secure the facts. Measure rather than estimate. Differentiate fact from hypothesis."

A biochemist: "One of the most difficult skills is to develop the ability to recognize—and then admit error."

And finally, a dermatologist: "Until you have gotten and weighed all obtainable facts, try to form no adverse opinion—above all, try to *express* no adverse opinion. Even then, before you judge, put yourself in the place of the other fellow."

No more quoting. You will now see what I meant when I said this is the language of bull, of all the hypocritical, tired clichés from which you have been liberated.

But we should bear in mind something. These are all persons who are "successes" in the very sense that you and I regularly use that word. They don't have to impress anyone any more. Their language may be conventional and their expressions ordinary, but any random inspection of these two enormous volumes will leave the reader with one dominant impression: Each of these persons is terribly in earnest. Each is trying to speak to others out of a long experience, which the world has labeled successful, and they all

feel that what they have to say is not what the world wants to hear today. The most poignant of the excerpts is from William Saroyan, "I'm 65. . . . I'm ignorant. I used to be angry about this. It is all right to be ignorant, just so you know it."

You spend here two years pouring over thousands of cases. In each you see how stupidly management acts, what it should have done. In such a godlike environment, it is easy to forget how ignorant each of us is. Time after time I watch the top MBA, placed on his first supervisory job, disintegrate in the face of his very first real decision. He has forgotten that he is ignorant, and that it is all right to be ignorant, just so he knows it.

The confident language of Game Plans and of Corporate Power and how to use or manipulate power and people is the language of the adversary approach to human relations. What you have heard in the excerpts I have read is a sort of final commitment to compassion, to humility, and to the idea that only selfless cooperation works. You will have to make up your own minds as to which environment you will choose to create as you embark on your careers.

During the active years of your business lives, I would suspect that an instability of long standing in American society will be resolved. I am not certain whether it will be a happy or an unhappy resolution but I am reasonably sure that this instability has lasted in the USA about as long as it can, and I am equally sure that the attitudes and goals of coming business leaders, namely you, will affect the final result and the national environment—one way or another.

Politically, we Americans are a democracy, and still fiercely committed to democracy, though we have various ways of defining it. Business, however, remains a monarchy. Some businesses operate as constitutional monarchies, some as absolute monarchies, and a very few as hereditary monarchies. My guess is that, given the rising forces of the times, these two systems, the political democracy and the business monarchy, will not, for too much longer, survive side by side unchanged. For whatever reason, education, the spread of information, or the natural evolution of ideas, the talk we hear today is for "participation," and for "a say in what happens." These are the words used in justification of terrorism by the African National Congress; they are heard from time to time on the shop floor; and they are heard in fairly strident tones from junior management, persons like yourselves.

In some form or other, the virus of participatory democracy will invade the organization of business during your active lifetimes. If this happens rapidly, while you are still in junior or middle management, you will cheer as it affects your relations with your superiors, and you will view with alarm its spread through the ranks below you. More likely, it will reach some kind of crescendo about the time you personally arrive at the top. A good many of you will be threatened by its coming, and will consider it to be aimed personally at you. At that time, you will find it hard to view the change dispassionately, but just now you can. So let's talk about it.

Going back to our earlier comments on current American society, it is clear that democracy can arrive in many forms, but it survives, if history is a reliable guide, not for very long. Already the American democracy has lasted longer than the Athenian democracy, and with our taste for adversary procedure, we may all too soon find ourselves paralyzed, unable to act, and tempted to give up on democracy.

An adversary democracy in business would, I imagine, fail very quickly. In an increasingly competitive world, a single business composed of individuals individually pursuing their own agenda would not last very long. A business, however, which learns how to tap all the knowledge and experience contained in its members, and through a collective judgment to achieve a focussed set of plans and goals, and as well thoroughly cooperative execution, even from those who didn't get their way, may be very hard to beat.

What might be the characteristic of an effective, durable, industrial democracy? I do not personally find them in the experiments labeled "co-determination" in Germany and England. These have a strong adversary character to them, and in Germany seem to me to have turned out to be mainly a cosmetic applied to the old system, which chugs along essentially unchanged. The characteristics of a successful industrial democracy are likely to be achieved primarily through a change in attitudes and tradition, and rather secondarily through changes in organization forms and systems.

Where do we start? For me, I believe the first rule is that all those who wish to participate and have a say *must think*, and not simply pop off. The words of Justice Brandeis, written over forty years ago, are still timely:

> "Democracy is only possible among people who think. . . . Thinking is not a heaven-born thing. . . . It is a gift men and women make for themselves. It is earned, and it is earned by effort. There is no effort, to my mind, that is comparable in its qualities, that is so taxing to the individual, as to think, to analyze fundamentally."

This rule will be hard enough to come by, and it will not happen unless you, as CEO, or manager, or foreman offer an example of it in your own lives, and, as well, work to create an atmosphere around you in which those responsible to you are encouraged and prodded to think, are heard when they voice their thoughts, and are given, not alone rewards, but rather serious and dignified attention and respect. This responsibility is not so much one which someone owes to you, as it is one which you owe to anyone who ever comes under your supervision.

There will be a second rule, and I will describe it with a word that is very probably most unpopular with you. The word is obedience. This word "obedience" curiously comes from a root which means "to hear." No business can operate unless its members hear each other. No business can operate, democratically or undemocratically, unless it can count on enthusiastic obedience in this root sense, obedience to fact, obedience to reason, obedience which goes, beyond the letter, to the spirit of a strategy or plan. The difference between obedience in the old and in the new will be that in a democratically organized business it will be obedience to rules, plans, and strategies in whose making each member can feel that he or she had an appropriate and relevant say, and not to such as are simply imposed without discussion or input.

Let us now mention a third rule: It is an expression of the cooperative as against the adversary approach, and to my mind it would go like this: When you work, you must work with and for others. You must identify less with yourself and more with the institution of which you are a part.

Now, such remarks may be comforting to you if you think they are addressed to your prospective bosses. They are not addressed to your bosses. They are addressed to *you*, and to the manner in which you will deal with the human beings who report to you and with whom you will have to deal.

It is one of the oldest clichés that business exists on trust. The more successful you are as CEO, the more decisions you will have to delegate. You cannot command that your subordinates think, work hard, carry out plans and programs with vigor and intensity. You will have to trust them to do it. You will succeed or fail according to how *they* do when you're not watching them. If they are more concerned with their personal career paths than with the corporation's success, you will be in trouble. If they are lukewarm in carrying out a program which is not to their taste, you won't be able to find out about it in time. Your best bet to be a successful CEO in businesses which are bound to become larger, in which decisions are steadily decentralized, in which broad participation increases, is to develop the philosophy and habits of action at the beginning of your career which you will have to be able to call from others at the peak of your career.

Is all this a long way from corporate environmental decision-making? I think not. The real difficulties of corporate environmental decision-making are clearer when we add a phrase and make it "decision-making in a participatory democracy." The chances of tackling successfully in a participatory democracy of 220 million people the kinds of enormous problems that have been described to us today look pathetically low. Nearly every emerging Third-World country has today chosen another way than the democratic way: one-party government, semi-dictatorial government, or straight dictator. Your generation will probably have a chance to prove or lose the democratic option, so formidable are our problems. You and I have the greatest stake in preserving this country as a functioning democracy. Only in such a state do we retain those freedoms whose loss would appall us and whose possession is taken for granted, freedom to talk un-afraid, freedom to move about, to choose a career—even the dangerous freedom to abuse freedom.

Democracies stand or fall by means of the attitudes and restraint and behavior of men and women rather than by means of organization, systems, and patterns. Wise men have known this for hundreds of years. Each generation learns it sooner or later. Those who learn it sooner produce for themselves golden ages. Those who learn it too late are the forgotten ones of history.

May I end with a quotation on the adversary environment which is the best and most timely one I know for Americans in 1980. It is from St. Paul, himself a businessman:

"Do not use freedom as an opportunity for selfishness. If you bite and devour one another, take care that you are not consumed by one another."

So—that ends it. You ladies and gentlemen will create your own environment. Whatever it may turn out to be you are condemned to live in it. The creating process starts right now. So—take it from here—and good luck.

Interview With
Jose A. Lutzenberger

HERMAN E. DALY

BRAZIL OCCUPIES HALF the continent of South America and is therefore responsible for the administration of a large share of the earth's ecosystem. The current Brazilian regime seems to have seven basic modes of dealing with the environment: (1) dig it up (2) cut it down (3) fill it in (4) dam it (5) burn it (6) plant it with monocultures and spray it with chemical biocides (7) overwhelm it with massive concentrations of people. This rather limited repertory of alternative forms of rape is partly an inheritance from the Portuguese who came for rapid, temporary exploitation rather than permanent settlement. It also partly derives from the imported modern ideology of growthmania and the consumer society, avidly exported by the United States. There are today, however, many Brazilians who are outraged at the unprecedented environmental destruction occurring in their country and are making an effort to stop it. Their leader and guru is José A. Lutzenberger, a Brazilian agricultural engineer of German descent who lives in Brazil's southernmost state of Rio Grande do Sul.

Lutz, as he is called by his many friends, is playing the same role in Brazil today as Rachel Carson played in the US in the early 1960s. It might be more accurate to say that he is the combined Rachel Carson, Paul Ehrlich, Amory Lovins, and David Brower of Brazil because he fights pesticides, overpopulation, energy waste, nuclear power, and in addition founded Brazil's strongest association for protection of the environment. (AGAPAN).

Lutz began his career working for a multinational firm as technical adviser on chemical fertilizers and biocides on three continents. Gradually, over a period of 14 years with repeated visits to the same places, it dawned on him that the net result of modern agriculture was to reduce the long run capacity of the earth to support life, and he was shocked by the mafiosi methods of multinational agri-chemistry. For someone who subscribes to Albert Schweitzer's "reverence for life" as a basic ethical principle, this is a painful realization. Instead of rationalizing, making

excuses, and looking only on the "positive side" of things, ten years ago Lutz, at age 44, quit his lucrative job, returned to his native city of Porto Alegre, and began making his living as a landscape architect. Later he founded a small consulting firm called Convivial Technology after the phrase of Ivan Illich. These activities earn him only a modest living because he devotes most of his time to unpaid environmental defense work. His inside knowledge of the pesticide industry and his personal experience with organic agriculture have made him the nemesis of the agro-industrial-chemical complex in Brazil, which is the world's third largest user of biocides.

I first met Lutz in January of 1976 while giving a course in economics and ecology in Rio Grande do Sul. Some of my students told me about him and took me to meet him in the seaside town of Torres, where he was making a state park and a demonstration organic garden. It turned out that he knew of me from having read my book, and since that is the fastest way to an academic's heart, we became instant friends.

Lutz speaks excellent English, as well as German, French, Spanish, and of course Portuguese. His library contains hundreds of books in numerous languages on ecology, agronomy, chemistry, physics, philosophy, theology, economics, and nearly everything else under the sun. He has the kind of broad knowledge and confidently imaginative intellect that today's universities seem to stifle rather than encourage. He is also an emotional man, and tears come to his eyes when he contrasts the loving care and appreciation of subtle harmonies and animal psychology of the organic farmer with the brutal and insensitive depradations of the monoculturalists. He can also get angry. But his emotion is always backed up by scientific understanding. Indeed, it is precisely because he understands better than others what is really happening that he feels the pain more than others.

Our friendship was renewed in November 1980 when I spent several days with him in Porto Alegre, after giving a short course there. I urged Lutz to write something in English for American environmental magazines. He said he just has no time. Even his books in Portuguese (*Fim do Futuro?* and *Pesadelo Atomico*) were edited by friends from speeches and short articles. I offered therefore to reconstruct our conversations and correspondence in the form of a written interview. He agreed to read it over and edit it. This is the result.

Daly—When I was here five years ago you were known locally as a somewhat quixotic figure with an exaggerated affection for trees. Today you are famous all over Brazil and receive ten times as many invitations to speak as you can possibly accept. What happened?

Lutzenberger—Since you were here we succeeded in creating a great amount of ecological consciousness, much more than we could have expected, especially in my profession, among agronomists. Back then I was still considered a fool among my colleagues, today I am a kind of guru for almost the totality of agronomy students in all of Brazil and among most of the agronomists active in their profession.

In Europe, the US, Australia, Japan, and Canada there is today a good and healthy, burgeoning movement of organic (biologically rather than chemically oriented) agriculture, but the average agronomist is unaware of it or fights it. Here we now have the opposite situation. There is almost nothing to show in practice, but most agronomists are anxious for change and frustrated for not knowing how.

By the way, the US Department of Agriculture in an official publication has now urged the development of organic agriculture in the US. That is an encouraging event.

Daly—I remember that beautiful demonstration garden you made in the park at Torres where you created a rich soil on top of pure sand, and had everything so well balanced that insects were automatically controlled. Did that serve as an example and convince some people?

Lutzenberger—My park in Torres is in the process of decay. Our state government did not renew my contract a year ago. Of course they don't like me. I attack them viciously for their stupid aggressions on the environment; but that is the only way to talk to that mafia, and I have to pay the price of their retaliation. They spend almost nothing on the park. It hurts me to see it now. But they have plenty of money for a petro-chemical center right next to Porto Alegre, upriver on the Jacuí, where we will get all the pollution into our drinking water.

Daly—But while the government was sabotaging your park, your colleagues elected you "agronomist

of the year." How did that come about?

Lutzenberger—It came about in spite of a bitter backstage fight by ANDEF (an agro-chemical lobby that includes some twenty multinationals). I was elected "agronomist of the year" in 1978. Then ANDEF tried to annul my prize. A new election was held and this time I won by even more, 414 to 6, with most of the agronomists employed in the chemical industry voting for me too.

Daly—That is very encouraging—but have things in general really improved by as much as your fame has increased?

Lutzenberger—No. It is a small victory and doesn't mean that anything has changed in Brazil regarding the wholesale destruction of Nature. You knew what is going on in the Amazon Basin. In the rest of the country the last remains of other ecosystems are now being obliterated. There has never been a biological holocaust such as this one in the history of Life. Thousands of species disappear every year without anybody noticing. If tomorrow the zebra, the elephant, the giraffe, or any other spectacular creature were to vanish forever that would be in all the papers, radios, TVs of the World. But every time a unique ecosystem is wiped out, and we had thousands in Brazil, uncounted endemic species go with it—mostly the small, less conspicuous forms of life, small vertebrates or invertebrates, insects, spiders, rare plants. Nobody registers their passing, nobody is interested. The Universe is poorer for every species that goes. Every lifeline in the Symphony of Evolution is a unique, irreversible historical process, that can be cut off but can never be resumed. Whether increasing ecological consciousness will in time provoke a reversal of tendencies remains to be seen. I can only hope so for our children's sake—for Life's sake!

Daly—Just what is going on in the Amazon Basin?

Lutzenberger—The most complex and wonderful of biomes is being burned, knocked down by dragging great chains between huge tractors, defoliated with Agent Orange, etc. Entire communities of plants and animals are being irrevocably lost, some before we have even catalogued them. In their place are being planted vast monocultures, which are inherently unstable; most don't last five years, and require massive doses of biocides and fertilizers that pollute rivers and lakes and kill wildlife.

Indian cultures are being wiped out. We think that "the Indians have no right to hold back progress." But what right, other than that of brute force, allows us to invade the Indians' world with heavy machinery, chain saws, and chemical defoliants sprayed by air-

Gerry Gardner

planes? Who is the real barbarian? North Americans might get some idea of the cost of this meretricious progress from the current cinema "Bye, Bye Brazil."

We have plenty of land in Brazil, so that we could postpone exploiting the Amazon until we learn enough about the marvellous patterns of life to do it intelligently and sustainably. We must restrain both our own greed and that of foreign companies. We have much to learn from the remaining Indian tribes.

Daly—With the bust of the "Brazilian economic miracle" and the worsening economic situation, that will be difficult.

Lutzenberger—Yes,the economic situation has never been worse in Brazil. Some few members of the military, which in 1964 had the greatest chance ever to create order, chose instead to become henchmen for multinational business. Inflation is now over 140 percent annually, and we owe more than 60 billion dollars while earning only 13 billion annually from our exports—more than half of which goes to service the debt, with the remainder being insufficient to pay for petroleum imports. So the debt will likely grow and inflation get worse. Nevertheless the mafia plans to build 60 nukes by 1995! Never before has one seen such madness! Fortunately they will not succeed. I put some hope, ironically, in the world depression that has already been triggered.

Daly—Within this generally bleak picture, many people are placing all their hopes on Brazil's alcohol fuel program, PROALCOOL. What do you think of it?

Lutzenberger—The alcohol program is another ca-

lamity. It will be in the hands of the international petroleum, automobile, and chemistry companies, a political disaster for Brazil. It will spread over the rest of Brazil the kind of feudal landholding system that disgraces the Northeast.

If today the Northeast is poor, if millions of *nordestinos* are forced to migrate to the stinking *favelas* of Rio, Sao Paulo, and Brasilia, it is because in their own region they were pushed out by sugarcane monoculture. In its current conception PROALCOOL threatens to extend this process of displacing people from the land—and displacing food crops with more profitable but less necessary, fuel crops. Of course it all has a kind of diabolical logic—it is all so rigged with subsidies, fiscal privileges, and free credit that is is difficult for normal folk to see through it. So you have a lot of good people, even some "ecologists," favoring the program.

Daly—Usually the migration of poor *nordestinos* is blamed on the periodic drought.

Lutzenberger—The key word there is *periodic*. Sure, a drought might be the proximate cause of migration, but the periodic droughts are a condition of nature to which traditional cultivation was well adapted. In the very few areas where a peasant culture was allowed to develop, in wet years they farmed the land distant from river beds, and in dryer years moved closer and closer to the river beds. Now with the monoculture that intelligent system was destroyed. The technocrat can't accept the wisdom of traditional restraints, and so he blames the drought and calls for great hydraulic projects, or more industrialization.

Daly—Getting back to alcohol—can't it be made by small producers employing people in the interior, and ultimately substituting a renewable resource for diminishing petroleum?

Lutzenberger—Of course, but it all depends on scale and rate of development, and beyond that on the structure of power in society. One could imagine a system of small-scale independent distilleries producing for local use, converting the *vinhoto* or slop into a good organic fertilizer. One could avoid large-scale monoculture and keep the population of cars below the level that could be "fed" on a sustainable basis, one could substitute public transport and bicycles for automobiles to a large degree—in short, we could live within an ecological budget. And we have plenty of other energy sources: low-head water power, wind, and biomass in direct combustion or through biogas or pyrolysis.

If our basic paradigm were the ecologically inspired one of a steady-state or homeostatic economy, then we could make good use of biomass energy. But in Brazil, as in all other countries, the basic paradigm is that of the ever-expanding economy which rides roughshod over ecological limits and tends to centralize power and promote only those technologies that are themselves centralizing. For example PROALCOOL, although it permits small distilleries to produce, requires them to sell to a centralized distributing agency.

Daly—I want to return to this general question of power and technology, but let's stick with PROALCOOL for a minute. What other effects will it have?

Lutzenberger—The sugarcane monoculture implicit in PROALCOOL is one of the many threats to the Amazon, and also to the Pantanal, the great swamp in Mato Grosso—one of the last natural paradises on earth. Of course alcohol production displaces food crops. Brazil already imports its staple food: black beans.

What will be the effect of PROALCOOL on the distribution of income? Food will be more expensive than it otherwise would have been, and auto fuel might be less expensive than it otherwise would have been. The poor spend a large percentage of their income on food and nothing on auto fuel. The middle and upper class spend a smaller percentage on food and a significant amount on auto fuel. On the consumption side, the effect on income distribution is regressive.

On the production side, we have similar concentrating effects already mentioned: feudal landholding patterns, large scale distilleries, and centralized distribution. It is hard to see how PROALCOOL can

avoid worsening an already unjust distribution of income and wealth. Unless we can break out of the paradigm of growthmania and megatechnology, even potentially good ideas—like exploitation of solar energy via biomass—become corrupted to serve the ends of growth and concentration of power rather than permanence, independence, and justice.

One further point about alcohol is that it is not the most efficient way to get energy out of biomass. Methane gas and pryolysis technologies convert more of the energy in the plant into final usable energy and can use more abundant plant material. Furthermore, we all knew that modern agricultural methods are highly energy intensive, and I know of no study which shows that the complete energetic balance of megatechnological production, distillation, and distribution of alcohol is positive. Even if it should turn out to be positive, the surplus will certainly be small compared to fossil fuels. So it is totally irresponsible to treat PROALCOOL as a new lease on life for the auto industry.

Daly — O.K., let's consider now this relation of power and technology.

Lutzenberger—We have a vicious circle between technological sophistication and concentration on the one hand and economic power on the other. The more complex and integrated the technology, the greater the demand for capital and the greater the need for bureaucratic management; the technocracy, in its turn, demands and promotes only those sophisticated and large-scale technologies that further concentrate economic power. That is why nuclear power or gigantic hydropower projects like Itaipu (12,000 MWe) are the favorites.

As a concrete example of this process, even on a lower technological level, consider the *caboclo* in the Amazon. Living on the river bank, he lives in plenty. From the river he gets all the fish he can use or dry for later consumption, the forest gives him an incredible variety of fruit the year round, and there is plenty of game. He has all the free fuel he needs. He complements his diet from small plantations of manioc, sweet potatoes, beans, and corn. He has a few chickens, sometimes a cow or two. The harm he causes the forest is minimal and well within its capacity for natural recovery. Now, some agricultural extension schemes, among other lunacies, are teaching him the methods of "modern" chicken farming, actually chicken or egg "factories." The "scientifically balanced" rations are formulated in Manaus, one thousand kilometers away, by big firms using imported corn, wheat or soybeans from the US and powdered milk from the Common Market. The broilers and laying hens are hybrid, of course, which means he cannot reproduce them himself. He remains dependent on the stock of some multinational firm in the US. Soon he will give up his traditional, locally adapted chickens that are immune to disease. In his "factory" he uses imported medicine, hormones, and antibiotics. The buyer of his product is the same one who supplies all the inputs. The little chicken raiser has absolutely no influence on prices either way. All the risks are his; all the advantages are with the big companies or multinationals. Of course this is not a scheme for improving food production, it is a scheme for creating dependence—a infrastructure for domination. This is really what "development" is all about.

The same is true when the *caboclo* is taught to grow tomatoes under plastic foil, with tons of soluble synthetic fertilizer—of course imported—and downpours of synthetic poisons, also imported. But most of the time he is simply displaced by immense agribusiness schemes that totally extinguish his paradise and send him to the slums in big cities far away. A very small percentage is used locally as cheap labor, under labor-camp conditions. In not so rare encounters, the big guy uses the machine gun on the "squatter" or the "ferocious" Indians.

This situation is representative, and what it means is that independent individuals who decide their own destiny are becoming an extinct species. They don't fit the pattern of megatechnology and the imperative of growth. The crowning irony, however, is that the energetics of mass chicken farming make it a net absorber of food energy available to humans whereas the traditional system, using local inputs not competitive with human food, was a net provider of food energy.

Another example of insanely centralized technology is project SANEGRAN, designed to provide sewage treatment for the 20 million people expected to inhabit Sao Paulo in the year 2000. The plan calls for one enormous central primary treatment station, the effluent of which will be carried by a single pipe, three meters in diameter, to Billings Lake, one of the few areas near Sao Paulo with any recreational value left. Can you imagine concentrating the crap of 20 million people into a single treatment plant? What happens when that plant breaks down? The pollution of Lake Billings and the waste of valuable organic matter are problems that our technocrats just refuse to take seriously. This crazy project has been approved, because in addition to concentrating waste, it concentrates power.

Daly—Do you think this tendency to concentrate power is connected with a philosophy of materialism?

Lutzenberger—No, I do not think we are materialistic at all—if we were, we would treat matter with more respect. Material things impose their own limits. The materialist wants his dinner, he may want a better dinner, but he has no desire for six dinners at once. Alan Watts said we are abstractionists, not materialists. We want the abstract power to command six dinners, not the actual six dinners. Money represents this abstract power which, unlike the real wealth for which it stands, can be accumulated indefinitely and be made to grow exponentially. Abstractionism, not materialism, promotes the concentration of power. GNP is an abstraction. If we thought of wealth in concrete material terms, we would realize the absurdity of an economy based on unlimited devastation.

Daly—Anyone in Brazil who criticizes the government as strongly as you do is likely to be called a "communist." What do you say in reply?

Lutzenberger—How could anyone with ecological understanding advocate communism? In capitalism you have a lot of little or large bandits, and you can play them off one against another and find some living space in the gaps, and the system can evolve. In communism you have one big centralized, all-powerful, unified mafia and nowhere to hide. Communism lacks the stabilizing negative feedback of a parliament, and of an independent conservationist movement. The communist countries are even more dedicated to megatechnology and growth than are the capitalists. The Soviet Union financed the Aswan Dam, and builds nuclear power plants, and makes supersonic airplanes to save a few minutes of the precious time of their elite class. In short, they do all the things that the Brazilian technocrats and their government want to do—I should be calling them communists!

We need something better than either communism or modern capitalism—namely an ecologically sane, homeostatic, steady-state economy. No system that depends on continuous growth can be ecologically viable. The fact that communism is worse should be cold comfort to those of us in capitalist countries. All centralization of power is bad.

Daly—Lutz, we have yet to consider the most fundamental and controversial environmental issue in Brazil: population. Twelve years ago I wrote an article on population issues in Brazil, and I am amazed to see how little the debate has progressed since then. Certainly there has been no major policy change such as took place in Mexico.

Lutzenberger—We desperately need birth control and a serious effort to reduce population growth. This is just elementary arithmetic, and if in Brazil we still have bitter debates about the need for birth control, that is caused not only by lack of knowledge of the facts, but also by ideological commitments and the crassest kind of class interest in maintaining an unlimited supply of cheap labor to promote ever-increasing concentration of power.

The upper and middle classes already practice birth control, but not the lower class. This incomplete democratization of birth control reinforces the inequality in the distribution of per capita income—or as the saying goes, "the rich get richer and the poor get children." Historically, the population explosion was almost always the result of the destruction of traditional culture by the conqueror. It's the alienated who give up demographic controls. For twenty or thirty thousand years the Indians lived in harmony with Nature; and even though the forest must have seemed unlimited to them, they were very conscious of the demographic problem and applied deliberate controls, including infanticide, when a tribe grew too large. Today, when you visit the villages of the "civilized" Indians, you see a tremendous population explosion and devastation of the environment.

Given its actual style of living and level of consumption, Brazil is already overpopulated in the sense that the current situation is unsustainable. In that sense the US is even more overpopulated than Brazil, and especially so if you count the depradations and waste of its suicidal armaments race with the Soviet Union.

Daly—That's a good point. And the US has yet to make any official effort to limit either its population or its per capita consumption. Nor have the US and the USSR agreed to eliminate a single bomb or missile from their arsenals. Until we do something ourselves, our preaching on population will not be taken very seriously.

Lutzenberger—Exactly!

Daly—Before we leave the subject of population, what role does the Catholic Church play in this issue?

Lutzenberger—The official attitude of the Catholic Church on this issue is truly retrograde, even though there are some enlightened individuals who are trying to change the Church's position. In other respects, the Church has recently become a force for social justice with its "option in favor of the poor." It may be, however, that all the Church's efforts to help the poor are largely cancelled out by the population growth that might be mitigated if it would just include access to birth control in its definition of social justice. Even if the government wanted to launch a birth control program now, it probably would hold back because it is already in a bitter fight with the Church on human rights issues.

Daly—Many people today say that environmental concern is an elitist hobby, and that it distracts attention from Brazil's more pressing problems of poverty and injustice, which require rapid growth for their solution. How do you answer these people?

Lutzenberger—I say that on the contrary, it is the growth mythology that has allowed us to put off questions of distributive justice. As long as faith in the myth of eternal growth of the "cake" persists we can say that those with the smallest slices are getting better off absolutely, even if not relatively, and that they should patiently wait for the cake to grow bigger before we redivide it more fairly because "premature redistribution" would hurt the poor by slowing down the rate of growth of the cake. Simple people believe this. Today in Brazil we are constructing a consumer society for 20 million people on the backs of the other 80 million or more.

But, when we finally realize that the cake is not growing and cannot continue growing—and that, fact, it is even shrinking—then no longer will we be able to avoid facing up to the demands for at least minimum justice in the distribution of income. For this reason, the myth of perpetual growth is assiduously maintained by those who no longer believe it themselves but find it in their interests that everyone else should believe it. Ecological concern and social justice are as inseparable as are the two faces of a coin.

Daly—Last question, Lutz. What principles must we build upon if we are ever to reverse this destruction and arrive at a sustainable homeostatic society?

Lutzenberger—First, we must arrest the process of desacralization of Nature and the exclusion from our code of ethics of all concern for anything not related or useful to Man. We must adopt Albert Schweitzer's fundamental ethical principle of reverence for Life in all its forms and all its manifestations. Second, we must accept a symphonic vision of Organic Evolution where Man is only one instrument in the orchestra. The idea of a symphony emphasizes cooperation, harmony, and mutual adjustment. In an orchestra, no instrument is insignificant; every instrument is complementary and indispensable to all the others. It's in this complementarity that the greatness resides. Third, we must rethink our technology. Today's hard technology, conceived in the interest of the powerful, must give way to soft technology conceived in the interest of Man and Nature. Man may be predestined to become conductor of the symphony, but only if he learns to obey its rules.

More Thoughts on Economics

BUSINESSMEN REGARD PROFITS as the elixir of life and are inclined to treat them reverently. They grow furious with those whom they accuse of regarding profits as a dirty word. Profits, they say, are the incentive for creativity and efficiency. Profits are the preserver of liberty. Lemuel Boulware, a retired vice-president of General Electric Company and a titan of tough bargaining with labor unions, said, "Profit, property, and freedom are inseparable....Profit benefits the non-owners much more than it does the owners of a business. Profit is even the poor man's best friend. It is the greatest engine of human betterment ever devised by man."

But non-true believers ask whether greater corporate profits and social welfare necessarily coincide. If particular companies' pursuit of greater profits means the rapid exhaustion of a scarce resource (such as soil or minerals), society may suffer, they say. Similarly, they add, the search for greater profits may influence foreign policy in dangerous or wasteful ways (as by maximizing arms sales to the Middle East or swelling the production of military hardware for national use or storage for future use).

In short, the cost-benefit ratio of individual firms, as measured by profits, does not necessarily correspond to the cost-benefit ratios for the nation or the world as a whole. The sum of optimal, profit-maximizing decisions by firms may or may not be the best decision for the society as a whole.

The toughest part of national and global decision making is measuring true costs and benefits; the same resources can be shifted to many different uses, and some costs (like that of pollution) are hard to calculate. It is also difficult to measure potential benefits, such as those of clean air, better-educated minds, a richer cultural scene or peace itself (within cities or between nations).

Practically speaking, even if one has a good idea of the national or global cost-benefit ratios and seeks to shift resources to better uses, it may be hard to get the people who control those resources to shift them or allow them to be shifted—because of habits or vested interests. A particular company or region doesn't always want to give up its defense orders; a labor union doesn't want to see jobs moved up to another region or country where the benefits might be larger for the society as a whole, but not for the individual union and its members.

Those who habitually praise the free-enterprise, profit, or market system don't like to submit to the discipline of the market when it affects their own interests adversely, even if only in the short run.

—Leonard Silk

OUR INDUSTRIAL SOCIETY is getting dangerously crowded, complex, and putrid. We urgently need a change in social values—a shift in our goals from increasing the quantity of production to improving the quality of life. Almost the whole of our society and its institutions, business and governmental, is geared to growth of the old kind; the shift can occur only if we have what has correctly been called "a Copernican Revolution of the mind." We have scarcely begun to think through what that would mean in terms of the use of resources, conservation, employment, education, income distribution, the location as well as the size of population, social and economic incentives and disincentives, structural changes in the economy and industry—if changing from quantity to quality were to become our dominant social purpose.

—Leonard Silk

FOUR BIOLOGICAL SYSTEMS — fisheries, forests, grasslands, and croplands—form the foundation of the global economic system. In addition to supplying all our food, these four systems provide virtually all the raw materials for industry except minerals and petroleum-derived synthetics. The condition of the economy and of these biological systems cannot be separated.

As the global economy expands at 4 percent per year, or 50-fold per century, pressures on the earth's biological systems are mounting. In large areas of the world, human claims on these systems are reaching an unsustainable level, a point where their productivity is being impaired. When this happens, fisheries collapse, forests disappear, grasslands are converted into barren wastelands, and croplands deteriorate.

The extensive deterioration of the earth's principal biological systems is not an issue of concern only to environmentalists. Our economic system depends on these systems. Anything that seriously threatens their productivity threatens the productivity of the global economy.

The world is not running out of energy, but it *is* running out of oil, and appears to be running out of cheap energy. As the price of energy rises, new sources will come into use. A world economic system where a barrel of oil costs $20 will look far different than one that evolved when the price of oil was less than $2 per barrel. Energy will be used sparingly and waste will be minimal. Far-reaching adjustments are called for not only in developing new energy sources but also in mobilizing scientific and engineering know-how to increase energy efficiency in every sector of the global economy.

The new inflationary forces arise from claims on the earth's resources of a continuously expanding global economy. As described earlier, at some point biological systems begin to deteriorate; oil wells begin to go dry; high-grade, easily accessible mineral reserves are used up; and there is no more fertile, well-watered cropland that can easily be brought under the plow. As the demand for the more scarce resources begins to outstrip supplies, scarcity-induced price rises result.

Diminishing returns on investments in basic sectors of the global economy, unprecedented inflationary pressures, and widespread capital scarcity—are all slowing economic growth. The global engine of economic growth is clearly losing steam. This slowdown did not originate in some sudden human failure to manage the economic system. Rather it is rooted in humanity's relationship to the carrying capacity of biological systems, the dwindling reserves of oil, the declining quality of mineral ores, and the ecosystem's limited capacity to absorb waste. In effect, the changing growth prospect reflects the constraining forces inherent in the earth's natural systems and resources.

In the more affluent societies such as Sweden and the United States, consumer desires are showing early signs of satiation. Young people in the upper-income groups in the United States place less emphasis today on the acquisition of material goods than did their parents. In Sweden, Goran Backstrand and Lars Ingelstam ask what Swedes could possibly do with the sevenfold increase in steel output and the tenfold increase in chemicals that a projection of the traditional 4- to 6-percent annual growth rates would yield. Further, they question whether Swedes would tolerate the environmental disruption such growth would imply when their essential material needs are already more than satisfied.

Formulating an economic policy for a sustainable society will be a complex process. Many of the old assumptions and guidelines will have to be discarded. A sustainable economic system will reflect explicit recognition of the need to stabilize the relationship between humanity and the earth's principal biological systems—fisheries, forests, grasslands, and croplands. In effect, this means devising comprehensive economic policies and plans that limit the offtakes or harvests from these systems to sustainable levels. The question is not whether the harvests will be limited. They will be limited—either through the exercise of foresight and careful management or through the eventual destruction of the systems.

The changes involved in accommodating ourselves to the earth's natural capacities and resources suggest that a far-reaching economic transformation is in the offing. The origins of the change are ecological, but the change itself will be social and economic. And the processes for achieving it will be political.

—Lester R. Brown

Cheryl Nichols

IN EARLY 1979, the U.S. Government greeted with great relief the report that unemployment had dropped to 5.7 percent. Ten years earlier, an unemployment rate that high would have been greeted with horror as socially and politically unacceptable. Unemployment in Europe in the late seventies reached levels not seen since the thirties. In the Third World, the proportion of the population unable to find productive work dwarfs the figures for the industrial world. Chronic high unemployment seems to have become entrenched in most of the world economy, and traditional measures for combating it appear inadequate or inappropriate—or both.

In the Great Depression of the thirties, the global economic machine broke down, throwing millions upon millions of people out of work. The current crisis in global employment is not the product of any such catastrophic malfunctioning of the economic system, and it is this fact that makes the current situation so alarming. It is possible for the world economy to tick along in what seems to be good health without providing livelihoods for vast numbers of people.

The social harm caused by high youth unemployment is perhaps even more serious than the economic harm. Young people are often cushioned by their families from the full brunt of individual poverty. Yet the legitimate fear of social observers is that if early experience in the labor market is characterized by frustration and a sense of inadequacy or uselessness, the resulting alienation may persist throughout a person's working life. —Kathleen Newland

IT IS ONLY IN this century that the majority of developed people have had even a first impression of the economic elbow room and social choice formerly available only to the wealthy. It may have made them not much happier in the deepest sense than their predecessors in the Trianon or in Caligula's Rome. But it is a vast improvement on serfdom or early industrialism, or the long depression or the rationed years of war. Must the cup be dashed to the ground after only the first sip?

There is a profound psychological obstacle to be overcome here, and continued stagnation with inflation will raise it higher still. But once again, the debate must be withdrawn from such extreme forms. Massive impoverishment is not proposed, nor a return to the Stone Age. At the most, the aim is an abandoning of the perpetual pursuit of "more" which is the root of inflation, the core of boredom, the rungs of a meaningless treadmill. Here perhaps our century is not entirely fixed in its materialist fantasies. It is precisely among younger people that the philosophy of

"enough" is making headway. It is they who head off to work in communes on the land and who often take the lead in urban renewal. It is among them that interest is growing in all the world's great ethical traditions, with their universal witness to the need for generosity and self-control. Above all, the young seem more alive to one of the primordial facts of the late twentieth century, the fact that merely to be born into the developed world is already to be a privileged member of a small, inconceivably endowed (and wasteful) elite. Indeed, it may be that it is through the growing, aching contrast between the fortune of the developed few and the misery of the vast mass of humanity that a stronger political and ethical commitment to world conservation and generosity can still be found.

—Barbara Ward

DECADES AGO, American companies began developing a new industry based on providing cool air to consumers. We call it the air-conditioning industry. Virtually everyone here, I suspect, lives in an air-conditioned home or apartment, drives an air-conditioned car, and works in an air-conditioned office. The manufacture of equipment to provide cool air has become a major source of profits, dividends, and jobs. Never have I heard any industrial leader, economist, or banker refer to the air-conditioning industry as non-productive.

And yet now, when a new industry—formed to manufacture, operate, and maintain equipment to produce *clean* air—comes along, it is termed "non-productive"—even though it, too, offers investment opportunities, profits, and jobs. —Russell Peterson

THE CONCERN OF the community at large is to ensure—by a guaranteed annual income, by a negative income tax, by increased social security—that the falling away of wages as machines replace human beings is not matched by a corresponding collapse in the community's purchasing power. If a concept is conservative enough for President Nixon to think of introducing it, we need not rush off with cries of "subsidized slacking" or anarchy let loose. No doubt a few people may prefer not to work—full time or part time—and here the social inventiveness of the community is required to provide the range of jobs in social services, in small-scale industry, in community efforts, which would not only take up the slack of possible unemployment but also extend a civilizing influence throughout societies.

—Barbara Ward

George Hall

Readings in Environmental Law

The law makes possible environmental victories that could not be won through political action, mobilization of public opinion, or any other means. An outstanding example is the Alaska pipeline case. In the context of the energy crisis, environmentalists' attempts to block construction of the pipeline were popular neither with politicians nor the public. Nevertheless, because the law was on their side, environmentalists won in court. Congress cynically passed a law permitting pipeline construction to proceed anyway, but that doesn't alter the fact that the law is a supremely important tool for environmental protection. Most other chapters in this book argue that there ought to be laws about this and that, so a parallel chapter on environmental law would tend to be highly duplicative. Instead, we offer here a number of writings on various facets of environmental law.

The Future of Environmental Law

JAMES MOORMAN

IN THE LAST DECADE we have witnessed the creation of a vast body of environmental law. During this brief and exciting era we have seen many environmental laws passed at the federal, state and municipal levels. Judicial environmental precedents have been cascading down from the bench in a torrent. So many environmental rules and regulations have been issued by the various agencies that lawyers have been unable to keep up with them. Vast bureaucracies have been created to administer these new environmental laws. Millions, yea billions, of dollars have been spent on the newly enacted schemes.

The structure of law that has been created in the last decade is indeed impressive, from the National Environmental Policy Act and the Clean Air Act right down to the actions of small towns like Petaluma, California. The question we must now ask ourselves upon assessing the future of this great body of law is whether it is adequate to deal with identified environmental problems.

A question like this cannot be answered with certainty. One can only guess. Standing here today, however, I would guess that we are closer to the beginning than we are to the end of the creation era of environmental law. I believe the creation of major new environmental laws will continue for at least another decade or more before we will be able to say that we have created a body of law adequate to deal with identified environmental problems.

I say this because I believe the law created so far does not in fact deal adequately with several fundamental problems. I contend that we have not yet come to grips through the law with certain problems of overwhelming importance. These problems are of such a magnitude that formulating adequate legal responses to them will be a long trial and error process.

1) *Ambient Problem.* The first environmental problem which I bring to your attention, and with which I contend that environmental law has not dealt adequately, is what I will call the "ambient problem." The ambient problem is the problem of the condition of humanity's media or ambience—the air one breathes, the food one ingests, the water one drinks, the light spectrum that bathes us, the panorama before our eyes, and the sound waves beating against our ears. It is a fundamental fact that we are biological organisms whose form is the result of an evolutionary process that occurred in a specific ambience. As such, we require that specific ambience for survival and can tolerate only limited alterations thereof. Despite this fundamental fact, we have unwittingly altered the ambient conditions in which we live. We have added a whole list of new chemicals to our medium—sulphates, nitrates, oxidants, etc. We have allowed chlorinated hydrocarbons to become a part of our fatty tissues. We have turned loose a pandora's box of polychlorinated-biphenals, fluorides, cadmium, asbestos, vinyl chlorides, and on and on the list goes. As a consequence, we have inflicted upon ourselves a whole host of major and minor ills and problems. This in short is the "ambient problem."

The most important thing that can be said of the laws we have passed to deal with the ambient problem, such as the Clean Air Act, the Water Pollution Act, and the Federal Insecticide Act, is that they do not deal adequately with the ambient problem. True, these laws have had their successes, but the ambient problem remains.

What is wrong?

For myself, I have come to the conclusion that the approach of the existing laws relies too heavily on complicated technical-legal schemes administered by bureaucrats. This approach has its uses, but it must be supplemented by another approach. One possible supplemental approach that appeals to me is one that has been much talked about in the environmental area, but which has not really been tried: the constitutional right. If we are to solve the ambient problem, then perhaps each of us needs a constitutional right for the protection and preservation of our ambient environment. The procedural scheme to implement such a right would, of course, be crucial to its efficacy. In order to make the constitutional right effective, for example, there would have to be a strong presumption in favor of the natural environment. Thus, if there is any doubt about a chemical, then it could not be broadly distributed through the market.

Can it happen? Can we really enact such a constitutional amendment? Proponents of the Women's Equal Rights Amendment have just learned that amending the Constitution is very difficult. Nevertheless, if the public comes to believe the problem is as serious as I believe it to be, then such an amendment would be feasible. A consensus against cancer and for a constitutional right can form and those with vested interests in uninvited additives will simply have to accept it.

2) *Population Problem.* The next problem the law has not responded to is the population problem. *Science* magazine carried a review of the world population and food situation by Lester Brown. Despite the wonders of the miraculous green revolution. Brown reported that the world's food supply has not kept up with the population growth and that we are facing an imminent crisis. As Brown puts it, the world is now living hand-to-mouth. The world is essentially without a food reserve; it has no reserve land to put into production; almost every country is now a net importer of food; North America is the only substantial exporter; the world fish catch appears to be past its peak and is falling. Yet despite these and other grim facts, world population continues to rise.

It seems clear that the population problems cannot be solved simply by increased food production efforts. Institutional and legal innovations are required to limit populations. The Punjab is in the process of enacting a law to require the compulsory sterilization of everyone between 15 and 45 with more than 32 children. When asked if people would complain about a loss of basic human rights, a Punjabi health official said such complaints had been received earlier about compulsory smallpox vaccinations, but that everyone eventually accepted such vaccinations as necessary for the good of all. He predicted that compulsory sterilization would be likewise so accepted and that it would soon become standard procedure throughout India.

Such a drastic direct population control will not, I hope, be required in the US, where we have one of the world's lowest birth rates. However, we cannot escape the population problem simply by maintaining a low birthrate. As we are sitting on virtually 80% of the world's surplus food production, we must choose to whom we are to sell it: this raises a large number of difficult "distribution" issues. Is the food to go to the highest bidder—that is to the OPEC countries, to Japan and to Western Europe? Or is it to be an instrument of foreign policy, perhaps even, as some suggest, a weapon? Thus, is the food to go to Russia as a reward and to be withheld from her as a punishment? Or is food to be an instrument of humanitarian altruism,

distributed to those in need in Bangladesh, the Sahel, and Ethiopia?

Distribution questions do not just apply to food supplies directly, but embrace the whole agricultural support system. As a consequence, we face a series of environmental issues we cannot escape. To what extent should we preserve agricultural lands and how do we do it? Should we allow the use of scarce fertilizer stocks on our lawns? Should we destroy a national forest in South Carolina to mine phosphates for fertilizer? To what degree should grains that could be consumed directly by the poor of the world be fed to livestock? What weight do we give to domestic inflation and domestic food prices in dealing with these problems?

And, if the problems of distribution were not difficult enough, we also face another type of "population" problem. It seems clear that no matter how we solve distribution problems, many hundreds of millions in the world are going to be deprived. We must assume that many of the deprived will not accept their fate, but will act. If the food does not come to them, they will go to the food. We must realize that the world's transportation and communication facilities have created a situation of amazing potential. World communications have spread a vision of plenty in our country to the less fortunate of other countries. Rising expectations and cheap transportation are creating a situation whereby tens, perhaps hundreds, of millions will have both the desire and the means to come to our country. The poor of Mexico are demonstrating quite clearly that our border is no barrier. And while we can always absorb a few million more, can we absorb the potential hundreds of millions that may choose to come?

The malnourished of the world, now perhaps a billion in number, may soon accelerate the great current of migration from hunger to the food of North America. At this point the law will face a terrible challenge: how to preserve the basis of our exportable surplus for the long term in the face of short-term misery and need.

3) *Development Problem.* The third problem I bring to you is the development problem. The epitome of the development problem is the appearance in fifteen short years of San Jose, as a pock on the skin of the planet. New cities have occurred throughout history, but the rapidity and destructiveness of contemporary development is a new planetary phenomenon and a cause for alarm. Right now the very process is at work in Kuwait where a Persian Gulf Los Angeles is being created with amazing rapidity. Anchorage and Fairbanks' populations were boomed at a tremendous rate by the pipeline. The growth of such places as Houston, Texas, is legendary. Such explosive development, I

think it is fair to say, is almost always an environmental and resource-conservation disaster. Contemporary development explosions result in air pollution, water pollution, the destruction of farmland, urban sprawl, and the extravagant wastage of energy and other resources.

There has to be a better way. I don't know what it is, but I do know that the Department of Housing and Urban Development has not found it. When I look at the bureaucrats' handiwork, whether in planning, land-use controls, or government development, I find their solutions inadequate and sometimes worse than unrestrained Houston's. This is a challenge of grand proportions that has not been met.

4) *Renewable Resource Problem.* The fourth problem is that of the destruction of our renewable resources. At this very moment we are depleting our fishing stocks, we are wasting our soil resources, and we are fast reaching the end of our timber stocks. Sadly, of all the environmental problems, this is the one we have been aware of the longest. At the turn of the century, this country went through a great wave of conservation concern and reform. We created a Forest Service, a Fish and Wildlife Service, a Soil Conservation Service, and other conservation agencies. However, through abuse and overuse, we continued to lose ground. The reason for failure, I suggest, must lie in part in the nature of our earlier solution to the problem.

Our twenty-thousand-man Forest Service now lets million-acre, fifty-year concessions to industry. Our Interior Department wrecks the salmon resources of the Pacific Northwest with dams to make electricity to make aluminum beer cans. Our Soil Conservation Service has become an agency which promotes the destruction of free-flowing streams. In brief, our solutions were administrative and bureaucratic and they have turned on us and bitten us.

What is the answer to this problem? I believe Professor Christopher Stone has told us: the fish, the trees, the living soil we depend on must have standing for judicial protection. They must have a legal status, which can be protected in the law.

This of course is not the whole of the answer. We must think long and hard about who the guardian *ad litem* for these living resources should be.
- It cannot be the worker who fells the tree;
- It cannot be the politician who counts votes;
- It cannot be the bureaucrat who will not risk his job;
- It cannot be the technical expert whose income derives from any of those orders I have just mentioned.

Who then is it to be?

At this point I have no solution save *everyman*—a universal guardianship of everyone and anyone, regardless of race, religion, color, species, or planet of origin, to step forward to protect the living resources of the earth.

5) *Non-renewable Resource Problem.* The fifth problem I bring to you is that of the wastage of our *non*renewable resources. Of these, the most important, of course, is the earth's reserve of hydrocarbons.

As best I can tell, our society remains deeply committed to the most rapid destruction possible of the earth's hydrocarbons. The supply of hydrocarbons, however, is finite and it is not at all clear that there will or can be a substitute. What is more, the world for many generations will need those hydrocarbons for health, happiness, and survival.

As far as I can tell, there is no justification whatsoever for our profligate use of hydrocarbons. The retreat from the automobile must begin at once, and all possible steps must be taken to bring our use of hydrocarbons down to a more modest and rational level.

Many things can and must be done. A very minor step would be an additional tax on gasoline. Each year thereafter I would continue to raise the gasoline tax. Such a measure would create the incentive necessary for far less use of gasoline. Of course people must be given time to adjust. There are many ways to attack the problem, but we must get started at once.

6) *Catastrophe Problem.* The sixth problem which environmental law has not dealt with adequately is the emerging problem of man-made catastrophes which can result from the use of Faustian technologies. By Faustian technologies I mean such things as nuclear power, followed by such wonders as recombinant DNA, laser death rays, and what have you. With the deployment of these technologies, we are now facing the prospect of accidents and sabotage on a grand scale. We have nearly had several nuclear blowdowns in this country already and there are rumors that the Russians have in fact had a blowdown.

So far we have dealt with this prospective problem by ignoring it. In the case of atomic energy, we have even passed a law to excuse reactor manufacturers and operators from liability. With the first large catastrophe, however, our present head-in-the-sand approach will end. Our liberal democracy will at that point be strained to the breaking point. Frankly, I don't know of a solution which permits both the broad use of Faustian technologies and our traditional liberties. The day after we lose Detroit, you and I may lose a good bit of our personal freedom. Monitoring may become a way of life. We may be unable to enter any metropolitan area, or to move about within one, without passing through numerous control points. We may be periodically seized and searched to a degree far

greater than we now are at airports.

The only alternative I see is for us to devise ways to severely limit and control the Faustian technologies. We must develop institutions that guide technology's development in such a way as to lessen, not heighten, the possibility of catastrophe. In short, we must control technology or control people. There is no other alternative except to risk catastrophe.

7) *The Problem of Other Species.* As a seventh problem, I bring to you and lay in your lap the problem of those other species who share our planet with us. So far we have not solved the problem of a decent and adequate environment for our co-tenants on this planet. We have, apparently, no adequate place for our brother the brown bear or for our sister the blue whale. The very ecosystems they depend on are relentlessly destroyed. Even the symbol of the nation, the bald eagle, is all but gone.

Our approach to this problem has been manifold. We have created national parks, wilderness areas, wildlife refuges; we have established fish and game departments; we have passed endangered species acts. There is nothing wrong with these efforts, except perhaps that we have not taken them far enough.

I think of the bald eagle as our miner's canary whose demise brings us warning that all is not right around us. We still suffer from an earlier arrogance that no species really matters except ourselves. This conceit may be our fatal mistake. The disappearance of other species may foreshadow our own disappearance.

8) *International problem.* Most of the problems I have raised with you are not America's alone. We share them with the world. It has been said before, but it is worth saying again: We have not solved the problem of international cooperation. Treaties, UN organizations, world courts, and what have you, are now insufficient to their tasks. We have only begun. I would not presume to tell you how we can do better, but I will presume to say we have not done well. We simply *must* do better.

We *must* prevent the destruction of such things as the Amazon forests, the ocean ecosystem, and East Africa's wildlife.

9) *The Problem of Future Generations* And last, most of the problems which I have raised relate not only to ourselves but also relate to future generations—to our children and grandchildren and beyond. Having adopted a little girl, I have this very much on my mind. We are clearly living too much in the present, too much for ourselves. We are not thinking sufficiently of our estate, the legacy we will leave.

What are we bequeathing? Exhausted resources, polluted lakes, destroyed rivers, wrecked soil? Are we endangering the basis of life on the planet—by broadcasting carcinogens and mutagens which risk the health and genetic stock of the future?

Our democracy is defective because we give the future no vote; our economy is defective because we exclude the future from the courts. Let us at least keep the future in our plans and give our successors a chance to survive. Let us construct rights for the future and duties for the present to the future.

The Evolution of Law

MARK HORLINGS

UNITED STATES ENVIRONMENTAL LAW evolved from existing doctrines to a remarkable extent and is administered by familiar institutions. Common law notions of trespass, nuisance, and eminent domain provided the focus for those first lawyers who happened also to be conservationists.

Most legislation either prohibits or promotes. This country's principal environmental legislation, however—the National Environmental Policy Act (NEPA)—seeks a process more than a result. Such process legislation doesn't dictate a particular decision, it mandates that decisions must be reached in particular ways. The assumption underlying process legislation is that good results usually flow from good procedures.

Prohibition makes sense when one is certain of assumptions (or is confirmed in one's prejudices). Process legislation appeals when one is uncertain about assumptions and needs a process to test them. Our principal prohibition statutes each says what it doesn't like, prohibits more of it, and authorizes regulations to improve things.

In contrast, NEPA requires not good decisions but the process of careful consideration in an open forum.

The central device of federal and state environmental policy acts is the impact statement. The laws require that an environmental impact statement, evaluating a proposed government action and its alternatives, be drawn up whenever the proposed action has important potential consequences. To the extent that impact statements are prepared defensively by officials already committed to a proposed project, the statements help only by providing ammunition for private groups opposed to certain government projects. That has proven to be immensely important, however.

The NEPA process is especially beneficial in situations of uncertainty. Looking back to the early 1970s, many environmental concerns did rest on uncertain bases. As more becomes clear, however, it may be time to cease testing assumptions and to enact prohibitions. It isn't useful to continue marshaling facts after conclusions become inescapable. The bottle and poptop can makers, for example, are happy for their industry to be studied as long as anyone likes—even at considerable cost to themselves. They are happy about delay because the time for restriction or prohibition of their throwaway trash is long overdue.

As NEPA matures, it becomes more common to find impact statements that are in technical compliance but are woefully inadequate in terms of true consideration of issues. Because the first generation of NEPA litigation proceeded simplistically—either you mentioned every contingency, in which case you were all right, or you didn't, in which case it was back to a fresh start—writers of impact statements often aim a paragraph at every possible environmental consequence and give in-depth consideration to very few. Such treatment may reveal soft spots to environmental activists, but it does little if anything to improve government agencies' decision-making processes.

Still, NEPA enjoys a flexibility and applicability that prohibition legislation cannot. When new threats are perceived, environmental assessments can be made without new hearings and legislation.

After watching the successes built around the environmental impact statement, those who believe environmentalism has gone too far are clamoring for *economic* impact statements. Unfortunately, current thinking about the cost of environmental protection is so badly askew that the accepted dichotomy is environment versus economics, and environmentalists tend to oppose economic impact statements. But the bad environmental choice is usually a bad economic choice as well, a general principle that helped environmentalists defeat dams in Grand Canyon and the American SST. Too many environmentalists shun economic analysis, feeling they should respond to "higher values." Impact statements could be used to educate snobs of all persuasions.

Following the Tax Model

There is currently some pressure to create new federal courts specializing in environmental issues. These would be modeled after the federal tax and claims courts. Some environmentalists have argued that their cases are necessarily complex and specialized, and that most judges cannot be expected to handle them adequately. Many nonenvironmentalists favor the idea in the belief that environmental cases are clogging the courts. The latter rationale reflects a desire to shove these concerns off into a corner.

Interest in special environmental courts waned after a Justice Department study showed that less than one-half of one percent of the federal courts' caseload dealt with environmental matters. The courts are clogged all right, but mostly with things other than NEPA.

Specialized masters to assist regular courts make more sense. What is complex about environmental cases is not the law but the facts, particularly scientific data, underlying the dispute. Special masters (or "friends of the court") with technical expertise could expand the general level of environmental awareness without the restriction of responsibility to an elite, specialized bar and judiciary.

To Protect the Right to Court

Environmentalists' one-half of one percent of the federal courts' caseload will get even smaller unless recent rulings hampering effective action can be corrected by legislation. The problems are Supreme Court rulings that (1) restrict the compensation of parties engaged in public interest litigation, and (2) reduce the practicality of class action lawsuits.

The end to reimbursement of plaintiffs in public interest litigation came as a bitter aftertaste to the Alaska pipeline fight. In *Alyeska Pipeline Service Company vs. The Wilderness Society, et al,* The Wilderness Society, the Environmental Defense Fund, and Friends of the Earth sued to block the Alaska pipeline. The conservationists won in the courts, but Congress repealed their victory by rewriting the law and declaring via statute that pipeline construction didn't violate NEPA. Afterwards, the plaintiffs applied for their legal expenses, based on a line of cases authorizing payments to "private attorneys general." The idea behind this doctrine is that plaintiffs who uphold the law save the government the costs of enforcement and deserve compensation.

In line with these precedents, the Court of Appeals awarded attorneys' fees to the conservation groups; the pipeline construction company was ordered to pay $100,000. The Supreme Court reversed, holding that to force one side in a dispute to bear the others' expenses was so contrary to American tradition that each instance must be specifically authorized by the legislature.

In overturning the series of cases that established the private attorneys general theory, the Supreme Court relied on an 1853 statute—since eliminated—promulgating the American rule that each side pay its own expenses. The Court held that long-accepted exceptions to that rule were interpretations of the 1853 statute—although cases involving the exceptions failed to mention the statute or demonstrate any awareness of its existence. A dissenting opinion argued that the private attorneys general doctrine was an exercise of the court's inherent power to do equity, and that the Supreme Court itself had never previously regarded awards of attorney's fees to be the exclusive province of Congress.

Alyeska hurt people outside the environmental movement: almost all public interest litigation on behalf of minorities, the poor, and consumers relied in part on the hope that a successful result need not be an expensive one.

Several statutes specifically provide for awards of legal expenses, and *Alyeska* will not affect cases brought under them. Federal air, water, and noise pollution laws give courts the option of awarding legal expenses, showing that Congress expected private enforcement to play a minor role in their implementation.

Two peculiar features of environmental practice justify special consideration of funding methods. First, most environmental cases seek injunctions, not damages; the lawsuits seek to stop threatened actions, not to be compensated for their consequences. If the court grants the injunction sought, the bulldozer goes away and there are no damages to collect; if the court denies the injunction, the bulldozer goes ahead and the damage is irreversible. The lawsuit usually dries up and blows away rather quickly in either case, and no damages are recovered from which to defray costs. Consequently, contingent fee arrangements, which let lawyers collect only when and if the client does, are refused by all but stupid or idealistic attorneys.

The second peculiarity of environmental cases is that they are changing in ways that require more data, more experts, and thus more money. In the early 1970s, the typical case forced consideration of environmental consequences upon defendants who contended that the law couldn't possibly be aimed at them. Typically, the defendant's case was extremely weak; failure to comply reflected arrogance as much as anything else. But now the "easy" cases are over. As compliance gets better, the cases get tougher. Omissions must be ferreted out; mistakes must be found; our experts must challenge theirs. Cases emerge from the law library and get into the field, at enormous additional expense.

The *Alyeska* decision will inevitably choke off much public interest litigation by environmentalists and others. Realistically, too, it is likely to skew the growth of environmental law, causing plaintiffs to frame their cases in ways that arguably bring them within one of the few statutes allowing attorney's fees. This is common practice, but a tactic likely to convert an otherwise good case into a loser.

There can be no mistaking the remedy for *Alyeska*—legislation. Immediately after the decision, a number of bills were introduced providing for expenses under specific statutes felt to be suitable for private enforcement. Some suggested blanket legislation authorizing payment in all cases brought to uphold important congressional policies. Private enforcement under the private attorneys general theory is not a perfect mechanism. A legal ombudsman, a formula allocating some fraction of the cost of promoting a project to the project's opponents, or public subsidy of the enormous costs of discovery [i.e., "compulsory disclosure, as of facts or documents"] in modern environmental cases might work better. But some remedy must be found, and quickly.

Class Action Suits

In similarly damaging precedents, recent Supreme Court cases all but eliminated the usefulness of class action suits to environmentalists. Generally, a class action allows multiple plaintiffs with similar injuries from a common cause to sue and share in a common recovery of damages.

In *Zahn vs. International Paper Company*, four lakeshore property owners sued for themselves and a class of 200 others, alleging that paper plant pollution had damaged their properties' value. The property of each of four named plaintiffs had suffered at least ten thousand dollars' damage, the minimum necessary to confer federal jurisdiction. The Supreme Court ordered dismissal of the class action, holding that not only the four named plaintiffs but every member of the class must be shown to have suffered at least ten thousand dollars' damage.

Environmental issues typically arise because the benefits of proposed actions are concentrated among a few with power to decide and the burdens are widely dispersed among many people who have no influence on the decision. It is because the benefits are concentrated and the burdens are shared that environmental controls have relied so largely on regulation and prohibition. Dispersed burdens could be aggregated by the many victims in class action suits and the overall net cost demonstrated. As a practical matter, the class action often provided the only way to defray the enormous costs of modern research, discovery, and proof. Finally, of course, class actions lightened the load on the courts, avoiding the constant retrials of the same basic facts by multiple claimants.

The Supreme Court has continued to chip away at the class action. A 1974 case required mailings to all identifiable class members even though that class—all odd-lot stock traders—numbered more than two million and the cost of pursuing the dispute was thereby pegged above two hundred thousand dollars.

The class action was one of the few effective remedies against the systematic little illegalities that threaten to nibble the underrepresented to death. Class actions afforded an ideal method of bringing together the costs of pollution in a single action. The remedy should be revived.

The only sure bulwark of continuing liberty is a government strong enough to protect the interests of the people, and a people strong enough and well enough informed to maintain its sovereign control over its government.

—FRANKLIN D. ROOSEVELT

Revitalized Institutions

Institutions besides the courts must enter the business of generating public information regularly and systematically. In early 1975, the Securities and Exchange Commission (SEC) held hearings to determine whether corporate disclosure rules should extend to environmental and social programs as well as financial data. The SEC hearings were prompted by a NEPA lawsuite brought by the Natural Resources and Defense Council.

The SEC is only 40-odd years old, but during that time, an enormous body of law and regulatory practice has grown up to standardize the preparation of financial information by American corporations. Most of the work of preparing and presenting this information falls upon the corporations controlling the raw data. Those corporations therefore develop internal expertise in financial disclosure. As a result, a large volume of periodic, systematic reports, in a standardized form approved by the SEC, is available to the public. The SEC watchdogs the preparation of reports and punishes violators.

Environmentalists should work to extend the scope of mandatory public disclosure regulated by a wider variety of institutions. Courts have jurisdiction over everybody, but they don't have continuing close relationships such as the SEC enjoys with the business community, the Interstate Commerce Commission with transportation industries, the Food and Drug Administration with pharmaceutical companies. The coziness that often develops between the regulated and the regulators is often criticized, but the potential for effective public disclosure through regulatory institutions is tremendous. If, as Brandeis said, "sunlight is the best disinfectant," just getting information to the public should be the first step. Refinements can be left to the future.

A Geneva Convention for the Environment?

If domestic environmental law is largely derivative, the international arena invites creative efforts toward shared concepts and strong institutions.

The kind of international behavior most similar to our treatment of the environment is war. Is, then, the base from which enforceable standards can evolve the Geneva Convention?

The major instances of international settlement of environmental problems—or more precisely, of compensation for damage already done—have involved special forums set up to settle specific disputes. Since the 1930s, at least, bilateral compacts have assessed damages and compensated victims. Canada and the United States settled a smelter pollution dispute through such a device, and the French and Spanish arbitrated a river-diversion case. These forums were not courts, with continuity and power to compel. They were created by and dependent for their continued existence on the problems they sought to resolve.

Decisions by the International Court of Justice or under the rules of the International Arbitration Association would be preferable, if only for the opportunity to build expert staff. Environmental cases have been submitted in both places, but at present, no international forum can compel its own jurisdiction. The opponents must stop squabbling long enough to agree on a forum. If you strip compulsory jurisdiction and the law of injunction from US environmental law, you are left with very little. That little is what one starts and ends with internationally.

In the US, environmental damage to individuals either goes uncompensated or must be compensated by the tort system. Success requires proof that the defendant did specified things that directly resulted in specified injury to the plaintiff. Proof is obviously easier when the victim gets hit by an automobile than when an asbestos worker turns out to have cancer or an urbanite suffers from emphysema. Statistics say that city living increases the risk of emphysema, but which of any number of polluting factories should pay?

The Japanese, often more practical than we, have been experimenting with a remedy since 1973. In that year, their Diet enacted a system for the compensation of the victims of industrial pollution. Under the law, Japan is divided into zones. Sufferers in zones where statistics indicate that pollutants led to an increased incidence of disease can be certified to receive compensation for medical expenses and lost wages. Funds for compensation come from graduated emission charges and a tonnage tax on cars.

Such a system permits compensation on the basis of scientific probability rather than legal evidence of causality. Usually, this is the best evidence that victims can muster. In dealing with cancer and other environmental diseases whose lengthy latency periods make their origins uncertain, no one can offer proof on the basis of traditional notions of causality.

Many environmentalists react negatively to schemes that allow polluters to weigh the costs of control against the expense of fines or compensation to victims. Compensation schemes like that adopted in Japan seem to constitute a license to pollute—often viewed as a license to kill, which in a sense it is. Nevertheless, such schemes deserve support—not to replace our tort system but to provide an alternative. To the extent that costs of pollution can be shifted from the public to those responsible for it, the incentive to find remedies increases.

In our country, to consider recourse to the legal system at all requires a certain optimism about the time available for change. Legislation takes too long, and the courts take longer. A step backward for each two steps ahead is standard. For the judicial system to contribute as much to environmental breakthroughs in the next decade as it has in this, proportionately more resources will be necessary as cases get tougher.

The principal value of the legal process lies in its ability to test for uncertain facts—not perfectly, but better than torture or other methods popular at one time or another. Like old age, the legal process looks better when you consider the alternative.

Law and Public Support

JAMES MOORMAN

I have serious reservations as to whether our complex conservation laws will ultimately protect the land from the ravages of expedient development in the face of the present world demand for resources.

The reasons for my reservations derive from the fact that our conservation laws do not have as broad a base of support as is necessary to sustain them over the long term. They are not accepted by a large and disgruntled body of the public.

Despite the obvious support for conservation and environmental protection as manifest in our law books, the dissenting mass of opinion that sullenly opposed each new conservation law has not been won over, to coin a phrase, in heart and mind.

The opposition to conservation laws believes such laws threaten their economic base and their freedom and liberty. Thus, we find labor leaders opposing environmental initiatives, ORV users balking at restrictions, ranchers opposing increases of grazing fees, loggers opposing a modest expansion of the Redwood National Park, fishermen insisting on the right to fish on porpoises. I recall when a stripmine control bill was being debated by the West Virginia Legislature a few years ago that one State legislator sought his constituents' views as follows: "Would you support a bill which would prevent you from doing what you wanted to do on your own land?"

An opposition founded in fear that a program threatens liberty and economic well-being is formidable indeed. The fact that Congress has rejected these fears and has passed conservation laws only means that battles have been won, not that the war has been won.

In order to combat the problems caused by the fact that their opponents fail to accept conservation controls in their hearts and minds, environmental citizen groups have followed a strategy of escalation. They have requested and won more and more stringent conservation controls. With every success along this line, however, rather than win acquiescence from their opponents, they have created even greater dismay, alarm, resentment and resistance.

What we have learned is that certain segments of society will not change their attitudes on conservation simply because Congress has passed laws. Instead they will do everything in their power to resist those laws.

—Thus they will continue to lobby strenuously to repeal or weaken the law.

—They will pour additional millions into PR campaigns to change public opinion.

—They will spend additional millions to hire an army of legal talent to search out every loophole, to challenge every implementing action, to seek out every opportunity for delay and to find every ground for challenging the law's validity.

If they comply, it will be at the last possible moment.

If they comply, it will be in the least possible degree.

If they comply, it will be under protest.

If they comply, it will be only after they have been beaten at every attempt to escape compliance.

If they comply, it is with everyone on notice that they will press on with their campaign to rid themselves of a law they view as burdensome.

I contend that under these circumstances, the land must lose sooner or later. The loopholes will be found, enforcement will at some crucial point come too late, repeals will eventually occur. The law alone is simply insufficient to ensure that the dissenting group will accept conservation.

What then is needed in addition to law? In brief, for the law to be effective it must rest on a basis of ethics and morality accepted and shared by society in general. If we are to ensure that conservation as a mode of conduct will be adopted, then we must convince people that it is the *right* thing to do and we must not rest simply on the proposition that it is what the law requires.

If a man believes he must protect soil in order to go to heaven, he is not going to hire a lawyer to find a loophole.

If a man believes his neighbors will look down on him if he wrecks a river, he is not going to hire a PR man to go talk to his neighbors.

If a man knows his conscience will hound him if he ruins a forest, he is not going to hire a lobbyist to petition the Almighty.

In brief, only when our society develops a broadly shared land ethic, leaving the law to deal with the small but ever-present minority of the anti-social, will we begin to gain ground, not lose it.

This idea is not original with me. Aldo Leopold's landmark essay on the Land Ethic was published almost 30 years ago, posthumously, in the first edition of *A Sand County Almanac*. At that time Leopold observed that the farmers in conservation districts only carried out those parts of the district programs which economically benefited them and let languish the balance. Leopold concluded then that this resulted from the farmers' perception that conservation was an economic matter, not an ethical one. I believe the problem of dissent today on conservation is just a matter of economics and is in no way a matter of ethics. Thus, opponents to conservation often view conservationists as just another group promoting its own interests, seeking to tie up land for its own use, rather than as a group promoting public policies for the good of the community as a whole.

I believe that if we are to weather our present crisis this misperception of conservation must change and conservation must become a broadly accepted land ethic instead of just a collection of imposed legal duties. Therefore, I believe it behooves us to re-examine Leopold's ideas.

In Leopold's view, ethics are "a limitation on freedom of action in the struggle for existence."

These limitations find their origin "in the tendency of interdependent individuals or groups to evolve modes of cooperation."

The "Land Ethic" simply enlarges our perception of the interdependent group to include soils, water, plants, and animals, or collectively, the land.

"In short, a land ethic changes the role of *Homo sapiens* from conquerors of the land community to plain members and citizens of it. It implies respect for his fellow members, and also respect for the community as such."

In the Leopold view, which I share, man is an interdependent member of the earth's biotic community. He cannot view himself as outside of that community. He is dependent upon the community's health. He must cooperate with the community to ensure the community's health so as to survive himself. He cannot act as the community's conqueror lest he simply conquer himself. Thus, as members of a community upon which we depend, we must cooperate with, rather than compete with, the land.

Leopold observed that, "There is a clear tendency in American conservation to relegate to the government all necessary jobs the private landowners fail to per-

form." He referred to the growth of government ownership, operation, subsidy and regulation. He did not question the appropriateness of the government role, but contended, as I do, that government cannot do the job alone. He made this point by suggesting that at some time government conservation, like the mastadon, will become handicapped by its own dimensions.

If Leopold had lived through the last 30 years to see how the government effort has grown beyond his wildest imagination; had he lived to see:

The Federal Water Pollution Act,
The Clean Air Act,
The National Environmental Policy Act,
The National Forest Management Act,
The Federal Land Policy and Management Act,
The Marine Mammal Protection Act,
The Coastal Zone Management Act,
The Surface Mining Control and Reclamation Act,

and dozens of others, he would have concluded from the growing complexity of these laws that he had been right 30 years ago: that government cannot control anti-land conduct—only an accepted Land Ethic can do that.

Leopold observed 30 years ago that the problem is acute. In much of the world he saw "a violent and accelerating wastage in progress."

He observed that "this almost worldwide display or disorganization in land seems to be similar to [a] disease . . ."

Leopold saw that the only solution was an end to violence against the land.

Only an accepted ethic, supplemented by law, can control the violence. We now are drifting into an era where the level of violence against the land is rising. That is indeed why Congress has passed laws such as the Surface Mining Control and Reclamation Act. Such laws alone, however, cannot control the violence, unaided by a land ethic.

The land ethic must reflect "an ecological conscience" and "a conviction of individual responsibility for the health of the land." An ethical relation to the land cannot "exist without love, respect, and admiration for land, and a high regard for its value."

To Leopold, "a thing is right when it tends to preserve the integrity, stability and beauty of the biotic community. It is wrong when it tends otherwise."

As did Leopold, I believe "our present problem is one of attitudes. We are remodeling the Alhambra with a steam shovel, and we are proud of our yardage."

We need a different, more sensitive criteria than yardage. It must be embodied in an ethic generally accepted. The survival of our land in the days ahead depends on it; our ultimate survival depends on it.

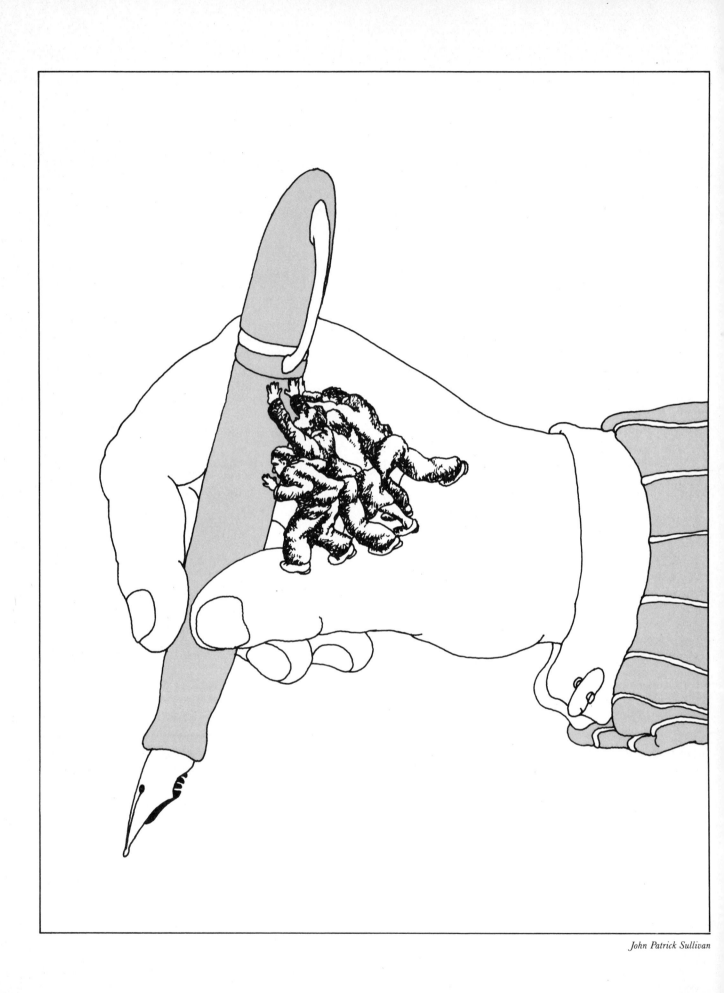

Citizens Appendices

How to Get Laws Introduced and Passed

The most insidious destroyer of democratic government is nonparticipation. People feel strongly about issues, but say to themselves: "I am powerless. What can I do to influence public policy?" This attitude has been a problem for centuries. Plutarch chronicles Solon as saying: "He shall be disfranchised who in times of faction takes neither side." Major societal problems will not be cured until there is much more universal participation in the political process. Laws *can* be influenced by people, working singly or in groups on public issues. Mastery of the complex machinery of the political process, however, is a necessary prerequisite. In order to effectively influence legislation, citizens must know when and how to apply pressure on their elected representatives.

How to Get Laws Introduced and Passed

ANN ROOSEVELT

IF A REPRESENTATIVE OR SENATOR were to answer truthfully the question, "What is the most important issue you are involved in?" the answer would probably be, "My own reelection." Survival, especially for members of the House, who are elected every two years, is of paramount importance. It dwarfs all other issues. Even Senators, who only need to campaign every six years, are well aware of the political maxim that one doesn't ignore the wishes of one's district for long and survive.

Primarily, it is this overriding concern with reelection that gives citizens power to influence the laws that will be formulated. Unfortunately, most people do not use their power to influence legislation, and thus Congressmen hear most frequently from paid industry lobbyists. (We will use "Congressmen" to mean both Representatives and Senators unless it makes a difference, in which case, we will distinguish between them.) In addition to the major corporations that employ full-time lobbyists, the Washington staffs of trade groups have for years served as conduits to explain to legislators what their members want. It is only relatively recently that public interest groups have employed Washington staffs to act in this capacity. The fact that so much consumer and environmental legislation was passed during the seventies speaks well for the effectiveness of these public interest lobbyists. Such measures as the Fair Campaign Practices Act, the Clean Air Act, the Eastern Wilderness Act, and numerous land protection bills would not have been passed in effective form without public-interest lobbying pressure.

If you do not live in Washington and yet you want to be effective influencing legislation, it is almost imperative that you join a national public interest group that is concerned with your issue and has an effective lobbying office in Washington. Enacting a bill into law is a long, tortuous process. For people outside of Washington to initiate ideas that ultimately become law, it is usually necessary to have a Washington liaison who can personally meet with legislators, be available for quick consultation, and keep the local individual or group aware of latest developments. The Washington staffs of consumer and environmental groups act as this contact for their members in the same way trade groups have acted for decades. Because legislative developments can move so quickly and because political savvy about the complex world of Capitol Hill is gradually built up over the years, the importance of affiliation with an effective national lobbying group cannot be overstated.

Another service that national groups provide is a legislative newsletter. Almost all groups have a publication that discusses the latest developments in legislation, who key Congressmen are, and how to influence them. The newsletter is an extremely important lobbying tool because local newspapers and TV do not provide in-depth analysis of legislation in Congress until it has either passed or failed. Potential amendments, for instance, are rarely discussed in the local press, even though an amendment may change the whole thrust of a bill. Thus, the legislative newsletter provides valuable information in addition to stimulating widespread interest in the issue.

The techniques that follow are basic lobbying strategies that you can employ to influence legislation.

To be effective, the first thing you must do is become knowledgeable about the issue. Once you have expertise, you have something very much needed by the overworked staffers on Capitol Hill—accurate information. Becoming knowledgeable is not the herculean effort it may seem; it becomes fairly simple if you get assistance from your Congressman.

First, find out if any legislation has been introduced or if hearings have been held on the issue. There is a service available to Congressmen called the Bill Status Office. The staff of the legislator merely telephones a Capitol Hill extension to learn from the computerized service what bills have been offered on a subject, whether hearings have been held, whether the bills have passed either house, etc. For a more detailed analysis of the subject and a more complete explanation of the bills, legislators can call on the Congressional Research Service. This service is located in the

Library of Congress and provides legislators with detailed information on any subject. Capitol Hill staffers can call the Congressional Research Service with a problem and a few days later receive a carefully prepared paper citing the pro and con arguments.

If your Congressman is willing, and most are, you can make use of these services to find out quickly if legislation has been submitted on your issue and what the points of contention are. Simply write your Congressman and ask him to ask the Bill Status Office to determine whether any bills have been held, and what has happened to the bills. If you would like a more detailed analysis of the bills, ask him to request that the Congressional Research Service, instead of the Bill Status Office, determine what bills have been submitted. Request background information on the pro and con arguments and citations of any relevant government studies that have been done on your issue. The National Academy of Sciences, for instance, does studies on almost every conceivable topic. Studies by government agencies provide background information that gives you expertise and can be used later on in the legislative battle.

Once you have received your Congressman's response, you can begin assembling the material you will need to become knowledgeable about the issue. Get the bills, any committee reports, and hearing records. Study them. Be sure to cite bills by their number, prefixed by HR for House of Representatives and S for the Senate. If the bill has been reported out of committee, ask that the committee report be included with the bill. This report gives a section-by-section analysis of major points in the bill and also explains the pro and con arguments advanced in committee debate.

The bills and committee reports can be obtained by writing to the House Document Room, Washington, D.C. 20515 or the Senate Document Room, Washington, D.C. 20510. Hearing records must be obtained from the committee that held the hearing, not from the Document Room.

Studying this material and doing independent research at your library will give you a good start. But what if there have been no bills introduced in your area of interest, or all the bills in existence embody bad principles? The answer, of course, is to write a bill of your own.

Introducing a Bill

Congressmen have at their disposal an Office of Legislative Counsel that drafts bills and amendments for Congressmen and committees. The Office will take bill drafts and outlines from a Congressman and put them into legal language suitable for introduction. It is partly because of the availability of this Office that so much legislation is now introduced. If you have an idea you want to expand into a bill, it is a relatively simple matter to contact your Congressman, get him to send your idea to the Office of Legislative Counsel, and then convince him to introduce the resulting bill. While some members of Congress refuse to introduce a lot of legislation, most are very willing to introduce well-thought-out bills for their constituents. The legislation that is introduced in this manner, however, usually ends up in the great burial ground of the Congressional committees and is never heard of again. It is relatively easy to get a bill introduced. To get it introduced in a way that will give it a good chance to become law is more difficult.

Old hands on Capitol Hill know that *who* introduces a bill and *which committee* the bill is referred to often determine whether or not the bill will become law. Only rarely will a bill become law if it is introduced by someone who is not a member of the committee that considers it. In fact, to give the bill the best chance, it is necessary to have someone introduce it who is a member of the *sub*committee that will consider it. In other words, there must usually be a champion of the bill working for it at both the subcommittee and committee levels.

Before asking a Congressman to introduce your bill, try to determine which committee and subcommittee it would logically be referred to. Get a copy of the volume entitled *Constitution, Jefferson's Manual, and Rules of the House of Representatives* from Superintendent of Documents, Government Printing Office, Washington, D.C. 20402. This book is published every session and describes the jurisdictions of House Committees. Unfortunately, it is not free; it costs $9.30 in paperback. A similar volume that describes Senate committee jurisdictions, *Senate Procedure, Precedents and Practices,* is available from the Government Printing Office for $8.10 in paperback.

Once you have determined which committee the bill will be referred to, get the *Congressional Directory* or some similar reference book from the library and find out who the members of that committee are.

The next step is to determine which member will be the most receptive to your viewpoint and the most influential on the committee. First, choose a member of the majority party. Minority members rarely have enough clout to get controversial legislation out of committee. Consider seriously a member who may be neutral on your issue but comes from your state. Usually you would choose your own Congressman because you would be able to use reelection pressures to get the bill pushed.

Another major factor in choosing a member to introduce your bill is that some members become specialists in certain areas. These members often consider themselves to be more nationally oriented, and because they are proud of their knowledge and reputation, will introduce bills concerning their specialty for citizens who are not their own constituents. Getting one of these specialists to introduce your bill means that you capitalize on the respect and influence that this member has.

Gerald McMurray, the Staff Director of the Housing Subcommittee of the House Banking and Currency Committee, once emphasized how influential specialists are: "If I had a bill in the housing area, for instance changing the block grant program, I would want the Housing Subcommittee Chairman Thomas Ludlow Ashley to introduce it because he is known as the one man in Congress who knows almost everything about our federal housing program. I'd expect a bill he introduced to have a good chance of passing because of the respect with which the other members view his knowledge. The advice I would give someone who wants to get a bill enacted into law is, "Try to get a specialist, a member respected by the other Congressman for his knowledge, to introduce it."

One easy way to get help in deciding who should introduce your bill is to contact the Washington staff of the environmental, consumer, or other public interest group that is most concerned with your issue. The staffs of these groups are familiar with the leanings of most Congressmen who are sympathetic to their views and are generally able to give good advice on who would be the most influential member of the committee.

Once you have found an effective member to introduce your bill, write to him proposing your idea. Include a draft of your bill and any supporting material you have been able to gather, such as scientific studies by government agencies, magazine or newspaper articles, statements by public officials, etc. The more polished and complete your package seems, the greater the likelihood that your bill will be introduced. Offer to get more background material and to explain your bill more fully if the staff wishes to telephone you. Include your telephone number. Finally, to maximize your chances, try to get endorsements from other people and groups for your bill.

Once a Congressman has agreed to introduce your bill, find out the name of the staff person in his office who will be handling the legislation. It is very important to become friendly with the Congressman's staff person assigned to your issue. It is this staffer who does the day-to-day work on the issue, and his opinion is respected by the Congressman. The only caveat is that congressional staffers, like the legislators themselves, are overworked. It is necessary to keep in telephone contact with them and to help them perform many tasks, such as assembling witness lists for hearings, preparing speeches, etc. On the other hand, there is a serious danger of alienating them if they are bothered too frequently. There is a fine line between keeping a staffer informed and bothering him.

Your relationship with the Capitol Hill staff is a professional, mutually beneficial one. Remain businesslike even in the face of delay. The staffer's schedule (or his boss's) will often force a delay. Unless procrastination has become chronic, remember that it is one of the facts of legislative life, and don't let it upset your relationship with the Hill staffer.

Once the mechanics of getting the bill introduced are completed, the process of expediting its passage through both Houses begins. At this point, traditional lobbying techniques must be used, so a digression to explain these techniques is necessary.

Lobbying

The key to lobbying is the efficient use of limited time and scarce resources. An understanding of the ramifications of the congressional committee system is essential to the concentration of lobbying effort.

Most basic work on legislation is done in the subcommittees and committees of Congress. The committee system is a timesaver. By working in only one or two areas throughout their congressional tenure, Congressmen do not have to learn basic facts every time they work on a new piece of legislation. To become an effective lobbyist, it is important to realize how influential the committee system is. It is not unusual for a member to stand up on the House floor when legislation is being considered and say; "I am against this amendment. We thoroughly discussed this issue during our committee debate and decided not to amend the legislation in this way." Sometimes he will even add, "I don't think you should vote for this because, if we are going to have committees in Congress, you should rely on their judgment in these matters."

Congressmen do rely on committee judgments. Usually, 90 percent of the issues in the bill are permanently resolved in committee. Of course, there are many exceptions. Some bills are completely revised on the floor. And some issues become so controversial that interest is high and many amendments are offered. But in general, the basic work is done at the subcommittee and committee levels, and only the most controversial sections of the bill are amended on the floor. Lobbyists wise in the ways of Capitol Hill realize this and concentrate their efforts on the committees. Extra effort expended on the relatively small number of committee members pays tremendous dividends when the time comes for a floor vote. For example, if you are successful in getting the committee to adopt your position, the committee's authority and prestige will help defend that position from attack on the floor. Even though you will use the following techniques at all stages in the political process, the bulk of your effort should be directed at getting a good bill reported out of committee.

Lobbying falls into two general categories: working with Congressmen's constituents and working with the media.

Organizing a Congressman's constituents to exert effective pressure on his opinion is the way public interest issues are won in Congress. At first, it may seem to be an impossible task; but as the issue begins to take hold, allies will be draw in to your position and it will become easier.

The first thing to do is to get the endorsements of national environmental, consumer, and public interest groups. Such endorsements will give you credibility and will impress upon local groups that your issue is important nationally.

Organization and background work are the keys to a successful legislative battle. You must plan your strategy carefully. Since the subcommittee and committee do most of the nitty-gritty work, they should be the focus of your attention. Contact the major local groups and branches of national groups in the districts of committee and subcommittee members and ask them to take a stand on the issue. Don't stop with environmental or consumer groups; labor unions, religious organizations, and fraternal organizations often can be persuaded to take stands on national issues. These groups sometimes have more impact than public interest groups. The broader the scope of groups supporting your cause, the more seriously the Congressman will consider it. When you have a broad coalition of support, it is difficult for him to say "those do-gooders are at it again."

Identify and recruit an interested person in each committee member's district. One way to find such a person is to ask the local branches of the national public interest groups for their recommendations. Material can then be sent to the person to disseminate to other interested people and groups. This contact person must be kept up-to-date on all developments and technical aspects of the legislation because he will also serve as your contact with the local press. Background papers, material suitable for use in pamphlets, etc., must be sent to this contact. He will be responsible for publicizing the issue, contacting local groups, organizing a letter-writing campaign, setting up a telephone network if possible, and coordinating the effort in the member's district.

Having an effective contact person in each district can often mean the difference between success and failure. Rafe Pomerance, President of Friends of the Earth and its former Legislative Director, describes one instance: "We knew Congressmen Dingell was going to offer an amendment in committee to gut the automobile emissions standards section of the Clean Air Act. But, because we had established contact people in each member's district, we were able to generate an outpouring of sentiment against the issue in five key districts. These five members changed their votes, and that proved to be the margin we needed to defeat the amendment."

One of the jobs that you and your contact people will have to undertake is to organize a letter-writing campaign. The basic means by which a Congressman

---

I know no safe depository of the ultimate powers of the society but the people themselves; and if we think them not enlightened enough to exercise their control with a wholesome discretion, the remedy is not to take it from them, but to inform their discretion.

—THOMAS JEFFERSON

---

keeps in contact with his district is the mail. Never underestimate the importance of letters. Telephone calls to the local office or even to Washington are often useful, but letters provide the basic demonstration of interest and expression of opinion concerning an issue.

The volume of mail a Congressman or Senator receives varies with many factors. Legislators from primarily rural areas usually receive less mail, but a speech or newspaper article may stimulate a large volume on a certain day. No matter how many letters are received, each one is opened, read, catalogued, and answered. Thus, there is a tally in every Congressman's office of voter interest and sentiment on different issues. The legislator is told daily, or at least weekly, how voter interest is running. He is told again before a vote.

Every Congressman knows that voters are often too apathetic to express their preferences in writing. When a person does take the trouble to write, the Congressman assumes that the writer's position must also beheld by a large number of other people in the district. In other words, he feels that every letter represents the sentiments of 50, 100, or even 500 voters in his district. A letter-writing campaign, therefore, is an important lobbying tool. There are certain techniques

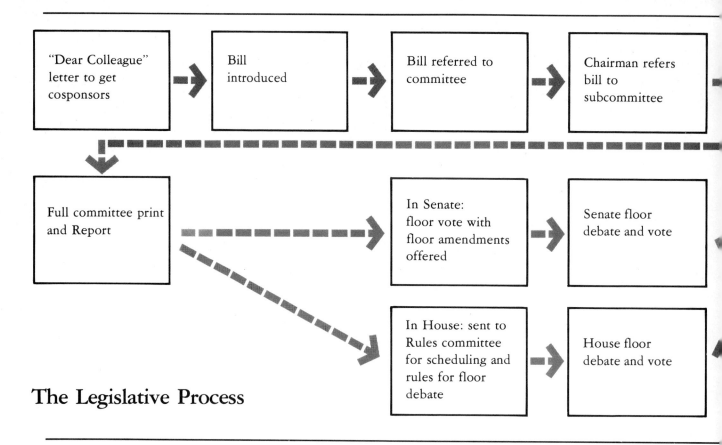

The Legislative Process

of letter writing that you should use and recommend to co-workers:

1. Always be courteous. You can disagree with a Congressman's position, but never be discourteous in doing so.

2. Try to keep the letter to one typewritten page. Complex letters are often put aside to be answered later and may lose their effectiveness. If you have more material than will fit onto one page, include extra background pages, but label them clearly as background and put your name and address on them in a corner. These pages will probably be routed to the staff person handling the issue and so will have more impact.

3. Do not write about more than one issue in each letter. That only confuses the staff and dilutes your impact.

4. It is better not to use a form letter provided by an environmental, labor, consumer, or other organization. It only takes a minute to write a few sentences of your own, and such a letter is much more effective. Try to add a few sentences about the issue's impact on the legislator's district.

5. If you write to a Congressman who is not your own, send a copy to your legislator and clearly indicate that you have done so on the bottom of your page.

Otherwise, your letter may bt routed to your own Congressman as a courtesy, and the legislator you want to influence will be bypassed.

6. If you are writing to criticize or praise a bill, be as specific as possible. If you do not know the bill number, try to describe the bill by its precise name, such as the "Eastern Wilderness Bill."

7. If you are writing about an amendment, try to include the bill number, who will offer the amendment, and what the amendment will do.

8. If possible, include in your letter some reference to the Congressman's past actions on your issue or some other related issue. Including this kind of reference shows that you are aware of his past record and that you are following the issue closely. If you write to the legislator and ask to be included on his newsletter list, you can become more aware of his attitudes.

9. Ask your Congressman to vote a specific way, support a specific amendment, or take a specific action. Otherwise you will get a "motherhood" response. He will say in a general way: "Of course I am in favor of clean air, adequate health care, or whatever you want." Then he may vote the wrong way. In order to be effective, you must be specific so you can hold him accountable for his actions.

10. It is always wise to try to meet the Congressman

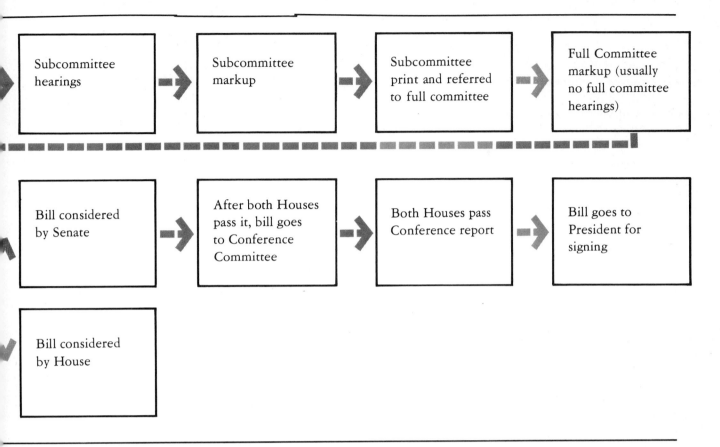

before you write to him. Then you can refer to your meeting in the first few sentences of your letter. Call his district office to ask for his schedule of office hours and public meetings.

Working With the Media

Since, initially, the congressional committee will be the basic unit you are working with, a good beginning is to go to your local library and get *The Ayer Directory of Newspapers, Magazines, and Trade Publications* or *Bacon's Publicity Checker* from the reference room. These books list the major newspapers throughout the United States. From one of them, you can extract a press list of the major newspapers in the district of each of the members of your committee. Such a list will prove very valuable as the campaign heats up. The next thing to acquire is the League of Conservation Voters charts of the voting records of Senators and Congressmen. By looking over these charts, you can deduce the political leanings of members of your committee. The charts can be obtained for $2.00 each from the League at 317 Pennsylvania Ave. SE, Washington, DC 20003.

The *Congressional Record* is also an important element in the legislative process. Reading it can be an enlightening experience, but it can also be used as a public relations tool. Congressmen can publish in the *Record* speeches, reprints of newspaper and magazine articles, etc., up to two *Record* pages in length. Then they can have these sections reprinted (subject, of course, to the approval of any copyright holders) at nominal cost. These *Congressional Record* reprints can then be sent to their constituents, to the press, or to anyone else the member wishes to receive them. If the member assents, it is possible for a group to pay the printing costs for these reprints and thus get reprints to send to its members. Sending out *Congressional Record* reprints is a good way to engender interest in an issue.

Letters to the editor of the newspapers in key members' districts are also good tools to stimulate interest in your issue. Send a copy of your letter to your Congressman at the same time that you send it to the newspaper. Then he will see it even if the newspaper does not print it. If it is printed, you will have an opportunity to write a follow-up letter to your Representative, including the printed letter. Be sure to ask the member to take some specific action, whether it be to ask the chairman to hold hearings, to support an amendment, or whatever you wish at the stage in the legislative process your bill is in.

Calling up editors and reporters of the local media in key Congressmen's districts to ask them to cover the issue is also a good way to influence legislation. Local newspapers and radio stations are usually much more willing to cover issues relevant to their Congressman or Senator than the national press, especially if you stress the local implications. Moreover, studies show that the local media are more influential in affecting people's opinions than the national media. Members of Congress are aware of this and pay particular attention to what is reported back home.

One of the best ways to influence a Congressman is not used as much as it should be. This is the use of praise when he makes a speech, offers an amendment, or takes a stand that is praiseworthy. Politicians hear a lot of criticism from the press and from constituents, but only rarely do they get praised. If a Congressman does something that is good for your cause or good for the environment in general, send him a letter thanking him. Either enclose a copy of the letter with a note to the local press, or even better, write a press release and send it to the newspapers in the Congressman's district. Praise him for his stand. Chances are good that the local media will pick up your press release and praise him also. If that happens, the Congressman will be very grateful for the favorable publicity in his home district where it can help him get reelected. The praise may encourage him to devote more time to your issue or even to become a specialist in it. After Senator Warren Magnuson wrote several consumer bills that became law, he was acclaimed in the press and by consumer groups. The praise had a salutory effect. Gradually he turned his committee, the Senate Commerce Committee, from a business-oriented group into a consumer panel.

Praising legislators publicly for their good works is a way to encourage them to do more good. But it is also a way to insure that your viewpoint will be taken seriously in future matters, since it conditions the Congressman to view you as an ally.

There are myriad ways to influence the media. The following is a partial list:

1. Assemble a press list and learn to write a good press release by studying books from your public library on press relations techniques and talking to reporters on your local papers.
2. Appear on local radio and TV talk shows and also get experts from local universities and organizations to appear.
3. Write feature stories and submit them to local magazines.
4. Try to get editorial support from local TV and radio stations. Contact the station managers and ask them to take a stand supporting your viewpoint. Have sufficient background material available. If you are successful, ask the station for a copy of the editorial and send it to the legislators.
5. Try to get local TV stations to do a documentary about your issue.
6. Contact other organizations in your key congressional districts and urge them to publicly support your position. Their support can be announced by a press release to the local media and by their newsletters to their members. Make sure they notify their Congressmen and Senators of their posi-

John McDermott

tion. It is very important not to forget to contact labor unions and other powerful groups that are principally concerned with your issue. These groups can be very influential with the local media and broaden your support.

7. Form local coalitions in key congressional districts. Formation of such a coalition is a newsworthy event and will be picked up by the local papers if they are properly briefed. Such a local angle on a national issue can help make it more relevant for the local press.

8. Visit local politicians and local political organizations such as the Young Democrats and Young Republicans. Ask them to make a statement on your issue and publicize it. It is a good idea when contacting local politicians and political organizations that do not have large staffs to include a sample statement they can release under their own name by slightly rewriting it. Other actions politicians could take include writing an article on the subject, appearing on local TV and radio shows, organizing other politicians, or testifying at congressional committee hearings. It is generally quite easy to get ambitious young politicians to take these actions because they will get publicity that will help in their future careers.

9. If there are public figures who have championed your issue in another part of the country, write to them. Ask them if they are going to be visiting your area in the future and if they would mind being interviewed by the press and making a statement on your issue. For instance, Pete Seeger, in his travels around the country giving concerts, is often interviewed on the subject of water pollution because he has become a spokesman for cleaning up New York's waterways. If it is explained that a key Congressman or Senator lives in the district, the public figure will often be willing to be interviewed because of the chance to influence public policy.

10. If you hear negative ads about your issue on television or radio, contact station managers about the possibility of getting free time to respond under the Fairness Doctrine. The station is only required to *sell* you time if the opposition bought time. In some cases, however, the station will decide that if you cannot pay for time, they will offer you some free, as a public service.

Until fairly recently, public interest issues were not publicized very much. Now everyone realizes the value of publicity to mobilize sentiment about an issue. Using your press list and organizing the constituents of key Congressmen are the two most effective ways to influence legislation. But lobbying techniques, to be useful, must be employed at different times in the legislative process. Thus, you must become familiar with the process by which a bill becomes law.

At almost every step in the legislative process, it is possible to lobby for your viewpoint. Just as a bill is introduced, if not before, cosponsors are sought by the member introducing it. You can help by writing to urge Congressmen or Senators to cosponsor the legislation. The mechanics of getting cosponsors is similar in both Houses. In the Senate, the members send out a "Dear Colleague" letter to all other Senators describing the bill and asking for cosponsors. Then the names of the cosponsors appear on succeeding prints of the bill. The House rules differ slightly although the "Dear Colleague" letter is the same. In the House, only 25 members may cosponsor a bill. The difference is theoretical, however, because other members who are in favor of the bill merely introduce identical bills. Getting a large number of cosponsors is important because the more cosponsors a bill has, the easier it is to get hearings on the bill. The chairman of the subcommittee or committee considering the bill has almost absolute power to determine if hearings will beheld. Naturally, he feels more pressure to call hearings if there are 50 cosponsors rather than five.

Once a bill has been introduced, it is referred to the committee that has jurisdiction over that issue. Then the bill is usually referred to a subcommittee for detailed consideration. It is possible, however, that the chairman of the full committee will not refer the bill to a subcommittee but instead will rule that the bill be taken up by the full committee.

When the bill is referred, the chairman of the committee or subcommittee decides if hearings will be held right away. If he sets a date for hearings, it is the job both of the staff of the Congressman who introduced the bill and of the subcommittee staff to organize a witness list. Depending on the complexity and scope of the bill, hearings can be set for 1, 2, 3, or even more days. Various kinds of witnesses are called: scientists, representatives of trade groups, public interest groups, government representatives, industry, and anyone with interest in the subject. They deliver testimony and answer questions from the subcommittee members. It is relatively easy to become a witness at a hearing. The staff person handling the witness list tries to get a broad representation of various points of view and so is anxious to find diverse individuals who are interested and knowledgeable.

Since most committees have very little money to pay travel expenses to Washington, they use two ways to get testimony from people unable to come to Washington on their own. The more common method is for people living far away to submit written testimony. Such testimony is included in the hearing record and is considered by the staff and legislators when making judgments about the bill. The other alternative is used, logically, when most of the witnesses would live outside of Washington but in close proximity to each other. This usually occurs when land bills are under consideration, or bills that would only affect one region. Field hearings are then held locally, congressional staff and legislators going to the area to take testimony.

Hearings are the basic medium of communication with the subcommittee, and their importance cannot be overstated. In addition to preparing testimony of your own and either submitting it in writing or delivering it in person, you should try to convince other groups and individuals who agree with your viewpoint to submit testimony. Congressmen or Senators not on the committee can testify, as can other politicians and public figures. Testimony from such individuals is valuable both because it is more frequently covered in the media and because legislators, obviously, pay close attention to influential people in their own profession. Try to convince other Congressmen and Senators and some local politicians to testify supporting your position.

Obviously, the hearing is an ideal occasion to release a statement to the press. Since members of the press usually attend important hearings, you can hand out a press release there that will often get picked up in a general story about the hearings. If it doesn't, such a release could still spark interest in your viewpoint and serve as background for future stories. Even if you cannot be at the hearing, it is wise to send your release out to your press list so it will arrive before the hearing takes place. At each point in the legislative process, every effort should be made to get your viewpoint into the press.

After the hearing, your bill could lie fallow indefinitely. Once again, lobbying techniques should be used to get a "markup." This term was coined because subcommittee members take a clean copy of a bill and mark it up with amendments. A markup is a working session. The bill is read, page by page, and the subcommittee members offer amendments and vote on them. when they have gone through the bill completely, they decide whether or not to vote out the bill as amended. Voting it out means they send a clean copy of the amended bill to the full committee.

If, after the hearing, no markup is scheduled, you should try to get influential members of the subcommittee, the full committee, and members of Congress in general to contact the subcommittee chairman asking for a markup. Letters to the subcommittee chairman, especially those from people in his district, are influential. Creating a climate of interest about the issue through publicity and through constituent pressure is very important. Once again, at this point in the process, having a liaison at a Washington public interest group can be very valuable. Your Washington contact can talk to staffers on Capitol Hill and determine which lobbying techniques would be most appropriate to help get the markup.

Once a markup is scheduled, it is imperative to determine what amendments will be offered and what counter amendments or strengthening amendments you would like to offer. Your Washington associates can find out, in general, what amendments will be offered. Contact between you and the Washington public interest group staff will have to be on a daily basis to determine strategy. Information will be needed for arguments in support of or against amendments. New amendments will have to be written and Congressmen found to introduce them. Lobbying pressure will have to be intensified. Here the background work that you have done establishing coali-

Elihu Blotnick

tions and contacting groups and influential people in the subcommittee members' districts will begin to pay off. You should be able to generate hundreds of telegrams and letters supporting your position by contacting various groups and individuals in key members' districts.

Work with the press should also be bearing fruit now. If you have generated interest in subcommittee members' districts, you can now follow up with a press release detailing the controversy in the markup. Another way of getting publicity is to have a local group in a key subcommittee member's district release a statement to the press. You want to create both constituent and media pressure to show that there is a ground swell of support for your position.

Once the subcommittee markup is over, even if you have been successful in getting strengthening amendments passed and debilitating amendments defeated, you will have to start over again when the bill is sent to the full committee.

The full committee can start the whole process again by calling a new set of hearings on the legislation as sent from the subcommittee and taking testimony from different people. In fact, this rarely happens. Usually the full committee goes directly to a markup of the subcommittee legislation. Depending on the members of the committee and the interest generated in the legislation, the full committee markup can be a pro forma ratification of the subcommittee work or a full-scale revision of the bill. Once again, the same lobbying techniques that were used to get a markup and to influence the subcommittee members will be used on members of the full committee.

Assuming that you have managed to get a good bill reported from the full committee, the next step differs between the two houses of Congress. In the Senate, the bill is scheduled for floor debate where amendments can be offered. In the House, the bill goes to the Rules Committee, which schedules it for floor action, sets limits on debate, and even determines whether or not amendments will be allowed. Nancy Matthews, legislative assistant to Congressman Richard Ottinger, explained how much power this committee has: "The Rules Committee is much more than a traffic cop regulating the flow of legislation. By limiting debate in different ways, the Rules Committee makes policy decisions which affect the floor vote. They can even kill a bill by refusing to give it a rule."

If the Rules Committee bottles up your bill, traditional lobbying techniques must once again be employed to convince the committee members that there is a need for the legislation. Organizational and constituent pressure from the members' districts and publicity about the committee's action have been effective in dislodging legislation from the Rules Committee in the past.

Once a bill has been scheduled for floor action, lobbying goes on at a fever pitch. Information on the bill must be disseminated as widely as possible. Try to get a story published in newspapers such as the *Washington Post* or *The New York Times.* Publicity at this time is very valuable. A couple of weeks before the 1974 Strip Mining Bill was to be voted on in the House, a public interest coalition notified former Congresswoman Patsy Mink that the Chamber of Commerce had received air time on various radio stations for a tape criticizing the bill. Representative Mink then wrote to a large number of broadcasters asking if they would present her rebuttal to the Chamber of Commerce tape. Less than a week before the vote, Congresswoman Mink's rebuttal was broadcast by 70 or 80 radio stations. This last minute publicity was probably a factor in the legislation's passing the House.

In addition to publicity, letters and mailgrams must arrive from all over the country. If you have done your background work well, long before the vote you will have placed stories in the newsletters of the major consumer and environmental organizations asking for supporting letters to Congressmen. As the vote approaches, you should contact the regional representatives of the major environmental and consumer groups asking their help in generating mail and Western Union mailgrams.

There is a last minute flurry of activity before the floor vote. Members of Congress who are knowledgeable and influential must be found to give speeches in support of the bill on the floor. You or the Washington public interest group staff might be pressed into service writing these floor speeches if the member's staff is too busy. Arguments against weakening amendments must be provided to key legislators. Strengthening amendments must be written and influential legislators must be persuaded to offer them.

The vote is the culmination of months of effort. Then, if your bill passes, the procedure begins all over again in the other house. Even after both houses have passed the legislation, the bill must go to a Conference Committee to iron out differences between the House and Senate versions. The Conference Committee is composed of members of the House and Senate committees that have worked on the legislation. The same lobbying techniques used to influence committee consideration can be used again to influence the Conference. Moreover, since the members are the same ones you worked with at the committee level, you should have a fairly good rapport with them.

When the Conference has reported out a compromise version of the bill, it once again goes to the floor of both houses. Approval, however, is a virtual certainty. Conference Reports are hardly ever defeated. Then the bill goes to the President for his signature.

The lobbying techniques described above may seem to be difficult and time-consuming. They are not. You may not need to apply pressure at every step in the process. Often a bill will take on a life of its own and sail through almost unopposed. Even with controversial legislation, allies will be drawn to your position and the work can be spread among various groups and individuals.

The important point to remember is that a single person can succeed in getting legislation enacted. A case in point is Dr. Abe Bergman of Seattle, a pediatrician with a social conscience. In 1966, Dr. Bergman boiled over because he was seeing children with severe burns from flammable clothing. He persuaded Senator Magnuson to accompany him on a tour of the burn ward at a local hospital. Magnuson promptly introduced a bill providing that standards be set to make children's sleepwear flame resistant. But Dr. Bergman did not stop with the introduction of the bill. He helped Magnuson's staff prepare a witness list and testified himself. As the legislation progressed, he continued to keep in contact with the staff and was available to assist in preparing background material. The legislation was enacted into law in 1967.

Then Dr. Bergman discovered that laws are not always enforced. The law provided that the Secretary of Commerce set the standards to make the sleepwear flame resistant. But the Secretary did not set the standards. Years passed and once again Dr. Bergman decided to act. He persuaded some people he knew at a local television station to make a TV documentary on the children's burn problem. As Dr. Bergman puts it: "If you are a public interest lobbyist and you don't have any money, you have got to use the media. The television documentary produced 3,000 letters in one day to the Secretary of Commerce. Senator Magnuson then made sure the Secretary saw the documentary, and the week after he saw it he signed the regulations."

Dr. Bergman is one example of a successful citizen lobbyist. Another could be you.

Preparing Your Arguments

GEORGE ALDERSON and EVERETT SENTMAN

WITHOUT GOOD ARGUMENTS your cause is dead. You need arguments to win the help and influence of other citizens, and you need arguments to influence your congressman.

In a legislative campaign, an argument is simply a reason why legislators should vote a certain way. Arguments are not necessarily the greatest determinant of a legislator's vote. A congressman may decide to do as you ask simply because you and your co-workers have built political support in his district for your cause. Yet even when he supports you for such political reasons, the congressman needs the arguments to justify his decision. He needs to justify it to himself, so he can feel comfortable with it. He also needs to justify the decision to the public if he is challenged by your opponents or by a rival candidate in the next election.

An argument must be logical, but it can also appeal to emotion. The logical content should predominate. An overemphasis on emotion runs the risk of alienating legislators and turning off many citizens who will feel patronized or demeaned by a purely emotional argument. People are generally flattered to be approached with a logical argument.

The combination of logical and emotional content was shown in the campaign against the SST subsidy. Opponents of the project argued that the government should not spend $1.2 billion to develop an airplane that would be patronized only by wealthy businessmen and the Jet Set. This argument had its logical side (Why spend all that money for a questionable purpose?) and its emotional side (an appeal to prejudice against the rich).

When you carry out a legislative campaign you need persuasive arguments, backed up by the most impressive evidence you can get. To meet this central need you'll have to find the information and put it in a form that will enlighten and inspire people. On many issues you'll be able to get the arguments and background information from national organizations that are active on the subject. Then it's your job to recast these arguments in terms that will mean something to your community. For instance, if you're working for an increase in federal aid to public libraries, you can get national arguments from the American Library Association, but then you'll have to find out how the increase would help your local libraries, because this is what will mean the most to your congressman.

Information itself is not an argument. In a campaign for an air-pollution control bill you might have a four-foot stack of scientific reports on the health effects and property damage caused by air pollution, but all this information won't do your cause any good in that form. No congressman or senator is going to read those reports, and few will even know they exist. The information must be put into argument form. Then you can cite those reports as the authority behind your arguments, and you may even be able to use them ceremonially at hearings or news conferences to impress people with the weight of your arguments.

Kinds of Arguments

There are basically four kinds of arguments used in legislative issues:

- Social Good: how your proposal will enhance people's lives
- Economics: how your proposal will make (or save) money, make more jobs, or stimulate more business
- Ethics: how your proposal is morally right and the opposing position is wrong
- Science and technology: an assertion that certain facts are true or a prediction of what will happen

A fifth kind of argument is often used in connection with the Senate's consideration of the President's nominees to federal judgeships, Administration posts, and regulatory commissions—the *personal argument*, concerning how a person is or is not qualified for the job.

To support the arguments, three kinds of evidence can be used:

- Uncontestable facts: those your opponents won't challenge
- Contestable facts: those you'll have to defend
- Opinions: the predictions or recommendations of experts and respected people

Preparing Your Arguments

The first step is to make an inventory of your arguments. Include every reason you can think of in support of your position. Then decide which of these arguments will be most persuasive to your senators and congressman and to the people in your community whose help you will need to influence these legislators—the public at large, active citizen groups, local politicians, local government agencies, local news media, locally respected citizens, and so on. Having chosen the most usable arguments, you'll be able to concentrate on preparing these thoroughly, giving less attention to the less usable arguments.

The entire inventory should be made not by you alone, but by your core leadership group, because it concerns the arguments all your leaders will rely on during the campaign. If the leaders have contributed to this basic preparation, they will have a stronger commitment to the campaign that follows. Besides, they may offer effective new ideas or different perspectives.

Inventorying All Arguments

After inventorying your arguments, proceed to inventory your *opponents'* arguments. Here again, consider which of these opposition arguments will be most influential on your legislators and on your opponents' cobelievers in the community. Then take stock of your responses to these arguments—how can you refute them or defuse them?

Don't neglect to think over how your opponents will respond to your arguments. If they have a strong rebuttal of your best argument, you'll need to prepare a strong rebuttal of *their* rebuttal.

As you review the arguments, consider how good the evidence is for each argument. If you have believable and authoritative evidence for an argument, chances are it will be taken seriously; if you don't, it won't. However, you can build up evidence by putting people to work researching the subject.

The argument inventory is a planning tool, showing you:

- Which of your arguments are not refutable.
- Which of your opponents' rebuttals need a prepared rebuttal
- Which of your arguments rest on slender or unimpressive evidence and therefore need further work
- Which of your opponents' arguments rest on slender or unimpressive evidence and therefore are vulnerable

Also review your argument inventory to see whether you have arguments in all four categories—social good, economics, ethics, and science and technology. If not, you may be missing a chance to broaden your appeal and thus gain more support.

Review the arguments to see if you have made a strong case that the issue affects your congressional district and state. Local-impact arguments are among the most effective when you're dealing with members of Congress, so don't neglect this subject if you can possibly make a good argument.

Support for Your Arguments

As part of your inventory process, draw up a list of your potential sources of support, and indicate which arguments will be needed to bring them into action.

After preparing this list, based on your knowledge of potential supporters, look at the subject the other way around, to discover new sources of support that you hadn't thought of before. Go through your arguments, asking yourself, "Who in our community would be concerned about this argument?"

This inventory process will give you a head start on your campaign, because you'll know where your strong points and weak points are. However, preparing your arguments is a process that never stops. During the heat of your campaign you may discover new sources of support—perhaps an affected neighborhood you had not known about, or a labor union that is concerned about your issue. When this happens, put somebody to work preparing the arguments and evidence that will bring this new support into action. On the other hand, your opponents may spring a new argument on you, in which case you will need to prepare a persuasive rebuttal fast.

This sort of argument preparation under pressure is normal to a legislative campaign. But you'll always do better if you start your preparations early and, as a result, can put all your group's time and effort at the peak of the campaign into tactical projects that will yield political support, instead of into research to plug the holes in poorly prepared arguments.

The argument inventory should be started at one of your group's first few meetings around the kitchen table. You can't afford to wait for ultimate perfection before kicking off the campaign. Indeed, the first things your group does in public should bring more supporters into the field who can help with the argument-preparation work. From start to finish, you must keep developing new arguments and new evidence, and keep poking new holes in your opponents' arguments. If you rest on your initial arguments and facts, people—especially politicians and news media—will start thinking your case is work. Keep asking yourself, "What can we do for an encore?"

Dredge deep for good arguments. Citizen groups

often base their campaigns on a few shallow arguments, and they run into trouble when the heat is on. Opponents will use their superior staff and money to try to defuse each of your arguments, and they will probably succeed in defusing some of them. By having plenty of arguments early in the campaign, you can afford to lose some.

If your opponents are likely to rely on technical or economic arguments to defeat your cause, your best bet is to put your own technical people and economists to work on the issue as soon as possible, preparing arguments of your own on the points that will be challenged.

Propose an Alternative

When your objective is to defeat something, such as a dam or a wrongheaded government policy, make one of your arguments the advocacy of an alternative. If you can avoid it, don't let your opponents paint you as irresponsible "aginners," because that can damage the credibility of all your arguments and may deprive you of community support you need in your campaign.

Many, many people who share your views will hesitate to join in a campaign that is purely against something. People will say, "They're just too negative!" The attitude seems to be that being against things is immature, irresponsible, and unrespectable. Remove this obstacle by advocating an alternative, and you'll open the door to all those who distrust "negativism" but otherwise would love to help.

The opponents of nuclear power, for instance, had great difficulty getting their point across in Congress in the early 1970s because the nuclear industry had so expensively and successfully convinced legislators and the public that there was no alternative. Antinuclear groups kept arguing that energy conservation and solar and wind energy were viable alternatives, and by 1976 these were taken seriously enough so that Congress began to look more critically at nuclear-power issues, abolished the Joint Committee on Atomic Energy, increased appropriations for solar and wind energy research, and weakened the Price-Anderson Act's federal subsidy of insurance for nuclear power plants. The growing acceptance of the alternatives to nuclear power was a major factor in this turnabout.

The Congressional Viewpoint

One of the most important results of your argument inventory will be the selection of arguments that will be most persuasive to your congressman and senators. You can make some good guesses, based on what you know of their past performance, and you'll learn more

as the campaign progresses through your conversations with the legislators themselves, with their staffers, and with local politicians who know them.

You may find that your three legislators are interested in completely different aspects of your issue. Perhaps your congresswoman will be most influenced by economic arguments, one of your senators by arguments concerning social benefits, and the other senator by ethical arguments. In this case, you'll have to include all three types of argument in your grass-roots campaign—indeed, diverse arguments will attract wider support among the public—but stress different arguments when you meet with legislators or arrange for local VIPs to call on them.

Debunking the Opposition

Just as important as having good arguments for your position is being able to refute your opponents'

Werner Muller/Jeroboam, Inc.

arguments. You need a good rebuttal not only for the legislators you're trying to influence, but for news media, local politicians, and even your own supporters. If your most committed volunteers keep getting asked by their friends, "How can you support a bill that would put 150,000 people out of work?" they will need to have a good answer, or you'll lose them.

There are several ways to handle opposition arguments:

1. Challenge the evidence the argument is based on. Never trust your opponents' facts. Go through them with a fine-toothed comb, looking for errors, misstatements, and faulty assumptions. Numerical data may have been based on faulty sampling or have been extrapolated from similar situations elsewhere. Get your experts to analyze opponents' facts and figures and shoot holes in them, if possible.

For example, in the campaign against the SST subsidy, the proponents of the SST claimed that 150,000 jobs were at stake. But when economists looked into this figure at the request of anti-SST groups, they found that only 20,000 workers were actually to be employed in the prototype program then at issue. SST proponents had taken a blue-sky figure of 50,000 workers that might be employed if enough SST aircraft were eventually ordered by the airlines, and had multiplied that figure by three, a standard multiplier reflecting general community services such as grocery stores, barbers, and taxi drivers patronized by the 50,000 workers.

You can also challenge opinions and predictions that your opponents are using as evidence for their arguments. To do so, you'll need experts. If you can recruit experts with more stature than those cited by your opponents, you'll be in good shape. But even if your experts are of less stature, you may be able to build them up through good use of the news media, good choice of a forum in which your experts will present their opinions, and by having your experts stress points that will appeal to those you want to influence.

In responding to your opponents' arguments, strive to give your senators and congressman an alternative, equally authoritative source of information and expert advice, so they can justify turning their backs on the information and advice your opponents have given them. Scientists, technicians, and other experts can serve this purpose, and so can government agencies— local, regional, state or federal.

2. Challenge the assumptions your opponents' argument is based on. Suppose you're working against a proposed dam which your opponents argue is needed to prevent floods from causing loss of life and property. If you can't disprove your opponents' figures on past losses of life and property (challenging their evidence), you may be able to challenge the assumption that the dam is the only way to prevent these losses. You might challenge the assumption that this advantage is worth the multimillion-dollar cost of the dam. You might also challenge the assumption that the dam will really prevent the losses. Assumptions can be the most vulnerable spots in an argument, because they are supposed to be accepted without question. If your opponents are smart, they will have built their arguments carefully to avoid relying on unproven assumptions; but if they haven't done so, they may be wide open to your challenge.

3. Challenge your opponents' choice of priorities. This is a way of dealing with opponents' arguments for which you don't have a strong rebuttal; it's a matter of making their arguments seem less important than yours. If you're fighting for a bill to control air pollution and your opponents claim it would work a hardship on the big auto companies, you might accuse them of being more concerned about General Motors' profits than about the health of the millions of people harmed every year by air pollution. Or, to strike a more positive note, you could stress throughout your campaign, "People before profits!"

4. Challenge the argument head-on. Especially useful in answering ethical arguments, which are not based on a showing of evidence, this response usually consists of strongly asserting a rival argument. For instance, in the controversy over abortion, the anti-abortion groups' ethical argument summed up by the slogan "Right to Life" has been challenged by those who advocate legal abortion with the argument that women have a "Right to Choose."

5. Look for inconsistencies in your opponents' arguments. Citizens fighting against electric power projects many times gained ground by pointing out that at the same time the power companies were arguing that they needed more power plants and dams, the same companies were spending millions to drum up new customers in the form of "all-electric homes" and energy-using industries; apparently the new power projects were not as necessary as had been claimed. (Only in the mid-1970s, when the energy shortage became a national concern, did the power companies stop this kind of advertising.)

6. Challenge your opponents' interests or motives. You may be able to undermine some of your opponents' arguments by showing that your opponents

Kent Reno/Jeroboam, Inc.

have an unworthy reason for their position, a reason that is not stated in their public arguments. For instance, in fights over proposed freeways it was discovered that many of the influential proponents had quietly bought land along the projected route, expecting to sell it to the highway department for a large profit. Exposure of such motives has helped to stop many highway and dam projects.

However, don't challenge your opponents' interests or motives unless you have good evidence for a charge. Unfounded accusations will damage your credibility, detract from the respectability of your cause, and could even be libelous.

Developing New Arguments

New arguments may be easier to find than you think. Most legislative issues are argued primarily on the national level, without getting down to how they affect your state, your congressional district, or your community. Every argument you develop that tells how the issue affects the people at home is in effect a new argument, and because it is about your legislators' constituents it may have more impact than national arguments.

Be on the lookout for arguments that will appeal to local people. You may discover sensitivity to an aspect

Every time we walk along a beach some ancient urge disturbs us so that we find ourselves shedding shoes and garments or scavenging among seaweed and whitened timbers like the homesick refugees of a long war.

And war it has been indeed—the long war of life against its inhospitable environment, a war that has lasted for perhaps three billion years. It began with strange chemicals seething under a sky lacking in oxygen; it was waged through long ages until the first green plants learned to harness the light of the nearest star, our sun. The human brain, so frail, so perishable, so full of inexhaustible dreams and hungers, burns by the power of the leaf.

The hurrying blood cells charged with oxygen carry more of that element to the human brain than to any other part of the body. A few moments' loss of vital air and the phenomenon we know as consciousness goes down into the black night of inorganic things. The human body is a magical vessel, but its life is linked with an element it cannot produce. Only the green plant knows the secret of transforming the light that comes to us across the far reaches of space. There is no better illustration of the intricacy of man's relationship with other living things.

—LOREN EISELEY

of the issue that you had previously considered insignificant. This is what brought new support for proposed wilderness areas in Colorado. Wilderness advocates had not seriously considered cattle ranchers to be potential supporters of wilderness; ranchers had usually opposed wilderness, even though cattle grazing is permitted in wilderness areas. But in 1974, through good local contacts, Colorado conservationists learned that the ranchers were more sympathetic to wilderness. Lacking roads, the ranchers said, wilderness areas were good protection against cattle rustlers, who nowadays need large trucks to haul off the booty. In addition, because wilderness is closed to motor vehicles, the cattle are not harassed by motorbikes and other off-road vehicles. Using these arguments, wilderness proponents won the support of key ranchers and thus gained some hard-to-get influence with Colorado congressmen.

An argument need not be based on a certainty. A mere possibility can be enough to gain support. Suppose you are working for legislation to increase federal funding of mental-health research. If a local university or college has done research in this field, you may argue that this institution could get more research funds as a result of this legislation. This could add the local slant that will get your congressman interested. If you can involve the relevant scientists at the university,

they may be able to get the university president to visit or phone the congressman in support of the bill.

Sometimes an argument may be hard to prove because there is little evidence on the topic or because the evidence does not have much stature. In this case, if you're convinced the argument is right, you may have to resort to the method laughingly referred to by scientists as "proof by vigorous assertion." That is, if you keep saying it often, and with conviction, it will begin to be accepted as valid. You hope that later your research teams will come up with better evidence, but meanwhile you've at least been able to keep the argument alive. An inadequately supported argument is highly vulnerable to challenge by your opponents, but as long as you don't rely on it too much and as long as your opponents can't use it to make you look foolish, it doesn't do any harm to use it.

Can you develop a new economic argument? Your opponents will probably claim that economics is on their side, but don't let them get away with it. Consider all the benefits and costs—who pays, and who benefits? Will jobs be lost or created?

The initial cost of a project you oppose may be dwarfed by long-term costs. See if you can make a reliable projection of the total cost over the life of the project. For example, in opposing the B-1 bomber project, the Federation of American Scientists observed that the U.S. Air Force proposal to build 244 B-1 bombers at a cost of $40 billion was less than half the total cost. Over twenty years, the real cost of building and maintaining 244 B-1 bombers would be close to $90 billion, according to the Federation.

Talk your issue over with experts in many relevant fields, because they may see vulnerable arguments that you wouldn't have noticed.

Getting the Evidence

The best arguments always are based on good, hard evidence—facts and opinions that show your argument to be valid. If you're working for an increase in Social Security benefits and you argue that the increase is·needed because recipients can't live on the present benefits, you'll have to offer some evidence to back up your claim. In this case the evidence might include the personal experiences of local people who receive Social Security benefits. It might also include a local economist's analysis showing that the benefits have not kept pace with inflation. It might include an informal poll of local Social Security recipients on the question of whether the benefits are enough to live on.

In developing and presenting the evidence for your arguments, always strive for *stature*. In a legislative fight, facts don't speak for themselves; they depend on the stature of their source. A fact is only as good as the person or institution it comes from, because every fact is likely to be challenged by your opponents. (The only exceptions are absolutely uncontestable facts such as that the sky is blue and that the Mississippi River flows into the sea.) Opinions, of course, depend completely on the stature of their source.

From Institutions

The best sources of evidence are experts and institutions active in your subject area but not directly associated with your cause. A university, a research center, or a government agency could fill the bill if you can find the right sympathetic person in that institution. On nationwide issues, national citizen groups usually provide this kind of high-statured information, but to make it more effective in your local campaign you will want to find respected local institutions to vouch for the facts. If you live in Utah, your congressman may have more respect for a professor at Utah State University than for one at Harvard.

Suppose you're working for a law to cut back on the use of cancer-causing substances. You would be able to get from national groups pertinent remarks by national cancer experts on the dangers of these substances. To add an effective local touch, approach the most respected medical people in your community and ask them to offer their views in support of your

objective. Give them copies of the national information and the best background data you have, and they should be able to make some cogent remarks on the subject, which you can then use both in your contacts with your senators and congressman and in your campaign for local support.

Some of the best evidence in legislative campaigns has come from short-term studies undertaken by scientists, social scientists, and economists at local colleges and universities. Their stature, expertise, and "ivory tower" position gives them an impact on legislators far greater than the equivalent nonacademician's. So when you see the need for better evidence—either facts or opinions—to support one of your arguments, the first thing to do is to sit down with a sympathetic local college professor and talk it over.

It's not enough to get studies done by university faculty. You want your study to reach news media, your legislators, and friendly local politicians. It's best to have the researcher release the report, preferably hand-delivering it to your congressman and senators and mailing it to a list of others which you've drawn up. Then, prompt local news reporters to ask for the congressman's reaction to the report—a move that ensures that he'll notice it.

Many universities have specialized institutes affiliated with them which share the university's faculty and may use advanced students as researchers under faculty direction. If the faculty of one of these institutes shares your viewpoint, it could be a good source of evidence.

By Yourself

Inevitably, much of the evidence for your arguments will have to be gathered by you and your co-workers. There isn't always a university or research institute on hand when you need evidence fast. Yet, if you—the issue advocate—say that something is a fact, you won't necessarily be believed, because the congressman will tend to think that you're just getting carried away with your cause.

When you know you've got a fact, don't relax until you've found a way to turn it into believable evidence. Suppose you're working on a bill that would provide federal aid to expand hospitals, and you know for a fact that all the hospitals in town have been turning people away for lack of beds. You have a fact, but how do you make it convincing evidence to the public and to you legislators? Several ways suggest themselves:

- Get the hospital directors to cosign a round-robin letter to your congressional delegation attesting to this fact, and have them release it to news media so the public will know.
- Have a friendly city council member call a hearing

on the subject and invite hospital directors, staff physicians, and patients to speak on the lack of space. Make sure news media cover the hearing.

- Get a friendly legislator or local politician to visit the hospitals when they are full to capacity, with reporters and photographers on hand to record the event.
- Get a few local physicians who use the hospitals to write up the situation and release it as a report to your congressional delegation by, say, the Elmsford Physicians' Study Committee.

These are just a few of the ways in which this particular fact could be established as believable, without going into further research on the point.

You never have time to research everything that will help. You have to decide which topics are most vital. In the hospital example above, it would probably be unproductive to devote long hours to deepening your facts for the argument that the hospitals need more space, because that will be quite believable. More crucial and harder to prove will be the fact that the hospitals have no source of funds other than the federal government to finance the needed expansion. Always focus your evidence-finding on what you think will be the most effective arguments and the most crucial facts.

Through Intern Programs

Knowing that you can convert bare facts into believable evidence enables you to use nonexperts to dig for the facts. You can do the digging yourself, you can get reliable volunteers to do it, or you can seek help through college intern programs. Many colleges and universities give undergraduates the chance to spend a semester working on social issues with a citizen action group. The students work full-time on your research tasks, and they receive college credit for it under an internship or independent study course. This is usually arranged through a professor in a relevant field of study. Intern programs usually want you to pay the students a subsistence salary, but they're used to cooperating with citizen groups that can't afford it. The four essentials in using interns are:

- Get students who share your viewpoint and thus will be strongly motivated to do the job well.
- Plan the interns' research tasks so they can be done in the time available and with the interns' level of skills.
- Be prepared to spend some time supervising the students as they get started on the project and periodically during their months with you.
- Keep them involved in your overall effort. Don't expect them to spend all their time in research,

because that can be deadly, but let them do more satisfying things from time to time, so they won't lose interest.

Interns can be among your best workers if you give them good supervision and keep them happy.

Using Case Histories

Real-life examples are essential to most legislative campaigns. In their daily routine, senators and congressmen constantly have to make decisions based on vague generalities and on nationwide data that are too vast to be readily understood. You can break through this routine and catch legislators' interest by telling how your issue has affected people. Good case histories can persuade a legislator to support your side. They can fortify a legislator who already supports you. And if you have a congressman who is a committeed opponent, case histories can bring him down from his cloud of generalities and force him to grapple with the realities you see in the issue.

A case history is simply the story of something that happened that is related to your issue. It could be as local and specific as, in a fight for a consumer protection bill, reporting that Mrs. Nussbaum on the corner had a flooded basement because fly-by-night plumbers installed faulty new plumbing and couldn't be located to fix it. Or it could be as earth-shaking as, in a campaign against a treaty with the Soviet Union, reporting the Soviet Union's past violations of treaties it had signed.

Senators and congressmen, as a rule, will be more influenced by case histories from their own state or congressional district because that is where their attention is focused, it is an area they know personally, and it is where their constituents live. Things that have happened elsewhere can be easily ignored, but things that have happened in one's own state or district must be heeded.

To take advantage of legislators' sensitivity to what goes on back home, built a collection of case histories on how the issue affects local people. Look for the most outrageous and unfair situations, which cry out for solution by the method you advocate.

There's always a temptation to work up case histories superficially, aiming for a long list of sketchy examples. This approach leaves you open to easy challenge by the congressman and by your opponents, because you can't answer questions about the details. Legislators have little patience with case histories that are merely a paraphrase of a brief newspaper story, so don't expect to get by with newspaper clippings. To avoid superficiality, take one or two of the best examples and develop them in depth.

The story of Mrs. Nussbaum's flooded basement, for example, could be expanded by obtaining copies of a receipt, sales slip, or contract given her by the fraudulent plumbers, a bill from the plumber who eventually stemmed the flood and identified the problem in the faulty installation, and a letter or approved claim from Mrs. Nussbaum's insurance company indicating the extent of damage from the flood. Get the dates and times of day: these are convincing details.

The documentation and blow-by-blow story need not be used every time you cite the case history, but you want your legislators to know you have the whole story. An informal report on a case history, with pertinent documents attached, could be turned over to your congresswoman when you have met with her, it could be mailed to her, or it could be submitted for inclusion in the record of a hearing on the subject.

When you use local case histories in your public arguments—in the newspapers, on television, or in your printed material—you'll stimulate other people to write to your congresswoman about their experiences with the issue. For instance, in a fight for stronger work-place health laws, if people see on television that Henry Tillman was unable to get a disability pension after his lungs were ruined by work in the cotton mills, others who have had similar work-place disabilities without adequate attention or compensation will get the idea of writing to their congressman about their own complaints. These can be the most powerful case histories of all because they arrive in the form of letters from people who have probably never written to a congressman before, telling about what has happened to them. These letters won't show great political sophistication and won't press for a commitment, but you can make up for that through other tactics. What these letters do is vital to your campaign—show the congressman that there *is* a problem affecting his constituents, and that they aren't going to forget about it.

Legislators and Their Staffs

You should also take the time to learn about your congressman and senators and their staffs. This will tell you a lot about their stances on other subjects, and from what background they view your issue. When you know the issues your congressman most strongly supports, you may think of a way to tie your cause to one of them. For instance, if you're campaigning for an increase in funds for family-planning programs and you discover that your congressman has been outraged at the high cost of the welfare program, you may decide to stress the argument that increased family planning will greatly reduce the welfare costs resulting from too many unwanted children.

To find out about your legislators' past record in Congress, use these sources:

- *The Almanac of American Politics* contains an overview of each legislator's record, a table of his votes on key issues, and a summary of how he was rated by specialized citizen groups.
- *Congressional Quarterly Almanac,* issued annually, contains an analysis and voting record for each major issue Congress acted on during the year.
- Your local newspaper's clipping file will cover your legislators' public pronouncements and involvement in local affairs over a span of many years.

Senators' and congressmen's biographies (the way *they* want them to appear) are printed in the *Congressional Quarterly.* To get a more critical view of your congressman, consider interviewing the candidate who ran against him in the last election. You may get a lot of vindictive remarks, but also a few good leads that can be very helpful. This way you may learn that the congressman has a close relationship with an industry that is among your opponents, or that he's friendly with some of your VIP supporters. Check out these leads carefully before you act on them.

Political reporters for local newspapers or television often have a buddy relationship with your congressman and senators, but they will sometimes tell you much about party factions that may be influencing a legislator's actions. If, for instance, your congressman is under the gun from a conservative faction in the party and knows he will be challenged by a conservative candidate in the next primary election, he may be taking more conservative positions this year in order to head off a split in the party. Learning this background, you would be able to plan your campaign accordingly—perhaps by framing your cause in more conservative terms or by getting local conservative VIPs to help.

Senators' and congressmen's campaign finances are open to public scrutiny through the Federal Election Commission, which will send you the reports you want upon payment of a copying fee.

The Senate and House of Representatives require their members to file financial statements annually. Some congressmen and congresswomen make it easier to see their statements by depositing copies in their field offices and by releasing their statements to local news media. With less cooperative congressmen, your only local source may be newspaper stories, which are likely to appear shortly after May 1, the deadline each year for members of Congress to submit their financial statements.

Be cautious in researching legislators' finances and personal backgrounds. They may hear about your inquiries from congressional employees eager to curry favor. This is even more likely if you are looking into their landholdings or court records at the county courthouse, because old courthouse employees have solid political ties. If you don't want legislators to know that your group is looking into their background, get someone to do this research who is not yet publicly associated with your group.

Presenting Your Arguments

You'll need to use two different approaches in presenting your arguments because you have two quite different audiences—on the one hand, your senators and congressman, on the other, your public supporters and those you hope to enlist in the campaign.

Your popular supporters will respond best to an argument presented dramatically, stressing the rightness and fairness of your proposal, as contrasted with the wrongness and unfairness of the opposite position. Evidence that symbolizes the issue can be important. In the fight to save the redwoods, contrasting pictures of intact redwood trees and pictures of logged-off redwood forests became the public image of the issue. In a fight for hospital construction funds, pictures of overcrowded hospital wards and admitting rooms might serve the same purpose. However, this symbolic evidence is only part of your presentation. You have to get the complete arguments out to your supporters, with enough background facts to make them usable.

Legislators like to think they consider the facts dispassionately and reach decisions on the facts alone. Actually, they are usually influenced more strongly by political pressure of the kind you can generate than they are by the arguments. But because legislators have this notion of calm, unbiased decision making, it's important to cater to it, primarily through your group's direct contacts with legislators—visits, letters, telephone calls—as opposed to contacts by individual citizens. Flatter the congressman by giving him a fact sheet on the issue that presents the arguments, with good evidence to back them up. The fact sheet should not be cast in terms of right or wrong or be emotional; your strong commitment and feelings will be clear from what you tell him in person. By leaving your passion out of the fact sheet, you will make it easier for the congressman and his staff to read your arguments without having to mentally edit out your value judgments. You want him to see that he can rationally justify his vote to himself and his constituents if he's ever challenged on it.

Every citizen group has a right to express its feelings on an issue. Citizens have emotions about issues, and these emotions are a tremendous political force because they are what motivate people to take action on legislative issues. Legislators also have emotions about issue. Indeed, you want your senators and congressman to share your emotional commitment to your issue, so they won't jump ship when your opponents put on the heat. But when you are in the touchy situation of asking a legislator to support your cause and he has not yet agreed to do so, just set your emotions aside for a few minutes—long enough to show him that your arguments can stand on their own, without emotion to prop them up.

Principal Authors

George Alderson, former legislative director of Friends of the Earth, is coauthor, with Everett Sentman, of *How You Can Influence Congress*.

Albert Bartlett is on the faculty of physics and astrophysics at the University of Colorado at Boulder.

Mildred R. Blake has served on the board of the United World Federalists. From 1971 to 1979 she represented Friends of the Earth at the United Nations. Before retiring in 1950, she spent 30 years as an advertising writer.

David R. Brower, a lifelong conservation leader, and subject of John McPhee's *Encounters with the Archdruid*, founded Friends of the Earth in 1969. In 1979, he became FOE's Chairman of the Board and publishing director. He was formerly Executive Director of the Sierra Club.

Kenneth Brower, son of David Brower, is author of *The Starship and the Canoe*, *Wake of the Whale*, *Earth and the Great Weather*, and *With Their Islands Around Them*. His writings have appeared in *Atlantic Monthly*, *Audobon*, *Paris Review*, and *Omni*.

Lester R. Brown is President and senior researcher with Worldwatch Institute. His latest book is *Transition: The Worldwide Effort to Create A Sustainable Society*.

Sharon Camp is Director of Education and Public Policy for the Population Crises Committee. A public interest lobbyist since 1971, she holds a PhD in Comparative and International Politics from Johns Hopkins.

Anne and **Clay Denman** both teach anthropology at Central Washington State University, where Anne is a professor and Clay is Chair of the Department. They were instrumental in founding the Small Towns Institute in 1969, and both still work for it, Clay as Executive Director and Anne as Editorial Director. The Institute provides information exchange for small communities with similar problems and opportunities.

Anne H. Ehrlich is Senior Research Associate at Stanford University, and coauthor of *Extinction, The Golden Door,* and *Ecoscience*. She is a director of Friends of the Earth.

Paul R. Ehrlich is Stanford's Bing Professor of Population Studies, coauthor of *Extinction* and *Ecoscience*, and author of *The Population Bomb*.

Lindsey Grant recently retired from the post of Deputy Assistant Secretary of State for environmental and population affairs. A career foreign service officer, he now works as a consultant on population and resources.

Joan Gussow is a consultant, teacher, and author on food, nutrition, and education. She is author of *Who Is Going to Eat the Breakfast of Champions?* and was a member of Senator McGovern's task force on world hunger.

Hazel Henderson is an economist with the Center for Alternative Futures in Princeton, New Jersey. She is the author of *Creative Alternative Futures*, *The Politics of the Solar Age*, and the forthcoming *Politics of Reconceptualization*.

John P. Holdren is Professor of Energy and Resources at the University of California and a coauthor of *Ecoscience*.

John Kauffman is a retired National Park Service planner. While with the Service, he led explorations by canoe on the Noatak and Kobuk Rivers, and was responsible for planning Gates of the Arctic National Park. He is author of *Flow East* and a member of the Wilderness Society's Governing Council.

Peter Lafen is a transportation specialist working with Friends of the Earth's Washington, DC office.

Marc Lappe is Chief of the Hazard Alert System, California Department of Health Services. His PhD is in experimental pathology.

Amory Lovins, Vice President of Friends of the Earth Foundation, is author of *Soft Energy Paths* and coauthor of *Energy/War: Breaking the Nuclear Link*. He served as FOE's representative to the United Kingdom from 1972-1980.

L. Hunter Lovins, a lawyer and forester from southern California, is an energy consultant, a founder of Tree People, and coauthor of *Energy/War: Breaking the Nuclear Link*.

Dan Luten, a former Shell Oil and University of California geographer, is a Director of Friends of the Earth.

Jerry Mander, a great figure in alternative and creative advertising, is author of *Four Arguments for the Elimination of Television*. He is currently working on a book about Indians and technology.

J. Irwin Miller is Chairman of the Financial and Executive Committee of Cummins Engine Company, Inc.

Stephanie Mills was called one of the young women to watch in the 1970s, by *Mademoiselle*. She has been editor of *Earth Times* and *Not Man Apart*, and is now associate editor of *CoEvolution Quarterly*.

Hugh Nash, son of World Federalist leader Vernon Nash, is a former editor and writer for *World Government News* and *Architectural Forum*, former editor of *The Sierra Club Bulletin*, and former Senior Editor of *Not Man Apart*. He has been with Friends of the Earth since 1970.

Stewart Ogilvy has been an editor for the Population Institute since 1972. He is active in World Federalist organizations, has served as advisor to Zero Population Growth, and is Honorary President of Friends of the Earth.

David Phillips is a wildlife expert working out of Friends of the Earth's San Francisco office.

Ann Roosevelt, former legislative director of Friends of the Earth, is now active in Boston-area politics and public interest work. She was an assistant editor for Random House (1970-1) and a science advisor to Senator Edward Kennedy (1972-3), before joining the FOE staff.

Gus Speth, a lawyer and environmentalist, was a staff attorney with Natural Resources Defense Council from 1970-1977. He served as Chairman of the Council on Environmental Quality under President Jimmy Carter and became a director of Friends of the Earth in 1981.

Wallace Stegner is author of *Angle of Repose* and *The Uneasy Chair*. He is a native Utahn, and one of our time's most eloquent spokesmen for the wilderness west.

John Tanton, an ophthalmologist from Michigan, is a past president of Zero Population Growth.

Mark Terry, author of *Teaching for Survival* and *Energy and Order*, is a founder of the Northwest School, an experimental educational facility in Seattle, Washington.

Russell Train was the first chairman of the US Council on Environmental Quality (1970-73), administrator of the US Environmental Protection Agency (1973-77), and President of the Conservation Foundation (1965-69). He is now cochairman of the Committee for 2000.

Mary Lou Van Deventer served as Managing Editor of *Not Man Apart* from 1975-77. She was a Writer/Researcher for California's Office of Appropriate Technology (1978-80) before becoming Associate Editor of *Sierra*, the Sierra Club Bulletin.

Stephen Wheeler handles MX lobbying for Friends of the Earth in Washington, DC.

Chuck Williams, former National Parks Representative of Friends of the Earth, is author of *Bridge of the Gods, Mountains of Fire*, a photographic homage to his home landscape, the Columbia River Gorge. He is currently leading the campaign to make the Gorge a National Scenic Area.